Beginning Visual Basic 5

Peter Wright

Wrox Press Ltd.®

Beginning Visual Basic 5

Published by Wrox Press Ltd. 30 Lincoln Road, Olton, Birmingham, B27 6PA , UK.
Printed in Canada
4 5 TRI 99 98 97

ISBN 1-861000-39-1

Trademark Acknowledgements

Credits

Author
Peter Wright

Additional Material
Rockford Lhotka
Alex Homer

Exercises and Solutions
John Smiley

Editors
Gina Mance
Chris Ullman

Development Editor
David Maclean

Technical Reviewers
Andrew Enfield
John Smiley
Rockford Lhotka
Owen Williams
Jon Bonnell
John Connell

Cover/Design/Layout
Andrew Guillaume

Copy Edit/Index
Wrox Team

Thanks

Peter Wright didn't write this book. Take a look at the cover and that's a strange statement, but take a look at the credits page and you'll see exactly what I mean. It's 2am in foggy England and on Friday the book will be complete bar the inevitable edits and amendments in the face of new betas. I didn't write this book. I wrote the text that comprises the ideas, the thoughts, the ideologies. I took the screenshots and wrote the code. Beside me, behind me, in front of me and above me, though, there were always a team of frantic editors, reviewers, designers, publishers and readers whose job it was to make damn sure that you are happy with what you just spent your hard earned buck for (if you are reading this in a store then that pang of guilt you just felt can only be eased by taking the book to the counter and handing over some cash). To them thanks, homage and unending gratitude are due.

First, my editors. Gina and Chris did a fantastic job in taking the ramblings of a binary hippie and turning them into a work of technical art. Without them this would be a set of Word files with text in no semblance of true order, screenshots in garish un-matching colors and spelling and grammatical errors to make most four year olds wince.

Then there's Dave Maclean. Here's a guy that called me up after seeing me post in a Compuserve forum with the idea that perhaps I'd make a good book author. He's lost a lot of hair since then, but his whip still hurts and his vision is still inspiring enough to keep me sat here till the early hours.

On the Microsoft side, an army of loyal Gateites keep the machine rolling and people like me supplied with a steady stream of toys. Special thanks though to Mike Pryke-Smith at Microsoft UK, not least for the interesting debate at VBUG a while back. Also to the team at Text 100 for providing copies of the software used to test various parts of the VB code (namely the OLE stuff) and of course to actually write this book; Quick plug – Office 97 ROCKS... buy it. Also, my thanks to the WPG Beta group at Microsoft US for ensuring that the betas arrived on time and for considering me worthy of messing with their new born babies.

Finally, away from the keyboard, my very special gratitude to Simon, Jenny, Adrien, Maxine and Euan. To Simon and Jenny for the beer, the laughs, the videos and the Python recitals. To Adrien for being cannon fodder in the latest multiplayer kill fest, and to Maxine for humoring two big kids need to kill, maim and destroy. To Euan for being profoundly Scottish and for your unerring ability to remind what enthusiasm really is. To all of the above for just being the world's greatest friends.

Slush fest over....read, enjoy, code and keep smiling. If you make a million based on the knowledge you gain from this book then please email me your name address and a signed affidavit to that effect.

This book is dedicated to one person, to my Gail Marie.

"How noble in reason! How infinite in faculty!
In form and moving, how express and admirable!
In action, how like an angel!"

William Shakespeare

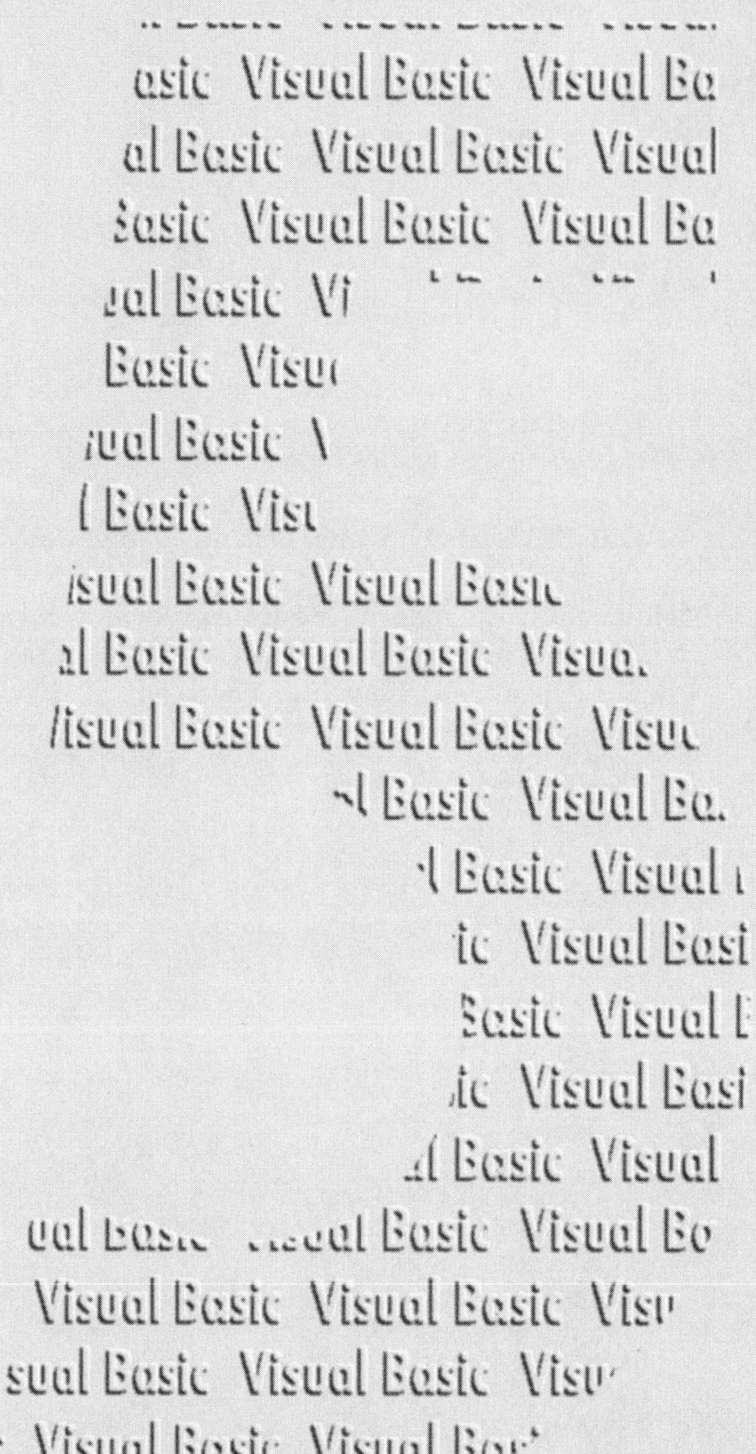

asic Visual Basic Visual Ba
al Basic Visual Basic Visual
Basic Visual Basic Visual Ba
ual Basic Vi
Basic Visu
ual Basic V
l Basic Visu
isual Basic Visual Basic
l Basic Visual Basic Visua
Visual Basic Visual Basic Visu
l Basic Visual Ba
l Basic Visual
ic Visual Basi
Basic Visual B
ic Visual Basi
l Basic Visual
ual Basic Visual Basic Visual Ba
Visual Basic Visual Basic Visu
sual Basic Visual Basic Visu
Visual Basic Visual Ba

Beginning
Visual Basic 5

asic Visual Basic Visual Ba
al Basic Visual Basic Visual
Basic Visual Basic Visual Ba
ual Basic Vi
Basic Visu
ual Basic V
l Basic Vis
isual Basic Visual Basic
al Basic Visual Basic Visua
Visual Basic Visual Basic Visu
l Basic Visual Ba
l Basic Visual
ic Visual Basi
Basic Visual B
ic Visual Basi
l Basic Visual
ual Basic Visual Basic Visual Ba
Visual Basic Visual Basic Visu
sual Basic Visual Basic Visu
Visual Basic Visual Ba

Introduction

Who's This Book for?

This book is designed to teach you how to write useful programs in Visual Basic 5 as quickly and as easily as possible. There are two kinds of beginners for whom this is the ideal book:

- You're a **beginner to programming** and you've chosen Visual Basic as the place to start. Great choice! Visual Basic is easy, it's fun and it's also powerful. This book will hold your hand throughout.
- You can program in another language but you're a **beginner to Windows programming**. Again, great choice! Come in from the cold world of C or whatever language you use and enjoy. This book will teach you how Visual Basic does things in terms you'll understand. Along the way, I'll give you all the background information you need on Windows programming to help you to develop really professional applications.

What's Covered in This Book?

This book is about the **Learning Edition** of Visual Basic. Newcomers with the Professional and Enterprise editions can also learn a great deal, but an explanation of the features specific to these two great packages is a little beyond the scope of this book.

Visual Basic is a big baby. We're not going to try and look into its every nook and cranny. What we *are* going to do is cut a wide path through the undergrowth to a suitable clearing where we can write our own programs.

Think of this book as a tour guide to Visual Basic country. You're only here for a short period, and it's never long enough (just like a real vacation). What you *don't* want is to go down every street in town. What you *do* want is the big picture, together with enough local understanding to enable you to find your own way around without getting into tricky situations. Sure, we'll look at some of the local highlights together, but these can only ever be a taster.

So what's in the tour? There are some things you have to know, like how Visual Basic programs fit together and what the main components are. All these fundamental building blocks are covered in detail. We then take a look at what you can actually do with Visual Basic. Just because something appears in Visual Basic doesn't mean it's in the book—we've only included those things that have a practical purpose. This book gets you where you want to go.

What's Not Covered in This Book

What we haven't put in this book is a lot of formal definitions and exhaustive lists of options. Visual Basic is a rich language, and each command has a welter of options. I'm just going to tell you what you need to know at the time. There are lots of good references, like the Visual Basic Manuals and Help Screens, that can give you all the minute detail. Alternatively, take a look at Appendix A which points you in the direction of some very useful Internet newsgroups, national user groups and other great sources of help and information.

I'm also not going to tell you how to actually use Windows. Throughout the course of the book, I assume you already know the basics of using a Windows program, such as how to select a menu option, or how to double-click something, and so on.

What You Need to Use This Book

Apart from a willingness to learn, you'll need access to a PC running Windows 95 and the Learning Edition of Visual Basic 5. You will also be able to complete a lot of the examples with the Control Creation Edition, which can be downloaded for free from the Microsoft web site (**`http://www.microsoft.com/vbasic`**).

All the source code for the examples in this book is shown in the chapters. You do not need any extra files to create the programs we discuss. However, if you do want to avoid the finger ache that comes with a lot of typing, you can download the examples from the Wrox web site.

`http://www.wrox.com`

Alternatively, if you don't have Internet access, you can purchase a CD-Rom with the code. See the page at the back of this book for details of how to order this.

Conventions

We have used a number of different styles of text and layout in the book to help differentiate between the different kinds of information. Here are examples of the styles we use and an explanation of what they mean:

Try It Outs - How Do They Work?

1 Each step has a number.

2 Follow the steps through.

3 Then read How It Works to find out what's going on.

Advice, hints, or background information comes in boxes like this.

- **Important Words** are in a bold type font.
- Words that appear on the screen in menus like the File or Window menu are in a similar font to what you see on screen.
- Keys that you press on the keyboard, like *Ctrl* and *Enter*, are in italics.
- Visual Basic code has two fonts. If it's a word that we're talking about in the text, for example, when discussing the **For...Next** loop, it's in a bold font. If it's a block of code that you can type in as a program and run, then it's also in a gray box:

```
Private Sub cmdQuit_Click()
   End
End Sub
```

- Sometimes you'll see code in a mixture of styles, like this:

```
Private Sub cmdQuit_Click()
   End
End Sub
```

There are two reasons why this might be so. In both cases we want you to consider the code with the gray background. The code with a white background is either code we've already looked at and that we don't wish to examine further, or when you're typing code in, this is code that Visual Basic automatically generates and doesn't need typing in.

- When a line of code has been split onto two lines because of space considerations, the continuation is marked with a ↳. When typing the code in Visual Basic, you should put any lines marked like this at the end of the code on the line above.

Note that VB5 does have its own line continuation character. It's a space followed by an underscore (_). I don't think this is very clear in print, so we've stuck with the bendy arrow.

These formats are designed to make sure that you know what it is you're looking at. I hope they make life easier.

How to Get the Most Out of This Book

This book is written as a hands-on tutorial. That means you have to get your hands on the keyboard as often as possible. Throughout the book there are Try It Outs! which is where you'll find step-by-step instructions for creating and running a Visual Basic program. This program illustrates the concept that's currently being explained.

I also use the Try It Outs! to teach you new concepts when it's better to see them in action first, rather than bury them in text. After each Try It Out! there is a How It Works section that explains what's going on. As the programs get longer, later in the book, some of the How It Works sections themselves get quite large. Please read them through, though. It's all part of the plan.

There are a lot of what technical writers call forward references in this book. These are where I say 'Don't worry about this difficult concept here. I'll explain it in Chapter *whatever*'. This kind of reckless behavior will preclude me from ever entering the Logical Writers Hall Of Fame, but frankly I don't care. What I do really care about is that you have exciting and interesting programs to play with as early as possible in the book, and to do that, I sometimes have to ask to you to take things on trust. Where I do use language elements that we haven't covered properly yet, I'll tell you. And believe me, they are all there later on, as promised.

At the end of each chapter is a list of my suggestions for ways to put the concepts you've just learned into practice. I've found that the best way to learn is to tinker about on your own, extending current projects and creating new ones. These suggestions are just that—suggestions—so use them if you want. Appendix C contains a list of proposed solutions for the exercises.

When you've finished the book, the one thing you can be sure of is that you'll be hungry for more. You'll have an excellent grounding in Visual Basic, but that's only the beginning. The whole world of Visual Basic development will be at your feet. To help you decide what to do next, I've put some unashamedly personal and opinionated advice into Appendix A -Where To Now? This includes references for further reading should you want to learn more!

Tell Us What You Think

We've worked hard on this book to make it useful. We've tried to understand what you're willing to exchange your hard-earned money for, and we've tried to make the book live up to your expectations.

Please let us know what you think about this book. Tell us what we did wrong, and what we did right. This isn't just marketing flannel: we really do huddle around the email to find out what you think. If you don't believe it, then send us a note. We'll answer, and we'll take whatever you say on board for future editions. The easiest way is to use email:

`feedback@wrox.com`

You can also find more details about Wrox Press on our web site. There, you'll find the code from our latest books, sneak previews of forthcoming titles, and information about the authors and editors. You can order Wrox titles directly from the site, or find out where your nearest local bookstore with Wrox titles is located. The address of our site is:

`http://www.wrox.com`

Customer Support

If you find a mistake, please have a look at the errata page for this book on our web site first. The full URL for the errata page is:

`http://www.wrox.com/Scripts/Errata.idc?Code=0391`

If you can't find an answer there, tell us about the problem and we'll do everything we can to answer promptly!

Just send us an email to `support@wrox.com`.

or fill in the form on our web site: `http://www.wrox.com/Contact.htm`

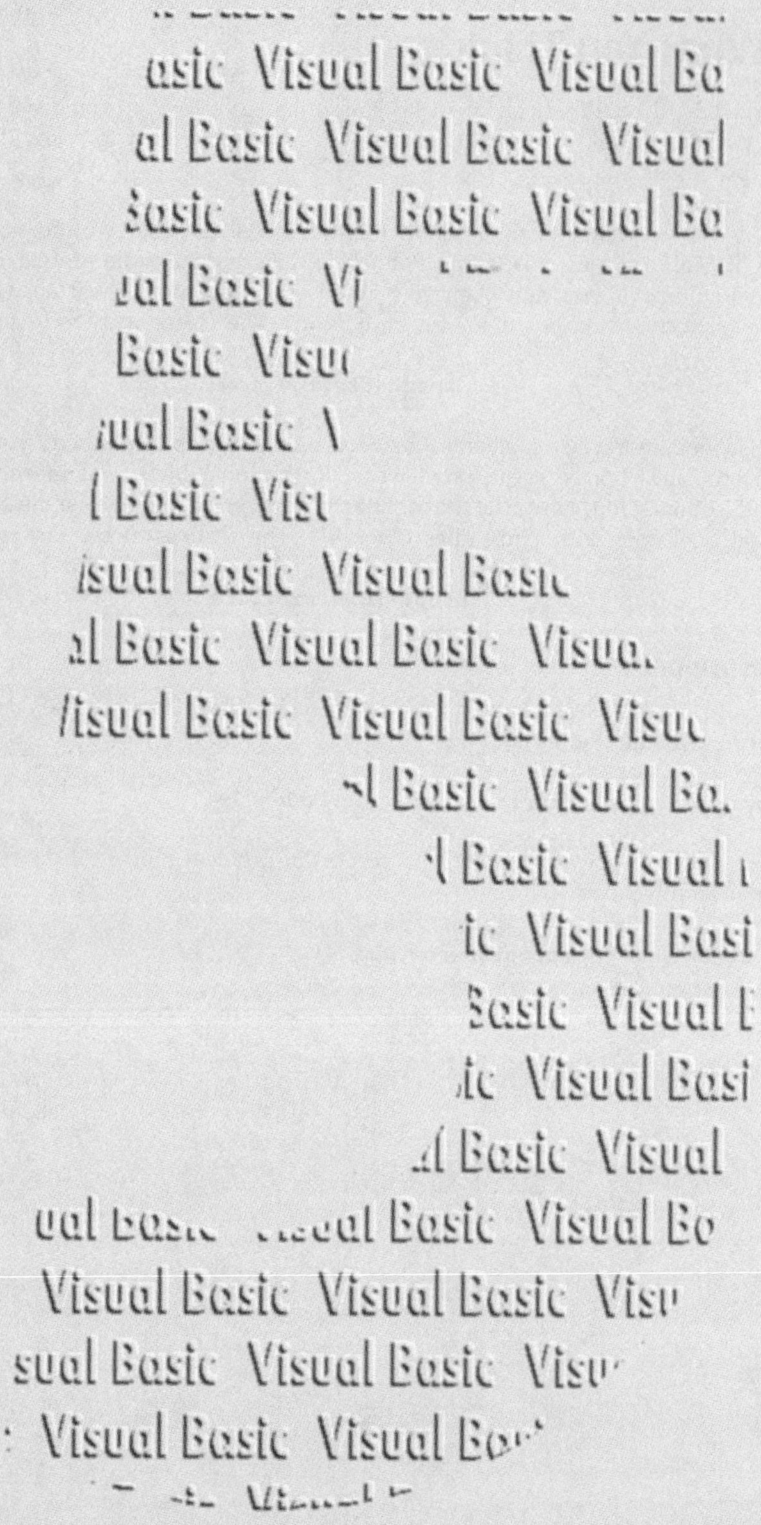

asic Visual Basic Visual Ba
al Basic Visual Basic Visual
Basic Visual Basic Visual Ba
ual Basic Vi
Basic Visu
ual Basic V
l Basic Vis
isual Basic Visual Basic
al Basic Visual Basic Visua
Visual Basic Visual Basic Visu
al Basic Visual Ba
l Basic Visual
ic Visual Basi
Basic Visual B
ic Visual Basi
l Basic Visual
ual Basic Visual Basic Visual Ba
Visual Basic Visual Basic Visu
sual Basic Visual Basic Visu
Visual Basic Visual Ba

Welcome to Visual Basic

As you will hear time and time again in this book and other journals, the best way to learn about something as interactive as Visual Basic is to actually sit down at a computer and try things out. In this chapter we'll kick off by getting comfortable with the Visual Basic environment, and then in the next chapter we'll have a go at creating a complete Visual Basic application from start to finish. The program we'll create will hardly be a program at all, but in experimenting with it you will get an all-round feel for what Visual Basic has to offer.

You'll see what VB5 looks like, and discover some of the ways it makes our life as programmers easier. You will learn how to start a Visual Basic project, save all the components of your program within a project, and get help while working. Along the way we'll look at some of the unique design features that make Visual Basic such an exciting programming tool.

In this chapter, you will learn about:

- The Visual Basic desktop
- How to start creating a program
- How to save and print out a program
- How to get help when using Visual Basic

A Quick Tour of Visual Basic

If you've used an earlier version of Visual Basic then you're in for a real treat. VB5 feels the same in many ways to its predecessors, but looks and performs in radically better ways. In this chapter you'll see just what we mean.

Fasten your seatbelt, we're going on a lightning tour of Visual Basic!

The Opening Visual Basic Screen

When you click the Visual Basic option in your Start menu to load and run Visual Basic, an array of windows, icons and scrollbars appears, overlaying the Windows 95 desktop. On top of that is the New Project dialog. This shows the different types of project that we can build with Visual Basic 5 Enterprise Edition, so don't worry if you have a smaller range of options.

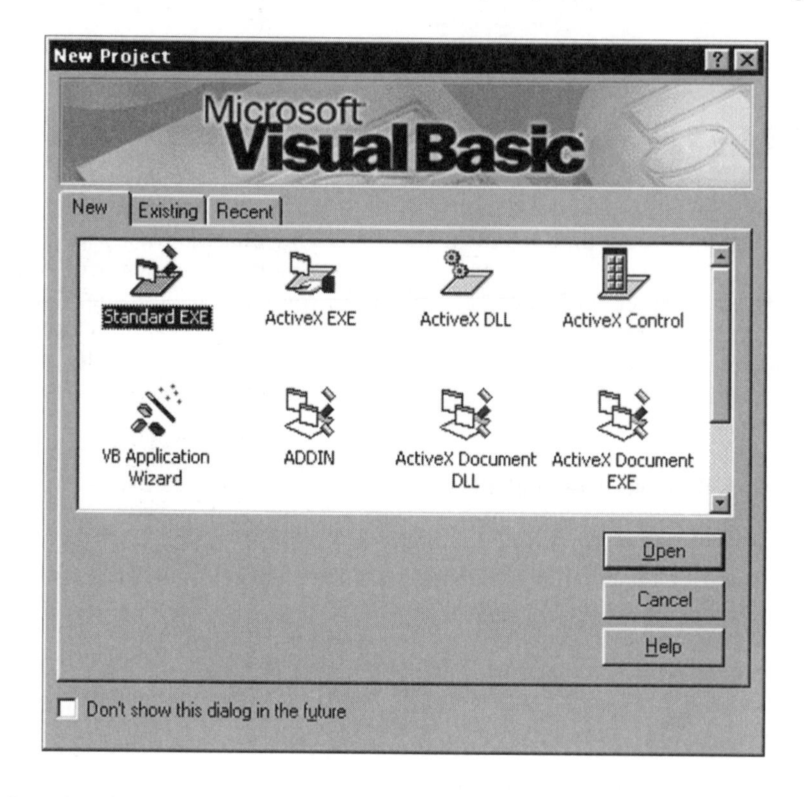

Select the Standard EXE option, this one will quickly become very familiar, and the main VB5 window now contains all the parts that make up the outline of a new program. Open the View menu, and select Code. This opens the window where we would enter the program code that makes our application actually do something useful. Your desktop will now look something like the next screen shot.

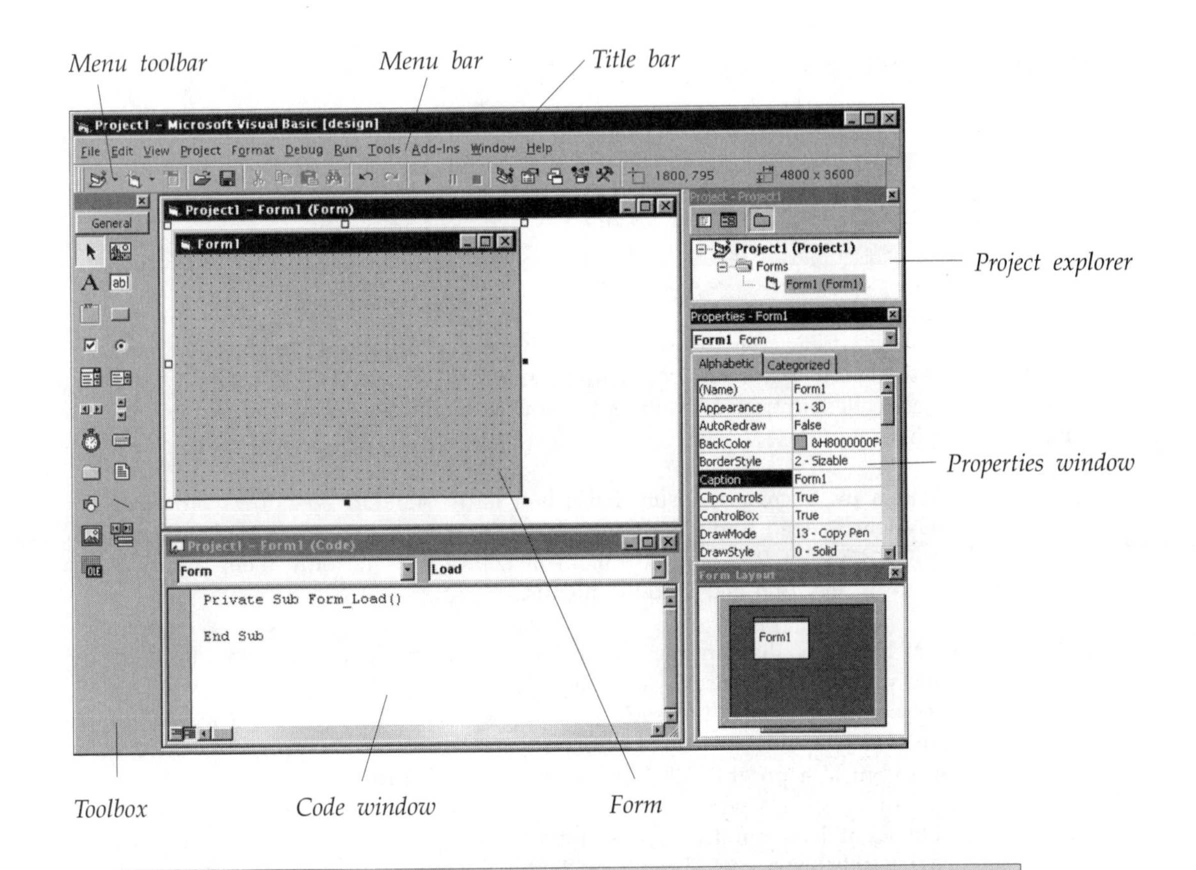

Don't panic if your screen appears different to the one pictured here. Visual Basic remembers how the windows and toolbars were arranged on the screen the last time it was used, and automatically sets itself up in the same way each time you run it.

As you will find out later on in this chapter, there are a great many things you can do to the Visual Basic environment to customize it the way you want it.

If you are used to earlier versions of Visual Basic, you'll also notice that there is a single background window, which contains most of the other windows. This is referred to as a Multiple Document Interface (MDI), and is the default for VB5. In earlier versions of VB you saw each window individually, and your desktop was visible between them—a Single Document Interface (SDI). If you prefer to work in SDI mode, you can select Options *from the* Tools *menu, and turn it on in the* Advanced *tab of the* Options *window. You can also control which windows are docked (i.e. attached to the edges of the main window) in the* Docking *tab of the* Options *dialog.*

Let's take a look at what all these windows and buttons mean.

Visual Basic Menus

At the top of the screen, just as with any other Windows program, you have the title bar and menus.

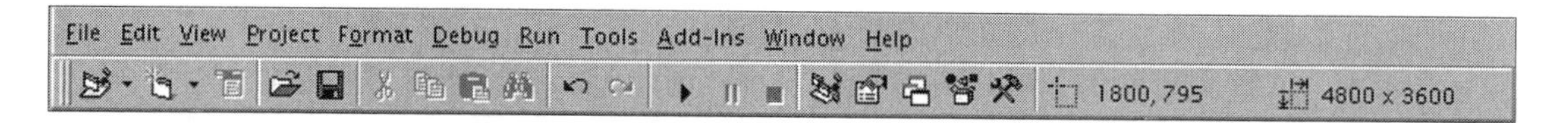

The title bar shows you that you are currently in Microsoft Visual Basic, and reminds you exactly what you are doing. On my screen, and hopefully on yours, the title bar reads Project 1—Microsoft Visual Basic [design]. This means that Visual Basic is currently in design mode of a project called Project 1, waiting for you to begin designing and writing your new Windows program.

Since it was written by Microsoft, Visual Basic is a fairly standard Windows program. The File menu allows you to load and save your work, the Edit menu provides familiar options to cut and paste sections of text, and so on. In fact, probably the only menu headings that appear unfamiliar are the Run and Add-Ins menus.

We'll cover all of the menu headings in detail later on in the book. However, the Add-Ins item is particularly interesting since it illustrates the power of Visual Basic. If you've used Microsoft Access before then you'll already have come across the concept of an add-in: it's a plug-in program which is able to take control of some aspect of the program you're using. In our case an add-in is a program that bolts on to Visual Basic and extends the way in which it works. An important point here is that not only is Visual Basic a powerful, extensible development tool, but that the add-ins that ship with Visual Basic were actually written in Visual Basic themselves. There's no better advertisement for the power of Visual Basic.

All of the menus work just as they would in any other Windows program. If you point at the File menu, for example, and click the left mouse button once, a list of options for dealing with files appears:

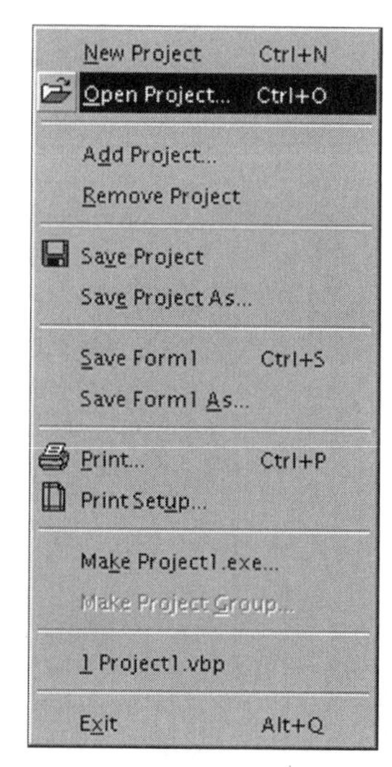

Don't worry too much at the moment about what all the menu headings and options mean—the easiest way to learn Visual Basic is by trying it out. And that's exactly what we're going to do.

The Toolbar

The toolbar is probably a little different in terms of its look and feel to anything you're used to. In the past, Microsoft, being the producers of Windows itself, was typically the one that we would look to, to determine the standards in terms of how our own applications should look and feel.

Visual Basic 5, like Internet Explorer 3.0 and Office 97, doesn't meet traditional guidelines on how a user interface should look and feel. However, Microsoft being Microsoft, this nonstandard behavior isn't too much to worry about. This is in fact Microsoft defining the look and feel of Windows applications in the future. You'll see a lot of things in Visual Basic 5 that just feel a little bit strange compared to earlier Windows applications you've used; these are invariably the changes that are taking place to the user interface standards across the board.

Enough—let's get back to that toolbar.

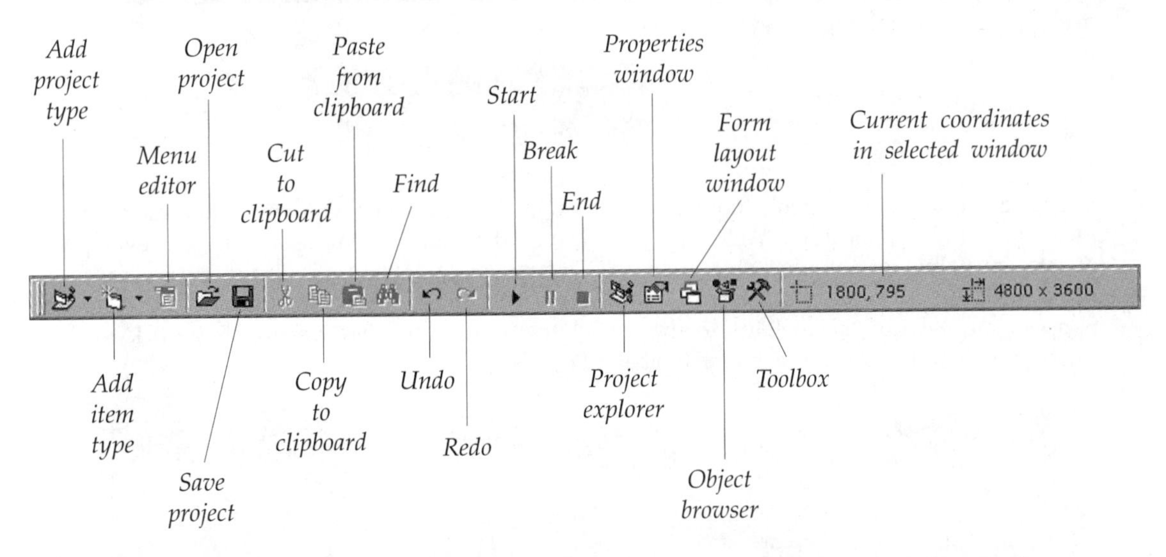

The icons on the toolbar provide an easy way for you to perform common operations without having to plow through the menus. For example, the leftmost icon does the same as the Add Project item on the File menu, while the rightmost icon does the same as Toolbox on the View menu. Again, don't worry too much about what all the buttons mean at this stage; you'll pick them up with ease when we write a simple program later on. For the time being though, you can get a simple explanation of each button by simply leaving the cursor over a button for a few seconds: a standard Windows tooltip pops up telling you what the button does.

Just to confuse matters though, this isn't the only toolbar that Visual Basic provides you with. If you take a quick peek at the View menu, you'll see an item there called Toolbars (strange that). Click on this and a submenu appears showing you a list of all the toolbars that are available from within Visual Basic.

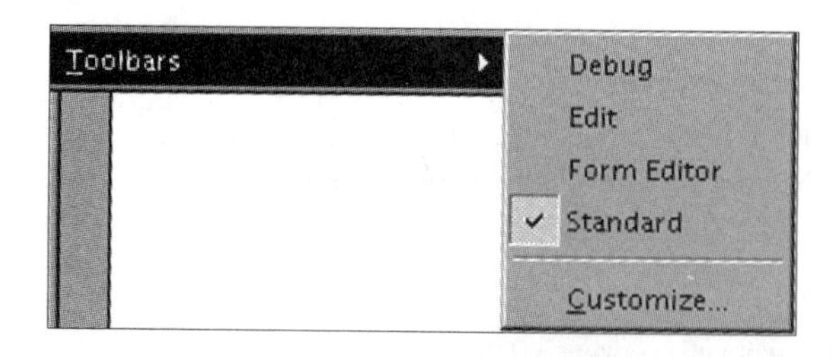

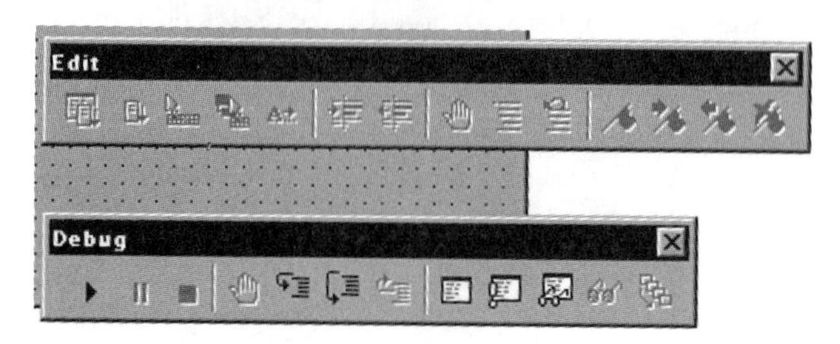

If you select all the of the items on this submenu, with the exception of Customize, then you should find yourself looking at three new windows floating around your desktop, each containing a new toolbar.

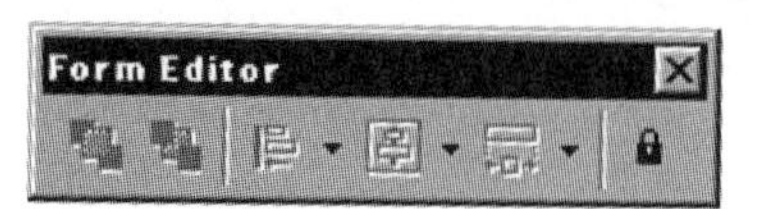

But hang on a minute! Aren't toolbars supposed to be something you find underneath the menu bar of an application? Well, traditionally yes they are, but more and more developers of late are going for this dockable approach—all the best toolbars are doing it this season.

Simply drag each of the toolbars to the top of the screen and, hey presto, they dock to the existing toolbar to produce a mega toolbar like this.

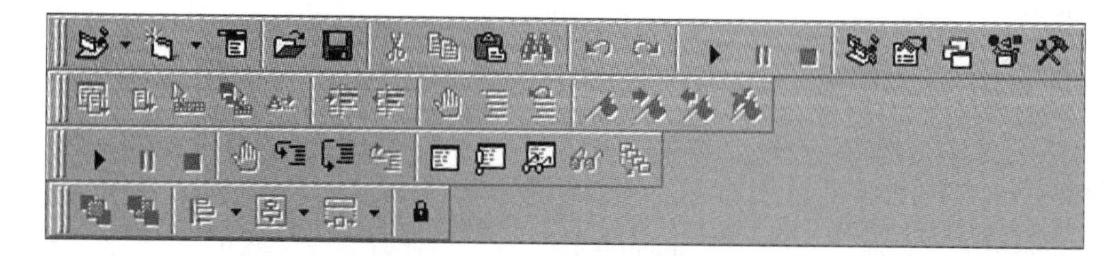

Notice that to the left of each line of icons there is a double bar. This is the drag point of the new format Windows toolbars. You can click and drag this double bar to slide the buttons left and right, as well as to move toolbars underneath other toolbars... it's tricky to explain and a lot easier to get the hang of yourself if you just go point and click for a while. Enjoy yourself!

Forms

In the center of the screen there is a blank window entitled Form1.

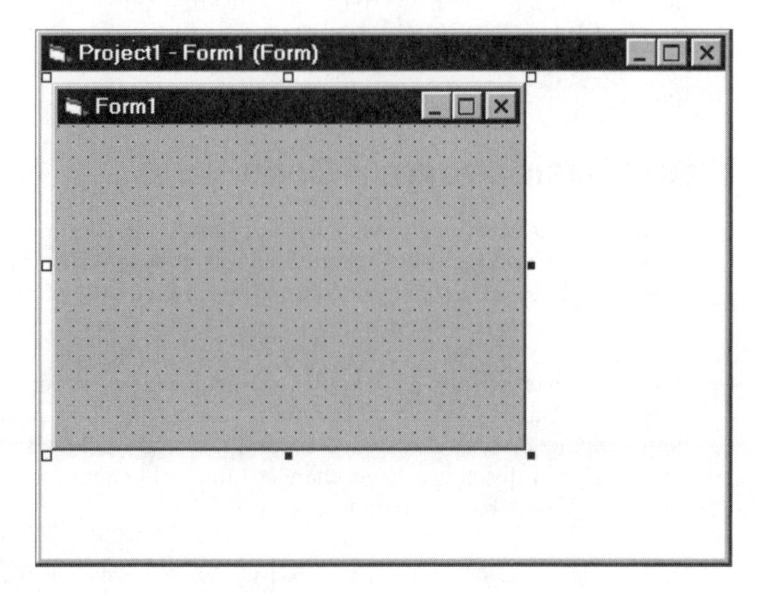

Forms are central to everything you do in Visual Basic. When your program is running, the user sees the forms as normal windows. In these windows the user selects menu options, clicks icons that you have drawn, or enters data into text boxes you have arranged.

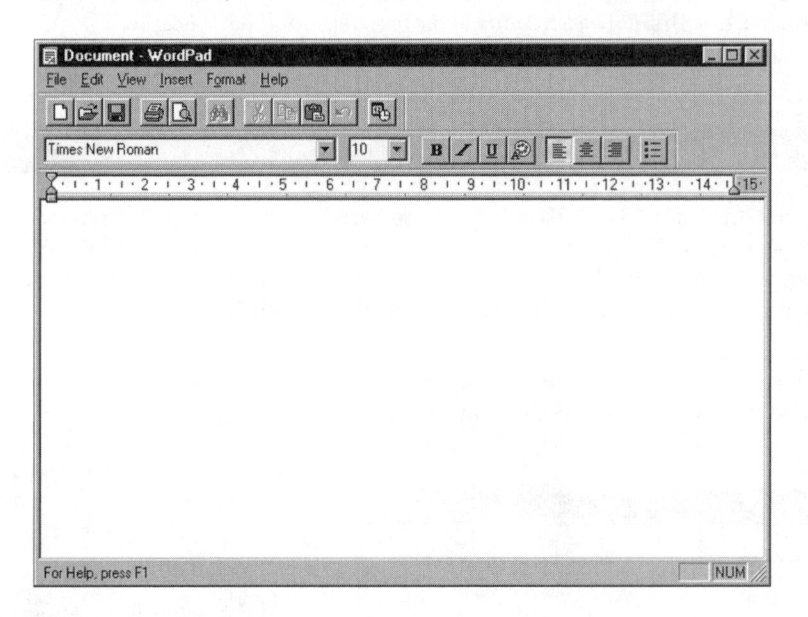

The window in which this typical application operates is derived from a form. It's your job as a programmer to get to such a point from the blank form you see on your screen.

We can compare the process of writing a Visual Basic program to the job of an artist. The artist starts with a blank piece of canvas. In our case this would be the form. The artist, equipped with a palette of different colors and brushes, then begins to lay down images on his canvas. In the same way, Visual Basic programmers lay down **controls**, such as command buttons, text boxes and so on, on to their 'canvas'—the form. When the work is complete, the artist exhibits his masterpiece to a waiting public who sees not a canvas sheet, but a painting. When the Visual Basic programs are complete, they are shipped to the user who sees the elements of a Windows application and not empty and confusing Visual Basic forms.

Visual Basic Program Code

There are two sides to forms: what appears in the Form window and what does not appear. Your user sees and interacts with the visible aspect. The invisible aspect is the form **code.** This is program text that you enter to tell the computer exactly what you want the program to do.

If you've never written a computer program before, code is the collection of English-like commands that tell the computer what to do step-by-step. In the past, programmers spent hours keying in page after page of program code before seeing anything actually work on screen. Thankfully, times have changed and the amount of traditional coding required in writing a Visual Basic program is very small.

If you've already come across other programming languages, such as C, Pascal or even the original BASIC, then you are in for an easy ride. The Visual Basic language is really a hybrid of these languages incorporating many of their best features, as well as features from older languages such as Algol and Fortran. However, the strongest influence in Visual Basic is, as its name suggests, the BASIC programming language. If you've already come across BASIC, the structure of the programs we'll write later on will appear very familiar, even if the commands themselves look somewhat alien.

Try It Out - Viewing the Code Window

As you saw when we first fired up Visual Basic, the Code window is missing from your screen by default. It doesn't normally appear immediately when you start Visual Basic, and we had to use the View menu to make it appear. There are three other methods by which you can achieve this; it's useful to know all of them, so we'll try each in turn.

1 Move the mouse over the form on your screen, and double-click the left mouse button. Once you've examined it, close the window using the far right button.

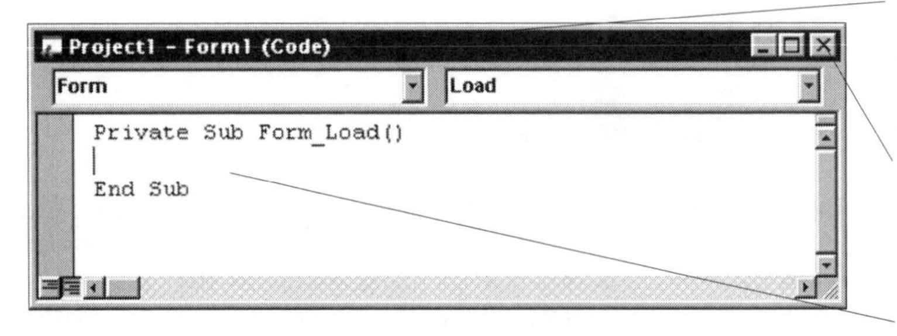

The code window will appear for whatever control or form you select, in this case your form labeled Form1.

Close the window by clicking the Close button in the top right corner of the window, or by pressing Alt-F4.

You type in code here.

2 You can also use function keys to open and close the code window. Move the mouse to the control or form whose code window you want to look at, and click the left mouse button once to select it, then press *F7*. Once again close the code window.

3 Or you can even use the Project Explorer to bring up the code window: if the Project Explorer isn't visible, select Project from the View menu. (The letter 'P' is the hotkey for that option.) When it appears, click on the name of your form once, and then click on the View Code command button. Once again, the code window pops into view.

View Code button

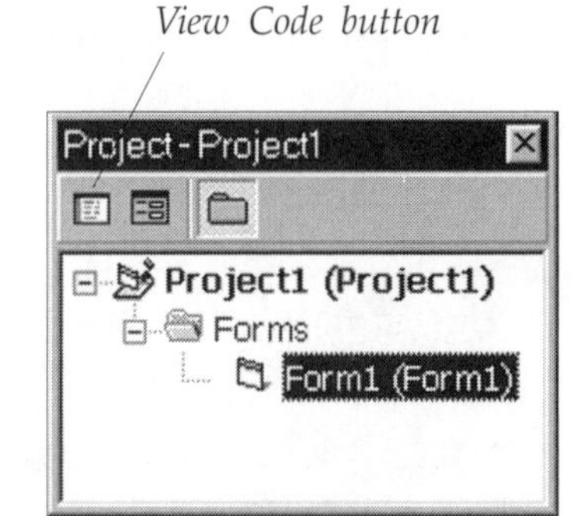

Notice how the title bar shows the name of the form you are writing code for.

Directly beneath the title bar are two list boxes showing specifically which area of the form this piece of code refers to.

Project1 - Form1 (Code)

Form | Load

```
Private Sub Form_Load()

End Sub
```

The two icons at the bottom left corner of the code window allow you to change just how much program code you see at any one time. The left button, the Procedure view button, limits the code displayed to just the section of code that you are working on. The right button, the Module view button, changes the code window so that it shows you all the code that relates to the form that you are working on—more on this later.

There's a lot more to the code window than you can see here. In previous versions of Visual Basic, programmers would type code into the code window and probably have a Visual Basic help file opened in the background so that they could keep on looking up the spelling of commands that they type, and the various ways in which they are used.

A lot of people complained that this way of working was slowing them down, and short of learning every single command and nuance of Visual Basic by heart, was there anything Microsoft could do to fix this? The solution was to add a number of pop-up windows to the code window. When you type code now, VB will actually pop up windows showing you the correct use of the commands you're typing, and even finish off typing those commands for you. This can be a godsend, even though the first reaction of many (including me) was to turn them off.

More on this later—remember, this is a whirlwind tour.

Controls and the Toolbox

The next stop on our whirlwind tour of the Visual Basic environment is the toolbox.

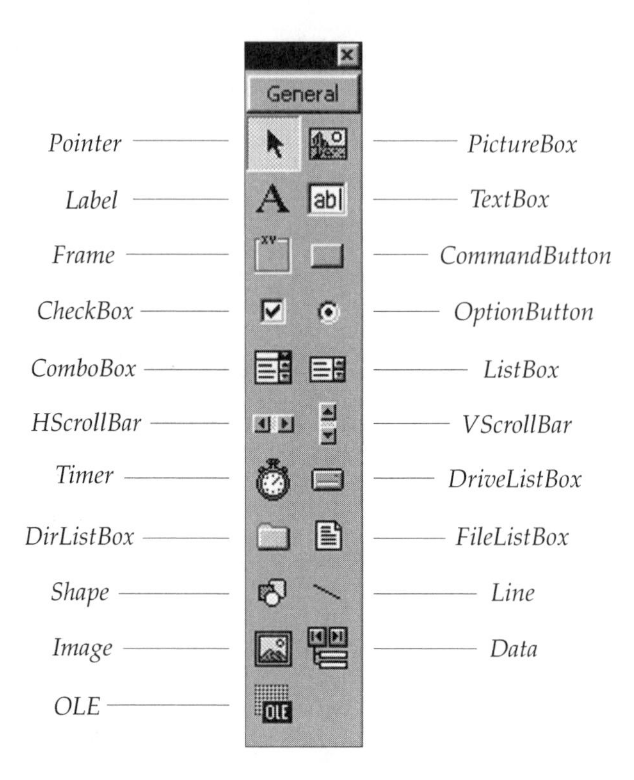

The toolbox contains icons for each control you can draw on your form. Controls put the **Visual** into Visual Basic. You use controls in Windows all the time: typing into text boxes, clicking option buttons and so on. In fact, almost every functional element of a Windows program is a control.

Each control, such as a text box or command button, has four aspects to it:

- A **graphical representation** that you see when you click on an icon in the toolbox and then place the control on to your form.
- **Properties** which govern the way it looks and behaves, determining for example its color, shape, size, the text that appears as a caption, and so on.
- **Methods**, which are code routines hidden away inside the control, and which can make it do something such as add items to a list box.
- **Events**, which are Visual Basic routines where you enter code to tell a control what to do when it is clicked, moved or dragged over.

Adding Controls Adds Power

If you're using either the Professional or Enterprise Editions of Visual Basic, you may find that there are a great many more icons in your tool palette than in the above screenshot. Enhanced 3D versions of many of the standard controls will be included, as will be controls for drawing graphs, playing sampled sounds, communicating over modems, animating icons and many more. However, we're going to concentrate on the Learning Edition. I also say 'may find' more controls, rather than 'will find' more controls, because like many other aspects of Visual Basic, the toolbox is totally customizable. More on this throughout the rest of the book.

One of the strongest features of Visual Basic is the way in which you can heighten its capabilities through the addition of more powerful controls. Controls that you add to the standard toolbox are known as **custom controls**, or ActiveX controls. In the early versions of Visual Basic the extension controls were known as VBXs. These VBX controls only really supported 16-bit development environments though, so when Microsoft released a 32-bit version of Visual Basic (VB4), the OCX standard was introduced. Due to internal politics though, OCXs have since been renamed ActiveX controls.

Many companies supply custom controls that greatly enhance Visual Basic. There are ready-built controls available which can achieve almost any kind of task, from displaying graphs to handling email and web pages—and once you master VB programming you can even write your own! Adding these controls to your project makes additional icons appear in the toolbox. The range of controls available is staggering, with companies supplying ActiveX controls to do everything from providing enhanced database support, to printing barcodes, or displaying the latest type of graphics file. Take a look at the toolbox below. This has a number of controls which aren't included with either the Learning or Professional Editions of Visual Basic.

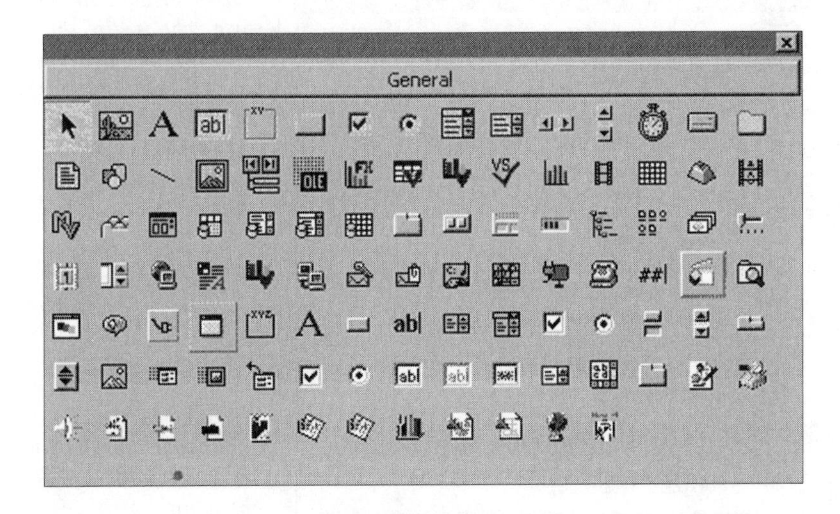

This is the full suite of controls and objects included with Visual Basic Enterprise edition. It's important to realize that the palette can contain not only ActiveX controls, but also objects from other programs, such as the Excel chart and Sheet icons on the bottom row.

As you can see, there's a strong chance that, as you add more and more controls and objects to the palette, sooner or later you're going to end up with one almighty mess which is very hard to navigate around.

Thankfully, Microsoft saw this problem coming. By right clicking your mouse over the palette a pop-up menu appears. Using this you can add new tabs to the top of the palette and then start to categorize your components a little better. Take a look at this.

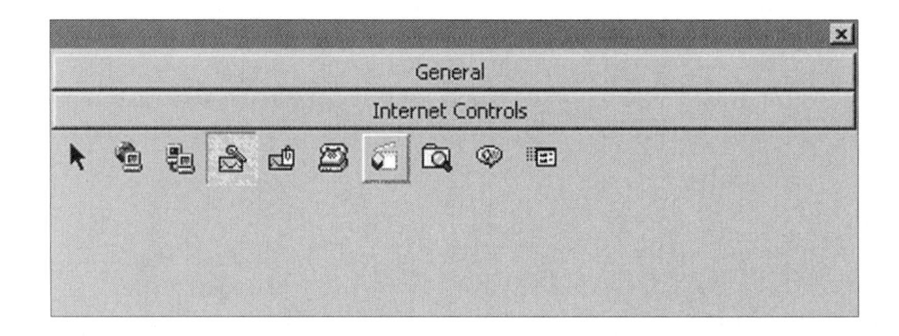

As we work through the examples in the book we'll come across places where the standard controls that Visual Basic puts into your palette just aren't up to the job in hand. At that point you will learn a little about adding tabs to your palette and adding controls and objects to the palette from the selection that all versions of Visual Basic kindly hide out of sight from you at startup.

The Project Explorer

To understand how useful the **Project Explorer** is you need to understand what makes up a project in Visual Basic.

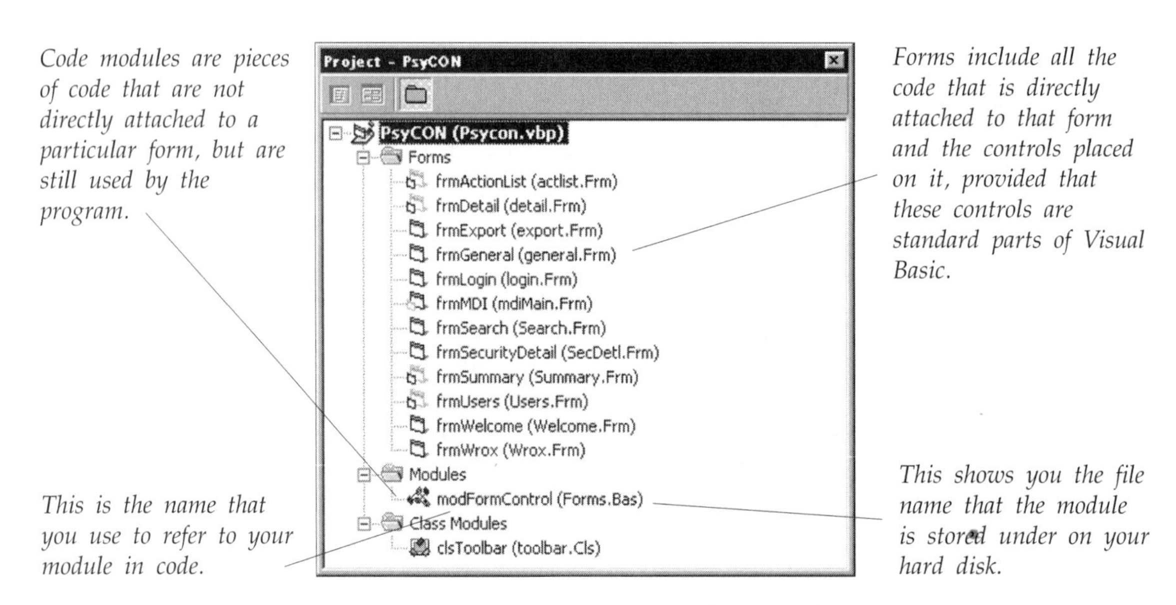

A project is a collection of forms, code modules and class modules (or classes). We've loosely covered what forms and code modules are, but class modules? Sounds ugly....

Class modules are one of the most important features of Visual Basic, introduced in version 4 to try to bring Visual Basic into the fabled realm of object-oriented development. We cover this whole area in a lot more detail in Chapter 7, but for the time being, think of a class as a template—a stencil if you like. You can even think of a class as being like a recipe, with which users can create the same chocolate cake over and over again.

It all sounds pretty horrific I know, but, as you'll see, it can be a great aid in simplifying your code and the problems your code is designed to solve.

Each form, code module or class module is stored on the hard disk as a separate file with its own file name. In addition, each module, class and form can have a different name that you use to refer to it in code. You can see this in our screenshot of the Project Explorer. The highlighted line shows the project file itself, with a filename of **`Psycon.vbp`**. Remember, everything—forms, modules, even the project itself—is considered an object in Visual Basic, in the same way that you might consider a button an object, or a list box an object... mind blowing huh?

The Project Explorer simply shows you a list of all the files in your project. By double clicking the name of a form in the Project Explorer, the form appears on screen. By highlighting a form in the Project Explorer and hitting the top left button—the View Code button—the form's code appears on screen.

In keeping with the Windows 95 standard, you can also select a file in the Project Explorer and press the right mouse button to bring up a menu with a range of options. This allows you to choose what you want to see, whether or not you want to save the file, remove it from the project and so on. Try it here and on other areas of the Visual Basic environment to see what I mean.

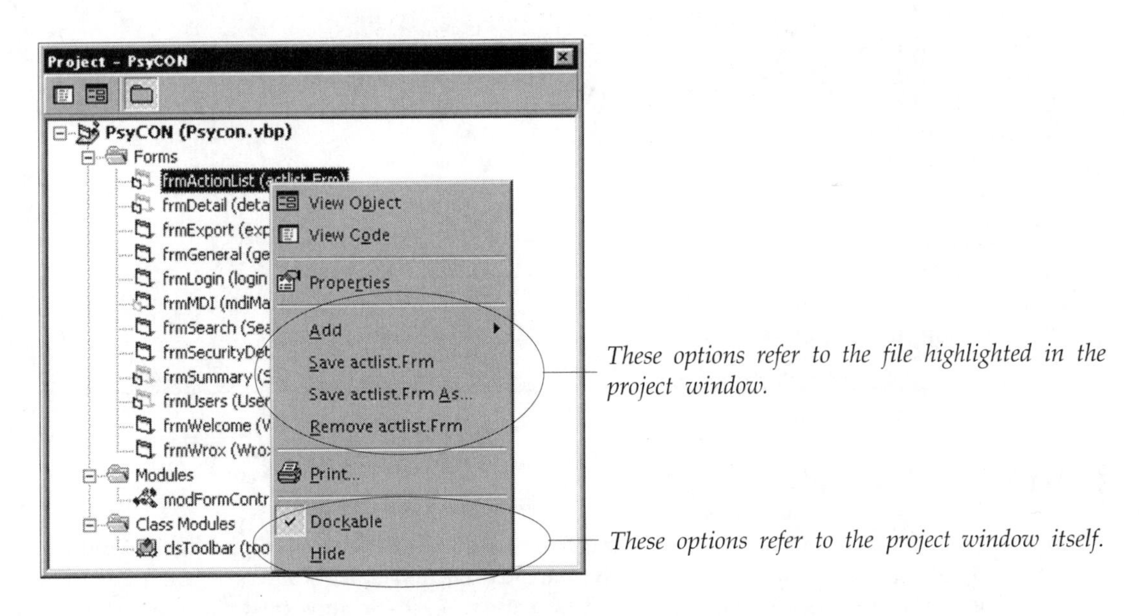

The Project VBP File

The Project Explorer is really a viewer for a file on your hard disk with the extension VBP. This is the Visual Basic **Project** file and tells Visual Basic that forms, modules and so on are used in your project. The project's file name can be anything you want, but it normally ends in the letters `.vbp`. It still works OK if you call it something else, but that seems a great way to sow the seeds of total confusion to me.

The file itself is a straight text file that contains the settings for all the environment variables and file names for the complete project, though you don't need to change it because VB looks after it by itself. It doesn't contain the actual project files in the way that say an Access MDB file does. You can open up a VBP file in Notepad and take a look. However, if you play with the settings and crash the system then that's your own fault.

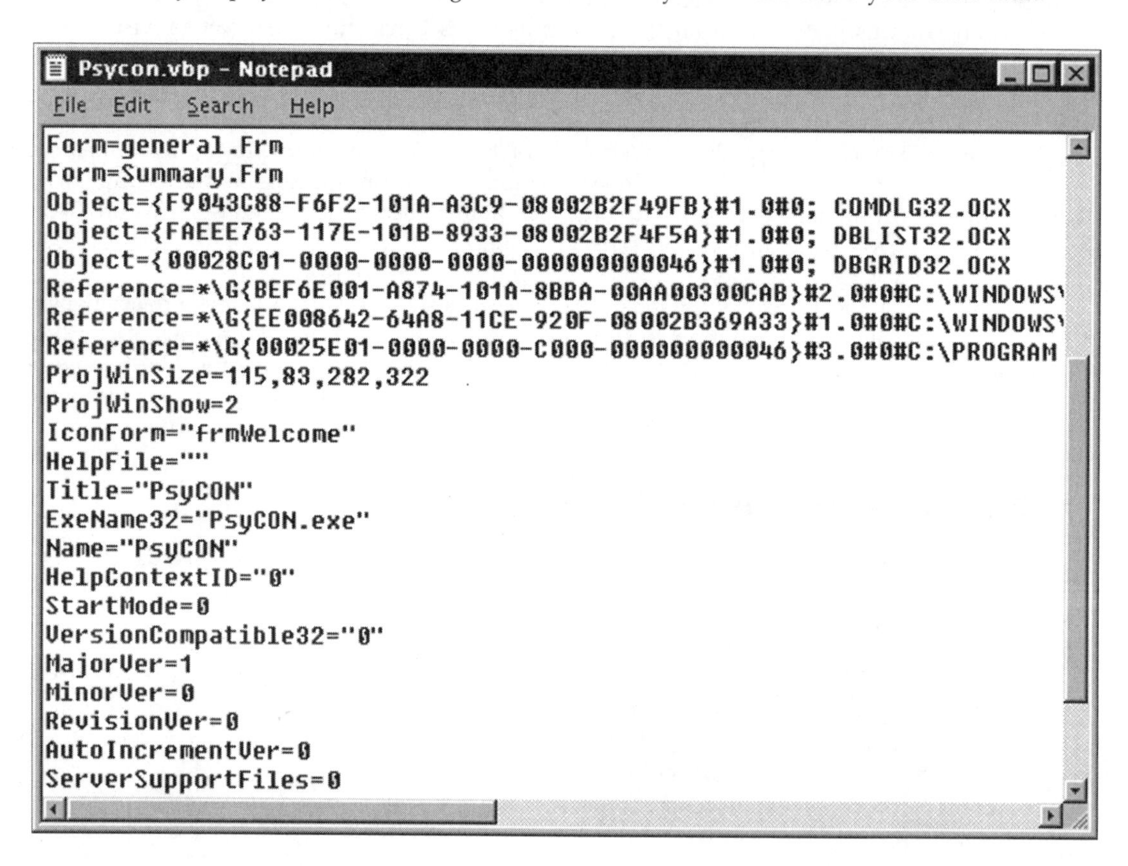


```
Form=general.Frm
Form=Summary.Frm
Object={F9043C88-F6F2-101A-A3C9-08002B2F49FB}#1.0#0; COMDLG32.OCX
Object={FAEEE763-117E-101B-8933-08002B2F4F5A}#1.0#0; DBLIST32.OCX
Object={00028C01-0000-0000-0000-000000000046}#1.0#0; DBGRID32.OCX
Reference=*\G{BEF6E001-A874-101A-8BBA-00AA00300CAB}#2.0#0#C:\WINDOWS\
Reference=*\G{EE008642-64A8-11CE-920F-08002B369A33}#1.0#0#C:\WINDOWS\
Reference=*\G{00025E01-0000-0000-C000-000000000046}#3.0#0#C:\PROGRAM
ProjWinSize=115,83,282,322
ProjWinShow=2
IconForm="frmWelcome"
HelpFile=""
Title="PsyCON"
ExeName32="PsyCON.exe"
Name="PsyCON"
HelpContextID="0"
StartMode=0
VersionCompatible32="0"
MajorVer=1
MinorVer=0
RevisionVer=0
AutoIncrementVer=0
ServerSupportFiles=0
```

Running Your Programs

Having had a quick look around, it's time to see just how easy it is to produce Windows programs using Visual Basic. In fact, we've already written a working program without doing anything. Seeing how we can run it is a great start for subsequent chapters when we write real Visual Basic programs.

The forms we use in our programs are not actually the passive background canvases that our earlier painting analogy suggested. With a multitude of different properties that can be manipulated, and a host of events to respond to, they are the foundation of your program. In the next chapter, we'll get a glimpse of what forms can do. For now, we're just going to see what the default form looks like.

Try It Out - Running a Form

1 If you don't currently have Visual Basic running, start it now by selecting it from the Windows 95 Start Menu, and select the Standard EXE project in the New Project window. (If you intend to work a lot with Visual Basic then it may be a good idea to make a shortcut to it on the Windows 95 desktop—consult the Windows 95 manuals or online help for information on how to do this.)

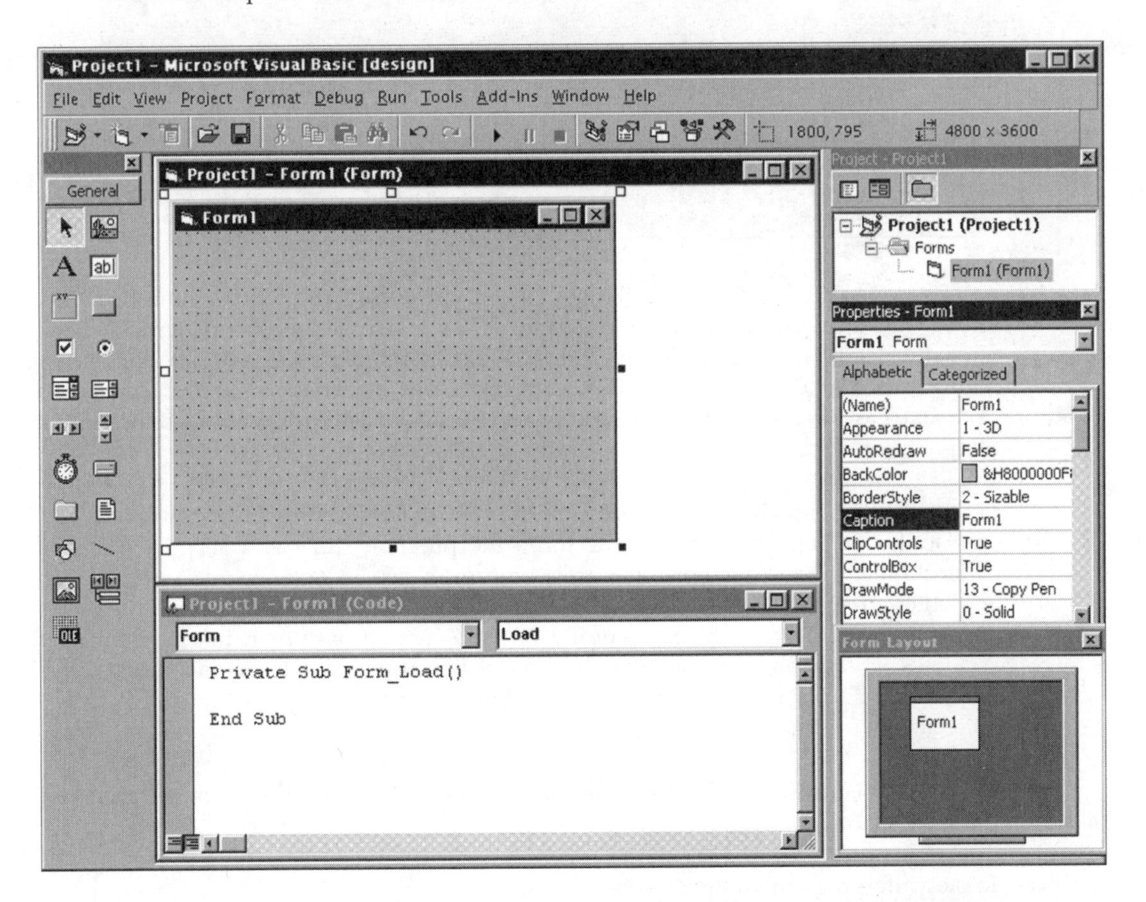

2 Although the form you work with in Visual Basic at design time is supposed to closely resemble the form in the final program, the reality is somewhat different. To see this, run the current project by doing one of the following:

- Either: Hit *F5*
- Or: Click on the Start button in the toolbar
- Or: Select Start from the Run menu

After a short pause the program will run and the main form will be displayed.

At this stage you'll notice three things. First of all the window looks almost identical to the way the form looks when you're in design mode, except the pattern of dots normally displayed over the form in design mode has vanished, and the border that normally surrounds the window in design mode has vanished. Secondly, the title bar of Visual Basic has now changed to show Microsoft Visual Basic [run] to indicate that the program is running.

The third difference is a little more subtle: even though we haven't written any code, or placed anything functional on the form, the program still has a surprising amount of functionality. You can move and resize the form just as you would a window in any other program. You can also click the minimize and maximize buttons in the top right corner of the form to dramatically increase its size or turn it into an icon on the Windows 95 taskbar. Also, clicking the control box in the top left corner brings up the standard Windows control menu, allowing you to quit the application, switch to a different one or again change the size of the window.

To write an equivalent program in a language such as C would require in excess of 150 lines of code.

3 To stop the program running, either:

- Click the End icon in the Visual Basic toolbar
- Close the window by clicking the close button in the top right corner
- Press *Alt-F4*

- Or select End from the Run menu

Although the program hardly seems worth the effort at this stage, you've actually accomplished what would take a C programmer hundreds of lines of code and hours of leafing through extremely technical documentation to accomplish. However, if this was a big project, say a customer order database or the next best-selling Windows game, you would probably want to think about saving your hard work to disk before something nasty happens and you lose the lot. Let's see how you can do this....

Saving Your Work

We've already looked at projects and seen how they contain the names of the files and modules that make up your application. How do these forms and modules get given file names, and how does your project get a file name?

Saving Your Project

As with most other Windows programs, Visual Basic has a File menu that contains the menu items to let you load and save. In addition, there is a Save Project button on the toolbar.

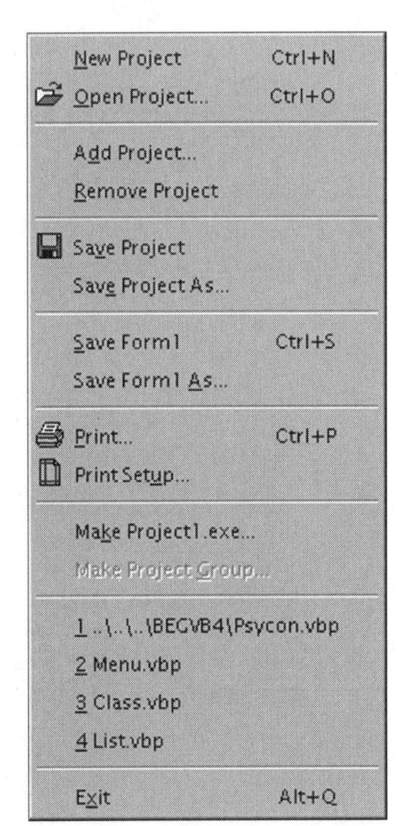

This allows you to save your work quickly at any point without having to fumble about with the menus. Take a look at Visual Basic's File menu.

Notice how many options there are to load, open or save something. Normally you would just use the Save Project menu item to save all your forms, including the properties such as position, size, color and so on, along with all your program code.

Try It Out - Saving Your Project

We'll now save the default project that Visual Basic has created for us, though it's unlikely we'll want to use it later! However, it shows you how we go about saving our projects.

1 Click on the Save Project menu item and a file dialog box will appear asking you to give your form a file name.

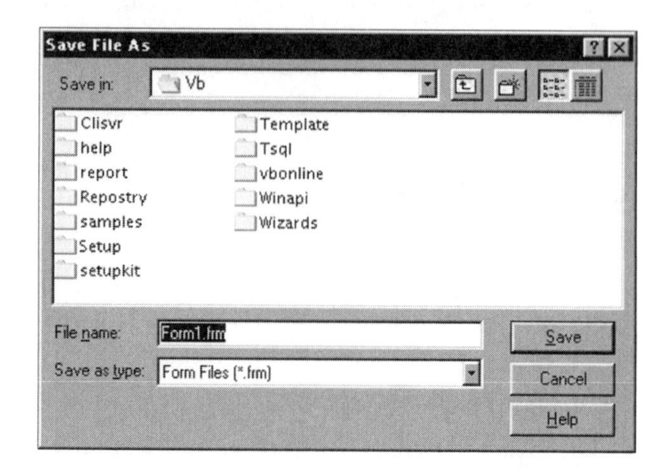

If you have more than one form or code module in a project, Visual Basic will put up a file dialog box for each one and display a name it thinks might be suitable for the form or module. If you want to change the name, click in the File name text box and type in an alternative.

2 Change the name of your form now. Click in the File name text box and enter **Firstfrm**. Don't worry about putting **.frm** after the name, as Visual Basic will do that for you if you don't provide a file extension yourself.

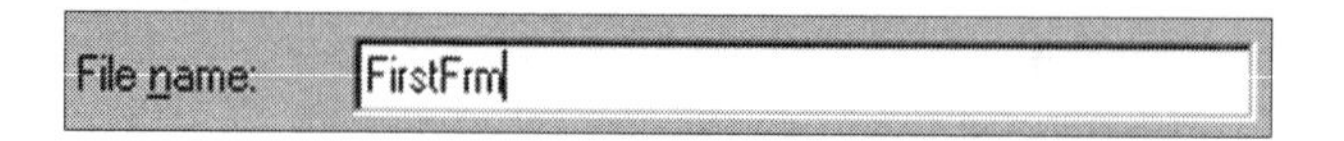

3 When you're happy with the file name for your form and the directory it will be stored in, click on the Save button. Visual Basic will now display a file dialog box for your project. This allows you to give a name to the project as a whole.

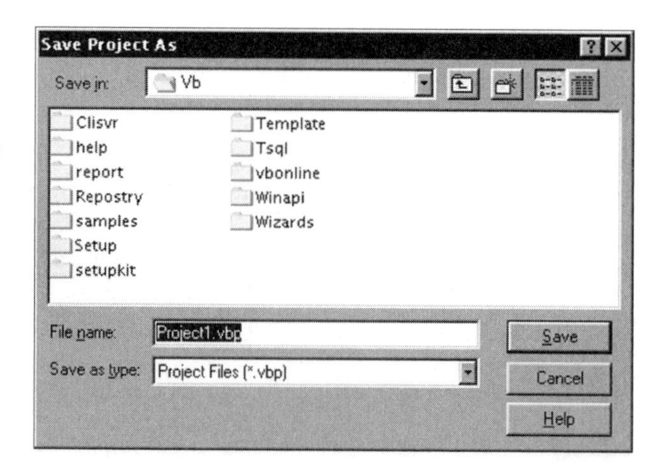

4 Visual Basic links the file names of your forms into your project, so that when you load up a project it automatically knows what all your forms and modules are called and where they are stored on your computer. Once a project has been set up, you can load and save all the components of your program in one go. For now just type in **`FirstPrg`** as the name of the project.

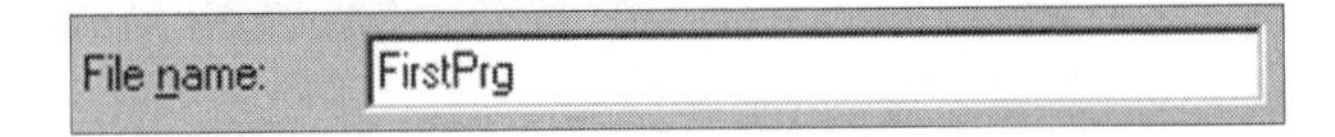

As with the form, Visual Basic will automatically tack a **`.vbp`** bit to the name. When you're happy, click on the Save button to go ahead and save the project.

5 Take a look at your File menu again. At the bottom of the menu you will now see the name of your project. This makes it very quick and easy to re-load your work whenever you come into Visual Basic—Visual Basic automatically remembers the names of the last four projects that you worked on.

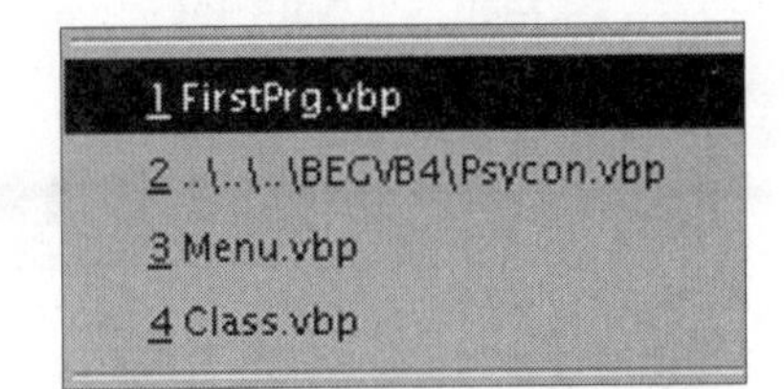

Once you've named all the forms and code modules in your project, saving your work becomes a much simpler task.

6 Try moving the form somewhere else on the screen and then reselect the Save Project menu item. You should notice the disk light come on for a short period of time, but this time Visual Basic won't show you any file dialog boxes. The reason for this is simple: as far as Visual Basic is concerned you've already named your constituent files, so it can just go away and resave them all with the names you set previously.

The next item on the menu is Save Project As.... *If you have previously saved your project, this enables you to rename it. Be careful though—all you're renaming is the project itself (the* **`.vbp`** *file that Visual Basic loads which contains a list of all your forms and code modules). You aren't renaming the forms or code modules themselves. Personally, I've never found a realistic use for this particular menu item, but no doubt somebody among us will need it.*

Ready-Made Projects

Until the release of Visual Basic 5, we were stuck with a product seriously lacking in wizards when compared to the rest of the Microsoft flock. Visual C++ programmers for example have app wizards and class wizards. Access developers have form wizards, table wizards and query wizards. Even Word has more wizards in one place than Stonehenge on a summer solstice.

Thankfully, VB5 has loads of wizards. So, just what is a wizard? Well, it's basically an electronic assistant. You tell them, simply of course, what you want, and they go away do it for you. It gives you the freedom to become a programming prima donna: 'No, let him draw the menu and toolbar again... I'm an artist!'

Try It Out - The Application Wizard

By far the biggest and best wizard in VB5 (we'll cover the others through the course of the book, don't worry) is the Application Wizard. We'll see what it can do.

1 From the File menu select New Project. When the project type dialog appears, rather than selecting the dreary drab Standard EXE, be daring. Click on the VB Application Wizard.

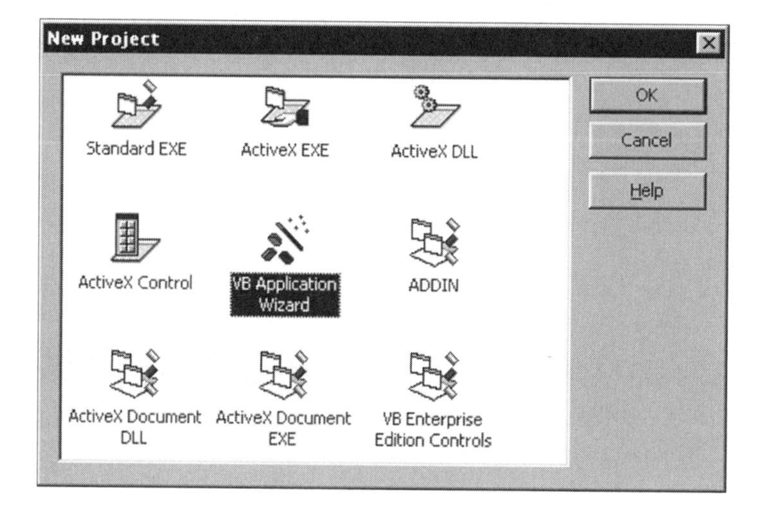

Depending on which version of Visual Basic 5 you have (i.e. Learning Edition, Enterprise Edition or Professional Edition), you might get less or more options than you see in this New Project Dialog, so don't worry if some seem to be missing from your own New Project Dialog.

2 The Application Wizard, in a nutshell, builds a complete skeleton of an application for you. The first time you run it, you'll get the usual friendly greeting that most wizards give, before it gets down to the serious business of coding magic. Click Next to move on.

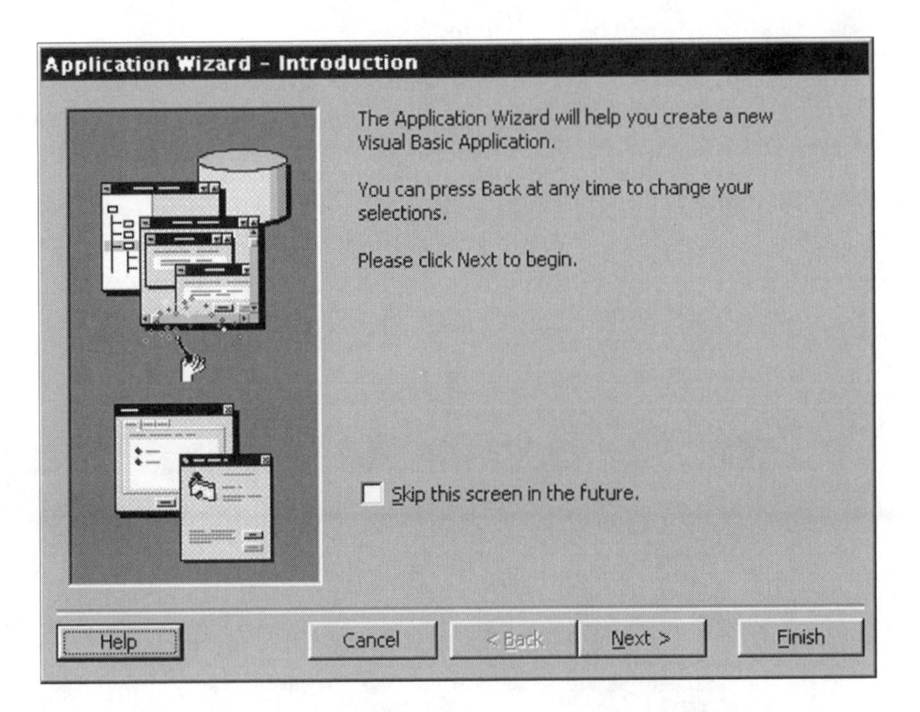

3 The next stage is to select what kind of user interface you want. For now leave it on Multiple Document Interface and click Next.

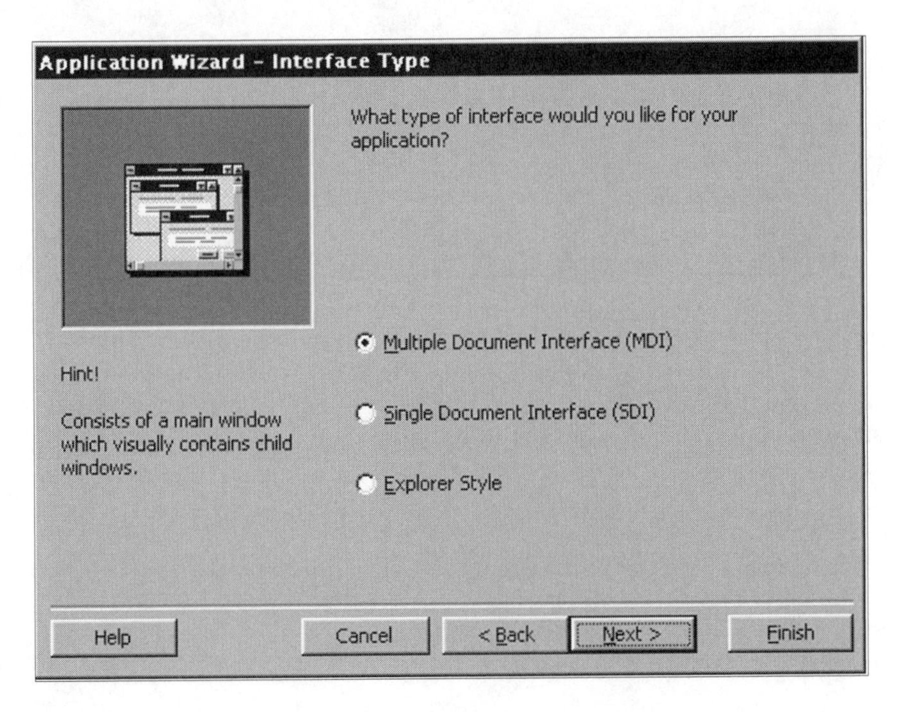

Multiple Document Interface is the same style of user interface as we find by default in VB5, with one large window being home to a number of smaller, child windows. Single Document Interface applications consist of nothing more than a single form with some controls laid on to give the user some functionality. Explorer Style applications look just like Windows file explorer; one window split in two, usually with documents, data and the like on the right, with lists on the left.

4 The next stage is to select what menus you want in your application. Of course, Visual Basic lets you create menus by hand yourself, but the wizard can add any or all of the standard Microsoft menus to your app in seconds without you lifting a finger. Again, leave the settings where they are and click on the Next button.

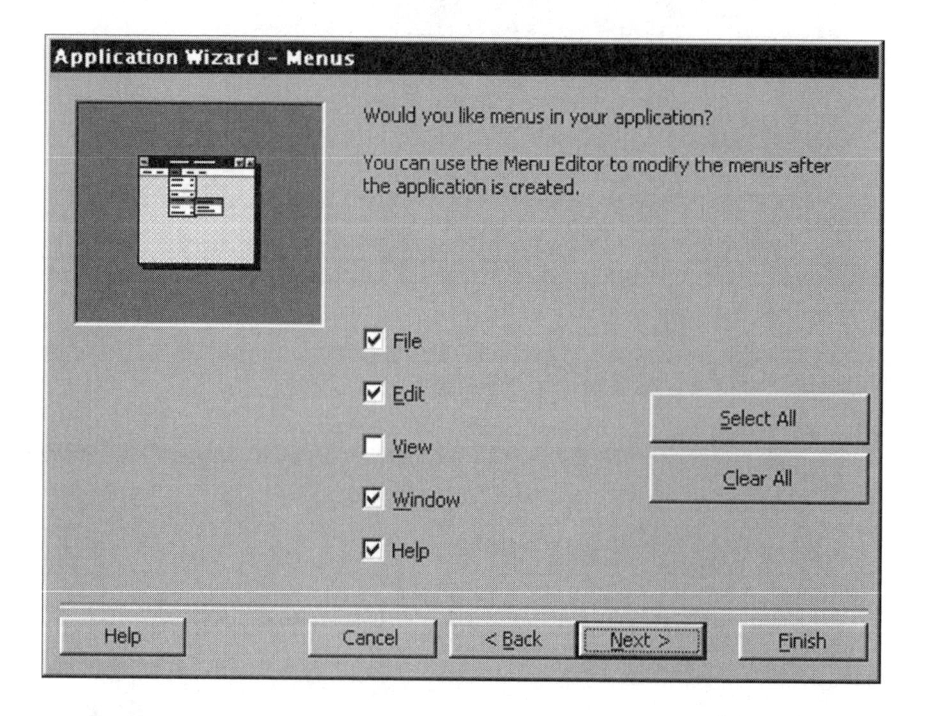

5 The next view asks about resource files. These really aren't within the scope of this book, but are covered in the next volume. Basically, you can store things such as sounds, graphics and text strings in files which you 'bind' to your application when you compile it. For now just click Next again.

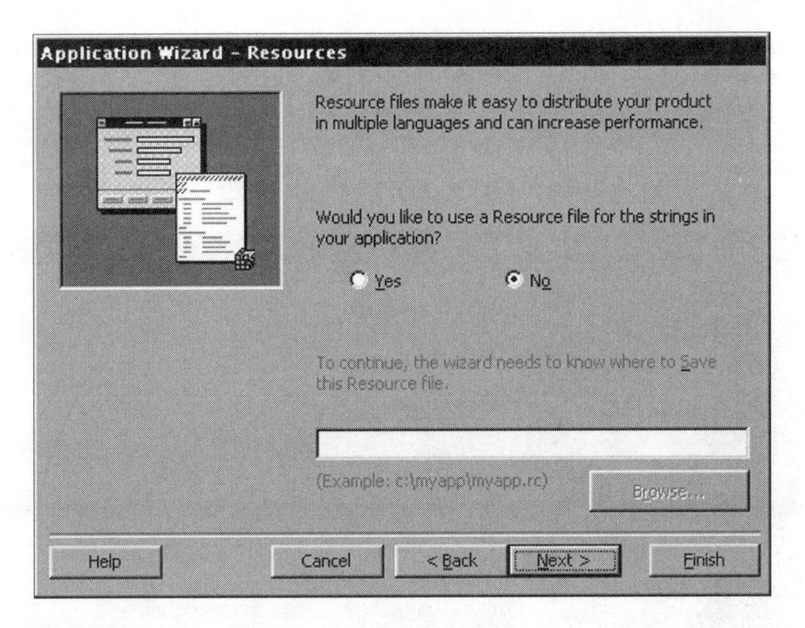

Using strings in a resource file whenever you want to display some text is very handy if you're developing software for an international market. Changing the language of the application is as simple as bolting on a new resource file.

6 In an Internet-enabled world, everyone will have a modem and a net account. In fact it's approaching that now with literally millions of people using their Windows PCs to connect to the Internet. With this in mind Microsoft has included an Internet browser option in the wizard so that your users can have access to your Internet web pages and support pages without ever having to leave your application. Pretty neat, huh? We'll take that. Select Yes and then click Next.

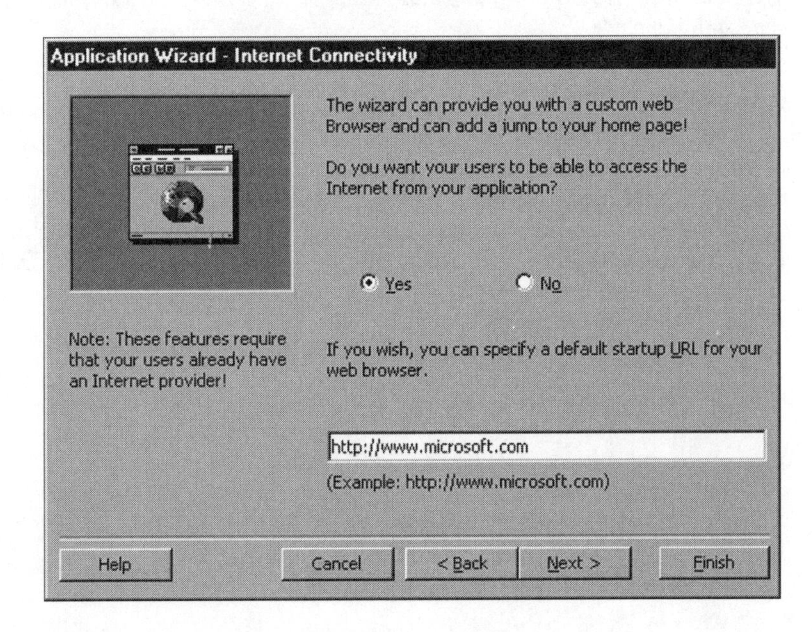

7 The Standard Forms part of the wizard allows you to add standard forms to your application. Need a custom settings dialog? Simply check the appropriate option. How about a splash screen to follow that login prompt? Just point and click, and it's yours. So, click all the check boxes and then the Next button. Isn't it amazing how easy this coding thing can be!

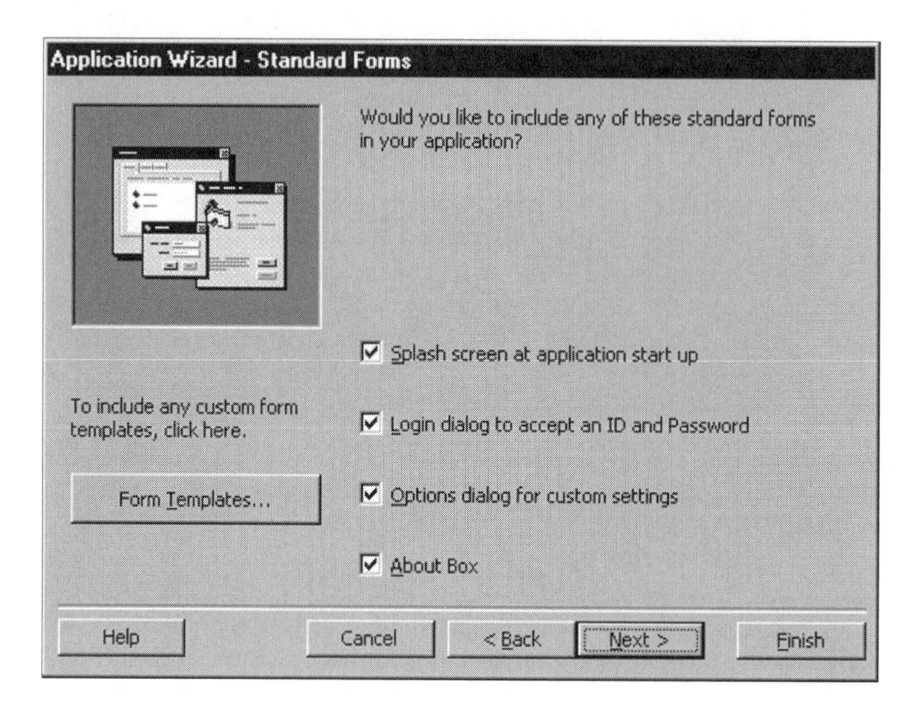

Visual Basic 5 also lets you create your own reusable forms. If you had already created some, you could click on the Form Templates *button on the wizard and select which of them you want to include.*

8 Many Visual Basic applications have an Access (or other) database where they store their data. The Data Access Forms page of the wizard allows you to specify which database you're using, and create fully functional database maintenance and browsing forms for your application by doing nothing more than pointing at the appropriate tables in the database. We look at this timesaving mechanism in a lot more detail later in the book. For now, though, just accept the default settings and click on the Next button.

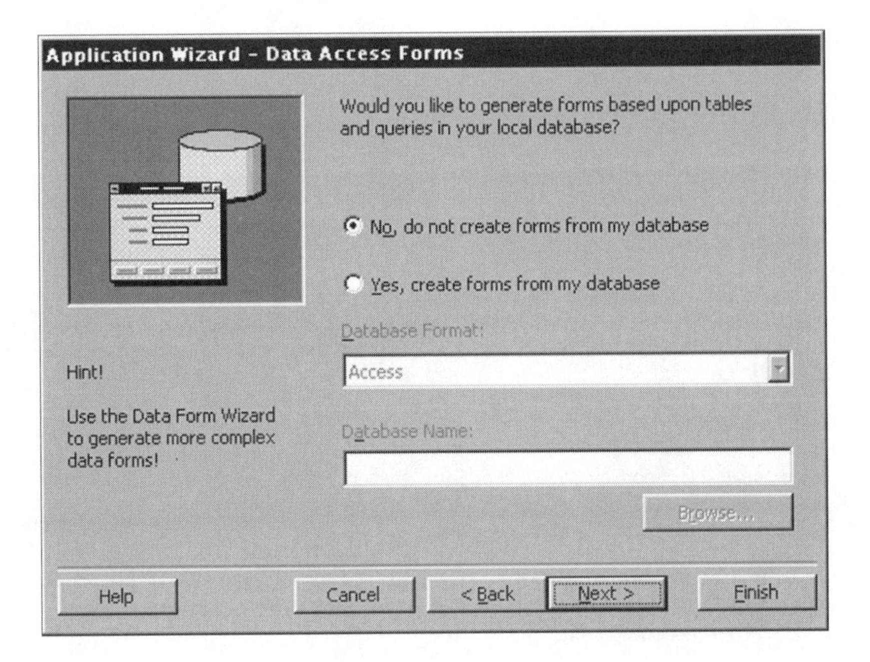

9 The final page lets you specify the name of your project, whether to save all the choices you made as the default ready for the next time you use the wizard, and whether or not you want to see a report on what the wizard has done. Click on the Finish button. It might take a while for this report to appear, but while you're waiting there's a lot going on, with the wizard basically taking control of VB and producing your application for you.

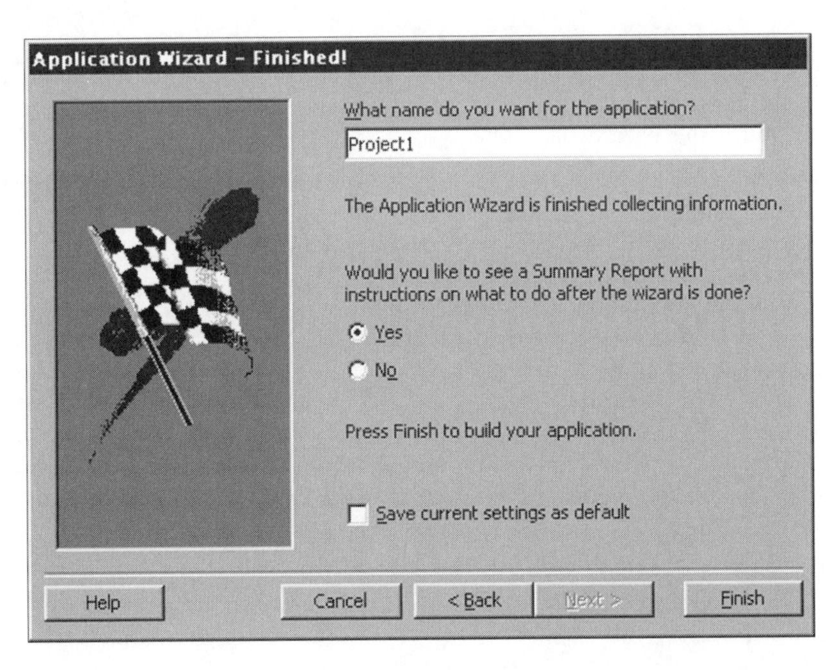

10 When all is done, a dialog appears telling you that the application has been created. Click OK and the Summary Report appears. In it, we can see what else is required to complete our application.

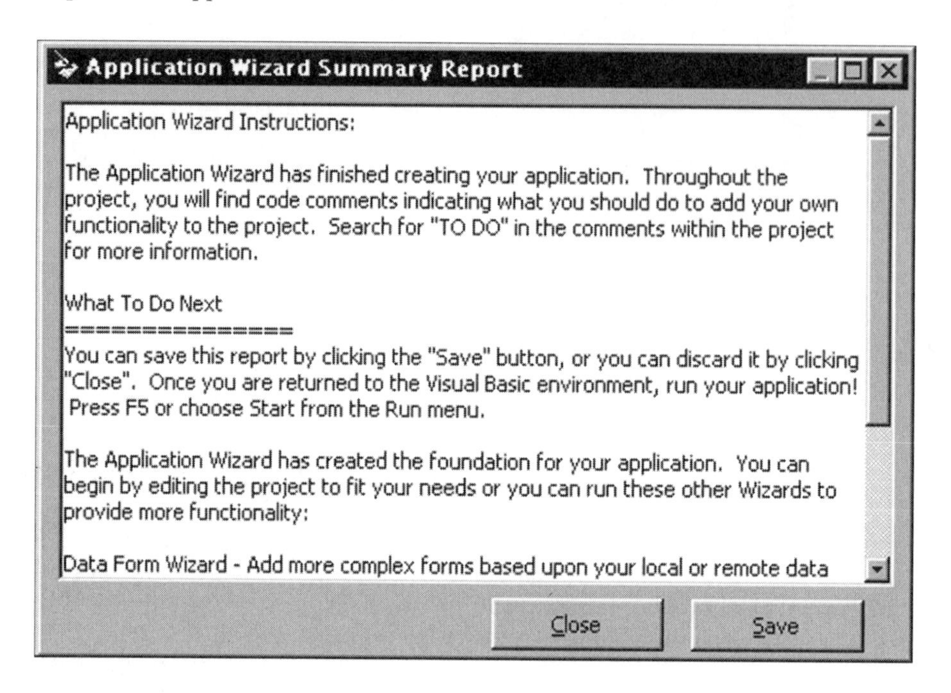

Looking at What the Wizard Has Done

When at last it is done, what you have is a semi-functioning program. You just need to write the code and produce the forms for the bits that the wizard didn't know about. That's the task for the next chapter, but in the meantime have a play with what we've created to see just how much the wizard has done.

Start the sample application by hitting the Run button on the toolbar, or by selecting Start on the Run menu. The first thing you see is a fancy splash screen as the application loads, followed by a log-in dialog. You don't need a password to get into the application at this stage, just click OK.

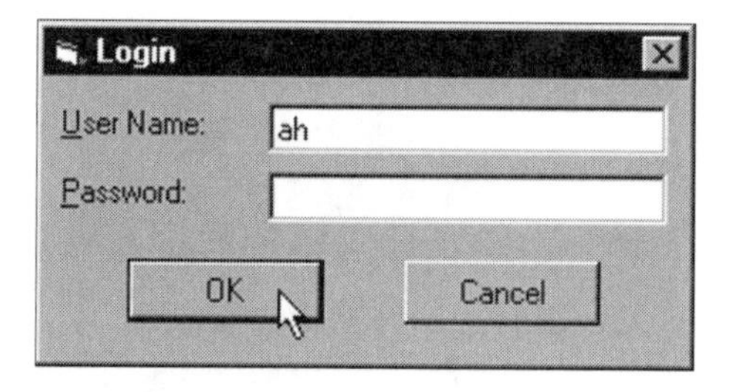

The main application window contains an editing window, and there are a surprising number of options on the menu and toolbars that the wizard has added for us automatically.

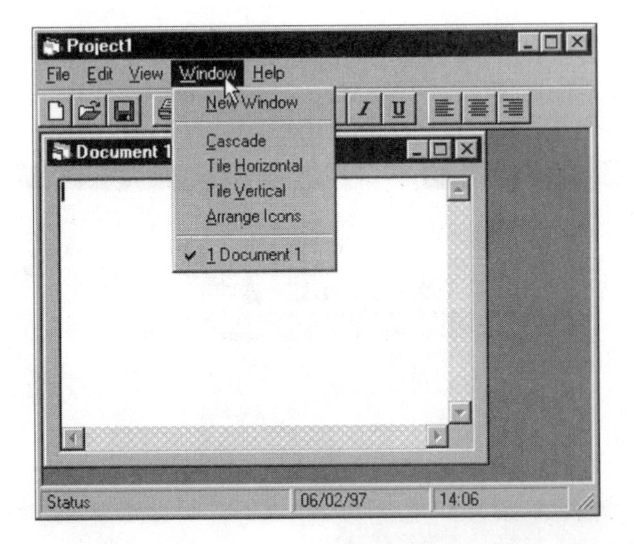

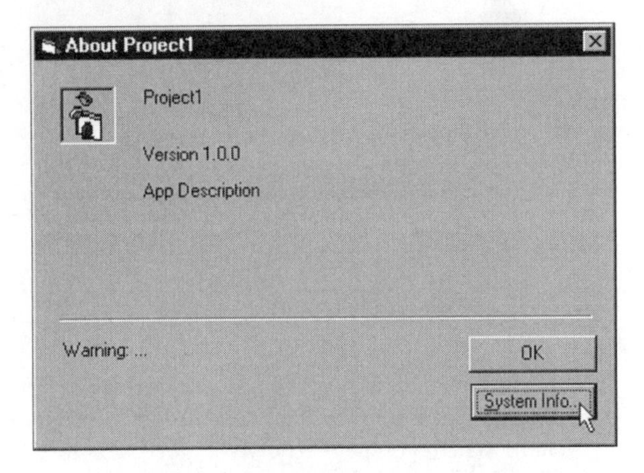

Open the Help menu, and click About Project1. This opens a skeleton About dialog, and it even has a button which will open Windows System Info application.

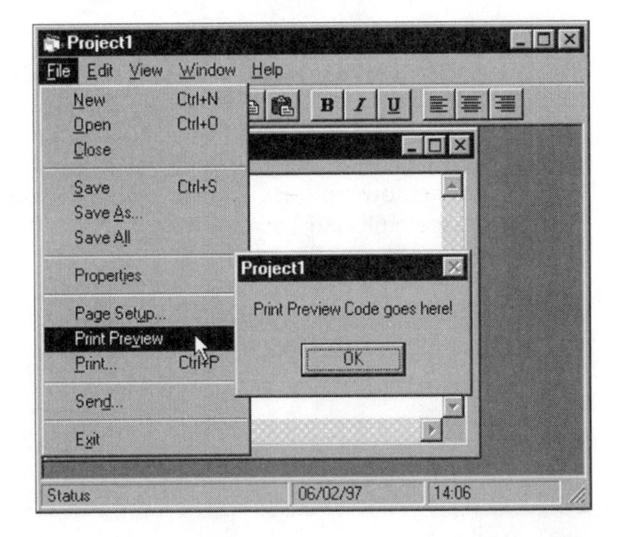

Of course, not everything is working. You can type in the editing window, but you can't open or save text. You just get a message that some more code is needed. And it's no good trying to print or preview it either....

In the wizard, we asked for our application to include Internet capability. Open the View menu and click Web Browser. Our application even has it's own web browser built in, though it's perhaps a little behind Internet Explorer 3 in terms of style!

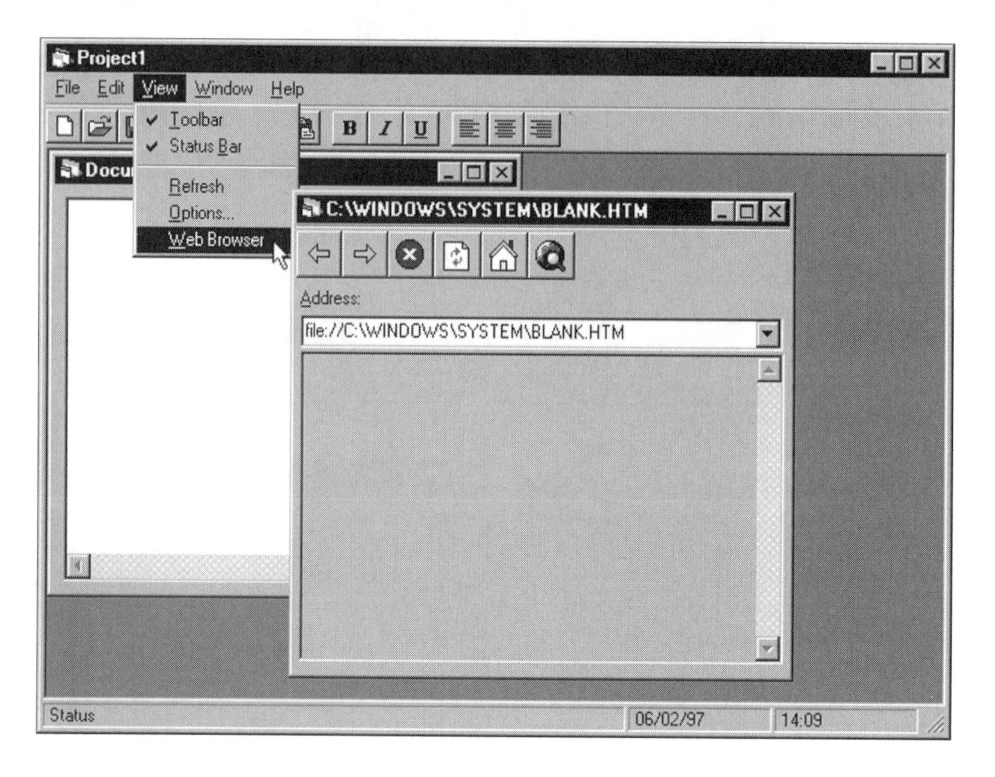

Still, we've got a surprisingly functional program from just making a few selections in the wizard. Have a play with it yourself and discover the other features that it already contains. Then, when you're ready, we'll get back to learning about Visual Basic again.

Working with Individual Project Files

So far we've just looked at the default Visual Basic project, consisting of just a single form and not much else. There are very few Windows applications that consist of just a single form or window, and so VB provides you with a wealth of menu items which you can use to drop pre-built and empty forms, and modules into your project. Don't believe me, huh? Take a peek at the Project menu.

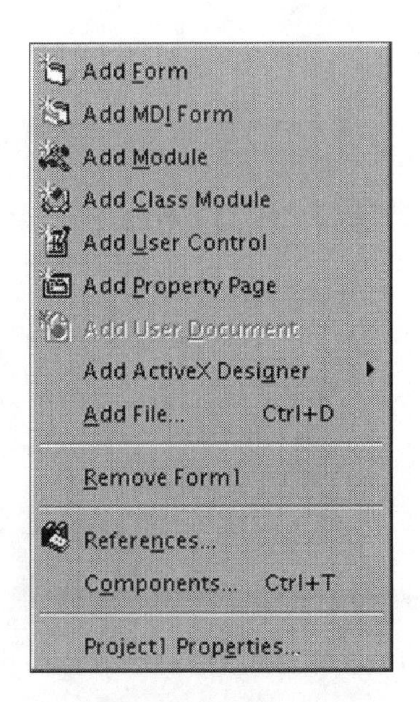

There are a great many items on the Project menu to allow you to extend your projects by adding new items into it. However, at this stage, we're just interested in the first four items (Add Form, Add MDI Form, Add Module, and Add Class Module), and the Add File item.

The first two items on the list allow you to add new forms to the project you're working on. The first is a standard, common or garden, plain old boring default format type form. The second though is kind of a super form, a form that contains other forms. We look at MDI applications later in the book.

The third and fourth items add code-only modules into the project. Again, we'll look at these later in the book.

The most useful though is the Add File item. In Visual Basic, it's very easy to break down your application into a set of totally disjointed standalone components. For example, a typical application may consist of a login form, a customer selection form, an invoicing form, an address labeling form, and so on. Each of these, if carefully designed, could easily be reused in other applications.

By saving these out to the hard disk, and using the Add File item on the Project menu you can quite easily add one such file into the current project.

Equally useful, though, is the ability to remove files from a project; you may have put a few forms into your project as test forms, for example, and then want to remove them. This can be accomplished in two ways. Either select the file you want to remove and choose Remove from the Project menu, or use the Project Explorer.

With Project Explorer, you simply select a file and then press the right mouse button to pop up a menu from which you can add a file into the project, save the files in the project, or remove them.

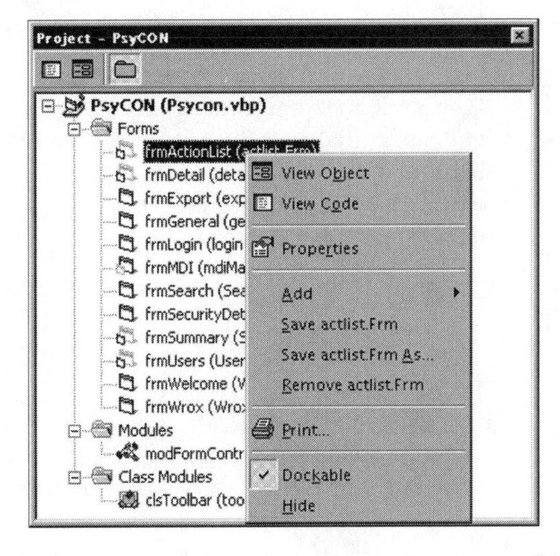

Printing out a Project

Although we're supposed to be moving more and more towards the paperless office, there's still no substitute in my opinion for a good stack of paper with your program on it when it comes to impressing the department manager, or simply hunting down that elusive bug. It's quite handy then that Visual Basic comes replete with project printing facilities. Take a look at the File menu once again.

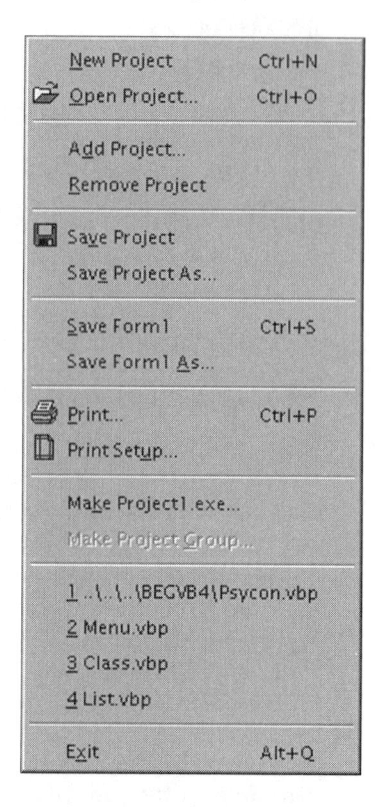

The Print Setup item is our first port of call. If you have had much experience with Windows applications, then you'll probably know what to expect when you click on this item.

Windows includes a number of common dialogs, which we can use from within our own VB applications, and which Visual Basic itself makes use of. The Print Setup dialog is one of them, and appears when you select Print Setup from the File menu.

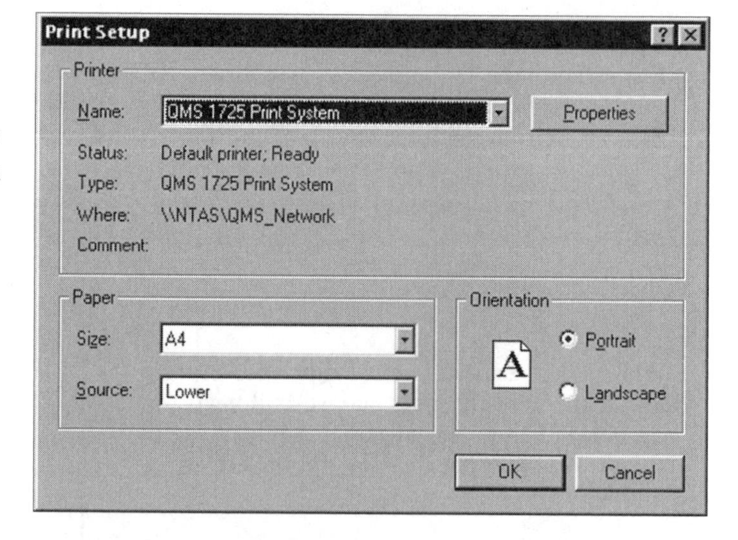

Using this dialog you can choose which printer to use (if you're lucky enough to have more than one available) and also specify various options that control the printout quality and style. For more information on this dialog, take a look at the Windows manuals themselves.

Once you've selected an available printer though, you can make use of the Print option on the File menu.

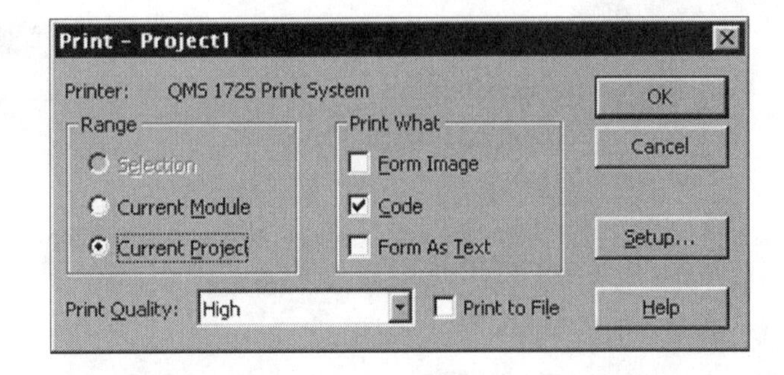

It's here that you choose which parts of your application to print out; you can specify whether to print out the selected chunk of code only, the currently selected module or the entire project. In addition to that, the Print What options allow you to tell Visual Basic whether the print out should be a graphical image of the forms in your application, just the application code, or a summary of all the form and module properties. The last option Form as Text, includes the properties of the controls on the forms. The Setup button, just as a point of interest, takes you back to the Print Setup dialog.

... and that's really all there is to it.

Getting Help

Visual Basic is a complex package. Not only must you master writing programs in the Visual Basic language, but you also need to master the Visual Basic environment, as well as reading the sometimes cryptic messages it can send you. Thankfully, Microsoft have supplied one of the best help systems of any development tool.

> *You might think it a bit strange for an author to be recommending that you use the Help system as much as you can. You bought the book to teach you Visual Basic and you don't expect to be told to go and look it up on a help screen. However, what you really want from me is the best way to get results, and that is a combination of this book (to teach you the techniques and give you the overview), and the help screens (for the itsy-bitsy references that are impossible to remember).*

Context-Sensitive Help

At any point while using Visual Basic you can hit *F1*, your panic button. This will activate the Microsoft Visual Basic Help system where you can obtain help and advice, as well as example program code for anything you come across whilst using Visual Basic.

Try this out now. Bring up the form's properties window, find the (Name) property and click on it. Now press *F1*. Visual Basic will display a page of text describing what exactly the (Name) property is and what it does.

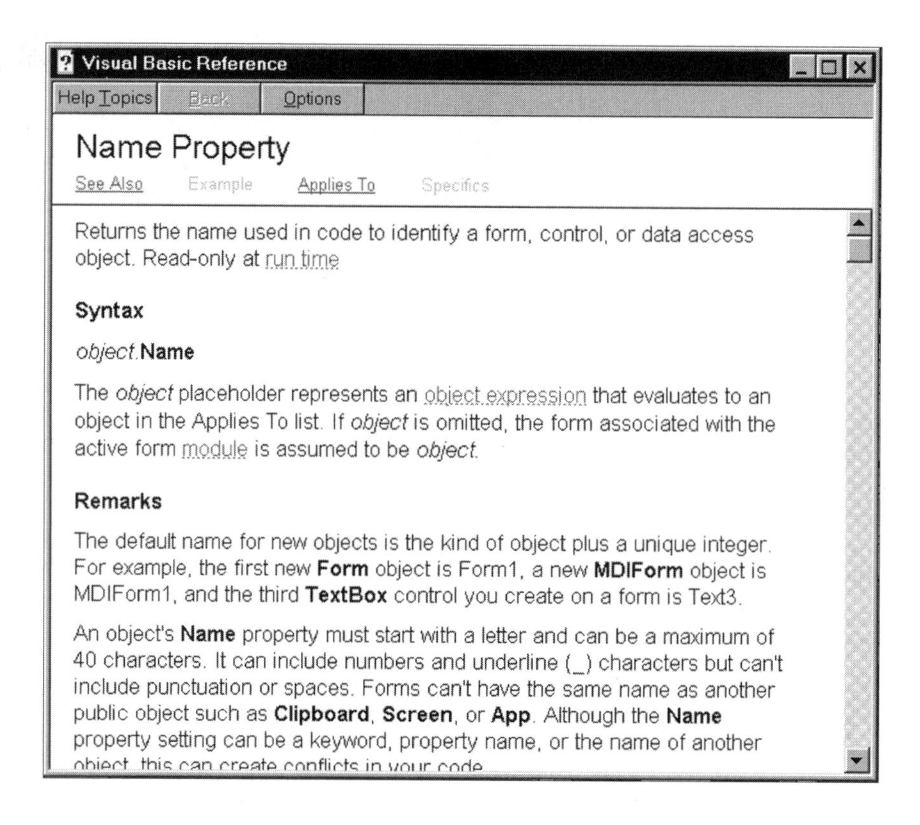

If you're a regular Windows user you'll have probably come across context-sensitive help before. Have a play with the help system for a while to get used to how it works. You may notice as you progress through the system that text in green appears. These items of text represent further topics that you can call up help on. If you click them, Visual Basic will whisk you away to another page of the help file to supply further reading, which itself may have green text enabling you to cross reference even further.

Searching for Help

Visual Basic also allows you to search for help on particular topics. Open up the Help menu on the Visual Basic menu bar and select Microsoft Visual Basic Help Topics. A tabbed dialog appears which allows you to search for help in a variety of ways.

The first page of the tabbed dialog that appears (Contents) allows you to find help by topic, and the other two pages allow you to search for help on a particular word. By far the most common way to access help is via the Index page.

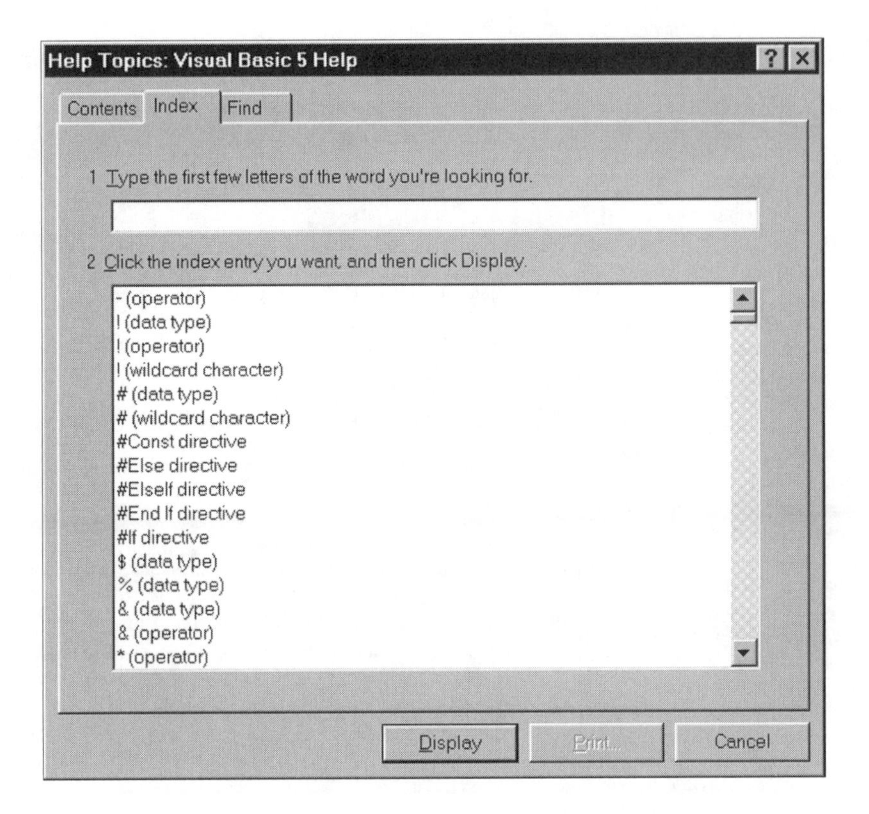

This lets you find a specific topic based on a keyword you enter, according to an index set up by the creators of the help file. Open up this dialog and type FORM into the text box. Notice that the list scrolls to the relevant point as you type each letter. Press *Enter* or click on the Display button now and a new window containing relevant topics will be shown. Double-click on an interesting topic (or highlight it then click Display) to view the help text itself.

The third page—Find—searches for text anywhere in the body of the help file. Because the first method is faster and more focused than the second, you'll probably find yourself using the Index page most of the time, but if you can't find what you're looking for there, then try the Find page for a more extensive search.

Books Online

Visual Basic 5 comes complete with all the program documentation on the same CD-ROM that you installed the software from. You can access it by selecting Search Master Index from the Help menu in Visual Basic.

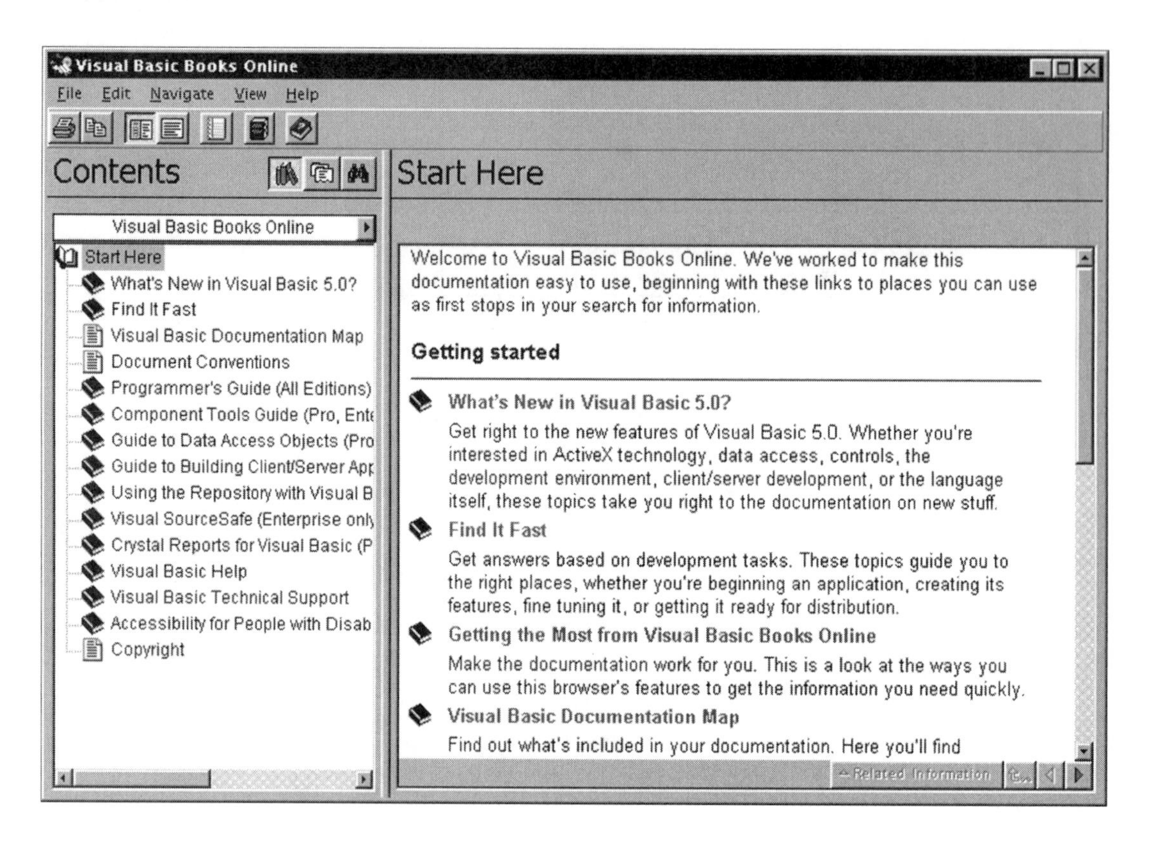

The left-hand side of the display is taken up with a list of the books included on the CD-ROM. Click these and the chapters appear, and then the subsections within the chapters, while all the time on the right the view changes to show the contents of the currently selected document.

On the whole, Books Online is extremely easy to use, and also includes its own tutorial. Books Online is also becoming more and more common as Microsoft strive to reduce the cost of shipping products by removing weighty paper manuals from the equation totally. Get used to it now—you're going to be seeing more and more of it in the future.

Summary

We've covered a lot of ground very quickly in this first chapter, so let's just recap on what we've done. We have:

- Explored the layout of the Visual Basic environment
- Learnt how to create a new project by starting Visual Basic
- Run and stopped a Visual Basic program
- Learnt how to use the Visual Basic help system

In the next chapter, we'll be taking a more in-depth look at what a form actually is—and we'll add some code to make it more like a program. Mind you don't expect too much just yet, we're still finding our feet, and familiarizing ourselves with the new VB5 environment.

Why Not Try...

1. Use the properties window to check out the properties of a Visual Basic form. How many properties exist for a form? What is the property that can be used to 'hide' a form.

2. Use online help to display the built-in function keys in the Visual Basic development environment. What are they?

3. How is a Visual Basic method different to a Visual Basic statement?

4. From the main menu, select Tools | Options | General, and change the Height and Width grid units. What effect does this have?

5. What are the default **`Height`** and **`Width`** grid units? Will changing them to 300 and 300 respectively increase or decrease the distance between the dots? Is the pattern saved with the project?

asic Visual Basic Visual Ba
al Basic Visual Basic Visual
Basic Visual Basic Visual Ba
ual Basic Vi
Basic Visu
ual Basic V
l Basic Vis
isual Basic Visual Basic
al Basic Visual Basic Visua
Visual Basic Visual Basic Visu
al Basic Visual Ba
l Basic Visual
ic Visual Basi
Basic Visual B
ic Visual Basi
al Basic Visual
ual Basic Visual Basic Visual Ba
Visual Basic Visual Basic Visu
sual Basic Visual Basic Visu
Visual Basic Visual Ba

Inside a Visual Basic Program

In the previous chapter we took a brief tour of the Visual Basic 5 environment, and saw how to manage projects and files as we come to build applications. We used the Application Wizard to create a partly functional program, and you were probably surprised at what it could achieve.

However, to create our own great programs, we have to understand how VB works underneath. I'm sorry to have to break this to you, but you won't find a Make Me A Millionaire Wizard to automatically create your next best-selling application. You have to do that yourself.

So in this chapter, we'll start by talking about the overall way that VB programs work, and take a good look at **forms**—the mainstay of any Visual Basic program. We'll look at how to customize your forms by changing aspects such as the background color and name of the form, by altering its **properties**.

Of course, simply being able to change the caption or border type of a form doesn't really make for a best-selling Windows program. Real functionality can only be added to your programs by adding code to your form. We'll look at how you can write code to handle the form's **events** as well. We'll even write a small amount of code. Finally, we'll create an executable program that can be run outside of Visual Basic.

In this chapter we'll learn:

- What event-driven programming is, and how it works in Visual Basic
- What Visual Basic forms are, and how to change the way they look
- How to go about programming properties
- How to write code to respond to events
- How to compile our first application

Objects and Events

In Visual Basic the majority of the code you write deals with a combination of two things: **objects** and their **events**.

- **Objects** in the real world can be anything from a television to a light switch. They serve specific functions such as displaying TV programs or illuminating your world. They can be made up from **collections** of other objects. A car, for example, is made up from wheels, chassis, engine and many other objects. In Visual Basic objects are the elements that make up your program's user interface. Forms and controls (such as command buttons) are all classed as objects.
- **Events** also have a real world equivalent. If you feel hungry, you'll eat a sandwich. If it starts raining when you're outside, you'll put up an umbrella. This is event-driven behavior. When a user does something such as click a command button in your program, Visual Basic translates this action into an event. It recognizes that a button had been clicked, so it labels it a `Click` event. You can write code to handle this event, which will do something like opening a message box every time the event occurs. This is an **event handler**—just the set of actions performed on a particular object, usually as a result of the user doing something.

Event-Driven Programming

Events are what set Windows programs, including your Visual Basic application, apart from other versions of the BASIC programming language, or languages such as C and Pascal. When a traditional BASIC or C program is run, the computer trots through the program code line-by-line—starting at the top, and following the specific route defined by the programmer to the end. In Visual Basic, the program starts by displaying a form or by executing a small fragment of code. However, from that point onwards, it's the user who determines which parts of the program code are run next.

A New Way of Thinking

Think about making a cup of coffee. In a traditional programming language you could write a program to make a cup of coffee as follows:

1. Fill kettle with water
2. Put kettle on
3. Place coffee in cup
4. Place milk in cup
5. Wait until kettle has boiled
6. Pour water into cup

This is pretty simple stuff to follow. A good way to think of the same task in Visual Basic is:

1 Show coffee, kettle, water, milk and cup to user

2 Let user make the coffee

The user can use each of the components shown, in whatever sequence he or she wants, in order to make the coffee. As a programmer in this situation, you would just provide small fragments of code to handle specific events. For example, when the user turns the kettle on, Visual Basic will run the code you have written to deal with that particular event, which would probably involve heating up the water and such like. The actual order of events required to end up with a cup of coffee is left to the user to decide, not forced on them by the programmer.

Object-Oriented Programming

In addition to event-driven programming, Visual Basic 5 supports a relatively new way of developing applications known as **object-oriented** development. If you are regular reader of serious computer magazines, then you will have already come across the term OOP many times. But what does it mean?

Well, traditionally, programmers would write programs that were called **structured** programs. The program would be designed to solve one big problem, but the programmers would break the problem down into smaller, more manageable problems and write small sections of code to solve each one.

OOP is the natural successor to this way of programming. Instead of simply breaking the problem down into smaller problems, OO programmers break the problem down into objects, each with a life of their own. For example, a Space Invaders game would typically have an `Alien` object. Just like an object in real life, this `Alien` object would have certain characteristics (**properties**) and certain functions that it is able to perform (**methods**). The programmer would then have to figure out what properties and the methods an object needs to bring it to life.

In the case of our `Alien`, the properties might include `X` and `Y` coordinate properties to define its position on the screen, along with `Move`, `Fire` and `Die` methods. Visual Basic lets you define templates for objects in the form of class modules. You can then turn these templates into real objects.

Defining the class is rather like talking to an alien and saying 'A human looks like this, can do such and such' and so on. Turning the class into a particular object (known as **instantiation** or creating an **instance** of an object) is like saying '...hey, and there goes one now!'.

We take a look at object-oriented programming in greater detail a little later in the book. For the time being you just need to appreciate that the whole concept of object-oriented programming in Visual Basic revolves around properties, methods, and events.

Properties

Every form and control has properties. Even some objects that you can't manipulate at all when you are designing and building your program, such as the screen and the printer, have properties. These are generally only available from within your application's code when it is running. Properties control the appearance and behavior of the objects in Visual Basic. These are some of the ways that forms can be customized using their properties.

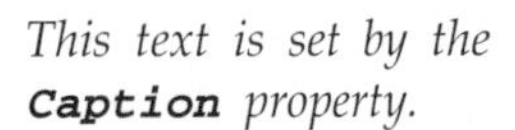

This text is set by the
Caption property.

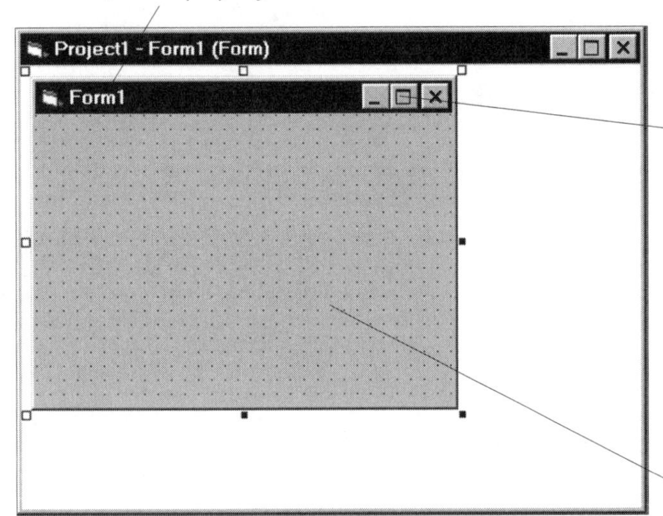

`BorderStyle` determines whether or not you can resize the window.

The position and size of the form on the screen is determined by its `Left`, `Top`, `Height` and `Width` properties.

The color of the inside of the form is set using its `BackColor` property.

One window we avoided mentioning in the last chapter was the properties window which, which allows you to do exactly that.

The Properties Window

The properties window allows you to set and view the properties of your forms and controls at design time (before you actually run your program).

*The **object box** tells you which control or form you are referring to. You can get a list of all the objects on your form by clicking the little arrow at the side.*

This property is highlighted, ready for editing.

Each property has a standard name. You can change properties in here manually at design time, or with your code at run time.

Forms have many properties—more than 40 that are available at design time, and even more at run time! There are more down here that you can get to with the scrollbars.

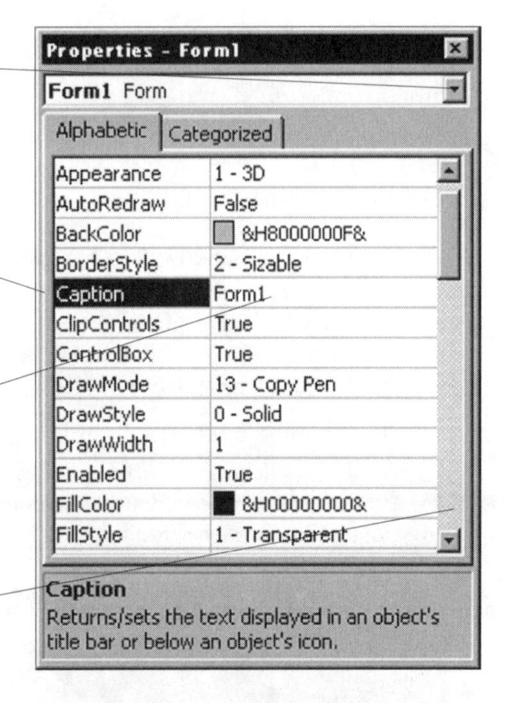

Also across the top of the properties window you will see two tabs. Normally when the project window comes into view it simply lists all the properties that are applicable to the current selected object (be that a form, a component on the form, etc.) in alphabetical order. However, you can click on the Categorized tab to see a more orderly list of properties.

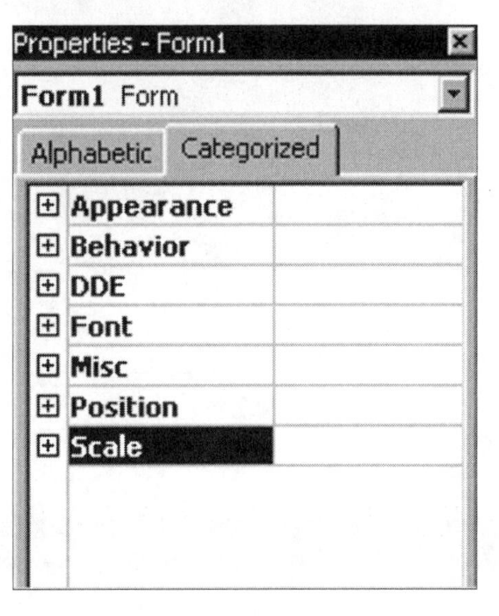

By clicking on the + signs next to each of the property categories, the list can be expanded to show the actual properties belonging to that category. This is a great mode to work in while you are getting used to Visual Basic, but you will probably find it easier to work in Alphabetic mode when you have got a grip on what's available in the properties window. Once you remember the names of the properties, you don't have to think about which category they come under. By far the best way to get to grips with properties, though, is to use them. We will do this in the next section.

Programming Using Properties

When Visual Basic is in design mode, we can take a look at the properties of the forms it contains. In this example, we're using the default project that is created when you select Standard EXE in the New Project window, after starting up Visual Basic or when you select New Project from the File menu.

If the properties window isn't visible, you can display it by:

- Clicking once on the form to select it as the current object, and then pressing *F4* to display the properties window with the properties for the current form. (You can tell when a particular window is selected as its title bar is highlighted.)
- Selecting Properties from the View menu.
- Right-clicking the form to bring up a pop-up menu, and selecting Properties from the bottom of it. Once it comes into view, don't forget that you can simply drag it on to another window or to the edge of the screen to dock it in that position.

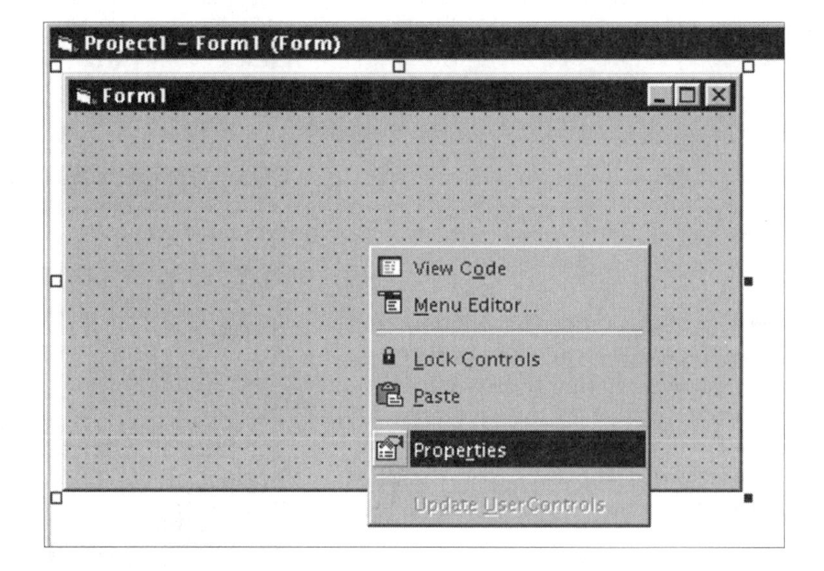

Try It Out - Changing a Form's Property

1. Click on the form to select it and then press *F4* to display the properties window. Make sure you are looking at the alphabetic list of properties. Move to the `ControlBox` property, either by using the scroll bar on the right of the properties window or by pressing *Shift+Ctrl+C*. This property defines whether a control box (the icon in the top left corner of the window that allows you to resize and close it) will be placed on the form at run time.

ClipControls	True
ControlBox	True
DrawMode	13 - Copy Pen

Pressing Shift+Ctrl+C *will move you to the first property in the list beginning with the letter C—if you keep on pressing this key combination, the highlight will move again and soon fall on the* **`ControlBox`** *property.*

2 To the right of the words Control Box you will see the word True. This means that there is a control box attached to the form at present. Change this to False by double-clicking the word True, clicking the arrow to the right of the property and selecting a value from the drop-down list, or by typing the first letter of the word.

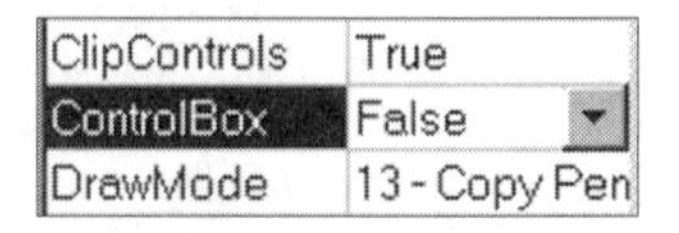

3 Did you notice that the entire title bar of your form changed? If you remove a control box from a form, then you also remove its icon and sizing buttons. If you run the program again at this point (press *F5*), you'll see the changes that you just witnessed in design mode carried through on to the form at run time.

You can still drag the form around the screen and resize it by dragging the borders.

However, there is no way to close the form now other than by clicking the End *icon on the Visual Basic toolbar. The Maximize and Minimize buttons are also gone, although you can still maximize it and normalize it by double-clicking on its title bar.*

4 Stop the program. Now find the property called **`BorderStyle`**. The text to the right of the property name should say 2—Sizable.

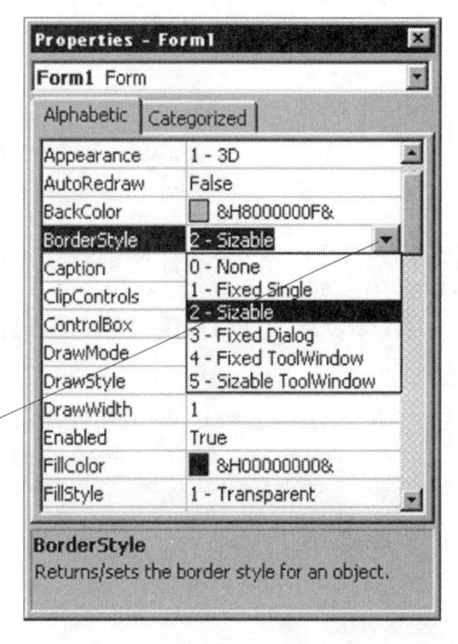

You can see all the alternatives for the property by clicking the arrow at the side to drop down the list box.

5 Keep double-clicking the **BorderStyle** field until it says 1—Fixed Single, or click on the arrow and select this option. Notice how the border style of the form itself changes as you cycle through the options on offer.

6 Now find the **Caption** property. Click on the text that says Form1 and press *BackSpace* to delete the current caption.

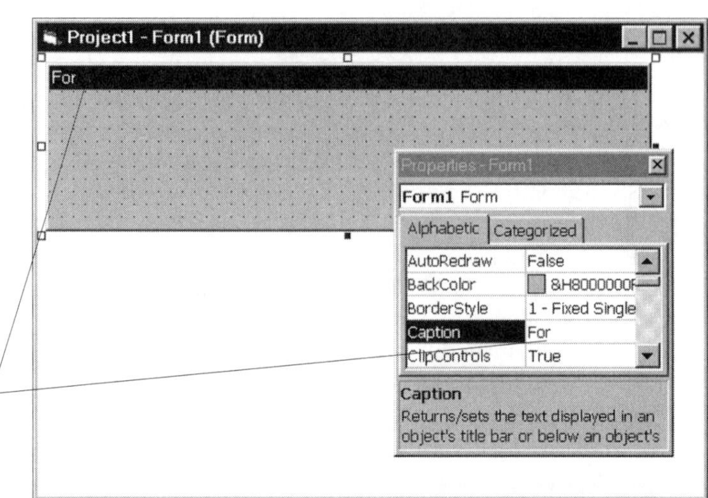

Just as when you changed the border style and removed the control box from the form, any changes you make to the form's caption are shown on the form in real time.

7 The rest of our form doesn't seem so different at design time. Press *F5* to run your application to see what it looks like at run time.

8 The result should be a plain box with a single line border round the outside. There is no way to move this window, resize it, or close it. Since you deleted the form's caption, Visual Basic automatically decides not to give the form a title bar. To stop the program click on the Visual Basic End icon again.

Changing Properties Interactively

Certain properties of your form can be changed without you even noticing it. For example, with Visual Basic in design mode, dragging the form to a new position, or changing its size will cause the **Width**, **Height**, **Top** and **Left** properties to change. This is an important point to remember. By simply moving the form around in design mode you are actually programming Visual Basic by telling it to display the form in a different position. If you resize the form, the window in the running program will adopt the new size; if you move the form, the window the user sees will appear in the same position on their screen as the form does on yours.

Bear this in mind if you are running in 1024 x 768 screen mode. Users who are limited to 640 x 480 won't appreciate seeing only half your form!

Where Code Fits in Visual Basic

OK, so we've talked about properties. We now need to start thinking about how we are going to get some code into our program, so that it actually does something. This diagram illustrates exactly how the user, your form and your form's event code all fit together in Windows.

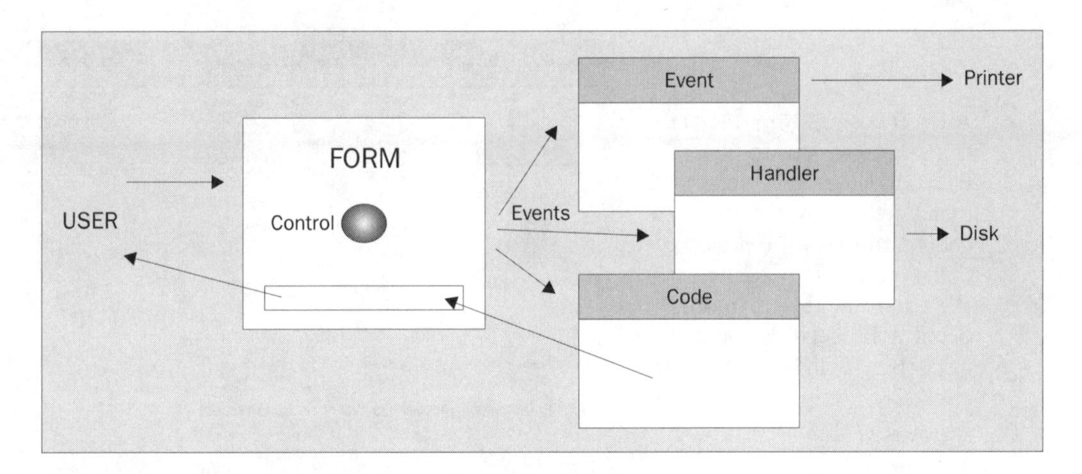

All controls in a Visual Basic program (such as text boxes, command buttons and forms) have a set of predefined events that you can add code to. With forms, for example, there is a `Load` event that is triggered the first time the form is loaded up and displayed. You can add code to this event to do various jobs at setup time, like positioning the form automatically, or displaying some standard values on the form and so on. There is also an `Unload` event that is triggered when the form is closed down. Each code fragment is called an **event handler**.

Event Handlers

Although each control and form in your project can respond to hundreds of different events, you don't need to write a single line of code unless you really want to. For instance, you may not want a command button to do anything when it's clicked—in which case you don't need to write anything for the `Click` event. You only need to write event code when you want something to happen in response to an event—Visual Basic is a very undemanding environment, which really lets you do as much or as little as you want.

Your First Visual Basic Event Handler

Time to write some code I think! As we have just mentioned, each form has certain events associated with it, one of the most important of which is the `Load` event. The `Load` event is triggered whenever a form is first loaded and just before it is displayed. A common use for this event is to set the values of properties for the form, or execute some code when it appears. We'll use this feature to create a simple program that places today's date on the form.

Try It Out - Writing an Event Handler

1 If Visual Basic is not running, then load it up now. If you have followed the examples so far and still have the skeleton form hanging around, then start afresh by selecting New Project from the File menu. Click No when asked if you want to save the current files.

2 After choosing New Project from the File menu, Visual Basic displays the Project dialog where you can choose the type of project that you want to create. We'll look at this in more detail a little later. For now, just select Standard EXE and click OK.

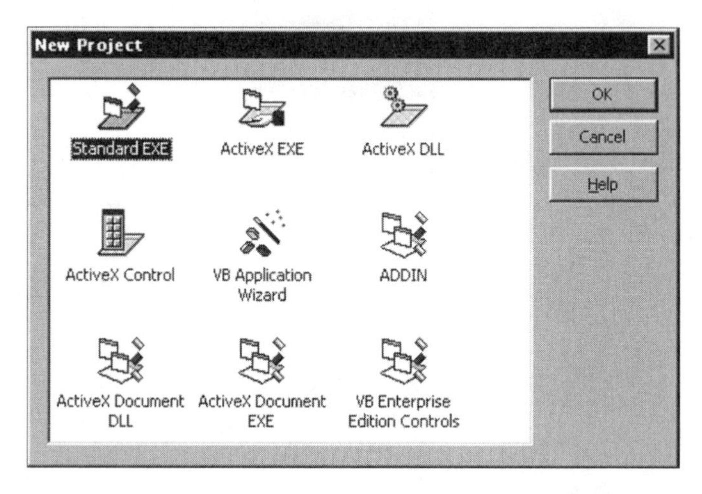

3 After a short pause you will end up with a new project complete with a clean, new form.

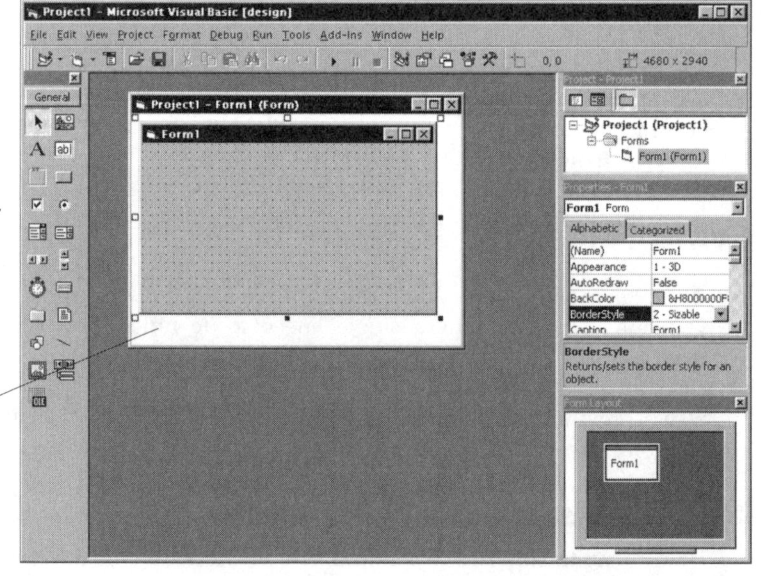

Resize the form so it looks like this.

4 Next, we need somewhere to display the date. The easiest way to do this in Visual Basic is to place a label control onto your form, and then put the value of today's date into it. To add the label control to your form, first click on its icon in the toolbox.

> *A control in Visual Basic is an object that sits on your form. They have particular functions. This sounds a bit general, but that's just what controls are—general. They range from buttons, to lists, to more specialized controls that access databases. Adding a control to your form allows you to use the facilities of that control in your program. We want to show some text on the form, and the label control will allow us to do that. Chapter 3 gives you a proper introduction to controls, but for now, just take it step by step, and we'll cover the bigger picture later.*

5 Now use the cross-hair cursor to draw a box on the form which is the shape and size you want for the label, holding down your mouse button all the time as you draw. In this case, make it about this size.

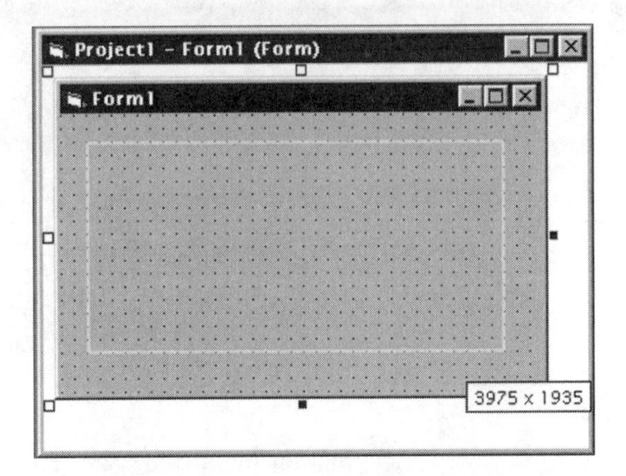

6 When it's the right size, release the mouse button and the label appears. Visual Basic has named the control `Label1`, the default name for a label control. We'll use this name to address the control in our code.

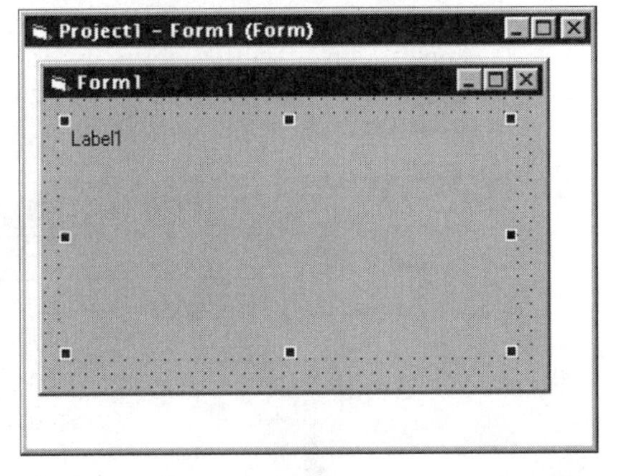

7 Let's run the program now for the hell of it and see what it looks like. Press *F5* or hit the Start button on the tool bar.

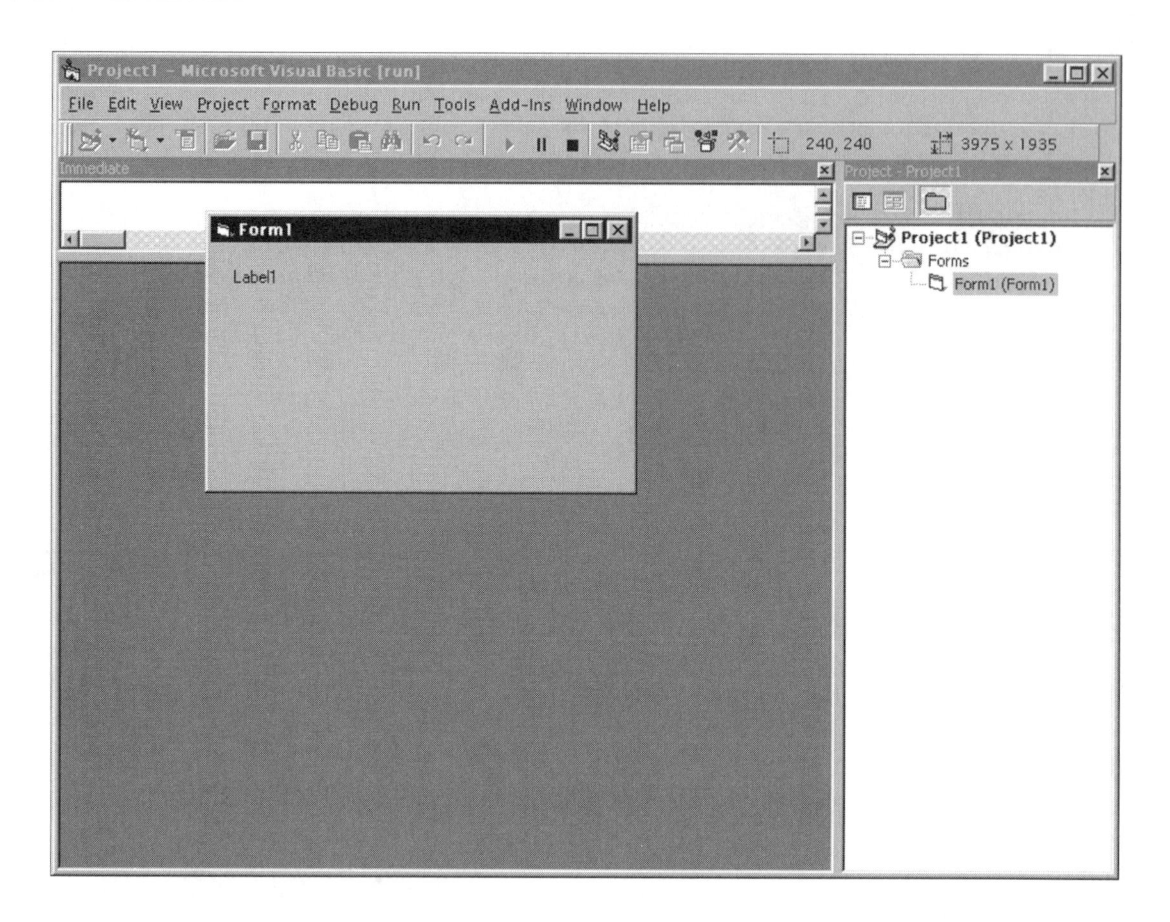

8 Stop the program by clicking the End button on the toolbar. We now need to add some code to the project to place today's date into the label. When you want to add code to a form or other object, the easiest way to display the code window is to simply double-click the object itself. A code window will appear with the top of the window showing the object that you double-clicked and a default event that you can write code for.

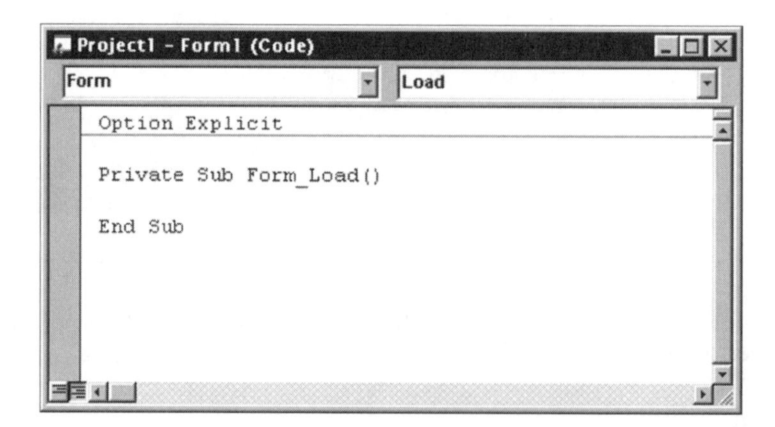

9 Clicking the down arrow to the right of the word Load will show a list of all the events that can happen to a form. For now though, just keep **Load** selected. The main area of the code window shows the code that makes up this event's handler. It's a normal subprocedure (i.e. a piece of code that performs a specific operation).

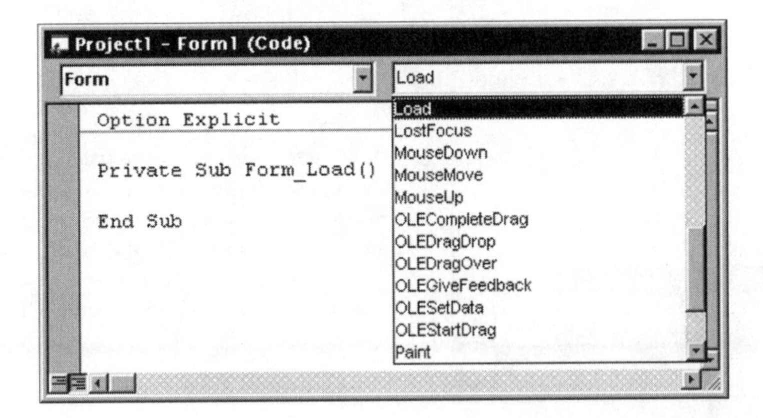

10 Click in the code window and type in code between the **Private Sub Form_Load()** and **End Sub** lines, so that the subprocedure looks like this. The code is explained in detail in the *How It Works* section that follows.

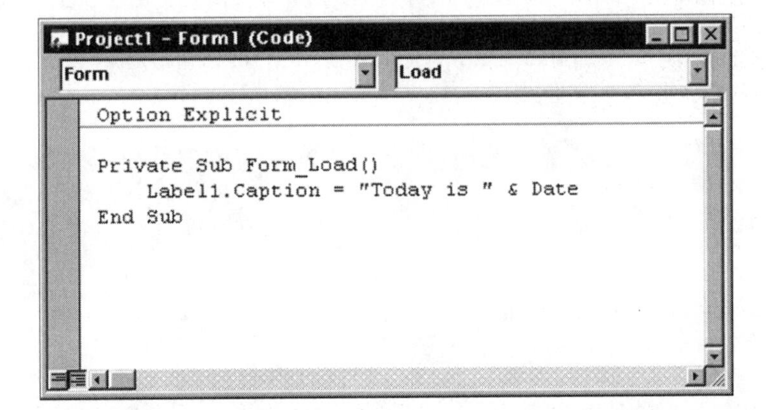

11 The final step to take is to make sure that the form appears centered on the screen at run time. In the bad old days we would have had to write a couple of rather confusing lines of code at this point, but no more. Simply make sure the form is selected, bring up the properties window, find the **StartUpPosition** property and set it to 2—CenterScreen.

*As you can see from the screenshot, there are a number of options available to you, including leaving it up to you where the form appears (**`Manual`**), leaving it up to Windows as to where the form should appear (**`Windows Default`**) or centering the form within its parent (**`CenterOwner`**). We look at that latter option in a later chapter where we cover MDI forms.*

12 Try running the program now by pressing *F5* or clicking the Start icon (from now on I will assume that you can remember how to run a program). The form will appear on screen as in the other examples, except now it will always appear dead center of the screen. In it is today's date.

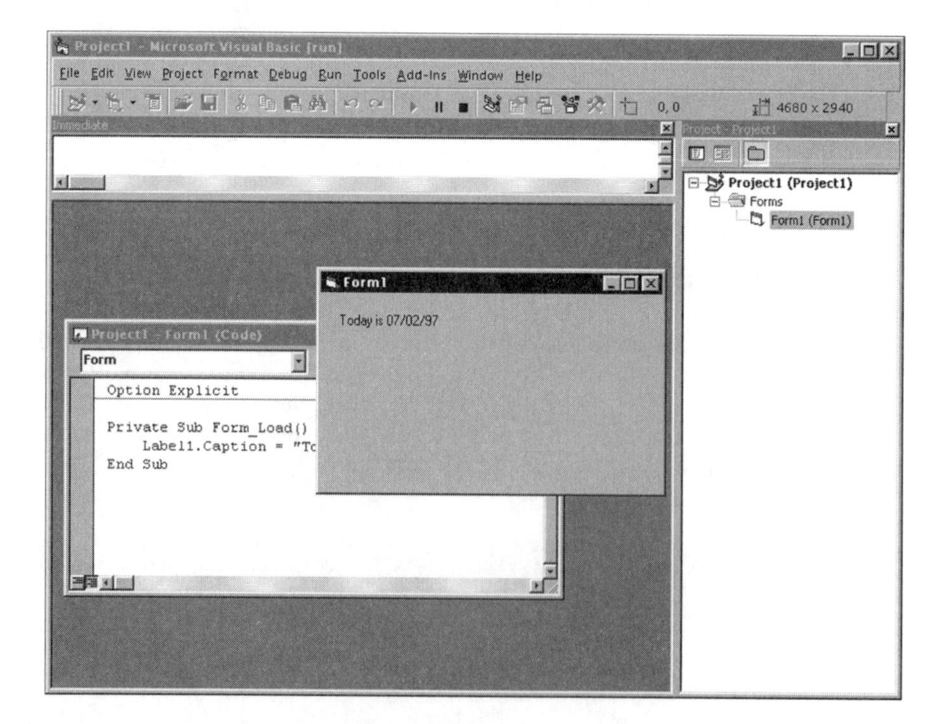

13 Stop the program running by clicking the form's close box.

In the future, I may not show you a screenshot of exactly how the code window should look. Use the list boxes at the top of the code window to find the object and event you need to write code for—you'll find it all too easy to just bring up a code window, type a couple of screens full of code and then find you have put it in the wrong event. Always check where you are, and where you should be!

How It Works

Let's take a look at the `Form_Load()` event line by line.

```
Private Sub Form_Load()

  Label1.Caption = "Today is " & Date

End Sub
```

The first line, `Private Sub Form_Load()`, tells Visual Basic where the code for the load event actually starts. The `Sub` command tells Visual Basic that the code is a **subprocedure.** There is another kind of code block in Visual Basic known as a **function** which we will cover later in the book. `Private` means that this piece of code is only visible to other bits of code attached to the same form or module. This is important and we'll cover it later when we talk about the big picture of what goes where in a project. For now, just ignore it.

The `Form_Load` bit is the name of the subprocedure. Visual Basic automatically names any event code you write to indicate the object it deals with, and the event that will trigger its execution: in this case `Form` and `Load.`

Although you can change the name of the procedure yourself, it's unwise to do so, since Visual Basic will be unable to relate the event procedure to the appropriate object. In our case, the code then won't execute when the form is loaded.

Two brackets `()` are used to hold things called **parameters**. These are values that are passed to a procedure to allow it to do its job, such as two numbers to be added together. In this case no parameters are needed. Don't worry about this now, it will all become clear later in the book.

The line of code that inserts today's date into the label looks like this:

```
Label1.Caption = "Today is " & Date
```

There's a lot of things going on here, not all of which it makes sense to explain at the moment. Put simply, the `Caption` property of `Label1` is set to hold a phrase (or **string** as it's officially known) that is made up of the words `Today is` and today's date, represented in our code as `Date`. The word `Date` is actually a built-in function of Visual Basic that goes and gets the date from the system clock inside your machine.

We tack it on to the end of the **Today is** bit using the ampersand (**&**) character, which tells Visual Basic to make it all into one string. The **Caption** property of the label holds the characters that are displayed in the label on the form at run time. These replace the word **Label1** that was the default value of the property we saw on the label at design time. Finally, the line **End Sub** marks the end of the subprocedure.

As I said, there's a lot going on here, but I wanted to throw you in at the deep end and show you how Visual Basic can make a little code go a long way.

Typing In Code

Newcomers often get concerned about the way their code looks in the code window.

As far as Visual Basic is concerned, as long as you spell the commands correctly and put spaces between each command, it doesn't really care how you go about arranging your code. If you type something incorrectly, Visual Basic will tell you straight away. For example, try deleting the **&** sign between **"Today is "** and **Date**. When you move to the next line, you get an error message box with some descriptive text of the error

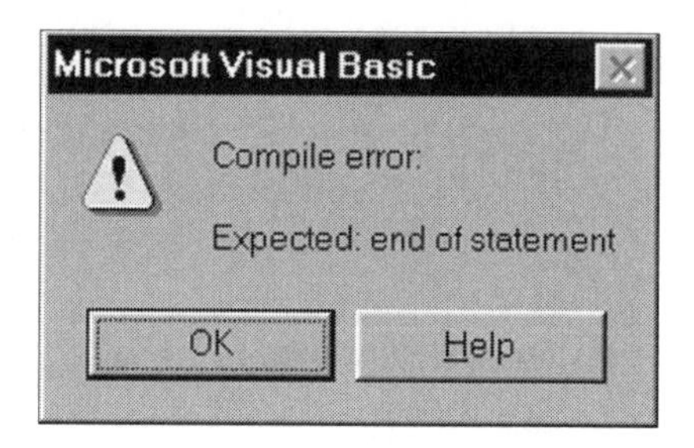

If you now hit the OK button on this dialog box, Visual Basic returns you to the code window and highlights the offending line. Change it back to how it should be: **"Today is " & Date**

As a rule, indenting using the *Tab* key makes blocks of your code stand out clearly. This is a real help when it comes to debugging. Note that single commands, such as those in the example above, must be kept on the same line. If you reach the right-hand edge of the code window when you are typing, don't panic—and don't press *Enter*! The code window will scroll to keep up with your typing. Often, if you do hit *Enter* in the middle of a line of code, Visual Basic will wake you up with an error message complaining that it can't understand what you are trying to say.

Visual Basic also helps you by doing its best to format all your lines of code in a standard way. It spaces out your code and adds capital letters to words it recognizes. This makes for neater and safer code. Even better, it can help you to complete lines of code by displaying the syntax of each statement as you type it, and suggesting values for various parameters. For example, as you type something like this, you see a pop-up window containing the full syntax of the statement:

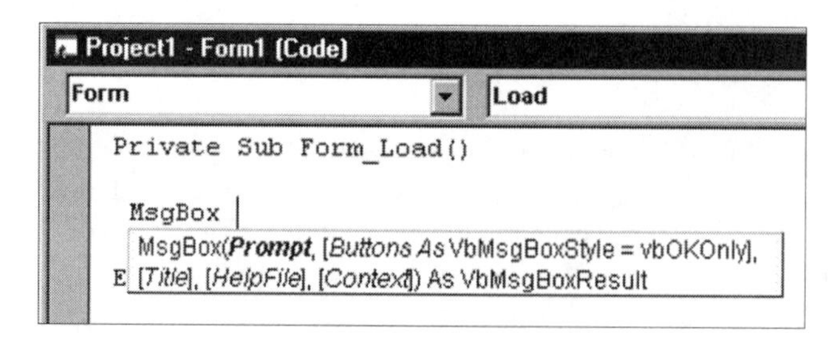

The other important issue when writing event code is not to delete the first or last lines of code—that is, the line beginning with **Sub** and the line that says **End Sub**. If you do delete them, Visual Basic won't know where your code starts and ends, so you'll have to retype them again yourself.

> *Did you notice how Visual Basic makes parts of each line a different color? Colors are used in Visual Basic to show you which parts of a line it recognizes as Visual Basic instructions. As you type in each line of code, Visual Basic automatically checks it to make sure it makes sense.*

Time To Say Goodbye

OK, so we can display the date. How about reacting to a different event. This time, we'll add some code that runs when the form's **Unload** event occurs.

Try It Out - Adding Code to the Form_Unload Event

Let's add some code to make the form say 'goodbye' when it's closed down. First of all, you need to get to the right routine in the code window.

1. If the program is still running, stop it. Then double-click on the form to bring up the code window. Click on the down arrow to the right of the word **Load**—at the top of the code window. The event list will appear as before.

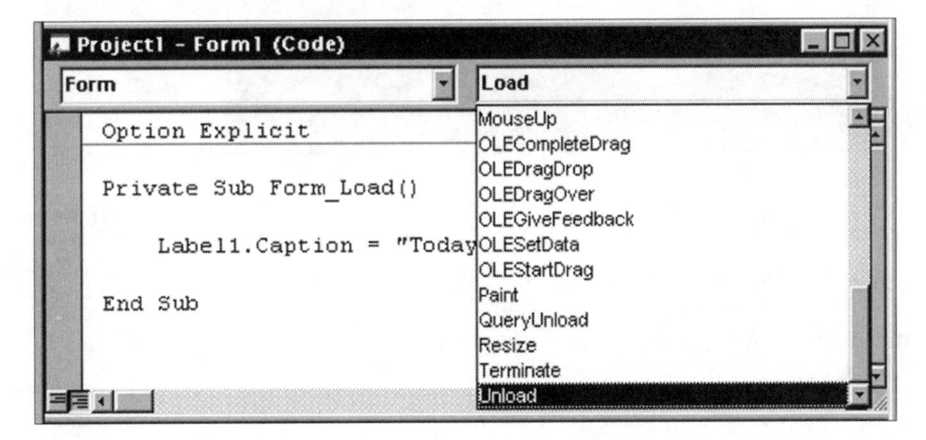

2. Use the scrollbars to find the word **Unload**, and select it. For the **Unload** event, the code should read:

```
Private Sub Form_Unload(Cancel As Integer)
    Msgbox "Goodbye!"
End Sub
```

The **MsgBox** line simply displays a message box with the word **Goodbye** inside. We'll cover message boxes in full later in the book. Basically though, a message box is simply a ready-made form for displaying messages to the user that they must respond to before carrying on. This is great for error messages and the ubiquitous 'You just formatted your hard disk' style of message.

3 Try running your program now. As before the form appears centered on the screen.

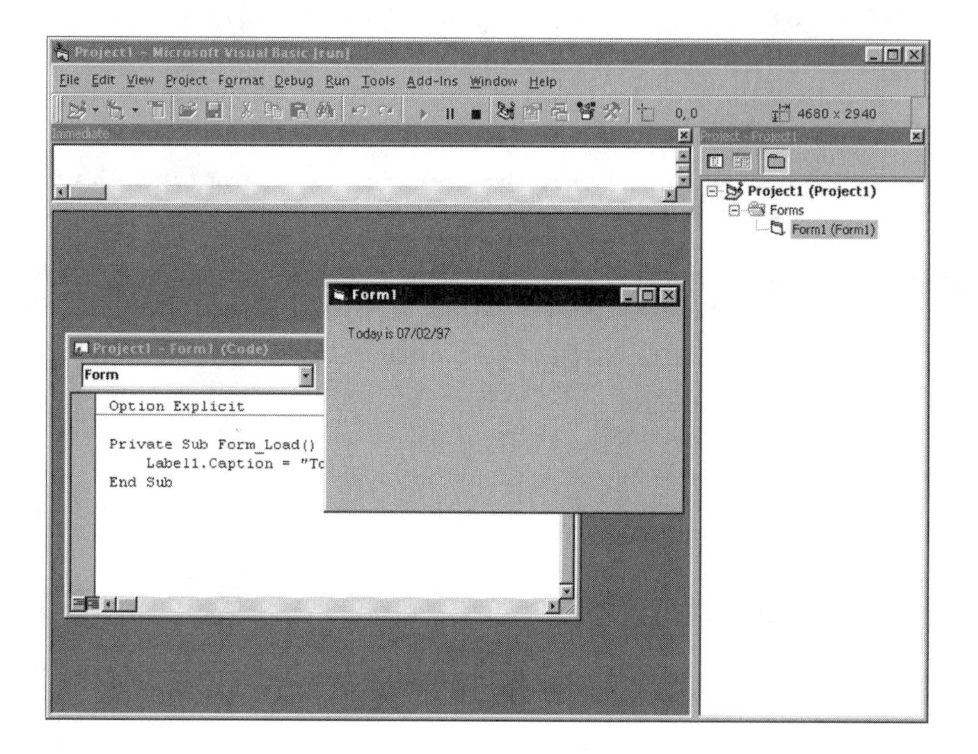

4 If you stop the program by double-clicking the control box on the form or using its close button, another window appears, (this time a message box), telling you 'Goodbye!'.

How It Works

You can change the way the message box looks and behaves from within your program, but our box is the plain vanilla version that contains only text and an OK button. Clicking the OK button will end the program.

Unlike the **Load** event, the **Unload** event does contain some parameters within the brackets, in this case **Cancel As Integer**. The word **Cancel** doesn't really mean anything—it's just a name that Visual Basic has given to the parameter to show what it does. The `As Integer` tells you that `Cancel` is an integer. Integers and other weird names are covered in the section on variables in Chapter 4. For now, all you need to know is that integer means whole number. By setting `Cancel` to a number, you can cancel the unload event. For instance, your code may not want the form to unload in a real program if the user needed to save some data first. If this all seems confusing then don't worry, it will become clear later.

That's it for our simple application—simple being the operative word here.

Making an Executable File

So far the program we have written has been run from within the Visual Basic environment by clicking on the Start icon or by pressing *F5*. Visual Basic wouldn't get far as a tool for serious developers if each user of a Visual Basic program had to go into Visual Basic itself to use the application. Visual Basic therefore provides a way to turn your finished programs into, effectively, stand-alone units that can be run by selecting them in the Windows Start menu, just like other programs.

When your program is complete and ready to go to the users (a long way off yet, I know), then it's time to make it an **exe,** or **executable file**. Turning your work of art into an **exe** is very easy.

The Visual Basic approach to producing an executable file is a little confusing. In fact, it was always confusing before—but it has become a little more confusing now, but for the better. Confused?

Interpreted vs. Compiled Code

Traditionally, programming languages got divided into two camps: **interpreted** or **compiled**. Compiled language users tended to look down on the interpreted masses. Interpreted languages had a reputation for detaching their users from the system, shielding them from the harsh realities of computer use and generally giving them a candy-coated introduction to programming. They are also a lot slower and a lot less slick than their compiled cousins.

The reason for this latter point is simple. Without going into too much theory of computer science, the PC sitting on your desk cannot, and never will, understand a word you say to it. If you could open her up, apply your fingers to some tracks on the circuit board, and tap out an electronic rhythm of 1s and 0s, then you would be approaching something that could be called communication (or lunacy).

Writing computer programs this way is tedious, error prone and archaic. We have evolved since the bad old days of toggle switches and now have these wonderful things called programming languages. A compiler takes your assembled mass of instructions and keywords and translates them into the electronic 1s and 0s that the computer needs in order to be able to go and do what you want it to do.

An interpreter, on the other hand, does not. It's a program that sits in between the machine itself and your program. When you run the program you are really running the interpreter which then happily trots through your code one line at a time, firing translated, interpreted statements at the computer in its mother tongue. It's a slow process.

Pseudocompiled Languages

Visual Basic was always a bit of a halfway house. When you compiled your applications in previous versions, they were always translated into an easier to deal with code called **P-Code**. Technically, this could be called compiling. However, you needed to ship a set of files from Microsoft with your application since the computer still could not understand this P-Code yet. The files you shipped interpreted it.

In VB5 we have a choice. If you have the Learning Edition of the language, then when you compile you essentially take the old-fashioned route. A program kicks in which translates your code into P-Code. When you run the application for real, a second program runs which interprets this P-Code into something that the computer can understand.

If on the other hand you have the Professional or Enterprise Editions of Visual Basic, then you can actually choose to do a real, proper compile. No hidden run-time interpreters with this one; your code gets compiled down to the something that the computer can understand natively, the result of course being that you end up with a much faster program than your interpreted buddies. OK, so you still have to supply some library files that your native code needs to carry out all its tasks. But so do C++ programmers—so don't let them look down their nose at you any more....

You can enable and disable this functionality from the Project Properties dialog.

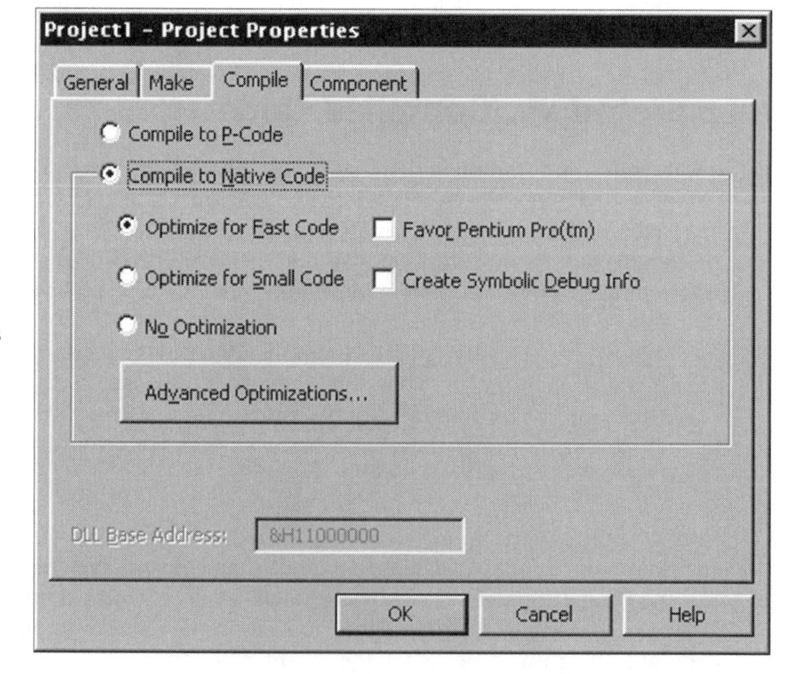

It's a little beyond the scope of this book to explain all of these options in detail, so take a look at the help files if you are curious. The rest of us are actually going to produce an executable program that can run outside of Visual Basic, without the aid of mirrors or a harness.

Try It Out - Creating an EXE File

1 When writing a program you may need to tell Visual Basic which part of your program to run first. To do this, select Project Properties... from the Project menu. A tabbed dialog appears which allows you to customize specific parts of Visual Basic and the current project. Click on the General tab now to bring up the general project options.

One of the first options on the project options dialog is Startup Object. By clicking the arrow to the right of the text box and selecting the name of a form in your project from the list provided, you can tell Visual Basic exactly where to start the program when you finally compile it. You'll notice that in addition to the forms in your project, there is also an option Sub Main. This allows you to start the execution of your application with code contained in a module rather than a form. Don't worry about this or the other options available for now, just get rid of the dialog by clicking on Cancel.

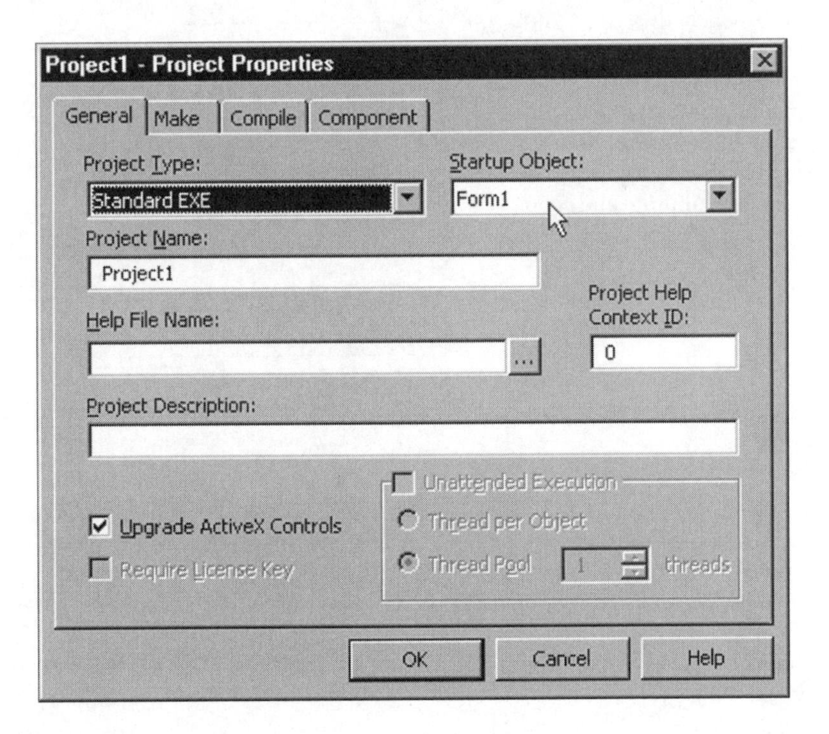

2 Now go to the File menu and select the Make EXE File... option. A dialog box appears asking you to enter a file name for your finished program, such as **`MyApp.exe`** or **`WroxWrite.Exe`**, and allowing you to determine where your file will be saved. In the file dialog, type in **`Test`** as the program name. Visual Basic will automatically add a **`.exe`** to the end of the name to produce an executable program called **`Test.exe`**.

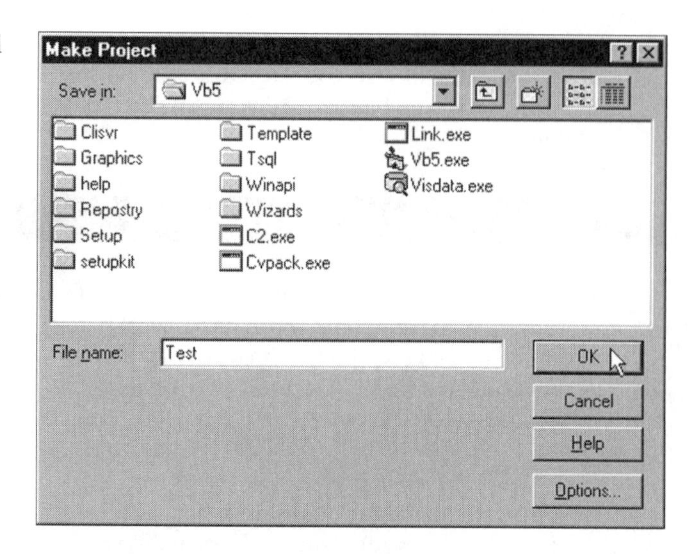

3 This dialog also contains a host of options, available by clicking on the Options... button. Click this now and give your program an **application name** by typing something into the Title box. This is the name of the program that will appear when it's running and you try to switch between it and other applications. It isn't necessarily the same as its file name. Let's call this program **`Today`**.

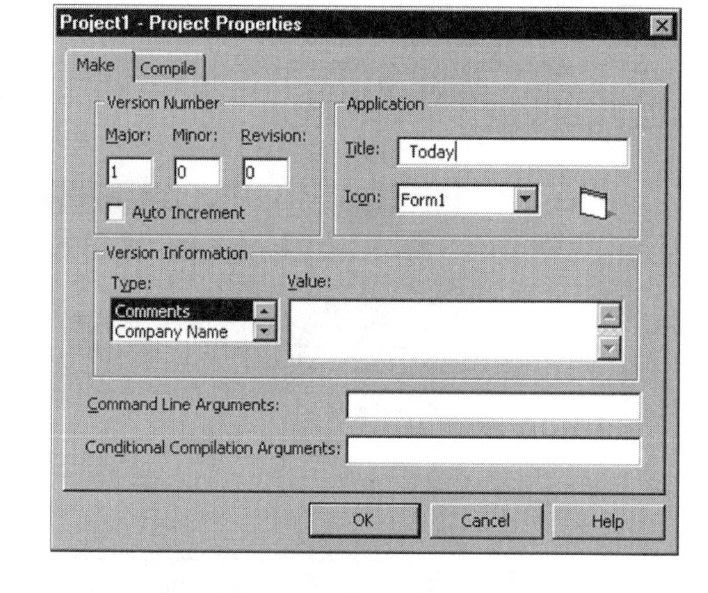

*As you can now see from this dialog, there's a lot more to an **`Exe`** file than meets the eye. The Project Properties dialog lets you embed information into the final executable, such as who wrote it, the version number, copyright information and so on. In these days of rife software piracy, this can be a godsend if ever you need to prove that a program you wrote belongs to you. You could also click on the Compile tab at the top of the dialog in the Professional and Enterprise editions of Visual Basic to change how the project actually gets compiled.*

4 Finally, hit OK in the Project Properties dialog and again in the Make Project dialog. Providing there are no obvious bugs in your code, Visual Basic will produce an **exe** file that you can then run.

5 Now we can try the program from outside Visual Basic, running as a native application. Open up My Computer or Explorer, navigate to the folder where you compiled the program, and double-click on its name. It runs just the same as it would inside Visual Basic.

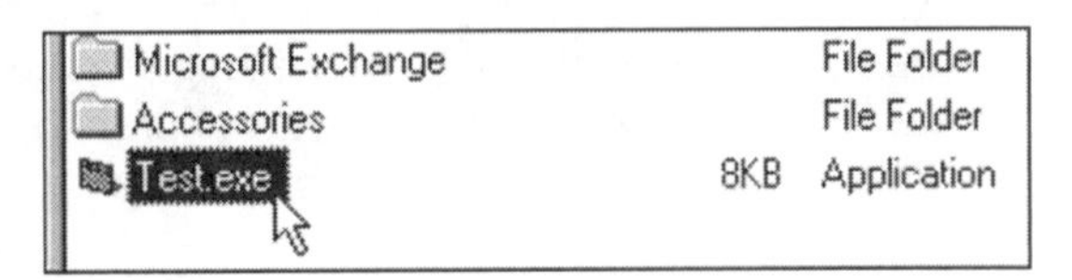

Changing the Program Icon

The program icon you see in My Computer or Explorer is a property of one of the forms in the project. By default it is the property of the first form to be displayed—the Startup Object we looked at earlier—but it can be changed to the icon of one of the other forms using the Project Properties dialog. That form's **Icon** property holds the name of an icon file which is displayed in the Windows Start menu for the complete application, when a shortcut is created to it on the Desktop, and when it's minimized to the Taskbar.

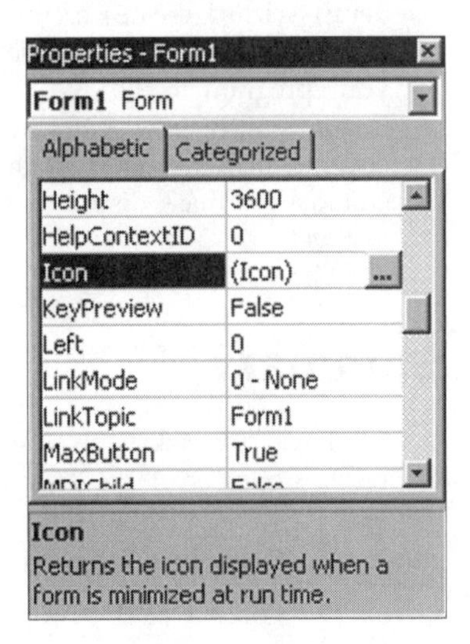

You can set the icon yourself, rather than accepting the default one as we just did, by bringing up the properties window of a form, moving to the Icon property and double-clicking it or clicking the **ellipsis** (three dots) button. A dialog box will appear asking you to select the name of an icon file. These usually end in **.ico**.

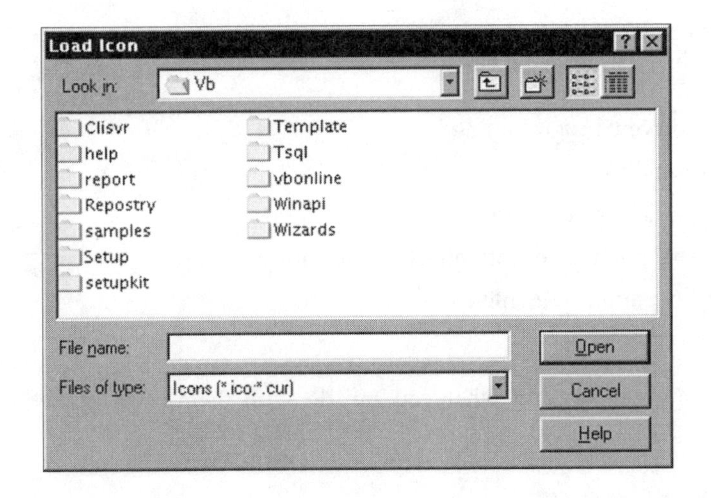

If you installed all the clip art and sample programs that came with Visual Basic, you will find a vast number of icons waiting for you in the `Icons` folder. Typically this will be **`\Visual Basic 5.0\Graphics\Icons`**. Once you have found what you want, just go through the same steps as before for creating an **`exe`** file. Then right-drag it onto your desktop from My Computer or Explorer to create a shortcut, and voilà! The icon of your choice!

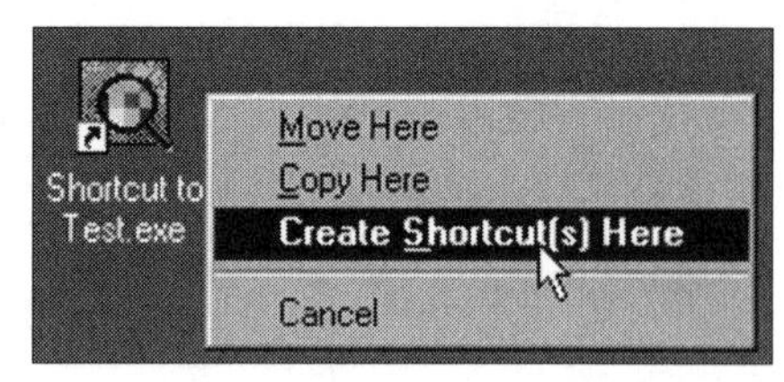

The Setup Wizard

When you're actually ready to send your program out to your users, you will need to make the installation process as simple as possible. Before the days of Windows, and in earlier versions of Visual Basic, this wasn't a desperately complicated task. However, since Visual Basic 3, and the advent of Windows 95 and Windows NT, life has become a lot more difficult. There are several DLLs and other supporting files that have to placed in the correct location on the user's system, without overwriting existing ones that may be newer. And, of course, there's the registry to worry about.

Visual Basic supplies a program called **Application Setup Wizard** to help you do this.

Setup Wizard creates an installation program for you that can lead your users through the process step by step. It also makes sure that you don't forget to give them any files, sets up your program in the Start menu, and makes the whole thing look a lot more polished than if you simply gave your users a scrap of paper telling them what to do. Setup Wizard is covered in detail later in this book when your projects become larger, and frankly, more suitable for mass distribution. **`Today`** is a good start, but I wouldn't give up your day job just yet.

Summary

We have covered a lot of ground very quickly in this chapter, so let's just recap on what we've done. Over the course of this chapter you have:

- Been introduced to event-driven programming
- Looked at the properties window
- Customized different properties on the form
- Added code to a form to respond to events affecting that form
- Compiled the program to make an **`exe`** file

At various points in this chapter you've gotten a taste of what you're going to learn in future chapters. First on the list are controls and what you can do with them. This is the subject of the next chapter.

Why Not Try...

1. Create a project with a form and a single command button. In the **`Form_Load`** event, use one of the command button's properties to hide the button at startup.

2. With the project you just created in design mode, press *F8*. Watch what happens. Keep pressing *F8* until the form is displayed.

3. Create an executable of this very simple project.

4. When you create an executable of your project, there are several options available to you. What option can be used to display the version number of your application releases?

5. Practice searching through an existing project for a text string. Load up the **`BIBLIO`** project contained in the Visual Basic sample directory. Double click on the form, and view the **`Form_Load`** event. Use the **`Find`** command in the Edit menu to search for all occurrences of the string "**`Unload`**" in the current procedure, module and project. Remember this lesson well, it can come in handy!

asic Visual Basic Visual Ba
al Basic Visual Basic Visual
Basic Visual Basic Visual Ba
ual Basic Vi
Basic Visu
ual Basic V
l Basic Visu
isual Basic Visual Basic
al Basic Visual Basic Visua
Visual Basic Visual Basic Visu
l Basic Visual Ba
l Basic Visual
ic Visual Basi
Basic Visual B
ic Visual Basi
l Basic Visual
ual Basic Visual Basic Visual Ba
Visual Basic Visual Basic Visu
sual Basic Visual Basic Visu
Visual Basic Visual Bas

Common Controls

Although forms are the mainstay of any Visual Basic application, they aren't much use without controls. Controls are the text boxes, list boxes, command buttons and so on that give your user something to interact with. They are also the means by which your program obtains and displays its data.

In this chapter we'll look at a complete application that contains some of the most common controls. We'll see how controls work, and how they fit into a Visual Basic program. In this chapter you'll learn about:

- How to select controls and place them on your form
- What controls really do
- How the command button control is used
- Why controls have properties
- Using other common controls such as text boxes, labels, option buttons, image controls and picture boxes

Working with Controls

To get started, we'll look at the general techniques for selecting and placing the different controls on your form. We'll then look at how the appearance and behavior of controls can be programmed using properties, much as we did with forms in Chapter 2.

We'll use the command button as an example of a frequently used control, but also run through some of the other common controls that you will use, such as **option buttons**, **check boxes**, **text boxes** and **image controls**. We'll also look at some of the problems these controls bring with them, and how to overcome them. First, however, we'll revisit our old friend the toolbox, which contains all of the controls that we're going to use in this chapter.

The Toolbox

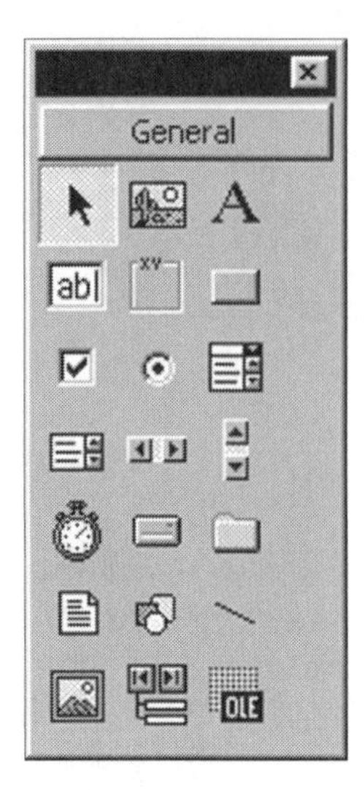

Just as with other aspects of Visual Basic, placing a control such as a command button or a text box on to a form is merely a question of pointing and clicking with the mouse. As we saw in Chapter 1, all of your controls are kept in the toolbox, waiting for you to put them on to your form.

The toolbox can be displayed by selecting Toolbox from the View menu, or by clicking on the toolbox icon on the main toolbar in Visual Basic.

Once displayed, you can move the toolbox around the screen by dragging its title bar, just like any other window. You close it by clicking the close button in the top right corner of the toolbox window. Again, in keeping with most of the other windows in the Visual Basic design environment, you can also right click over the toolbar to display a context sensitive menu. This, among other things, lets you tell Visual Basic whether or not you would like to make this dialog dockable.

Placing Controls on to Your Form

In Chapter 2, we placed a simple label control on to a form to display today's date. Let's do it again, this time with a command button.

Try It Out - Placing Controls

1 Start a new project by selecting New Project from the File menu.

2 The New Project dialog appears. Choose the Standard Exe option, as shown:

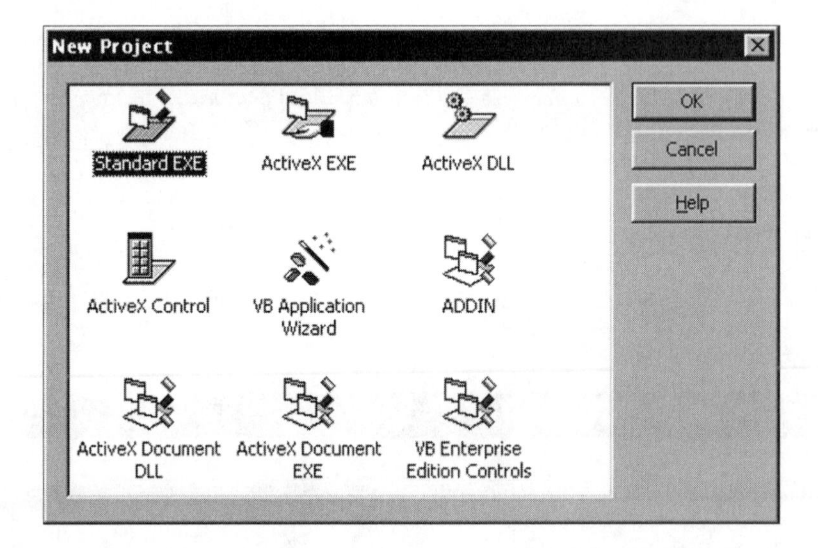

3 Once you have your new project created, and the blank form is on display waiting for you to draw on it, select the control you want by clicking on its icon in the toolbox. In this example, we want the command button. Don't forget that if you get lost, you can simply move the mouse pointer over the icons in the toolbox to have a pop-up tip appear, telling you what you are pointing at.

4 Move the cursor to the place on the form where you want the control to go, and draw the control by holding the left mouse button down and dragging the mouse. A rectangle will appear on the form representing the size of the control.

When you're happy with the size, just release the mouse button and the control will be drawn on to the form.

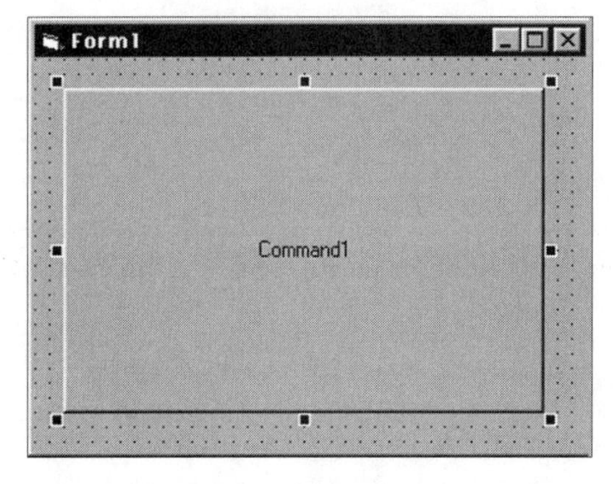

5 You can now click on the control itself and drag it around until you're happy with its position.

Alternatively, if you need to move a control around the form small step at a time, you can do so by holding down the Ctrl *key and using the cursor keys on the keyboard. Each press of an arrow on the keyboard translates to a movement of just one dot on the screen in the indicated direction.*

Resizing Controls

Even after a number of controls have been added to the form, it's still possible to move them around or resize them.

Try It Out - Resizing Controls

1 Clicking on a control you have already drawn selects that control and displays the controls **resize handles**. These are small black boxes on each edge and each corner of the control.

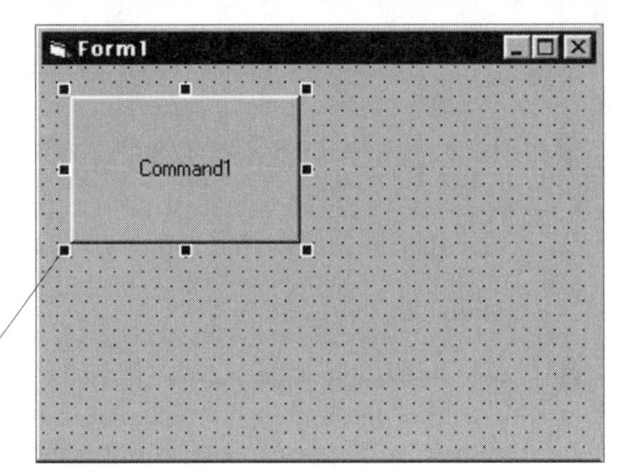

Clicking on these buttons and dragging the mouse around causes the control to change size.

> ***Some controls cannot be changed in size, while others have preset minimum heights or widths below which you can't go For example, a combo box should always be high enough to display one line of text.***

2 Sometimes it's faster to double-click on a control in the toolbox and allow Visual Basic to put it on the form at the default size and position. You can then resize and move it around. Visual Basic lays each control one on top of the other in the default position, so they can be a little hard to find if you don't move each one as you place it.

Just as with moving controls, you can also resize a selected control on a step by step level. Instead of holding down Ctrl *and pressing the arrow keys though, hold down* Shift *and press the arrow keys. Each click of a cursor key results in a small change in the size of the selected control.*

The Alignment Grid

To help you position the controls neatly, Visual Basic provides an **alignment grid**. This is the grid of small black dots that covers your form. The grid can be changed in size or removed completely using the General tab on the Options dialog (remember from Chapter 1 that you can bring up the Options dialog by selecting Options... from the Tools menu).

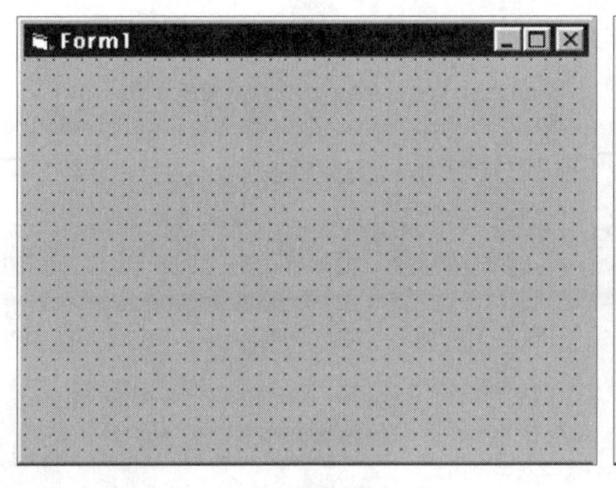

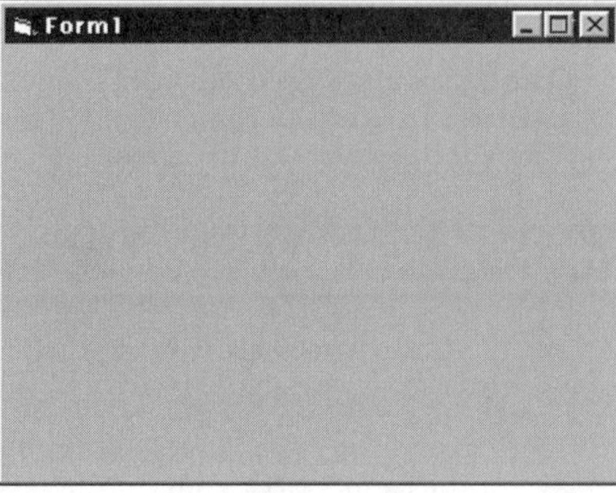

With a grid *Without a grid*

Try It Out - Changing the Alignment Grid

1 Select the General tab on Options dialog (once again, you can bring this into view by selecting Options from the Tools menu).

The first four options on this box allow you to set up the size of the grid, decide whether or not you want the grid shown, and whether or not Visual Basic should force you to place controls on grid points (Align Controls To Grid). You can change all these options to suit your requirements.

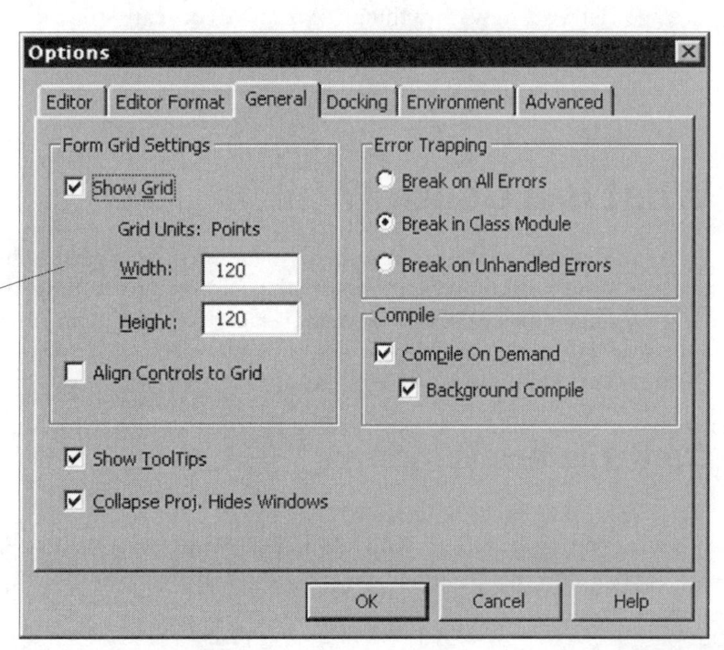

I tend to use quite a fine grid (height and width both 150). This allows me a great deal of flexibility when moving my controls around, yet still lets me line the controls up neatly on the form rather than in a cluttered mess. Some people don't like using the grid at all and turn it off at the first possible instance. Do whatever you feel happy with!

Control Locking

Once your form is festooned with controls, it becomes very easy to drag them out of alignment by accident. Fortunately, the Visual Basic environment provides a control locking feature that freezes all your controls on a form into place.

Try It Out - Control Locking

1 Place a few randomly chosen controls on to your form from the toolbox and size and position them as you see fit.

2 Choose Lock Controls from the Format menu (or if you have the Form Editor toolbar on display then click on the padlock icon).

3 Now try and move the controls around. You get the little resizing handles, but they're white and won't let you move anything. (Actually, you can still move or resize them using *shift* or *ctrl*.)

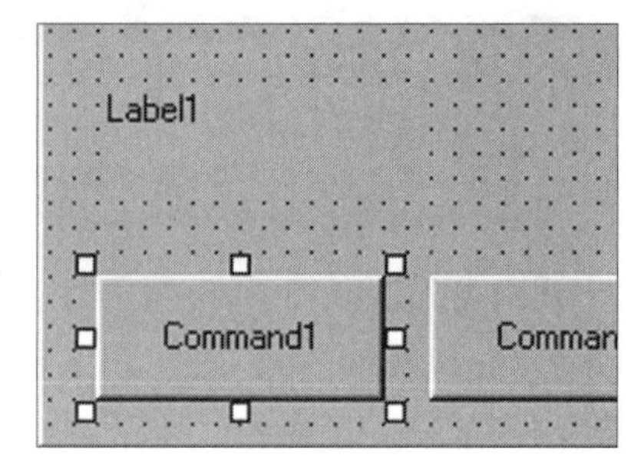

What is a Control?

While controls might just appear to be nice looking graphics on your form, if their purpose was purely decorative, then Visual Basic would be little better than a fancy painting program (quiet at the back there!). However, the real power of Visual Basic comes as a result of the **functionality** that's built into each control (i.e. what each control can actually do). Let's take a look at what controls can actually do.

Controls are Windows

A control is really a window that has a program running inside it. This is no different to what you are used to with your own Windows Desktop. To run a new application, you open a new window. This application will take control of that window and invest it with its own appearance and functionality. A Visual Basic control takes control of a window in a rather more extreme fashion than an application, but it's essentially the same.

A control is therefore a lump of prewritten code inside a window which can be dropped into your own program. It incorporates into your own project the functions which that code provides. The software industry has been eagerly awaiting these kind of standard components for many years in order to speed up the process of writing software.

Visual Basic introduced the idea of **custom controls**. Before this, each programmer would write almost every line of code in an application from the ground up. This meant that there was a large amount of repetition of coding which had no doubt been done by other programmers in other projects. Although we consider Visual Basic to be truly revolutionary, it's only a result of what has happened in every other industry. Your PC is made up of components from dozens of different manufacturers, each specializing in producing one particular part. What makes Visual Basic controls special isn't the idea of re-useable software components alone—these have existed in different incarnations for many years. It is, rather, the elegance with which each control can be customized to, and integrated with, your particular application.

A custom control, or ActiveX control is a component that extends the functionality of your current environment over and above the controls that you already have in your tool palette. By adding more ActiveX controls to your system, you're actually increasing the power and usefulness of your Visual Basic environment. The fact that you can add controls also means that each installation of Visual Basic tends to be totally unique—every developer has their own preference for which ActiveX controls should appear in their Visual Basic toolbox.

These controls are ActiveX enabled, which means can easily be used by many other ActiveX enabled applications within your desktop, such as the Office suite, Internet Explorer and so on. These controls are usually created by software vendors and come as part of new software packages or can be downloaded from the Internet for free or for a small fee.

Properties and Events

You interact with a control by using three types of hook: properties, methods and events.

- **Properties** are a collection of parameters you can set to control the way a control looks and behaves. If controls were people, properties would be characteristics like height, weight, fitness and programming skills.
- **Methods** are things that the control can do. If a person were a control they might have a method to Eat.
- **Events** are the things you can do to a control that it will recognize and be able to respond to. Each control has a set of events it understands. You will be relieved to hear that controls respond to a far narrower range of events than people do. You also don't have to persuade or encourage controls to do anything—you just click on them with the mouse.

Each control has its own set of properties, methods and events that make it useful for particular purposes. To make this a bit clearer, let's take a look at probably the most common control of all, the **command button**.

Command Buttons 

Second only in popularity to the text box, and unsurpassed for its sheer simplicity and lack of charisma, is the command button. I talk in terms of simplicity, because although command buttons are incredibly useful and enormously widespread throughout the world of Windows, they can only really do one thing—click. You point at them with the mouse, click the left mouse button and voilà, a **click** event occurs. In fact, so enormously popular are the command buttons that Microsoft even extended their functionality a tad with VB5. Now, not only do command buttons click, but they can click while displaying a small picture or two... neat huh?

Events

Of course there are other events that a command button can respond to, but the majority of them all center around whether or not the button is being clicked. Events such as **MouseDown** and **KeyDown** are useful in detecting exactly what the user is trying to do to the command button, and with which weapon. Essentially, however, it's all a question of clicking.

Properties

Once you start to think about controls as windows, it becomes easy to see why they have properties, like forms do. Both have **Height** properties, **Font** properties, **BackColor** and so on. You can also use our old friend, the Properties Window to resize, change the color and fonts of controls.

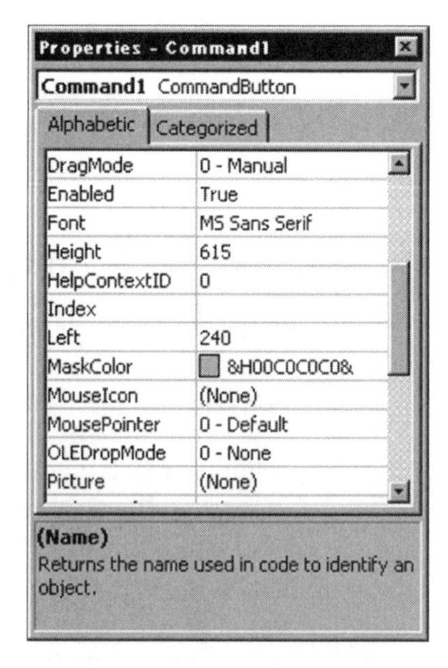

Let's change the properties of a command button now, to alter the way in which it functions.

Try It Out - Using Command Button Properties

1 Create a new Visual Basic project by selecting New Project from the File menu. As usual, make sure that you select Standard Exe from the project types on offer. Once the project has been created, select the command button icon from the toolbox and draw a command button on the form.

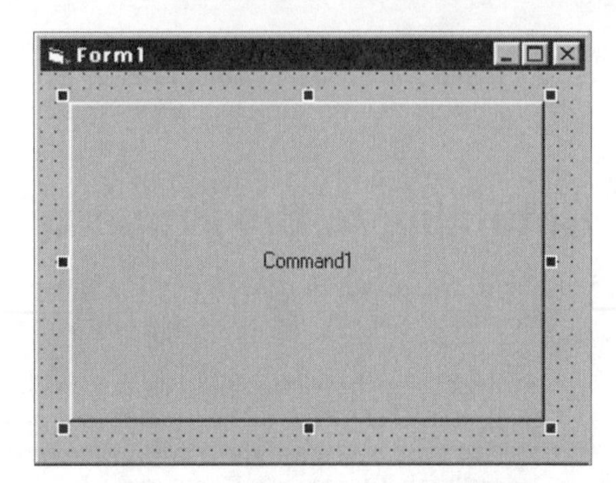

2 Let's actually make the control button do something this time—we'll make it beep whenever it's clicked. To do this we need to display the code window and type in some code.

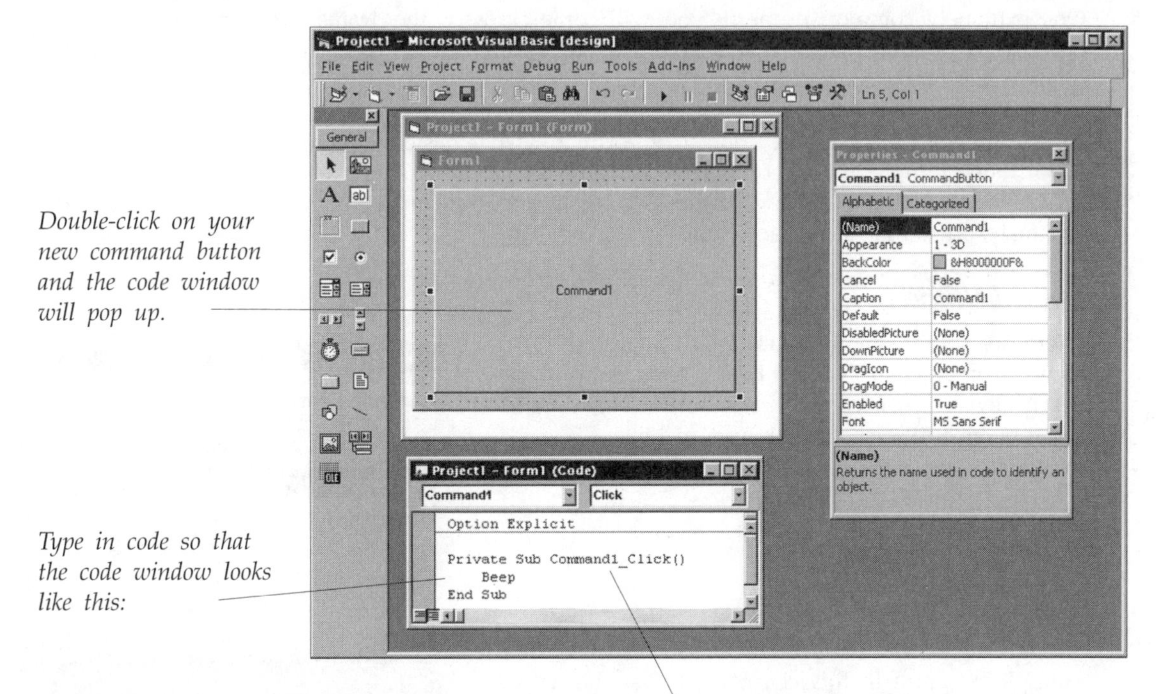

Notice that the text inside the code window says **`Private Sub Command1_Click()`***. This means that we are looking at the code that will occur whenever the command button,* **`Command1`***, is clicked. We cover code in a lot more detail a little later in the book, so don't fret if you can't understand the strange words and symbols. All you need to know is that we are going to be writing code which Visual Basic will run whenever this command button is clicked.*

3 Now try running the program by either pressing *F5*, selecting Start from the Run menu, or by clicking the run icon on the main Visual Basic toolbar.

If you now click the command button you'll find it beeps, because the code you typed into the command button's click event tells it to. When you have had enough of the program, you can stop it by pressing *Alt-F4* or by clicking the end icon on the toolbar.

Returning to the Property Market

Before we go any further, it's worth talking a little more about properties, especially some of the more common ones.

In order to make Visual Basic as easy to learn as possible, Microsoft was kind enough to give most of the controls in Visual Basic similar properties. For instance, all controls have an Enabled property, most also have a Visible property and so on. This makes it worth speaking generally about properties and controls before delving into specific instances.

The Name Property

One extremely common property you will come across is the Name property. This is used in order to write code which will differentiate between each of your Visual Basic controls. In other words, each control is given a name.

Whenever you create a new control or form in Visual Basic, a default name is automatically given. For example, when you start up a new project in Visual Basic, the default form is called Form1. When you draw the first command button on to that form, it will be called Command1, the next Command2 and so on.

Standard Names

There are some common standards for giving a name to your controls. Text boxes, for example, are nearly always prefixed with `txt`, forms begin with `frm`, option buttons with `opt` and so on.

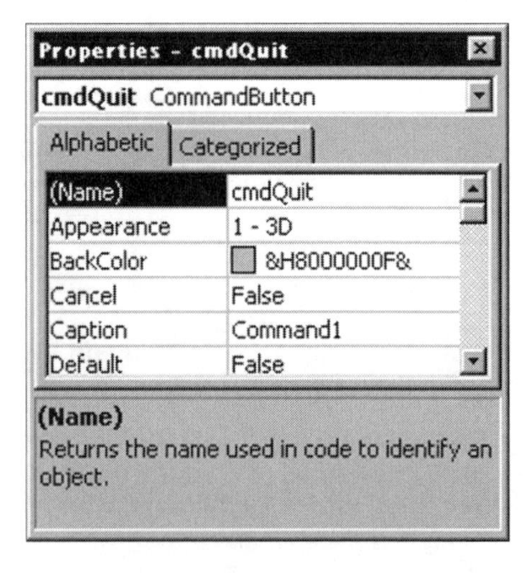

A full list of these is given in Appendix B, but you'll come across many of them as we cover the example program in this chapter. At first the names may seem a little strange, but the end result is that they do make your code a lot easier to read and understand.

For example, if you have a line like:

```
optDrive.text = "D:"
```

Visual Basic won't like it. This is because option buttons don't have a **Text** property. Once you get used to working with Visual basic this sort of mistake is easy to spot since the name of the control indicates that it's an option button.

Of course, if you wanted to name a drive control optDrive, then that's entirely up to you. Visual Basic only complains if you try to use properties that don't belong to certain controls, such as a Text property with an option button. If this happens, Visual Basic gives you an error message and lets you go away and fix the error.

In the final analysis, Visual Basic doesn't really care what you call your controls—it's quite happy for you to name them all A, B, C, D etc. However, that doesn't really make your life as a programmer very easy. Sticking to a standard way of naming your controls can make your life a lot more hassle free, especially when you have to come back to the code in a few months time to maintain it or fix a bug. By that time you probably won't have a clue what the code does. The last thing you need at that stage is to waste time trying to figure out what the control and variable names mean.

Caption and Text Properties

Each control on a form in Visual Basic has to have a unique name, unless you deliberately place them in a group called a control array. You can assign the name yourself using the standard naming convention from Appendix B, or you just accept the default name that Visual Basic gives you. This is really a private name between you the programmer, and the control. When you run the program the name will be invisible to the user.

There are, however, two other text labels that can be assigned to certain controls and which will display that text on screen. These are the Caption and Text properties.

The Caption Property

Captions are usually found on objects such as forms, frames and command buttons. A caption is simply a piece of text that is displayed on screen to give the object some kind of header or title.

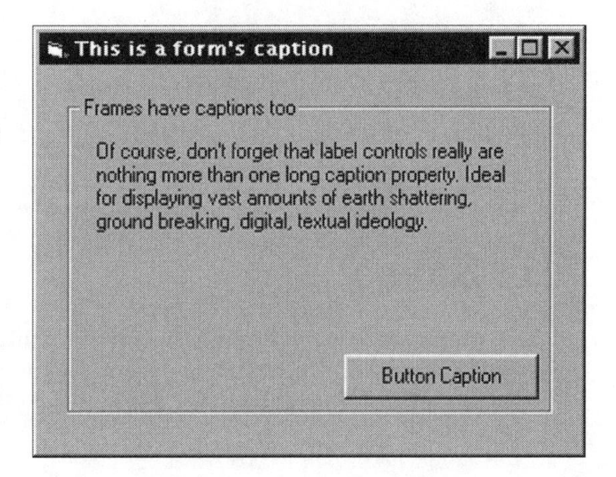

In the case of the command button, the text is actually displayed in the center of the command button itself.

The Text Property

The Text property is somewhat different. This is normally found on controls that can accept data entry from the user, such as a **text box** or **combo box**. By setting the Text property, you are actually telling Visual Basic what to display on screen in the text entry area. The following line of code is what we'll use when building our graphic file viewer sample. Remember our first question about the text box? This code makes the file name appear in the file name text box by assigning it to the **TEXT** property of the text box.

```
txtFileName.TEXT = filFileNames.Path & "\" & filFileNames.filename
```

We'll see how this works in detail when we look at the label and text box controls later in the chapter.

Shortcut Keys

There is another interesting feature of the Caption property, which in fact applies to any control which can have a caption. Look closely at the wording of the caption on the following button.

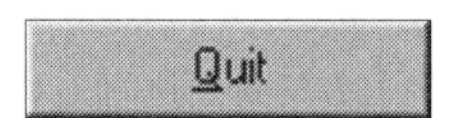

*Notice how the letter Q is underlined. This is called a **hot key**, and it means that by pressing Alt-Q when the program is running, you can trigger the Quit button click event without having to move the mouse to point and click.*

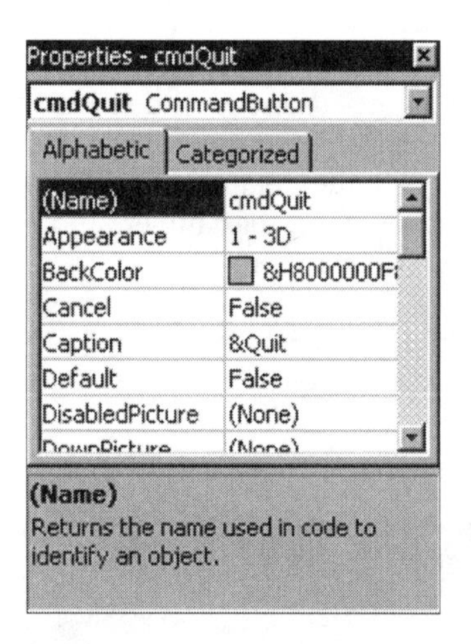

Hot keys can be set up on any control that can have a caption by simply placing an & sign in front of the letter you want underlined.

From a user's point of view this makes your programs much easier to use.

Text Boxes 

Text boxes are one of the most common controls found in any Windows program. They provide an area on screen into which the user can enter information and where you can also display information to the user.

The area inside these controls behaves like a DOS text screen of old. Like many of the other controls in Visual Basic, much of the hard work with text boxes is done for you. In a great many cases, all you need to do is simply place a text box on to a form before your users start entering data. Visual Basic and Windows automatically handle all the complex stuff such as displaying the characters which the user types, inserting and deleting characters, scrolling the data in the text box, selecting text, cutting and pasting text and so on.

It's so easy in fact, there's nothing stopping us trying it out!

Try It Out - Text Boxes

1. Start a new project in Visual Basic by selecting New Project from the File menu. (Again, don't forget to select Standard Exe from the selection of project types that appears.)

2. Select the text box control from the toolbox and draw a text box on the default form.

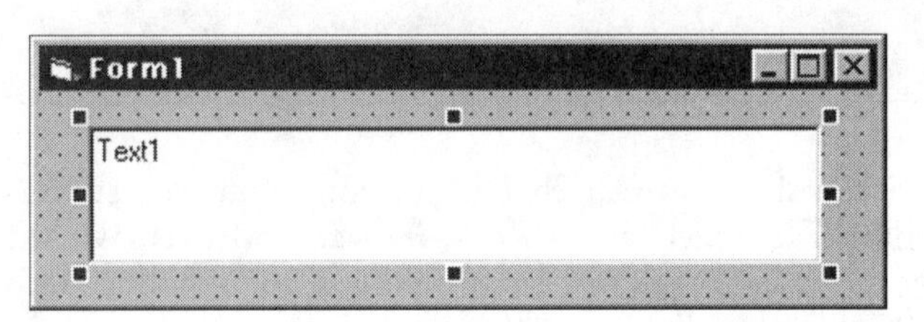

3. You can radically change the way a text box looks by using its **`Font`** property. This handy little property lets you change absolutely everything you could ever want to change about the style of the text in the text box.

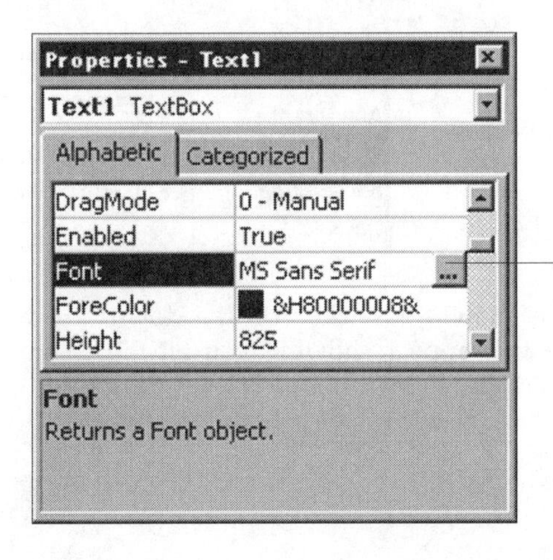

Click on the command button with the little dots to the right of the font property and a font dialog box will miraculously appear.

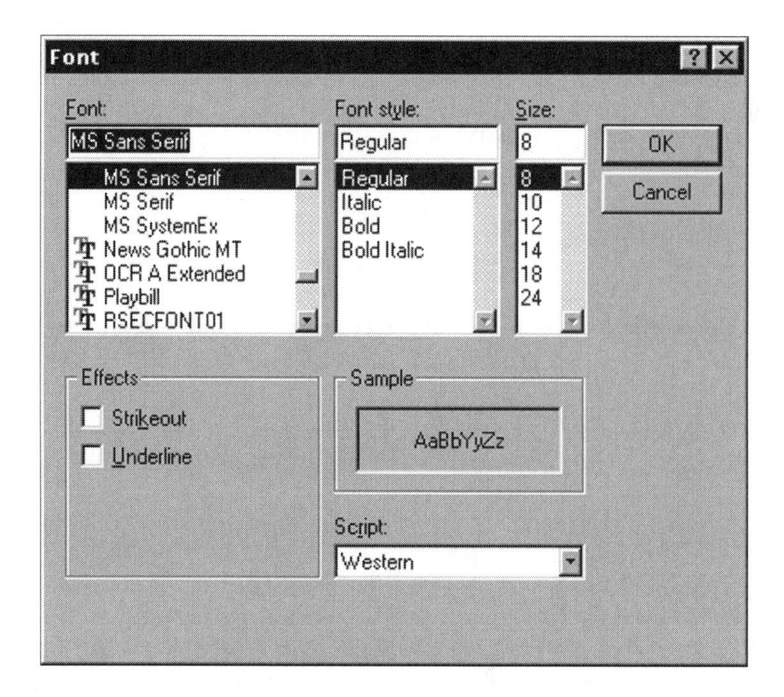

Using this one dialog you can change the font name, its style (whether or not it is bold, underlined, italicized and so on), its size and even whether it appears as subscript or superscript—all by doing nothing but pointing and clicking. The only stuff you can't do with this dialog is set up the font colors.

Color… there is more than one? Sure, you can change the background color of the text (the color behind the writing), and the foreground color (the color of the actual text). To accomplish this you use the background and foreground color properties.

4 Find the **`BackColor`** property in the properties dialog box for the text box.

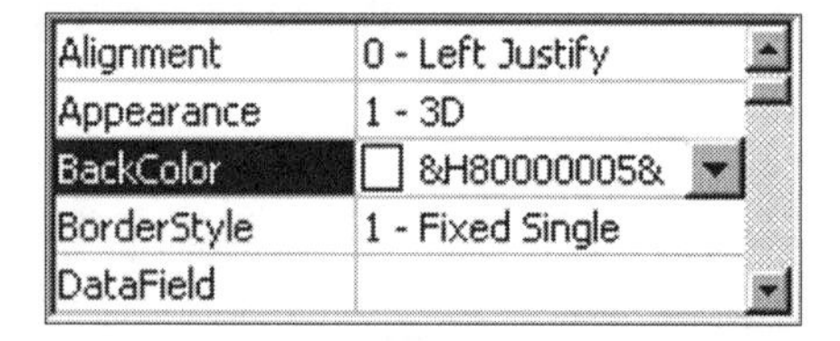

5 Don't worry about the complicated value shown—just click on the down arrow to the right of the property and a color dialog will appear showing you all the colors that are available. To select one, just point and click—try it!

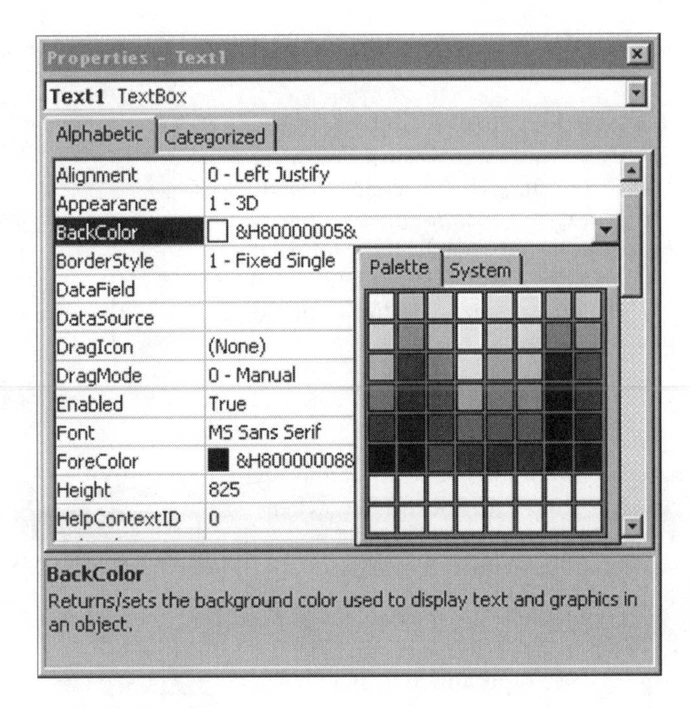

Notice that the color popup that appears has a couple of tabs across its top, one saying Palette, the other saying System. In the screenshot the Palette popup is selected meaning that a nice selection of colors is shown. If I had selected the System tab, then the colors on display would have been limited to those set up as system colors using the Windows control panel's Desktop settings.

That's really all there is to it. We'll take a look at fonts and colors in more detail in Chapter 11 - Graphics. For now though, let's move on to some of the other more common properties of the great text box.

Text Box Properties

The most important property of a text box is the **`Text`** property. We can change this at design time in the properties window, or at any point your program can examine the **`Text`** property to see exactly what is in the text box on screen, or it can be used to change text on the fly. And the latter feature exactly what we're going to take advantage of right now!

Try It Out - Changing Text On The Fly

Just to make things a little trickier we're going to prevent the user from changing the text in the text box by his/herself, to prove there's no cheating involved.

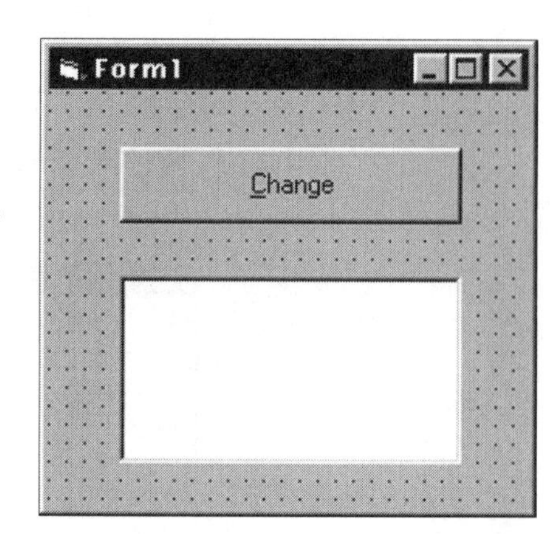

1 Start a new Visual Basic project and select Standard EXE and place a command button and a text box on the form. Change name property of the command button to **cmdChange** and the text box to **txtDisplay**. Also change the caption of the command button to &Change and blank the Text property of the text box. The form should currently look like this:

2 Now change the MultiLine property of the text box from false to true. This means that when the end of one line is reached, the text box will wrap the text around on to the next line.

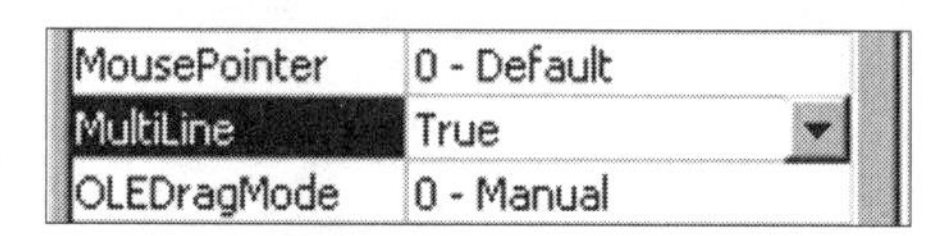

3 Next changed the Locked Property to True. This means you can't type anything into the text box.

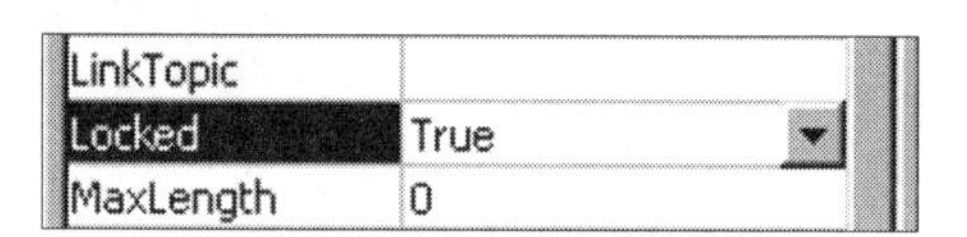

4 Double click on the Change button and add the following line to the event code:

```
Private Sub cmdChange_Click()

txtDisplay.Text = txtDisplay.Text + "Hello!"

End Sub
```

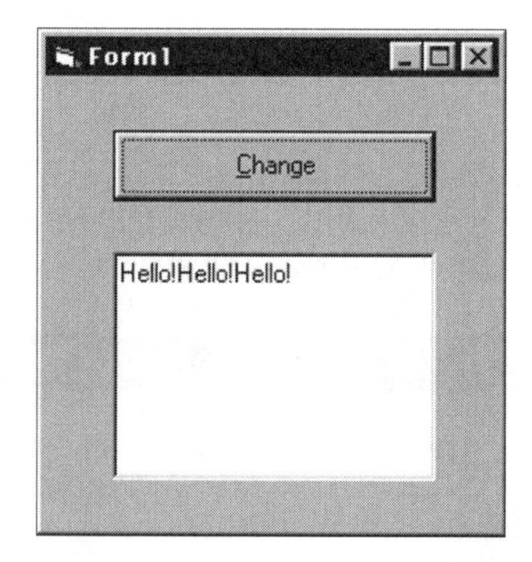

5 Now run the program, and although you can't alter anything in the text box by typing into it, if you press the Change button, it adds a line of a text to the text box every time you press it.

How It Works

The program is simple enough, it just takes the **`Text`** property from the text box and displays the word 'Hello!' every time the Change button is clicked. We use the **`Locked`** property to stop the user from entering any data into the text box and the **`MultiLine`** property to ensure that the word is displayed on the next line and on the one after.

Checking User Input

Really the only thing text boxes can't do without your help is check the data that the user enters. Problems occur because a text box allows the user to key in more information than can be displayed, and to enter alphabetic data when your program only really wants numeric information and so on.

By default the text box allows you to type in data that is larger than its width. When this happens the text box scrolls to show you the next section. You can also scroll it yourself by placing the cursor inside the text box and using the arrow keys to move left and right. This can be great when you need such a feature, but it can make your interface look badly planned.

Visual Basic provides a property to help us get round this. Setting the MaxLength property to anything other than 0 limits the amount of data that can be keyed in. Try it: set the MaxLength property to something silly like 5 and run the program. Now select the text box and start typing. You can only enter 5 characters. Stop the program and change the **`MaxLength`** property back to 0. If you run the program again you will find that you can enter as much text as you want.

Text Box Events

I keep on saying **displays data** and **enters data** for the text box when really it would be more logical to say that a text box holds and displays **text**. Well, despite the somewhat misleading name, text boxes don't only hold text. They can hold punctuation marks, numbers, arithmetic symbols—in fact anything you can produce by pressing a key, the text box can display. This can become a little bit of a problem if, for example, you needed the user to enter a number, and only a number.

Try It Out - Getting Data From a Text Box

Let's look at a program that does check what is entered into a text box.

1 Start up a new project in the normal way, and when the default form appears, add two labels, two text boxes and a command button to it. Delete the default entry in the **`Text`** properties of both text boxes, so that they appear blank on the screen. The form should look like this:

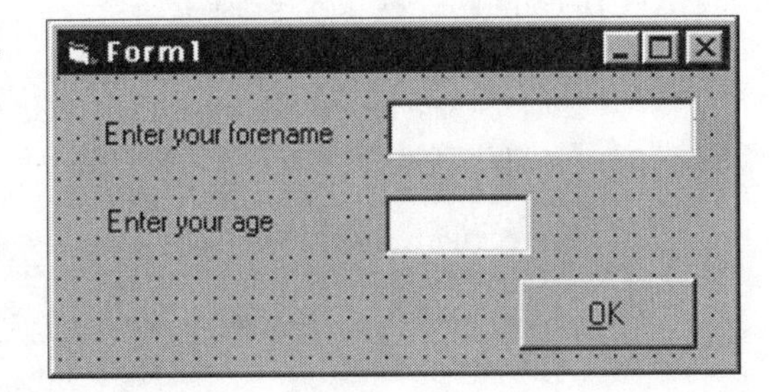

2 The two text boxes should be named (using the Name property of course) **txtForeName** for the top one, and **txtAge** for the bottom one. The label controls should be named **lblForeName** and **lblAge** respectively. Also, name the command button **cmdOK** and the form **frmMain**. Then set the **MaxLength** property of the age text box to 2.

3 Double click the command button to bring up the code window and add the following line.

```
Private Sub cmdOk_Click()

    MsgBox "Input accepted!"

End Sub
```

4 Run the Program and enter a letter into the age text box and observe what happens.

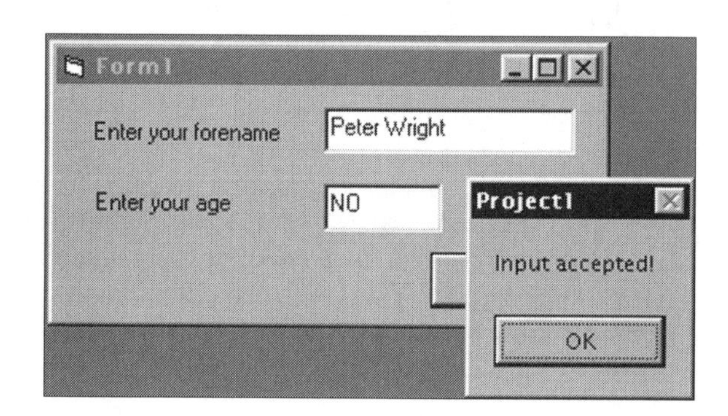

That's the problem, nothing does. Your input is accepted blindly whether you enter a number or a set of letters. It doesn't prevent you from entering completely nonsensical input such as numbers in your forename or letters in your age.

We're going to fix that now. Then after that we're also going to check that when the user hits the OK button that they have actually entered any data in both the name and age text boxes and not just left them empty.

Try It Out - Adding Code to the KeyPress Event

The best way to check data as it's entered is using the **KeyPress** event. This is triggered for a text box whenever the user presses a key that's displayed in the text box and tells us the **ASCII** code for the key pressed.

> *Each character on your keyboard has a unique number, called the ASCII (pronounced as-key) code. Using this we can check that the right keys have been pressed, and we can also tell the* **KeyPress** *event to ignore certain keys. Convenient, huh?*

To help you, Visual Basic also has a complete list of these ASCII codes built in. Select **Microsoft Visual Basic Help Topics** *from the* **Help** *menu, switch to the* **Index** *page of the dialog that appears and enter the word ASCII. Then click the* **Display** *button and Visual Basic will search its help topics and display the results. The result, called the ASCII character set, shows you a complete list of all the characters and their associated codes.*

So, let's enter the code we need for this program. We will be using the **`txtForeName_KeyPress`** event.

1 Stop the program from running if it still is, and double-click the Forename text box on the form to bring up the code window. When it appears, click on the arrow next to the word Change and select KeyPress from the list of events shown. The code window should now look something like this:

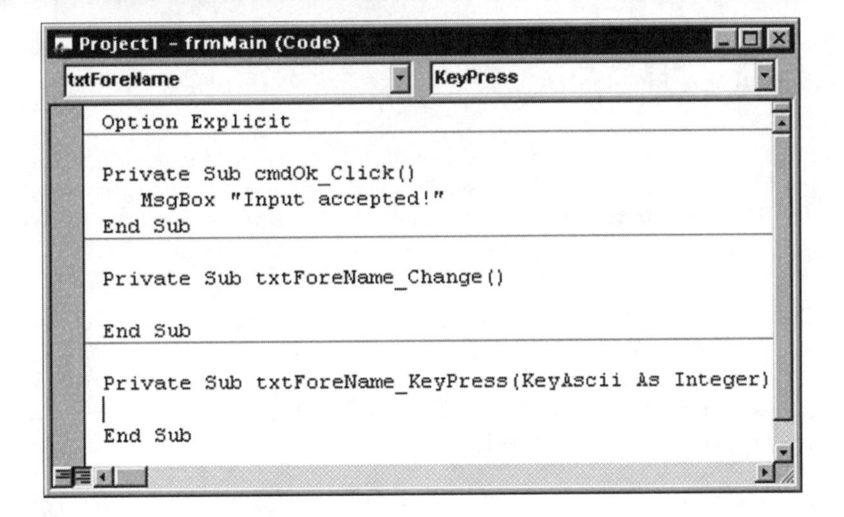

2 Let's add a line to the event to check which key was pressed and deal with it. Conveniently, the ASCII codes for the numbers 0 to 9 all run in sequence, so our event code to catch them is fairly simple. Add a line to the event code so that it now looks like this:

```
Private Sub txtForename_KeyPress(KeyAscii As Integer)

If KeyAscii >= Asc("0") And KeyAscii <= Asc("9") Then KeyAscii = 0
EndIf

End Sub
```

3 Now if you run the program you'll find that you can't add a number into the text box. Pretty convenient huh? Unless your name happens to be C3PO or R2D2!

How KeyPress Works

The first line of code:

```
Private Sub txtForename_KeyPress(KeyAscii As Integer)
```

marks the start of the event code. It tells us and Visual Basic where the code for dealing with the `KeyPress` event starts, and also lets us know the name of the control whose `KeyPress` event we are writing code for. The first line of the `KeyPress` event has the phrase `KeyAscii As Integer` in it. `KeyAscii` is called a **parameter**—it's a way for Visual Basic to give your code a value which it can use to figure out what's going on. You'll come across it frequently!

In the `KeyPress` event, `KeyAscii` holds the ASCII number of the key that was pressed. For example, if the user pressed the A key, then `KeyAscii` would equal 65. The line

```
If KeyAscii >= Asc("0") and KeyAscii <= Asc("9") Then KeyAscii = 0
```

uses the `KeyAscii` parameter to check whether the key pressed was valid. It does this using the Visual Basic `Asc` function.

> ***A function is a piece of code, in this case built into Visual Basic, that takes something from your code, processes it away on its own, then returns a new value. The `Asc` function allows us to get at the ASCII value for a symbol. So saying `Asc("0")` will give our code the ASCII code for the character 0.***

We can then compare whatever is held in `KeyAscii` against the value returned by `Asc` to determine whether or not the key pressed was numeric or not.

Finally the `>=` symbol means *is greater than or equal to* and the `<=` symbol means *is less than or equal to.* Armed with this knowledge, the line of code actually reads:

If the parameter `KeyAscii` is greater than or equal to the ASCII code of '0', and less than or equal to the ASCII code of '9', then set `KeyAscii` to 0.

Setting `KeyAscii` to 0 in the `KeyPress` event has the effect of cancelling the key just pressed. All the other characters will still work though.

Try It Out - Verifying Input into the Age Field

We can use a similar technique for the age text box. In this case we want to keep the numbers and ignore everything else. The code goes into the `txtAge_KeyPress()` event.

1. Stop the program running.

2. View the code window for the age text box, either by double clicking the age text box on the form, or by selecting `txtAge` in the left dropdown list box in the code window.

3 When the code window appears, select the **KeyPress** event.

4 Add the following line to the event handler code:

```
Private Sub txtAge_KeyPress(KeyAscii As Integer)

If KeyAscii < Asc("0") Or KeyAscii > Asc("9") Then KeyAscii = 0
EndIf

End Sub
```

Now if you run the program, you'll find that the age text box only accepts numbers, and ignores spaces, letters or any other character you decide to hit. In addition, because the MaxLength property has been set to 2, you won't be able to enter an age of more than 2 digits in length—the chances of a 100+ year old reading this book and using Visual Basic is pretty remote, so I'm confident I can get away with this.

You should also be aware that the backspace character also has an ASCII code which will also be ignored by this code. This is an issue that we'll have to deal with later.

Checking for an Empty Text Box

Now all we need to do is check that the user has actually entered something in the text boxes when the OK button is hit. We've already seen that the Text property lets us see what is in a text box, so if the Text property equals " ", then obviously the user has entered nothing. In Visual Basic, " " is how you would check to see if a piece of text actually contains nothing. This is commonly called an empty string.

Try It Out - Checking for an Empty Text Box

1 If the program is running, stop it and double-click the command button to bring up its click event code.

2 Replace the current code with the following few lines of code, and the program is complete.

```
Private Sub cmdOK_Click()

  If txtAge.TEXT = "" Then
    Msgbox "You must enter your age"
    Exit Sub
  End If

  If txtForename.TEXT = "" Then
    Msgbox "Enter your name please"
    Exit Sub
  End If
```

```
    End

End Sub
```

The code checks the value of each text box to see if anything was entered. In either case, if nothing was entered, a message box is put on screen with an error message in it. Then the `Exit Sub` line exits the event code. Event code like this is normally called a **subprocedure**. We cover what **subprocedure** really means later in the book.

In actual fact, our example never reaches the line `End Sub` because either the one of the text boxes contains nothing, in which case the `Exit Sub` finishes the event routine for us, or both text boxes contain something in which case the `End` statement terminates the program.

We can make the program even better by using a command called `SetFocus` to move the cursor to the offending text box. Focus is a tricky subject best discussed in a separate section, so I'll leave it to the end of the chapter.

Label Control 

The **label** control is the perfect complement to the text box. The text box is one of the few controls that doesn't have a caption of its own, so a label is used to place some text on the form near to the text box to show exactly what it represents.

Label Properties

Just as with the text box, the style of the label font can be changed with the `Font` property. You can even add a border around a label to make it appear to all intents and purposes the same as a text box. This is done by changing the `BorderStyle` property in the same way as you did with the form in the last chapter.

Label Events

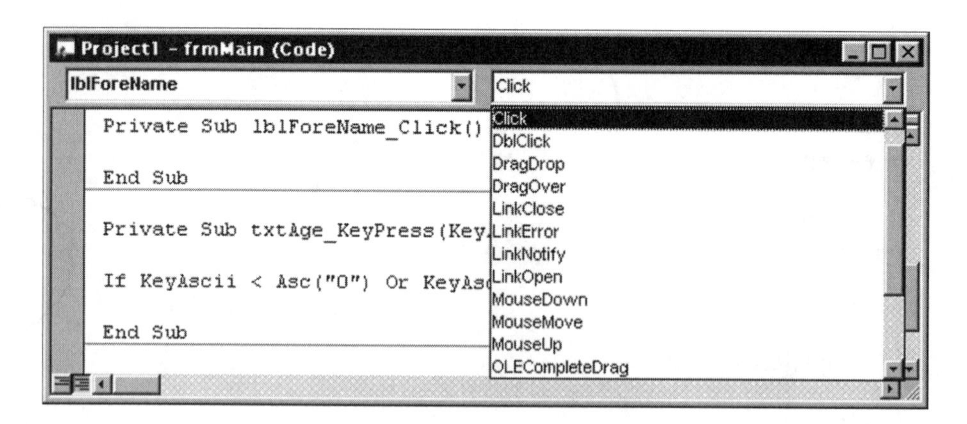

Labels are **lightweight** controls—they use less system resources, such as memory, and they need less processor power to manage them. This is simply because Visual Basic doesn't have to worry too much about the user entering data in them, resizing them and so on. However, while they may be lightweight from a Windows management point of view, they are up there with the best of them when it comes to event handling.

Labels can respond to the full set of events, with the obvious exception of events such as `KeyPress`, since the data in the label caption wouldn't take input like a text box does. One of the most common events coded for labels is the `Click` event. For example, in a banking application you may have a client's personal details, such as their address, on the screen. Adding code to the `Click` event of the label that says `Address` could be used to bring up another form showing the other addresses that the customer may have lived at over the years.

Other programs tend to use label `Click` events as backdoors—ways into a program if all else fails. I recently came across one such program, which, if you double-clicked the `Password` label on a particular form, allowed you to change or reset the password—very convenient for forgetful users!

Check Boxes

Check boxes allow you to present on/off, true/false options to users. Think back to school—remember the old multiple choice questions? Well, a check box is similar to the squares that you ticked to indicate your answers.

Try It Out - Check Boxes

1 Create a new Visual Basic project. When the default form appears, select the check box from the toolbox.

2 Double-click the check box icon to draw a check box on the form at the default size and position.

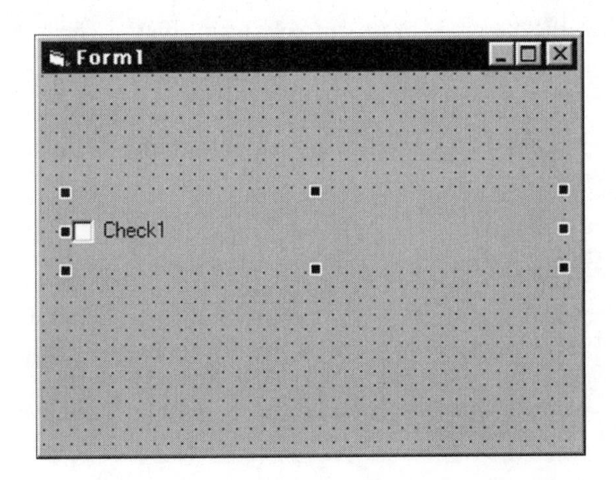

3 By default, the caption of a check box appears to the right of the box. You can change this by changing the **Alignment** property. Bring up the properties window and find the **Alignment** property. By default it is set to 0 - Left Justify, meaning that the box, not the text, is on the left. Double-click this property to change it to 1 - Right Justify.

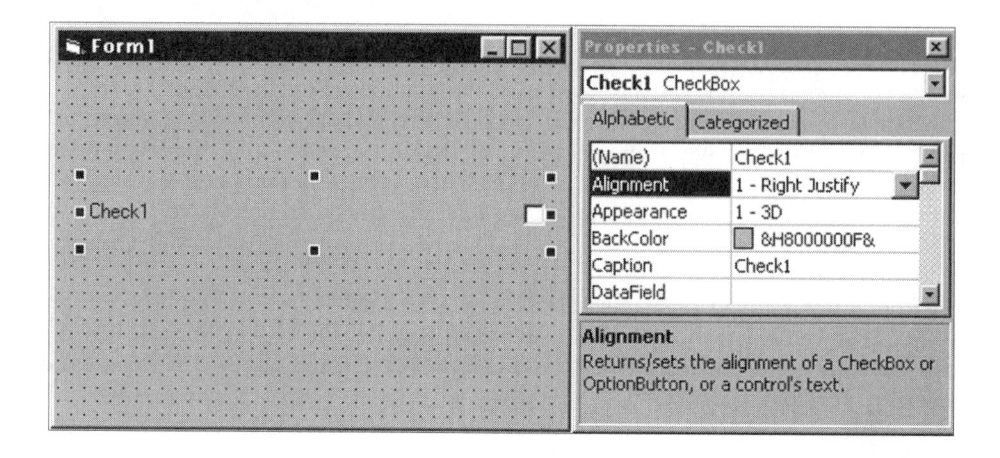

4 Add a couple more check boxes to the form so that the form now looks like this. Don't forget to change the **Alignment** property of each.

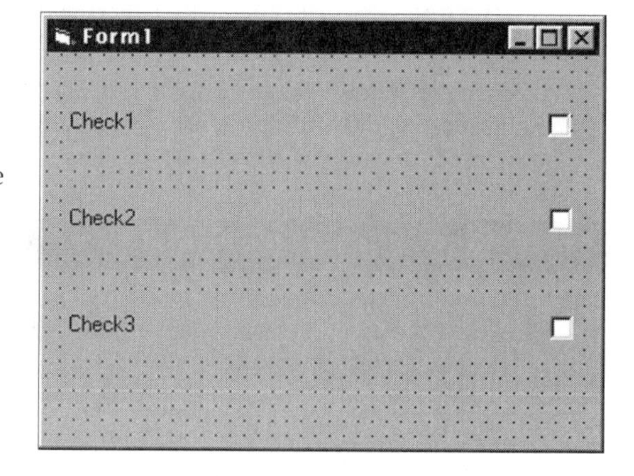

5 Now try running the program. You can select any of the check boxes independently of the others.

Check boxes are independent of each other, which means that checking one does not affect any of the others on the form.

Check Box Events

There aren't many events that can be used with a check box, and by far the most important is the **Click** event. This triggers both when the user points and clicks on the check box and when the user presses the hot key combination. You can add code to the **Click** event to do something based on the status of the check box at that time. However, you can't just insert the action you want performed into the **Click** event directly, as the clicking action could either **select** or **deselect** the option, depending on what state the check box was in beforehand.

To really make use of check boxes, you have to use the **Value** property.

The Check Box Value Property

The current status of a check box can be examined using its **Value** property.

Value Property	Status of Check Box
0	Unchecked
1	Checked
2	Grayed out, disabled

Let's write a small program to look at the Value property of a check box while the program is running.

Try It Out - Checking the Check Box

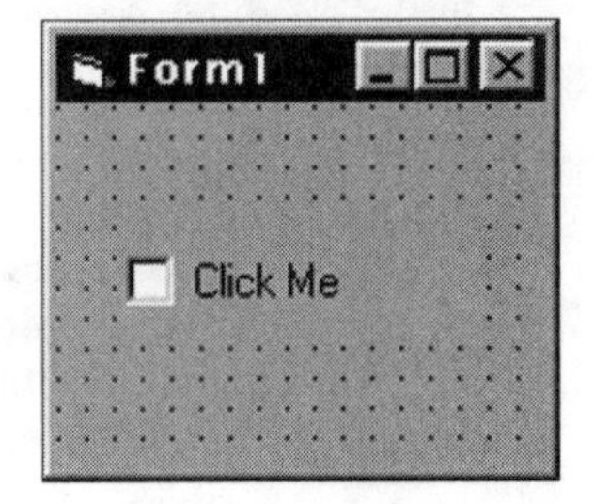

1 Create a new Visual Basic project and draw a check box on to the default form. Add a caption, as shown.

2 Still in design mode, double-click the check box to bring up the code window. Add the following line of code as shown below. We'll be using VB's Message box function (**msgbox**) to display a message when the control is clicked.

```
Private Sub Check1_Click()

    MsgBox "The value is now " & Check1.Value

End Sub
```

3 Now try running the program.

Each time you click on the check box a message box will appear showing you what is in the Value property of the check box. If the check box is checked, then Value will be 1. If it is not checked then Value is 0. The only value you won't see here is 2, which you get when the check box is disabled.

*The fact that the check box can be grayed out can be the cause of some very worrying bugs. Let's imagine you let the user check the box and then disable it to prevent them doing it again—at that point you can't determine in your program whether or not the check box was actually checked, since the value you will get from the **Value** property will be 2. Beware of this!*

Option Buttons 

Option buttons are a close cousin of the check box. They are also an on/off switch for various options. The difference is that option buttons are **mutually exclusive**. They can be grouped together to allow a user to select **either** one thing, **or** another thing, **or** another. The amount of **or**'s depends on the number of option buttons you group together. They are very useful in database type applications to let the user quickly choose one from a number of options in a list.

All the option buttons on a form or in a frame (more on these later) work together: clicking one option button clears all the others. It's like the station selector on a radio, where pressing the button for a new station makes the old one pop out. In fact, they are also known as radio buttons.

Try It Out - Option Buttons

1 Create a new Visual Basic project. When the default form appears, select the option button from the toolbox.

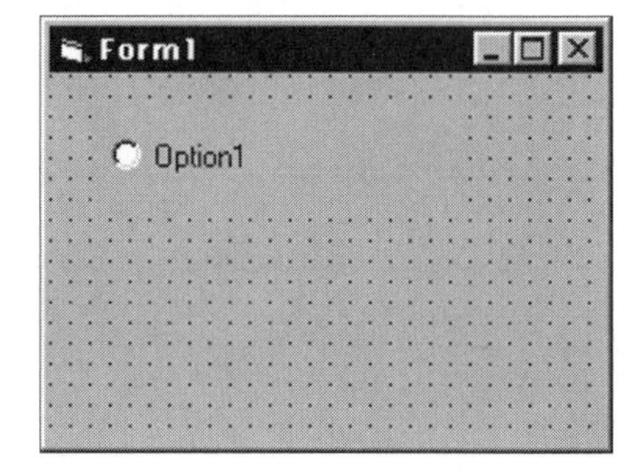

2 Double-click the option button icon to draw an option button on the form at the default size and position.

3 Like the check boxes we saw earlier, the caption of an option button appears by default to the right of the button. Just as with the check box, this can be changed by using the option button **`Alignment`** property. Bring up the properties window and find the **`Alignment`** property. Double-click this property to change it to 1 - Right Justify.

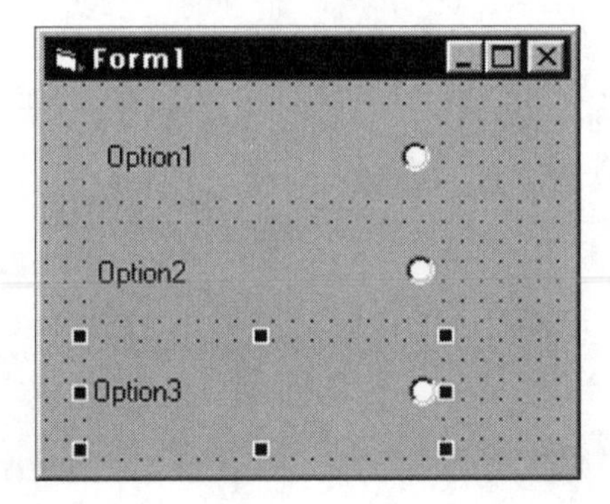

4 Add a couple more option buttons to the form so that it now looks like this.

5 Now try running the program.

Any option buttons placed directly on to a form or into the same frame cancel each other out. If you select one, all the others are deselected. Try it out—with the program running, try clicking on each of the buttons in turn and you'll see the result.

Other than that, the option buttons work in the same way as check boxes, the only exception being the way the Value property works. Instead of have three possible values (0, 1 or 2), option buttons only have two: true or false. If the option button value is set to true, then the button is set, otherwise it is not.

Picture Boxes and Image Controls  

Visual Basic provides two controls specifically for displaying graphic images: the **picture** control and the **image** control. These controls are both very powerful and each has advantages and disadvantages over the other. In this section you will get an overview of both, how they work and what they can be used for. Later, in Chapter 11, we will go into each of them in much more detail. For now, however, it's just a brief glimpse.

Using the Picture and Image Controls

The most important property of both the picture box and the image control is the **`Picture`** property, which determines which image file is loaded into the control. If you display the properties window and double-click the **`Picture`** property, Visual Basic will display a file requester and ask you to select the file which you want displayed in the control.

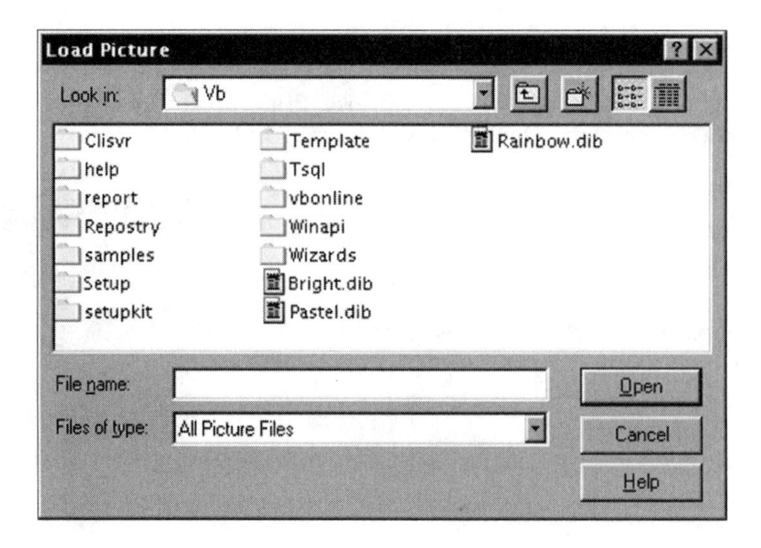

Image File Formats

You can load a number of different kinds of graphics files into the picture and image controls.

Image File Type	File Extension	Description
Bitmap	`*.BMP`	The traditional Windows format for graphics. Windows Paint is the usual source of these images, which can be used for everything from clip art to icon symbols.
Windows Metafile	`*.WMF`	Normally a graphic file drawn with a structured drawing package, such as Microsoft Draw. Good for clip art in a program since metafiles take a lot less memory than any other format.
Graphics Interchange Format	`*.GIF`	A graphic file most suited for simple images, such as geometric objects or large amounts of color. It's popular on the Web as file sizes tend to relatively small.
JPEG	`*.JPG`	A graphic file often used with photographic or artistic images, which allows the file to be greatly compressed in size but still maintain acceptable image quality.
Icon	`*.ICO`	Small icon graphic, such as those found on toolbars.

You can load a picture into an image or picture control either at run time or at design time. The sample we're going to build starts with no pictures in the controls and will use code to load selected graphics into them.

Picture and Image Controls Compared

An image control is one of a collection of controls known as **lightweight** controls, some of the others being the line control, shape control, and label. In a nutshell, lightweight controls require less system resources (such as computer time and memory) to manage them than other controls do, for example, the picture box, the command button or the heaviest of them all, the grid. The reasons for this are fairly complex, but from our point of view it is the limitations of the image control compared to the picture control that are of interest.

- **Images** cannot be placed on top of other controls, unless they are first placed inside a container object such as a frame or picture box. Also, they cannot receive focus at run time. We cover focus a bit later.
- **Picture boxes** are much more functional than image controls. They can be drawn anywhere and they can receive the focus, which makes them very useful for creating your own graphical toolbars. They can also act as container controls, which means you can place other controls inside them, almost like a form within a form.

In Chapter 11—Graphics, you'll learn how to really put these two controls to work.

More Common Properties

Many of the controls presented in this chapter have properties in common. We looked at some of the simpler ones at the start. However, having gained some more knowledge about specific controls, we can now get a better understanding of more advanced properties such as Enabled.

The Enabled Property

As we've said, check boxes can have three states from the user's point of view. These are **selected**, **deselected** or **grayed**, meaning disabled. A check box, like most other Visual Basic controls, has an Enabled property to control whether it can be selected on the form at run time. The Enabled property can only ever be one of two values as far as Visual Basic is concerned: true (meaning on), or false (meaning off).

*If you've programmed in C or Assembler before, then you'll be used to the words True and False. For the rest of us, this may seem awkward—why not simply use the words Yes and No? This is, unfortunately, one of the many areas of programming where jargon has crept in from the bad old days of binary and machine code programming. It stems from something called **Boolean logic**. We'll look at this in more detail much later in the book, but for now I'm afraid you're just going to have to get used to it.*

Setting Properties at Run Time

We've seen in this and the last chapter how to set properties at design time by using the properties window. It's also possible to set them up from within your program code. In fact this is one of the easiest ways to make your programs come alive.

__Design time__ is the time when your program is not running and you are placing controls on to your form and writing code. __Run time__ is when you have clicked the run button and your forms and controls respond to events by running the relevant procedures.

Disabling Controls

Imagine the user has just entered some text, the result of which is that you want to disable two command buttons, named Command1 and Command2. In your code you would simply write:

```
Command1.Enabled = False
Command2.Enabled = False
```

Visual Basic would then gray out the command buttons to indicate that they no longer work, and your user would be unable to click them.

Enabling Different Controls

When the **`Enabled`** property is used to turn an object off, the effect is visible on screen. Text boxes, command buttons, list boxes and menu items all tend to appear grayed out, indicating to the user that they no longer function.

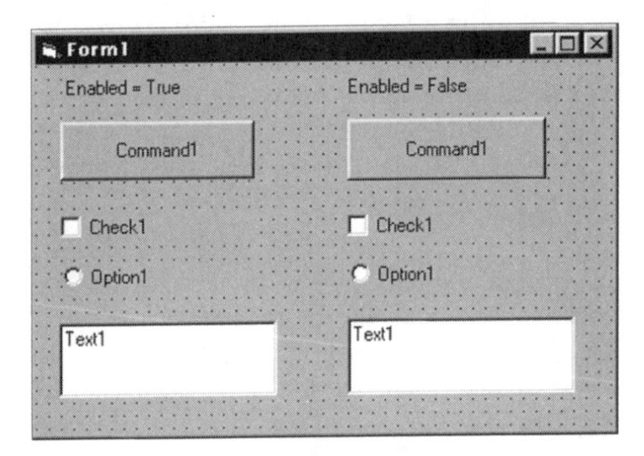

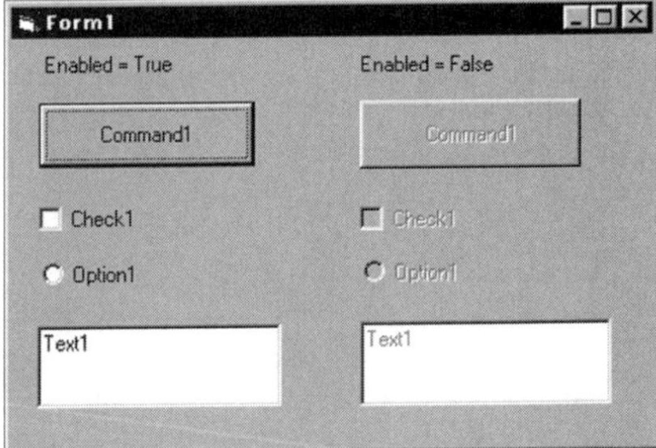

Try It Out - Enabling Controls

We'll now look at how you can enable and disable controls at run time with the click of a button and just one line of code.

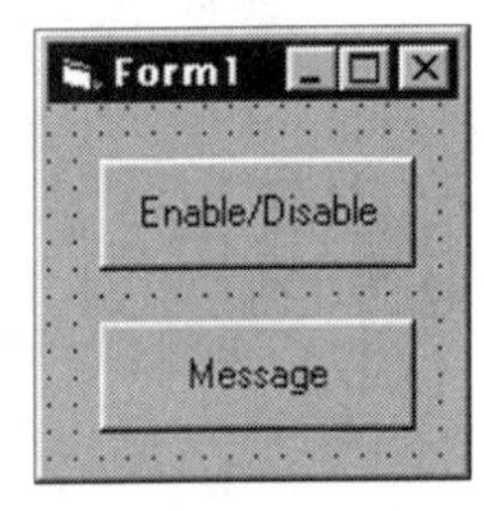

1 Create a new Visual Basic Project, select Standard EXE and then place a two command buttons on the form. Name the top one **`cmdEnable`** and the bottom one **`cmdMessage`**. Set the top command button caption to read Enable/Disable and the bottom one to read Message.

2 Double click on command button **cmdEnable** and add the following line of code to the button's click event:

```
Private Sub cmdEnable_Click()

    cmdMessage.Enabled = Not (cmdMessage.Enabled)

End Sub
```

3 Double click on the command button **cmdMessage** and add the following line of code to this button's click event which just displays a message box.

```
Private Sub cmdMessage_Click()

    MsgBox "Hello!"

End Sub
```

4 Run the program and click the message button. The follow dialog appears:

5 Click OK to make the dialog disappear and now this time click on the Enable/Disable button. The Message button goes gray and no longer responds to your clicking.

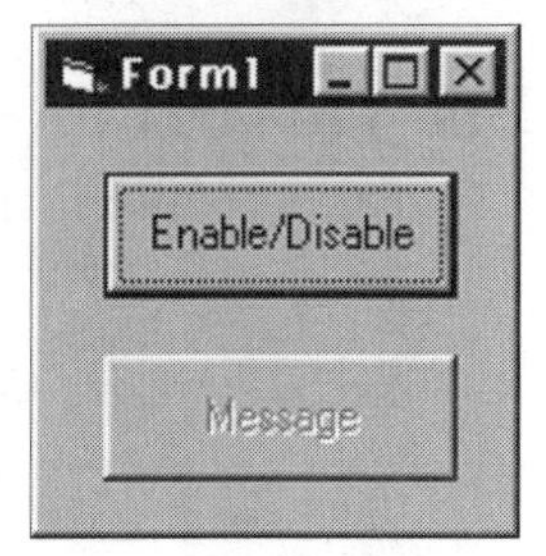

If you press Enable/Disable again, it comes back to life once more.

How It Works

Basically the whole program revolves around the single line in the click event of the Enable/Disable button:

```
cmdMessage.Enabled = Not (cmdMessage.Enabled)
```

There's just one part of this line which might be confusing and that's the word **not**. It's all very simple though, all that the line does is take whatever the **Enabled** property of the Message command button is, reverse it. As we commented earlier, the Enable/Disable button can only ever be true or false. If the **`Enabled`** property is True then it is changed to not true (i.e. false), and if it's false it changes it to not false (i.e. true). It's as simple as that. So every time the Enable/Disable button is clicked, the **`Enabled`** property is reversed.

The Visible Property

Another common property which operates in a similar way to Enabled is Visible. Setting this property to false makes the control disappear from the screen. In the case of a container object such as a form or frame, all controls within it would also disappear when the program is run.

Focus

Earlier on we mentioned focus—surprisingly this has nothing to do with karma or the summoning of an inner force to accomplish a goal! In Windows, focus tells us which control is currently selected when the program is running.

You've already seen this in practice throughout the chapter, although you might not have noticed it. Take our last example, when both buttons are enabled, press the *Tab* key and you will see the highlight move from control to control. Wherever the highlight lands, that is the control which currently has the focus.

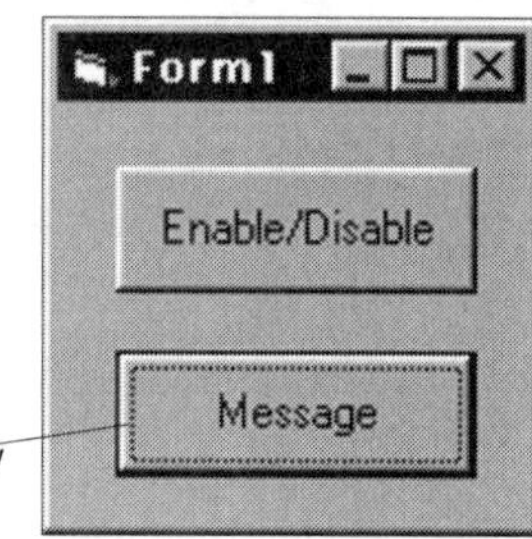

The dotted line around the control means it has the focus. The next action you perform, like a click or key press will go to this object.

The TabIndex Property

Focus is really useful on a form that has a lot of separate fields requiring data entry. Many experienced typists prefer to move about the form using the *Tab* key, rather than taking their hand off the keyboard to use the mouse. You control the order in which the controls receive the focus using the TabIndex property.

When the project is running, keep pressing *Tab* and you will see the highlight move from control to control. If you stop the program running and bring up the properties window for those controls, you will see the TabIndex is 0 for **`cmdEnable`** and 1 for **`cmdMessage`**. Indeed if there were more controls on the form they would have higher TabIndex values.

Whenever you change a TabIndex property, Visual Basic automatically re-orders the rest. Again you can see this if you bring up the properties window for the Message command button. Set the TabIndex of this to 0 and rerun the program. This time the Message button gets the focus first, and if you look under the properties window you will see that **`cmdEnable`** now has a TabIndex of 1.

Using Focus at Run Time

You can also move the focus from within your program code. For example, if the user enters some bad data, you can move the focus back to the offending control by using the **`SetFocus`** command.

Try It Out - Controlling Focus

You can track whether or not a control has focus through the **`Gotfocus`** and **`Lostfocus`** events. Now, this is where the problems start to creep in.

1 Start up a new project and drop some controls on the default form so that it looks like the login form shown. Delete the default entry in the Text property of both text boxes, to make them blank. Make sure you name the userid text box **`txtUserid`** and the password box **`txtPassword`**—that way the code I am about to get you to type in will work.

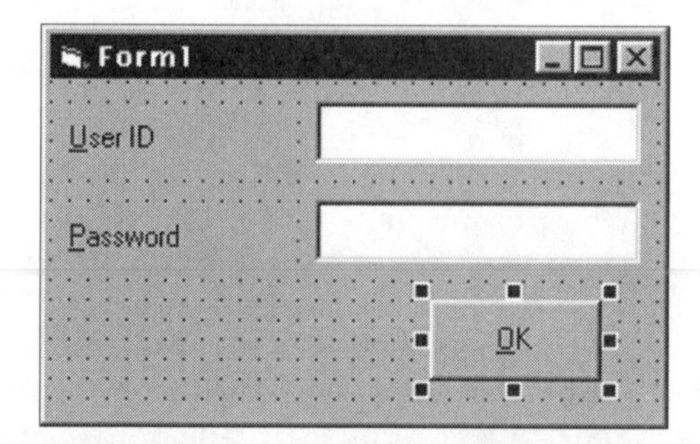

2 The program has two text boxes, one for a Userid, the other for a Password. Double click on the userid text box and use the events combo box to find the **`LostFocus`** event—we are going to add some code into this. When you have found it, type some code in so that the **`LostFocus`** event handler for that text box looks like this.

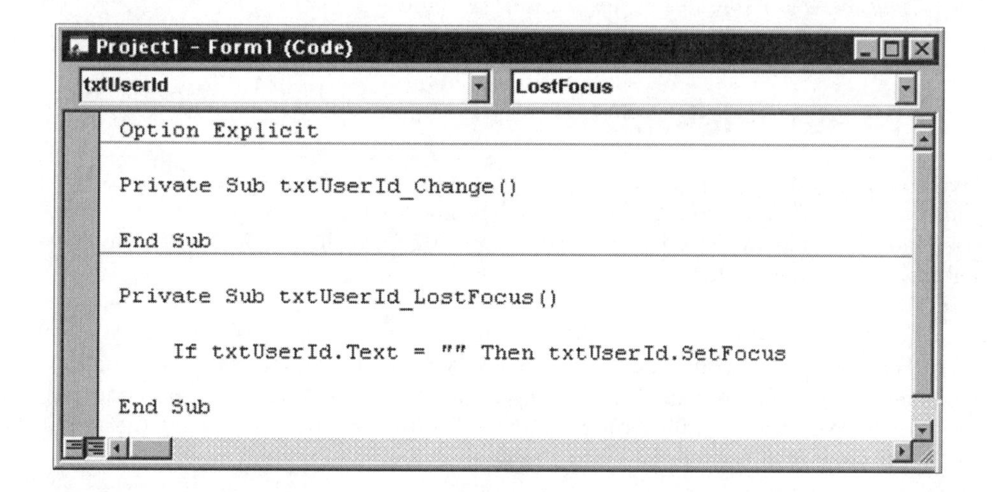

If the control loses focus (for instance, the command button was clicked or the user moved to the Password box) without entering any data, this **Lostfocus** code will set the focus back on to itself.

3 Run the program and try moving off the Userid box without entering anything. You will see the cursor snap straight back into the Userid box, forcing you to enter something—no problems there!

Now imagine we want to do the same to the Password box.

4 Back in design mode, double-click the Password box to bring up the code window and select the `LostFocus` event. Now change the code so that it looks like this:

```
Private Sub txtPassword_LostFocus()

    If txtPassword.Text = "" then txtPassword.SetFocus

End Sub
```

Now we have a problem. For one control to lose focus, another has to gain it. If you run the program now and try moving off the Userid box, the program will hang up; it will lock itself into a loop which you can only stop by pressing *Ctrl-Break*.

What happens here is that as Userid loses focus, so Password gains it. The Userid box then says 'Hang on...you didn't enter anything', and grabs the focus back, causing the Password box to lose focus itself. The Password box then does exactly the same as the Userid box just did.

> *For this reason many programmers don't use the `LostFocus` or `GotFocus` events at all, and especially not for text box validation. The preferred route is to use the `KeyPress` or `Change` events. However, if you must use `LostFocus` then there are ways around the problems, as you will see later.*

For My Last Trick...Ole!

We have covered a lot of ground in this chapter—taking you hopefully from the position of someone who knows nothing about Visual Basic to someone who is at least able to draw a user interface, and even add a little code to bring it to life. Now it's time to have some fun with a funky thing called OLE.

In a nutshell, what OLE lets you do is embed entire applications and their data within your own. For example, if you have Microsoft Word 6 or later, then you can actually cut and paste an entire document from it into a Visual Basic application with no code. At run time the user is then able to fully edit and interact with the text they see in the application, just as they would as if it were in Word itself.

It sounds too good to be true.

Try It Out - OLE

1 Create a new project. When the new form appears, select the OLE control from the toolbox

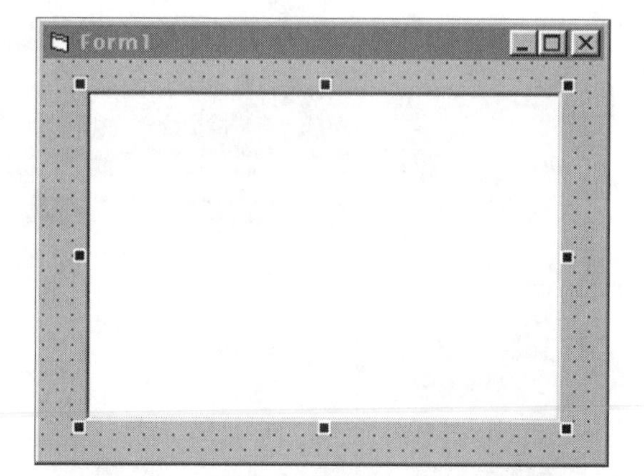

2 Draw it on to your form just as if it were any other control.

3 After a short pause, a dialog will appear asking you what kind of OLE object you intend to play with. The dialog will list all the OLE applications your version of Windows knows about.

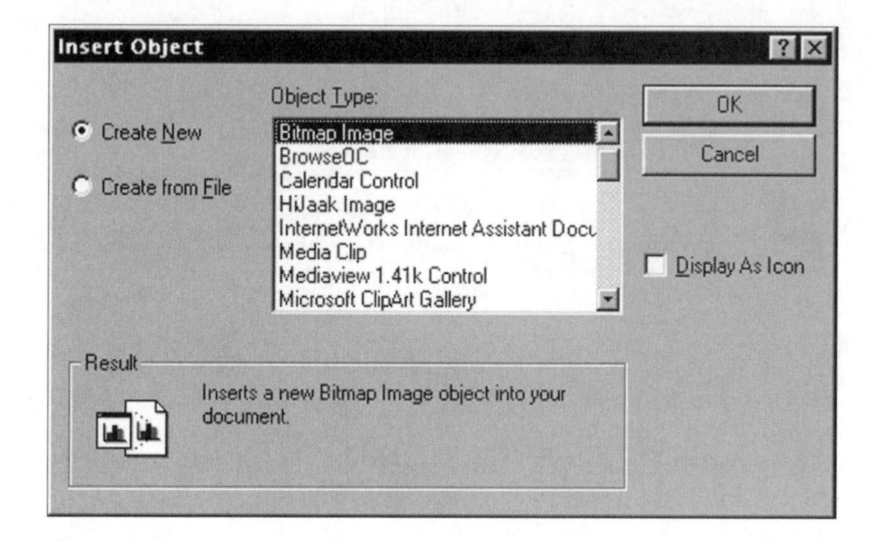

Choose Microsoft Word Document.

4 After some bumping and grinding (I never said OLE was fast), you should see something quite strange happen. Take a look over the page.

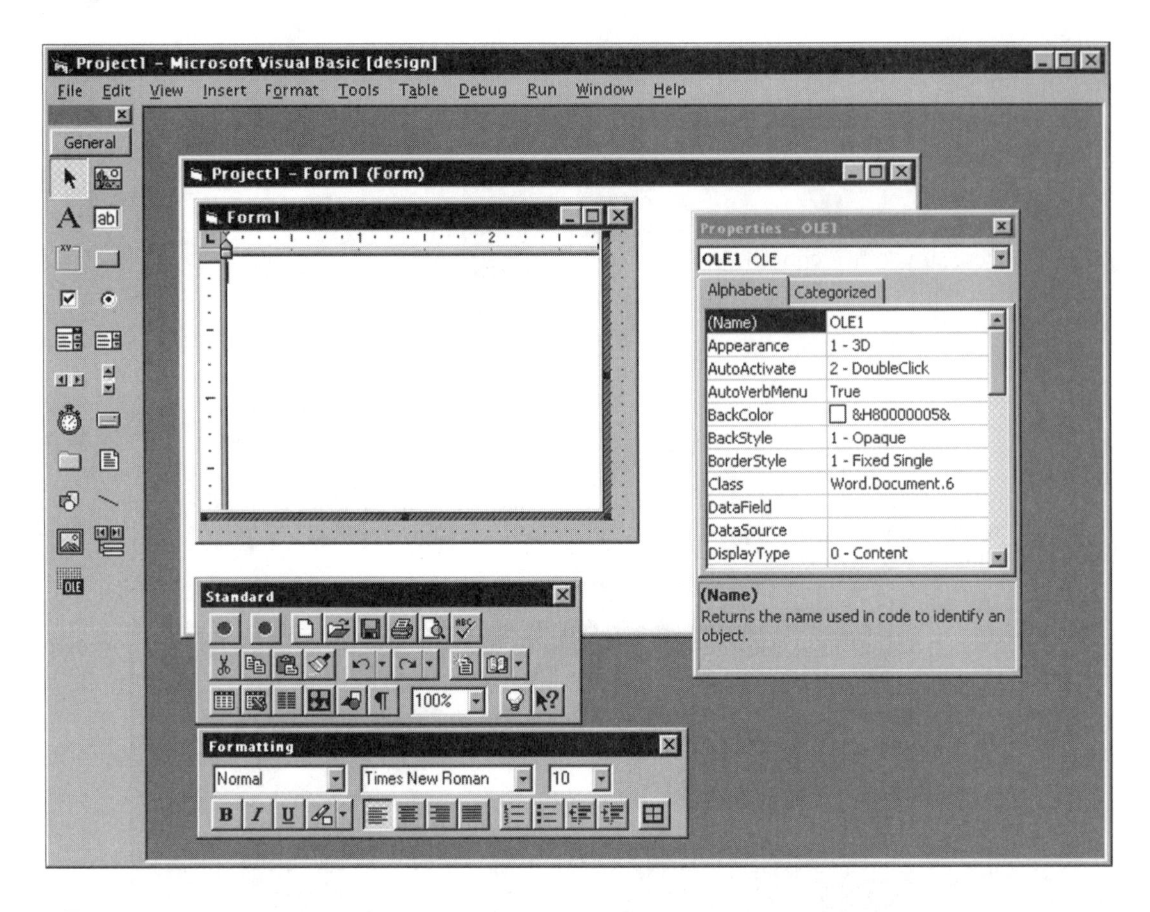

5 Notice the toolbars and the different menu. These are Word toolbars and menu items, assuming of course that you have Word installed on your computer. However, you must undock the toolbars in Word first. Because Word supports something called in-place activation, VB is able to provide all of Word's functionality from within your very own Visual Basic application. Try running the program by clicking on the Run icon, or by pressing *F5*, then double-click in the OLE box.

You can now type away and format as though you have a mini-version of Word running.

How It Works

In actual fact, you do have a mini version of Word running! What OLE does is load in the parts of MS Word that you need to support the feature set that the control gives us, and then runs this alongside your Visual Basic program. Windows 95 sits between the two applications and makes sure they work together happily.

You don't need much imagination to see how powerful this can be. Microsoft themselves see Visual Basic as 'glue' to stick OLE components together with custom applications. Any application that is OLE-compliant can be plundered for functionality.

So What, Really, is OLE?

From what you have seen to this point, OLE would appear to be nothing more than a system for embedding another application in your own. If you have ever used OLE in earlier versions of Windows, then you'll probably be aware that you can also use OLE to embed or link data from another application into your own, and at runtime have a small copy of that application run whenever the user decides that they want to edit that data.

However, this is only a tiny fraction of what OLE really is. In fact, it shouldn't really be called OLE any more, because the Object Linking and Embedding side of things is just a fraction of the total functionality of OLE in Windows 95.

As you'll see a lot later in this book, OLE allows you to totally take control of another application, using something called Automation. In terms of your code, dealing with the other application really looks no different to the way you might deal with a control on one of your forms. OLE also provides us, the programmers, the means to wrap functional objects up in self contained units that can be reused over and over in applications in the same way that you might use an ActiveX control to add functionality to your own applications. Imagine developing a security front end that handles all aspects of logging into your company's database and then distributing this to all your users as an OLE object. Any programs they have on their machines which need some kind of secure front end can be modified with very little effort to use your new security object, reducing the amount of code duplicated on each machine, and also reducing the support burdens on yourself.

NT4 (and the update to Windows 95) take this even further, by allowing us to distribute objects around the network, and basically hold them in a central locations so that all the network user applications simply wander out over the network activating objects for their own use on whatever machine they reside on. The future is here...

We go into a lot more detail on OLE later in the book. However, the whole subject does have a bit of a nasty smell about it for many programmers since it is supposed to be so hard to use from a programming point of view. As you can see, this is no longer the case.

Summary

In this chapter you have seen how to use some of the more common controls in Visual Basic 5, and acquired a good foundation in terms of dealing with controls, properties and form design which we can build on through the rest of the book. Specifically you learned about the following:

- How to use text boxes, option buttons, check boxes, command buttons, picture and image controls
- How to change properties in your code
- How to validate a text box
- Some of the problems that come with text boxes, option buttons and control focus
- A little about the wonderful world of OLE

However, if you've read all the reviews and listened to all the rumors, then you'll know that we've only scratched the surface here with this summary of controls. In later chapters, we cover some of the more complicated controls that require a little more knowledge of coding in VB in general—such as list boxes, grids and so on. In terms of visual controls, one really powerful feature of Visual Basic 5 is its ability to actually create the controls that you use in your projects to build up those gleaming user interfaces. We also look at how you can do that in later chapters. But first we have to prepare the ground, and for that we are going to take a closer look at the code behind forms in Visual Basic.

Why Not Try...

1 Create a project which contains a form with a single command button. At startup, have the form display the command button with no caption. Write code so that if the command button is clicked, the caption changes to the word ON.

2 Create a project which contains a form with a single command button. Write code so that when the button is clicked, it moves 100 twips to the left of its current position. Use the `Print` method of the form to display the current coordinates of the button in the form window. What will happen when the button moves off the edge of the form?

3 Create a project which contains a form with a single command button. In design mode, change the caption to OK. In the `Click` event for the button, place code to center the button within the form. Now, rename the command button to `cmdOK`, Look for the code you just placed in the `Click` event of the command button. Where has it gone?

4 Create a project which contains a form with two command buttons. Set the caption of button #1 to Tom. Use an ampersand (&) to make the T in the caption a 'hot key'. In the `Click` event of button #1, display a message box indicating that Tom has been selected.

Set the caption of button #2 to Terry. Use an ampersand to make the T in the caption a 'hot key'. In the `Click` event of button #2, display a message box indicating that Terry has been selected

Run the project. Press *Alt+T*. Which message box is displayed?

5 Create a project which contains 2 text boxes. Upon startup, which text box receives focus? Can you change this?

asic Visual Basic Visual Ba
al Basic Visual Basic Visual
Basic Visual Basic Visual Ba
ual Basic Vi
Basic Visu
ual Basic V
l Basic Vis
isual Basic Visual Basic
al Basic Visual Basic Visua
Visual Basic Visual Basic Visu
l Basic Visual Ba
l Basic Visual
ic Visual Basi
Basic Visual B
ic Visual Basi
l Basic Visual
ual Basic Visual Basic Visual Bo
Visual Basic Visual Basic Visu
sual Basic Visual Basic Visu
Visual Basic Visual Ba

Writing Code

It's now time to bring your programs to life and make them think for themselves. Designing forms and adding controls isn't enough. Among other things, your programs need to be able to make decisions, and run different bits of code depending on what the user does.

In this chapter we'll look at some of the building blocks of Visual Basic programming. If you've programmed in BASIC, C or Pascal before, then most of this will be familiar.

You will learn:

- How to make simple choices, by using **`If...Then`**
- How to select from several different options
- How to repeat sections of code, by using **`For...Next`** and **`Do...While`**
- How to combine all these language features into working Visual Basic programs

Writing Code in Visual Basic

In the first three chapters you gained an understanding of the main components of a Visual Basic program, so let's just recap:

- **Forms** are the framework on which you build your interface.
- **Controls** are the building blocks from which you construct that interface.
- **Event subprocedures** are the glue that binds these components together and makes it into a system that achieves what you want.

One of my objectives in this book is to try and get you up and running fast, with practical and interesting programs. To do this, I've thrown you in at the deep end. You saw your first lines of code in Chapter 2, using the **`Form_Load`** event to display the date, and the **`Form_UnLoad`** event to display a message box wishing you good-bye.

Now, I'm afraid, the party's over and it's time to get down to some serious programming. The next two chapters are about the techniques you need to write effective event handlers and other types of code.

- In this chapter we'll explain how to structure your program code so you can make choices and respond to different events and conditions.
- In Chapter 5, you'll find out how to represent data in your code, and what you can do to that data to get the required results.

These two subjects are fundamental building blocks for programming in Visual Basic. You'll learn all sorts of other things along the way, including the rich set of built-in functions that Visual Basic offers. We'll throw all of these in, as and when appropriate. For now though, if you're going to get to grips with writing code in Visual Basic, you need to understand its structure and the way we use data within it. So, let's make a start!

Putting Code into Modules

Imagine, for example, that you wanted to check the characters that your user was entering into a text box, like we did in Chapter 3. If you only have one text box, then that's no problem. Unfortunately, however, most real-life forms have lots of data entry points, so you could end up typing in the same code for each one. There has to be a better way, and sure enough there is—**modular programming**.

Up to now, all the code we've written has been directly contained in the event handlers of various controls and objects. As these objects are themselves placed on to forms, all our code has been inside forms. Modules are very different.

Whereas the code in a form normally relates specifically to that form, code in a module can be **public**. It can be called on by any other code in your project, and isn't normally tied to any one control or form. So in the case of checking text box input, you could create a public routine in a module called, for example, `CheckInput`. You could then call that central routine whenever you needed it.

Functions and Subprocedures

When breaking down your program into modules, you have a choice between placing your code in functions or subprocedures.

- **Functions** usually consist of code that does something specific and then returns a result to the part of the program that called it. For example, the `Sin()` function in Visual Basic does exactly this. You pass a number to it, and it gives you back a result that is the mathematical sine of the original number.
- **Subprocedures**, on the other hand, don't tend to return results. They just do something. The `Unload` method, which we used earlier to unload a form, is actually a subprocedure. There's no way to check whether the form is actually unloaded or not, apart from just looking at it.

So far, all the Visual Basic code you've written is for event subprocedures. When a command button named `Command1` is pressed, Visual Basic runs the `Command1_Click()` event **subprocedure**. Your code in that subprocedure usually does something, like changing the display, but it doesn't tend to pass anything back to Visual Basic.

The Big Picture

Forms, modules, subprocedures and functions are all related. But just what exactly are they? Well, you already know about **forms**—they are the elements of your programs onto which you can draw controls to build up a program's user interface.

Behind all the graphic excitement you have **event code**. This is code which does something in response to the user triggering an event, such as clicking on a command button, moving the mouse, and so on. This event code is actually a subprocedure.

Think about making a cup of coffee. `Making_Coffee` is the application. Filling up the kettle, putting coffee in the cup, and stirring the coffee are all subprocedures. You don't have to learn how to fill the kettle each time you want to make some coffee. `Filling_The_Kettle` is stored in your head as a subprocedure. It's the same in your Visual Basic application. If you have a common block of code that is used over and over, then put it in a subprocedure.

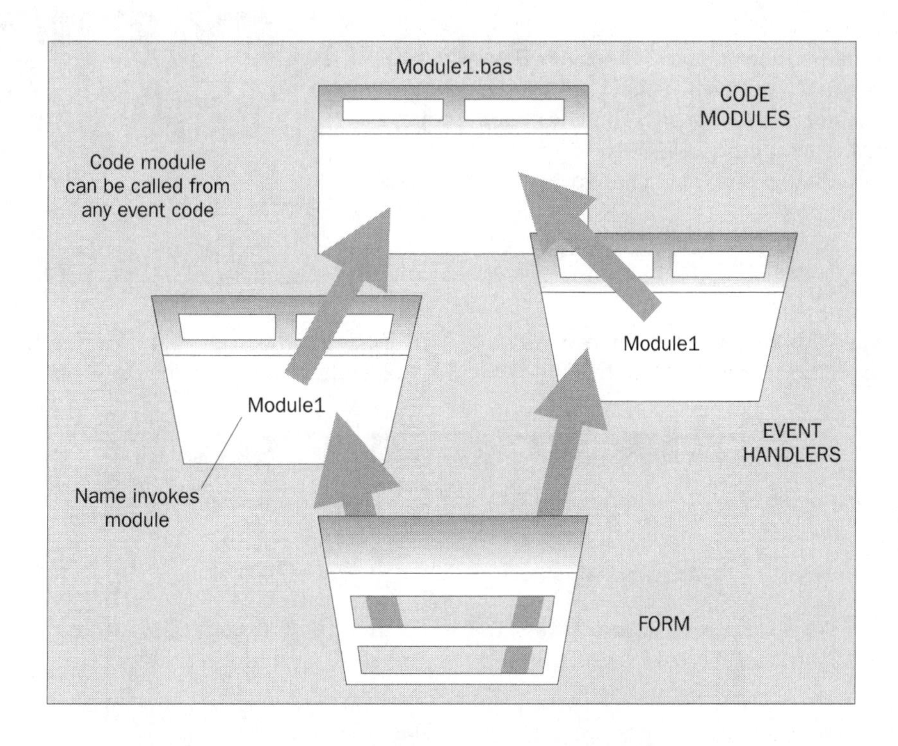

Functions are very similar to subprocedures except for the fact that they return a result. When you make a cup of coffee, you may not be able to find the coffee jar, so you would call out to your partner to locate it for you. Only then would you be able to get the coffee jar. In Visual Basic, you would use the **`Partner_Find_Coffee`** function to locate the coffee. Then your **`Get_Coffee`** subprocedure would go to wherever the **`Partner_Find_Coffee`** function told you to go.

Imagine a form that has no visual manifestation, just subprocedures and functions. If you can picture this, then you can picture a **module**. Modules provide a way for you to write code that can be used throughout your entire system. Normally, subprocedures and functions in a module are **global,** meaning that they can be called by code anywhere else in your application.

If you're still a little confused, don't worry. We'll cover functions, subprocedures and modules in a lot more detail as you work your way through the book.

Try It Out - Adding Subprocedures

In Chapter 2 we wrote a program that displayed the date in the center of the screen. Centering the form was easy—we just changed a property. However, suppose you want to display a form in a customized position, such as a third of the way down and across the screen. Wouldn't it be nice if we could just call a subprocedure that would automatically place the form where we want it?

1 Create a new project, choosing Standard EXE as usual, and add a label as we did in Chapter 2. Double-click on the **`Font`** property in the properties window to bring up the font dialog box, and change the font to 18 point bold.

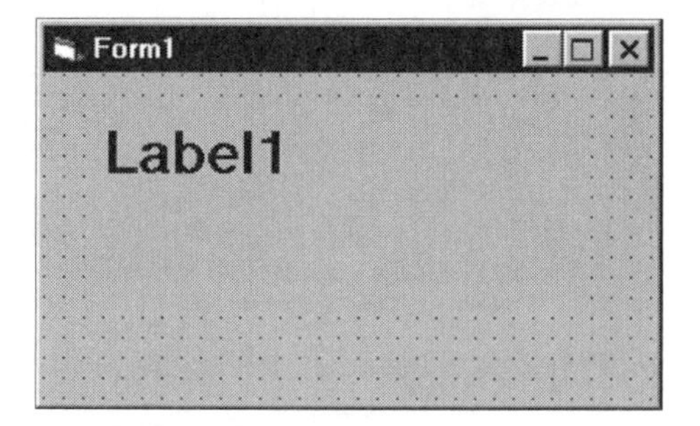

2 Now double-click the form or press *F7* to bring up the code window for the **`Form_Load`** event. Add the following line of code to display the date on the label:

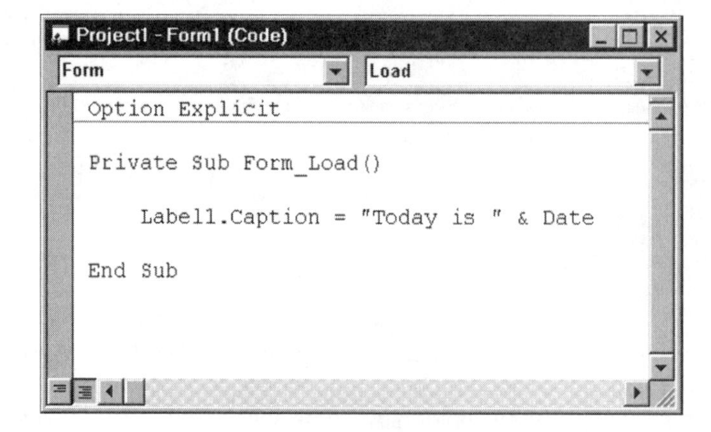


```
Option Explicit

Private Sub Form_Load()

    Label1.Caption = "Today is " & Date

End Sub
```

3 Now let's create the subprocedure that will position the form on the screen. Click on the arrow at the top of the window next to Form, and select (General) to move to the (General) (declarations) section. To add a new subprocedure simply type the following line beneath the words **Option Explicit**.

*The words **Option Explicit** appear because we've asked Visual Basic to make us declare all variables. We'll cover this in detail in the next chapter. For now, ignore it.*

```
Private Sub Place
```

Press *Enter* and Visual Basic will automatically put in the lines that mark the start and end of the new subprocedure, and then wait patiently for you to type something meaningful.

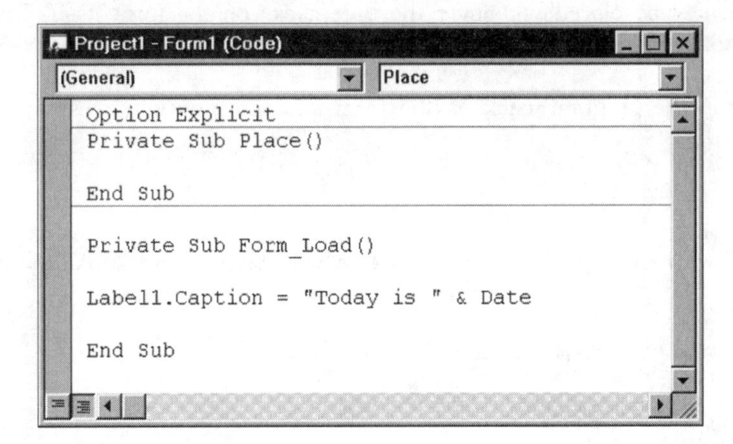

4 Type in code so that the **Place** subprocedure looks like this:

```
Private Sub Place()

    Form1.Left = (Screen.Width - Form1.Width) \ 3
    Form1.Top = (Screen.Height - Form1.Height) \ 3

End Sub
```

5 All that's left to do now is to call the subprocedure. From the top left combo box, select **Form** and then find its **Click** event. Then type in a line of code so the event handler looks like this:

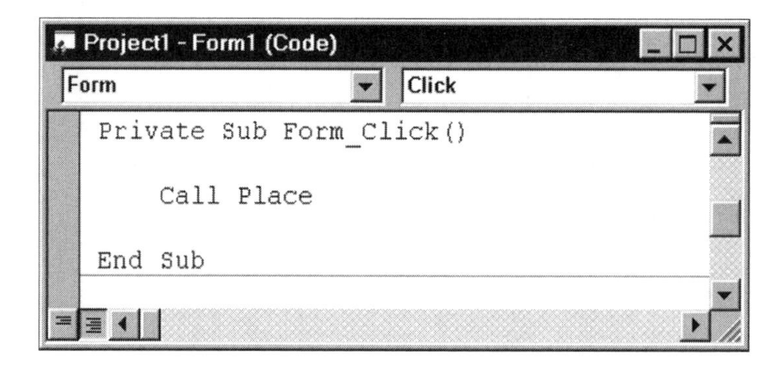

The **Call** command tells Visual Basic that we want to call a subprocedure. In our case **Call Place** tells Visual Basic to run the subprocedure called **Place**. This will cause the form to be placed whenever the user clicks on the form itself—any area of the form not already covered with some other control, that is.

6 Now run the program, click on the form and see how it moves to the position you specified.

How It Works

Call is really a hang over from the days of Visual Basic 1 and 2. Although you can use it, and it does make your code a lot easier to read, you could equally well have said:

```
Private Sub Form_Click ()

    Place

End Sub
```

Since **Place** isn't a keyword, Visual Basic knows that you're trying to call a subprocedure.

> ***Keywords** are words that have special meanings in Visual Basic, such as **Call** or **GoTo**. They are used for things such as commands. You can't use them in your code for your own purposes, as Visual Basic won't allow it.*

Where's the Form?

When you use modules, you can actually choose not to show any form at all when your program starts. Instead, you can run code in a module directly. If you want to interact with your users, however, you'll have to create a user interface on the fly. Modules are normally used as a backup to forms. They provide common code that all the forms can use. Just to illustrate the point, though, let's write a program with no forms at all.

Try It Out - A Program with No Forms

1 Start a new project and choose Standard Exe as the project type. As you know, all new projects in Visual Basic are created with at least one form already in them. From the View menu select Project Explorer to bring up a list of all the files in your project. The only one at this point is, of course, Form1.

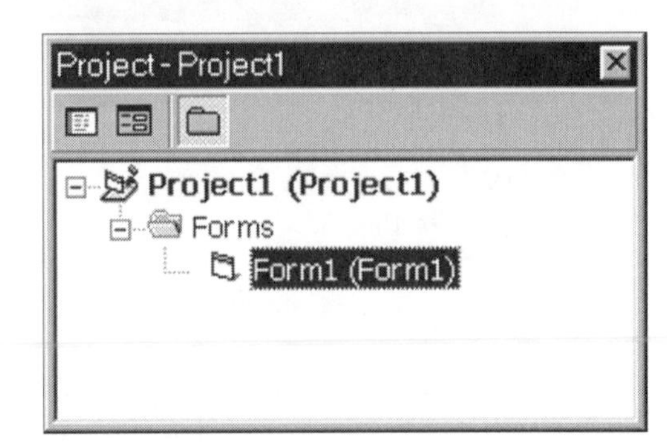

2 Select this line by clicking it once, then from the Project menu select Remove Form1. If you have made any changes to the form since it was created then Visual Basic will ask you if you want to save those changes, otherwise it will simply remove the file leaving you with an empty project.

3 We now need to add something into the project which can hold code, otherwise there's no point in having a project at all. In the case of this example we need to add in a code module. You can add a code module to the project either by selecting Add Module from the Project menu, or by dropping down the Add icon on the standard toolbar, and selecting module from the list shown. Do one of these things now.

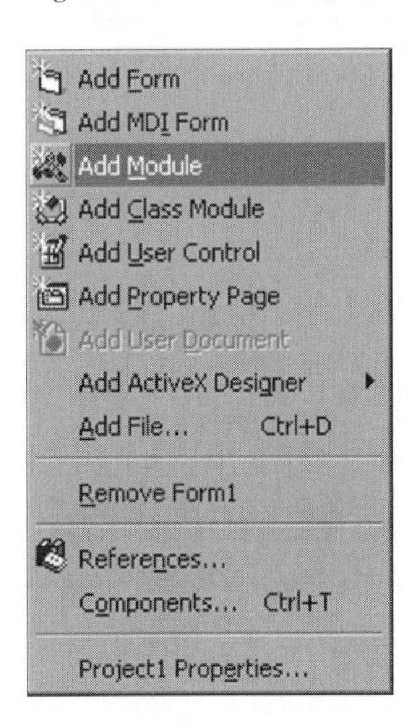

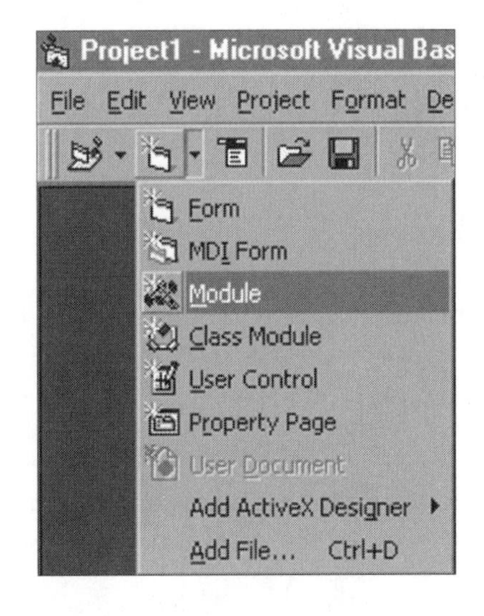

Be sure that you choose Module from the lists, and not Class Module. Class modules are very different beasties to the one we're after and we cover them in a lot of detail a little later in the book.

4 When you select Module, the Add Module dialog pops up:

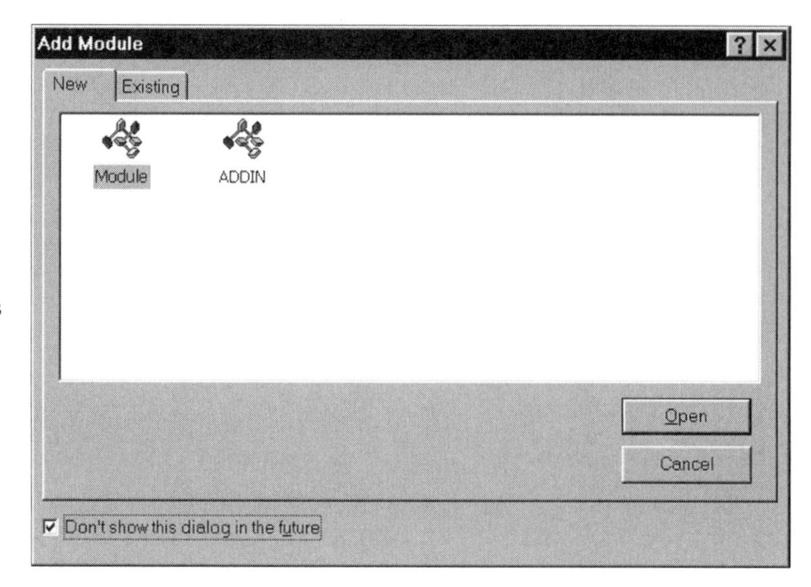

If you like, you can tick the Don't show this dialog in future box, so that you won't have to go through this stage next time. Whether you do this or not, select Module and click on the OK button.

5 As soon as you create a module, a code window pops up for it. Remember, modules are forms but without the visual side.

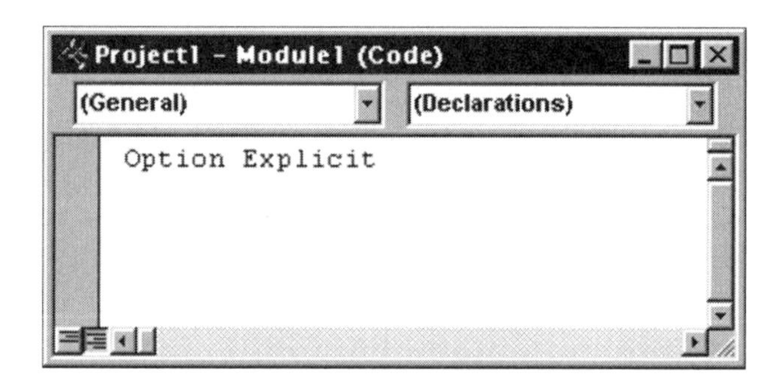

6 For a program with no forms, you need to have a subprocedure called **`Main`** in a module, to act as the replacement for your main form. Click in the code window now and create a **`Main`** subprocedure.

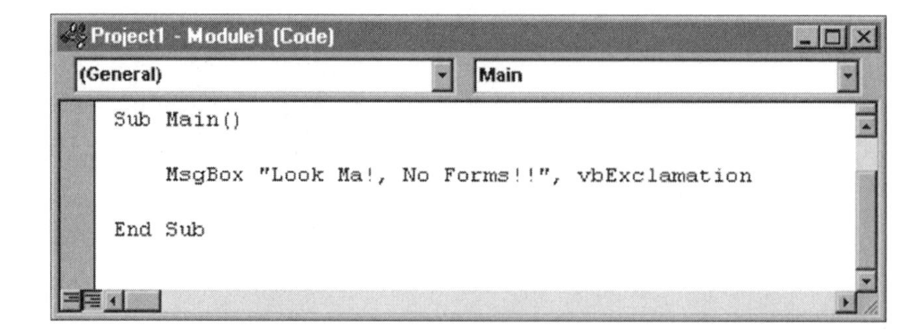

*Visual Basic names this **Main** in the top right combo box automatically.*

7 Whenever you create a project that has no forms, Visual Basic instinctively knows to run the **Main** subprocedure when the program starts to run. If you click the run button now, up comes the message box.

We used a form of the **MsgBox** statement here. The only things we told the command were to show the text **"Look Ma!, No Forms!!"** and to make the box a simple type with an exclamation mark. The constant **vbExclamation** tells Visual Basic the type of box we want. Message boxes get the full treatment in Chapter 10.

Running an Application that has Forms and Modules

There will be times when you'll need to run a **Main** subprocedure in an application that does have forms. When this happens you need to actually tell Visual Basic to load up your module first, rather than the first form you created. You do this using the Startup Object option. Select Project Properties... on the Project menu to bring up the property pages for the current project.

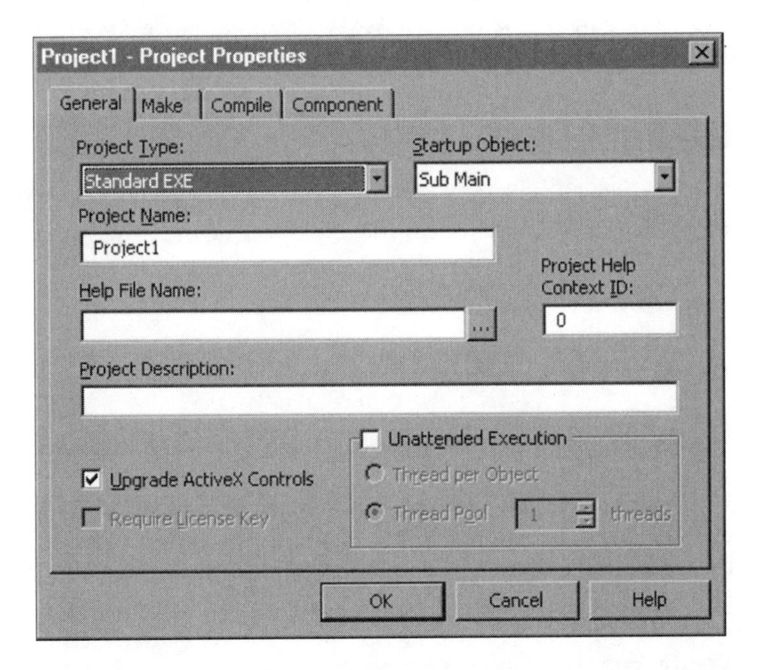

Here the Startup Object option is set to Sub Main, meaning that the **Main** subprocedure will be run before anything else. If you had a project with a number of forms, you could select any of the forms to be run first instead.

Doing it in Public or in Private?

In the code examples up to this point, and in many more to come throughout the rest of the book, you'll notice the word **Public** or **Private** placed at the start of subprocedures or functions. What does this mean?

As you already know, Visual Basic projects are actually made up of forms for the user interface and code modules that perform background and common tasks. Each of these units is self-contained. They have their own data and their own code. **Public** and **Private** enforce this.

Public subprocedures are declared like this:

```
Public Sub <subprocedure name>
Public Function <function name> As <return type>
```

A routine declared as **Public** is accessible from throughout the whole program. For example, code in **Module1** could be called by code in **Form1**, or indeed any other form or module. More often than not, if you need a piece of code to do something throughout the whole project, then **Public** is what you want.

Private, on the other hand, is totally the opposite. If you stick a **Private** routine inside a form, then only other code in that form can use it. For example, let's say you have a two-form application and you create a **Private** routine in **Form1**. At that point, the only code that can legally call this routine is code in **Form1**. Calling it from **Form2** will just cause an error. So what's the point? Well, life would certainly appear to be simpler if everything was **Public**. That way you wouldn't have to worry about having to keep track of what's where. **Private** subprocedures, however, have certain inherent advantages:

- They use less memory, in particular less of the crowded bits of memory.
- If everyone in a town came out on to the street at the same time, then things would get crowded.
- They protect parts of your code that you don't want to be affected by operations outside the module.
- They let you use the same names over again in different modules.

Of course, this is just an overview. We use both **Public** and **Private** routines throughout the entire book, and cover them in a great deal of detail in Chapter 7, *Creating Your Own Objects*, where it fits best. In both the next chapter and in Chapter 7, we'll see how variables fit into the public and private landscape. Next though we turn to the problem of getting your program to make a decision.

Making Choices in Programs

Two of the most important parts of any programming language are its decision-making and branching capabilities. These terms need some explanation.

Decision-Making

In a subprocedure, your code will normally start to run at the first line of code and proceed down through the rest until it meets either an **Exit Sub** or an **End Sub** statement. The word **Sub** is short for **subprocedure**, which is the name Visual Basic gives to a single block of code.

For example, many applications include a Quit command button. When this button is clicked, the application shuts down. The simplest event code you would find for this command button being clicked is:

```
Private Sub cmdQuit_Click()
   End
End Sub
```

Decision-making takes place when the program code decides to perform a particular action *provided* that a certain condition is met. As a programmer, you first of all have to test the condition, then write the code that needs to be executed in response.

Think about the Quit command button again. Although the event code does the job just fine, it could make a safer exit. What would happen if the user hit the Quit button by accident? The application would close down and—if they had forgotten to save their work—your poor user would lose the lot. Decision-making can get around this problem:

```
Private Sub cmdQuit_Click()

    If WorkSaved = False Then
       MsgBox "Save your work first!"
    Else
       End
    End If

End Sub
```

With just a few extra lines of decision-making code, your users become happy bunnies. When they hit the Quit button, the code checks to see if their work is saved. It does this by checking the value of a variable called **WorkSaved**. If the work hasn't been saved, then our old friend the **MsgBox** is used to display a message to that effect. Otherwise, the application ends as before.

> *If you want to run this fragment of code yourself, then add the line* **WorkSaved = False** *directly before the* **If** *statement. It's really intended to work as part of a larger program where the value of* **WorkSaved** *would have been set elsewhere.*

Branching

Branching occurs when the program code takes control of itself, and decides that the next line to run is in fact ten lines back, or a hundred lines further on.

Decision-making and branching are closely related. The code won't normally branch to a different line unless a decision has been made saying that it should do so. Think about a trip to the beach. Given that everything goes to plan you:

1. Drive to the beach.
2. Find a pleasant spot.
3. Relax for the rest of the day.
4. Pack up your stuff.
5. Drive home.

Decision-making comes into play if you live in a country like England, which has no roof! In that case you:

1. Drive to the beach.
2. **If** the weather is rotten, **Go to** step 6.
3. Find a pleasant spot.
4. Relax for the rest of the day.
5. Pack up your stuff.
6. Drive Home.

The same techniques apply with Visual Basic. You lay out your code in the order you want things to happen. You then use condition statements like **`If`** to check things are OK. If they aren't, then **`Goto`** or **`Call`** statements can be used to branch to another part of the code.

Over the course of this chapter, you'll learn everything you need to know about **`If`** statements, **`Goto`** and **`Call`**—so don't panic if it isn't all completely crystal clear straight away.

It is possible to jump off to another line of the program without having tested any condition. In general, however, this is regarded as bad programming practice and I'll explain why in the course of this chapter.

Decision-Making

There are various ways to make choices and selections in code though they all come back to the same basic action—testing whether or not something is true. As you'll see over the next few pages, you will sometimes be glad of a way of handling a decision-making process that is more elegant than a long and complicated line of **`If...Then`** statements. This is where methods such as **`Select Case`**, which we'll be looking at later, come into play.

Testing for Conditions with If...Then

The simplest way to make a decision in a program is using the **`If...Then`** statement. You may remember that we've already used this in some of the examples earlier in the book. Hopefully, everything that you've seen already will now begin to fall into place. Let's try out some code to see how the **`If...Then`** statement works.

Try It Out - The Basic If Statement

Many business applications have some form of security built in to prevent unwanted users from playing around with information they shouldn't have access to. Normally, you use the **`If...Then`** statement to check the user's name and password before letting them go any further.

Let's see how to do this.

1 Start a new Visual Basic project.

2 Bring up the properties window for the default form by pressing *F4*. Change the **`Caption`** property to Please enter your password.

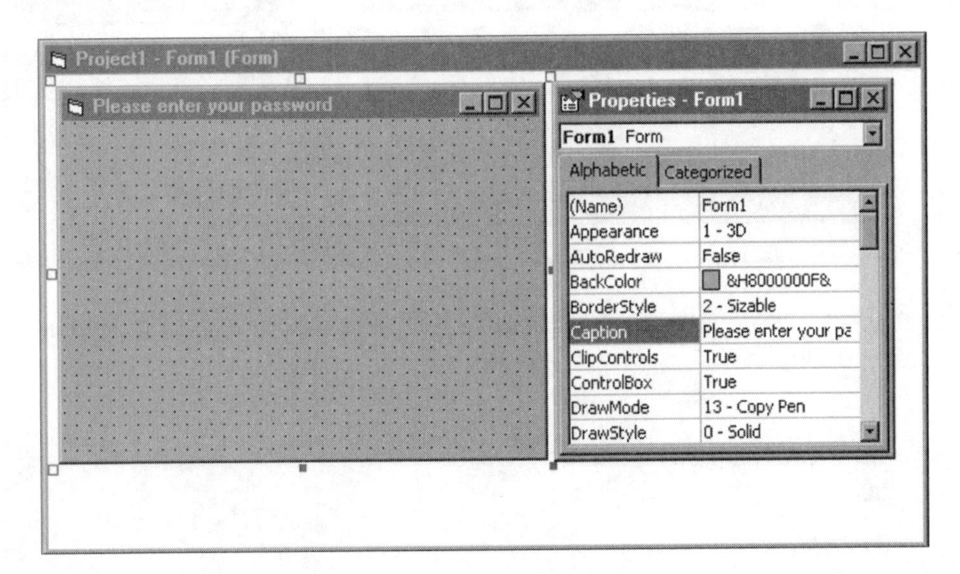

3 Draw one text box and one command button on the form. Resize the form and move the new controls around so that your form looks something like this:

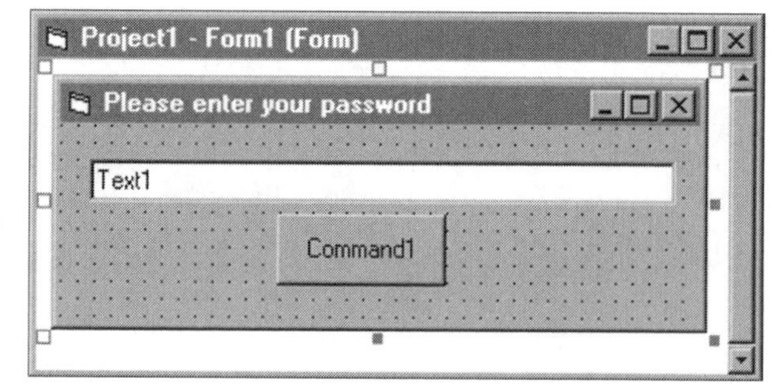

4 Select the text box and bring up its properties window. Find the **`PasswordChar`** property and set it to an asterisk (*). See how the text box caption is replaced by ****.

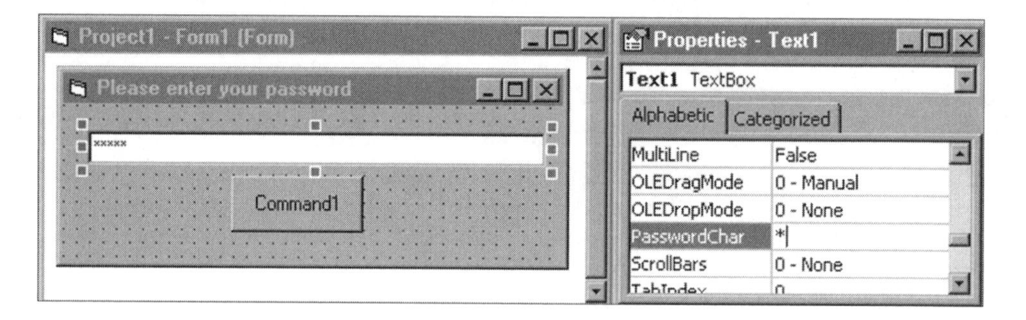

5 Then find the **`Text`** property and blank it out: select the property by clicking on it, then press the *BackSpace* key on your keyboard, followed by *Enter*. This removes the ***** from the box.

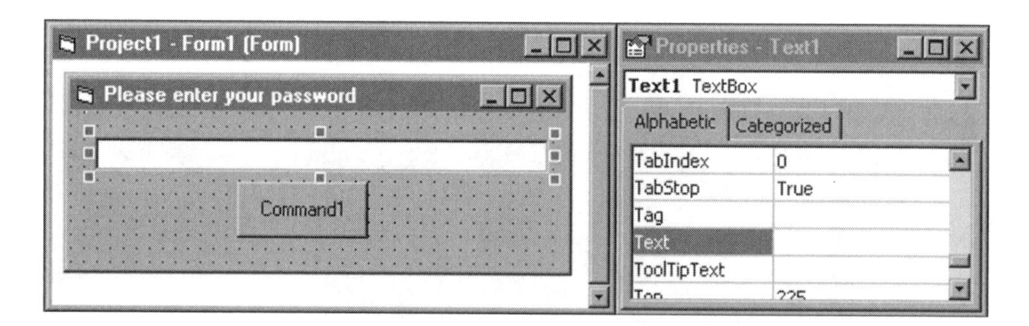

6 Select the command button, bring up its properties window and set the **`Caption`** property to OK.

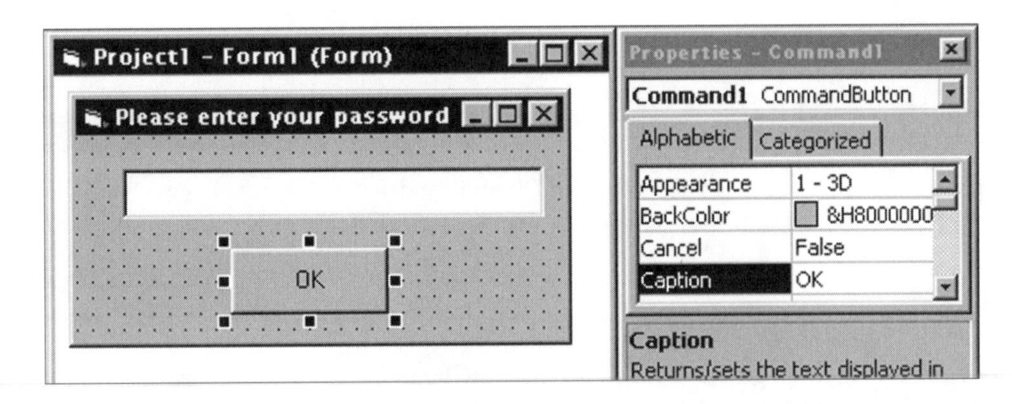

7 Now we can write some code. When the program runs, we want the user to key in their password, then hit the OK button. At that point, an **If...Then** statement will check the password and display the results in a message box on the screen. Double-click the command button to bring up the code window. Type in code so that the command button's **Click** event looks like this:

```
Private Sub Command1_Click()
 If Text1.Text = "letmein" Then
        MsgBox "Great - password accepted!"
        Unload Form1
        End
    Else
        MsgBox "Sorry, that's wrong, try again!"
        Text1.Text = ""
        Text1.SetFocus
    End If
End Sub
```

*When referring to the **Text** property of **Text1**, I have taken care to use the full syntax for the sake of clarity. You could, however, miss off the **Text** property name completely and just use **Text1**—by default Visual Basic will assume this refers to the **Text** property. Notice also how we're unloading the form explicitly before we end the program. If this were the main form in our application, unloading it would end the program anyway, but there's no harm in being sure.*

How It Works

Try running the program. If you typed all the code in correctly then the program will run after a short pause. Click in the text box and type Fred.

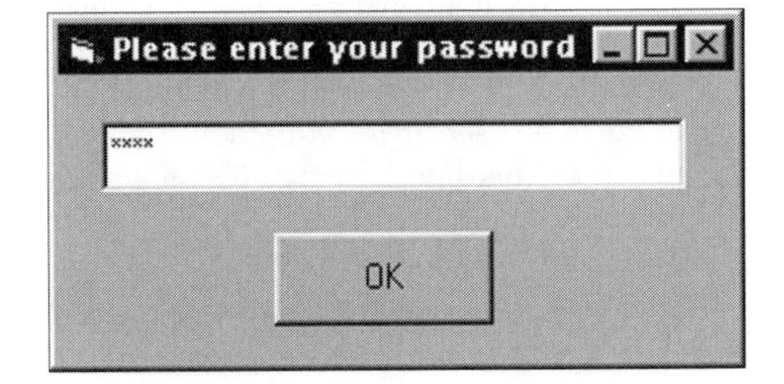

Stars appear in place of the keys you press on the keyboard. This is what setting the **PasswordChar** property to * does for you.

Having entered Fred, click the command button and a message box appears telling you to try again.

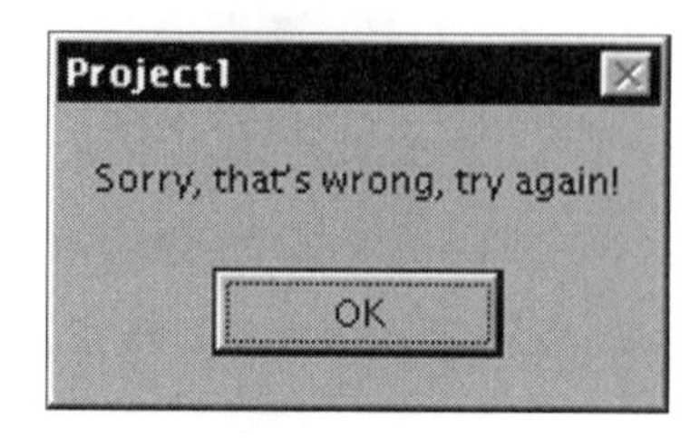

Get rid of the message box by clicking the OK button, then type letmein into the text box and click the command button again. This time the password is accepted and the program ends.

The **If...Then** statement in the above example consists of a number of parts:

- Straight after the word **If** there is the condition we want to test. In this example the condition is **Text1.Text = "letmein".**
- Immediately following the condition is the **Then** part, which tells Visual Basic what to do if the condition is met.

Take a look at the code again. Translated into plain English it says: *if the value of the text box is 'letmein' then unload the form and end the program.*

The **Else** statement, and the code following it, tells Visual Basic what to do if the condition isn't met. In the example, this part of the command actually means: *otherwise, display the message 'Sorry, that's wrong, try again!' and move the cursor back to the text box.* The **Else** part of the statement is actually optional—you could just have an **If...Then** statement that only does something if the condition is met.

The two lines of code:

```
Text1.Text = ""
Text1.SetFocus
```

clear the previous text ready to accept your next attempt, and set the focus back onto the text box.

You should note that by default, comparing text in Visual Basic is case sensitive. This means that it matters whether you use capitals or lower case letters in the text. If you had typed LetMeIn, it would have been rejected as an incorrect password. If you want to make Visual Basic case insensitive, you should add the statement **Option Compare Text** to your code. Just type this line into the (General) (declarations) section of the form or module you want it to apply to.

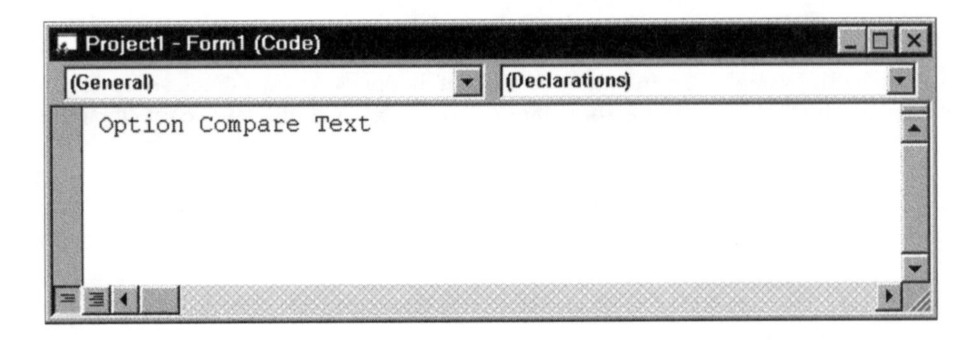

To return to the default, you need to use **`Option Compare Binary`**. As this is the default, you don't actually have to type it in. Deleting the line you just added will do fine.

Defining the Conditions You Want to Test

This actually leads us nicely on to **conditional expressions**. It's pretty obvious what the `=` sign means in the previous example, but what if you want to test for two numbers not being equal, or a number that is higher than another? By changing the equals sign in the example, you can test for many different conditions.

The complete list of symbols that you can use to test conditions is:

Symbol	Meaning
=	Is equal to
<>	Is not equal to
>	Is greater than
<	Is less than
>=	Is greater than or equal to
<=	Is less than or equal to

For example, **`If Age > 21 Then Admit_Entry`**, would read as *If age is greater than 21, then admit entry*. Here **`Admit_Entry`** represents some code you want executed if the condition is true.

*The code **`Admit_Entry`** can either be a few lines of Visual Basic code tucked right there in the same event handler, or it can be code contained in its own code module, separate from this handler. In the second case, this block of code is called a **subprocedure**, and simply writing its name, **`Admit_Entry`**, causes Visual Basic to jump to that code and execute it there and then. Modules and subprocedures are inherently bound up with controlling program flow, and we'll look at them in more detail later in this chapter. Before that though, let's finish our review of the ways to test conditions in Visual Basic.*

Testing Multiple Conditions

This is all fairly straightforward stuff—but what happens when you need to test for more than one condition before doing something? An example could be a correct password and the person's age to be greater than 21.

Visual Basic lets you use the words **And** and **Or** in order to make your complex conditions easier to read in code. In this example we could have an **If...Then** statement that says:

```
If Age > 21 And Password = "letmein" Then Admit_Entry
```

Normally with an **If...Then** statement, you check for a number of conditions and tell Visual Basic whether you want to do something if all the conditions are met (using **And**), or if only one condition is met (using **Or**). You can group tests together by using parentheses on the **If...Then** line. For instance, with a line like this:

```
If Age > 21 and Password = "letmein" or Password =
↳"Supervisor" Then Do_Something
```

it's not immediately obvious what the code does. Does it do something if the **Age** is greater than 21 and the password is **"letmein"** or **"Supervisor"**? Or does it do something if the password is **"letmein"** and **Age** is greater than 21, or if the **Password = "Supervisor"**? Confusing isn't it?

By using parentheses the code becomes much more readable and the results a great deal more predictable:

```
If (Age > 21 and Password = "letmein") or Password = "Supervisor" Then
↳Do_Something
```

This **If...Then** line will do something if the password is **"Supervisor"**, or if **Age** is greater than 21 and the password is **"letmein"**. The brackets separate the tests into smaller groups, so the **If** line treats:

```
(Age > 21 and Password = "letmein")
```

as one test, call it test A, and:

```
    Password = "Supervisor"
```

as another test, call it test B. The **If...Then** line will then work as long as A ***or*** B is true.

> *When we get a long line of code, I've broken it onto two lines using a (symbol. This isn't part of Visual Basic. When you type the code in, you should ignore the symbol and put all the code on one line. There is in fact a continuation character in Visual Basic. When you want to break a line of code put a space followed by an underscore _ character. I haven't done this in the book because I don't think you'll see a _ as clearly as a ↳.*

Multiline If Statements

It's already obvious that the line of code gets longer and longer as the condition gets more and more complex. There's another way to use the **If...Then** statement that can help make the code a little more readable.

With the multiline **If...Then** statement, the code following the word **Then** is spread over one or more lines. The **End If** command tells Visual Basic exactly where the conditional code ends. Let's try the example again:

```
If (Password = "letmein" and UserName = "Peter") or
    ↳LoggedIn = True Then

    Allow_Access
    Update_User_Log
    Display_First_Screen

End If
```

By using the multiline **If..Then** *statement, you not only make your code a lot more readable, but you also place a lot more functionality into it. In this example, providing the appropriate conditions are met, three subroutine calls are made instead of just one.*

Multiline If...Else Statements

Just as with the single line **If...Then,** the multiline version lets you use the **Else** statement to give Visual Basic an alternative course of action:

```
If (Password = "letmein" and UserName = "Peter") or
    ↳LoggedIn = True Then

    Allow_Access
    Update_User_Log
    Display_First_Screen

Else

    Deny_Access
    Erase_HardDisk
    Electrocute_User

End If
```

Multiple Alternatives Using ElseIf

Under normal circumstances you're limited to just two courses of action with an **If...Then** statement:

- The code that executes if the condition is met.
- The code following the **Else** that executes if the condition fails.

With multiline **If...Then** statements, though, you can perform further tests depending on the result of a prior test. For this you need to use **ElseIf**.

ElseIf enables you to build complex decision making code that can take any number of courses of action.

```
If <condition> Then
   ...
   ...
ElseIf <condition> Then
   ...
   ...
ElseIf <condition> Then
   ...
   ...
Else
   ...
   ...
End If
```

The code following the last **Else** statement is run if all the other conditions on the **If** and **Elseif** lines fail.

Try It Out - Multiline If...Then Statements

Before we can go any further and start to really explore the world of multiline **If...Then** statements, we really are going to need a program to try them out with. So, we're going to create an application that allows the user to enter a filename in the text box, and when they click on the View the File button, runs the appropriate Windows program to deal with the filename they enter. This can all be done using a multiline **If...Then** statement. So let's get started:

1 Begin a new project in VB and add a label control, one text box and a command button to it so that it looks like this:

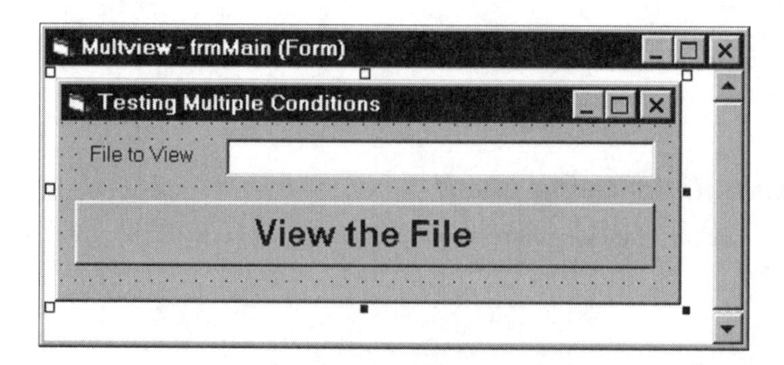

2 Blank out the text box, then name the controls as follows:

Control	Name
Form	`frmMain`
Text box	`txtFile`
Command button	`cmdView`

3 Double-click on the command button to bring up the code window, and enter code so that its **`Click`** event handler looks like this:

```
Private Sub cmdView_Click ()

    Dim sExtension As String
    Dim iReturnValue

    sExtension = UCase(Right$(txtFile.Text, 3))

    If Dir$(txtFile.Text) = "" Then
        MsgBox "Sorry, I couldn't find that file!" & vbCrLf
         ↳ & "It may be hidden.", vbExclamation
        Exit Sub

    ElseIf sExtension = "TXT" Then

        iReturnValue = Shell("Notepad " & txtFile.Text, 1)

    ElseIf sExtension = "BMP" Then

        iReturnValue = Shell("PBrush " & txtFile.Text, 1)

    End If

End Sub
```

Now try to run the program. For the filename enter the path and name of a text file that you have on your hard disk (if you don't have one then use Notepad now to create a text file called, for example, **`c:\test.txt`**) and then click the button. After a short pause you should see Notepad load up with the text file inside it.

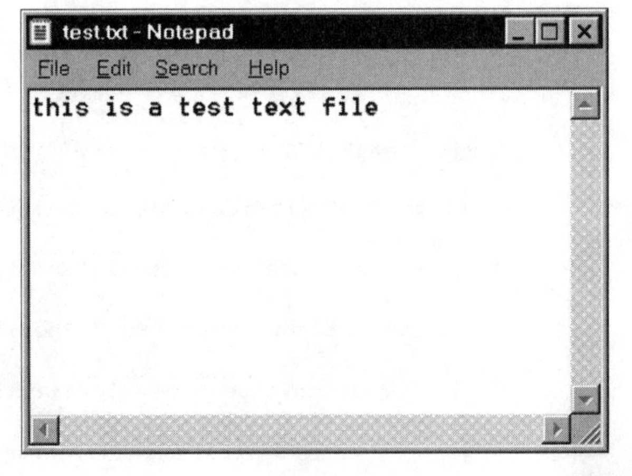

If you had entered the name of a picture file, ending in **.bmp**, then the code you entered would cause Windows PaintBrush to load up and show the file contents.

> *Note that* **Shell** *depends on the application being available in one of your Windows system's folders to work. PaintBrush is an old Windows 3 program, but is included with Windows 95, and stored in your Windows folder. Newer programs, such as WordPad and MS Paint are stored in your* **Program Files** *folder instead.*

The program isn't yet complete. If you select a file ending in **.bat**, then nothing happens. You'd expect it to load that file into Notepad in the same way as **.txt** files. Also, the program is currently unable to deal with **.wav** (sound samples) files and **.mid** (MIDI soundtrack) files and **.avi** (video clip) files. So, as this is the age of multimedia, in just a moment we'll add these features and also make the program tell us when something has gone wrong, rather than just sitting there blankly when it doesn't recognize the file type. First, though, let's find out what's going on under the hood.

How It Works

Have another look at the code you just entered. Looks daunting, doesn't it? We'll take it step by step.

```
Private Sub cmdView_Click ()

    Dim sExtension As String
    Dim iReturnValue
```

The two lines that begin with the keyword **Dim** set up some variables. These are places in memory to temporarily hold data. We cover variables in the next chapter.

```
        sExtension = Ucase(Right$(txtFile.Text, 3))
```

This next line takes the 3 right-most letters of the selected file name (i.e. the file extension) and makes sure that all the letters are changed to upper case. It then stores the result in the **sExtension** variable. For example, if you selected **ReadMe.txt**, this line would take the **txt** bit, and convert it into upper case letters if it isn't upper case already. The result is stored in **sExtension**.

```
    If Dir$(txtFile.Text) = "" Then
        MsgBox "Sorry, I couldn't find that file!" & vbCrLf
          ↳ & "It may be hidden.", vbExclamation
        Exit Sub

    ElseIf sExtension = "TXT" Then

        iReturnValue = Shell("Notepad " & txtFile.Text, 1)

    ElseIf sExtension = "BMP" Then

        iReturnValue = Shell("PBrush " & txtFile.Text, 1)
```

```
    End If
```

The main part of the code is the **If...Then** statement. This is a multiline version, which first checks whether the file selected actually exists, and then checks the **sExtension** variable to see if it recognizes the file type. If it does, then the appropriate program is loaded up using the **Shell** command, and the file is displayed.

Dir$** allows us to check whether a file exists. The **Dir$ command returns either the name of the file if it is found, or **""** if it's not. So the line:

```
If Dir$(txtFile.Text) = "" Then
```

will do something if the file name in the text box can't be found on the disk. **Shell** is a command in Visual Basic that lets us run another program. The program name and any other parameters are held in the parentheses after the word **Shell**. For example:

```
    iReturnValue = Shell("Notepad " & txtFile.Text, 1)
```

runs up Notepad and displays the **ReadMe.txt** file, whose name you may have entered. The **1** in the code tells Visual Basic that when the program is run it should be displayed in front of our Visual Basic program. You could equally well have **Shell** run a program out of sight in the background, or just display a taskbar button for it.

Shell actually returns a value to your code that you can check to see if everything worked OK. In this example, though, we just dump whatever **Shell** returns into the **iReturnValue** variable, and don't actually use it.

Try It Out - Adding More File Types

Let's now extend the program and make it handle other graphics, sound, and video files as well.

1 In the code window, click on the line above the words **End If** and type in this:

```
ElseIf sExtension = "WAV" or sExtension = "MID" or sExtension =
    ↳"AVI" Then
   iReturnValue= Shell ("MPlayer " & txtFile.Text, 1)
Else
   MsgBox "Sorry, I don't know how to handle this file type",
vbExclamation
```

> *If you're using Windows NT, instead of Windows 95, you must substitute* **MPlay32** *for the word* **MPlayer** *in the code above.*

As you saw before, the code after the **ElseIf** will only be run if all the initial **If...Then**, and the other **ElseIf...Then** parts fail. Now if you run the program, you'll be able to deal with graphics files and multimedia files, such as **Wav**s and **MID**s as well.

The **Else** command that you entered displays a message box. **Else**, as opposed to **ElseIf**, normally lets you tell Visual Basic what it should do if the **If...Then** fails. In this case, though, **Else** tells Visual Basic what to do if *all* the **If...Then** and **ElseIf...Then** lines fail.

2 Finally, let's make the program treat **.bat** files the same as it does **.txt** files. Move to the line that says:

```
ElseIf sExtension = "TXT" Then
```

Change it so that it now reads:

```
ElseIf sExtension = "TXT" Or sExtension = "BAT" Then
```

and the program will then be able to read **BAT** files.

I'll make no bones about it—this is a difficult program to throw at you now. Don't worry if it doesn't all fall into place immediately as a lot of what's in it will be covered in later chapters. I just wanted to give you a useful application here and now. When you're done editing this, though, you'll have an application that we can, and will, rely on later in the chapter. Save it to your hard disk with a name of ***ShowDone.vbp****.*

Getting Selective

If you play around with conditions and **If...Then** statements long enough, you'll soon end up tying yourself in knots with code consisting of line upon line of extremely similar looking **If..Then...Else...End If** statements. **If...Then** is great for one-shot tests and simple two-state decision making (**If** *a* **Then** *b* **Else** *c*). But when things start to get really messy, it's time to reach for the **Select Case** statement.

The Select Case Statement

There comes a point in any program where the **If...Then** command is simply not up to the job. Imagine, for example, a menu on screen—not your normal Windows style menu, but a simple list of numbered text entries. Let's say there are seven of them. If the user presses number **1** on the keyboard, then you want the first option's code to run. If they press **2**, then a different part should kick in, and so on.

Using **If...Then** you would have something like this:

```
If KeyPress = "1" Then
   'code for option 1
Else If Keypress = "2" Then
   'code for option 2
Else If Keypress = "3" Then
   'code for option 3
```

```
Else If Keypress = "4" Then
   'code for option 4
Else If Keypress = "5" Then
   'code for option 5
Else If Keypress = "6" Then
   'code for option 6
Else If Keypress = "7" Then
   'code for option 7
```

Looks a mess, doesn't it? If computers are so great at making repetitive tasks simple, then there must be a more elegant way of doing this kind of test. There is—using the **Select Case** statement.

Try It Out - Select Case in Action

Remember the awful multiline **If...Then** statement in **ShowDone.vbp**? Using **Select Case** that code could be so much nicer. But before we launch into a fully blown breakdown of how it all works, let's type some code.

1. In Visual Basic, load up the **ShowDone.vbp** project again. When the form appears, double-click on the View The File command button on the main form to see its code.

   All the **ElseIf** lines relate to the **sExtension** variable—checking the extension of the selected file and running the appropriate program. This is ideal hunting ground for **Select Case**. (Finger ache time).

2. Change the code so **Select Case** is used, like this:

```
Private Sub cmdView_Click()

   Dim sExtension As String
   Dim iReturnValue

   sExtension = UCase(Right$(txtFile, 3))

   If Dir$(txtFile) = "" Then
      MsgBox "Sorry, I couldn't find that file!" & vbCrLf
      ↳ & "It may be hidden.", vbExclamation
      Exit Sub
   End If

   Select Case sExtension
      Case "TXT", "BAT"
         iReturnValue = Shell("Notepad " & txtFile.Text, 1)
      Case "BMP"
         iReturnValue = Shell("PBrush " & txtFile.Text, 1)
      Case "WAV", "MID", "AVI"
         iReturnValue = Shell("MPlayer " & txtFile.Text, 1)
```

```
        Case Else
            MsgBox "Sorry, I don't know how to handle this file type",
             ↳ vbExclamation
    End Select

End Sub
```

All that's involved here is moving the **End If** line to underneath the words **Exit Sub**, then changing all the **ElseIf**s to **Case**, and adding a **Select Case** statement. Finally, then, run the program.

How It Works

Select Case tells Visual Basic that we want to check against one specific variable, in this case **sExtension**. The **Case** lines that follow tell Visual Basic what to do if the variable equals the value following the word **Case**. This value is written in quotes if it is text.

Notice how, if you want to check for more than one value, you simply separate the values in the **Case** statement with commas:

```
Case "TXT", "BAT"
```

This is the same as saying:

```
If sExtension = "TXT" or sExtension = "BAT" Then
```

but with the obvious exception that the **Case** statement is easier to read, and takes a great deal less typing that the traditional **If *xxxx* Or *xxxxx* Then...** construct.

In the above example, if we were only interested in files ending in **TXT**, then the **Case** statement would look like this

```
Case "TXT"
```

There's no need for commas here, just the single value that you want to check for.

Selecting Options Based on Different Conditions

As well as being able to check a single value or a number of values, the **Case** statement can also check running ranges of numbers, such as 1–5, or 100–200. Let's say you wanted to check if the variable contained a number in the range 10–15; your **Case** statement would look like this:

```
Case 10 To 15
   Here is the code
   That you want to execute
   If these values are true
```

Another difference to the normal **If...Then** statement is that **Case** statements can't contain the name of the variable you are checking, so you couldn't say **Case Index > 10** if **Index** is the name of the variable in the **Select** statement. Instead, you should use the word **Is**. **Is** refers to the variable you're checking, so it's quite legal to write:

```
Case Is > 100, Is <= 500, 999
```

This checks for values greater than 100, or less than or equal to 500 or equal to 999. Remember that the variable name is held on the **Select Case** line. The **Is** keyword checks the value of the variable against the condition, so **Is > 100** means: *if the variable is greater than 100.* As before the commas mean or, so the above line actually says: *if the variable is greater than 100, or less than or equal to 500, or equal to 999 then do something.*

Selecting Strings

You can use **Case** in exactly the same way to deal with text. If you use the **To** clause, Visual Basic does an alphabetic comparison on the two strings:

```
Select Case sPassword
   Case "Apples" To "Pears"
      ...
      ...
End Select
```

This example would cause your case code to run if the value of the **Password** string falls alphabetically between **"Apples"** and **"Pears".**

*When you do comparisons between text strings, Visual Basic deals with the comparison in a semi-intelligent way. First of all it looks at the case of the letters in the string. A capital letter such as **G** is treated as coming before its lower case equivalent **g**. So if you were to compare **Peter** and **peter**, in alphabetical sorting order, **Peter** comes first.*

*This type of comparison occurs for every letter of the string. The result is that Visual Basic handles strings properly so that **Apple** comes before **Pear**, **Aardvark** comes before **Arachnid**, and so on. Beware, though—**Aardvark** is quite different to **aardvark** as far as Visual Basic is concerned.*

For My Next Trick - Loops

Conditional statements such as **If...Then** and **Select Case** are great for running pieces of code that are based on just one condition. However, the real beauty of computers has always been their ability to do a great many repetitive operations in a fraction of the time it would take a human to do the same thing.

This is where loops come into play. Think back to your schooldays. You've just entered class late for the 12th time and forgotten your homework for the 10th time. The teacher is naturally a little upset and in a fit of fury orders you to write down 'I must stop being a complete failure' 1000 times. There we have it—a boring, odious task that a computer could perform with no hassle. The only thing to remember here, though, is that the well-programmed computer probably wouldn't have been late for class in the first place.

A **For...Next** loop is what we need here. This enables us to run a block of code a set number of times. In the case of our little childhood problem, the code in question would simply write the words 'I must stop being a complete failure' 1000 times.

Try It Out - The For...Next Loop

1 Start a new, Standard EXE project in Visual Basic. Double-click on the form to display its Code window.

2 Select the **Form_Load** event and type in some code so that it looks like this.

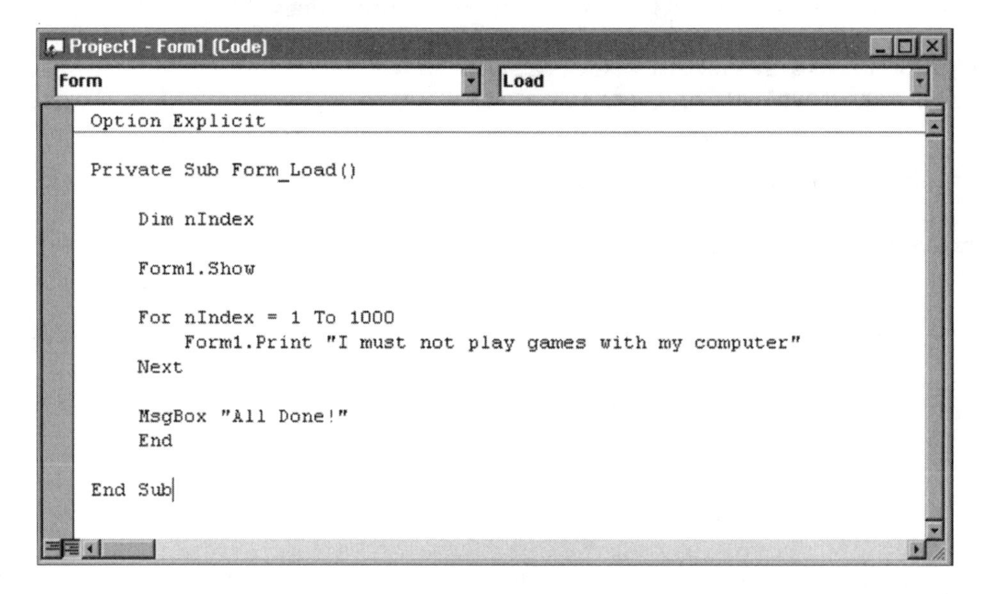
Project1 - Form1 (Code)
Form
Load
Option Explicit
Private Sub Form_Load()
Dim nIndex
Form1.Show
For nIndex = 1 To 1000
Form1.Print "I must not play games with my computer"
Next
MsgBox "All Done!"
End
End Sub

3 Run the code and you'll see the message appear on the form 1000 times. A message box then appears telling you that the program has finished. We'll cover the **Print** command in more detail later, but for now this is quite straightforward, I think.

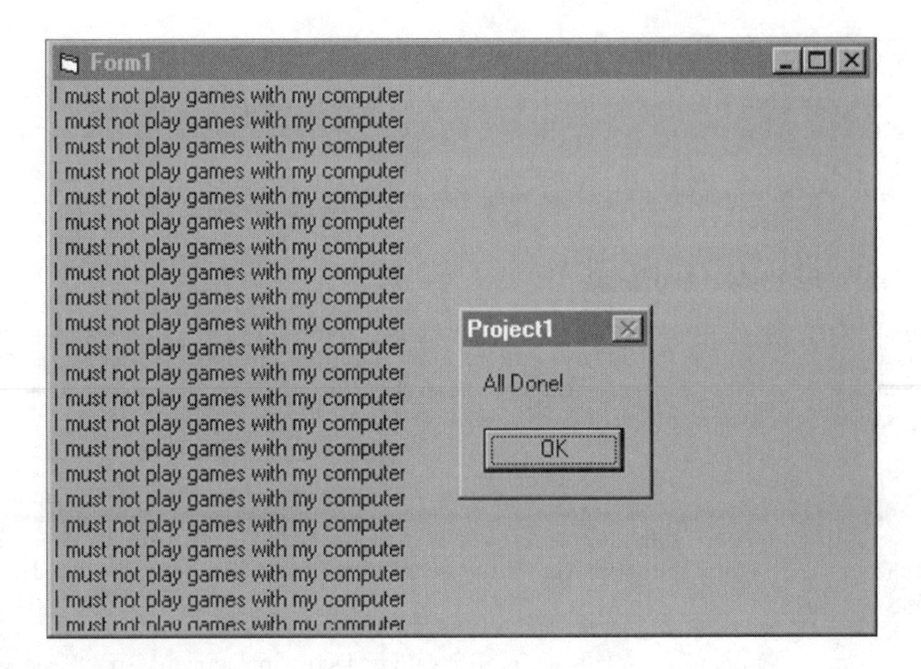

How the For...Next Loop Works

The line `For nIndex = 1 to 1000` is the start of the `For...Next` loop, which is what we're interested in. The `Next` statement shows where the loop ends. All code placed between the `For` and the `Next` commands is executed on each pass or iteration of the loop.

Of all the looping commands in Visual Basic, the `For...Next` combination is the only one that has been inherited from the first ever version of the BASIC language. This is because `For...Next` is easy to use and is surprisingly powerful.

How Index Variables Control For Loops

`For...Next` loops use a numeric variable as a **counter** to keep track of the number of times the loop actually needs to run. In loop-speak this variable is often called an **index.**

We tell Visual Basic that `nIndex` is a variable at the start of the routine, with the line

```
Dim nIndex
```

A variable is a container for a piece of data to which you can assign a label, called a variable name. You can change the value of a variable at run time, which is why it's useful for counting loops. We'll be looking at variables in more depth in the next chapter.

By saying `For nIndex = 1 to 1000` we're telling Visual Basic to load the variable `nIndex` with the number `1` to start with. By default, `1` will be added to it at each pass through the loop's code until it equals `1000`. As soon as the variable goes outside the range `1` to `1000`, the loop exits and the code following the `Next` statement is run.

*You should really place the name of the index variable after the word **`Next`** (i.e. **`Next nIndex`**). This makes the code a lot easier to read and follow, particularly if you have a number of **`For...Next`** loops nested inside each other. In our example, however, there is only one **`For...Next`** loop, so it's obvious that the **`Next`** command relates to the preceding **`For`**.*

Controlling the Index Variable

In our example, the **`For...Next`** loop increments the index variable by **`1`** on each iteration. This is the default setting for a **`For...Next`** loop. It can be changed by placing a **`Step`** statement at the end of the **`For`** statement. **`Step`** tells Visual Basic how many to add to the index variable on each iteration. We can see that:

```
For nIndex = 1 to 1000 Step 50
```

tells Visual Basic to start with the value of **`1`** in **`nIndex`** and add **`50`** to the index variable on each pass. As before, the loop will exit as soon as the value of **`1000`** is exceeded in **`nIndex.`**

By far the most common use for **`Step`** is in creating decreasing loops. Visual Basic will automatically add **`1`** to the index variable every time, so a statement like:

```
For nIndex = 1000 to 1
```

wouldn't actually work as the index variable would attempt to begin at a value greater than the one it's supposed to finish at. The code within the loop wouldn't actually execute before the program exited the loop. The statement:

```
For nIndex = 1000 To 1 Step -1
```

would work, since the **`Step`** clause tells Visual Basic to add **`-1`** to the index variable on each pass.

Leaving a For Loop

Visual Basic provides a command for leaving a **`For...Next`** loop prematurely. Placing the command **`Exit For`** inside a loop will cause it to stop immediately. The code will continue running from the line directly following the **`Next`** statement. This works in much the same way as **`Exit Sub`** does to leave a subprocedure.

An Aside on Naming Your Index Variables

It's a long-standing tradition that index variables in **`For`** loops are usually called **`I`** or **`J`**, or even **`X`** and **`Y`**. Despite what other books or magazines might have you think, this is extremely bad programming practice. It stems from the limited choice of variable names that were available in Fortran, a language that was a predecessor of BASIC. In Fortran, all integer variables began with the letters **`I,J,K,L,M`** or **`N`**. The **`X`** and **`Y`** names presumably come from terse mathematicians.

If you defined a variable, then you undoubtedly had a reason for doing so. Furthermore, if you started a **For...Next** loop, then there was a reason for that as well. Always give any variable a meaningful name. If you have a **For...Next** loop that is counting records in a file, then call the index variable **nRecordsInFile**. If you have taken the time to bring a variable to life, then take the time to christen it properly too. When you return to your code to make changes to it in a month or a year's time, the variable name will make the code much more readable. You should be able to get a hint from the index variable's name as to exactly what the loop itself is doing.

Showing a Form as it Loads

You'll notice that we've used the **Show** command in our earlier example to make sure that the form is visible, before we start to **Print**. If it weren't, nothing would appear. Loading a form with the **Load** command simply sets aside some memory to hold the form's graphics, code and controls. It doesn't actually make the form appear on screen.

The form will normally come into view at some point after the end of the form's load event. I say 'at some point', because the code in the **Load** event could go off and do a hundred or more other things such as setting up variables to hold data, or doing some calculations in loops. The form will only become visible when all the code is complete, and Visual Basic has the time.

The **Show** method gets around this by forcing Visual Basic to bring the form into view. It's always good, from a user's point of view, to put a **Show** command in a form's **Load** event. If something appears on screen almost straight away, your users won't start panicking and think that your program, Windows, or both, have crashed.

It's all a matter of psychology—if users can see something happening, then they stop counting the seconds it takes for your program to actually do something useful. This is the purpose of the splash screen we saw in the application created by Application Wizard in Chapter 2. You could take another approach and **Show** a small form containing a message such as Please Wait—Loading Data.

The Do Loop

The **For...Next** loop is a venerable remnant of the original BASIC language. Visual Basic is an evolutionary product that has adopted many of the best commands and attributes of other leading languages such as C and Pascal, and married them to its BASIC roots. The **Do** loop illustrates this point well, as it's based on a similar structure found in Pascal.

The **Do** loop is an alternative way to repeat a block of code. You can achieve the same results using various combinations of the **For...Next** loop, but sometimes using **Do** makes your code more elegant and intuitive. At the end of the day however, it's a question of style.

There are three types of **Do** loop: those that run forever, those that run while a condition is being met, and those that run until a condition is met. These are covered by using the

Do...Loop, Do...Loop While and the **Do...Loop Until** commands. There aren't many real uses for a loop that runs forever, so we'll just be considering the other two of them here.

Do...Loop While

Let's go back to the password example from earlier on in the chapter. It's OK to electrocute the illegal user and throw them out of the system, but sooner or later you'll run out of living users. You really want to give the user a second, or maybe even third chance. Enter stage left the **Do...Loop While** loop.

Try It Out - Three Tries for the Password

1 Create a new project in Visual Basic, and just as before remove the default form that appears, replacing it with a code module. When you add the code module into the project the code window pops up, which is handy, because it's time for you to type in the following **Main** subprocedure.

```
Sub Main()
    Dim nRetries As Integer
    Dim sPassword As String

    nRetries = 3

    Do
        sPassword = InputBox$("Enter the password and click OK")
        nRetries = nRetries - 1
    Loop While sPassword <> "letmein" And nRetries > 0

    If sPassword <> "letmein" Then
        MsgBox "You got the password wrong - Access denied"
    Else
        MsgBox "Welcome to the system - password accepted"
    End If
End Sub
```

Try running the program now. Remember, because there are no forms in this project, Visual Basic will look for a subprocedure called **Main**, which is convenient since that is really what you just typed into the code module. When the program runs, it displays the following:

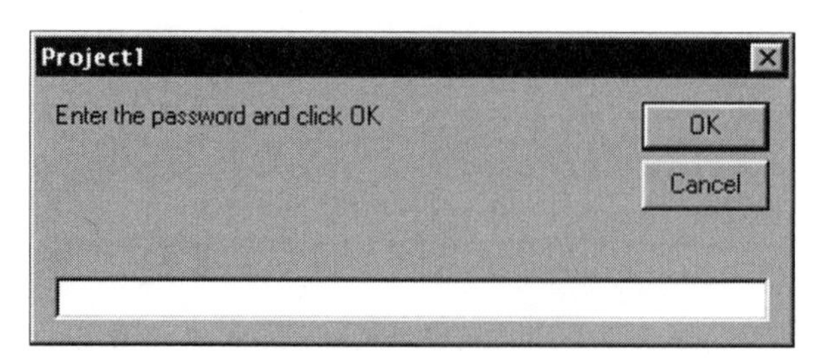

Try entering a password. Each time you get it wrong the program displays the same dialog box, asking you once again to try and log in with the correct password—so much more humane than simply frying your users, but undeniably less fun too.

2 On the third wrong attempt, the program ends. Clicking the OK button will return you to design mode.

3 Before we take a look at the code, save your work. We will be coming back to this project in a moment so give it a name we can all remember, like **Passdo1.vbp** for example.

Let's take a look at that code.

How It Works

First of all we need to declare two variables. This tells Visual Basic what these variables are going to be used for, i.e. what kind of data you're planning to store in them.

```
Dim nRetries As Integer
Dim sPassword As String
```

Here, **nRetries** is a number that counts the attempts that have already been made at guessing the password, while **sPassword** contains the text string that is the current guess.

> ***Dim** is used to declare or dimension these variables. Don't worry about this too much, as we'll discuss it in more detail in the next chapter.*

Next we have the loop. The **Do** command marks the start of the loop code. Just as **Next** marks the end of a **For** loop, the **Loop** keyword closes a **Do** loop. The **While** clause tells Visual Basic to run the code as long as the users keep getting the password wrong and the user still has a number of retries left.

```
Do
   sPassword = InputBox$("Enter the password and click OK")
```

The first line of the loop places an input box on the screen with the words Enter the password and click OK on it. Like the message box, an input box is another of Visual Basic's built-in features. However, this one accepts input from the user and then puts that input into a variable of your choice, in this case **sPassword**.

We then reduce the number of tries left by one:

```
nRetries = nRetries - 1
```

If the password was wrong, and there are retries left, the line:

```
Loop While sPassword <> "letmein" And nRetries > 0
```

sends the program back round the loop again.

When the loop ends, one of two conditions must be true. Either you ran out of tries, in which case the first message box is displayed:

```
If sPassword <> "letmein" Then
   MsgBox "You got the password wrong - Access denied"
```

or you got the password right, in which case the second message box is displayed:

```
Else
   MsgBox "Welcome to the system - password accepted"
```

Input boxes and message boxes are covered in detail in Chapter 10. What's important here is the **Do..Loop While** code.

Do...Loop Until

Maybe three attempts to get a password right still isn't enough. Maybe your users are management personnel, or worse still, executives. Enter stage right the **Do...Loop Until** loop.

If we use **Do...Loop Until**, we can keep the loop going for as long as it takes the user to enter the right password. Let's replace that **Do...While** loop in **Passdo1.vbp** with a much nicer **Do...Loop Until** for the management types.

```
Sub Main()

   Dim nRetries As Integer
   Dim sPassword As String

   nRetries = 3

   Do
      sPassword = InputBox$("Enter the password and click OK")
      nRetries = nRetries - 1
   Loop Until sPassword = "letmein"

End Sub
```

If you try running the code, you'll see how the **Loop Until** clause keeps the loop going until the user finally gets the password right. To stop the program running, press the *Ctrl* and *Break* keys or enter the correct password.

Where to Test in the Loop

It's worth noting at this point that although up to now we have placed the **While** and **Until** clauses after the **Loop** keyword, they can also be put straight after the **Do** command. Apart from the obvious syntactical differences, doing this actually changes the way the code itself runs.

Placing the clauses **While** or **Until** after the **Loop** statement causes the loop code to run at least once. It encounters the **Do** keyword, does its business, and then looks at the **Loop** line to see if it needs to do the whole thing again. Placing the clauses after the **Do** statement means that if the condition isn't met, then the loop code is ignored totally, and the next line that's run is the one immediately following the **Loop** command:

```
Do While 1 = 2

   'This code will NEVER run

Loop
```

Finally, just as with the **For** loop, the **Exit** keyword can be used to drop out of a **Do** loop prematurely. In this case the exact statement you need is **Exit Do**.

In Windows version 3, if you have a loop that does nothing but calculation (in other words it never updates the screen or asks for user input), it was possible to make any other programs that were running grind to a halt. This was because pre-95/NT versions of Windows waited for the program that had the focus to give control back to the operating system. In Windows 95 and Windows NT, the operating system allocates each program in turn a proportion of time, but suspends it again automatically when it's time is up.

However, if your code is quite happily chugging away in a loop doing nothing but calculations, then your application will appear to lock up—even though Windows will still allocate time to others. So users working with your program will soon get bored. OK, you can show them an hourglass, but you might want them to be able to select other forms, or enter values for the next calculation, at the same time. Your application becomes more responsive, and anyway it helps to keep users awake.

The **DoEvents** command is a way of achieving this. Simply place a **DoEvents** command in your loop and whenever it's encountered, your program will tell Windows to update the interface, and do anything else it has to, before your original code can continue. Chapter 6 explains how you can use **DoEvents** and something known as the **idle loop** to not only create system-friendly programs, but also to create extremely responsive programs your users will love.

The While...Wend Loop

The final type of loop in Visual Basic is the **While...Wend** loop. To be totally honest, I can see only one reason why Microsoft included this loop in Visual Basic—for compatibility with earlier versions (and perhaps to keep WordBasic, C and Pascal programmers happy!). It's exactly the same as the **Do...While** loop, but without some of the flexibility that particular loop offers. Indeed, even the Programmers Reference manual states that it's better to ignore **While...Wend** and head straight for the **Do...While** loop.

For this reason you'll only see **Do** loops used in the more complex code examples later in the book. For those of you who desperately want to use the **While...Wend** loop, here's our password code rewritten:

```
While sPassword <> "letmein"
    sPassword = InputBox$("Enter password")
Wend
```

It's basically the same as a **Do...While** loop, except that the word **Do** is missing and a **Wend** has replaced the **Loop** statement. The other difference between the two types of loop is that you can't exit a **While** loop using an **Exit** command. The only way out is to change the variable that the **While** loop is testing so that you make the condition fail, and the loop stop.

Jumping Around With GoTo

There have been hundreds of pages of press and book coverage devoted to the evils of the infamous **GoTo** command. For those who have never heard of the term, **GoTo** is a command that lets you jump from one part of your code to another. It's as simple as that. Not a voodoo doll in sight!

The History of the Crime

In the early days of BASIC, before subprocedures and functions came along, **GoTo** provided an easy way to break your code into manageable chunks. You could write some code to perform a common function and use **GoTo** to run it from anywhere within your program simply by saying **GoTo**, followed by a line number denoting where that code began.

The problem with **GoTo** was that your code could soon end up looking a real mess with **GoTo**s all over the place and no real indication of where they actually led to in functional terms.

When subprocedures and functions came along, under the banner of structured programming, the aging **GoTo** command was dropped like a proverbial hot brick amidst comments such as 'It promotes spaghetti code' and 'It increases the likelihood of bugs creeping into the system'. You can actually write a program without ever touching **GoTo.**

When to Use GoTo

However, **GoTo** is actually a necessary command. Visual Basic's built-in error handling command **On Error** requires the keyword **GoTo**. When your Visual Basic program is running for the first time, errors will normally occur. You may come across values in your controls that are too big for Visual Basic to handle. In a database program, your code might have trouble actually talking to the database, especially if your users belong to the typical breed that have a habit of deleting things with their eyes shut.

On Error provides a way for you to catch these errors in your subprocedures and run a piece of code to handle them, rather than having your program crash all over the floor. For example the line:

```
On Error GoTo ErrorHandler
```

tells Visual Basic that in the event of an error occurring in the program, it should go to the part of the subprocedure named **ErrorHandler** and run the code from there.

> *Handling errors that crop up during run time is a whole subject in itself, and is extremely important if you're going to distribute Visual Basic applications to other users. Take a look at Chapter 8,* Debugging, *for a full explanation.*

If you have a valid and legitimate reason to use the **GoTo** command (such as when handling errors), then by all means do so. Used wisely it won't ruin your program and it won't damage your street credibility. Once again, though, always use the right tool for the job.

Jumping to a Label

Before you can use **GoTo** you need to define a label. A label is a name you can assign to a point in your code. You define a label by simply typing a name on a line and placing a colon (**:**) immediately after it.

If you define a label called **Code1** for example, you can jump to the code following your label by saying **GoTo Code1.**

```
Private Sub A_subprocedure()

    GoTo Code1
        ...
        ...
        ...
Code1:
        ...
        ...
End Sub
```

Problems start to occur when you have a `GoTo` followed by another `GoTo` and so on. A surefire way to test for overuse of the `GoTo` command is to try drawing straight lines on a listing of the code in your project between all the labels and the `GoTo`s that call them. If you end up with a jumbled mess of crisscrossing lines, then you've overdone it and would be well advised to simplify your code. This line-drawing approach is where the term 'spaghetti coding' comes from.

Just one more analogy before we close the subject of `GoTo`*. Two men, each with a hundred thousand nails and a thousand small pieces of timber are given identical plans to build a house. The first man builds a tumbledown shack that, quite literally, tumbles down. For generations afterwards the man's offspring refuse to use wood and nails to build houses, since they are unsafe to live in. The second man however builds a fine house out of the materials and lives happily ever after.*

The moral of this tale is that it's not the tools and materials that a man uses which create disasters, it's his naiveté and lack of skill. A badly written program is a badly written program, not an indictment of the tools used to write the program in the first place.

Summary

In this chapter you've learned about loops, decision-making, jumping and modules. These are three of the most fundamental aspects of writing Visual Basic code. We've covered:

- How to define conditions in `If` statements and loops.
- How to write single-line and multiline `If` statements.
- How to add code modules to your project. How the `Select Case` statement can help you check one variable for a range of values.
- How to use a `For` loop to run parts of your program a specific number of times.
- How to use `Do` loops, and the significance of the `While` and `Until` clauses.
- How to make safe use of the `GoTo` command.

In the next chapter, we'll learn about how to represent data in your Visual Basic programs. You've already used simple data-like strings and loop counters; now you'll learn about what other kinds of data Visual Basic supports.

Why Not Try...

1. Create a project which contains a form which can be used as a "login" form to an application. Place a label, a text box and a command button on the form. Ensure that the text box receives focus on startup. Place code in the **`Click`** event of the command button, so that the entry in the text box is validated against a password you have selected. (Use a simple **`If`** statement). If the password is correct, then display a message box congratulating the user on their correct choice.

2. Modify the project from Exercise 4-1. This time, use an **`Else`** statement to display a message box warning the user that they have typed in an incorrect password.

3. Create a project which contains a form, a text box, a label and a command button. Write code, using the **`Select Case`** statement, that accepts a character into the text box, and determines whether the character is a vowel. In the label, display a running count of the number of vowels entered.

4. Modify Exercise 4-3 to count consonants as well.

   Hint: You'll need to add another label to display the second count.

5. Create a project which contains a form and a text box. Set the **`MultiLine`** property of the text box to true. Set the **`ScrollBars`** property of the text box to Vertical. Use a **`For...Next`** loop in the **`Form_Load`** event to print out the multiplication tables from 2 to 12 in the text box.

   Hint: You will need to use nested For...Next Loops.

asic Visual Basic Visual Ba
al Basic Visual Basic Visual
Basic Visual Basic Visual Ba
ual Basic Vi
Basic Visu
ual Basic V
l Basic Vis
isual Basic Visual Basic
al Basic Visual Basic Visua
Visual Basic Visual Basic Visu
al Basic Visual Ba
l Basic Visual
ic Visual Basi
Basic Visual B
ic Visual Basi
al Basic Visual
ual Basic Visual Basic Visual Ba
Visual Basic Visual Basic Visu
sual Basic Visual Basic Visu
Visual Basic Visual Ba

Making Data Work For You

The programs you write focus around one thing—data! From a programmer's point of view there are two aspects to handling data. Firstly there's the user interface—the forms you create and the controls you draw on them. This interface must allow the user to enter the data your program needs easily and efficiently. Secondly, your program has to process that data to produce the results you want.

Visual Basic incorporates a number of ways in which you can both hold and manipulate data inside your applications. Once the work is finished, you can either kick the results back out to the user interface, or store them somewhere more permanent, such as on the hard disk or on paper.

This chapter is about how to handle data once it gets inside your program. You will learn:

- What kinds of data Visual Basic can work with
- How to use scrollbars to input numeric data
- How to use date and time information in your programs
- What strings are, and what you can do with them
- How to build your own data objects using Visual Basic
- When variables are valid in a project with more than one form and when they are not

Data and Visual Basic

A **variable** is a space set aside in your applications where you can store temporary information. This could be anything from a piece of text to represent a user name, to a simple number holding a count of the number of times a user has performed a certain operation. The important thing here is that variables are *temporary* stores for your data. They are used to hold the information your program needs to do the job in hand. As soon as your program ends, your variables vanish, taking the data they contain along with them.

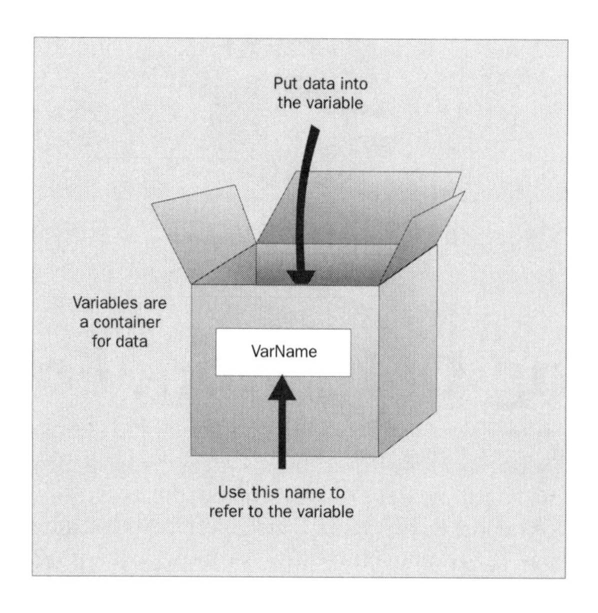

Using Variables

When you first set up a variable you have to give it a **name**. From then on you can examine the data in that variable, change it, delete it and so on, by referring to it by name. You don't need to worry too much about the work Visual Basic has to do behind the scenes in terms of actually storing the data somewhere.

Let's look at an example. Imagine you need to store someone's age somewhere. You could create a variable called **Age** and store a value in it by typing:

```
Age = 24
```

Later, the number stored in **Age** could be used in calculations to get further numbers to store in other variables, or it could even be assigned to a control property. You may, for example, have a form containing a text box to display someone's age, called **txtAge**. You could display the contents of the **Age** variable in the text box simply by saying:

```
txtAge.Text = Age
```

If you've ever done any programming before, you won't need much introduction to variables. Even if you are new to programming, you'll find the concepts here straightforward. In fact, in the first four chapters of this book you have already come across almost as many variables as you will ever need. For example, in Chapter 4 we used a variable **nIndex** as the **counter** when creating a loop:

```
For nIndex = 1 to 20
    'Do Something Here
Next nIndex
```

In this kind of simple context, variables are really quite intuitive. What we'll do in this chapter is focus on the ways that Visual Basic uses data, examining in detail only those features that are peculiar to Visual Basic.

Declaring Variables

In many BASICs, including Visual Basic, simply having a command that says **`Age = 24`** is enough to create a variable called **`Age`** which can hold numbers. Similarly, saying **`Name = "Peter"`** is enough to create another variable, this time called **`Name`**, which can hold text, or more specifically alphanumeric characters. This is known as **implicit** declaration.

The **explicit** method of creating a variable is slightly more verbose. We have to first tell Visual Basic that the variable exists by declaring it using the **`Dim`** command. With **`Dim`**, you have to give your variable a name immediately, and you have the choice of telling Visual Basic what kind of data that variable will hold. This is known as setting the **data type**.

> *Explicit declaration, while it may be a little more long-winded, is actually the best method to use. It prevents confusing bugs at runtime that are difficult to track down and even more difficult to fix.*

Choosing the Explicit Declaration Option

The way Visual Basic expects you to define variables is determined by an entry on the Editor tab of the Options dialog. The Require Variable Declaration entry on that dialog means that you must tell Visual Basic which variables you are going to use before you actually use them.

The Require Variable Declaration option toggles Visual Basic between implicit declaration, where it automatically declares variables for you, and explicit declaration, where it needs variable declarations from you before a variable can be used.

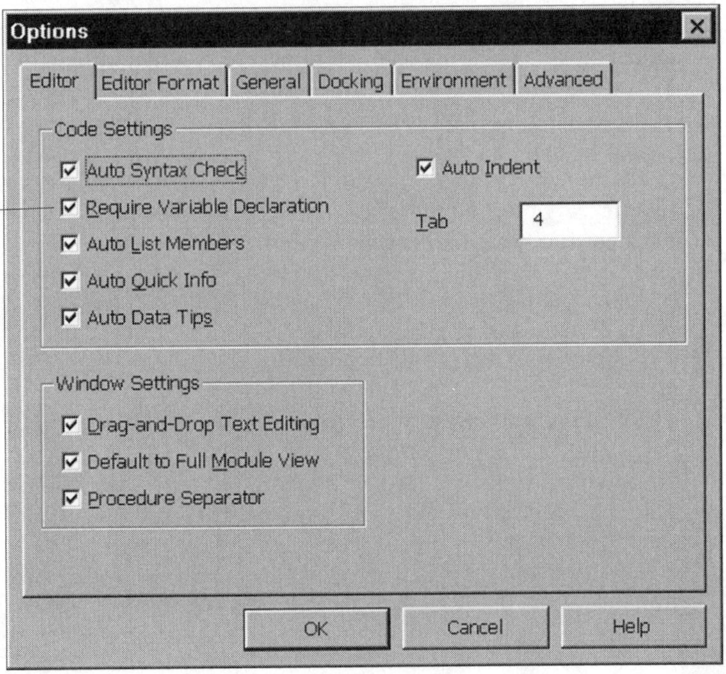

For explicit declaration, you need to make sure that this option is ticked before you start a new project or create any additional forms or modules in a project. Visual Basic will then insert the words **`Option Explicit`** in the General Declarations section of any module or form—it's this **`Option Explicit`** command that makes Visual Basic force you to declare your variables before use.

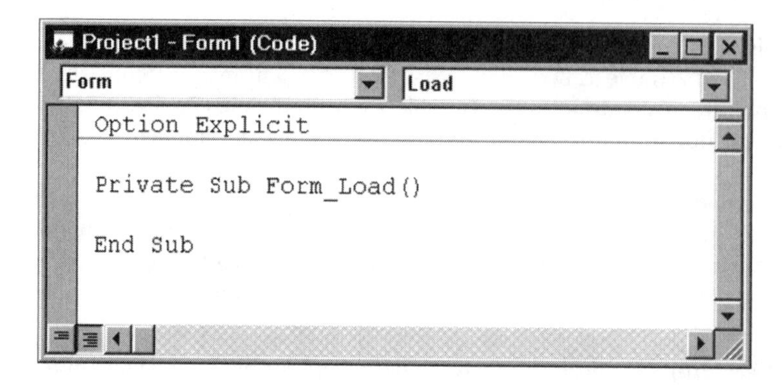

Remember that to make the change effective, you have to open a new project after changing to the explicit declaration option. Once you have set this up though, it remains set up forever, or at least until you decide to turn it off.

You can also type the **`Option Explicit`** *line into any existing form or module code windows yourself if you wish.*

Constants

Variables, as the name suggests, are places in your program where you can hold items of data that are going to change. However, you'll frequently find a need for a more stable kind of runtime storage. This is what **constants** are for. They're rather like a variable in a bomb-proof glass case—you can look at it, but there's no way you're going to mess with it.

Constants are great for improving the readability, and hence maintainability, of your code. Imagine a game, for instance, where you need to use a simple **`For...Next`** loop to move ten aliens around the screen:

```
For nAlien = 1 to 10
   Call MoveAlien(nAlien)
Next
```

There are no problems with this on its own, but what if the rest of the program had other loops that went from one to ten to do various other tasks? There could be loops to check if an alien wants to fire, die, or make a sound. What's going to happen when someone tells you the game is too easy and you need to put twenty more aliens in it?

Under normal circumstances you'd have to trot through all the code in your program hunting for loops from one to ten. If you'd used a constant, however, you would only have one line to change.

```
' To increase the number of bad guys, change this constant declaration
Constant NUMBER_OF_ALIENS = 10

For nAlien = 1 to NUMBER_OF_ALIENS
   Call MoveAlien(nAlien)
Next
```

Notice how the name of the constant is typed in capitals. Visual Basic is pretty laid-back about what you want to call your constants and variables, but it is common practice to set up constants with names that are all capital letters. That way, just by reading through the code, you can easily see which parts of your program are using variables and which are using constants.

Types of Data in Visual Basic

If Visual Basic is the only programming language you've used, or even if you came here from QBasic, then you could be forgiven for being oblivious to the idea of there being different types of data. So far, almost all the variables we've looked at have behaved the same, regardless of the kind of data they store—be that words, numbers, or whatever.

However, these false assumptions have to change now. Visual Basic, like most of the more advanced languages, does have **data types**. This means that you can create variables that will only accept one type of data. These are the traditional fare of **typed** programming languages like C and Pascal. We haven't worried about them up to now, as you've been using a feature called **variant data types**, which allows you to avoid this kind of typing.

A Variable for all Seasons - The Variant

Variants are variables which are named in the same way as any other variable, but which are a jack of all trades when it comes to actually storing information. You can store literally anything in a variant and it won't moan at you. From a beginner's point of view this is great. You could store text in a variant variable one minute, numbers the next, and dates a short while later. You don't have to worry about whether or not the variant can cope, or whether you are matching the right type of data to the right variables.

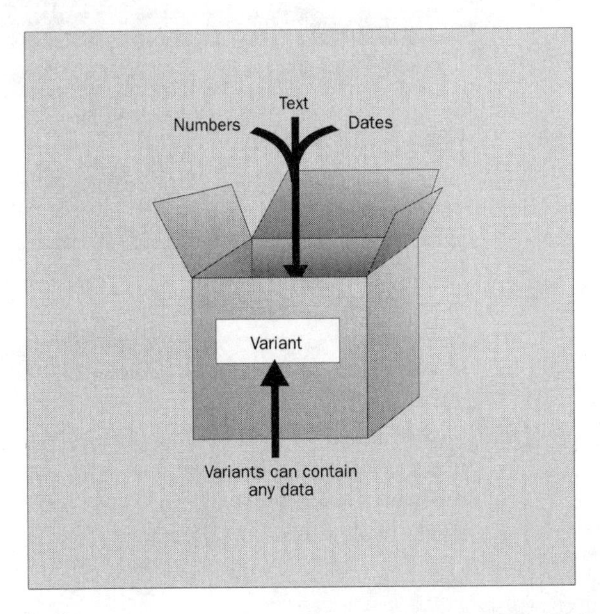

Try It Out - Variants and Typed Variables

Variants have a number of specialized uses apart from being the lazy programmer's data stash. For example, you can check the contents of a variant to find out what kind of data a user has entered. This is done using, for example, the **`IsDate`** and **`IsEmpty`** functions.

Let's try out the **`IsDate`** and **`IsEmpty`** functions with a short example.

1 Create a new project in Visual Basic in the usual way, and resize the form so that it looks like the one in the screenshot. For the sake of completeness, set the caption up as well, using the properties window.

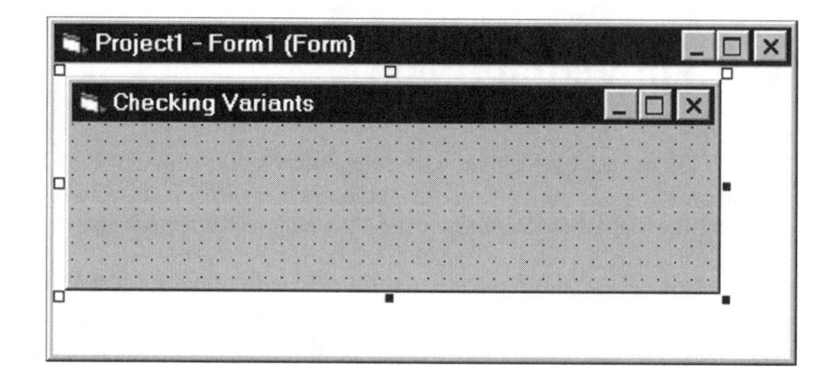

2 Next drop a label and a text box on to the form as shown. Remove the default entry from the **`Text`** property of the text box.

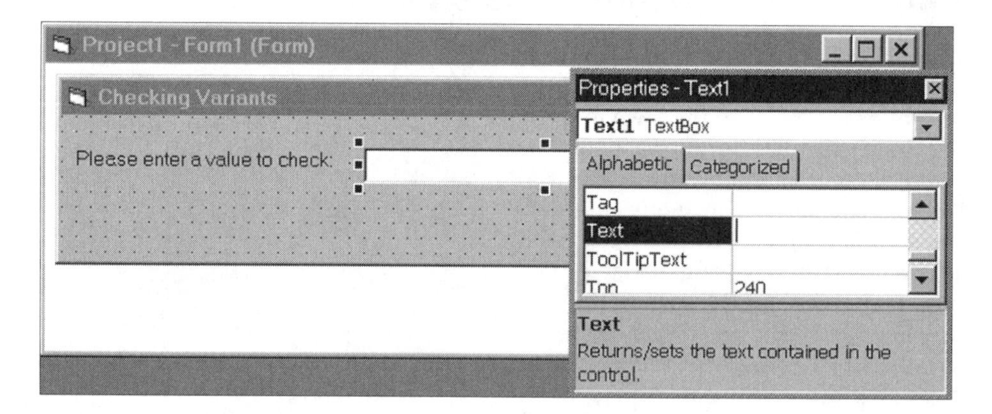

3 Nearly there. The final stage before we can write some code is to put another label underneath the other two, but with its caption cleared out. Also make sure you name this label **`lblType`**; that way there is absolutely no chance of us confusing the two labels at runtime.

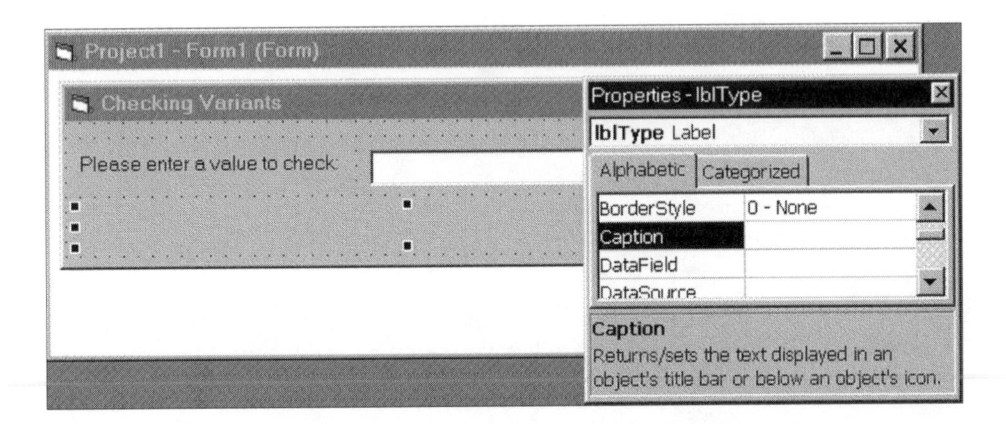

What we are going to do here is display some text in this latest label control to show the type of data that the user just entered into the text box above. We can do this quite easily because Visual Basic includes a number of special commands that are designed to report back on the type of data held in a variable.

4 The only thing we need to do in code, then, is to use the second label to display a message showing the type of data entered into the text box as it is being entered. Double-click the text box to bring up the code window for the text box's **`Change`** event. Type in code so that the **`Change`** event looks like this:

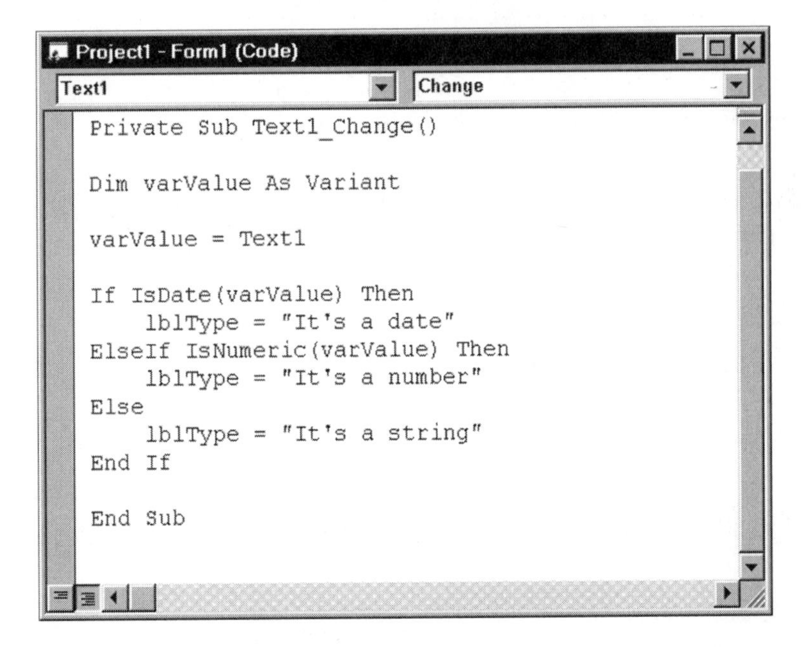

5 Now try running the program and keying something into the text box. As you key in values, the label beneath the text box shows you the type of data you have entered.

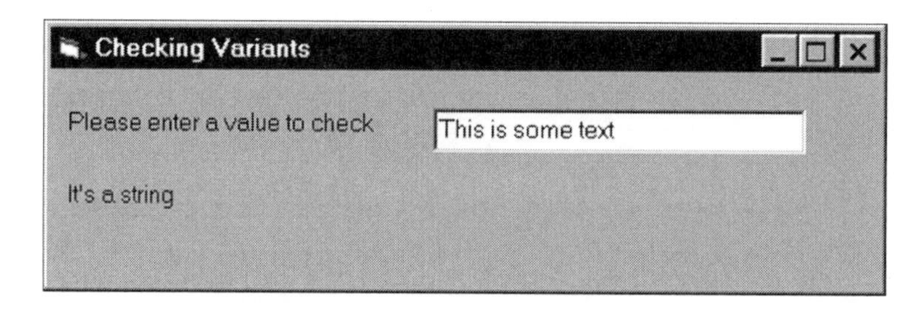

6 Try keying in text, mixing text with numbers, or entering a date. The **IsDate** and **IsNumeric** functions will detect what you're doing, and your code will use these functions to show on screen exactly what's going on.

7 Finally, save the program you just created as **Variant.vbp**—we will be coming back to it in a moment.

How It Works

The **IsDate** and **IsNumeric** functions return either **True** or **False** to your code, depending on whether or not the value in the variant can be converted to a date variable or a numeric variable. In our example, a multiline **If...Then** statement is used to check first for a date, then a numeric value. If both checks fail, the program assumes that what you've entered must be a mixed text and numeric value, which can only be stored in a string variable. We'll look more closely at strings later in the chapter.

In the example, the value of the text box is copied into the variant **varValue** before any of the checks are done. This is actually good programming practice. Visual Basic can deal with values in variables a lot quicker than with values in properties, such as the **Text** property of the text box.

In practice, the **Text** property is a variant itself, although Visual Basic always treats the data in it as text. This means that you could use the **IsDate** and **IsNumeric** functions on the text box if you wanted to check the data that the user is entering without having to key in extra code to copy the property to a variable:

```
    If IsDate(Text1.Text) Then
```

will work just as well as the code we used in the example.

If you play around for a while you'll notice that the **IsDate** function accepts a variety of weird date formats as being valid. For example, I have never known anyone who would write the date 66/6/15, but it's accepted. Weird!

*The name **varValue** uses the prefix **var** to indicate that this is a variant type variable. See Appendix B for a guide to Visual Basic naming conventions.*

When to Use Variants

The flexibility of variants has a price though, and there are two drawbacks to using a lot of variant data types. One is slower processing, and the other is safety.

- Each type of information in Visual Basic (be it text, numbers, decimal numbers, Yes/No values) is stored in a different way. Variants know instinctively how to cope with each type of data, but first of all they have to go through a short process to determine what the data actually is. You don't see this happen, but the net result is that variants can actually slow your program down.
- Variable typing isn't just an excuse for overcomplicated programming. It can play a big role in preventing errors, and it does this by allowing you to restrict the number of things you can do to a variable. You can't, for example, find the square root of a name. We'll look at how this actually works a bit later on, but for now just remember that the more Visual Basic knows about your data, the more it can help you.

> *So why use variants? Firstly, because they make life incredibly easy, and secondly, because often you don't have the choice not to. Many of the control properties you come across are variants themselves (e.g. the* **`Text`** *property of a text box) as are many of the values returned to you by Visual Basic commands and keywords. For these reasons, it's important to understand variants and how they work, even though it's best to avoid them wherever possible.*

Checking the Contents of a Variant

Since variants can hold almost any kind of data, Visual Basic has a special function we can use to determine what kind of information is in the variant. This is more comprehensive than the **`IsDate`** and **`IsNumeric`** functions that we just looked at. The **`VarType`** function returns a number that corresponds to the data type stored in the variant at that time.

Try It Out - Checking the Contents of a Variant

If it isn't still loaded, load up the **`Variant.vbp`** project that you created earlier (the one that displays the type of data you enter into a text box).

1 Double click on the text box to bring up the code window, then alter the code so that it reads as follows:

```
Private Sub Text1_Change()

    Dim varValue As Variant

    If IsDate(Text1) Then
        varValue = CVDate(Text1)
```

```
    ElseIf IsNumeric(Text1) Then
        varValue = Val(Text1)

    Else
        varValue = Text1

    End If

    Select Case VarType(varValue)

        Case 5
            lblType.Caption = "Type 5 - Double"
        Case 7
            lblType.Caption = "Type 7 - Date"
        Case 8
            lblType.Caption = "Type 8 - String"

    End Select

End Sub
```

2 Now run the program and try typing in a proper date:

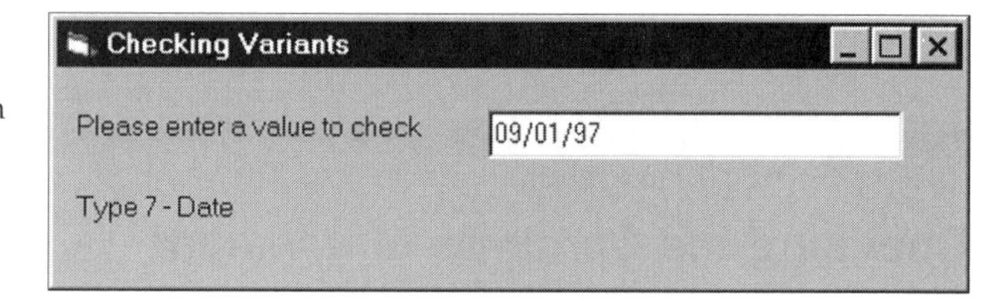

How It Works

Instead of putting the text box value straight into a variant, the code first checks to see if the value is either a date or a number. If it's a date, this condition is true:

```
    If IsDate(Text1) Then
```

And if it's a number, this condition is true:

```
    ElseIf IsNumeric(Text1) Then
```

Remember that at this point **`Text1`** is just a string with any possible combination of letters and numbers. Depending on whether Visual Basic thinks the string is a date or a number, one of two conversions is performed:

- The **`CVDate`** function takes a valid date from **`Text1`** and converts it into a variant of type 7. Visual Basic then places it into **`varValue`** and always treats it as a date.
- Or the **`Val`** function takes the number from the variant and outputs a double precision number which can be stored in a variant, or in most of the other number data types.

At this point, **varValue** contains a date, a number, or a string. These are the only possible things you can type into a text box. Next, the **VarType** function looks at what kind of variant **varValue** is, and returns a number that describes exactly what's in it. The possible return values, and what they tell us about the type of variant are:

Value	Name	Contents of the Variant
0	Empty	There is no data in the variant
1	Null	The variant has no value, which is different to it being empty
2	Integer	A whole number between -32768 and 32767
3	Long	A whole number between -2,147,483,648 and 2,147,483,647
4	Single	A normal, everyday decimal number
5	Double	A decimal number which is either *very* big, or has a huge number of decimal places
6	Currency	A decimal number with 4 decimal places
7	Date/Time	A combination value holding some particular date and time
8	String	A piece of text
9	OLE Object	This is advanced stuff. It's a lump of program, but ignore it for now
10	Error	This tells you what kind of error occurred
11	Boolean	A true or false value
12	Variant	This is an array of variants
13	Non OLE object	Another different type of code lump
14	Decimal	A decimal (power of 10) type value
17	Byte	A binary value
8192	Array	An ordered table of values (see later)

All that remains is for a **Select Case** block to put the corresponding message in the label:

```
Select Case VarType(varValue)
    Case 5
        lblType.Caption = "Type 5 - Double"
    Case 7
        lblType.Caption = "Type 7 - Date"
    Case 8
        lblType.Caption = "Type 8 - String"
End Select
```

Numbers in Visual Basic

Variants are great but, as we said earlier, using them is not great programming practice due to their lack of discipline and system overhead. The alternative to using variants is to define a data type for a specific kind of data.

Visual Basic has a number of different data types for storing numbers. The type you use depends on whether you want to store whole numbers (1, 2, 3, 4) or decimals (1.234, 2.345), and on how big or small you expect the numbers to get.

Integers and Longs

Integer and **long** variables allow you to store whole numbers. They are also the fastest of all the data types available in Visual Basic, and integers are excellent for use as counters in loops. However, integers can only hold a number between -32768 and 32767. For this reason, they aren't that suitable for holding numbers such as account numbers, or ID numbers in a database—where you could have hundreds of thousands of records. For large whole numbers, the long data type should be used, as this allows you to play with numbers from -2,147,483,648 to 2,147,483,647.

More Precise Numeric Types

When **decimal** values are needed, for instance in scientific applications, you'll need to turn to **single** and **double precision** numbers. To be honest, **single** is probably as far as you will need to go as these allow you to store decimal figures in the billions range, and at very high precision. If you know anything about scientific notation, then the exact range is -3.402823E38 to 3.402823E38. If you need to go above and beyond that, and deal with extremely high precision numbers, or numbers in the zillions, then opt for the **double** data type.

> *Predictably, handling double variables takes a lot of work on the part of Visual Basic, so using them can be slow.*

The final numeric data type is the **currency**. Despite the name, currency variables aren't just there to deal with cash. The currency data type is a numeric data type with a fixed number of decimal places, in this case 4. If you store a value with more than 4 decimal places in a currency variable, the extra decimal places are truncated—simply cut off in their prime. So the number 123.456789 would become 123.4567.

So currencies are nothing more than single and double values with a fixed decimal point. There isn't that much more to tell. If you intend to have calculations in your program that need a fixed number of decimal places, then use currency. Otherwise, integers, doubles, singles and longs are all perfectly adequate. However, currency types can help to prevent rounding errors, which can occur with other number types.

Declaring Numeric Variables

Declaring any of these number variables is straightforward. Simply type **`Dim`** followed by the name you wish to give the variable. Then type **`As`** followed by the data type.

```
Dim cNetPay As Currency
Dim fDragCoefficientOfHullAtWarp1 As Double
Dim lUnitsSold As Long
Dim iCounter As Integer
Dim fRoyalty As Single
```

When you declare a variable, Visual Basic automatically allocates a default value. Unlike many other languages, which leave the value of new variables as 'undefined', Visual Basic sets numbers to zero (and strings to `""`) when you first create them.

> *You can also declare variables using the keywords* **`Static`**, **`Private`** *and* **`Public`**. *These tell Visual Basic something about the life and scope of your variable. We'll cover these later in the chapter.*

Working with Numbers

As you would expect, Visual Basic lets you do arithmetic with numbers. You can add them using `+` and subtract with `-`. Many newcomers to programming get a little confused when it comes to division and multiplication though. Take a look at the keyboard and you'll see there's no multiply or divide sign. Instead you use `*` to multiply and `\` and `/` to divide. Why 2 divides?

Well, just as you can have decimal and integer variables, so you can divide to produce decimal and integer results:

- The `/` sign does decimal division; doing `5 / 3` in code will give you the answer you would expect: `1.666666666667`.
- Doing `5 \ 3` in code gives you `1`; the decimal part of the number is truncated (cut off) to give you an integer result.

Integer division runs quicker in code than its decimal equivalent. It's worth bearing this in mind if you need to do division inside a loop of any kind. The loop will run significantly faster with an integer division `\` than it would with a decimal division `/`. If you remember, we used `\` in Chapter 4 to find the screen width. You can't have fractions of a pixel, so that was a good idea.

Using Scrollbars to Input Numbers

In the introduction to this chapter, we differentiated between the way data flows in and out of your program, and the way that data is then manipulated inside your code. Good programming makes these two work in unison, so that the user interface you create gets the data you need from the user in the most direct and intuitive manner. Choosing the right tool for this is half the job.

If you want numbers from your user, then you have several choices of control. For numbers that have a defined and specific value, such as your age, a text box is the best choice. If, however, you want the user to alter the value of a variable bit by bit, then scrollbars are ideal.

When to Use Scrollbars

Scrollbars are ideal when your user has to give you a ballpark value, and they want immediate feedback about the result. For example, take a look at the volume control in Windows 95:

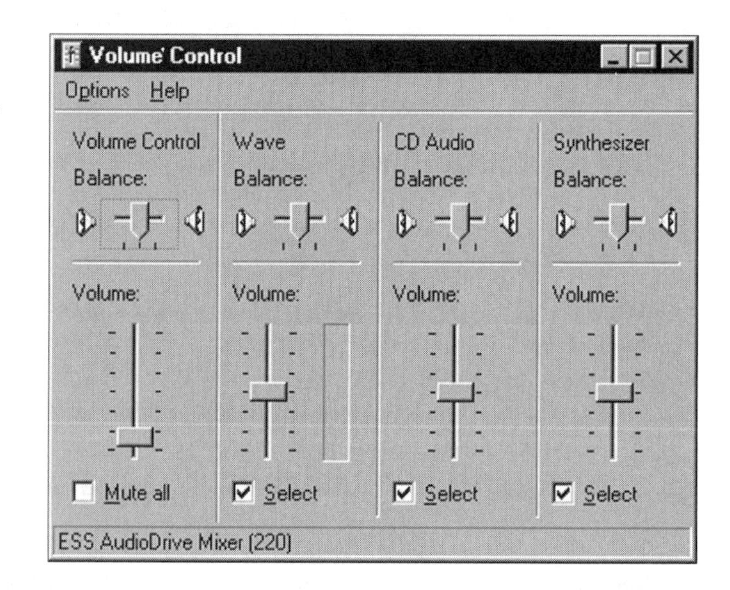

With something like volume, it's better to present the user with something approximate, but familiar, than to present them with a text box asking for an exact figure. It's hard to relate the number 255 to a loud volume, but easy to look at a slide with the slide control at one end of the bar and see that it is turned up as far as it can go.

How Scrollbars Work

For many beginners, scrollbars can be a little daunting. They aren't something that you can easily relate to the real world and they provide a very abstract method of obtaining information from your users. For this reason many beginners ignore them completely, assuming that something that looks complex really is complex. In reality, nothing is further from the truth. Indeed, scrollbars are one of Visual Basic's easiest controls to master.

Play around with the scrollbars in some of the Windows applications you own, or even the ones attached to the windows in Visual Basic, to get a feel for what properties and events must be lurking in there.

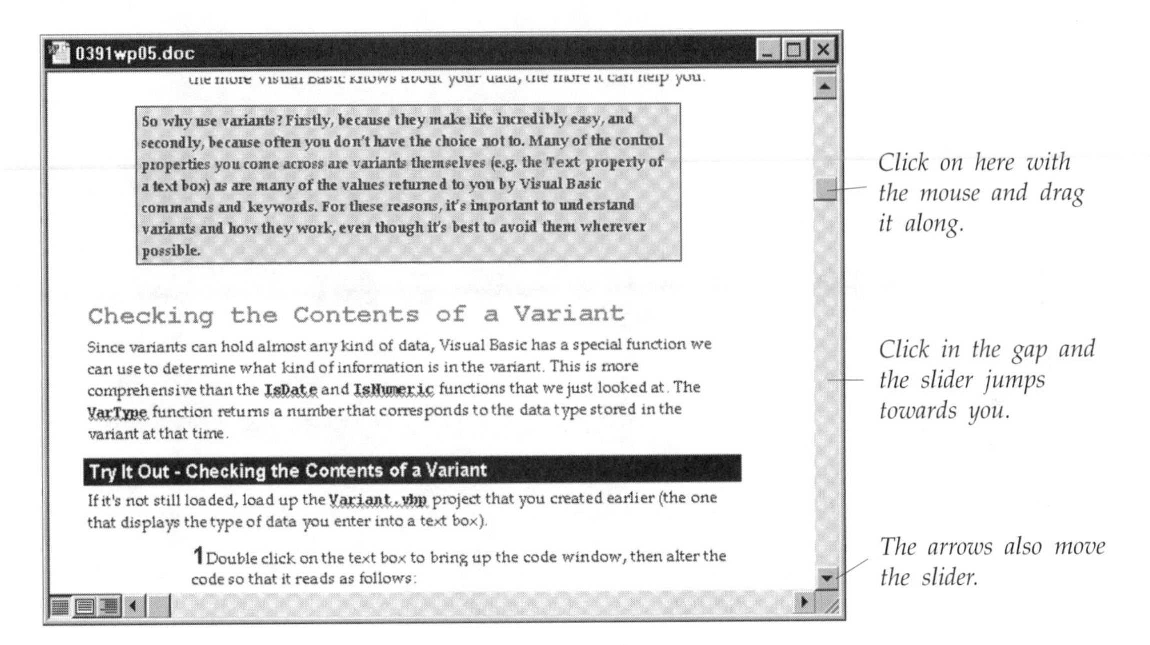

Let's see how this all works in real code.

Try It Out - Using Scrollbars

1 Start a new project in Visual Basic.

2 Select the horizontal scrollbar button and draw a scrollbar on to your form as shown.

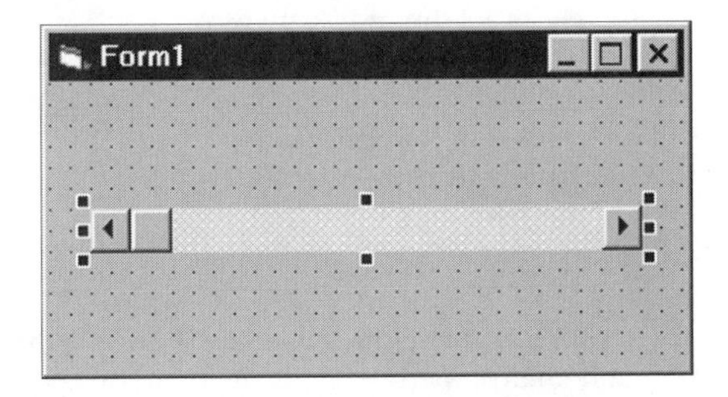

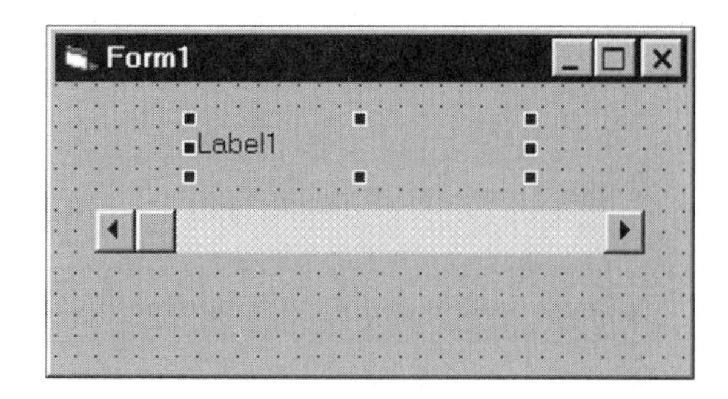

3 Now place a label above it on the form.

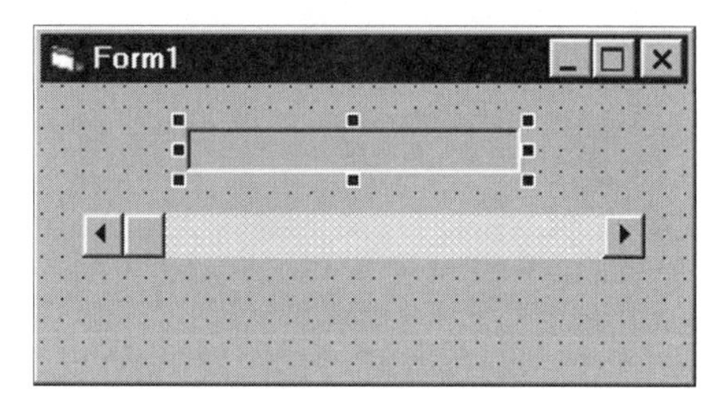

4 When you have drawn the label, bring up its properties window. Give it a `BorderStyle` of `1` and erase the `Caption`.

> *As long as you have the `Appearance` property set to **1 - 3D** (the default), setting the `BorderStyle` like this puts a nice 3D border around the label, so that it looks almost identical to a text box. This is a great way to display data in simulated text boxes so that the user can't change it.*

5 In order for Visual Basic to determine a value for the position of the slider, we need to tell the scrollbar what its maximum and minimum values are. Select the scrollbar and bring up its properties window. Find the `Min` and `Max` properties of the scrollbar and set `Min` to `0` and `Max` to `10`. This gives our scrollbar a range of 0 to 10.

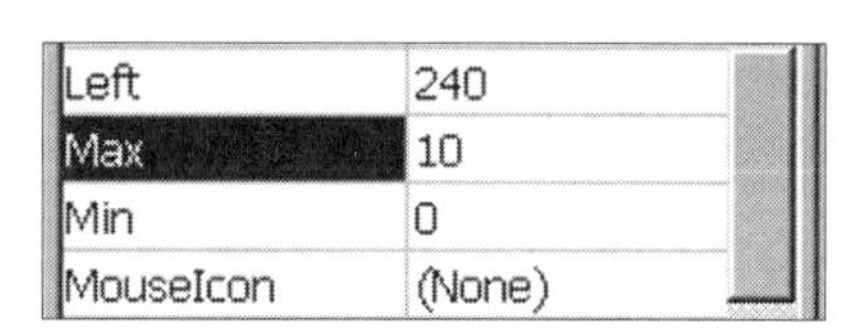

Left	240
Max	10
Min	0
MouseIcon	(None)

6 At run time, if the user clicks in the area between the slider and an arrow, a value called `LargeChange` is added to the current slider value to make the slider jump. Find the `LargeChange` property and set it to `5`. This will cause the slider to jump in steps of 5 if the user clicks between it and an arrow.

Index	
LargeChange	5
Left	240
Max	10

7 Finally, when the user clicks an arrow, a value called `SmallChange` is added to the current slider value. Find this property and set it to `1`. By setting the `Min`, `Max`, `LargeChange` and `SmallChange` properties, we have told Visual Basic how the scrollbar should work.

8 The next step is to display the current value of the scrollbar in your label whenever the scrollbar is changed. Double-click on the scrollbar to bring up its code window. By default, the **Change** event appears. Type in this code:

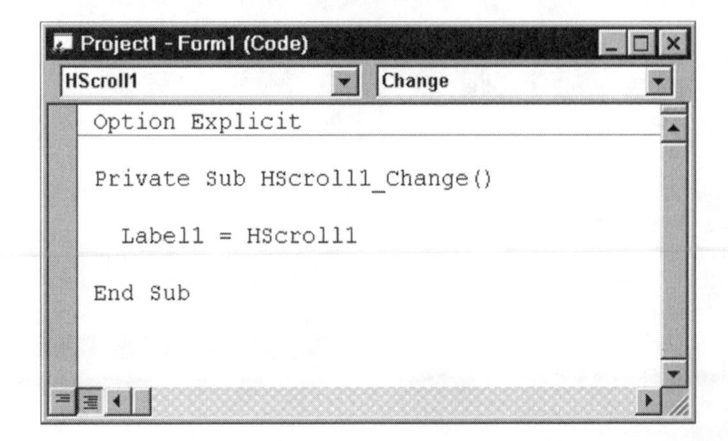
Project1 - Form1 (Code)
HScroll1
Change
Option Explicit
Private Sub HScroll1_Change()
Label1 = HScroll1
End Sub

9 Now run the program.

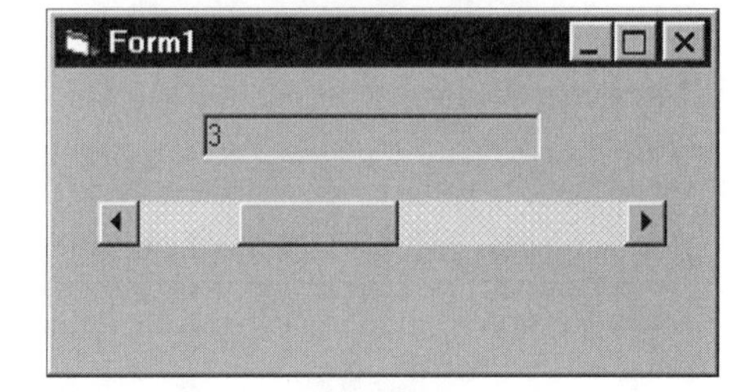
Form1
3

> *Notice the size of the drag point in the scrollbar—its huge! The size of the drag bar represents the ratio between **LargeChange** (remember you set this to 5) and **Max** (which you set to 10).*

How It Works

With the program running you can see the effect that the properties we set have on the scrollbar. When the slider is at the left end of the scrollbar the value is `0`, at the right end it is `10`—these are the values you placed into the `Min` and `Max` properties.

If you click between the slider and an arrow, the value of the scrollbar changes by `5`. Click on one of the arrows, though, and the value changes by `1`. These are the values you put into the `LargeChange` and `SmallChange` properties.

The `Change` event to which you added code places whatever is in the `Value` property of the scrollbar into the caption of the label. These properties are both the default properties of their respective controls, so you don't have to explicitly refer to them in your code. The `Change` event occurs whenever a change occurs to the scrollbar, for example when an arrow is clicked, or when the slider is dragged and released.

There is an alternative place to put this code. The **Scroll** event reflects the changes to the scrollbar as they happen, rather than after they have happened, as is the case with the **Change** event. Stop the program running and bring up the code window for the scrollbar again. This time, use the top right combo box to select the **Scroll** event.

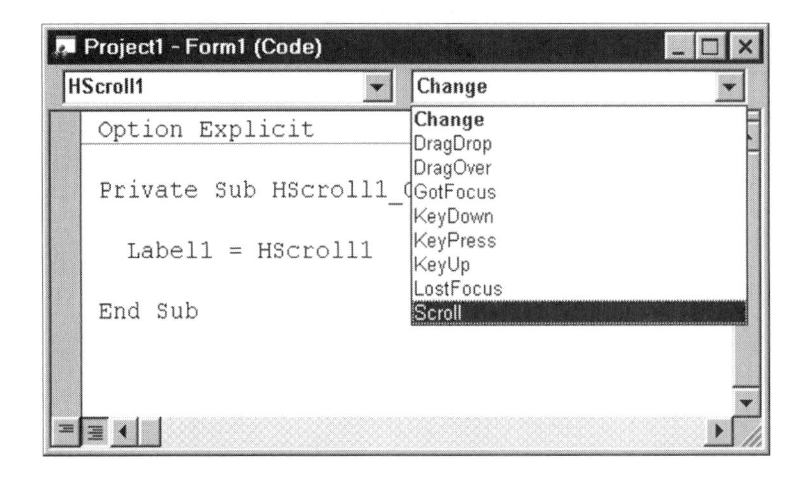

Add this line of code again:

```
    Label1 = HScroll1
```

Now run the program again and try dragging the slider around. This time, each time the slider moves, the label changes, regardless of whether or not you've actually let go of the slider. However, if you delete the line of code from the **Change** event, you will see that the code in the **Scroll** event only works when you are dragging the sliding bar itself around.

This is a little like the latest versions of Word where if you drag the vertical scrollbar up or down, a tooltip appears, telling you which page you're on.

String Variables

String variables are predominantly used to store and manipulate text. Numeric variables can only hold numbers, whereas strings can hold both numbers and figures—although they are both treated as text. The following are all strings:

```
sFirstName = "Peter"
sAddress1 = "28 Code Gulch"
sDateOfBirth = "5/8/88"
```

Declaring Strings

Strings can be declared in a number of ways. Most of the built-in data types that Visual Basic supports have a special abbreviation code attached to them. In the case of strings, this is the dollar `$` sign. This abbreviation is actually known as a **type declaration character**. Despite its long name, it does a straightforward job. If you dimension (`Dim`) a variable and attach the appropriate type declaration character to the end of the variable name, Visual Basic will automatically create a variable of the required type.

Let's say we wanted to create a new string variable to hold someone's name. Using the longhand method, we'd have to write:

```
Dim sName As String
```

With the shorthand method the amount of code is reduced—but so too is the readability of the code:

```
Dim sName$
```

The small `s` *at the start of the name tells you this is a string. Take a look at Appendix B for a guide to naming variables.*

Use Quotation Marks for Text

Whenever you place data into a string variable, you must enclose it in quotation marks. This lets Visual Basic see which parts of your program are supposed to be variable names, and which parts are constants (numbers, letters, text and so on). It's an important point to remember and actually brings us back to the `Option Explicit` phrase we met a while back. Without the `Option Explicit` phrase, a line like:

```
sFirstname = Peter
```

would compile without any problems. Visual Basic would assume that `Peter` is a string variable, the contents of which you want to copy to the string variable `sFirstname`. However, this is far from what we actually wanted to do, which was to place the name `Peter` in the string variable itself:

```
sFirstname = "Peter"
```

Had the `Option Explicit` facility been turned on, then the first example wouldn't have got past the Visual Basic compiler. You'd have been given a Variable not defined error message.

Remember—you can switch the `Option Explicit` *facility on by selecting Options... from the Tools menu and checking Require Variable Declaration on the Editor page.*

Explicit Declaration Prevents Bugs

Why is it so important to have this option turned on, especially as implicit variables require less code and thought than explicit ones? Well, take a look at this code:

```
Sub Problem_Proc()
    sO10 = InputBox$("Enter your name")
```

```
    MsgBox "Your name is " & s01O
End Sub
```

This is a very simplified piece of code, but it has a pretty serious bug in it. If the subprocedure was embedded in a couple of hundred other lines of code, the bug could become very hard to track down. Basically, the code is supposed to get the user to enter their name and then display their name on screen in a **MsgBox**. The variable used to store the name that the user enters is called **sO10.** However, no matter how hard you try, the program won't work. Instead it will keep on displaying the message Your name is, but without any name!

The reason for this is that I have misspelled the variable name in the **MsgBox** statement. In the first line of code I implicitly created a variable named **sO10** (letters **s** and a capital **O**, plus numbers **1** and **0**). However, in the **MsgBox** code, I refer to a variable called **s01O** (letter **s**, numbers **0** and **1**, and *letter* capital **O**). Visual Basic doesn't care—it just goes ahead and creates two variables, each with slightly different names. If I'd been using **Option Explicit**, the program wouldn't have run and Visual Basic would have pointed the bug out to me immediately.

Working with Strings

Dealing with text in string variables can become a little tricky, so Visual Basic has a full set of very useful string handling functions that allow you to break down the string and examine parts of it.

The first function is **StrComp**, which is designed to compare two strings and return a number telling you what the comparison is between them.

Try It Out - Comparing Strings with StrComp

1 Start a new Visual Basic project and remove the default form from the project by selecting Remove Form1 from the Project menu.

2 Create a new module by selecting Add Module from the Project menu.

3 In the code window that appears, type in code so that the code window looks as follows. Type the first line (**Public Sub Main()**) under the **Option Explicit** line that appears when you display the code window; Visual Basic will automatically create a **Main** subprocedure for you.

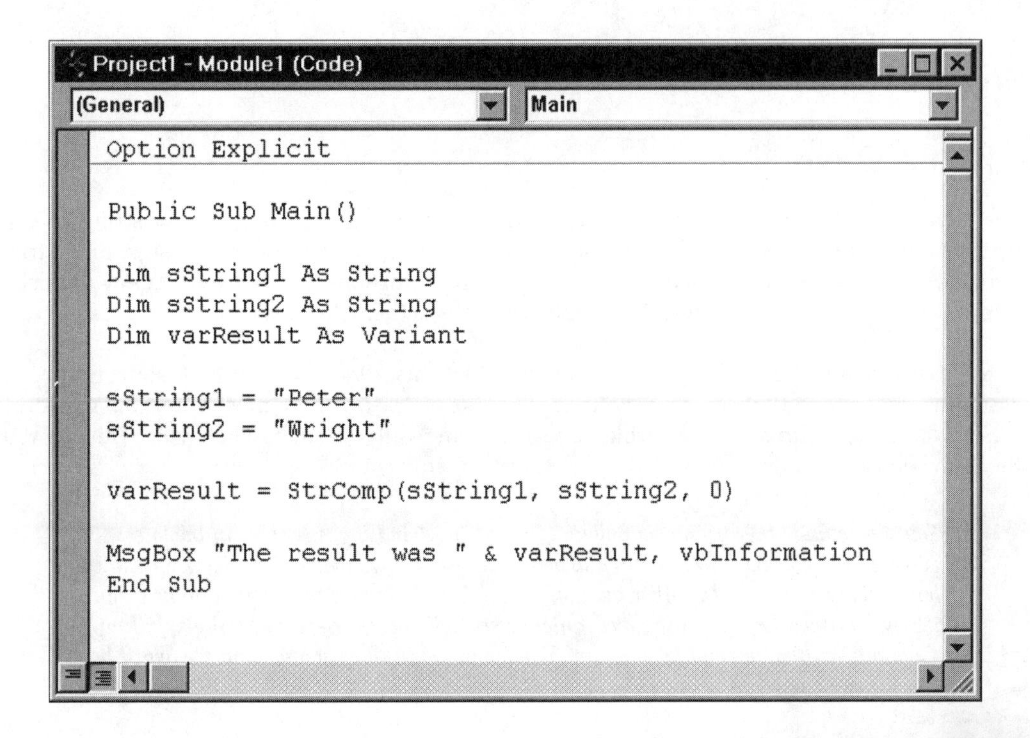
Project1 - Module1 (Code)
(General)
Main
Option Explicit
Public Sub Main()
Dim sString1 As String
Dim sString2 As String
Dim varResult As Variant
sString1 = "Peter"
sString2 = "Wright"
varResult = StrComp(sString1, sString2, 0)
MsgBox "The result was " & varResult, vbInformation
End Sub

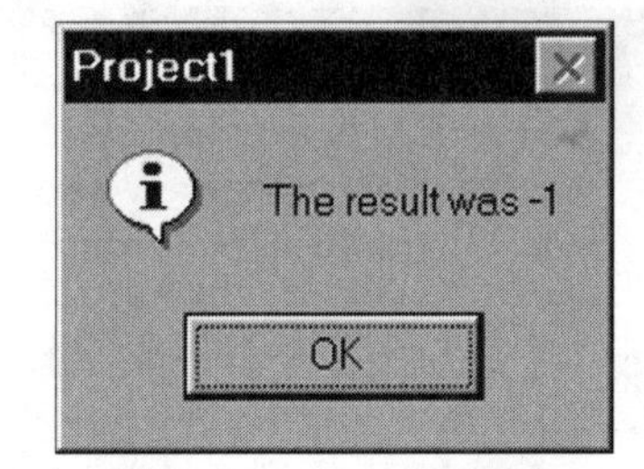
Project1
The result was -1
OK

4 If you now run the code a message box appears, telling you that the result of the comparison was **`-1`**.

How It Works

The numbers returned by **`StrComp`** can be tested using **`If...Then`** or **`Select Case`** statements to determine how the strings compare. The results will be:

- **`-1`** if the first string precedes the second alphabetically (**`A`** comes before **`B`** and so on)
- **`0`** if they are the same
- **`1`** if the first string comes after the second alphabetically
- **`Null`** if one of the strings compared was **`Null`**

Since **`StrComp`** can return a **`Null`** value, you can see why we declared the **`varResult`** variable as a variant. The number **`0`** at the end of the **`StrComp`** statement tells Visual Basic to do a case-sensitive comparison:

```
varResult = StrComp(sString1, sString2, 0)
```

If the number were anything other than `0`, this code would do a case-insensitive comparison.

Changing Case

The **`LCase$`** and **`UCase$`** functions enable you to change all the letters in a string to either upper case or lower case. Both functions return a string which you can assign to a string variable using the `=` sign. There are two alternative functions, **`UCase`** and **`LCase`**, which return variants of type `8` (strings), so you can assign them to variants.

Often a string function will have two versions like this. One, without a `$` sign, is for assigning the returned value to a variant. This is the easiest and most common version. The other, with a `$`, returns only a string. Use the string only version when you want to reduce the number of variants you use in the interest of efficiency.

> *You'll also find other versions of many of the string-handling functions in the latest version of Visual Basic. Windows allows you to use strings where each character can be one of several thousands, rather than one of the 256 characters we are used to using in the Western world. These are called **unicode** strings; there are special string handling functions with names ending in a capital* `B` *for use with these strings, but we won't be considering these here.*

Try It Out - Changing Case

1 Start up a new project. Remove the form and add a new module to it, as we did in the previous example.

2 Enter code into the code window so it looks like this:

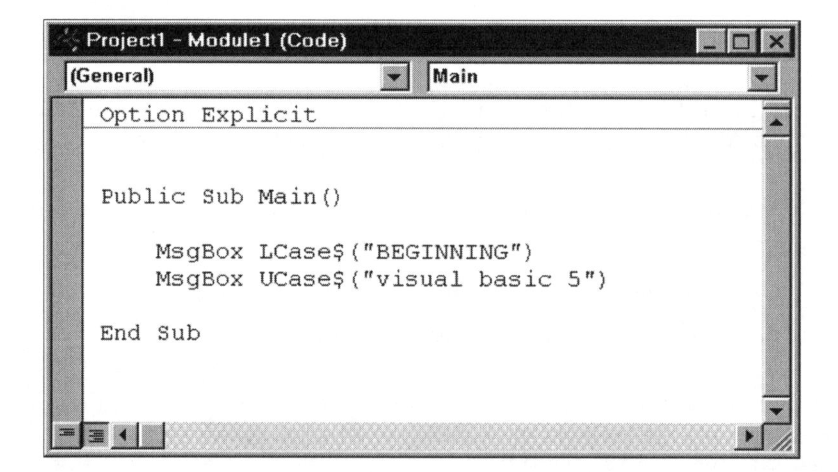
Project1 - Module1 (Code)
(General)
Main
Option Explicit
Public Sub Main()
MsgBox LCase$("BEGINNING")
MsgBox UCase$("visual basic 5")
End Sub

3 Run this code. See how the **`LCase$`** and **`UCase$`** functions change the case of all the letters passed to them.

The first message box says beginning, whilst the second says VISUAL BASIC 5. They are different to the actual strings passed to the two message box functions.

Searching Strings

The two things you'll need to do most frequently to strings are searching and dissecting. Visual Basic comes with a daunting array of functions especially for doing just these things: **`Mid$`**, **`Left$`**, **`Right$`** and **`InStr`** are a few.

The simplest of these is **`InStr`**, pronounced *in-string*. **`InStr`** allows you to search one string to see if another one appears in it. If a match is found, Visual Basic returns a number to your code that is the position of the letter in the first string at which the second string appears. If the search fails then all you get back is `0`.

Try It Out - Using InStr to do Simple Searching

1 Start up a new Standard EXE project and add two text boxes, two labels and a button to your form. Blank out the text boxes so the form looks like this:

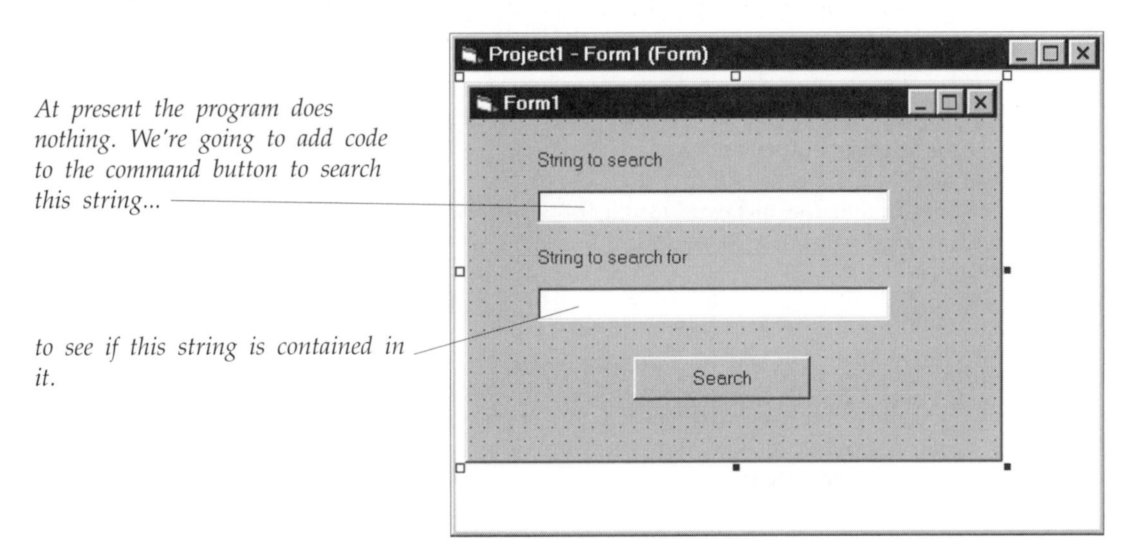

Name the top text box **txtSource** and the one underneath **txtSearch.** Also name the command button **cmdSearch**—it's good practice to name your controls and makes the code a lot more readable.

2 Now double-click on the command button to bring up the code window. Type in code so that the command button **Click** event looks like this:

```
Private Sub cmdSearch_Click()
    Dim iIndex As Integer

    iIndex = InStr(txtSource.Text, txtSearch.Text)
    If iIndex = 0 Then
        MsgBox "The search string could not be found!", vbInformation
    Else
        MsgBox "The search string was found starting at position " &
    ↳   iIndex, vbInformation
    End If

End Sub
```

3 Now run the program. Enter source text in the top text box and then type the string text you want to search for in the bottom text box.

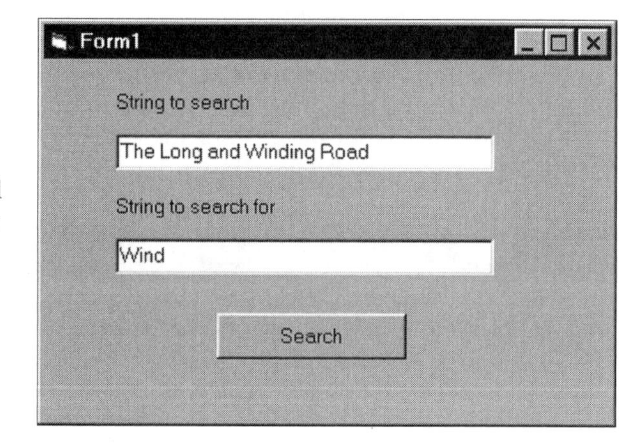

4 Hit the Search button and a message box appears telling you whether or not the text was found, and at which position in the top string it was found.

How It Works

Let's take a look at the code that makes this application useful. The first line declares an integer variable **iIndex** to hold the position of the second string, **txtSearch.Text**, in our first string, **txtSource.Text**.

```
    Dim iIndex As Integer
```

iIndex will be zero if no match is found. The next line is the one that counts as it contains the **InStr** function:

```
    iIndex = InStr(txtSource.Text, txtSearch.Text)
```

Here, we simply assign the result of the **InStr** function to the variable **iIndex**. The two strings we're dealing with are held in brackets straight after the **InStr** function. The first string, be it a variable, a property (as here), or a piece of text in quotes (e.g. **"source string"**), is the string you want to search *in*. The second string is the value you want to search *for*.

The remaining lines examine the value that **InStr** returned, and display the appropriate message box. If **iIndex = 0**, then **InStr** couldn't find a match and you will see the message: The search string could not be found! Otherwise, the value of **iIndex** is displayed.

```
If iIndex = 0 Then
    MsgBox "The search string could not be found!"
Else
    MsgBox "The search string was found starting at position " & iIndex
End If
```

InStr is great for doing simple searches. However, if you really want to pull some strings apart, then you need to look to the **Mid$**, **Left$** and **Right$** functions. Using these three functions, you can write code that can examine portions of a string.

Try It Out - Taking Strings Apart

In the following program we'll get the user to enter their forename and surname and then use the **Left$** and **Right$** functions to separate the two words. First of all, though, we'll need to create the project itself.

1 Create a new Standard EXE project in Visual Basic and add three labels, three text boxes and a command button to it, so that it looks like this.

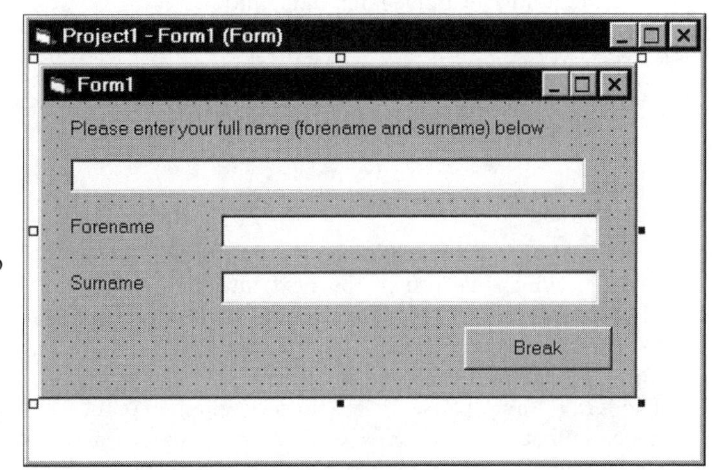

So that the code you are about to enter actually makes sense, make sure that you name the top text box **txtName**, with the two underneath named **txtForename** and **txtSurname** respectively.

2 Double-click on the command button to bring up the code window for its **Click** event. Type in code so that the **Click** event looks like this:

```
Private Sub Command1_Click()

    Dim iPosition As Integer

    iPosition = InStr(txtName, " ")

    If iPosition = 0 Then
        txtForename = txtName
        txtSurname = ""
    Else
        txtForename = Left$(txtName, iPosition)
        txtSurname = Right$(txtName, Len(txtName) - iPosition)
    End If

End Sub
```

3 Now run the program and enter your name. When you press the command button at the bottom of the form, the name is split into two parts. For the sake of completion, you may want to set the **Locked** property of the bottom two text boxes to **True** to ensure that you or anyone else who comes to use the program can only enter data into the top text box.

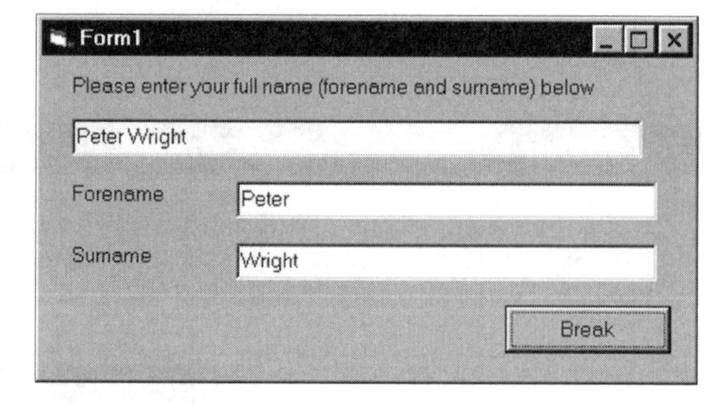

4 Before we go any further, stop the program running and save your work as **Names.vbp**—we will be returning to this project in a moment.

How It Works

The first two lines of code should be pretty familiar. The **Dim** line sets up an integer variable, which we use in the next line to find the first space in the name you entered. Most people enter their forename and surname separated by a space, so we can use **InStr** to search for this.

The **If...Then** clause checks to see whether or not any spaces were entered. If there are none, so that **iPosition = 0**, then the program assumes that no surname was entered and copies the text you typed into the forename box only.

If a space was entered in the name, these two lines of code are run:

```
txtForename = Left$(txtName, iPosition)
txtSurname = Right$(txtName, Len(txtName) - iPosition)
```

The first line uses the **Left$** function to pull some text from the left of the string entered. The number of characters to pull, and the string to pull them from, are passed as parameters to **Left$**. In this case, the string is the text property of the text box, and the number of characters to pull is held in the **iPosition** variable. Remember, we used **InStr** to find the space. If a space was found 5 characters into the string, and we pull the 5 leftmost characters from the string, then we'll actually get everything up to and including the space.

The **Right$** function works in exactly the same way. You tell it which string you want to pull characters out of, and how many characters to pull. The difference, as you probably guessed, is that **Right$** pulls characters from the right-hand side of the string, whereas **Left$** pulls them from the left-hand side. Previously, we used the **iPosition** variable to determine how many characters to get. This won't work with the **Right$** function. If the string is 25 characters long and the space is the 5th character in, then saying **Right$(txtName, 5)** wouldn't give us the desired answer, so some math is needed.

The Len Function

The **Len()** function can be used to find out how long a string is. So if the space was found at character 5, and the string is 25 characters long, **Len(txtName)—5** gives us **20**. In the code above, this would mean that we'd pull the rightmost 20 characters out of the string. It looks complex initially, but it's really very straightforward.

The Mid$ Function

The third function that I mentioned earlier is the **Mid$** function. Where the **Left$** and **Right$** functions can be used to pull text from the left and right-hand sides of a string, **Mid$** lets you pull chunks out from anywhere in the string.

Mid$ works in a similar way to the other two commands. You pass it the text you want to pull stuff out of. However, instead of just telling it the number of characters to pull, you tell it which character to start at, and how many characters you want to pull starting from there.

Try It Out - Extracting Strings Using Mid$

1 If you still have the previous project open, you can modify what you have just written. If not, then load it back from your hard disk (you did save it didn't you!).

2 We could have done everything we just did using only the **Mid$** function. Take a look at this:

```
Private Sub Command1_Click()

    Dim iPosition As Integer

    iPosition = InStr(txtName, " ")

    If iPosition = 0 Then
        txtForename = txtName
        txtSurname = ""
    Else
        txtForename = Mid$(txtName, 1, iPosition)
        txtSurname = Mid$(txtName, iPosition + 1, Len(txtName) -
    ↳   iPosition)
    End If

End Sub
```

3 Now run the program and you will find that it works in exactly the same way.

How It Works

The two lines that have changed are:

```
txtForename = Mid$(txtName, 1, iPosition)
txtSurname = Mid$(txtName, iPosition + 1, Len(txtName) - iPosition)
```

The first parameter you pass to **Mid$**, just as with **Left$** and **Right$**, is the text you want to manipulate—in this case the **Text** property of **txtName**. The next parameter is the first character you want to pull. Finally, we pass the number of characters that **Mid$** should return. The returned string is saved in the two labels on the form, just as before.

The Date and Time Data Type

Date and time values are handled rather uniquely in Visual Basic in that both are combined together into a single value. Visual Basic automatically handles the conversion from this single value into a meaningful number for us to read.

```
Dim dDateTime As Date
```

Try It Out - A Visual Basic Clock

The current date and time can be obtained using the Visual Basic keyword **Now**.

1 Start a new project and place a label on to your form. Double-click the label's **Font** property and make the label really big and bold.

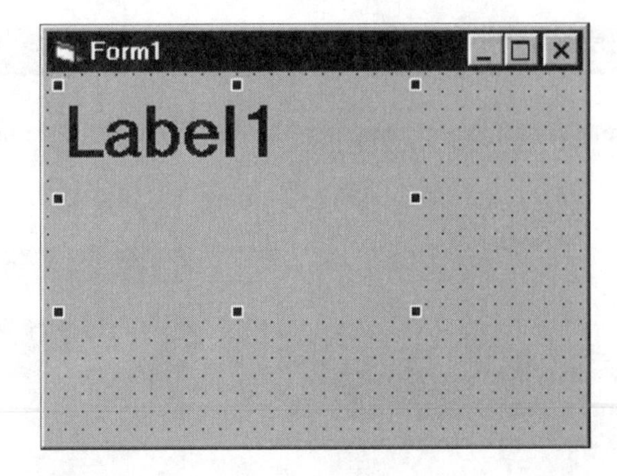

2 Double-click on the form itself and, when the **`Form_Load`** event pops up, change it so it looks like this:

```
Private Sub Form_Load ()
   Form1.Show
   Label1.Caption = Now
End Sub
```

3 Run it. Hmmm... not so easy—our clock seems to have stopped.

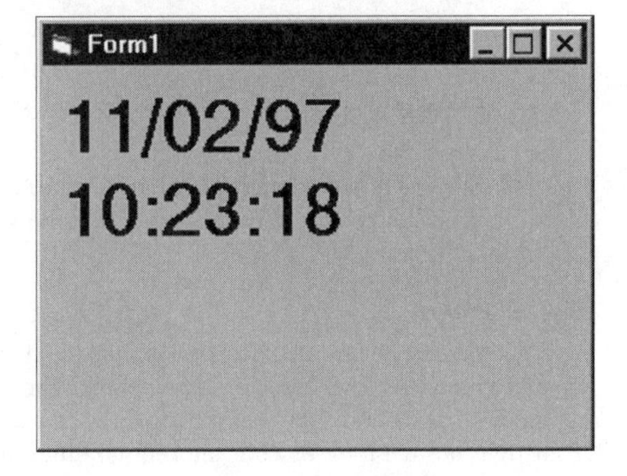

Note that the format this appears in depends on the settings in the Regional Settings dialog box in your Control Panel.

How It Doesn't Work

The time doesn't change of course. All it does is load the current time into the label at form load time. To make the time change, you need to use a **timer** control to change the caption of the label at regular intervals.

Try It Out - Adding a Timer

1 Stop the program running and bring up the form. Select the timer control in the toolbox.

2 Place the timer anywhere on your form. This is a hidden control that is only visible at design time, so it doesn't matter where you put it.

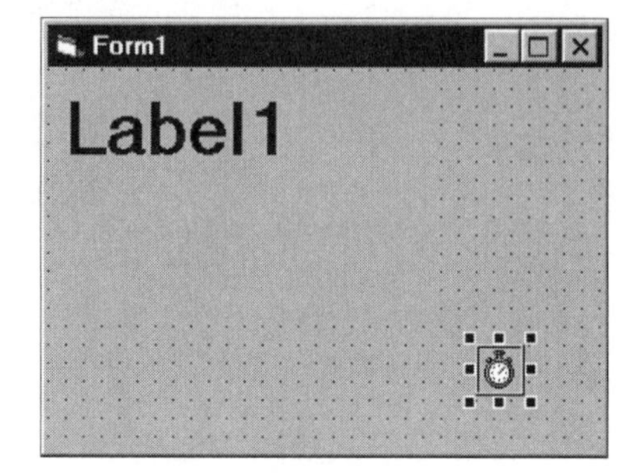

3 Double-click on the timer to bring up its **Timer** event and add this code.

```
Private Sub Timer1_Timer()

    Label1.Caption = Now

End Sub
```

4 Set the timer **Interval** in its properties window to, say **100**, then the clock will keep time smoothly. Run the program and everything is fine.

How It Works

The **Timer1_Timer()** event is activated at regular intervals, the period of which is determined by the **Interval** property. The interval is measured in milliseconds, so **100** is a tenth of a second. The **Timer** event is the only event that the timer supports. It allows you to execute a block of code at regular intervals, such as updating the current time.

Breaking Now Down into Parts

Obviously much of the work you do with date and time values will inevitably involve breaking a value down into its component parts, for example day, month, year, hour, and minute. Luckily, the categories I just listed are also the names of Visual Basic keywords that allow you to break a date and time field down into these parts. For an example of how some of these functions work, let's make up a new project.

Try It Out - Breaking Down a Date and Time Field

1 Start up a new Visual Basic Standard EXE project, just as before, but this time put two label controls and a timer on to the form so that it looks like this:

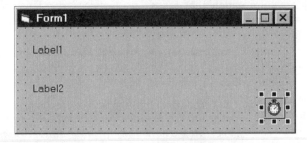

2 Set the timer interval up to **`100`** again, and then double click on the timer to bring up its code window with the **`Timer`** event showing, ready and waiting for us to type some code in.

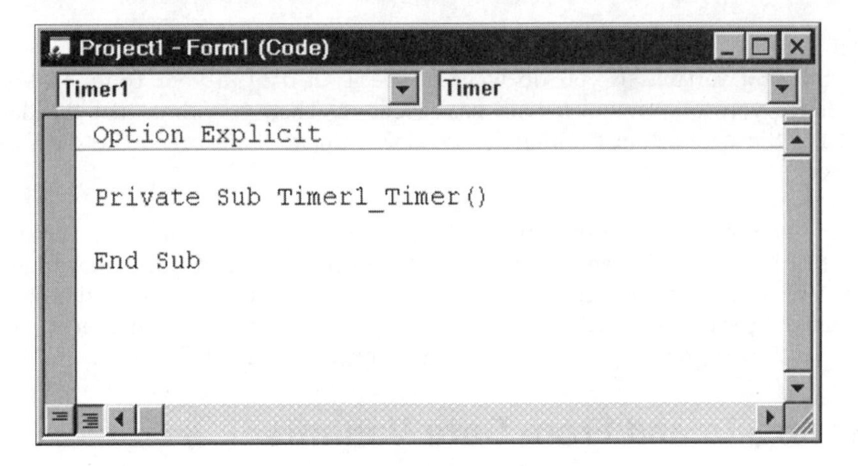

3 Enter code into the event routine so that it looks like this.

```
Private Sub Timer1_Timer()
    Label1 = "We are " & Minute(Now) & " minutes, " & Second(Now) &
    ↳   " seconds"
    Label2 = "into hour " & Hour(Now) & " of day " & Day(Now) &
    ↳   " of the month"
End Sub
```

4 Try running the program now and you will see today's date and time broken down according to each time and date function that we put into the **`Timer`** event.

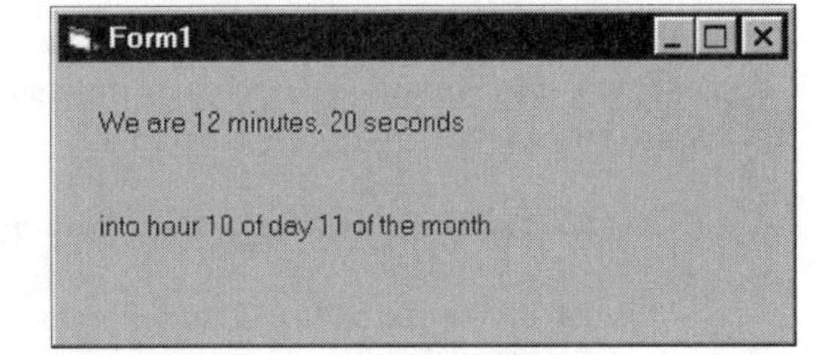

How It Works

The value of **Now** has been broken down in order to space out the display, and to leave off information that wasn't really necessary. This acts as a good illustration of some of the date parsing functions. All of them work in roughly the same way. You just state:

```
<variablename> = <functionname>(<dateandtime>)
```

and away Visual Basic goes.

> *Note that this is not what you actually type in. In practice you would substitute each of these for your own variable name and so on.*

```
nHour = Hour(Now)
nDay = Day(#01/01/94 12:00#)
nYear = Year (#01/01/1994#)
```

As you can see, it's also possible to feed dates to these functions explicitly, without needing to use the **Now** variable. If you do want to specify a date in your code, all Visual Basic needs is for you to surround it with hash signs **#**. Then providing that the date is legal, i.e. it matches the date settings under the Windows Control Panel, then the date will be accepted and used.

Dates are strange things to deal with. Unlike strings and other number variables, specific parts of a date variant mean specific things. You may want to pull a day number out to find out what day of the week a specific date falls on. You may have the day, month and year stored in separate variables, and want to bring them all together in a date variable. Visual Basic has a range of functions specifically to help in these cases.

Converting To and From Date Variants

The **DateSerial** function allows you to convert a day, month and year value into a date variant. For example:

```
Dim datDate As Date
datDate = DateSerial (1970, 03, 04)
```

This code puts the 4th of March 1970 into the variant **datDate**. The format of the **DateSerial** function is **DateSerial (<*Year*>, <*Month*>, <*Day*>)**. This is an extremely useful function that we'll return to in later chapters.

Earlier on you saw how to use the **IsDate** function to see if the value in a variant can be converted into a date. The actual conversion of the date is where the **DateValue** function comes into play:

```
If IsDate(varText) Then datDate = DateValue (varText)
```

The format of the **DateValue** function is straightforward. You simply say:

```
<variable name> = DateValue ( <variant or property> )
```

You may at this point be wondering what the point of the **DateValue** function really is. If you can hold a string in a variant, or even in a string variable, and check to see if it's a valid date; what's the point of going to all the trouble of converting the date to a date variable? The answer is math!

Working with Variant Dates

Once you have a valid date in a date variable, you can use the **DateAdd** and **DateDiff** functions to do some simple math on it. If you want to know what the date will be in two weeks time, use the **DateAdd** function. If you want to know how many days there are between today and the date an invoice was printed, then you can use the **DateDiff** function.

Both functions work in a very similar way, in that you need to tell them the units you're dealing with. For example:

```
datDate = DateAdd ( "d" , 7, datDate)
```

adds 7 days to the date in the **datDate** variable.

```
nDifference = DateDiff ("d", datDate1, datDate2)
```

This puts the difference in days between the dates in **datDate1** and **datDate2** into **nDifference**. The **"d"** in both cases is known as the **interval** and could be any one of the following:

Symbol	Unit of Time
yyyy	Years
q	Quarters
m	Months
y	Day of the year (1 is 1st January etc.)
d	Days
w	Weekday
ww	Weeks
h	Hours
n	Minutes
s	Seconds

The Null and Empty Values

The **Null** value and keyword are rather special. The **Null** value is used to indicate **unknown** data and is most commonly found in database applications. Consider filling in a form on paper. The form asks you for your surname, but you leave it blank by mistake. When the company that uses the form processes it, they get a blank surname area. Since your surname can't realistically be nothing, they tell their database that your surname is unknown. In Visual Basic we use **Null** for just that purpose.

Only variants can hold **Null** values. If you try to assign **Null** to a string variable, you'll get an error. You can assign **Null** to a variant with the simple phrase *<variable>* **= Null.** Checking to see if a variant contains **Null** is a slightly different matter, and requires the use of a Visual Basic function called **IsNull.** Here's an example:

```
If IsNull(varVariable) Then MsgBox "Variant is null"
```

The **IsNull** function returns a value of **True** or **False,** so it makes code like the line above pretty easy to read. I could have written:

```
If IsNull(varVariable) = True Then MsgBox "Variant is null"
```

but that begins to make the code a little cryptic.

The **Empty** value is in some ways similar to the **Null** value, except that whereas the **Null** value indicates unknown data, **Empty** indicates that a variable has never had a value put into it. The **IsEmpty** function can be used to test for **Empty** in the same way that **IsNull** can test for the **Null** value.

Collections of Data

In a larger application, such as a payroll system or even a game, by far the most important data you'll need to deal with will be held in groups of one kind or another. For example, you may not want to deal with employees by holding their name, address, IRS number and so on, in different variables—when it's much more convenient to deal with an employee as a **group** of related data. The **Type** command in Visual Basic lets you create such groups.

In a game you may need to keep track of which aliens are alive, and which are dead. This kind of group is called an **array**. This is a list of variables, all with the same name and data type.

Let's look at the **Type** command first.

Type Declarations

As I said, the **Type** command lets you define a group of variables and give them a common name. You could have an **Employee** type to hold an employee's name, address and so on. In a game you might have a type defined to hold information about the bad guys, such as the name of the graphics file that holds their image data, their coordinates, energy and such like. If you are used to C or Pascal, then you'll feel at home with **types**. In C you have the **struct** keyword which does the same thing, whilst in Pascal you have **records**.

Take a look at this fragment of code:

```
Type Employee
    lEmployeeNo As Long
    sSurname As String
    sForenames As String
    varBirthDate As Variant
EndType
```

This declares a type called `Employee`, which holds some of the data you might associate with an employee. Declaring a type like this only declares a template for a new variable. It's like telling Visual Basic 'This is what a variable of type Employee would look like'. Having created the `Type`, you then have to create a variable from it:

```
Dim CurrentEmployee As Employee
```

This declares a variable of type `Employee`, which has already been set up by the `Type` statement. `CurrentEmployee` itself doesn't hold any data that we are interested in. It's the actual parts of the type that we use. In code you can set what is in each part of the `CurrentEmployee` data. You do this by placing the name of each **element** of the type after the new variable name:

```
CurrentEmployee.lEmployeeNo = 1
CurrentEmployee.sSurname = "Wright"
CurrentEmployee.sForenames  = "Peter"
```

Arrays of Data

A **type** groups a collection of possibly different data types together under one name. **Arrays**, on the other hand, let you create lists (or collections) of a single data type. What you get with an array is really a number of variables, all with exactly the same name, but with different data. So you could have an array to hold the values of cards in a deck. Each element of the array, or individual item of data in its own right, is differentiated from the rest by something known as an **index**. Index simply means an identifying number.

If you want to declare an array instead of a normal variable, it's easy. You just put brackets after the variable's name, with a number inside them saying how large the array should be:

```
Dim nArray(100) As Integer
```

This sets up an array called `nArray`. The array consists of 100 integer numbers. You can get at these numbers to see what they are, or to set them to different values, like this:

```
nArray(2) = 50
nArray(50) = nArray(0) + nArray(99)
```

Have a look at the last line of code in that example. The first element of an array is numbered 0, with the last being one less than the size of array you asked for. So, if you set up an array of 100 elements, they will be numbered 0 to 99.

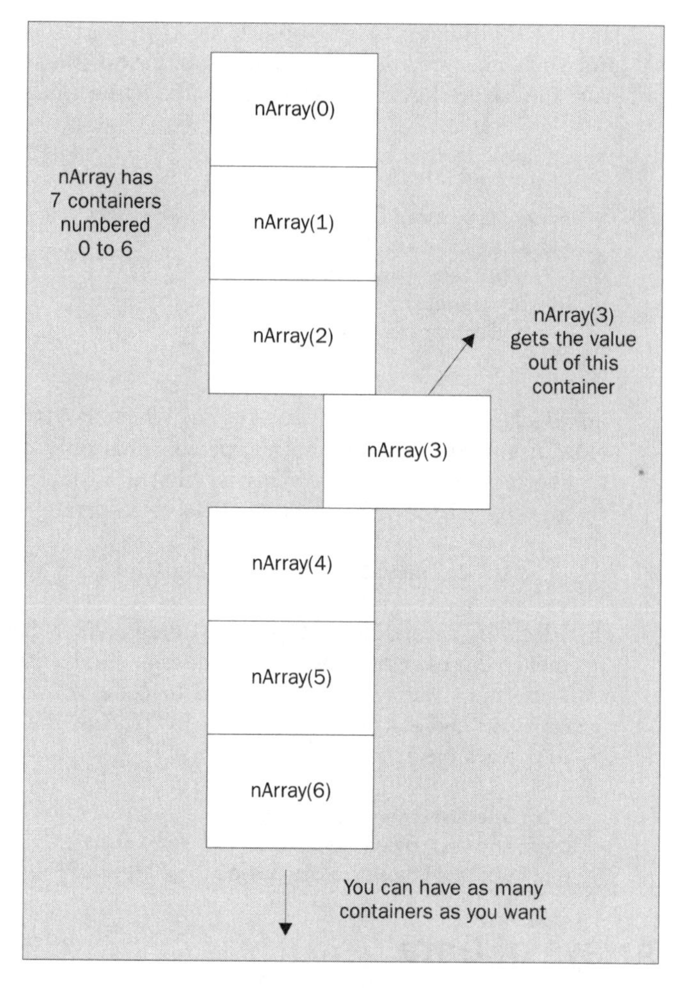

Arrays don't always have to start with an index number of 0. You can declare an array to start at any number you like. For example, **`Dim nArray (-12 to 28)`**.

Re-Dimensioning Arrays

Arrays have been with us since BASIC first hit a computer screen. However, something Visual Basic can do which very few other versions can, is change the size of an array once it has been declared. Previously, if you asked for a 100-element array, that's what you got. If you needed to change its size, then you'd have to stop the program and change the code. This can get very annoying!

In Visual Basic you can **`ReDim`** an array to change its size up or down. In addition, if you use the **`ReDim`** command in conjunction with the word **`Preserve`**, you can even change the size of an array without destroying the data contained inside it.

One of the most common uses for this is in games, or any other application that needs to deal with random data. Being able to change the size of an array at run time is often used for increasing the number of bad guys in a game, or adding more bullets to the screen. In a serious application it's great for creating random amounts of data to throw at a program for testing. Each piece of data could be held in an array, with the exact number of items of data determined at runtime, changing the array with **`ReDim.`**

Try It Out - Declaring and Re-Dimensioning Arrays

1 Start a new project in Visual Basic. Double-click on the default form to bring up the code window.

2 Type in code so that the **`Form_Load()`** event looks like this:

```
Private Sub Form_Load()

    Dim nRandoms() As Integer
    Dim nLoopCounter As Integer
    Dim nArraySize As Integer

    Form1.Show

    Randomize
    nArraySize = Int(Rnd(1) * 10)
    ReDim nRandoms(nArraySize)

    For nLoopCounter = 1 To nArraySize
        nRandoms(nLoopCounter) = Int(Rnd(1) * 1000)
        Form1.Print "Element " & nLoopCounter & " = " &
          ↳ nRandoms(nLoopCounter)
    Next

End Sub
```

3 Run the program you see a random number of random numbers printed on to the form.

4 Select the Restart option from the Run option and you'll get a different set of random numbers. The array is also resized randomly to hold these numbers. Select Restart again to generate more sets:

How It Works

The first line of code **`Dim nRandoms() As Integer`** sets up an array with no elements in it. Two other variables are then set up: one (**`nArraySize`**) to hold the size of the array, the other (**`nLoopCounter`**) to hold a counter to step through each element of the array later on.

The line **`Form1.Show`**, as you saw in the previous chapter, forces Visual Basic to display the form on screen as soon as possible. Remember, the **`Load`** event just loads the form up into memory, it doesn't actually display it. We need to **`Show`** the form in order to **`Print`** on it. Without the **`Show`** command, all you would see at the end of the program would be a blank form. Try removing the line yourself to see this.

After showing the form, the **`Randomize`** method is used to set up Visual Basic's random number generator. We'll look at random numbers later, in the chapter on graphics, so don't worry too much about what this and the **`Int(Rnd(1) * 10)`** statements do. The net result is that a random number between **`0`** and **`10`** is put into **`nArraySize`**. This is used in the next line to **`Redim`** the array:

```
    ReDim nRandoms(nArraySize)
```

The rest of the code steps through each element of the array, using the **`For...Next`** loop to put a random number into each element and then print that element on the form.

There's a bit of a problem with using **ReDim** in this way. Imagine the situation where you have 100 employee names held in an array and you suddenly decide you need 101. You could **ReDim** the array to make it bigger, but when you do a **ReDim**, any data in the array is lost forever. We need to find a way of **preserving** the data held in the array when it's resized.

Preserving Array Data

You may need to **ReDim** an array and preserve the contents of it quite frequently. You may have an array of record IDs in a database for instance. What happens when the user adds a new record to the database? The answer is that you use the Visual Basic **ReDim Preserve** keywords.

ReDim Preserve works in exactly the same way as the **ReDim** statement on its own, the only difference is that you now say **ReDim Preserve** instead of **ReDim.**

```
Dim nArray(100) As Integer
ReDim Preserve nArray(200)
ReDim Preserve nArray(400)
```

Now the data already in the array will still be there after you change its size. Of course, if you make an array smaller, you lose the stuff in the part that's not there any more!

Multidimensional Arrays

It's possible to have multidimensional arrays, where there is more than one index. All you do is add another number to the declaration like this:

```
Dim nMultiArray(100,100) As Integer
```

You can then address each element of the array as you would a one-dimensional array, only this time there's another index to change.

Using For Each...Next

Using a normal **For...Next** loop is the traditional method of getting at the elements in an array. However, Visual Basic 5 also includes a **For Each...Next** loop which is designed specifically for peering into arrays (and collections, which you will met later in the book).

The syntax is really quite simple:

```
For Each <variant> In <arrayname>
   ...
   ' Code to deal with the variant, which is actually the current
   ' element of the array
   ...
Next
```

The syntax is remarkably similar to a normal **For...Next** loop, the difference being the use of two variables on the **For** line: the array name itself, and a variant to hold the value of each element.

When the loop runs, it moves through each element of the array, putting its value into the variant that you would have declared before you started the loop.

You can then deal with the variant just as if it were an element in the array, but without the hassle of having to remember which element you are dealing with.

The For Each...Next Loop

Our earlier example, using the **For Each...Next** loop, looks like this.

```
Private Sub Form_Load()

    Dim nRandoms() As Integer
    Dim varElement As Variant
    Dim nArraySize As Integer

    Form1.Show

    Randomize
    nArraySize = Int(Rnd(1) * 10)
    ReDim nRandoms(nArraySize)

    For Each varElement In nRandoms
        varElement = Int(Rnd(1) * 1000)
        Form1.Print "Value is " & varElement
    Next

End Sub
```

How It Works

Gone is the **nLoopCounter** variable we had before, to be replaced by the **varElement** variant.

In the loop itself, the first line sets **varElement** to a random value, just as before. However, by setting **varElement**, you are actually setting whichever element the loop has reached in the array. This is because the **For Each** line effectively tells Visual Basic that instead of using the array itself, we are going to use our own variable (in this case **varElement**).

The second line in the loop simply prints out the random value that you just set.

The result is a bunch of code that is not dramatically smaller than the one we had previously. However, it is a great deal more structured and, with experience, a lot easier to read.

We will cover the `For Each...Next` loop later in the book in more detail since it also applies to something known as **collections**.

Variable Scope

Variables have a limited visibility, and the data they hold can only be accessed whilst the variable is still in view. The most obvious time that a variable goes out of view is when your program stops. When you restart it, all your variables are set back to their initial values.

This is known as **scoping**. As long as a variable is **in scope** you can write code to change it, display it and so on. When the variable goes out of scope, all the information becomes unavailable and the programmer can no longer write code to deal with that variable. Ending an application makes all variables go out of scope, but there are less extreme cases than this. Variables that you declare in one module are normally only in scope when that module is running. It's possible to circumvent this by creating static or global variables, but on the whole, variables live and die with their parent modules.

This can be a little confusing, so let me explain some more. You have four types of variable scope:

- Global
- Module level
- Local (procedure level)
- Static

Imagine that you are looking out of a submarine periscope from inside a particular module:

Global variables are those that you'll always be able to see. If the world is your program, then no matter where you are, the periscope will always show you the sky and the water. No matter where you are in your program you can always see, use and update global variables.

Module level variables can be thought of as icebergs. It doesn't matter where you are in the two Polar Regions, you will always be able to see icebergs. However, you can only see the icebergs that are in the same polar region as you. Module level variables are only available to you if you are running code in the same form or module that they were declared in.

Local variables are like seagulls in the sky. As far as you are concerned, they exist only while you have the periscope fixed on them. In your programs, local variables and their contents only exist in the subroutine or function in which they were declared.

Static variables are like seagulls that have landed on your submarine. They are always in the same position, each time you bring the scope round to a certain angle. As soon as you move the scope off them they no longer exist, but move it back and they're still sitting there just as before. In your program, static variables, like local variables, can only be used in the procedure or function they were declared in. Move out of the subroutine or function and the variables can no longer be used. However, when you come back to that subroutine, the static variables are still there, with exactly the same values as before. Local variables change—they lose their contents and have to be rebuilt.

A variable's scope is determined by where and how the variable is created. We've already seen how to use **`Dim`** to declare variables. Using **`Dim`** creates local variables whose scope is within the subprocedure or module in which they are created. In order to understand what this really means, we need to take a look at how to create projects that have more than one form.

Using Variable Scope

All the projects we have looked at so far only have one form.

- A variable that is declared inside a procedure attached to that form using **`Dim`** is **local** to that procedure, and can not be accessed by event handlers for other objects on the form.
- A variable that is declared using **`Dim`** or **`Private`** in the **`General Declarations`** section of a form can be accessed from any procedure attached to that form.

In the previous chapter, we learnt how to create subprocedures that can be called from code within a form, even though they are contained in a separate module, a **`.bas`** module. We do this by declaring the procedure as **`Public`**

```
Public Sub DoThis()

End Sub
```

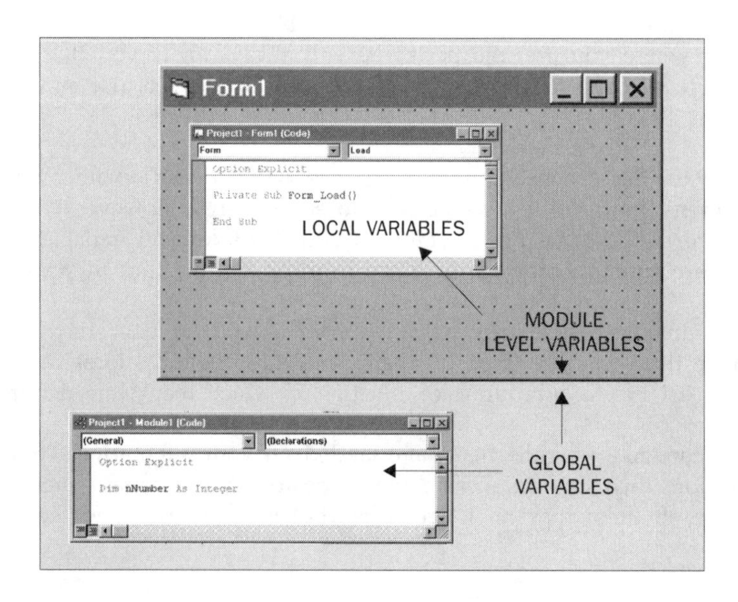

If you declare a variable in the general declarations section of a **.bas** module using **Public**, you will be able to use it all over the project, in whichever form or module you like. This is a **global** variable.

That's a lot of theory. Let's see how it works.

Local or Private Variables

A variable declared within a sub procedure or function with the **Dim** keyword is said to have **local** scope. It can only be accessed by code within the same function or subprocedure. This gives rise to some interesting problems. Because a local variable can only be accessed from within the subprocedure or function it was created in, it's possible to have more than one variable in a program with the same name and all with different values. This little gem of a bug-haven is known as **name shadowing**.

Try It Out - Same Name, Different Place

1 Create a new Visual Basic project, delete the default form, and create a new code module.

2 Enter the following in the code window:

```
Sub Main()
   Dim nNumber as Integer
   nNumber = 12
   Call Proc2
   MsgBox nNumber
End Sub

Private Sub Proc2
   Dim nNumber as Integer
   MsgBox nNumber
End Sub
```

3 If you now try running the code, you'll see a message box with a 0 in it. This is the value of **nNumber** in Proc2. Click on the OK button and another message box appears with the number 12 in it. This is the value of the **nNumber** variable in the **Main** subprocedure. Confused? Just imagine what it gets like with a couple of hundred instances just like this.

To summarize then, local variables are created in subprocedures and functions. They can only be accessed from within the routine they were created in. Identically named variables in other functions live a totally separate existence and have their own values.

Module Level Variables

In contrast, **`Private`** or **`Dim`** can also be used to create variables that can be used by all the code in a form or module. Each form or module has a section outside of any procedure or function that is known as the **Declarations** section. It's here that **module level** variables can be created. You can see this section by bringing up a code window on any form or **`.bas`** module, and selecting (General) (Declarations) from the combo boxes at the top.

Creating a variable here using the **`Dim`** statement makes that variable and the data it holds accessible by every procedure in this particular form or module. Procedures in other forms or modules can't see these variables and, as before, can have identically named form or module level variables of their own.

Try It Out - Module Level

1 If you still have the module from the previous example open, then open up the code window. If you don't, then start a new project, remove the form and add a new module.

2 Declare **`nNumber`** as a global variable in the General Declarations section of the module like this.

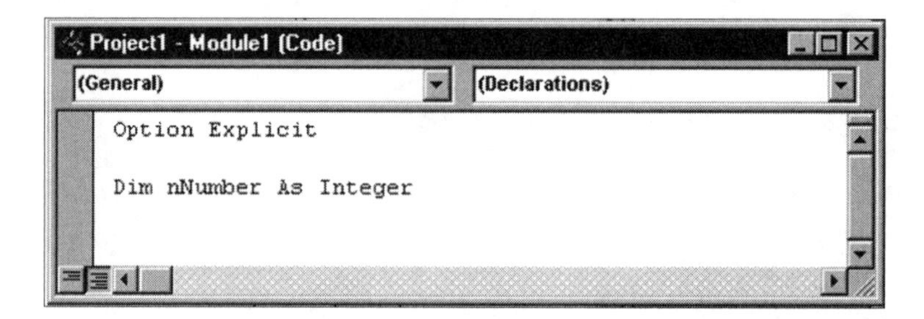

3 Then either type this all in afresh, or just remove the **`Dim`** statements from the code you typed in previously.

```
Sub Main()
   nNumber = 12
   Call Proc2
   MsgBox nNumber
End Sub

Private Sub Proc2
   MsgBox nNumber
End Sub
```

4 Run the program. The message box shows the same result both times. The variable **`nNumber`** is now a module-level variable, and so holds its value all the time the program is running.

You can declare this variable using either **`Dim`** *or* **`Private`**. *You can also do exactly the same thing in the general declarations part of a form module. Using* **`Private`** *probably gives a better description of what is happening.*

Static Variables

The information held in a module level variable is **static**. This means it remains in existence for as long as your application is running. There are ways of killing off module level variables in forms, and we'll look at how to do this in Chapter 14, *Object Variables*.

The **`Static`** keyword can be used to create a similar type of variable. Statics hold their data for as long as the application is running, but are only visible and can only be used by the code in the procedure in which they were created. So, really, they are safe local variables. They obey the same rules as any other local variable, but they don't forget their data when the subprocedure or function ends.

Statics are declared in exactly the same way as if you were using **`Dim`**, but instead of typing **`Dim`**, you type **`Static`**:

```
Static nNumberOfRuns
```

A typical use of a static variable is for keeping track of values in a **`Timer`** control's event, which occurs on a regular basis. Each time the code runs, it can use the same values as last time. When the **`Timer`** event code finishes, and is out of scope, the values don't disappear—as they would if they were declared using **`Dim`** or **`Private`**.

Global or Public Variables

The final scope of variable you'll come across is the **global** variable—which you can create, surprisingly enough, with the **`Public`** keyword. Global variables can only be created in the Declarations section of a code module. Forms can't create global variables at all. The data held in a global variable is accessible by every line of code in the application, and can therefore be quite useful for maintaining information used throughout your application.

A common use of globals is to hold the name of the program's current user. Any code that needs to access this can do so with no problem at all. As with static, local and module level variables, you create a global one by typing the word **`Public`**, followed by the name of the variable.

```
Public sUserId
```

Although variables you declare in the General Declarations *section of a form are normally only visible throughout that form, you can in fact access such a variable from outside by including the form name as part of its reference. For example, if you declare a variable like this in the general declarations section of* **`frmHomeForm`**:

```
Public varFormLevel as Variant
```

Then you can access it from another form or module by using the name:

`frmHomeForm.varFormLevel`.

Which Type of Variable Should I Use?

Each type of variable scope brings its own problems with it. Global variables are considered to be too unstructured and uncontrolled to use very much in a program. If all your variables were global, then the chances are that a bad piece of code in one procedure could cause many others to function badly, by updating a global variable with the wrong value.

While local variables are better in theory, they can also cause their fair share of problems. Too many local variables in a procedure can cause an Out of stack error message to crop up which will crash Visual Basic. However, this isn't normally a problem and only affects procedures that have an extremely large number of variables defined in them.

Statics can solve the stack problem since they use their own private area of computer memory to store their values, which is totally separate from that used by the local variables. Static variables, however, can cause problems if you forget that, in a procedure, a static never forgets *its* data. You should never assume that a static variable will be empty, or contain empty values.

We'll cover more of the big picture about forms, modules and functions later on in the book. For now, just accept that passing data around needs thinking about.

Variable Scope Quick Reference

Type	Declaration	Where	Scope
Local	**`Dim varName as varType`**	In each event or subprocedure	Can only be used in the procedure in which they are declared.
Private (Module Level)	**`Private varName as varType`** or **`Dim varName as varType`**	In (General) (Declarations) section of the form or module	Can be used in all procedures in that module.
Public (Global)	**`Public varName as varType`**	In (General) (Declarations) section of a code module only	Can be used in all modules in the whole project.
Static	**`Static varName as varType`**	In any location	Scope depends on where it is declared. Data is preserved out of scope.

Summary

In this chapter you've learnt how to represent and use data inside your Visual Basic programs. We covered:

- How to declare variables, and the benefits of forcing explicit declaration
- The use and limitations of the variant data type
- What other kind of data Visual Basic understands, including numbers, dates and strings
- How to use Visual Basic's rich set of string handling functions
- When and how variables are in and out of scope

Why Not Try...

1 Modify the project from Exercise 4-2. This time, deny the user entry to the system unless the day of the week is a weekday.

2 Create a project with a form and a command button. In the **`Click`** event of the command button, initialize a string with lower case letters. Use a loop to change every other character to upper case. Use the **`Print`** method of the form to display the modified string.

3 Create a project with a single form, a text box and four command buttons. Initialize the text property of the text box to "". When **`Command1`** is clicked, perform a test to determine if the text box is "empty". (This is a common task in data validation.) What is the best way to accomplish this task?

In each of the remaining 3 command buttons, declare a single variable. In **`Command2`**, declare a variant, in **`Command3`**, an integer, and in **`Command4`** a character variable. Use an appropriate test to determine whether the variable is "empty". Again, what is the best way to accomplish this task? Without explicitly initializing these variables, how do they being their "life"?

4 Create a project with two forms and a command button on each. Declare a variable on **`Form1`** so that when the button on **`Form1`** is pressed, its value can be displayed, but it cannot be displayed when the button on **`Form2`** is clicked. Then, change the variable scope so that its value can be displayed when the button on **`Form2`** is clicked. Finally, change the variable scope so that if the button on **`Form1`** is clicked, a running total of the button clicks is maintained and displayed.

5 Create a project with a form, a text box and 2 command buttons. Have the user type an entry into the text box. Use the **`Mid$`** in **`Command1`**, and the **`Right$`** in **`Command2`** to display the last character of the **`Text`** property of text box.

asic Visual Basic Visual Ba
al Basic Visual Basic Visual
Basic Visual Basic Visual Ba
ual Basic Vi
Basic Visu
ual Basic V
l Basic Vis
isual Basic Visual Basic
al Basic Visual Basic Visua
Visual Basic Visual Basic Visu
l Basic Visual Ba
l Basic Visual
ic Visual Basi
Basic Visual B
ic Visual Basi
l Basic Visual
ual Basic Visual Basic Visual Ba
Visual Basic Visual Basic Visu
sual Basic Visual Basic Visu
Visual Basic Visual Ba

Using List Controls

Many applications, particularly those that deal with data, need to present lists of information to the user. A personnel system, for example, may need to present the user with a list of job categories or department names when entering employees into the system. A strategic space game may need to present a list of appropriate weapons to the player on the fire control screen. All these facilities can be easily implemented in Visual Basic through the use of various types of list and combo boxes.

Visual Basic offers a rich variety of list controls. These controls are quite straightforward, and can make laying down the skeleton of your application seem easy. This chapter will introduce the list box and combo box controls, and show you how to make them operate effectively, and in unison.

This chapter covers:

- What the Visual Basic **list box** control can do
- What the Visual Basic **combo box** control can do
- How we use list boxes in our programs
- How we use combo boxes in our programs

We'll start with a look at the types of list controls we can use.

What's on the Menu

List boxes allow your user to choose a control from a list of options that you put up in the list box window. The user can only choose what you allow them to see. Here's an example of a list box control. You can see that it's a simple, single window, with the items listed one after another:

Choice Number 0
Choice Number 1
Choice Number 2
Choice Number 3
Choice Number 4
Choice Number 5
Choice Number 6
Choice Number 7
Choice Number 8
Choice Number 9

Combo boxes *can* look like list boxes, with an extra text box control incorporated into them. In some cases only this text box part is visible on the form, and list is not visible until the user actually clicks on the down-arrow button to display it.

Combo boxes come in three styles—**drop-down combo**, **simple combo**, and **drop-down list box**.

- The **drop-down combo**, style `0`, is like a text box with a list attached. The user can either type their own value into the text box part, or select an existing one from the list. They have to actually choose to show the list of options by clicking on the down arrow.
- The **simple combo**, style `1`, always shows the list of options to the user, but again the user can enter their own value in the text box.
- The **drop-down list box**, style `2`, looks like the **drop-down combo**. The list isn't displayed until the user clicks the down arrow. However, this time, the user can only select from the list of options. Typing in the text box scrolls the list to the matching value and highlights it.

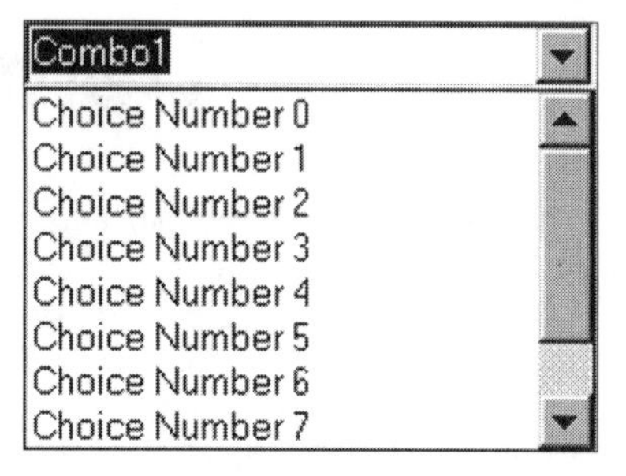

All the controls you've seen here are accessed from the tools palette in the usual way, just like any other kind of control in Visual Basic.

List box control

Combo box control

We'll look at each of the different kinds in turn, and see them in action in a Visual Basic project.

Using Visual Basic List Boxes

List boxes are ideal when you want to present a list of choices to the user, and restrict their choice to that list alone. If you only have a short list of choices, you could, in theory, use a collection of option boxes. The list box, though, is a far better choice because:

- It displays the options as a continuous list, so users see that they are picking one option from a list.
- You can control how much space the control takes up on your form by sizing the box at design time.
- You can add and remove items from the list using code far more easily than with option buttons.
- Unlike option buttons, you can set up a list box to allow multiple selections to be made in it.

Let's have a look at using the list control.

Try It Out - Creating List Boxes

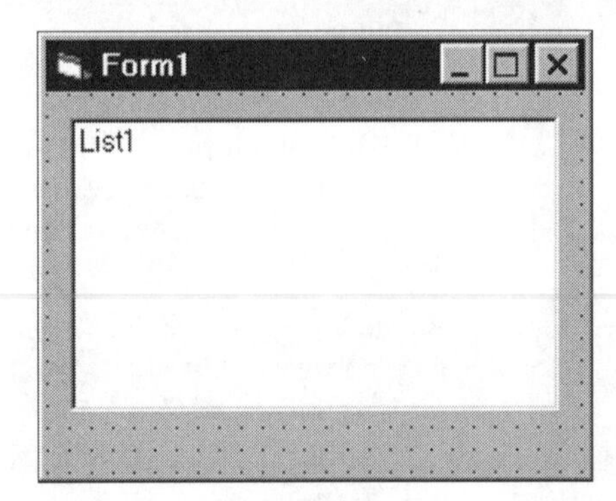

1 Create a new Standard EXE project in Visual Basic in the normal way. Then draw a list box on to the form that comes with your project, so that it looks like the one here:

2 Next, double-click on the form (not the list box you've just drawn) to bring the code window into view, showing the code for the form's **Load** event. Let's add some code to this event to fill the list box with some information.

```
Private Sub Form_Load ()
   Do While List1.ListCount < 100
      List1.AddItem "This is Item Number " & List1.ListCount
   Loop
End Sub
```

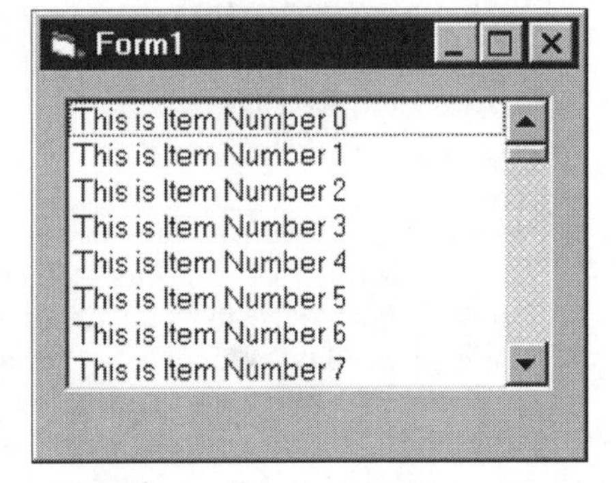

3 Finally, run the program to see the results.

4 The list box displays the items that have been added by the code in the **Form_Load()** event. Because there are too many items to display in the box, Visual Basic automatically adds a scroll bar down the side.

How It Works

The only code that does any real work in this application is the code that you added into the form's **Load** event. This code used the list box's **AddItem** method to create the list. If you bring up the **`Form_Load()`** event in the code window, you can see how this works:

```
Private Sub Form_Load ()
   Do While List1.ListCount < 100
      List1.AddItem "This is Item Number " & List1.ListCount
   Loop
End Sub
```

As the list box is empty at the start, this loop starts with **`ListCount`** as zero, and labels the first entry as Item 0. **`ListCount`** is simply a property of the list box, updated automatically by Windows, which always contains a count of the total number of items in the list.

> ***As with arrays, one of the quirks of these kinds of controls is that the item numbering always starts from 0. In this example, the number of the last item will always be 99.***

The **`AddItem`** line places a new item in the list box, made up of the string **`'This is item number '`** followed by the **`ListCount`** property of the list box. In our example it works like this:

```
List1.AddItem "This is Item Number " & List1.ListCount
```

You may have noticed something else very weird about the list box: when you first ran the program the list box shrank a little. Why? Well, normally, the list box will round its height down so that it can fit an exact number of lines on display. This is all due to the **`IntegralHeight`** property.

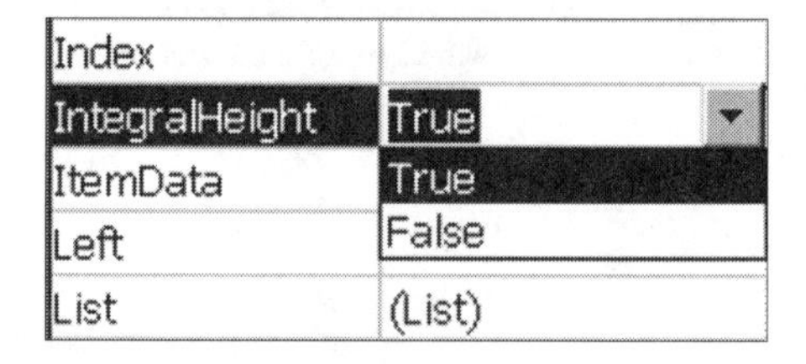

By default, when you put a list box on to a form, this property is set to **`True`**, which means that the list box will resize itself to fit an exact number of lines on display. Setting it to **`False`** lets the list box retain its dimensions—but as a result, you may end up with only part of the bottom line being displayed. Check this out:

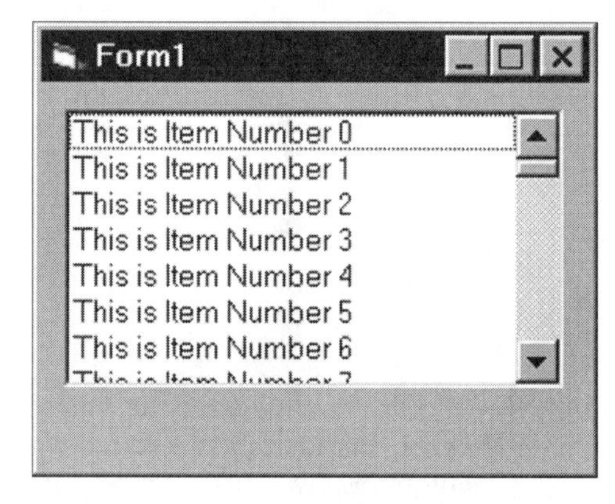

The property can only have two values—**`True`** or **`False`**—which you select in the normal ways: either by double clicking the property in the Properties window, or by dropping down the list of alternatives.

Sorting Items in a List Box

By default, the items in a list box are displayed to the user in the order in which they were added to the list. So if you had code that said:

```
List1.AddItem "Zebra"
List1.AddItem "Camel"
List1.AddItem "Elephant"
```

Then your list box would look like this:

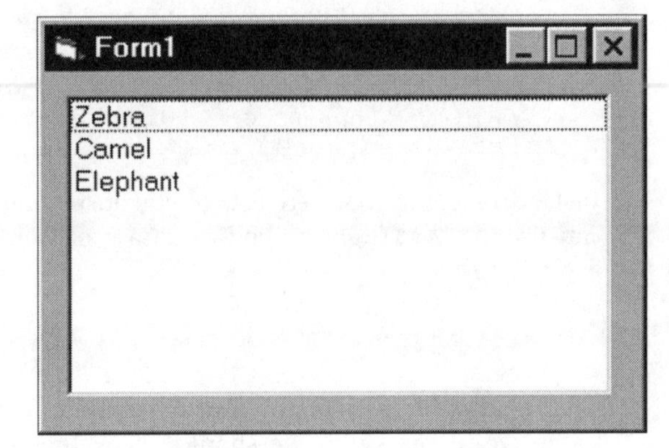

As list boxes go, this is fine. It shows all the items, and the user can make a selection with no problem. Well almost. Users are funny creatures who tend to expect a little more of your applications than they actually put in the program specifications. If you had a list of 1000 clients displayed in a random order like this, they would get upset fairly quickly.

The solution is close at hand. List boxes have a property called **Sorted**, which can be set to either **True** or **False**.

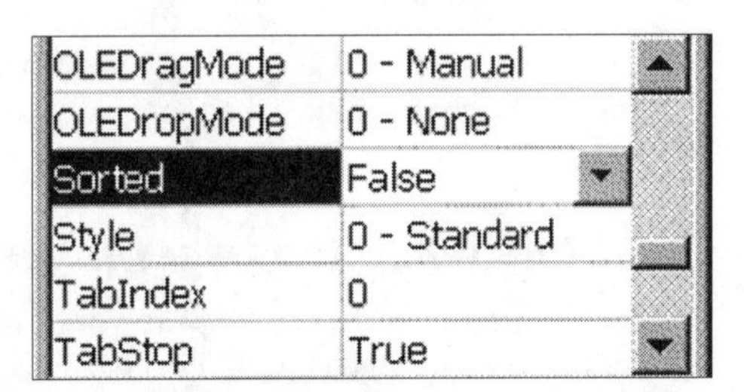

By setting the **Sorted** property to **True**, any items you add to the list are automatically sorted. This gives our users what they are after:

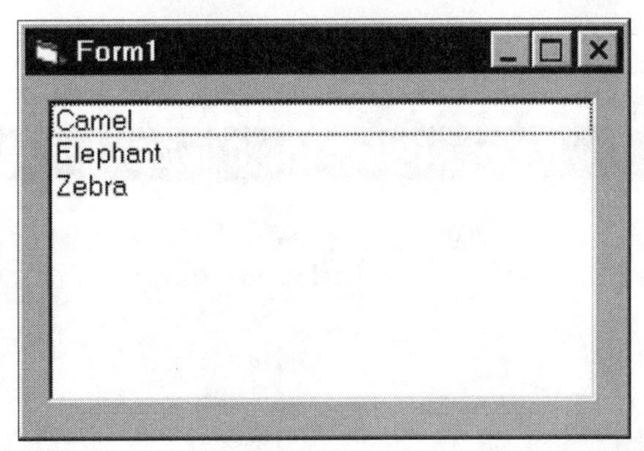

> *The **Sorted** property can only be changed in design view. You can't change the sorting of a list while your program is running.*

Sorting, however, does have a rather unfortunate drawback, in that it takes Visual Basic a little longer to add each item to the list. If you're dealing with large lists, say hundreds of items rather than tens, this can add a lengthy delay to your program code (yeah, yeah—except for the smart aleck at the back with the P6).

> *One way to get around this delay is to put a **DoEvents** command into the loop that builds the list box. That way the screen will be updated throughout the course of the loop. It will take your code longer to fill the list, but the user will see the list growing.*

Instead of using a sorted list, if you just want to insert an item in a particular position, you can use the **AddItem** method you saw earlier, and specify the position you want it to appear in:

```
List1.AddItem "A New Item", 3
```

This places the item in the fourth position, and its **ListIndex** will be **3**. To make sure the value we use is valid, we should check that it is less than the existing **ListCount** property:

```
nNewPosition = 6
If List1.ListCount > 6 Then List1.AddItem "A New Item", nNewPosition
```

Selecting Items in a List Box

Once you've put a list of options up in your list box, the user needs to be able to select one, or perhaps more than one, and you need to be able to get that selection into your code.

Detecting When the User Makes a Selection.

Let's start by taking a look at some of the events that list and combo boxes support to enable you to detect when something happens to the list. By far the most useful event to use is the **Click** event. This occurs whenever the user selects an item from the list. Once a **Click** event has occurred, you can examine the **Text** property of the control to see exactly what was selected.

Try It Out - Using the Click Event with List Boxes

1 Following on from the last Try It Out, double-click on the list box to bring up its code window and select the **Click** event.

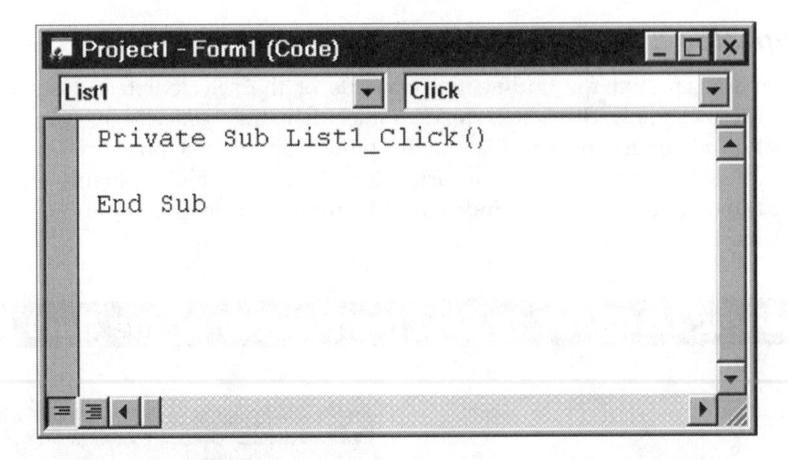

2 Add a **MsgBox** command so that your event code looks like this:

```
Private Sub List1_Click ()
   MsgBox " Selected : " & List1.Text
End Sub
```

3 Save the program as `List.vbp` (we'll be using it again in a little while), then run the program. Whenever an item on the list is selected, the **Click** event occurs and displays a message box showing you the item you chose.

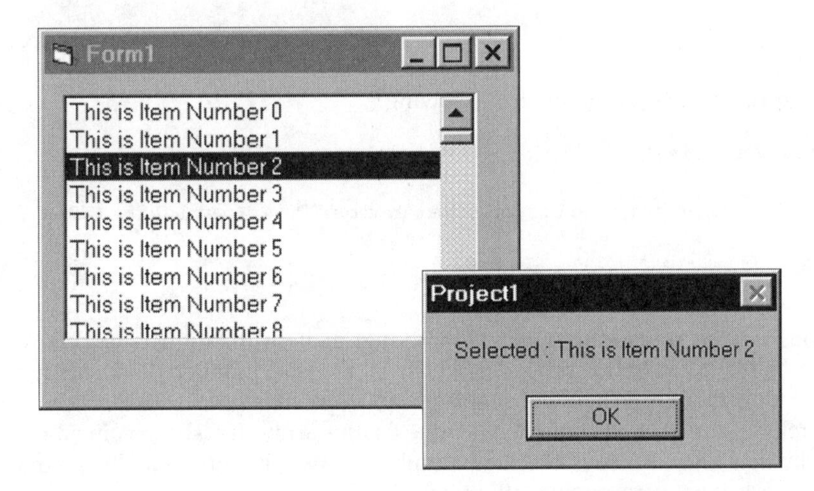

How It Works

It's extremely simple to find out what was selected if you use the **Text** property. This applies to all styles of list and combo box. The property contains the currently selected item from the list. If no item is selected, then the **Text** property will contain a blank string **" "**. In combo boxes, though, as you'll see later, the **Text** property could also contain text the user has entered rather than selected. As far as list boxes are concerned, it's the value of the item selected.

Identifying Specific Entries in the List

The **Text** property is good for finding the contents of the selected item. Sometimes, however, we want to know the actual *index*, rather than the *value*, of an item. As with most other information about list boxes, this can be pulled up from a property—in this case **ListIndex**. All list controls maintain an array called **List**, which contains all the items in the list. **ListIndex** is used like the index of an ordinary user-defined array, to access the individual elements in the list.

Try It Out - Using ListIndex to Find the Number of the Item Selected

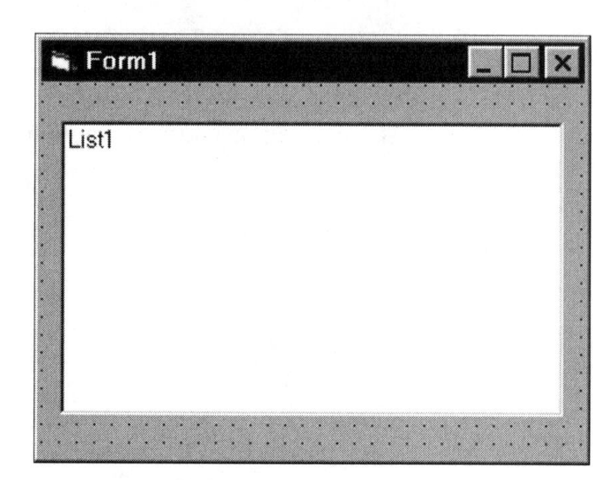

1 If the program **List.vbp** is still running, stop it to get back to Visual Basic design mode.

2 Change the **Click** event to the following:

```
Private Sub List1_Click()

   MsgBox "You have selected Item number " & List1.ListIndex

End Sub
```

3 If you run the program again now, clicking an item in the list will show you the value of the **ListIndex** property, which is also the number of the item you selected. Watch out, though. When the message box says 'You have selected item number 2', it is just telling you the position of that line in the array. It's sheer coincidence that the text in that line also says it's item number 2. Well it's not actually a coincidence—I did it to check you were paying attention.

Removing Items from a List Box

The **RemoveItem** method, as the name suggests, allows you to remove items from the list. You must specify the number of the item you want to remove after the word **RemoveItem**. Typing:

```
   List1.RemoveItem 5
```

removes item number **5** from the list box. Remember though, that since items in the list box are actually numbered from **0** upwards, item **5** is actually the 6th item in the list. Aren't computers wonderful!

ListIndex is commonly used with the **RemoveItem** method to remove the currently selected item from the list, as you'll see in the next example. We can also use the **Clear** method to remove all the items from the list.

Try It Out - Removing Items from a List

In this example, we'll try out the **RemoveItem** and **Clear** methods. To get rid of all the items in a list box named **List1**, we simply say:

```
List1.Clear
```

The items will vanish almost immediately. Let's try an example.

1 Create a new project in Visual Basic and draw a list box and two command buttons on to the form like this:

2 Bring up the Properties window of each command button and change the **Caption** property of Command1 to Clear and Command2 to Remove.

3 Add the following code to the **`Form_Load`** event to add 100 items into the list:

```
Private Sub Form_Load()

   Do While List1.ListCount < 100
      List1.AddItem "Item " & List1.ListCount
   Loop

End Sub
```

4 Now add code to the Clear command button's **`Click`** event to clear the list box contents:

```
   List1.Clear
```

5 Finally, add the following line to the Remove button's **`Click`** event:

```
   List1.RemoveItem List1.ListIndex
```

6 That's all there is to it. Now run the program:

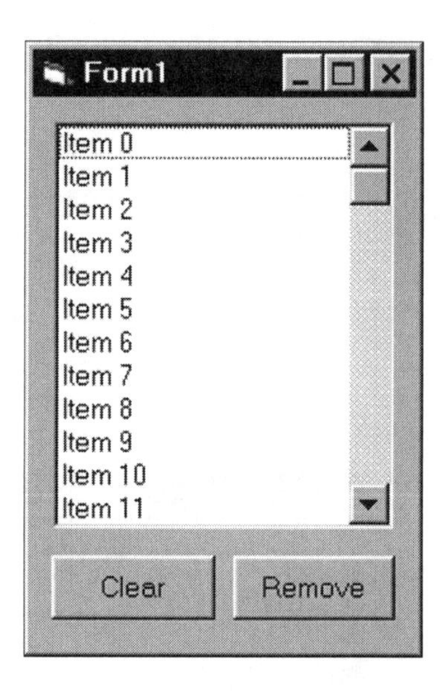

7 Select an item in the list and press the Remove button. The selected item will vanish and the ones below it will automatically shuffle up to fill the gap.

8 Now try hitting the Clear button. All the items in the list box are immediately cleared, leaving you with an empty control.

How It Works

We have filled the list box name **`List1`** with a list of items, just like the last example. To remove them all again, we just use the line:

```
List1.Clear
```

Removing individual items is a little more complicated. We need to know which one is selected, so we can remove just that one. We saw how to get the index of the selected item earlier:

```
List1.ListIndex
```

So to remove just that item we use:

```
List1.RemoveItem List1.ListIndex
```

If you try to remove an item without giving an index number, you'll get a syntax error. If you try to remove an item using an index that doesn't exist, you'll get a run time error.

Selecting Multiple Entries

In all the examples so far, we've used the **simple select** method for selecting items from lists. With simple select, the user can only ever select one item at a time. List boxes do, however, allow users to select more than one item.

With an order entry system, for example, you could have a list box showing you which invoices are waiting to be paid. You might want your users to be able to select all the invoices that were paid off today, and click a button to remove them from the list all at once. If so, you need the **`Multiselect`** property.

The MultiSelect Property

The mode you use for making selections from a list box is controlled by the **`MultiSelect`** property. This has three possible settings:

Setting	Description
`0`	**Default**. Allows the user to select only one item at a time.
`1`	**Simple multiselect**. Each item the user clicks is selected, so clicking on three items means all three become selected. Clicking on a selected item again deselects it.
`2`	**Extended multiselect**. With this method, just clicking an item works the same as Setting `0`. However, holding down *Shift* when clicking selects all the items between the previous selection and the current one, and holding *Ctrl* down while clicking makes the list box work in the same way as Setting `1`.

This property can only be set from the properties window at design time.

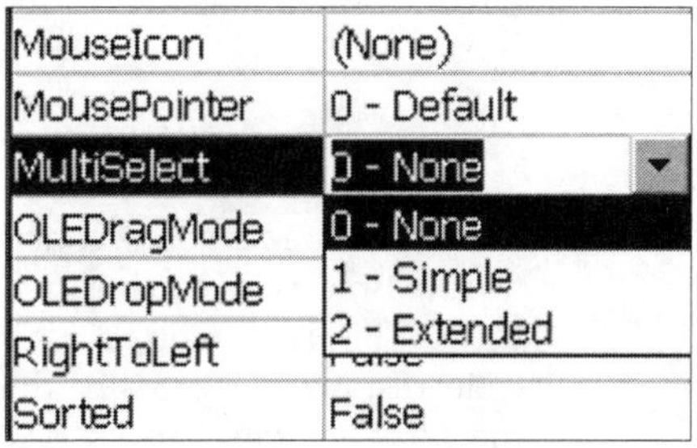

MouseIcon	(None)
MousePointer	0 - Default
MultiSelect	0 - None
OLEDragMode	0 - None
OLEDropMode	1 - Simple
RightToLeft	2 - Extended
Sorted	False

Try It Out - Simple MultiSelect

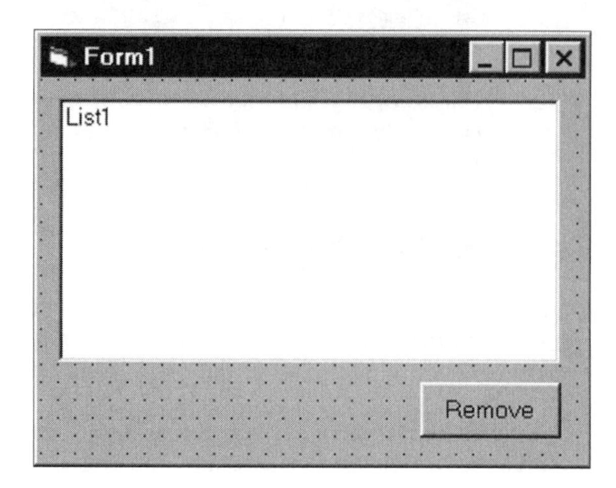

1 To see how this works, let's build another simple application. Create a new Standard EXE application, and draw a list box and button on to the form. Change the button's caption to Remove.

2 Bring up the form's **Load** event and change it so that it reads like this:

```
Private Sub Form_Load()
   Do While List1.ListCount < 500
      List1.AddItem "Item " & List1.ListCount
   Loop
End Sub
```

You should be able to guess what this code does by now; it just loads in 500 items into the list box when the form loads up so that we have some data to play with.

The next step is to set up the select mode of the list box so that we can do some extended selecting on the items it contains.

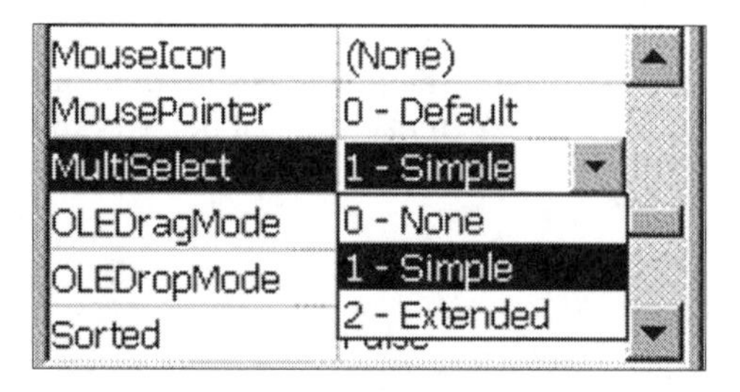

3 Select the list box then go to the properties window and find the **MultiSelect** property. Drop down the list of options and select 1-Simple.

4 Finally, let's add some code to the button on the form. What we want to be able to do at run time is select a range of items in the list box and then hit the button to remove them. This is actually a lot easier than it sounds, although the first time you see the code responsible it really does look quite horrendous. Double click on the button on the form to bring up its code window and then change the button's **Click** event so that it looks like this:

```
Private Sub Command1_Click()

    Dim nEntryNumber As Integer
    nEntryNumber = List1.ListCount

    Do While nEntryNumber > 0

        nEntryNumber = nEntryNumber - 1
        If List1.Selected(nEntryNumber) = True Then List1.RemoveItem
        ↳ nEntryNumber

    Loop

End Sub
```

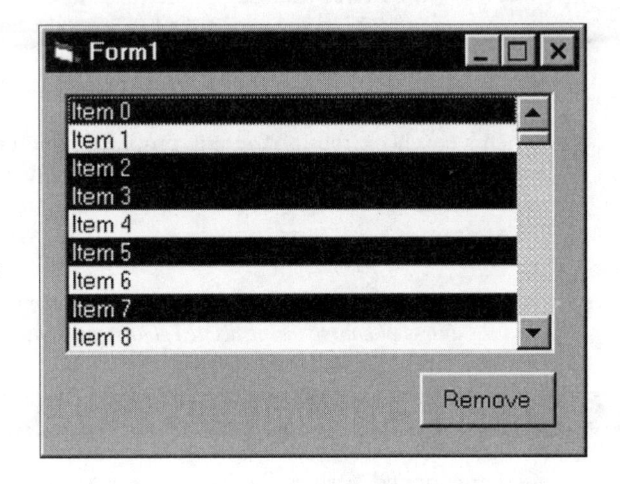

5 Now save the application and then try running it. After a short pause, providing you typed everything in correctly, the form will come into view. The form contains a single list box with 500 items in. Select a few entries and then press the button.

How It Works

When the command button is pressed, the loop goes through the entries in the list, examining the **Selected** property to see whether or not the item has been marked as selected. If it has, then the **RemoveItem** method is used to get rid of it.

First, a variable called **nEntryNumber** is set up to hold the number of the item in the list that is to be checked. The total number of items in the list is found from the list box's **ListCount** property, and placed into this variable.

```
Dim nEntryNumber As Integer
nEntryNumber = List1.ListCount
```

We have to check the last item in the list first and work backwards, since every time you delete an item, the **ListCount** property goes down by one. If you tried to work up through the list, you'd tie yourself in knots, as your code could end up trying to check items that no longer exist. Inside the **Do** loop, we decrease the entry number each time round:

```
Do While nEntryNumber > 0
    nEntryNumber = nEntryNumber - 1
    ...
Loop
```

Now we need to figure out how to see if an item is selected. As well as the **List** array that holds the values of the items in the list, list boxes also have a **Selected** property—which is also an array. In this case, it has an entry for each item in the list, but the values it holds are just **True** if the item is selected, or **False** if not. To find out if an item is selected, then, all you need do is check the **Selected** item with that index. If it has been clicked with the mouse, then **Selected** is true and the item is deleted using **RemoveItem**, and the code loops round to check the next one.

```
Do While nEntryNumber > 0
        nEntryNumber = nEntryNumber - 1
        If List1.Selected(nEntryNumber) = True Then List1.RemoveItem
           ↳ nEntryNumber
Loop
```

When you check the **Selected** property, you need to include the number of the entry you want. You can think of **Selected** as an array of Boolean values, each of which can be either **True** or **False**, depending on the state of the corresponding item in the list box's own array.

After a multiselect, the **Text** *property of the list box contains the last item selected, unless of course we've deleted that item from the list.*

Try It Out - Extended MultiSelect

As I mentioned earlier, there's also a way to select multiple items without having to laboriously click each one. This is known as **extended multiselect**. Let's see how it works.

1 Stop the last program and bring up the properties window for the list box.

2 Find the **MultiSelect** property and change it to 2—Extended.

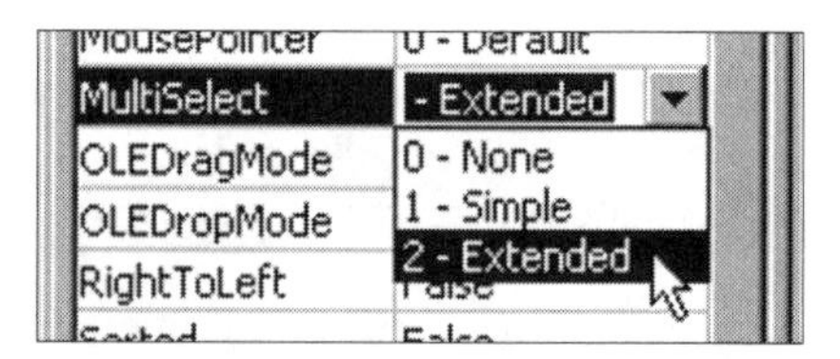

3 Run the program again.

4 Click on the top item in the list, then hold down the *Shift* key and click on another item further down. All the items between the top one and the next one are selected automatically.

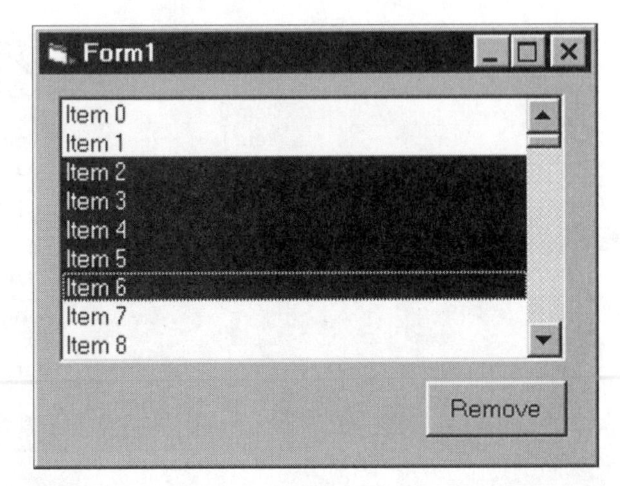

5 Now try selecting another item even further down, this time holding the *Ctrl* key down while you click. This selects an item in a similar fashion to the way simple multiselect works.

Once the items are selected, the corresponding elements of the **`Selected`** array are set to **`True`**, enabling you to process them just like we did in the previous example.

Displaying Multiple Columns of Entries

List boxes have a further advantage over combos, in that they can display multiple columns of information. This is controlled by the list box's **`Columns`** property.

Try It Out - Multiple Columns

1 Stop the program and bring up the properties window for the list box again.

2 Type the number **`2`** into the **`Columns`** property.

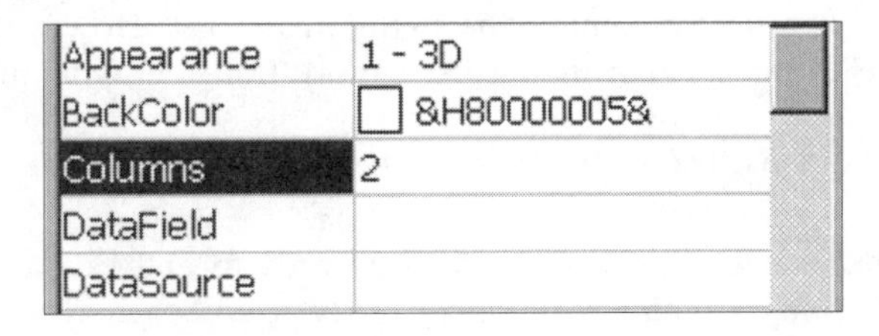

3 Run the program again.

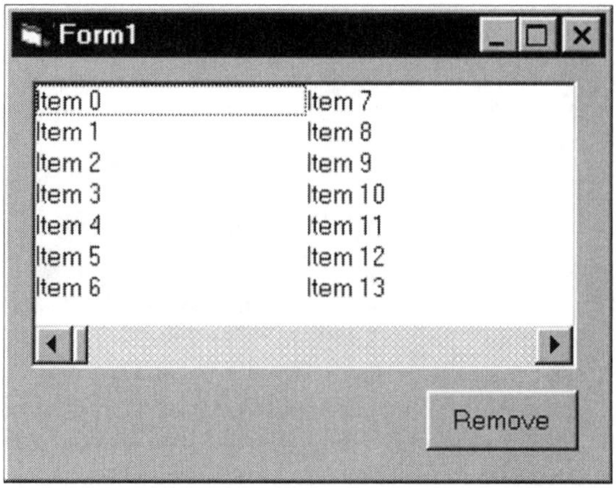

How It Works

The program works the same way as before, but now the information in the list box is in two columns instead of one. The scrollbar that was previously on the right-hand edge of the list box is now at the bottom, allowing you to scroll across the columns, rather than up and down the list.

> *The **`Columns`** property determines how many columns are visible in the list box at one time, not the total number of columns. At run time, you can change the value of the **`Columns`** property to change the column width. However, at design time, you can only change it back to **`0`**, which makes the list into a normal single-column one again—because this needs a vertical scroll bar not a horizontal one.*

Using Visual Basic Combo Boxes

Combo boxes are extremely close cousins to list boxes. Nearly everything you can do to a list box, you can also do to a combo box. Items can be removed with the **`RemoveItem`** method, added with the **`AddItem`** method, cleared with the **`Clear`** method, and sorted by setting the **`Sorted`** property to true. They also have the **`List`** property, like the list box, which is really just an array containing the items in the list. However, there's no **`Selected`** property, because selecting an item in the list simply transfers it to the integral text edit box.

So, if combo boxes and list boxes are so similar, what are the advantages of each one?

- A **combo box** provides your users with an area to enter data and the option to see a list of suggestions. Combo boxes are usually used where you might use a text box for user input, but want to also show a list of possible options.
- A **list box**, on the other hand, is very similar to a grid without columns. The list is always shown, and the user can only select items from the list. There is no data entry portion attached to a list box.

Combo boxes come in three flavors: **drop-down combo boxes, simple combo boxes** and **drop-down list boxes**. These flavors, or styles, can be selected by changing the `Style` property of the combo box when it's on the form—as we saw at the beginning of the chapter. Here we'll create a few and see them in action.

Try It Out - Creating Combo Boxes

1 Start up another new project, and when the default form appears double-click it to display the code window for the form's `Load` event. In a moment you are going to add a combo box to the form, so we can start by adding the usual code to the form's `Load` event, so that it looks like this:

```
Private Sub Form_Load()

    Do While Combo1.ListCount < 500
        Combo1.AddItem "Item " & Combo1.ListCount
    Loop

End Sub
```

2 Now select the combo box control from the toolbox and draw a combo box on the form. If you try and change the height of the box, it will snap back to one line deep.

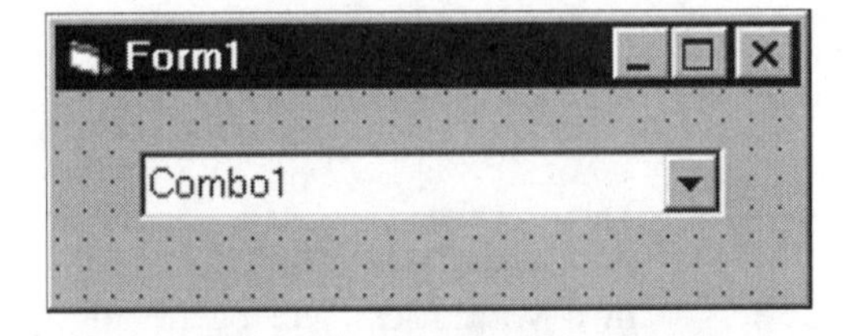

3 Run the program. When the form loads up, you can either type text into the text area of the combo, or click the down arrow to display a list of possible options.

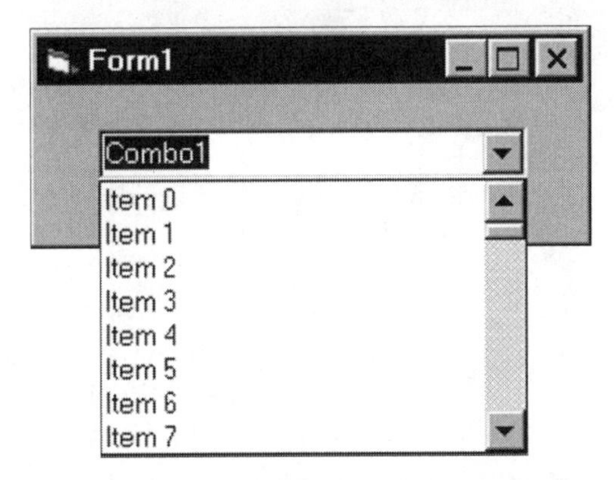

4 Stop the program now. Bring up the combo box's properties window and find the `Style` property. Change the style from the default drop-down combo box to 1-Simple Combo.

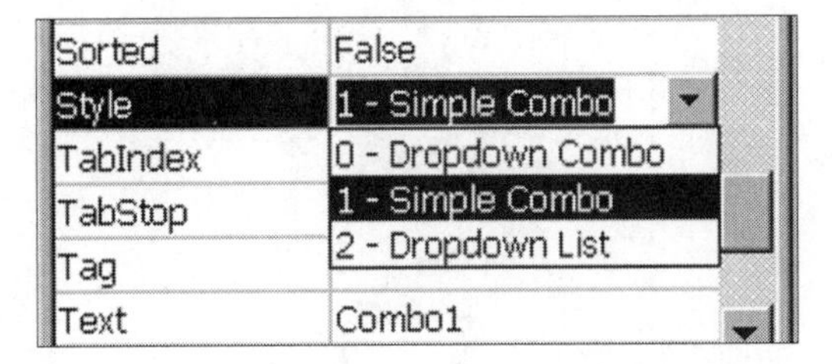

5 See how the arrow on the combo box on the form vanishes automatically. Now re-size the combo box so that it looks like this:

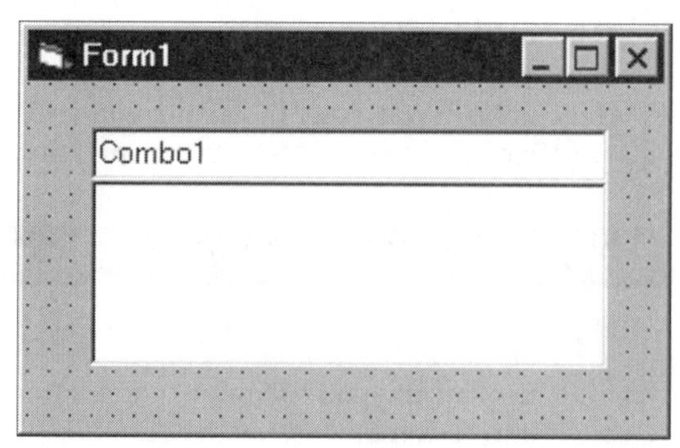

6 Run the program again. As before, you can type any text you want into the combo box, or select an item from the list. Unlike last time, though, the list is displayed all the time.

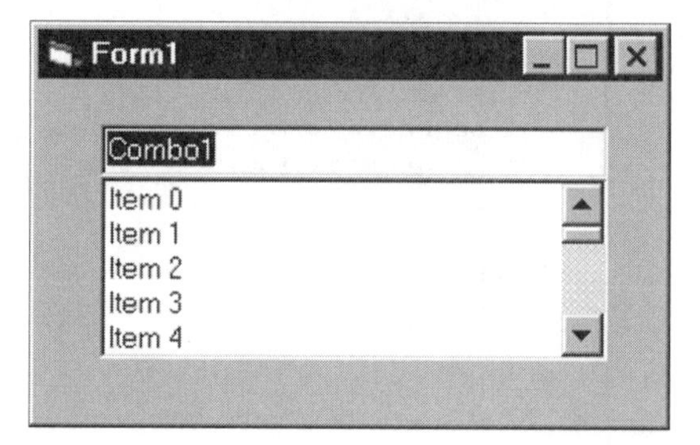

7 This is called a **simple combo** box. Because the list is always displayed, you must size the combo box at design time so that at least the top of the list is visible. If you don't, then your users will be unable to select anything from the list.

8 Stop the program, and this time change the `Style` property to 2-Dropdown List box. This type of combo box looks identical to the first drop-down combo box.

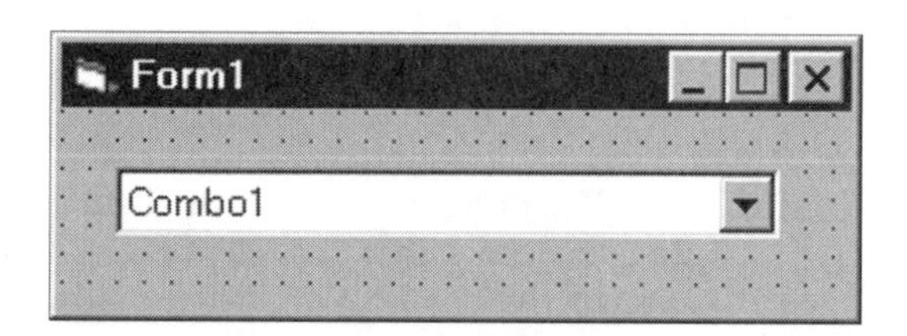

9 Run the program again. The drop-down list box will only let you select items that are in the list—you can't enter your own text.

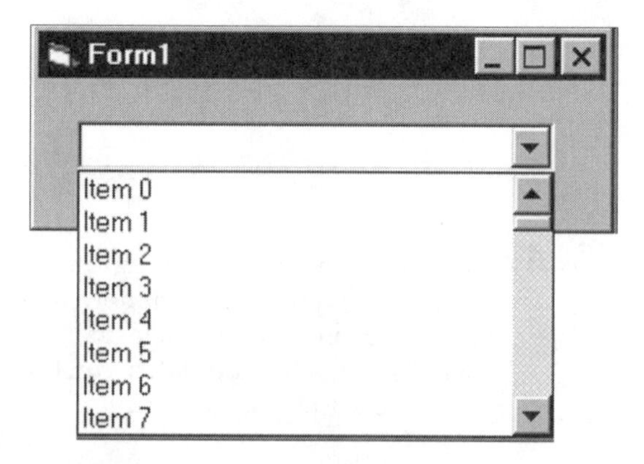

10 Type the letter I. The combo box will automatically find the next entry in the list beginning with I and display it. Keep pressing I, and it will display the next entry, and so on.

> *Of course, this only works here because all the entries in the list begin with the letter **I**. If they began with the letter **A**, you'd have to press **A** to cycle through the items!*

Combo Box Events and Properties

Although there are a great many similarities between combo boxes and list boxes, there are quite a few differences between the events and properties they both support. Let's look at the events first.

Clicking and Changing

A combo box consists of two parts: a text entry box and a drop-down list. Therefore, it has several events that are like those available for text boxes. For example, it has a **`Change`** event. You can use this to see when the user has actually altered the text in the text box by typing something in. It's worth noting that the **`Change`** event only occurs when the user types something into the text box part of the combo. When they select a new item from the list a **`Click`** event occurs.

Dropping Down the List

The **`DropDown`** event is another of the combo box's events, allowing you to catch the point at which the user clicks the arrow and causes the drop-down list to appear. You can use this to change the items in the list dynamically, while your program is running. For example, if the user can enter items into other controls in your program, you can build up a list of values for the combo box only when they actually open it, instead of wasting time doing it each time the other controls change. Of course, this only makes sense for a drop-down combo box or drop-down list box. In a simple combo box the list is always visible, and there is no **`DropDown`** event.

Retrieving the Text

On the properties side, the **`Text`** property with a combo box kills two birds with one stone. It lets you see not only which item the user has selected, but also whether they typed something in instead of making a selection. You can use this property to see what they typed.

```
sNewEntry = Combo1.Text    'what the user typed into a combo's text box
```

Combo boxes also have a **`List`** property—the array of items displayed in the list—and a **`ListIndex`** property, which contains the index of the currently selected item. Plus, the number of items in the list is given by the **`ListCount`** property. However, they don't have a **`Selected`** property array. With a list box, **`Selected`** is handy for letting the user do multiple item selections. Since combo boxes only ever let you choose one item at a time, there's no need for a **`Selected`** property—just check the **`Text`** property to see what the user wants to do.

Setting the Selection

Both list boxes and combo boxes allow you to set the index of the currently selected item in code. All you do is assign the appropriate value to the **ListIndex** property. For example, to select the third item in a combo box named **Combo1** you can use:

```
Combo1.ListIndex = 2
```

This allows you to set the selection in a list or combo box to a particular item when your program starts (in the **Form_Load** event after you've filled the list) or at any time afterwards.

Remember that the **ListIndex** always starts at zero, and if none of the items are selected, the **ListIndex** will be **-1**. Also, if you want to loop through the list, remember that the **ListCount** property returns the actual number of items in the list, which will be one more than the index of the last item. So to loop through the list you need to use:

```
For nLoop = 0 To Combo1.ListCount - 1
    sThisItem = Combo1.List(nLoop)
Next
```

One other property that both list and combo boxes have is **TopIndex**. When the list is too long to be displayed in its entirety in the list, Visual Basic adds scrollbars to it. **TopIndex** contains the index of the item that is currently at the top of the visible list. It also allows you to scroll the list yourself. This is useful, because setting the **ListIndex** property selects the item specified, as well as scrolling it into view. Setting the **TopIndex** property doesn't select the item. For example, the following line uses the **TopIndex** property to scroll the list down by **10** items:

```
Combo1.TopIndex = Combo1.TopIndex + 10
```

> *If you want to detect when the user scrolls the list, you can react to the* **Scroll** *event for a list or combo box. This works like the scrollbar control we saw in Chapter 5. It's not particularly useful, but you may find a use for it.*

Mouse and Key Detection in List Boxes

Sometimes, you'll want to react to **mouse events** in your list boxes. Like most other controls, list boxes allow you to catch **MouseDown** and **MouseUp** events. Your users can click and drag the mouse to scroll through the entries in a list box, so these events allow you to see where the mouse is currently pointing, and to catch the points at which the user presses and releases a button. You'll see more ways of using mouse events later in the book.

There are also events that occur when a key is pressed, which you can react to. By adding code to these, you can get more idea what the user is doing with your list box than is available in the usual **Click** event. Here's a simple example.

Try It Out - Detecting MouseUp Events, and Shift, Ctrl and Alt Keys

For this example, we'll use the **List.vbp** project we created earlier. If you forgot to save it, go back to the first example in this chapter to create the form with the list box on, and add the **Form_Load** code that fills it with some values.

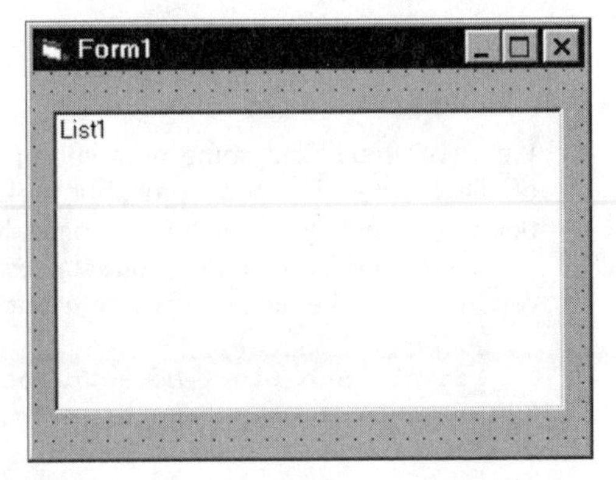

1 Open the project **List.vbp** we created earlier.

2 Double-click on the list box to open its **Click** event handler in the code window, and delete the code for this event.

3 In the top right of the code window, select the **MouseUp** event and type in the following code:

Project1 - Form1 (Code)

List1 | MouseUp

```
Private Sub List1_MouseUp(Button As Integer, Shift As Integer, X As Single, Y As Single)
   Dim sMsg As String

   sMsg = "You clicked the list box"
   If Button = vbRightButton Then sMsg = sMsg & " using the right mouse button"
   sMsg = sMsg & vbCrLf & "at a point " & X & " across and " & Y & " down"
   If Shift > 0 Then
      sMsg = sMsg & vbCrLf & "You held down the "
      If Shift And 1 Then sMsg = sMsg & "Shift "
      If Shift And 2 Then sMsg = sMsg & "Ctrl "
      If Shift And 4 Then sMsg = sMsg & "Alt "
      sMsg = sMsg & "key(s)."
   End If
   MsgBox sMsg

End Sub
```

4 Run the program, hold down the *Shift*, *Alt* and *Ctrl* keys, and click on the list box with the *right* mouse button (not the left one). You get a message box like this:

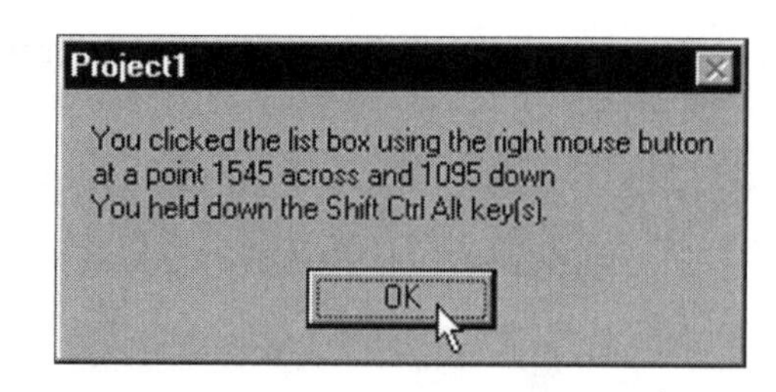

How It Works

Well, we've sneaked some new concepts in again, just as you thought you'd got to the end of the chapter. The code probably looks a little odd, because as well as introducing the **`MouseUp`** event, we've included some **bitwise**, or **binary arithmetic**. Let's work through the code. First, notice that the **`MouseUp`** event has several parameters. Windows sets these to certain values before it calls our event code.

```
Private Sub List1_MouseUp(Button As Integer, Shift As Integer,
        ↳X As Single, Y As Single)
```

The first one tells us which mouse button was clicked. We can compare it to the Visual Basic built-in constants **`vbLeftButton`**, **`vbRightButton`** and **`vbMiddleButton`** to see which one it was.

Button Constant	Value	Description
`vbLeftButton`	**1**	Left button was clicked
`vbRightButton`	**2**	Right button was clicked
`vbMiddleButton`	**4**	Middle button was clicked

In our code, we see if the right button was clicked, and insert some text into the message string **`sMsg`** to show that we noticed:

```
sMsg = "You clicked the list box"
If Button = vbRightButton Then sMsg = sMsg & " using the right mouse
↳ button"
```

The second argument in the **`MouseUp`** event tells us whether the *Shift*, *Alt* or *Ctrl* keys were held down at the same time. This is a bit more complicated, so we'll come back to that in a minute.

The other two arguments are the relative X and Y coordinates of where we clicked inside the list box. So we can continue our routine by collecting these, and putting them into a string ready for our message box:

```
sMsg = sMsg & vbCrLf & "at a point " & X & " across and " & Y & " down."
```

*The **`vbCrLf`** causes a line break.*

OK, so we can't put it off any longer. To find out whether the *Shift*, *Alt* or *Ctrl* keys were held down when the mouse was clicked, we can check the value of the **`Shift`** parameter in the **`MouseUp`** event. The problem is that the user can hold down more than one button, so we can't just test it like we can with the **`Button`** parameter.

Visual Basic defines three **mask constant** values, which we use with **`Shift`**:

Constant (Shift)	Value	Description
`vbShiftMask`	**1**	*Shift* key was held down
`vbCtrlMask`	**2**	*Ctrl* key was held down
`vbAltMask`	**4**	*Alt* key was held down

So if both the *Shift* and *Alt* keys were held down, the value would be **`1 + 4 = 5`**. If it was just the *Ctrl* key, the value would be **`2`**. We could test all the possible combinations, but there is a far easier way.

Introducing Bitwise, or Binary Arithmetic

We can store more than one 'value' in a single variable if each value only needs to equate to Yes or No, or True or False. You may be aware that computers use **binary** methods to store data, so any value in memory consists solely of a set of ones and zeros. Here's an example:

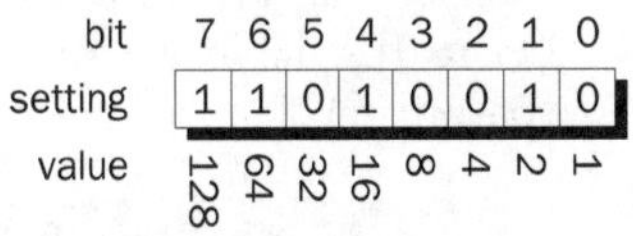

bit	7	6	5	4	3	2	1	0
setting	1	1	0	1	0	0	1	0
value	128	64	32	16	8	4	2	1

You usually work from right to left when using bitwise arithmetic, and in this case we have bits 1, 4, 6, and 7 set (i.e. they are equal to 1). Adding up the equivalent values, 2 + 16 + 64 + 128, we can see that our 'variable' is storing the value 210. The maximum value that we can store in eight bits is 255—but, of course, we can always use more bits.

The trick with bitwise arithmetic is to think of our variable as storing individual ones and zeros rather than a number like 210. We can set individual bits to 1, and clear them (back to zero) using a selection of special operators as well as simply adding or subtracting numbers. The two most popular bitwise operators are **`AND`** and **`OR`**. These take the two values we present them with, and examine them one bit at a time before returning another value based on how the individual bits in the two originals compare.

`OR` sets the individual bits in the result if the equivalent bits in either one OR the other of the originals is set. **`AND`** sets the individual bits in the result only if the equivalent bits in one AND the other (both) of the originals is set.

So when Windows sets the value in the **`Shift`** parameter, it uses the OR operation. For example, if the *Alt* key is held down, it effectively uses the code **`Shift = Shift OR 4`** to just set bit 2, like this:

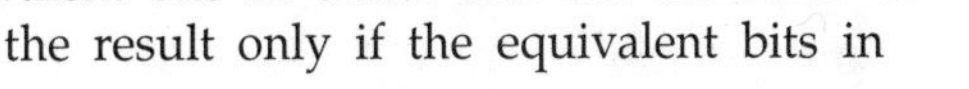

0 0 0 0 OR 0 1 0 0 = 0 1 0 0

The bonus is that, if any of the other bits were already set, they don't change. So if the code had already set bits 0 and 1, to indicate that the *Shift* and *Ctrl* keys were held down, we get:

0 0 1 1 OR 0 1 0 0 = 0 1 1 1

This is how we can check individual bits, and hence individual keys. You can also see why the constants are called **mask** values. To see if a particular bit is set, we use **AND** with the relevant mask constant, which you can think of as masking out the other bits. It only sets the resulting bit if both of the original bits are set, so the expression **Shift AND 1** will clear all the other bits, without changing the one that indicates if the *Shift* key was pressed, like this:

0 1 0 1 AND 0 0 0 1 = 0 0 0 1

This is why the mask constants are 1, 2, and 4, rather than 1, 2, and 3.

So, looking at the code we used, you can see that each **If...Then** statement will only be **True** (i.e. have a value not equal to zero) if that particular bit is set in the **Shift** parameter. Hence, we can tell if that key was held down:

```
If Shift > 0 Then
    sMsg = sMsg & vbCrLf & "You held down the "
    If Shift And 1 Then sMsg = sMsg & "Shift "
    If Shift And 2 Then sMsg = sMsg & "Ctrl "
    If Shift And 4 Then sMsg = sMsg & "Alt "
    sMsg = sMsg & "key(s)."
End If
MsgBox sMsg
```

In fact, as you'll now have guessed from their values, the constants for the **Button** argument also work the same way. However, only one mouse button can be clicked at a time, so we only ever get one of the bits in the **Button** value set at a time. This is why we can explicitly test the value using the constants, rather than having to **AND** them.

Reacting to Mice and Keys

But why do we need to worry about what's happening in **MouseUp** events? Well, as you've seen earlier, the **Click** event doesn't tell us anything about what's actually happening in our list box. The user can click using the mouse or the keyboard (by scrolling with the arrow keys and pressing the space bar).

However, the **MouseUp** event tells us a lot more. Now, we can react in different ways, depending on which other keys were held down, and which button the user pressed. For example we might decide to display a shortcut menu when they right-click with the mouse, or when they hold the *Shift* key down while pressing the space bar.

You'll see how we can use menus in Visual Basic in Chapter 9.

We can use the other list box events **`KeyDown`** and **`KeyUp`** to cope with detecting key presses rather than mouse clicks. They also provide a **`Shift`** parameter showing which other keys were held down at the same time. Of course, these key events don't give us a **`Button`** parameter, or X and Y coordinates.

No Mouse Events in Combo Boxes

Note that the mouse events are *not* available with the combo box. This isn't really too much of a problem, though. List boxes present lists of information to the user, so being able to detect the mouse events can be quite handy for popping up information about items without actually selecting them. Combo boxes, on the other hand, only use the list to present a list of valid choices to the user.

Summary

In this chapter, we've looked at how we can use list boxes and combo boxes to present information to our users in a simple, structured, and easy-to-understand way. There are different types of list and combo boxes, which we specify by setting various properties for the control. We also saw a little of how binary arithmetic lets us examine the values of individual bits in a variable, rather than thinking of it as a whole single value.

Specifically, you've learned:

- How to create and fill different types of list box
- How to detect which item is selected
- How to select and delete multiple entries
- How to detect mouse and key events
- The basics of bitwise arithmetic

We've now looked at all the basics of how we work with the basic controls available in Visual Basic, and how we write our own code routines to handle them—and our users. In the next chapters, we're moving on to some new aspects of working with Visual Basic. Of course, you'll see the controls and methods we've introduced so far in this book being combined with these new techniques.

Why Not Try...

1. Add a list box to a form and fill it in design mode, using the **`List`** property of the list box.

2 Modify the above exercise by deleting the entries in the `List` property and loading the list box at run time using the `AddItem` method. Load it with the letters of the alphabet (capitals).

3 Modify the list box created in the exercise above so that the `IntegralHeight` property is set to false (the default is true). See how the last row of data is cut off in the middle? Is there an `IntegralHeight` property for a combo box?

4 Create a combo box with a drop-down style and fill it with some entries. With this style, the user can type their own selection into the combo's text box, though this doesn't affect the displayed list. Change this so you can add user entries to the list at run-time.

5 What is the difference between the `Change` event and the `Click` event in a combo box?

asic Visual Basic Visual Ba
al Basic Visual Basic Visual
Basic Visual Basic Visual Ba
ual Basic Vi
Basic Visu
ual Basic V
l Basic Vis
isual Basic Visual Basic
al Basic Visual Basic Visua
Visual Basic Visual Basic Visu
al Basic Visual Ba
l Basic Visual
ic Visual Basi
Basic Visual B
ic Visual Basi
al Basic Visual
ual Basic Visual Basic Visual Ba
Visual Basic Visual Basic Visu
sual Basic Visual Basic Visu
Visual Basic Visual Ba

Creating Your Own Objects

This chapter was written for the Professional and Enterprise Editions of VB5. If you're using the Learning Edition of VB5, you'll still find this chapter of great interest but you should download the alternative Try It Outs from the Wrox web site:
`http://www.wrox.com/ftp/beginning/0391chp7amnd.zip`

This chapter is about the mysterious world of objects and object-oriented programming. Microsoft has a vision for us poor, lowly, humble developer types: a vision of component-driven programming. You need security—just plug in a security component. You want to add some awesome multimedia facility—just plug in the awesome multimedia facility component. You'll be pleased to know that this chapter isn't about buying an expensive stash of components, though; it's about how you can write your own.

In this chapter you'll learn:

- What an object is, and how to make one
- What class modules do
- How to create your own properties and methods

This chapter will give you the tools to create your own Visual Basic construction kit.

OOP!

When I wrote the last edition of this book, Microsoft had just added class modules to Visual Basic for the first time, and introduced us to what was seen by many to be something of a bandwagon: the world of OOP. Today though, OOP is no longer a buzzword, nor is it just something uttered after dropping a Ming vase on the floor. It's an essential part of application development and something that you've really got to get to grips with now, before it's too late.

OOP is an acronym for **object-oriented programming**. It's a bit of a mouthful, but the concept is really quite a good one. In the bad old days we would write linear code. Your program started at line 1, trotted through a couple of hundred other lines of code, then finished somewhere near the bottom. This was great until some bright managerial type realized that programmers make mistakes and are allowed to get away with it. How can these mistakes be reduced, if not eliminated?

Another bright spark, this time a programmer, decided, "Hey, we could break the program down into lots of little programs and piece them together". And so the structured programming approach, adopted by many languages today, was born. Instead of one big program containing horrendous mistakes, we ended up with lots of little programs, each with lots of small mistakes.

Of course, the managerial types got even more concerned at this and came up with the idea of bringing programmers into the real world. It's rather like having invited the in-laws round for lunch the day after you held a wild party—it seemed a good idea at the time, but there's an awful lot that can go wrong.

With OOP, you write a program based around real-world objects. For example, if you were writing a salary package, the objects you would be dealing with would be **departments** and **employees**. Each of these objects can have properties: for example, an employee has a **name** and **number**, a department has a **location** and a **head**. In addition, there are methods that the salary department may want to apply to these objects—once a month it may decide to apply a **pay** method to the employee objects. OOP programs are written in the same way: you decide which objects you need, what properties they should have, and the methods that you will want to apply to them.

In this way, you soon build a program consisting of stand-alone objects. These objects could incorporate and build on functionality offered by other objects, or they could be totally unique. For example, a **building** object in our new salary package would be totally different to anything else, whereas a **management** object would be nothing more than an **employee** object, with the additional properties and methods needed to deal with an ego.

So, how does all this translate to Visual Basic? Let's find out.

Objects in Visual Basic

Visual Basic is a late-comer to the world of object-oriented programming, and many would say it's still not really there. To me, this is the voice of the jealous purist—probably a C++ programmer. Visual Basic 5 is still lacking in some of the features that the C++ programmers take for granted, but it has moved closer than ever before to being a complete object oriented development system.

The strength of VB lies in its component model—the way that each part is itself an object. For example, the toolbox is loaded with objects that you can add to your program at will, and customize for the job in hand. You can also add more components to your projects, in the form of ActiveX custom controls. These are objects that someone else has written.

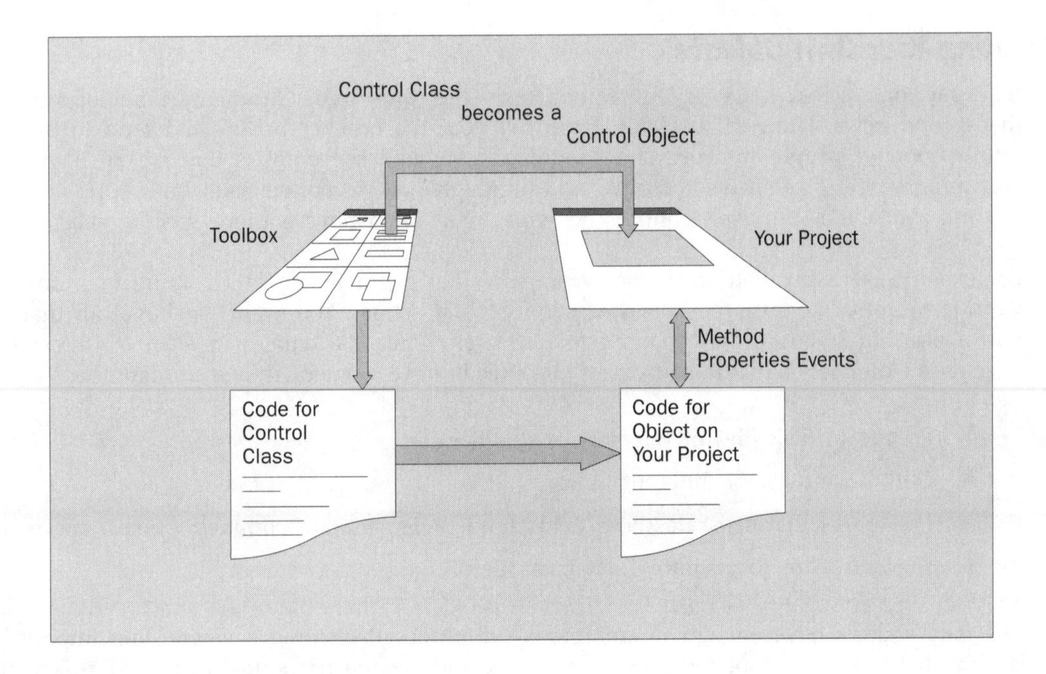

These objects all have some common characteristics:

- They have a generic function that is defined enough to be understood, but flexible enough to be useful. A button control makes things happen, but it can appear and behave differently depending on the way we've set it's properties, and the code we use to react to its events.
- They interact with the outside world using properties, methods, and events which are defined within the object. The combination of these is called the **interface**, and is all the user needs to know about them to use them successfully in their projects.
- You can have as many of them in a project as you like, and you can have many instances of the same type of object.
- You don't know, and don't need to know, what the code does inside the object to make it work. Objects provide a good method of hiding the way the task is implemented, and the way it handles its data, from the user.
- Because users only see the control object, you can change the way it works inside without upsetting the programs that use it—as long as you keep the interface consistent.

In fact, this is a pretty good set of criteria for designing objects from the ground up. The programmers who created the toolbox controls, which we've already seen, would have used these kind of principles to create useful controls such as the list box.

Creating Your Own Objects

It's a fact of life that not everyone wants to do the same thing. From my point of view, that's good news: I like to surf and, I can tell you, the beaches in England tend to be a little empty (of people *and* surf, stop laughing). Anyway, the point is that we all have our own programming problems to solve, and although generic objects like those supplied with VB and available as ActiveX controls are great, you often have a more specific need.

For example, let's say you work for a company that has a lot of data coming in from various sources, like customers, on-line services, and so on. You want to shovel all that data into a nice database file that you can review later. While the data is in a lot of different formats on disk, each of the sources or data feeds have a lot of things in common:

- They're in disk files of one sort or another
- They have a lot of different fields
- The marks that separate these fields tend to be similar—commas, quotes, spaces etc.
- They all want to go into a database file

The data sources have enough in common to think about creating a single data import control that you can adapt for each type. You could set the properties of the control to the type of data that was coming in, and then tell the object which database to use as a destination. Then a simple

```
DataImportObject.GetThatStuff
```

method would send it off to parse the incoming data into the database.

If all this sounds too good to be true, it isn't. You can actually create this kind of object yourself using Visual Basic. The only drawback is that you can't just decide what kind of object you'd like, and hope the object fairy comes along and adds it to your toolbox. You have to create all the code inside your object yourself. The good news is that, after you've done it once, you can use that object over and over again, without ever having to look inside it. And of course, other programmers can use it in their projects as well—you've just become a 'software components vendor', so you should be a millionaire next week.

The object templates that you create yourself are called **class modules**. Until the release of Visual Basic 5 we were really constrained quite a lot in the kind of objects we could create. We could create class modules and share them around the other Visual Basic developers in the team. If we wanted to get a little bit more ambitious, then it wasn't too much trouble to make these objects available to other applications through the use of OLE (more on this later). However, this didn't produce objects that could be used in a Web page, or even plugged into the Visual Basic toolbox. If we wanted to create our own plug in controls, then we really had to power up a nearby C++ compiler and go fry our brains.

Visual Basic 5 though changes all this. The techniques you learn in this chapter to create classes and objects in your own application also apply in a large portion to the creation of ActiveX controls as you will see in Chapter 17.

Class Modules

In the projects we saw in previous chapters, when we've had a piece of code to run repeatedly, we've created a stand-alone subroutine or function, and called it from wherever in the project it was required. If we wanted that code to be available in more than one form, or to be reusable in other projects, we placed it in its own module.

In contrast, the code in a class module is never run directly. The class module acts as a blueprint for an object. Think of objects as being the things created from classes by using the **New** statement. In order to implement a class you must create a object from it.

Here, the object is created from the class called **MyClass**, and the object variable **MyObject** provides a reference we can use to work with it:

```
Dim MyObject as New MyClass
```

This places an object called **MyObject** into your program. The statement says 'create a **MyObject** variable based on the blueprint called **MyClass**'. And if the class **MyClass** was the data import class that we discussed earlier, we could then use its methods, such as:

```
myObject.GetThatStuff
```

From here on, it looks a lot like any other control, for example:

```
datTitle.Refresh
```

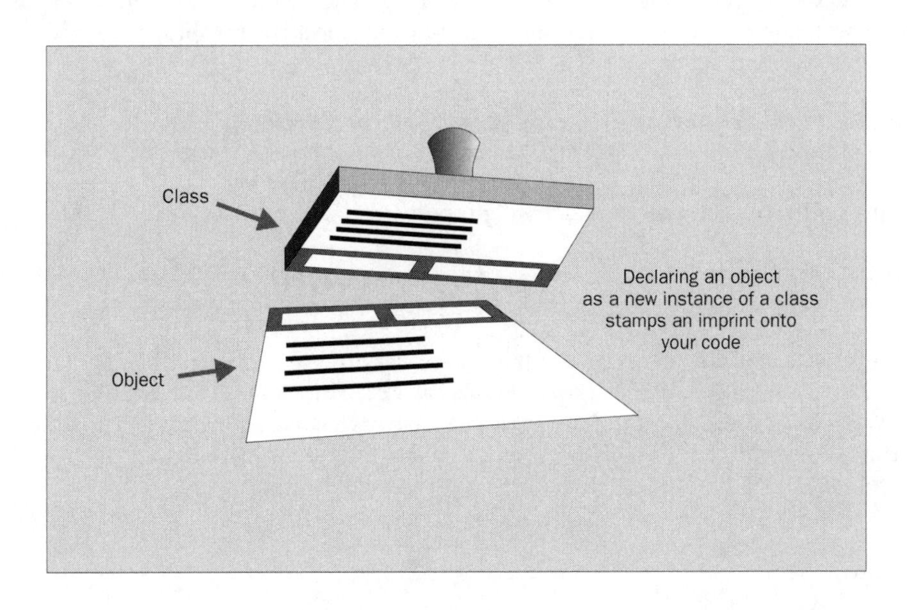
Class
Object
Declaring an object
as a new instance of a class
stamps an imprint onto
your code

*You'll often hear the term **instantiate** used to describe the action of creating an object from a class. The object is said to be **instantiated** from the class.*

You can find a good illustration of the relationship between an object and its class in the Properties window. If you look at the combo box at the top of the window, you'll see something like this:

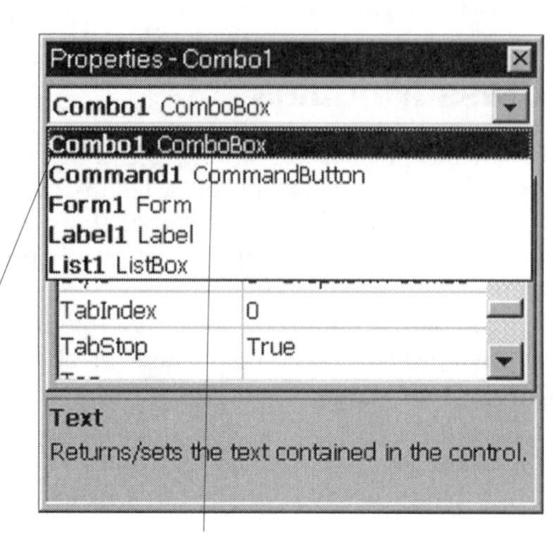

This is the name of the object itself. In OOP-speak, this is the instance of the class.

This is the class from which the object is derived. For visual controls, it's the name of the control in the toolbox.

You can create an unlimited number of objects from a class in a project, in the same way you can create multiple controls. The way that each individual instance of the same class behaves depends on how you set its properties and use its methods, exactly as it does for a control.

Class Properties and Methods

It won't have escaped your attention that, when working with objects in Visual Basic (and here we're talking control objects), there's a blurred line between **properties** and **methods**. Consider these two statements:

```
Form1.Visible = True      'set the Visible property to True
Form1.Show                'call the Show method
```

It seems arbitrary that one should be a property and the other a method. Why not have:

```
Form1.MakeInvisible       'call an imaginary MakeInvisible method
Form1.Hide = True         'set an imaginary Hide property to True
```

The truth is that inside the code for the `Form` class, these would be handled in almost the same way. By setting a property, you invoke a `Property Let` event handler, which then goes away and makes the form invisible—if that's what is required. As you'll see later, this can run a lump of code inside the object. Calling the `Show` method directly runs a similar lump of code, but this time not via a property event handler.

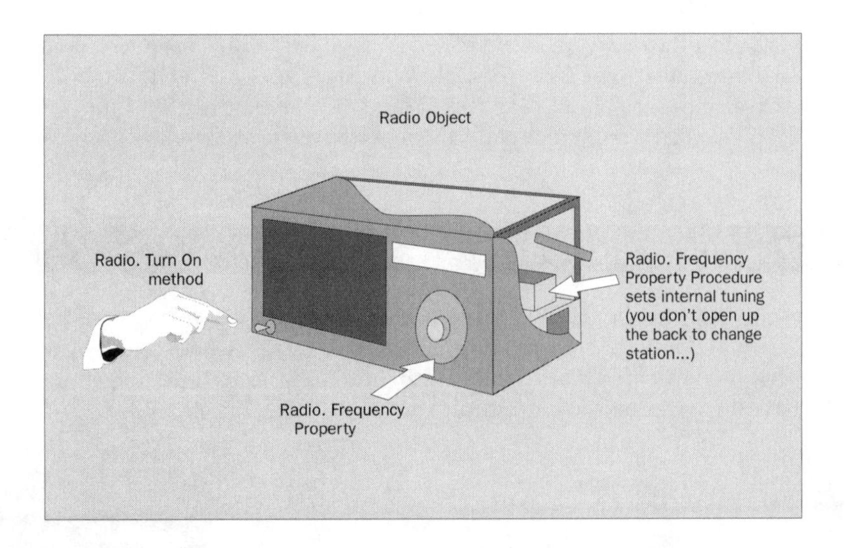

The whole point here is that, inside a class, you have *both* **method** procedures and **property** procedures, which you can use to do almost anything you like. It's only you, as the designer, who makes the decision to implement a **MakeInvisible** method rather than a **Show** method, or a **Hide** property instead of a **Visible** property. Of course, it won't make you very popular with other programmers who use your objects—they'll most likely expect the 'standard' kinds of properties and methods that other Windows objects and controls implement.

However, we've gone on too long in the abstract. What we need to do now is to see a class in action, and make one of our own.

Designing Classes

In this section, we're going to go through the process of creating a class that will move a small box around on the screen. Before we go any further, though, I want to tell you a little story. *If you came to VB5 from VB4 then READ THIS:*

When Microsoft first decided to include class modules in Visual Basic 4, they were nasty crude things that really looked like nothing more than a confusing code module. In VB5, things have changed. Class modules are powerful things that support almost everything you would expect to find in an object-oriented development system.

For example, you can create controls which can be combined into VB (and other languages) development environments, and look to the world just like any other control. Their properties will appear in the Properties window, and their events in the drop-down lists in the Code window.

On the flip side, though, they can get quite complex—and in a package aimed at rapid development, complex is bad.

Microsoft isn't stupid—they saw this and decided to include an absolutely stonkingly good utility in Visual Basic called the Class Builder. Why does this matter to you? Well, it doesn't, other than to drive home just how easy VB is, and how much fun this new version is to work with. I'll still walk through the code in detail afterwards, but in the meantime, prepare to be dazzled.

Try It Out - Creating a Box Class

OK—what we are going to do here is write a class to 'wrap up' a box on screen. This will enable us, later on, to draw a box on a form, erase it, move it and so on—just by using the properties and methods of this class. Pretty neat huh? The exact amount of code that you are going to have to write to accomplish all this is just two lines!

1 The first step, of course, is to create a new Standard EXE Visual Basic project, as usual. When this is done, take a look at the Project menu.

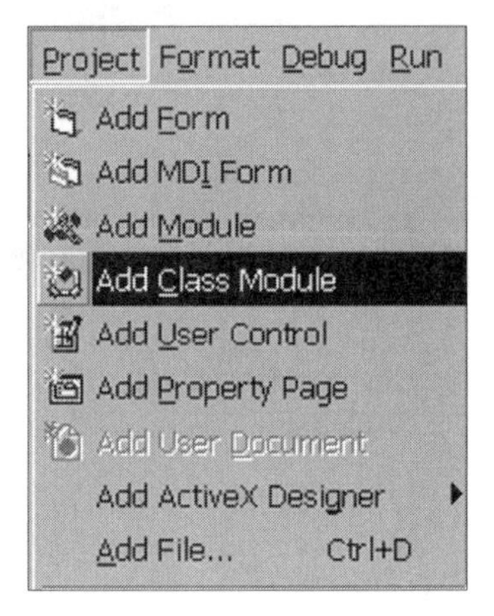

2 You can add a class module to your application by selecting Add Class Module from the list. Try it now, and the Add Class Module dialog will appear:

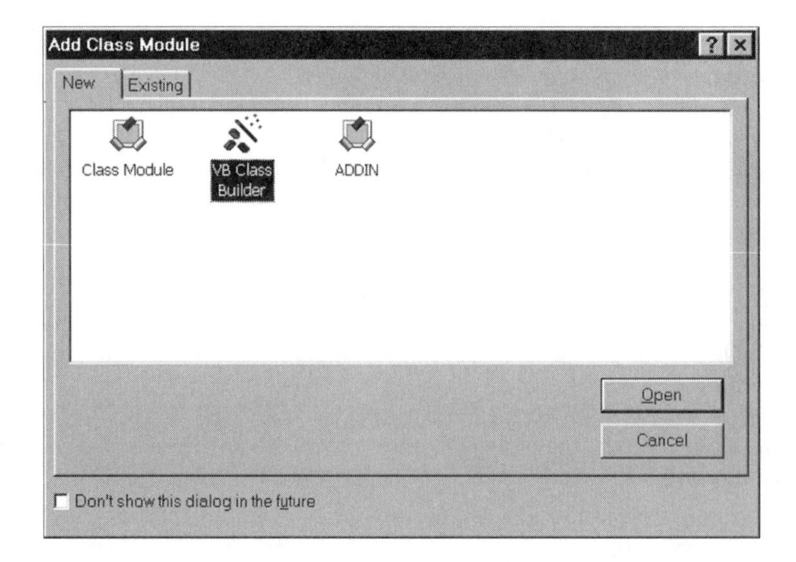

3 While there are three options presented, we'll ignore the third option as we cover it much later in the book. This leaves you with only two choices: you can either create a class module and edit it the traditional, old fashioned way by selecting Class Module and clicking OK, or you can select the VB Class Builder and let it do all the hard work. So assuming, like me, you like an easy life, select the VB Class Builder option and click OK. After a short pause the class builder will appear on your screen:

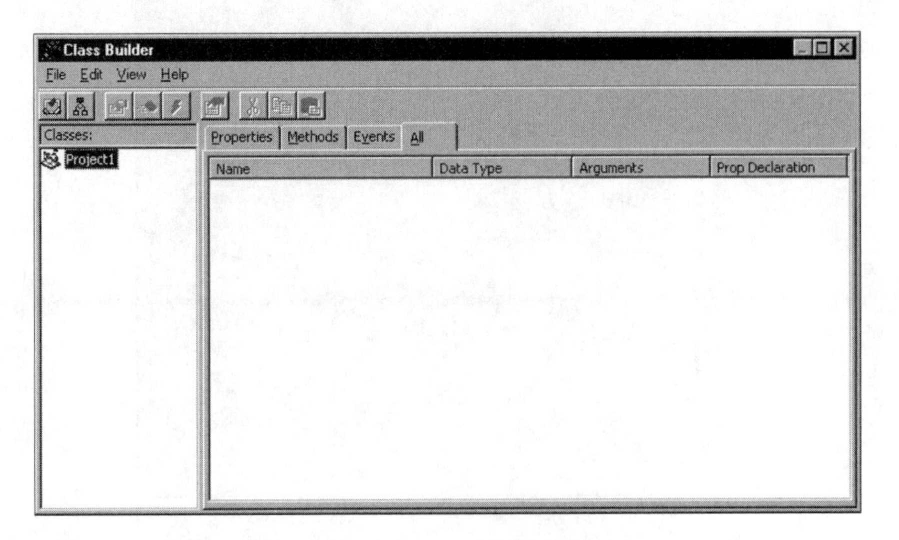

Many programmers, particularly those set in their ways, resent tools which detract from the physical amount of work they have to do, and I have to admit that I used to be one. However, there really is no reason in the world not to use the class builder whenever you need to create a new class. Writing class modules by hand is time consuming, boring, and error prone, whereas using the class builder you stand a good chance of getting it right first time.

4 The first step is to create a class itself. In our case we want to create a `box` class, a class that at run time we can turn into a visible box object on the form. To do this, click on the far left button on the toolbar, or select the File | New | Class menu options.

After a short pause the Class Module Builder dialog will appear, waiting for you to fill in some vital information about the class that you are working on.

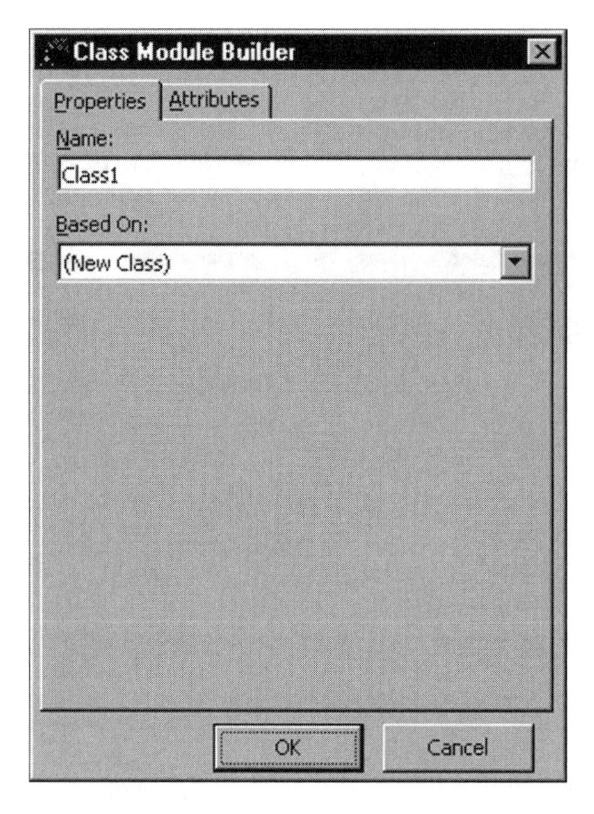

5 We're going to create a brand new class from scratch, so select the (New Class) option in the Based On combo, and enter **clsBox** as the name for your class. Then click the OK button to return to the class builder.

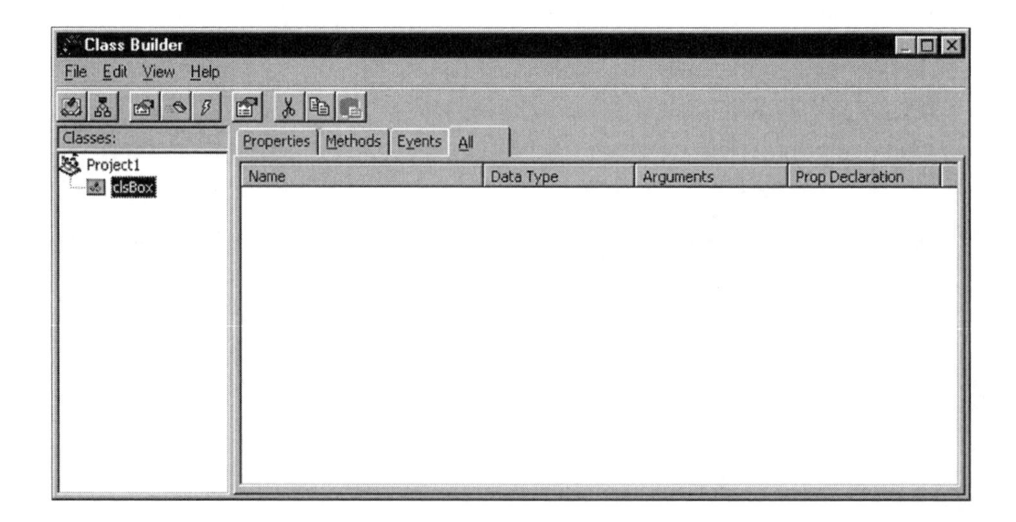

Notice how the display has now changed to show the new class that you have just created. All we need to do now is add some properties and methods to the class, and maybe an event or two, to turn it into something useful.

6 Let's start off with the properties. In order for us to draw a box, there are just four properties inside the class that we absolutely have to be aware of: the box's top and left coordinates (we'll call them **`X`** and **`Y`**), and the box's width and height (which we will call **`Width`** and **`Height`**). To add in a property, all you need to do is either click on the new property button, or right click on the class and select New Property from the pop up menu that appears.

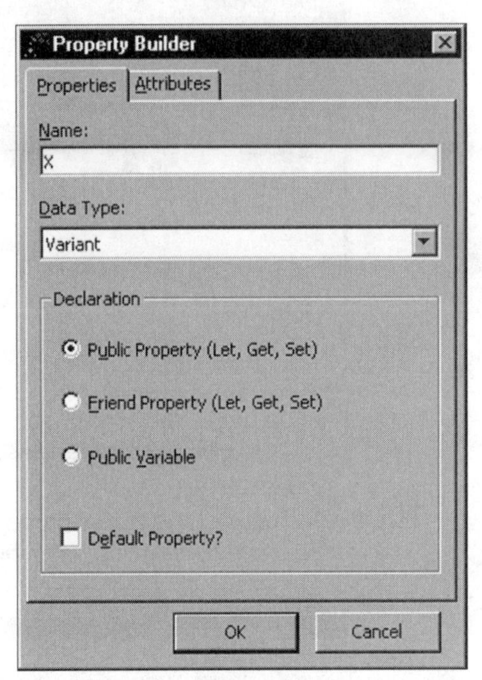

7 Again, after a short delay, the Property Builder dialog appears, looking really quite similar to the class builder dialog we saw a little while ago. Enter the **`X`** into the Name box—which is what we'll use to refer to this property in code. This is going to be the **`X`** property that tells the class where the left hand edge of the drawn box should appear.

8 The Data Type: combo box is where you can choose the type of data that the property can hold. By default this is a variant. In the case of our **`X`** property, though, we know that the property is only ever going to hold a single number, so just drop down the list of data types and choose Integer.

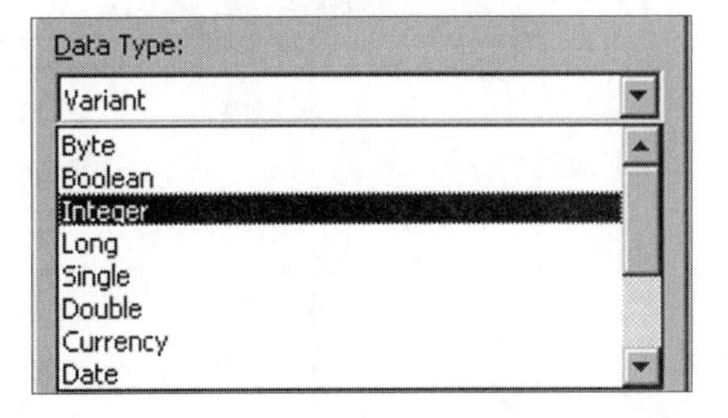

If you're an impatient type, note that a quicker way of selecting your choice is to tab to the Data Type *box and press the first letter of the data type you want—for example, in this case you would press I.*

9 Finally, the Declaration frame is where you choose how to define the property, or more specifically its **scope** within the class, and any objects you create from it. Leave this set to Public Property and click OK to return to the class builder. The main display changes again, this time to show you that you have a new integer property in the class, called **X**.

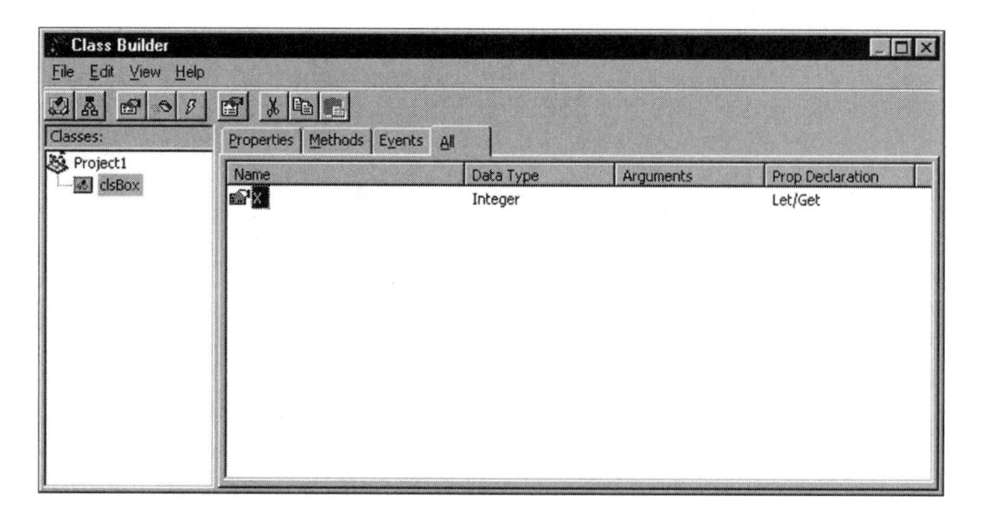

10 Finally, create three more properties called **`Y`**, **`Height`** and **`Width`**. Set them all to integer and define them as public properties.

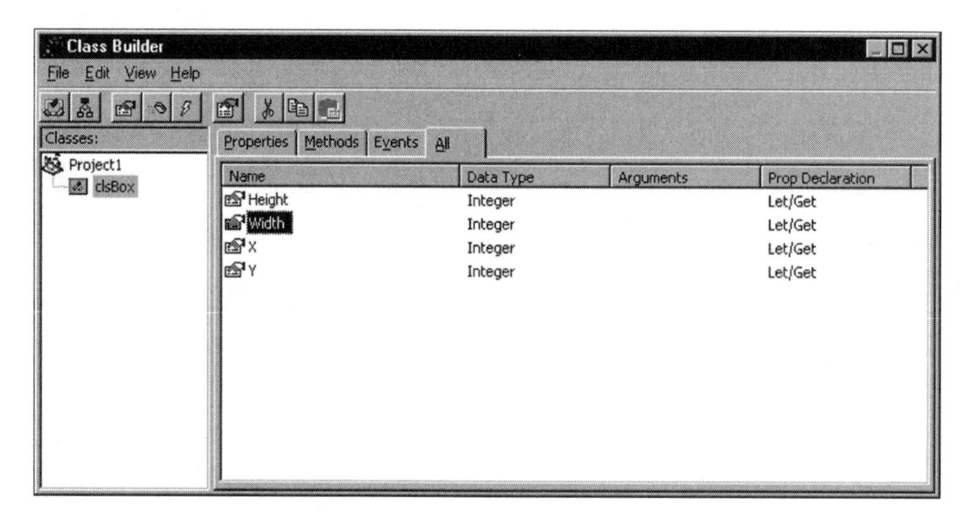

How It Works

When you create a class you are actually defining the template for what will later become an object, just like any other object in your application such as a form, or a control on a form. Like these other objects, the classes you create need to be given properties, methods, and events that they can respond to. The class builder just automates a boring and repetitive process that previously had to be done by hand.

Public Properties and Variables

We'll now take a closer at one of the options we selected in the Property Builder dialog. It asked you to define the property in one of three ways:

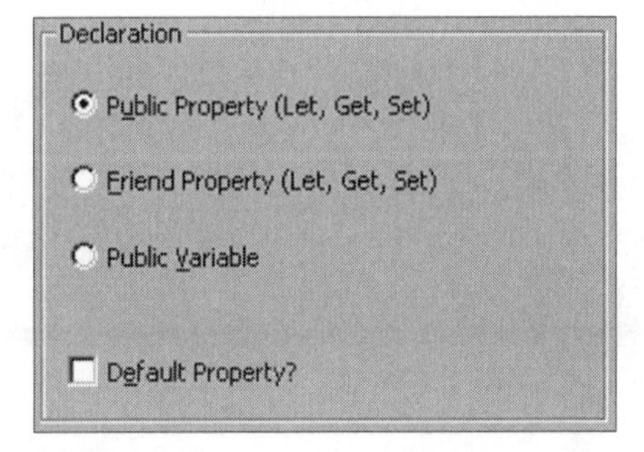

The first choice—creating a **public property**—is probably the one you will use most often, and is what we have used in our class. A public property is one that any code that creates an object based on this class will be able to use. **Friend properties** are really only useful when we deal with writing our own ActiveX controls, and we'll talk about this in detail in Chapter 17. The last option allows you to declare the property as nothing more than a **public variable**. It's important at this point then to outline the distinction between a public property and a public variable.

A public **variable** inside a class is just like any other public variable, except that when you deal with it in code it looks like you are dealing with a property. For example, if we declared our `X` property as a public variable, and later declared an object called `MyBox` based on this class, then we could have a line of code that said

```
MyBox.X = 1000
```

As you can see, the reference to `X` here looks just like we are dealing with a normal property on any other object or control. But what we're doing is allowing the user of our object to set `X` to whatever value they want.

If we had declared `X` as a public **property**, it would look exactly the same. But in the background there is a batch of code that is run each time the property is written to (i.e. changed). In this code, we can decide if we like the value that the user has specified, and if not, do something about it.

Using properties instead of public variables to provide access to the data in a class means that you can make sure no corrupt data gets into the class—by writing validation code into the property code. In fact properties are infinitely more useful when you need any kind of processing to take place when the user reads or writes to them. For example, updating the `Color` property of a custom text box object could require that the object instantly change on screen, something that simply can't happen with a variable.

Try It Out - Adding Methods to the Class

At this point our class is almost ready to go. It has all the properties we need, and just requires a couple of methods: one to draw the box (**`DrawBox`**) and another to erase it (**`ClearBox`**). In both cases, the methods will take a single parameter which is the object that we wish to draw on—it could be a form, a picture box etc., so a generic object is fine.

1 Adding methods to a class is just as easy as adding properties. Right-click on the class itself in the class builder and select New Method, or click the New Method button on the toolbar.

As always, after a short delay, a Method Builder dialog will pop into view.

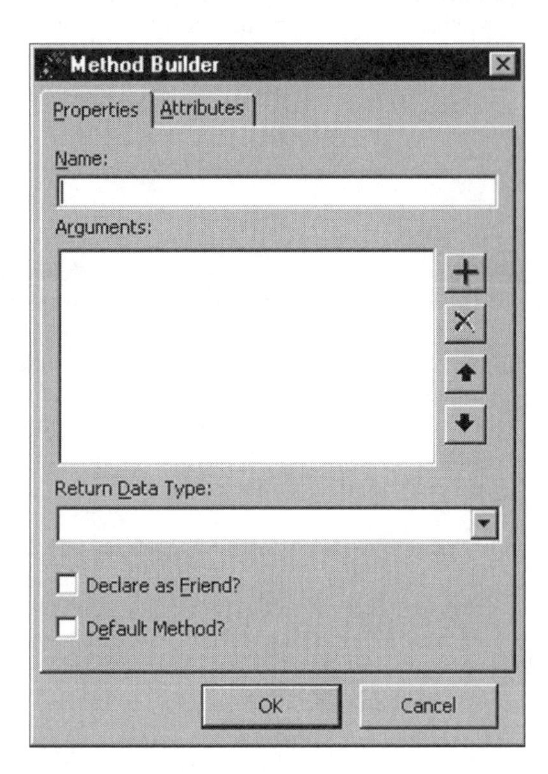

Notice anything familiar here? As you spend more and more time developing your own Windows applications, you'll find that producing a consistent user interface is half the battle in terms of winning users over to your cause. Microsoft has done just that, by ensuring that all the dialogs in the class builder, Visual Basic, and even Windows always look vaguely familiar and very similar. That way you, the user, have less to cover on each step of the learning curve—and you get up to speed with the application in question faster.

2 To add our first method, start by typing its name—**`DrawBox`**—into the Name box.

3 This routine is going to need a single argument—the object that we want to draw on. To add this in, just click on the plus sign to the right of the Arguments list box and the Add Argument dialog will appear.

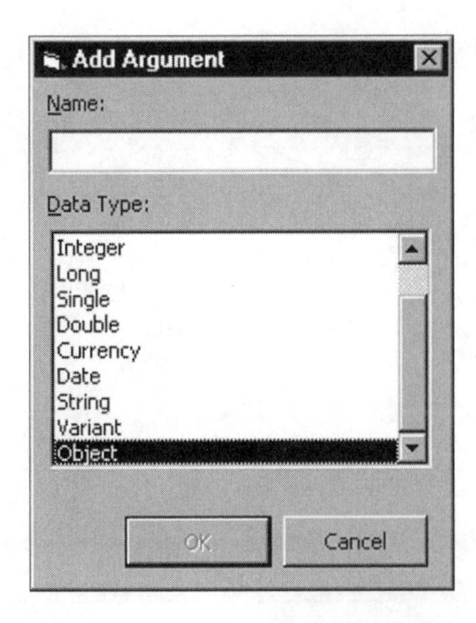

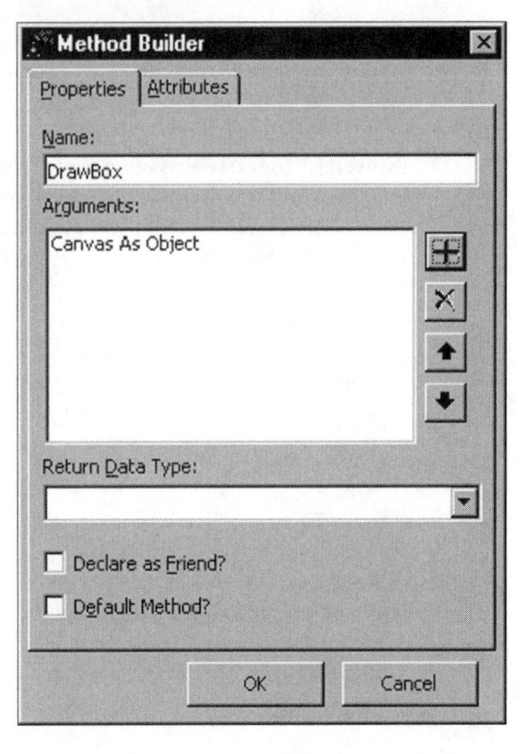

4 Scroll down the list until you find the argument type you want, in our case Object, and fill in the Name property of the argument as **Canvas**, since we are, after all, going to be drawing on it. (**Canvas** is just the name we'll be using to refer to the object in our code, like we do when defining parameters in a normal subroutine.) Then click OK to return to the Method Builder. The new parameter is now displayed in the arguments list.

5 At this point, you've really defined a subroutine—a method of the class which takes a parameter, but which returns nothing. You could drop down the Return Data Type combo box, and select a data type from the list that appears, to turn this method into a function—but for our example that really isn't necessary. Just click on the OK button to add the method to the class.

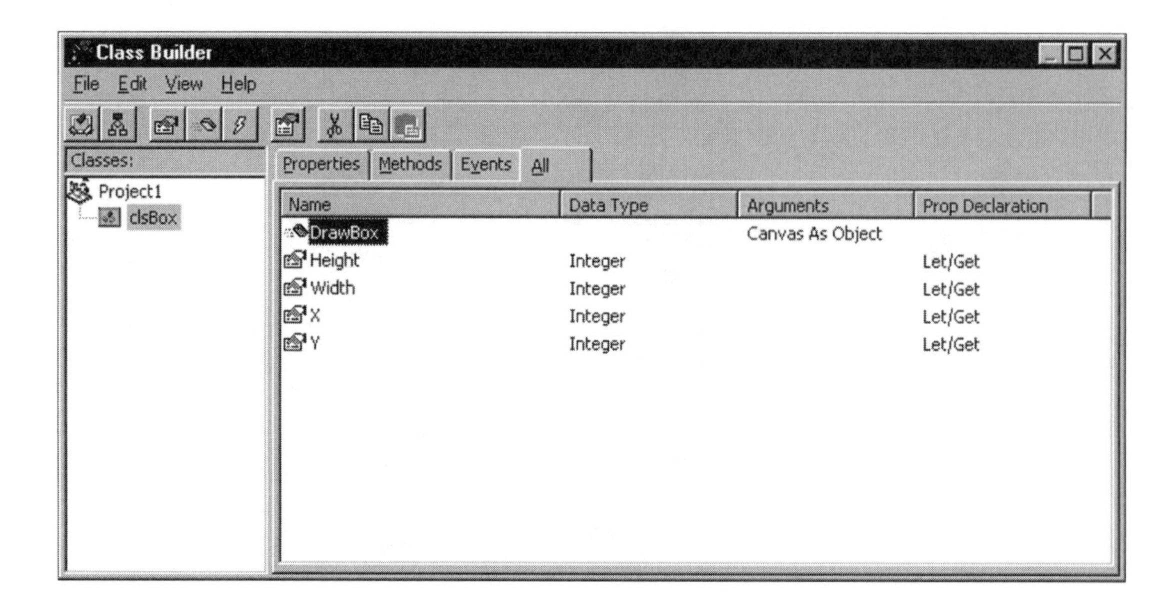

Once again, when you return to the main class builder dialog, the new item you have added to the class is clearly visible in the list, albeit with a different icon to the properties that you added a little earlier.

6 Now add the **`ClearBox`** method to the class as well. Just as with the **`DrawBox`** method, this takes a single object as a parameter and returns nothing. Name the argument **`Canvas`** again. When you are done, simply click on the OK button in the method builder to return to the class builder.

7 Finally, close the class builder down by clicking on the normal close icon in the top right hand corner of the window. The class builder will automatically pop up a dialog, asking you if you want to update the project.

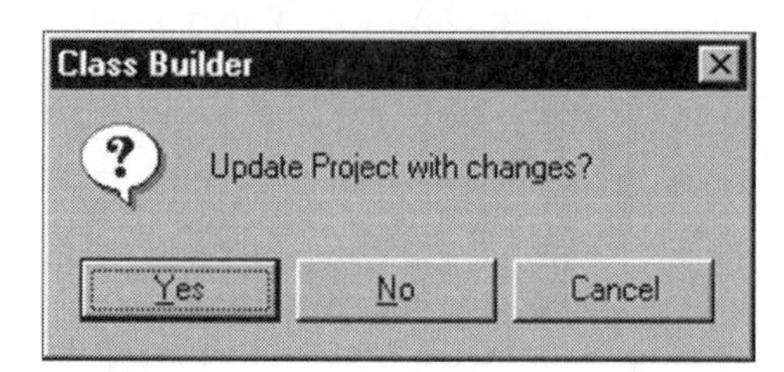

8 Clicking on the No button would cancel all the hard work we have just done, while clicking on the Cancel button would return us back into the class builder. What we want to do is to click on the Yes button to add the new class to the project, and to put into it all the properties and methods that we just set up. Do it, and you'll see what I mean.

9 If you now go to the Project Explorer and double click on **`clsBox`**, you can view the code for that class.

10 Now take a brief stroll through the code, and you will see that all the code for the properties seems to be in place (don't worry about exactly what it all means—we'll take a look in a little more detail in just a moment). In fact, the only code that would appear to be missing from the project is the code for your two methods, **`DrawBox`** and **`ClearBox`**.

11 Now it's time to write those two lines of code that I promised you at the start of all this, in order to complete the class. Find the **`DrawBox`** method in the class and modify the code so that it looks like this

```
Public Sub DrawBox(Canvas As Object)

    Canvas.Line (mvarX, mvarY)-(mvarX + mvarWidth, mvarY +
    ↳  mvarHeight), , B

End Sub
```

This code just calls the standard VB **`Line`** method, using our **`Canvas`** parameter. This parameter is simply a reference to an object that will be specified for the parameter, when the method is called from our code later on. **Line** is a method of the form object (and other controls and objects) which will draw a box on the form if we include the final **B** parameter.

12 Last thing—find the **ClearBox** method in the class, and modify its code so that it looks like this

```
Public Sub ClearBox(Canvas As Object)

    Canvas.Line (mvarX, mvarY)-(mvarX + mvarWidth, mvarY +
    ↳  mvarHeight), Canvas.BackColor, B

End Sub
```

13 You now have a fully working box class. We'll add some code to it in a little while to test the whole thing out, but for the time being save just that file as **clsBox.cls**, by selecting Save clsBox As... from the File menu—you're going to need to come back to this class later on in the chapter.

Understanding the Class Module

While you may always choose to stick with the class builder for creating your classes and the majority of the code inside them, it's still worthwhile knowing exactly what is going on behind the scenes in those code modules, and understanding what each part of the code actually means and what it does.

After a while you will find that the code is, on the whole, self-explanatory. Blocks of code that are **Public** are accessible by any code outside of the class, and are usually used for the methods and properties that define the interface of the class, and subsequently any objects you create based on it.

Private code is strictly internal. A **Private** routine in a class module, for example, can only be called from within another piece of code inside the class module. A **Private** variable in the class can only be examined and written to by code in the class, not by anything outside of the class.

It's pretty easy to see that subroutines and functions in the class actually become **methods** when the class is used to create an object, but what about those property things? ...there's so many new keywords to learn and understand. Take a look at the code the class builder created to put our **X** property into action

```
Public Property Let X(vData As Integer)
'used when assigning a value to the property, on the left side of an
'assignment. Syntax: X.X = 5
    mvarX = vData
End Property
```

```
Public Property Get X() As Integer
'used when retrieving value of a property, on the right side of an
'assignment. Syntax: Debug.Print X.X
    X = mvarX
End Property
```

Think back to the controls you place on a form for a moment. In your code, you can write values to some of the properties and read values from others. There are also some that you can both read and write to. When you define your own properties in a class module, you need to write code which handles the writing of a value to a property, and the reading of a value from a property. These are the **Property Let** and **Property Get** routines that you can see in the code snippet above.

- The **Property Let** routine is the code that is called when someone tries to assign a value to a property, in this case the **X** property. It really works in the same way as a normal subroutine; a parameter is passed across, which is the value that the user wishes to store in the property. It's then up to your code to store that value somewhere—most commonly in a private variable within the class.
- The **Property Get** routine, on the other hand, is the code that is run when someone tries to read the value stored in a property, and as such it returns a value—just like a function in Visual Basic. In this instance, the value is pulled from the **Private** variable defined earlier in the class, and returned in the same way that a function would return a value.

These two routines work great when dealing with standard data types such as a variant, string, integer and so on. However, if you need to define a property to hold an object, then instead of a **Property Let** routine, you have a **Property Set** routine. The class builder will automatically handle setting this up for you, if necessary.

The only real differences are the way the property procedure's parameter is defined, and the way it's called from our program. In this case, the parameter will be an **object**, so we have to declare it as such. For example, we might want to have a property which defines the font to be used for drawing text on a form:

```
Public Property Set Font(ByVal New_Font As Font)
    mvarFont = New_Font
End Property
```

To set our object's **Font** property from our application, we just send a **Font** object to it. However, to make sure VB knows that the **Property Set** procedure is to be used, we add the **Set** keyword when we set the property, like this:

```
Dim myFont As New StdFont  'StdFont is the VB class name for a Font
↳ object
myFont.Name = "Courier"
myFont.Bold = True
Set MyObject.Font = myFont 'calls the Property Set procedure
```

The interesting bit here, is that you can see how we're using someone else's class to create a **Font** object to pass to our class! In this case, the class is **StdFont**, and it belongs to Visual Basic. You'll see how we bring classes to life like this is the next section. But first, a bit more abut properties...

Protecting Your Properties

One of the biggest advantages of using properties, as we hinted earlier, is that we can protect our objects from out-of-range values. The default code that the class builder created (with some comments removed) looks like this:

```
Public Property Let X(vData As Integer)
    mvarX = vData
End Property
```

As long as the user supplies a valid integer value, the internal value of the property, **mvarX**, will be set to that value. They can't set it to **"Hello World"**, because the parameter is declared as of type **Integer**, and they'll get a compile error in their project.

However, consider if they set it to **-7983**. Where will the box appear? Certainly not visible on the form. We can prevent this by rejecting any values that we don't like the look of:

```
Public Property Let X(vData As Integer)
    If vData > 0 Then mvarX = vData
End Property
```

Now, our object will ignore any negative values set in the **X** property.

Read-Only Properties

We can also make our properties **read-only** if required. While this isn't much good with our **X** and **Y** properties, it might be useful if we were calculating a value, such as the length of the diagonal, inside our object. We would want to allow users of the object to read the length, but we wouldn't want to allow them to change it.

To do this, we just remove the complete **Property Let** routine from our code. If it's not there, the user can't set the value of the property, but the **Property Get** routine still allows them to retrieve the existing value.

Bringing the Class to Life

Remember, a class is nothing more than a template, just like an integer is nothing more than a data type. If you wanted to deal with an integer in your code, for example, you would need to declare a variable to Visual Basic and tell it that the variable is going to hold integer values:

```
Dim MyAge As Integer
```

The same applies, kind of, to classes. In order to actually use the class, we need to create an object based on the class at run time. Let's take a look at that **Box** class again. We'll create a **Box** object and draw it on to a form.

Try It Out - Creating a Box Object

1 If you still have the project from the last exercise loaded then great, just double click on the form to bring up the Code window, and away we go. If you don't, then simply create a new Standard EXE project, add the class module we were just working on (you did save it didn't you?) to the project by selecting Add Class Module from the Project menu, clicking on the Existing tab of the dialog that appears and then finding the saved class.

2 Double click on the form to bring up the Code window. Drop down the events combo box and find the **Click** event; we are going to write a bit of code to deal with the new object, which will be run when the form is clicked.

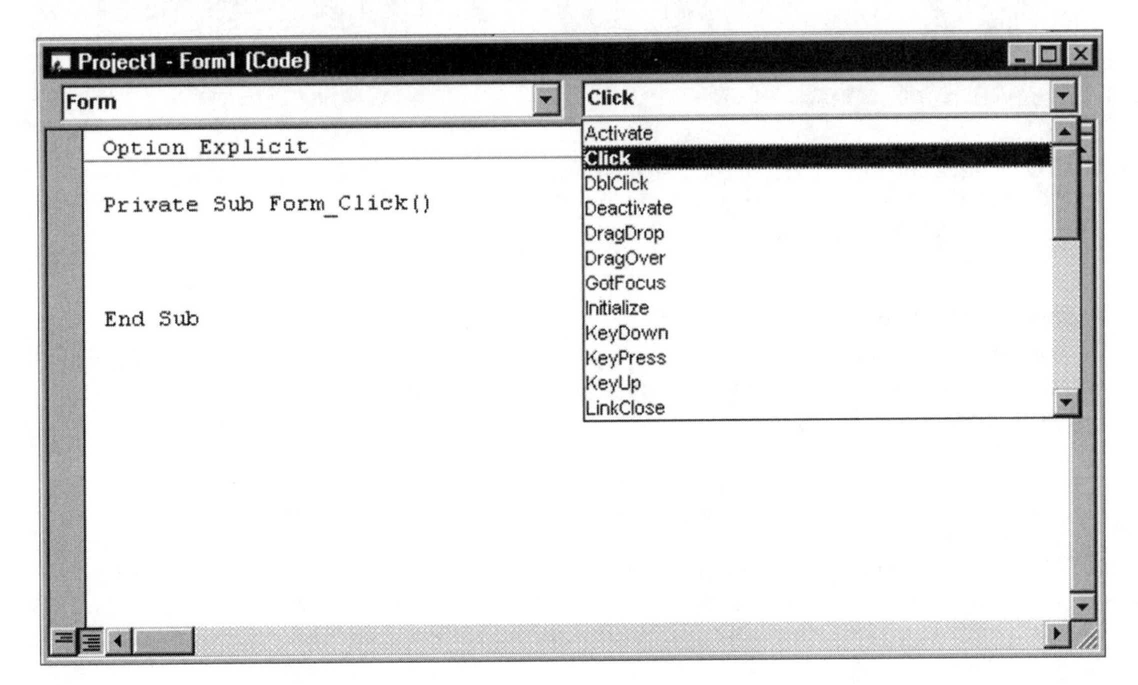

3 Before we can actually make use of all the code in the **clsBox** class, we need to turn the class into an object. A simple **Dim** statement is all we need to get this done, so add the following to the form's **Click** event:

```
Dim A_Box As New clsBox
```

This tells Visual Basic to set up a new object variable called **A_Box**, which is going to hold a new instance of the **clsBox** class. The **New** keyword is important since, without it, VB would think you are trying to create another copy of an existing **clsBox** object. When you try to refer to it, you'll get an error.

4 Now that the object has been created, we can add a few more lines of code to actually set the values of some properties within our new object, and then call its **DrawBox** method. Add to the code in the **Click** event so that it now looks like this:

```
Private Sub Form_Click()

    Dim A_Box As New clsBox

    With A_Box

        .X = 0
        .Y = 0
        .Width = 1000
        .Height = 1000
        .DrawBox Me

    End With

End Sub
```

5 That's all there is to it. Run the program and click on the form when it appears, and—as expected—our box will come into view, all under the control of a neat class we defined with only two real lines of code.

How It Works

The **With** keyword marks the start of a block of code that deals with a single object, in this case our new **A_Box** object. Within that block, to call a method belonging to the object or deal with one of its properties, we just need to prefix the method name or property name with a period.

The first four lines of code in the block simply setup the **X**, **Y**, **Width** and **Height** properties of our **A_Box** object, to define the position and size of the box that is about to be drawn. Then, the **DrawBox** method is called. Remember that this takes an object as its parameter, and simply draws on that object. In this instance the object we are passing across is called **Me**, which is a short-hand way of referring to the current form—the form whose event code is running.

But wait! What about that **ClearBox** method? We could really demonstrate the versatility of objects and classes by calling **DrawBox** and **ClearBox** in a loop to animate the box...let's try it.

Try It Out - Animating the Box

1 Stop the program running and double click on the form to bring up the code window. Add an integer declaration to the top of the click event, like this:

```
Private Sub Form_Click()

    Dim A_Box As New clsBox
    Dim nIndex As Integer
```

2 Now change the **With** block so that it includes a loop, and the total event handler looks like this (remembering to remove the line **.X=0**):

```
    With A_Box

        .Y = 0
        .Width = 1000
        .Height = 1000

        For nIndex = 0 To 1000
            .ClearBox Me
            .X = nIndex
            .DrawBox Me
        Next

    End With

End Sub
```

3 Run the program again. Now when you click on the form at run time you'll see the box slide across the form. All done with very little code, thanks to the bulk of the work being wrapped up neatly inside a class.

Optional Parameters

You can write methods in objects, and even property procedures, that have **optional parameters**. Let's have a think about why you'd want to do this.

Wouldn't it be great if, with the **DrawBox** method from **clsBox**, we had the option of specifying a color when the box is drawn? This would not only increase our artistic scope when drawing the box, it would also enable us do away with the **ClearBox** routine altogether. We could simply invoke the **DrawBox** method again in the same place, using the background form color to make the box disappear.

Alternatively, we could even keep the interface definition of our object the same (remember how this is important from earlier in the chapter) by leaving the method definition in place, but just calling our new version of **DrawBox** directly from it with no color parameter. Then, any programs which used the old version will still work.

Try It Out - Passing Optional Parameters

1 Stop the program running and, in Project Explorer, double click on **clsBox** to bring up the code for the class again. Take another look at the **DrawBox** and **ClearBox** methods.

```
Public Sub DrawBox(Canvas As Object)

    Canvas.Line (mvarX, mvarY)-(mvarX + mvarWidth, mvarY +
    ↳ mvarHeight), , B

End Sub
```

```
Public Sub ClearBox(Canvas As Object)

    Canvas.Line (mvarX, mvarY)-(mvarX + mvarWidth, mvarY +
    ↳ mvarHeight), Canvas.BackColor, B

End Sub
```

Here we have two methods that are basically identical. The only difference between them is that **ClearBox** specifies a color when it erases the box on the screen, and **DrawBox** does not.

2 Highlight the **ClearBox** code by dragging the mouse over it. Then delete it.

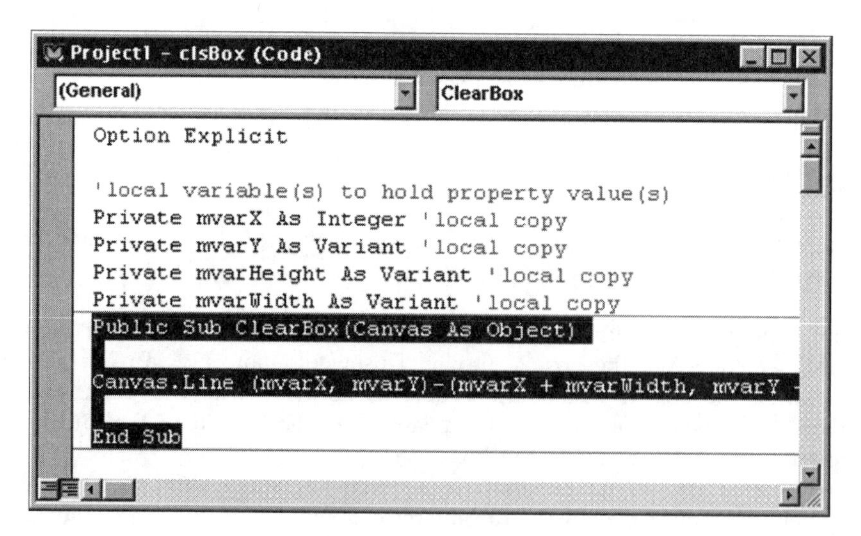

3 We'll now make a couple of changes to the **DrawBox** method to make it take a color as an optional parameter. Change the code so that it looks like this:

```
Public Sub DrawBox(Canvas As Object, Optional lColor As Long)

    If IsMissing(lColor) Then
        Canvas.Line (mvarX, mvarY)-(mvarX + mvarWidth, mvarY +
      ↳  mvarHeight), , B
    Else
        Canvas.Line (mvarX, mvarY)-(mvarX + mvarWidth, mvarY +
      ↳ mvarHeight), lColor, B
    End If

End Sub
```

4 At the moment (with no **ClearBox** routine), the program won't compile as there's a reference to **ClearBox** in the form's **Click** event. To rectify this, just take the line with the reference out and replace it with the highlighted line below.

```
Private Sub Form_Click()

    Dim A_Box As New clsBox
    Dim nIndex As Integer


    With A_Box

        .Y = 0
        .Width = 1000
        .Height = 1000

        For nIndex = 0 To 1000
            .DrawBox Me, Me.BackColor
            .X = nIndex
            .DrawBox Me
        Next

    End With

End Sub
```

5 Now run the program. There's no visible difference, but the program itself has shrunk a little in size. While this makes very little difference to a small program like this, it could make all the difference if the object was bigger, and if it was used in more places within the code.

6 If you haven't already done so, then now would be a great time to save the project so far to disk—we'll add to it in the next section.

How It Works

There's an additional parameter now, **lColor**, which is listed in the **DrawBox** declaration. However, since it's preceded by the word **Optional**, there's no requirement for the programmer to supply a value for it when calling the method through code.

```
Public Sub DrawBox(Canvas As Object, Optional lColor As Long)
```

So, how do you determine, in your method, if the programmer has actually used an optional parameter? That's where the **IsMissing()** function comes in. **IsMissing** is a VB function that will tell you, by returning **True** or **False**, if an optional parameter has been passed to your code.

In the method above, we say:

```
If IsMissing(lColor) Then
```

If the optional parameter isn't passed to the procedure, **IsMissing** returns **True**; if it is passed, **IsMissing** returns **False**. This way, you can write code to perform differently, depending on whether or not the parameter was passed. In the code above, if it was passed, then it is used in the **Line** method to specify a color, otherwise the **Line** method is called without any color value.

There's just one important point about optional parameters which we need to note. Optional parameters must be specified as the last parameters in the subroutine's declaration. For example, this won't work:

```
Public Sub MyRoutine(Optional sName As String, nAge As Integer )
```

but this will:

```
Public Sub MyRoutine(nAge As Integer, Optional sName As String )
```

A Cautionary Note

Using optional parameters absorbs a few extra processor cycles, but gives you a great deal of flexibility. You could also take the view, though, that they provide you with just enough rope to hang yourself.

One of the reasons for moving towards structured programming, and object-oriented programming, is to make your life easier when it comes to reading, understanding, developing and maintaining your code. Optional parameters effectively remove the safety net, allowing you to write almost freeform code 'I think I'll use this parameter here, but I can't be bothered here'.

When using them, it is very easy to tie yourself up in knots, especially when it comes to debugging your code. I have seen numerous projects here at my company, Psynet, where the programmers have been using these VB5 features and later found themselves debugging by superstition, adding a parameter here, leaving it off there and so on, in the hope that the code will work.

These features are great for producing your own reusable, multipurpose objects and components, but they really should be used with care in everyday programming. Ask yourself this—is there a benefit to using them in the routine I am writing, or would my code be better for ignoring them? In our earlier example, they were great at reducing the size of the code. However, you could also say that the code would be more readable if we had left the `ClearBox` routine in.

The simple rule, then, is use common sense. Treat optional parameters with more than a little respect.

> *VB now also supports indefinite parameters, which let you pass a variable sized array of parameters to a function. I have yet to find a good use for this, so I haven't bored you with it.*

Using Events

One of the newest features of Visual Basic 5 is the ability to define our own **events**. Think back to our `Box` class. What sort of events would it be nice to have embedded in a `Box` object? How about a `Draw` event so that we could update something else on screen each time the box got drawn, or a `Move` event so that we could take a peek at the properties to make sure the box hasn't vanished off the edge of the screen?

All this and more is possible at last, and very easy to implement, especially if we drop back into our old friend, the class builder.

Try It Out - Defining Events

1 Run up the class builder once again by choosing the Add Class Module option from the Project menu. We are not really going to add yet another class module to the project but by selecting this menu item we gain easy access to the Class Builder option through the Add Class Module dialog.

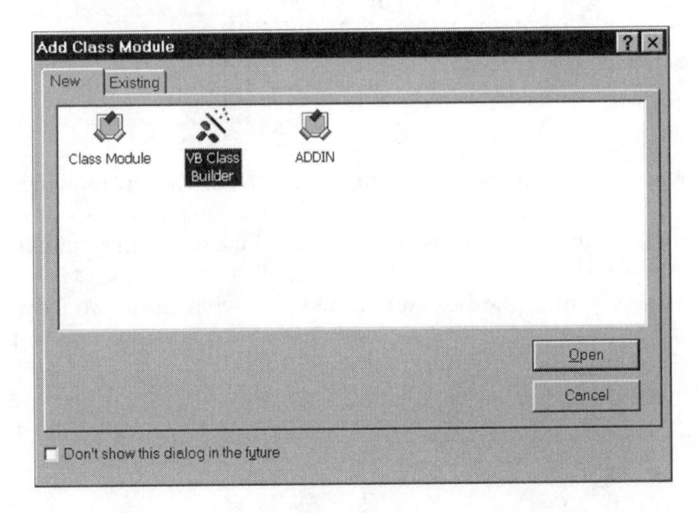

2 Once the class builder has loaded up, select our **`clsBox`** class and then either click on the Add Event button, or select File | New | Event on the menu bar.

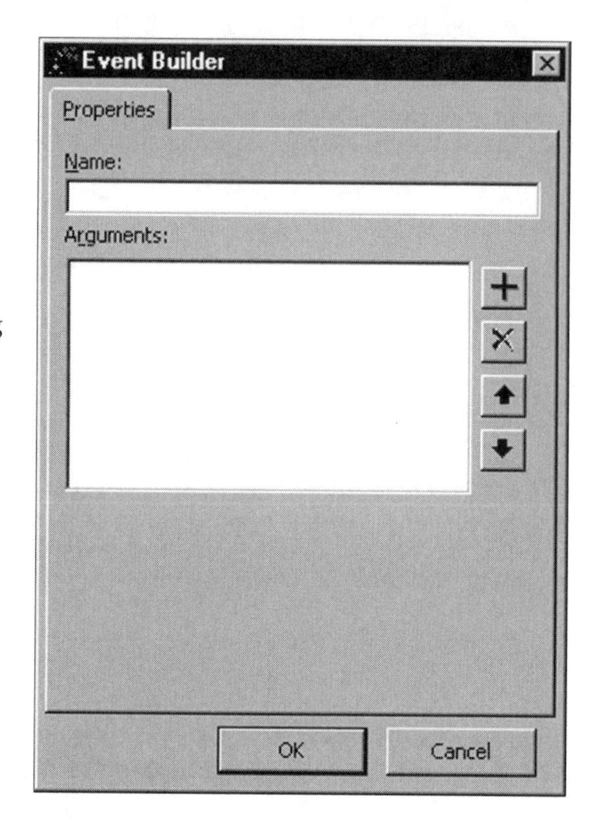

As you might expect by now, a dialog appears asking you to enter information about the event that you would like to create.

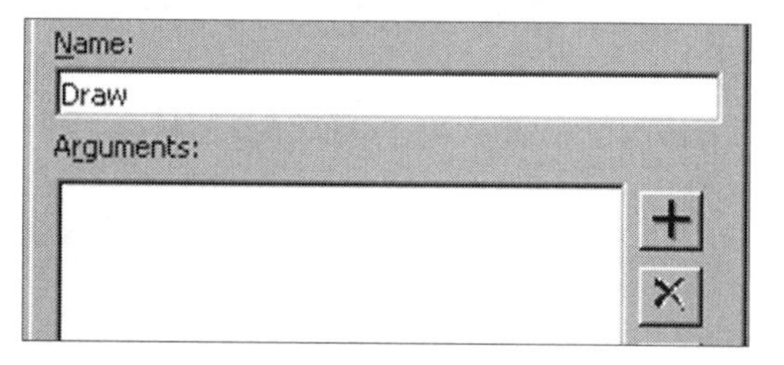

3 We are going to create an event that gets triggered every time the box is drawn on the screen, so enter the name Draw in the event builder's Name: box.

4 Next, we need to list the arguments, if any, that the event will include. This probably sounds a little confusing because now, for the first time, we are looking at writing code from an 'inside VB' viewpoint, rather than from the point of view of a VB user. Try to keep a clear head, though, and think logically. The **`Draw`** event is going to be triggered every time the box gets drawn, so what information would someone responding to that event like to know? Well, a good bet would probably be the **`X`** and **`Y`** coordinates of the box.

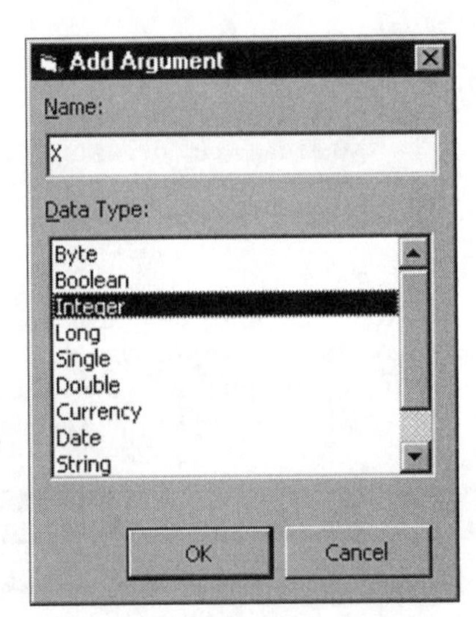

Click on the + sign to add the first argument, and fill in the dialog that appears as shown.

Here we have called one of the arguments to the routine **X** and told the class builder that this will be an integer.

5 Now click OK and do the same again for the **Y** coordinate. When you are done, click on the OK button on the Event Builder dialog to return to the main class builder form.

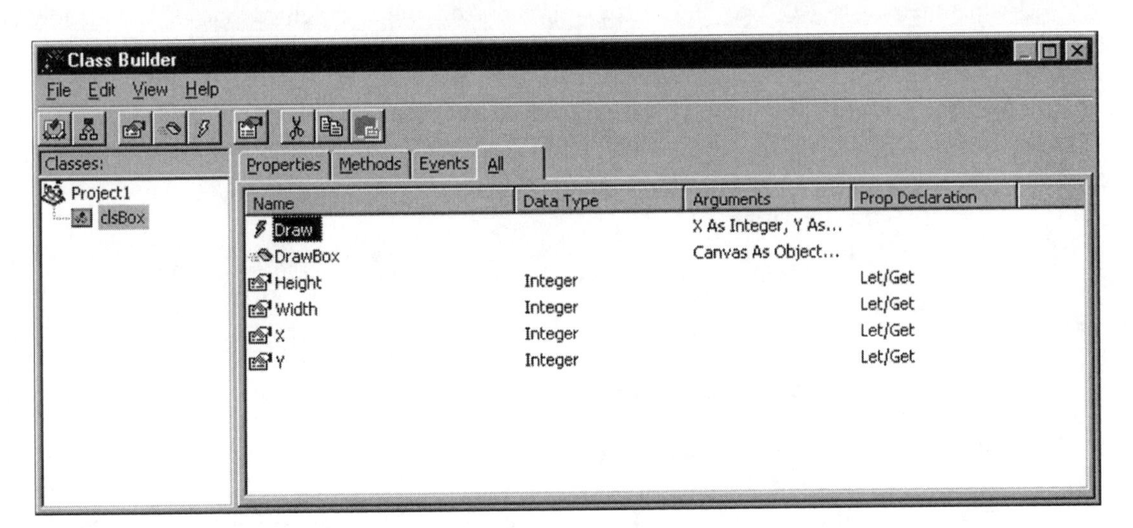

6 Now we have an event in the list of members of the class. Close down the class builder and let it update your project.

Now take a look at the class module, to see what the class builder did:

```
Option Explicit

'local variable(s) to hold property value(s)
Private mvarX As Integer 'local copy
Private mvarY As Integer 'local copy
```

```
Private mvarWidth As Integer 'local copy
Private mvarHeight As Integer 'local copy
'To fire this event, use RaiseEvent with the following syntax:
'RaiseEvent Draw[(arg1, arg2, ... , argn)]
Public Event Draw(X As Integer, Y As Integer)
    ...
    ...
```

Notice the three new lines you have. These declare the event according to the information you supplied to the class builder. However, we're not quite there yet. Those of you still awake will probably have asked at this point 'How does VB know when to raise the event, i.e. when to trigger it?'. The simple answer is ... it doesn't—you have to tell it.

Try It Out - Raising Events

We want the new **Draw** event to be raised whenever the box gets drawn on the form. This requires us to add a couple of lines of code to some pre-existing routines.

1. Find the **DrawBox** routine in the class module and add a line of code to the bottom of this method to tell it to raise a **Draw** event. Add the highlighted line of code below so that your method looks like mine.

```
Public Sub DrawBox(Canvas As Object, Optional varColor As Variant)

    If IsMissing(varColor) Then
        Canvas.Line (mvarX, mvarY)-(mvarX + mvarWidth, mvarY +
      ↳  mvarHeight), , B
    Else
        Canvas.Line (mvarX, mvarY)-(mvarX + mvarWidth, mvarY +
      ↳  mvarHeight), varColor, B
    End If

    RaiseEvent Draw(mvarX, mvarY)

End Sub
```

2. Take a look at our form's **Click** event once again. There are a couple of things that need changing here. Remove the line that creates our **A_Box** object from the **Click** event and add a line into the General Declarations section of the form, so that the code in your form starts out like this

```
Option Explicit

Private WithEvents A_Box As clsBox

Private Sub Form_Click()

    Dim nIndex As Integer
```

```
With A_Box
...
```

3 Add a line of code to the **`Form_Load`** event like this

```
Private Sub Form_Load()

    Set A_Box = New clsBox

End Sub
```

Easy enough. Now when the form loads the object gets created and the rest of our code should run without any other changes. Now we can add the event handler. Some of you may still be wondering *HOW*? How can he go ahead and just add an event handler now, for something he has made up. Have you ever heard the phrase 'Big Brother is watching you'?

4 Drop down the object combo in the code window.

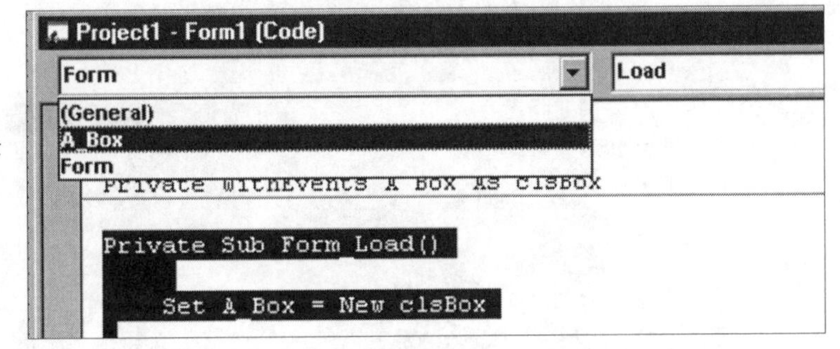

5 Visual Basic was watching everything you just did. It saw you create an object **`WithEvents`** in the Declaration section of the form, and saw you define the object and its events. For that reason you can now select it from the object combo in the Code window. Do it now.

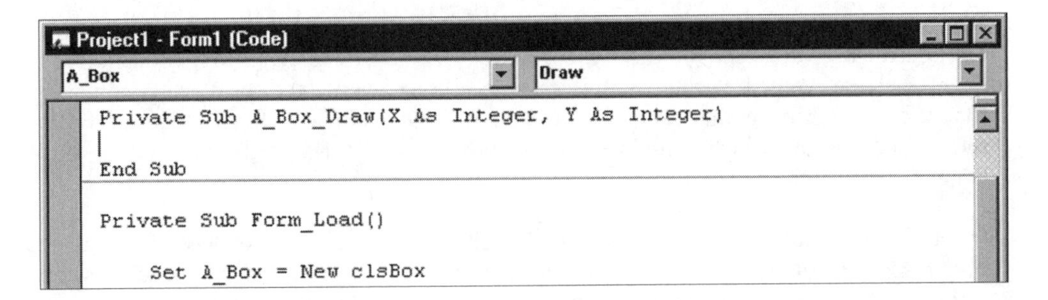

As soon as you select this object, notice how the event combo automatically changes to show the **`Draw`** event that you defined. You can now write code into the window to handle the event—just as you would any other normal event.

6 Let's just drop a **Print** command in here to print the coordinates of the box to the debug window, i.e. the Immediate Window that sits just out of sight at run time, and lets you can keep an eye on what's going on with your project.

```
Private Sub A_Box_Draw(X As Integer, Y As Integer)

    Debug.Print "The box just got drawn at " & X & ", " & Y

End Sub
```

7 Finally, run the program. Click in the form and watch the box slide across the screen. In the background while this is happening, you should be able to see the Immediate Window (or debug window) filling up with the text you are printing in response to the Box's **Draw** event.

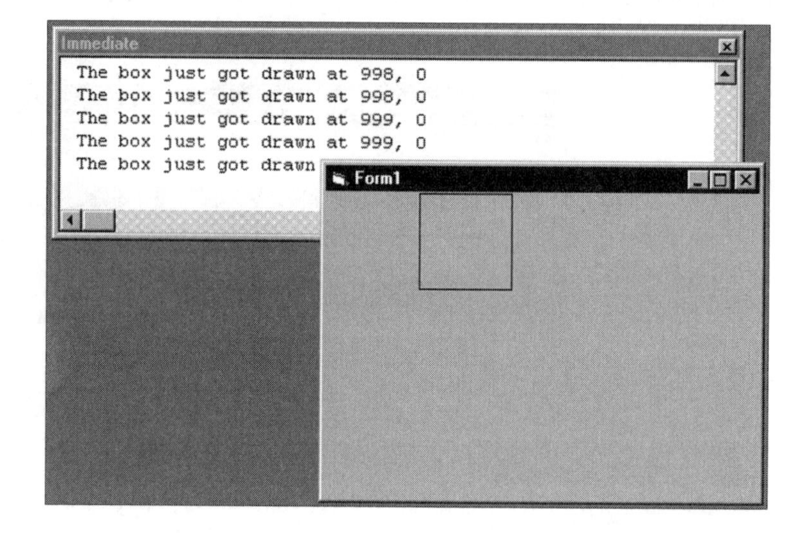

How It Works

We just used the **RaiseEvent** method to tell Visual Basic 'Hey ... something just happened—fire an event for me'. Then, all we needed to do was to tell Visual Basic the event that we wanted raising, in this case the **Draw** event, and pass across any arguments that the event has. In this example we sent the two values of the two property variables **mvarX** and **mvarY**, which contained the X and Y coordinates of the box, to the new **Draw** event.

In order to be able to handle events of an object of our own, we needed to declare the object slightly differently. First, it had be declared in the form (or a module) as **Private**, rather than being private to a particular routine. Secondly, we had to use the word **WithEvents** instead of **Dim**.

```
Private WithEvents A_Box As clsBox
```

So we removed the **Dim** declaration from the **Form_Click** event handler and added a new line to the declarations section of the form. The new declaration used the **WithEvents** keyword to tell Visual Basic that we are declaring an object that has events attached to it, and that we intend to write a little code to deal with those events. Notice also that the **New** keyword was removed.

When you write

```
Dim A_Box As New clsBox
```

you're effectively telling Visual Basic not only that you are going to be using an object based on **clsBox**, but also that VB should go away and allocate some memory for that object and create it. However, due to a limitation in VB5, this can't be done when we use the **WithEvents** keyword. Instead we have to create the object ourselves separately, by adding a line to the **Form_Load** event, and let Visual Basic 5 do the rest.

Finally, we added a **Print** line to the new event just to check on what was happening when our program was executed. That's all there was to it.

Congratulations! In the space of one relatively short chapter, you have created your own graphical class, added properties and methods to that class, added a custom event, and written a custom event handler. That little lot would send your average novice C++ developer insane within 15 minutes. Give yourself a hefty pat on the back.

Seriously though, we really have covered a lot of ground in this chapter and you may be getting a little worried that you are going to forget it all. Don't worry, you aren't going to, because OOP is here to stay in VB5 and everything you do, both on your own and through the rest of this book, will rely on the OOP principles we have just covered to one degree or another.

Summary

We've introduced some stiff new concepts in this chapter. In this way, it's a little different to other parts of the book—where the hard part is wading through the richness of Visual Basic's command set. What matters here is getting your head around the idea that your whole program is built on objects, some of which come in the box, and some of which you can write yourself.

We covered:

- What an object is in VB
- How controls are special types of objects
- How to create a simple class
- How to implement property procedures and methods
- How to use classes in your code
- How to produce your own events
- How to raise an event
- How to declare an object **WithEvents**

Why Not Try.....

1. We are going to create a TrafficLight class. Start by using the Class Builder to create a class called **`clsTrafficLight`**.

2. We want our class to draw a traffic light on the form and then turn different lights on in response to the user clicking one of a set of command buttons.

   Give the TrafficLight class the following properties: **`Height`**, **`Width`**, **`X`** and **`Y`**, which are all integers, and **`RedLight`**, **`YellowLight`**, and **`GreenLight`**, which are booleans. Also add the following methods: **`DrawLight`**, **`ClearLight`**, **`TrafficGo`**, **`TrafficStop`**, **`TrafficCaution`**. Each of these routines should take a single argument—the object that we are going to draw on. Call this **`Canvas`**. Finally, add one more method called **`LightOn`**, and give it two arguments—**`Canvas`** and then an integer argument called **`Interval`**.

3. Add code to initialize the **`X`**, **`Y`**, **`Height`** and **`Width`** properties. Then write the methods: **`DrawLight`** and **`ClearLight`** should be fairly self-explanatory—they should draw a traffic light (3 squares in a row will be fine) and clear it from the form. **`TrafficGo`**, **`TrafficStop`** and **`TrafficCaution`** turn the green, red and yellow lights on respectively while turning the others off.

4. Create a form with several buttons. Include buttons which will, when clicked, create and destroy the traffic light, as well as buttons which will show the light to permit traffic to go, stop, and proceed with caution.

5. Finally, modify the TrafficLight class to run on automatic: place a timer on the form, and have the traffic light cycle through red, yellow and green.

asic Visual Basic Visual Ba
al Basic Visual Basic Visual
Basic Visual Basic Visual Ba
ual Basic Vi
Basic Visu
ual Basic V
l Basic Vis
isual Basic Visual Basi
al Basic Visual Basic Visua
Visual Basic Visual Basic Visu
l Basic Visual Ba
l Basic Visual
ic Visual Basi
Basic Visual B
ic Visual Basi
l Basic Visual
ual Basic Visual Basic Visual Ba
Visual Basic Visual Basic Visu
sual Basic Visual Basic Visu
Visual Basic Visual Ba

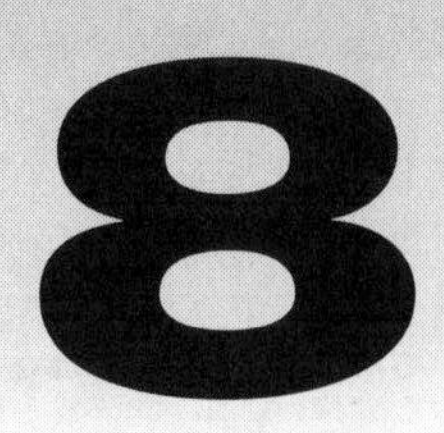

Debugging and Good Design

This chapter is about the reality of programming in an unpredictable world. So far we've made some unsustainable assumptions about Visual Basic programming: you'll never make mistakes in your code, users behave impeccably, you have all the time in the world. Well, it's now time to get out of the playpen and see what we can do to increase our chances of actually getting working programs out in time, in real life.

This chapter covers:

- How to organize your code into small reusable blocks to reduce the chance of errors and increase your efficiency
- How to write maintenance-friendly code (which is easy to change when you come back to it later)
- How to handle events that you didn't really expect at run time without crashing your program
- How to debug programs that don't work

Writing Programs that Work

To write code that works, you first have to have a good plan. Then, you have to write your code in such a way that the errors are minimized and easy to find. Then, you have to be able to find any errors that do occur and remove them, or else be prepared to deal with them at run time.

Designing Safe Programs

The bigger a program becomes, the more likely it is that you will introduce bugs into it. Think about this—if you write a three-line program that takes a number from the user, checks that it really is a number and then displays it on screen, it should be pretty easy to test it. You could even go as far as to tell users that the system is totally bug-free—it's only got three lines of code so that's not too difficult to do.

Now think about this—you have just spent the past 9 hours sitting at a keyboard, typing in roughly 900 lines of code. The code takes a number from the user, checks a database to find a match, loads up some records to do some calculations, multiplies the original number by the number of records you've found, adds in your age in minutes and displays the number on screen whilst playing the Star Spangled Banner! Easy to guarantee no bugs in that little lot? No, not really!

You could test it by running it, over and over and over again. You could hand it to other people to test, who, like you, would run it for days and days and still find no problems. Then, the fateful day comes—you give the system to a paying customer who inadvertently enters a decimal number where everyone else had assumed that whole numbers would be used. Result: the program crashes in a heap and you have one very upset customer on your hands—and no pay check.

So where did we go wrong? If you can guarantee that 3 lines of code will work with no problems, why not 6, 12, 24, 58 or even 900? The reason is something called **cohesion**. The first example has 3 lines of code, and performs one specific function: it checks a number to see if it is OK, displaying it if the check went without a hitch. The second example performs a number of totally different functions: it gets a number, finds some records, does some sums, and plays music.

The first routine has very strong cohesion. It's a very small program consisting of just one routine that performs one, and only one, function. The second example has very weak cohesion. The whole program is dependent on the operation of a single part. Imagine if your whole house was on one electrical circuit, with a single fuse for all the outlets. Every time one outlet blew, the whole place would go down. Instead, each area has its own circuit. When one circuit goes down, not only can the rest of the house carry on, but the repair man only has to check a small number of outlets to find the fault.

To increase your chances of success, it's better to write programs that consist of smaller blocks of code, each of which has strong cohesion. Each small block of your program should do just one thing, and do it well. If the 900-line program had been written so that it consisted of eighteen 50-line routines, it would be much easier to deal with. You could check and debug each of the eighteen routines rather than the one big program!

Visual Basic programs can be broken down into separate modules called **subroutines** and **functions** (which are collectively described as procedures or subprocedures) to achieve this.

Designing Efficient Programs

Using modules to create libraries of useful routines has great benefits in terms of programming efficiency, as well as avoiding errors. Placing code that you use repeatedly into separate modules, or better still, into reusable classes, can ultimately save you hours of typing and design. This code can then operate both in a single project and across all the projects you work on.

If, for example, you have a very data-intensive application that has a lot of fields into which the user has to type information, you may want to verify the input to each field as it's entered. It makes sense to place a routine that verifies this input into a single central routine, rather than rewriting it over and over again in the event handler for each individual control.

Once you've written this input verification routine, you could then attach it to other projects that require input checking, without having to rewrite it.

Planning for the Unpredictable

No matter how well you design and structure your program, things will happen that you didn't expect, or that happen so rarely that you can't consider them a normal event for your program to deal with. As football coaches love to say, 'It's all out there waiting to go wrong'. Users press strange key combinations, disk drives crash for no reason (try putting a disk in—it helps...), networks go down mysteriously. The list of possibilities is endless. The only thing you know for sure is that it's your fault when your program crashes, even if the file-server got hit by a meteorite in midflow.

Therefore, it's a good idea to build in some code that makes an attempt to deal with unforeseen events. Visual Basic provides some help, by giving you the chance to deal with run time errors in your own way, rather than just throwing up its hands immediately and crashing your program.

Making Your Code Work

'It's a bug in the system, sorry......the computers are down, we can't find your records until Monday.....no, no—it's a computer fault, can't be helped, we'll fix it as soon as we can!' Sound familiar? They are all common excuses that everyone comes up against when dealing with companies that use computers. When banks overcharge, they blame computer errors, mail order companies blame the computer when your order goes astray, employers blame payroll systems when excess tax is deducted, or too little is deducted and the tax man finds out.

There are very rarely any true *computer* errors. Computers always do exactly as they are told. If, in an invoicing system, you tell the computer that the total amount your customers should pay is the bill *minus* sales tax, it's not the computer that gets it wrong, it's you! So, how can we cut the bugs (as they are known) out of the applications we write?

The answer to all these questions is that you can't. The more controls you add to your Visual Basic applications, and the more code you write to respond to events, the higher the likelihood is that you have written bugs into your system. You can be sure that these bugs will do their best to remain hidden until:

- You need the program to do something urgently
- You demonstrate the program to someone who may want to buy it
- You let someone else use it

The tricks and tips you'll come across can't guarantee that you'll never send a system out with bugs. Debugging and structured programming aren't safety nets for programmers—they're damage limitation techniques. If you're an employed programmer, then think yourself lucky that you're in one of the few professions where you *can* make mistakes and get away with it. Thankfully, the same isn't true about doctors. Do it too often, though, and your employers will soon start to think again about your pay check!

Write Understandable Code

Ultimately, the best way to reduce bugs in a system is to design it properly. However, this is a book on programming. All programmers, including me, detest writing thousands of flowcharts and reams of text explaining what a system should do, preferring instead to dive straight in and start writing code. So what we'll concentrate on here is how to reduce the bugs, and write **nice** code, rather than how to design the perfect system—there are some excellent books around on system design. For the time being, leave the analysis to the analysts, and the fun to us!

In even the simplest of systems, there are literally hundreds of possible routes your code can take in response to a user doing something, expected or otherwise. To be able to keep that little lot in your head all the time when you're developing is simply not feasible. For this reason, it is an excellent idea, when looking at a programming problem, to see how it can be broken down into smaller, more manageable chunks of code, or even reusable objects.

In Chapter 4, you learned how to create small subprocedures that could be used to perform specific jobs in response to certain conditions.

```
If nChoice = 1 Then
    DoThis
Else
    DoThat
EndIf
```

In this example, **DoThis** and **DoThat** are subprocedures that are called, depending on the value of **nChoice**. This is called **structured programming**, and makes your code easy to follow and control. As we mentioned in Chapter 2, Visual Basic also allows you to make use of OOP (object-oriented programming—similar in many ways to structured programming, but much more powerful). Well, developing your application from an OOP standpoint can literally save you hours at debug time, as you will see by the end of this chapter.

Just to appease any stray C++ programmers, we'll admit that Visual Basic isn't actually a truly OOP language. But it is object-based, and allows us to embrace most of the useful OOP techniques.

Passing Parameters to Subroutines and Functions

Subroutines and functions don't have to accept parameters. A procedure that clears all the entries from a list box doesn't need to be told anything other than *Do it!* Likewise, a function that gets the current date and time returns a value without the need for a parameter. However, subroutines and functions that are at all flexible, will accept a variety of parameters.

For example, in a general procedure that centers a form on the screen, you could define a form object variable and pass it to the procedure:

```
Public Sub CenterForm(frmThisForm As Form)
```

You could then call this procedure from any event code:

```
Sub Form_Load()
   CenterForm Me
End Sub
```

Often, you may need to pass a subprocedure several parameters. For example, you may need to create a procedure that writes some data out to a database. In this case, it could be helpful to pass each element of data that you want written out as a parameter:

```
Public Sub WriteEmployeeData (sEmployeeName as String, nDepartmentID
    ↳as Integer, nAge as Integer)
:
:
End Sub
```

There are two ways in which parameters can be passed to functions and subroutines. The easiest method is the one we've seen in the examples so far: **passing by reference**. The other method is called **passing by value**, and has some benefits in terms of protecting your data, though it is a little more complex.

Passing Parameters By Reference

When you pass by reference, you just declare the parameter in brackets after the subprocedure or function name:

```
Public Sub DisplayEmployee(nEmployeeID As Integer)
```

Here, the **nEmployeeID** parameter is passed by reference. This is the default for all Visual Basic parameters. What it actually means is that if we have code in the subprocedure which changes the parameter, for example **nEmployeeID = 100**, then the original value of the parameter that's passed to **DisplayEmployee** will itself be changed. This can be useful, but it can be a real pain if you forget about it. Let's see what I mean in some real code.

Try It Out - Problems with Passing By Reference

1 Create a new project in Visual Basic and remove the default form that appears by selecting Remove Form1 from the Project menu.

2 Create a new code module and, when the Code window appears, type in this subprocedure:

```
Private Sub SubProc(nNumber as Integer)

    nNumber = 9999

End Sub
```

This sets up a subprocedure called **SubProc** which sets the parameter it receives to the value 9999.

3 Move the cursor to the line following the **End Sub** statement and insert the following **Main()** subprocedure.

```
Public Sub Main()

    Dim nAge As Integer
    nAge = 24
    MsgBox "The age is currently " & nAge
    SubProc nAge
    MsgBox "Age is now " & nAge

End Sub
```

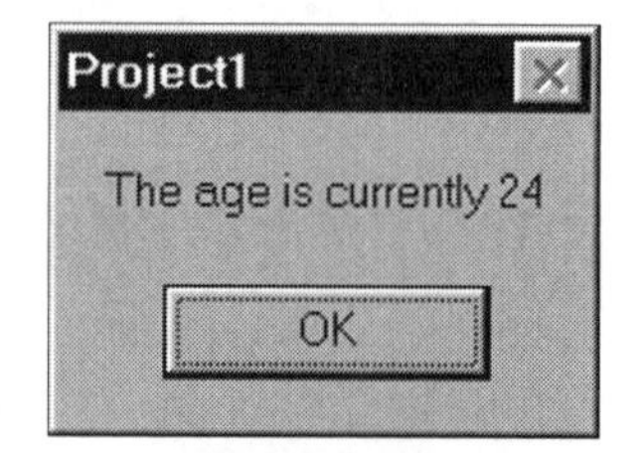

4 When you've typed everything in, run the program. A message box appears, showing you that the current value of the **nAge** variable is **24**.

5 When you click OK in the message box, the next line of code calls the **SubProc** procedure. A message box then appears showing you that **nAge** has been changed to **9999**.

This highlights the problem of passing by reference. The procedure has access to the original variable, so any changes made to the parameter also affect the original variable that was passed in the first place.

Sometimes this can be useful, however. It's a convenient way of getting a function to return more than one value to the code that called it. You specify all the values as parameters, and inside the function you can change any of them.

Try It Out - Passing Variables By Value

Let's change our last example to pass a variable by value, rather than by reference.

1 Find the **SubProc** procedure that you just typed in.

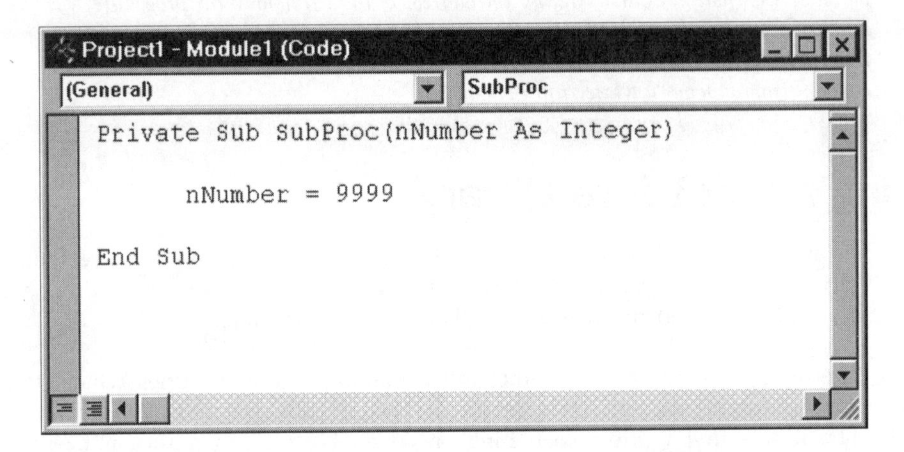
Project1 - Module1 (Code)
(General)
SubProc
Private Sub SubProc(nNumber As Integer)
nNumber = 9999
End Sub

2 Change the **Sub SubProc** line at the top so that it reads like this:

```
Private Sub SubProc(ByVal nNumber as Integer)
```

3 Run the program again.

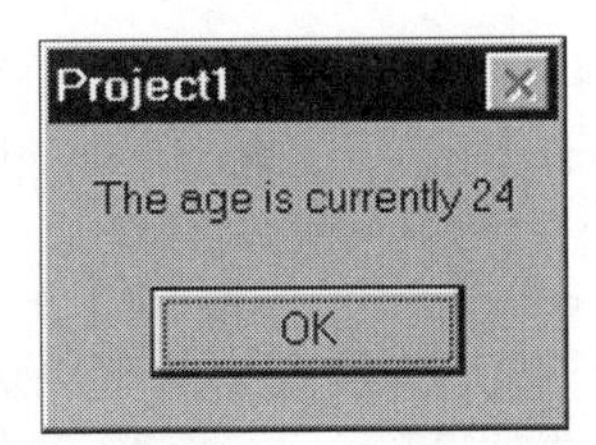
Project1
The age is currently 24
OK

Project1
Age is now 24
OK

The message box now pops up the same value of the **nAge** variable both times. Passing a parameter by value does just that—it passes the value of the parameter, not the original variable itself.

Passing By Value Reduces Bugs

The main reason to use **ByVal** wherever possible, is that it can reduce the likelihood of bugs. It only takes a small lapse in concentration to assign a value to a parameter passed by reference, when in fact you didn't really mean to. This can have a domino effect as the value is passed back to the code that called the subprocedure, or on to other subprocedures and so on.

You will also find the **ByVal** keyword being forced on you when you come to deal with **API calls** later in the book. When you deal with Windows' Application Programming Interface (the API), passing a parameter by value when you meant to pass by reference, or vice versa, can crash your computer—or, more likely, your client's computer.

> *The only drawback with using **ByVal** is that it consumes more resources than passing by reference. Instead of just sending the address of the variable to the procedure, VB has to make a copy of the variable in another area of memory first, then pass the address of this variable. So passing variables by value can slow your code down, and cause it to consume more memory while running.*

Building a Procedure Library

One of the most useful aspects of Visual Basic modules, is that you can use them to create **code libraries**. We have already seen how you can write procedures (including both subroutines and functions) in such a way that they are reusable.

A code library is a collection of modules, all containing useful routines which you can bolt on to new applications as and when required. Theoretically, the code would have been fully tested when it was first written, so bolting on code like this can reduce not only your coding time, but also the potential number of bugs in your system. By placing useful procedures in a separate module, we can add this module to other projects and use these procedures over and over again.

To build up a code library effectively, you need to ask yourself a number of questions whenever you write code in your programs:

- Can you envisage a use for this procedure in other applications?
- Does the code assume anything? For instance, does it rely on global variables, forms or controls with specific names? If it does then change it!
- How can you make the procedure as crashproof as possible? Add error checking, add code to check the parameters, add code to deal with errors or call an error-handling routine from another of your libraries.

The overriding principle of Visual Basic is that you should try to build your applications out of components where possible, and this doesn't just mean fancy custom controls. You can build up your own useful library of components as a reusable class module, from just a few forms and modules.

Handling Errors at Run Time

Applications, and more importantly users, are never perfect. In any large program you write, there'll always be logic errors which can crash the system, or events like users pressing certain key combinations, that you had never imagined could happen.

Thankfully, Visual Basic incorporates very powerful means for you to trap errors. There are literally hundreds of possible errors that Visual Basic can catch and deal with. Describing them all in detail here would take a long time, but what we'll do is look at the generic methods involved in trapping and dealing with these errors.

One important nuance of meaning to bear in mind is that an error in the Visual Basic sense doesn't quite have the negativity normally associated with the word. Errors are the system's way of signaling to you that a set of events has taken place that is unforeseen in your code. Thanks to the informative way that Visual Basic tells you about what's going on, an error is more a request for a response than an invitation to find a new career.

The Err Object

When your code comes across something that doesn't fit in with its expectations, it can't operate properly. Programs don't think for themselves—they only do what you tell them to do. In order to deal with the situation created by an error, we need to know what kind of error it was. Some errors can be handled by your program directly, by writing a procedure that puts things right, while some are just too bad to recover from. We need to narrow the field down from just any old error.

There is a built-in object in Visual Basic called **`Err`** which has numerous properties that let you find out the error number, the error message, where the error came from, and so on. These properties form the starting point for error handling routines. Once we have identified the type of error, we can choose whether or not to deal with it.

The properties of the error handler that we're interested in are:

Property	Description
`Number`	Default value. Lots of numbers corresponding to different errors.
`Description`	Short description of the error. More to tell users about it than for use in your code.
`Source`	Identifies the name of the object that generated the error, again more for information.

It's clear that, from a code point of view, what's important is the number of the error. Let's look now at how you trap an error, and then see what to do with it.

The On Error Command

If you were to type in this next bit of code, it would result in the error message Divide by zero being displayed.

The **On Error** command lets you tell Visual Basic where to go when an error occurs. Each subroutine or function in which you want to trap errors needs to have an **On Error** statement in it. The syntax for **On Error** is pretty straightforward:

On Error Goto <*label*>

Where <*label*> indicates the line to jump to.

To tell VB that we're using a label to identify a point in our code, we add a colon (**:**) to the end of the label. For example, take a look at this procedure:

```
Public Sub Division()
    On Error Goto ErrorHandler
    Print 12 / 0
    Exit Sub

ErrorHandler:
    MsgBox Str(Err.Number) & ": " & Err.Description, , "Error"

End Sub
```

The code in this little error handler simply displays details of the error in a message box. The first line, **On Error Goto ErrorHandler**, tells Visual Basic that if an error occurs, it should **Goto** the label **ErrorHandler**, which is defined a little later in the procedure. Take a look at the code from **ErrorHandler:** onwards. It creates a message box containing the error number and description. Both are properties of the **Err** object, and are set automatically by Visual Basic when an error occurs. After the message box, the subroutine ends.

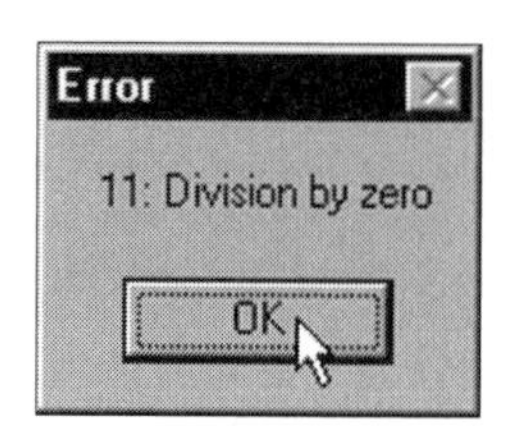

Did you notice the **Exit Sub** above the **ErrorHandler:** label as well? Normally Visual Basic trots through the code in a subprocedure or function line by line, starting at the top and working its way down. Obviously, you wouldn't want the error handling code to run if no errors were met, so **Exit Sub** is used here to get out of the subroutine without displaying a pointless message box.

Once the procedure finishes, and execution passes back to the code that called it, error handling is automatically turned off. So, you need to use an **On Error** statement in all the procedures where you explicitly want to handle an error yourself.

If there is *no* error handler in the procedure, VB will exit from it and use the error handling code in the procedure or code that called it. This continues until it finds a procedure that does include an **On Error** statement, or until there are no more procedures to examine, in which case it uses its own internal error handling code and stops your program executing.

Using `On Error Goto 0` *in the code effectively turns off the error handler. This could be used if you wanted to handle errors yourself in part of a procedure, then let VB handle any others later on. However, you should really handle all errors yourself.*

Using Error Handling Effectively

Errors are an essential part of the communication between your program and the machine. Used well they can be very powerful. Let's consider an example where error handling is fundamental to the success of a program.

Let's say you're creating a module that you want to keep as generic as possible so that you can use it again. The module searches through a form and prints out the current values of all the controls that have a **Text** property, in the Immediate Window. This is only an example. Once you've captured the text, you can do anything you like with it.

We don't want to pass the names of every control on the form to the module as that would be a real pain. Instead, we'll pass the form as an object variable and then cycle through the controls collection looking for the ones with a **Text** property.

Error handling comes into play to cope with the fact that not all objects have a **Text** property. When you get an error, you can examine its number in the **Err** object. If this is **438** (Object does not support this property or method) you can just carry on with the next control on the form. If any other error occurs, the routine ends. This way, you can use a single loop to check the whole form.

We can use an **If...Then** statement to examine the error number, and to tell VB to carry on and ignore the error we use the **Resume Next** statement in our error handler. The code to do this would be something like:

```
Public Sub SearchText(frmHostForm As Form)

    On Error GoTo NoPropertyError

    Dim objControl As Control
    Dim nResponse As Integer

    For Each objControl In frmHostForm.Controls
        Debug.Print objControl.Text
    Next

Exit Sub

NoPropertyError:
    If Err.Number = 438 Then Resume Next

End Sub
```

If you add this code to your project, all you have to do to call it is to write **SearchText**, followed by the name of the form it applies to. If it's the current form, then **SearchText Me** is fine.

Adding Error Handling to Your Apps

There are several other properties of the **Err** object, but really they are more than a little beyond the scope of a beginner's guide. However, if you plan to ship an application you have written, then there are a number of considerations you need to take into account about the error handling:

- First of all, errors nearly always occur when you least want them to, no matter how much you test the app first. The golden rule to follow is that if you're writing code for an event which uses controls and properties in any small way, add an error handler. It's a good idea to spend a little time writing a generic error handling routine,which you can call from any error handler anywhere in your program—this could handle specific errors that you think the app might throw up, and deal with the rest using some generic code.
- You must deal with any errors that occur while the program is running. Even a message box appearing before the application is allowed to continue is better than the standard Visual Basic way of displaying the error message, then crashing out.
- If you're dealing with databases, write some code to make sure that any transactions you have running are rolled back in the event of an error. If you're dealing with the API, then the same applies—write some code to release any API resources you have allocated, or you will end up with a nasty memory leak. More on this in Chapter 17.
- Never underestimate the user, and more than this, never underestimate the damage a single fatal error can do to your reputation and the confidence the users have in your application.

Debugging - Kill All Known Bugs Dead!

Let's lay our cards on the table. Programming any computer with any language can be a real pain. Sure, when things go well, everything's rosy. You type the code in, design your forms, run the program and everything works first time. Usually, though, the reality is somewhat different—I'm beginning to sound a little like the merchant of doom, I know.

A more likely scenario is that you start to type the code in and Visual Basic keeps beeping at you, and flashing up annoying message boxes telling you that you've missed a bracket or misspelled a Visual Basic keyword.

Visual Basic Debugging Tools

One thing which has always stood BASIC in good stead in the programming community, is the ease with which developers can pull their programs apart. Since BASIC is predominantly an interpreted system, the code you write is never handed over to the complete mercy of the machine to do with as it will; instead it is passed to another program, an interpreter, which is responsible for using your program to instruct the computer what to do. It is thus extremely common to find debugging facilities built directly into this interpreter—it already knows what state your program is in at any point in time, so who better to ask the questions we need answered?

If BASIC in general has always been kind to programmers with its debugging possibilities, then Visual Basic 5 is a veritable Fairy Godmother. VB not only assists you in tracking what is happening in the application while it's running, but also helps you debug as you write, through its automatic syntax checker and the various auto-fill wizards which help you remember keywords and syntax as you type the code. You have probably already seen these facilities in action in the exercises we have covered in the book so far. Just to fill in the blanks, though, and answer any still unanswered questions, let's take a look at how VB actually helps you write code.

Helping You Write Code

Select Options... from the Tools menu. You've seen the dialog that appears before, and it should be quite familiar to you since it allows you to customize much of the way Visual Basic works to suit your own personal tastes.

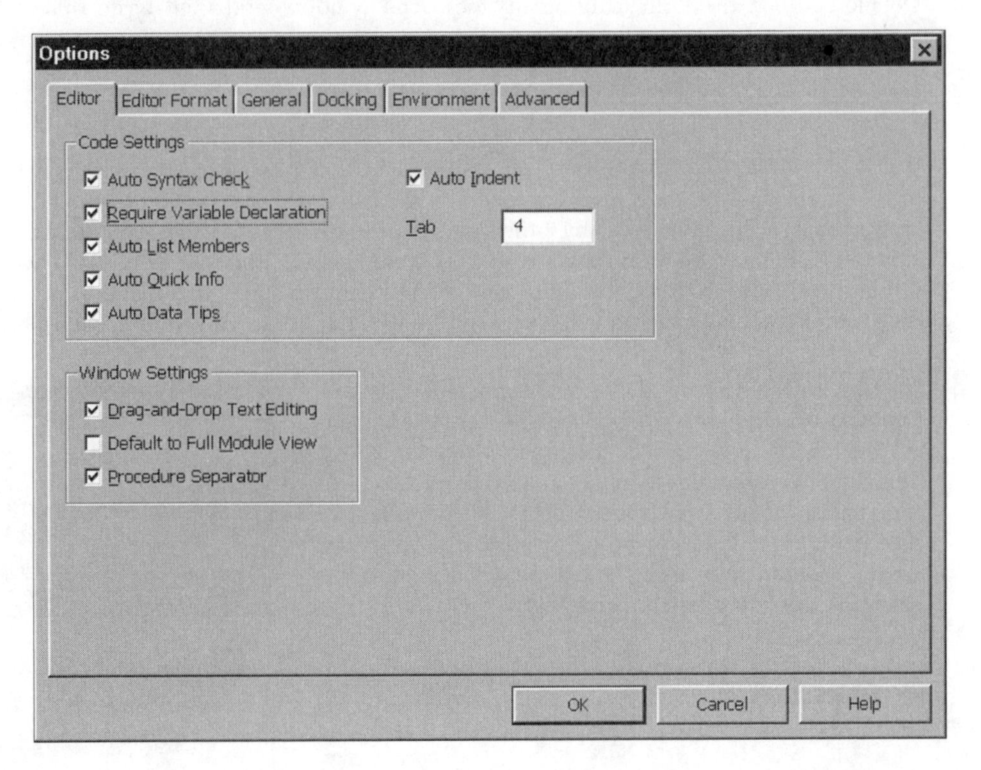

The items that we're most interested in this time round are the ones to the left inside the Code Settings box. Most C++ developers have a set of options in their compiler that allow them to change just how picky their compiler is, and thus how many errors it will throw out depending on their coding style when they go to compile their code. In many ways, the options you see here are the Visual Basic equivalent, allowing you to customize just how picky Visual Basic is at design time.

If you turn on all the options you may find that in the early part of your learning VB, the development environment is frustratingly picky. Trust me though—if you have all these things enabled while you learn VB then you will pick up some very good habits that will stand you in good stead later on, when you do know a little bit more about what you're doing. Let's take a look at all of these in detail now, and see exactly what they mean.

Try It Out - The Auto Syntax Check

The Auto Syntax Check is the most basic setting, and really is a godsend when you're learning Visual Basic. It highlights errors that might otherwise stop your program compiling, but it does this at the same time as you actually write the code. Let's take a look at what a difference it makes.

1 Select Options... from the Tools menu, turn off the Auto Syntax Check option, and then close the dialog down.

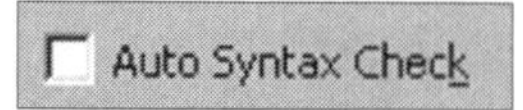

2 Double click on the form to bring up the Code window, and then write this code into a form's **Load** event.

```
Form1.Left=
```

With Auto Syntax Checking turned off, as soon as you press the *Enter* key, VB will highlight the line of code in red to show you that there is a problem with it. However, it won't give you any other information about what the error is, and will even let you carry on writing code. If you were deep in thought while you were writing the code, it would be quite easy to miss the mistake you made—only to have the compiler give you a rude message when you hit *F5* to run your masterpiece.

3 Go back to the Options dialog and turn Auto Syntax Checking on, and then go back to the code. As soon as you hit the *Enter* key in the Code window, VB immediately complains—giving you a lot more information about what the problem is, and taking the cursor right back to the buggy line of code you wrote. You can then fix it, and that will be one less error for the compiler to throw out.

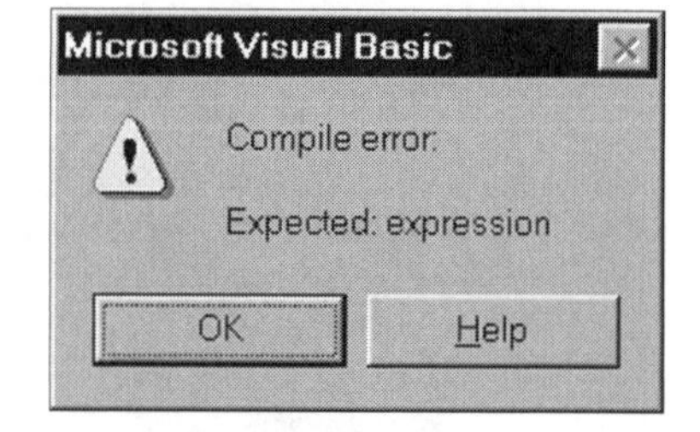

In this case the error was simple; VB was expecting us to put something after the = sign, because **Form1.Left=** doesn't really mean anything to VB without a value to the right of the = sign.

Try It Out - Keeping Track of Variables

The next item on the Options dialog, Require Variable Declaration, we met back in Chapter 5 when we looked at variables. Aside from helping you keep track of your variables by forcing you to declare them before using them, this option can save some really nasty errors from occurring. Take a look at this.

1 First select Options... from the Tools menu, turn off the Require Variable Declaration option, and close the Options dialog.

2 Open up a new project, double click on the form when it appears, and enter the following code into the form's **Load** event, making sure that you type it correctly (i.e. type **MyValve** for the last part of the **MsgBox** line).

```
Private Sub Form_Load()

    MyValue = InputBox("Please enter your name")
    MsgBox "Hi there, " & MyValve

End Sub
```

3 Now run the program and type in a name:

4 It doesn't quite work, and in a large program with several hundred lines of code it could be very hard to see why. What it's supposed to do is ask you to enter your name, and then when you have done so it's supposed to say 'Hi there, ' followed by the name you entered. But as you can see something is wrong. Press OK and stop the program running.

5 The problem is that the first line of code uses the **InputBox** function in Visual Basic to prompt the user to enter their name, and stores it in the **MyValue** variable. However, the message box statement that follows displays the contents of **MyValve**, spelt with **v** instead of a **u**. To emulate the Require Variable Declaration option, simply go back and add the line Option Explicit (which is basically all this option does) under the General Declarations section.

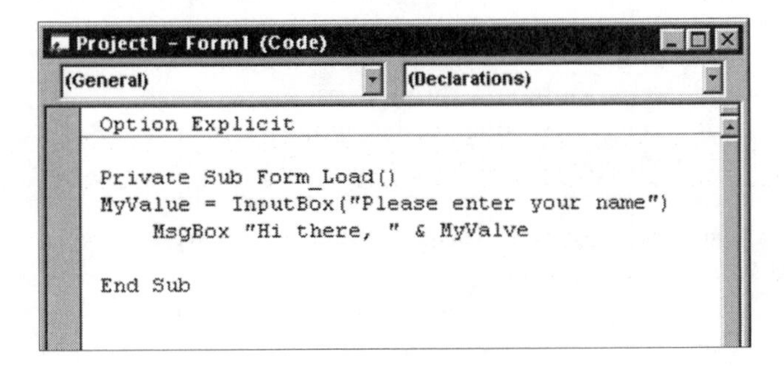

6 Now go back and run the program. At compile time, the system throws out:

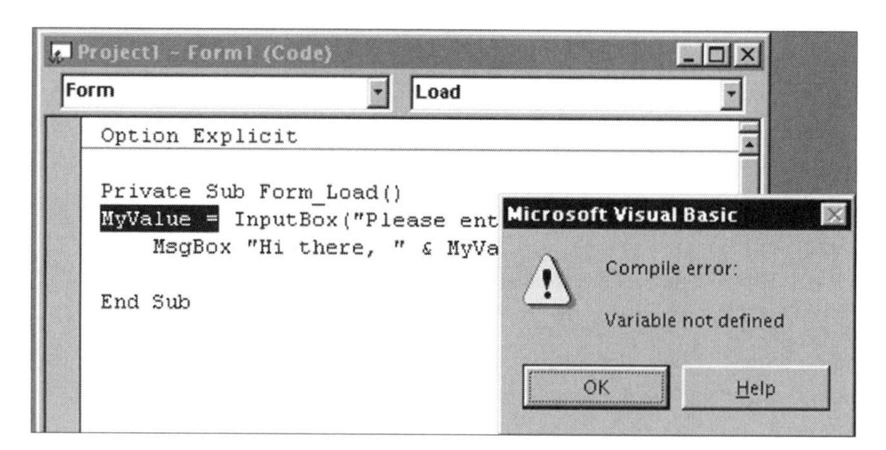

It does this first for the **MyValue** variable (spelt with an **u**) since we haven't **Dim**'med it anywhere, and then (if you do put in a **Dim** statement) for the **MyValve** variable for the same reason. In older versions of BASIC, but thankfully not Visual Basic, that particular problem was really quite common, and would frequently stop inexperienced programmers in their tracks for hours. Although it forces you to program a little more rigidly, turn Require Variable Declaration on—it's worth the extra effort.

> *There's actually a bit of a limitation in Visual Basic when using this option, which I mentioned back in Chapter 4. When you turn on the* **Require Variable Declaration** *option, what actually happens is that Visual Basic inserts the words* **Option Explicit** *at the top of any* new *form, module or class that you create. However, it doesn't put it at the top of any* existing *forms in your project. In those forms, you'll have to insert* **Option Explicit** *by hand yourself.*

Providing Code Hints

A new feature in Visual Basic 5 is its ability to provide you with hints, as you write your code. There are hundreds of properties, methods, functions, and objects in Visual Basic, and I would guess that there are probably millions of different ways of combining them all. That's a lot of information to hold in your head.

In previous versions of VB, what we were left with was a development environment that really wasn't much of a help when it came to writing the actual code, and which in turn encouraged errors and bugs by not helping us. Programmers were forced to spend hours thumbing through page after page in the manuals, or frequently resorting to the online help in order to refresh their memories of how command X worked, or for the spelling of parameter Y. The options shown here almost totally eliminate that, and help to reduce compiler errors when the time comes to run the application.

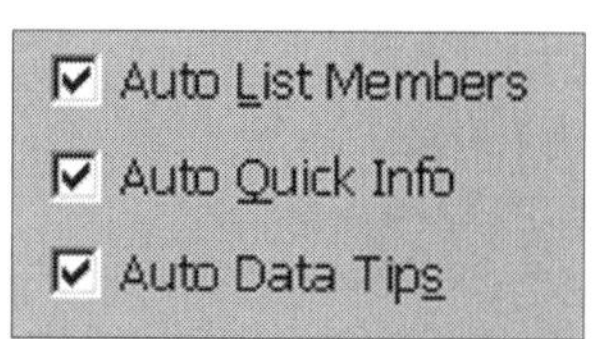

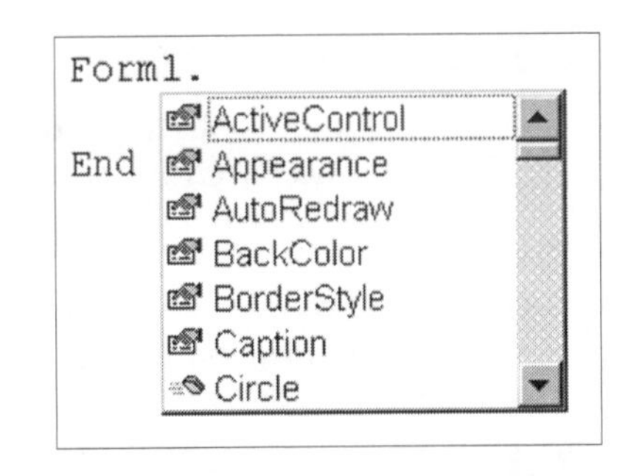

Despite the somewhat cryptic names, they really are all quite easy to understand. Enabling Auto List Members means that whenever you deal with an object or a class in your code, VB will pop up a list box beneath the line of code that you're working on to show you the methods and properties that belong to that object or class, like this.

More often than not you'll use this list just to refresh your memory. However, if you prefer to save yourself all the typing you can, you can simply click on a member in the list or use the arrow keys to select an option and then press *Tab* or *Space* to let Visual Basic fill in your code for you.

> *If you press Return, you'll be moved to a new line. In general, this isn't what you want. It's better to get used to just selecting the property or method with the arrow keys (or by typing enough characters to uniquely identify it) then typing a space instead. Think of it as though VB had typed the property or method for you, and you were just adding the space before the next keyword.*

The Auto Quick Info option is similar to the Auto List Members option but instead will display a list showing you the syntax for any method you use, the same syntax summary in fact (but without all the preamble) that you would get by looking up the method or function in online help.

```
MsgBox
MsgBox(Prompt, [Buttons As VbMsgBoxStyle = vbOKOnly], [Title], [HelpFile], [Context]) As
VbMsgBoxResult
End Sub
```

I have to admit that initially I found this to be a real pain, and very offputting since it can obscure other code in the module. However, once you get used to it, there's no denying that this really is one of the most powerful aids in VB5.

It's worth noting here that if you do decide to disable these features, you can still fall back on them in times of great stress by simply pressing *Ctrl-I* for Quick Info and *Ctrl-J* for Auto List Members.

The final item, Auto Data Tips, does the same as the other two, but is used when you declare variables, showing you a list of matching data types that can be used in the declaration.

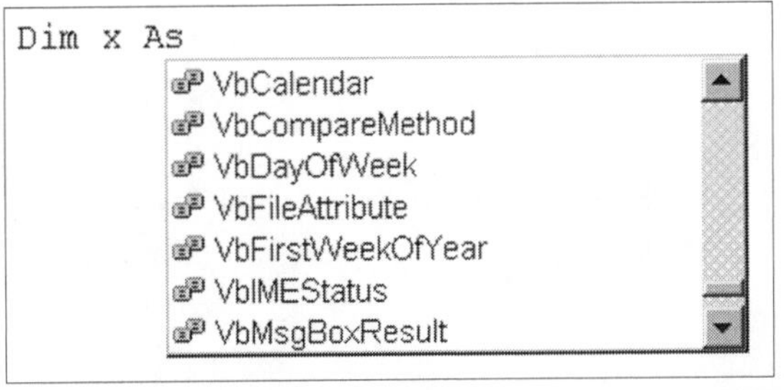

Debugging at Run Time

As well as the all the cool toys that Visual Basic provides you with at design time to reduce the risk of errors, it also provides a plethora of tools to figure out just what went wrong when you finally do get the program running.

These tools work when your application is paused, or in **Break** mode. Before we go any further, it's worth explaining how to put the program into this state. There are actually several ways you can do this.

The first, and probably the method you will use initially, is automatically done for you. If your code has a serious problem, then it will put itself into break mode, and usually cause an error message to be shown.

To move to break mode yourself, you can either select Break from the Run menu, or click the break button on the standard toolbar. Alternatively, you can press the key combination *Ctrl-Break*.

> *It's also possible to put the* **`Stop`** *statement into your code, which causes VB to enter break mode at that point. However, as you'll see later, there are better ways of stopping our code at a required position.*

When the program is in break state, you'll see that the Run button and Stop button are enabled, and the Break button is disabled, since the application is already in the break mode.

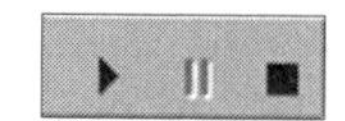

With the program in this state, we can start to really explore what's happening in our code.

The Immediate Window

The Immediate Window is where most of your work in break mode will take place, providing you with a means to execute commands ad hoc, examine and change variable contents, and generally mess about with everything that's going on in your application at the point in time where it stopped.

Looks pretty harmless really doesn't it? Well, let's look at the power underlying that simple interface then.

Try It Out - Using the Immediate Window

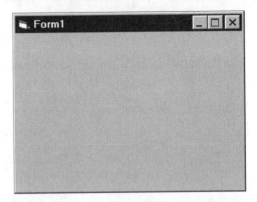

1 Create a new, Standard EXE application, and without adding any code, run it. After a short pause while the program compiles, your application's main form will appear.

2 To put the program in break mode, so that we can use the Immediate Window, either select Break from the Run menu, click on the Break icon on the toolbar, or press *Ctrl-Break*. Almost immediately there should be a flurry of disk activity before the Immediate Window pops into view. (Incidentally, if your environment is set up a little differently from mine and the immediate window doesn't appear on its own, you can also bring it into view by selecting it from the View menu.)

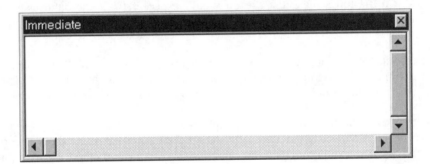

3 At this stage, the program is very much like a patient lying on a surgeon's table. The Immediate Window is your equivalent of a scalpel, allowing you to slice into the unconscious program, move things around, and generally mess about peeking and poking to see what happens. For example, type this into the window and press *Enter*:

```
Print "Hi there!"
```

What you can do in the Immediate Window isn't limited to running simple methods like **Print**, though. You can also update any properties which may be available to your program code at the point it stopped, as well as any variables. Let's have a look at the form's properties to see this in action.

4 At the moment, your application's form should be sitting quietly in the background, behind the Immediate Window. Let's maximize it. Type this into the immediate window and press *Enter*:

```
Form1.Windowstate = vbMaximized
```

As soon as you hit the *Enter* key on your keyboard, your application's form grows to take up the full screen, just as you would expect it to. If the Immediate Window vanishes from view at this point, you can bring it back quite easily by pressing *Ctrl-G*.

The Immediate Window lets you type in commands, just as you might into the Code window at design time. The obvious difference, though, is that in the Immediate Window these commands are run straight away, instantly letting you see the results on screen.

In the Immediate Window you can call simple methods (such as **Print**), as well as any function or subroutine in your own application. Being able to print the value of variables or properties is very useful, and you can also use a shorthand method of a question mark (**?**) instead of **Print**:

```
? sMyValue
```

is the same as:

```
Print sMyValue
```

However, you can only enter one line of code to be executed into the window. For example, you might want to list all the values in an array called **aThis** so that you can examine them—a lot easier than typing a **Print** command for each one. To do this you use a **For...Next** loop, but you have to use the 'colon' syntax to get it all on one line:

```
For nLoop = 1 to 100 : Print aThis(nLoop) : Next
```

Visual Basic allows you to put more than one statement on a line, by separating them with colons. However, it's considered bad practice in normal code because it not only makes your code hard to read, but can also result in single-word commands or statements being treated as line labels if they are at the start of a multistatement line.

Despite this limitation though, its pretty easy to picture just how powerful and useful the Immediate Window can be as a debugging tool; you'll find yourself relying on it time and time again.

Watches

Although you can use the **Print** command in the Immediate Window to display the contents of a variable or a property, the Watch window provides a great deal more versatility.

Basically, at run time, the Watch window displays the contents of any variable, property or expression that you care to feed into it, and can also be used to stop your program dead in its tracks when a specific condition appears. For example, you may want to put your application into break mode after the 50th pass through a loop. Let's take a look.

Try It Out – Using the Watch Window

1 Create a new Standard EXE project, as usual. When the default form appears, double click it to bring up the code editor and select the form's **Paint** event.

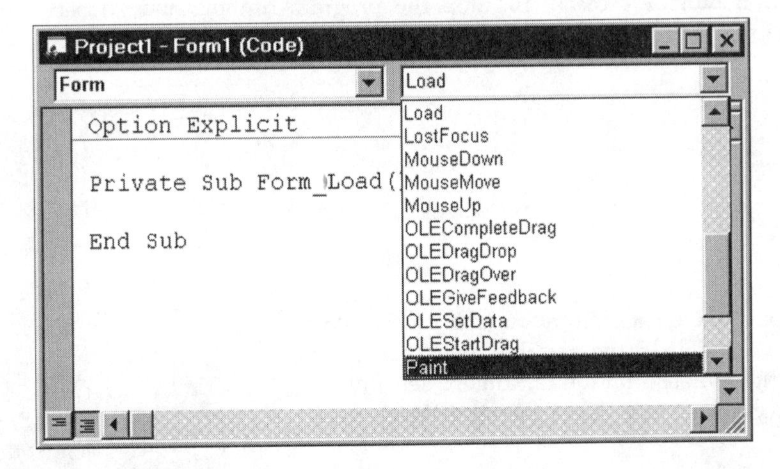

2 What we're going to do here is add a small loop that prints some text on to the form every time Windows decides that the form needs painting (i.e. when it first appears, when it is covered then uncovered, when it is resized, and so on). Add the following code to the event handler:

```
Private Sub Form_Paint()

    Dim nCounter As Integer
```

```
    For nCounter = 1 To 25
        Print nCounter
    Next

End Sub
```

3 Now run the program and you'll see a list of numbers appearing on the form, like this.

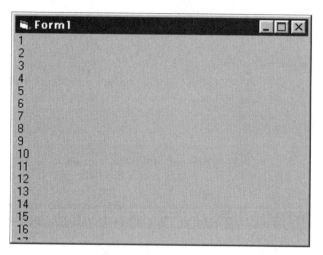

4 Using a Watch though, we can stop the program at a predetermined point, for example when **nCounter** exceeds **10**. Stop the program running and go back to the Code window.

5 If you double click on **nCounter** on the **For** line, to highlight the variable, and then press the right mouse button, a context sensitive menu will appear. Select the Add Watch item.

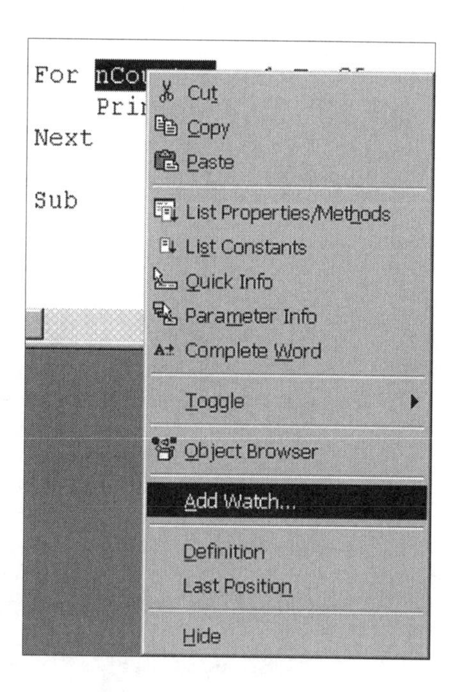

6 The Watch dialog appears, asking you for information about exactly what it is you wish to do. The two most important areas of this dialog are the Expression text box at the top, and the Watch Type frame at the bottom. By changing the expression and the watch type in this dialog, you can tell VB that you want to just keep an eye on a variable's contents in break mode, that you want to stop a program running when a variable hits a certain value, or that you want to stop the program running every time the variable changes.

If we were just going to watch the expression, perhaps to keep an eye on a variable's contents at run time, then we would just leave the expression box as it is—showing the variable's name. However, we want to stop the program running as soon as the counter hits `10`, i.e. the tenth pass through the loop, so change the Expression: text box so that it looks like this:

Add Watch
Expression:
nCounter = 10
OK
Cancel
Help
Context
Procedure: Form_Paint
Module: Form1
Project: Project1
Watch Type
Watch Expression
Break When Value Is True
Break When Value Changes

This means that the expression we're looking for is '`Counter is equal to 10`'.

7 When the counter hits `10`, we want to put the program in break mode (in a real world application one reason for this might be so that we could use the Immediate Window again to start exploring the state of the program). To do this, just change the Watch Type to Break When Value is True, and then click on the OK button.

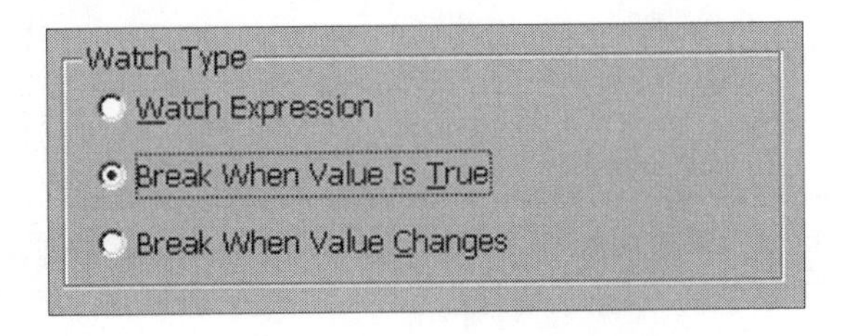

8 As soon as you do this, the Watch dialog will vanish, and the Watches window will appear showing you a list of all the watches currently set up.

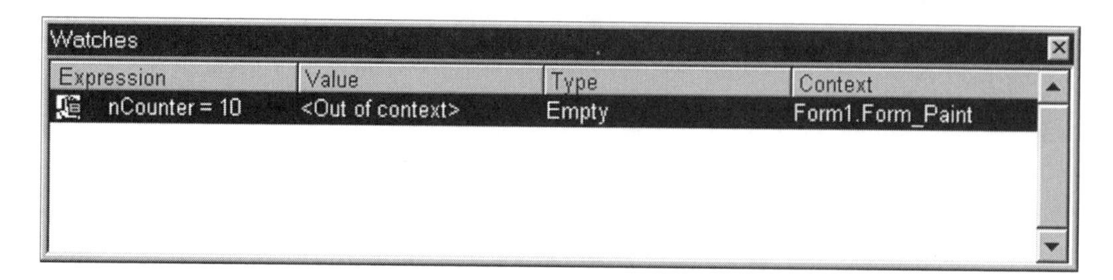

The Watches window shows you the expression itself, the current value of the expression, the type of data in the expression, and the context in which the expression will become active. Notice how, at the moment, the Value and Type are set to <Out of context> and Empty respectively. Because the program isn't running at the moment, the expression is out of context—it basically means it's not valid since it's out of scope. Because it's not valid and doesn't really exist at this point, it's also deemed to be empty.

9 Now run the program.

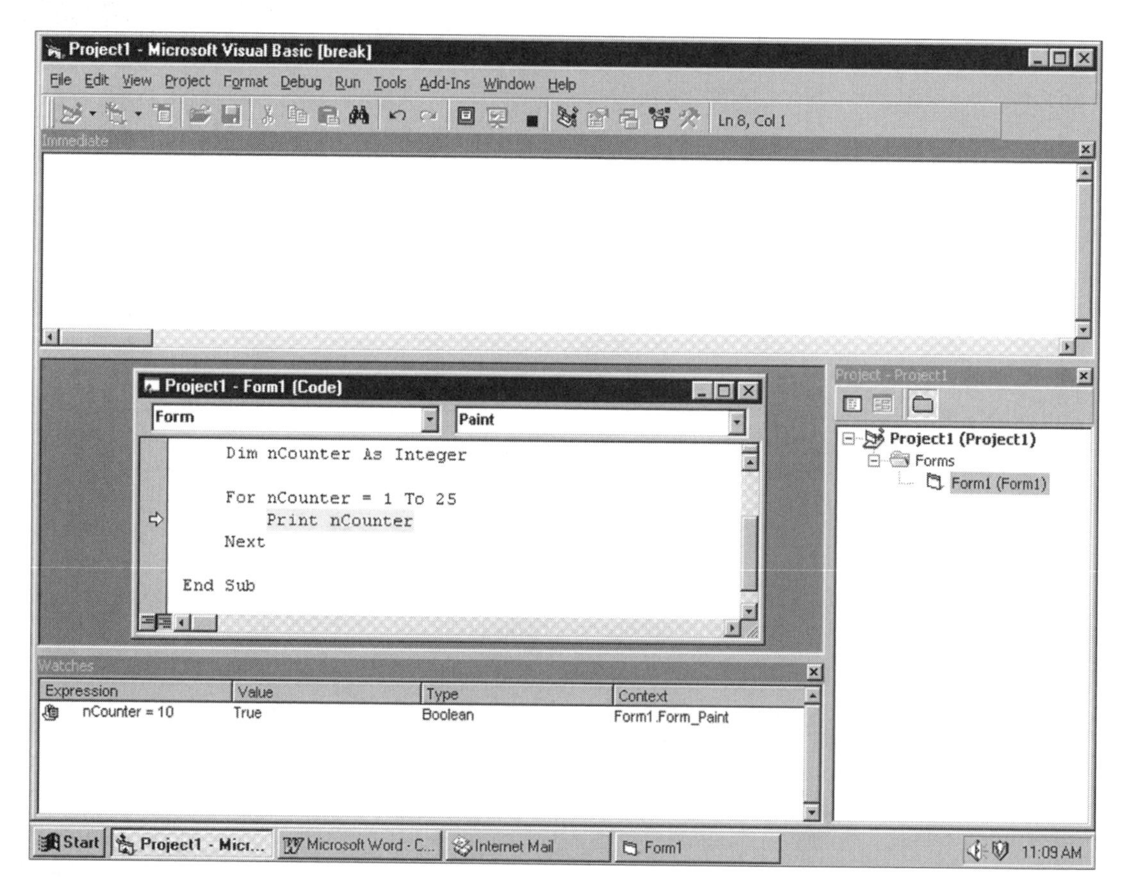

The Watches window will activate properly once the program comes to a halt (on the tenth pass through the loop). Notice how the value of the expression is now shown as **True**. How can that be? Surely the value of the expression is **10**, since we're looking at the counter variable **nCounter**? Well, in a word, no.

When you set up the watch you told Visual Basic that the expression you wanted to watch was **nCounter = 10**, which is a comparison, a Boolean (true/false) comparison in fact. When **nCounter** is equal to **10** then the expression is considered to be **True**. At any other time the expression is considered to be **False**. That's exactly what the Watches window thinks as well, which is why it set the Type to Boolean, and the Value to **True**.

Did you notice the other things that happened when the program stopped this time? Take a look at the Code window, and you'll see a highlight on the next line of code that will execute, in this case the **Print** statement. That's quite common; Visual Basic will always highlight the next line of code to be run, when a program goes into break mode. You should also have noticed that the Immediate Window popped up too, just in case you wanted to try some things in there to get a little more information about the state of the program.

Leave the program in this broken state for a moment because this is an ideal state to look at the **Step** commands that VB supplies.

Try It Out – Stepping Through Your Code

There are a number of things you can do with the program in this broken state; you can either stop the program totally, let it continue running normally, or, if you like, you can take control and step through each line of code in the program in turn, nice and slow. This can be a great way to get a feel for what a section of code is doing, and is a very useful technique when debugging.

1 Assuming that you followed the previous example, the program should currently be in break mode, with the highlight on the **Print** line in our print loop.

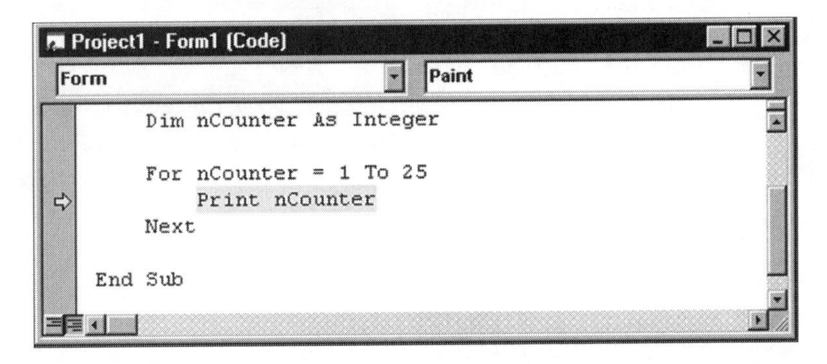

2 Let's get rid of the watch statement that we had in there previously. To do this, just right click on the statement icon in the watch window and select Delete Watch from the pop-up menu that appears.

3 In its place, we're going to add in a simple watch on the **`nCounter`** variable, so that as we step through the program code line by line, we can see exactly what's going on.

Just as before, double click on the **`nCounter`** expression in the code window and then right click to bring up the pop-up menu that you use to add a new watch. The Add Watch dialog will appear, just as before.

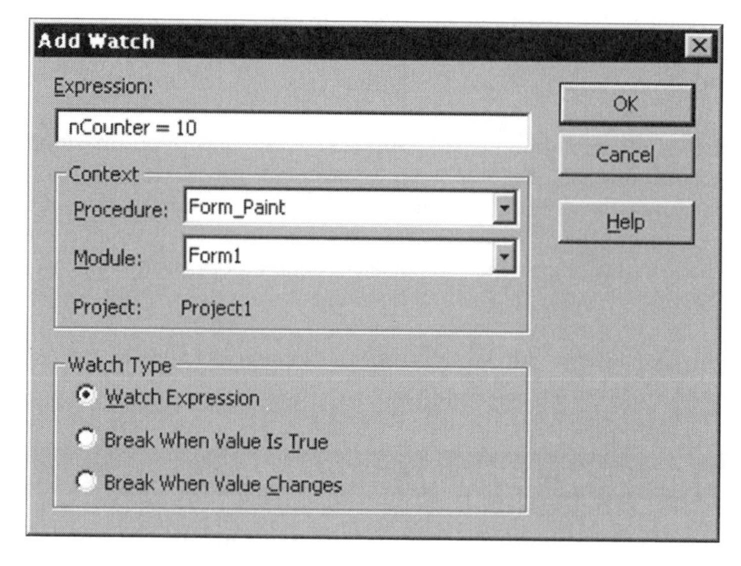

4 This time, leave the dialog exactly as it is—all we want to do is watch the **`nCounter`** variable as we step through the code. Just click the OK button. The Watches window will update to show you the new watch expression, this time showing you that we're looking at an integer variable called **`nCounter`** that has a current value of **`10`**.

5 Now drop down the View menu for a second and click on Toolbars, then select Debug from the submenu that appears.

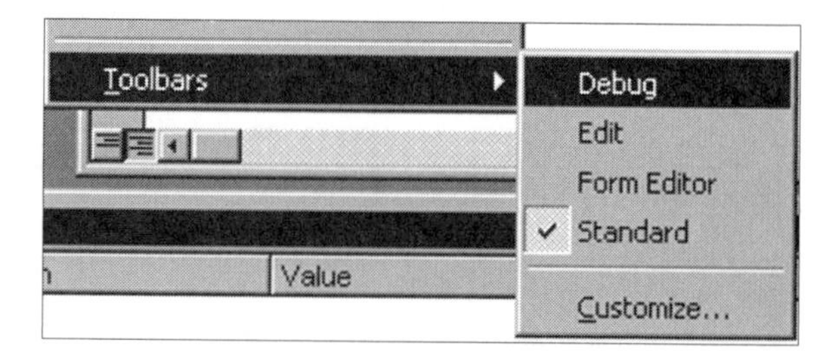

The Debug toolbar, complete with all the code stepping icons, will appear. This is what we'll use to step through our code.

6 Click on the Step Into icon.

In the code window you'll see the highlight move to the next line of code—the **`Next`** statement.

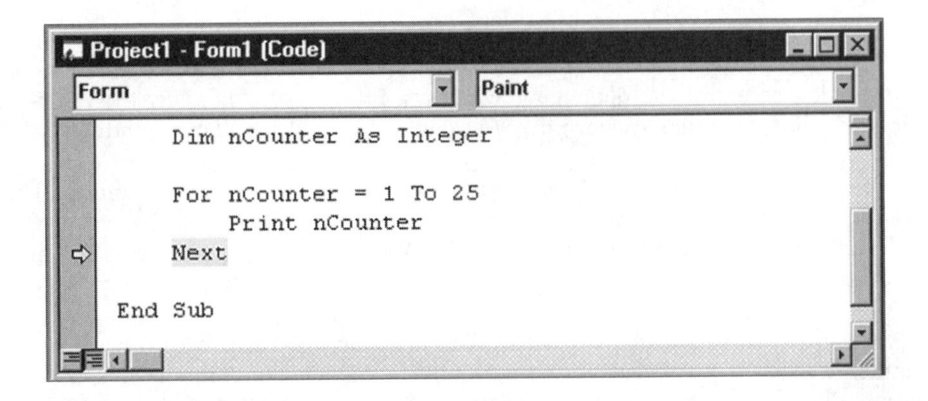

Click again and it will move back to the **Print** statement, i.e. the next statement that is to be executed. If you now look at the Watches window, you'll see it has updated the value of **nCounter**. Keep clicking to see how the code changes the value of **nCounter** as the program is executed.

Using the Variable Value Tooltips

Visual Basic 5 has also added another useful way of getting information about the values of variables while your program is in break mode. If you select a variable name in the Code window, while that variable is in context, a **Tooltip** appears showing its value. For example, here we've stopped the code while the **Form_Load** event is taking place, and filling a list box with values.

Just double-click the name of the variable to select it, then wait....

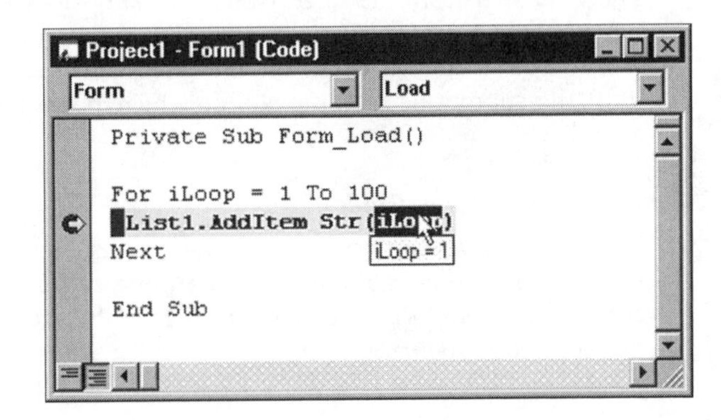

The Step Options

The debug toolbar provides you with the options you need to step through your code.

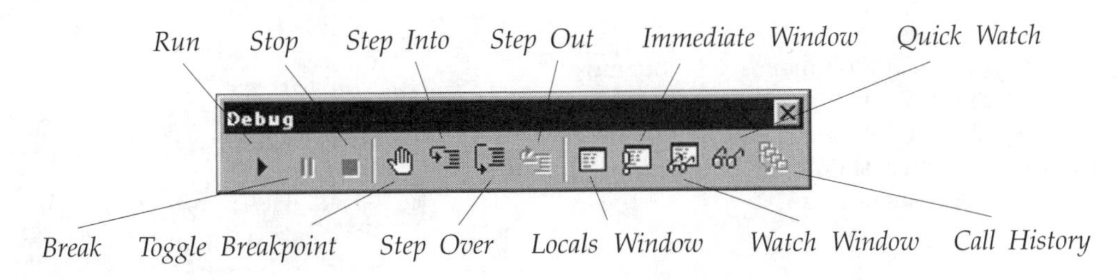

The first three icons on the toolbar should be quite familiar. They are the same icons that you find on the Standard toolbar—which run, break and stop a program. The far right-hand group of icons control the debugging windows, bringing up the Locals window (more on this later), the Immediate Window, the Watches and the Quick Watch windows.

The icons we're most interested in, though, are the ones in the center group. The first icon lets you toggle breakpoints in your code—lines on which the program will drop out of run mode and into break mode no matter what. We look at breakpoints in a lot more detail in a moment.

The next three icons are the step icons. The first one, the Step Into icon, is the most commonly used. It just executes the currently highlighted line and moves the highlight to the next line to be executed. You used this just now. Incidentally, you could also just press *F8* to accomplish the same thing.

The next icon across is the Step Over icon. Imagine a scenario where instead of a simple loop like the one here, you have a loop running a collection of subroutines and functions that you've written yourself. If you were using the Step Into method, then each time you clicked the icon, the Code window would change to show the code for the highlighted subroutine, and then proceed to step you through that. After a while this can become more than a little tedious, especially if you're already happy that the subroutine in question is fully debugged and working. In that case you would click on the Step Over icon, or press *Shift-F8* to just run the subroutine in one go without having to step through each line of code.

The final step icon, the Step Out icon really does the opposite of Step Into. If, as in the hypothetical example above, you had stepped into a subroutine where you really didn't want to be, then you could hit the Step Out button, and the code would run as normal until the subroutine is complete, at which point the program would be left in break mode again.

Controlling the Step Order

Before we move on, just click on the Debug menu for a second because there are three more related commands there, which aren't represented by icons on the Debug toolbar.

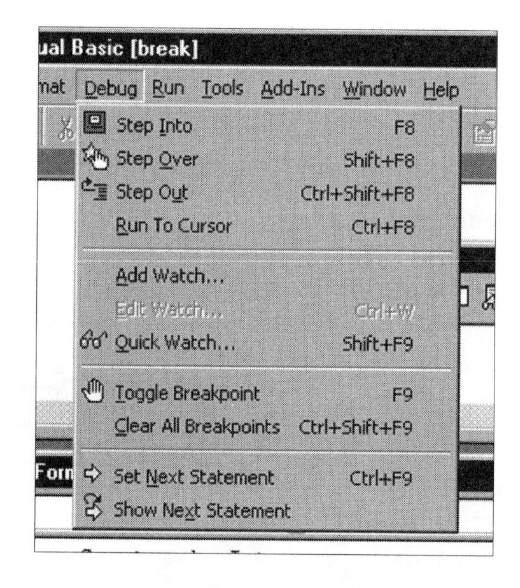

Although the step commands let you move through the code in a slow motion version of how it would run at full speed, they offer no real control over what should be run next, or for how long the code should run.

The Run to Cursor, Set Next Statement and Show Next Statement items on the Debug menu get around these limitations. They are all very easy to use as well.

As the name suggests, Run To Cursor tells VB that you want it to run the program up to the line where the cursor is, and then go back into break mode. To use it you just click on a line and either select this option on the Debug menu, or press *Ctrl-F8*.

There are times, though, particularly when dealing with larger programs, when it's easy to get lost in the Code window—and find yourself quite a distance away from the current line of code. Selecting Show Next Statement gets around this, instantly changing the code window to show you the next line of code that will execute.

There are also times where something may have gone wrong, and the next line of code that VB is going to execute isn't necessarily the line of code that you want it to execute. In these instances, all that's required is for you to click on the line that you want to run next, and then either press *Ctrl-F9*, or select the Set Next Statement option from the Debug menu. The highlight will instantly move to the line containing the text cursor, allowing you to run the program, or just step through it, from that point.

It's hard to get a feel for all these features in a small program like the one we're working with, but they all represent a powerful set of tools for getting to grips with larger programs. If you like, try loading up one of the sample programs that come with Visual Basic itself, and use the debugging commands we've already covered to get a feel for how the code is put together.

Breakpoints

When we looked at watches a short while back, one of the things we covered were watches that would put a program into break mode when a certain expression was met. We used:

```
nCounter = 10
```

There are times, though, where you need to stop a program at a specified point in time—whatever happens, and regardless of everything else that has already happened in the code. An example I found recently was in developing a game. There was a bug in the code that only occurred when the last guy alive died, and the code to display the level scores appeared. The most realistic way to look at this code was to put a **breakpoint** in that code, and then play the game.

Breakpoints stop a program no matter what, and so this meant that after the game had been playing a while, and the end of the level was reached, the breakpoint was triggered and we could then walk through the code and take a look at what went wrong.

Breakpoints are, as with most of the other debugging tools in Visual Basic, very easy to use. Just click on a line of code and either select Toggle Breakpoint from the Debug menu, click on the Breakpoint icon on the debug toolbar, press *F9*, or simply click in the gray bar to the left of the line of code. The result is that the line of code you're looking at changes color to show that a breakpoint has been set:

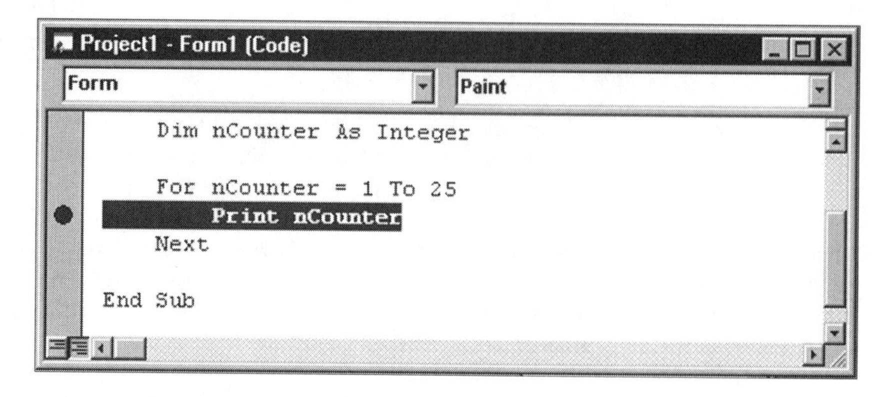

Whenever that line of code is hit at run time now, the program will drop down into break mode allowing you the chance to either pull it apart with the Immediate Window, or to add watches, single step the code, and so on.

Get used to breakpoints—they can be a godsend.

The Locals Window

Wouldn't it be great if there was a way to get a big picture view of all the variables in a routine, and what their values are, without having to go to all the trouble of setting up breakpoints and watches? Well, thankfully, in Visual Basic 5 there is, and it's called the Locals window.

Try It Out - Using the Locals Window

1 Start up a new project in Visual Basic and write in this code for the form's **Paint** event:

```
Private Sub Form_Paint()

    Dim nCounter As Integer
    Dim nTotal As Long

    For nCounter = 1 To 25
        nTotal = nTotal + nCounter
    Next

    Print "The total is " & nTotal

End Sub
```

2 Then set up a breakpoint on the **Print** line, and run the program—it just calculates a running total in a loop, but when it's done the breakpoint will cause the program to stop.

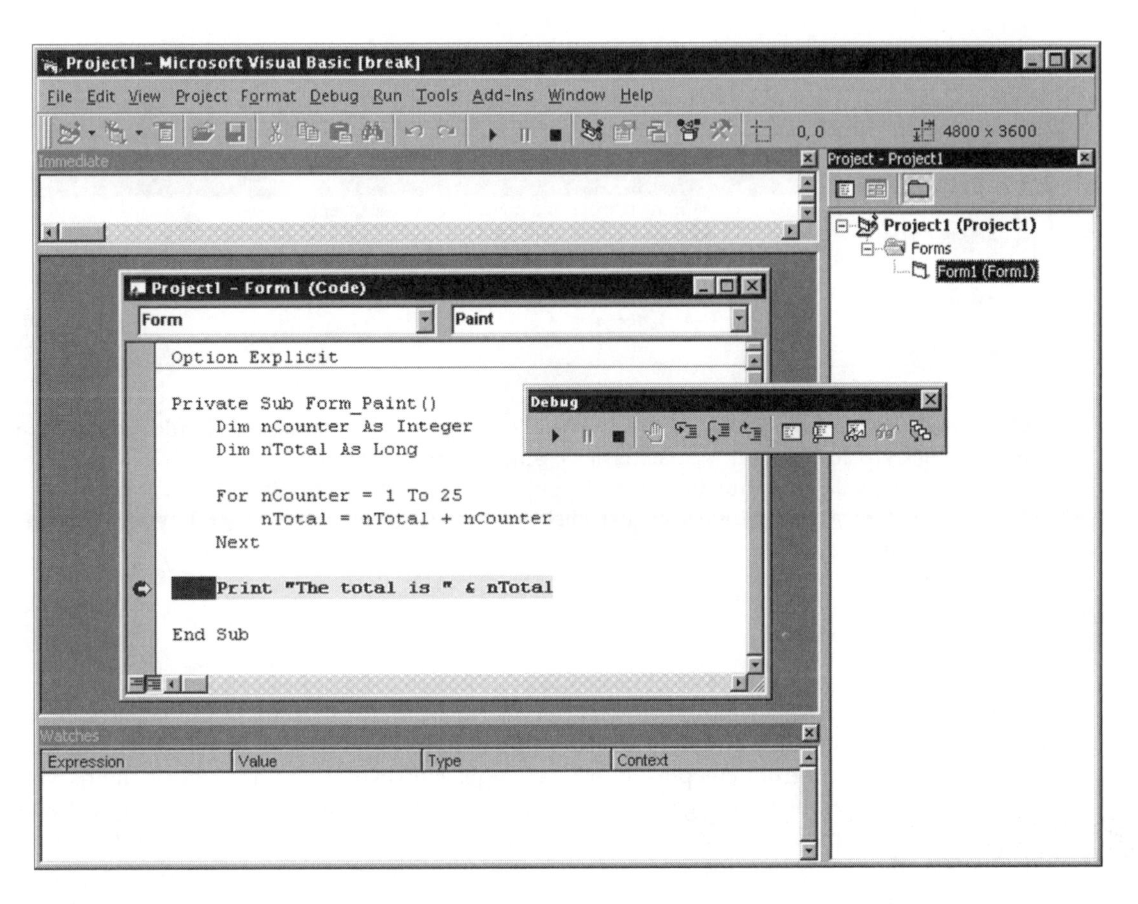

3 Now click on the Locals Window icon on the Debug toolbar, or select Locals Window from the View menu. The Locals Window will appear, showing you all the variables that are local to the code where the program stopped.

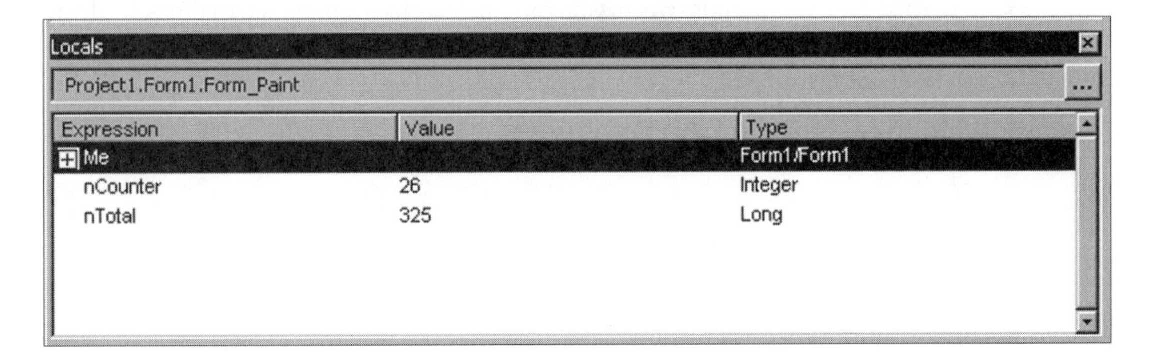

Not only is this a lot easier than dealing with a lot of watches, but it also enables you to instantly see any local objects, such as the **Me** object at the top of the window, as well as the variables. You can also click on the + sign next to **Me** (which refers to the currently active form or object), and see all its properties and their settings.

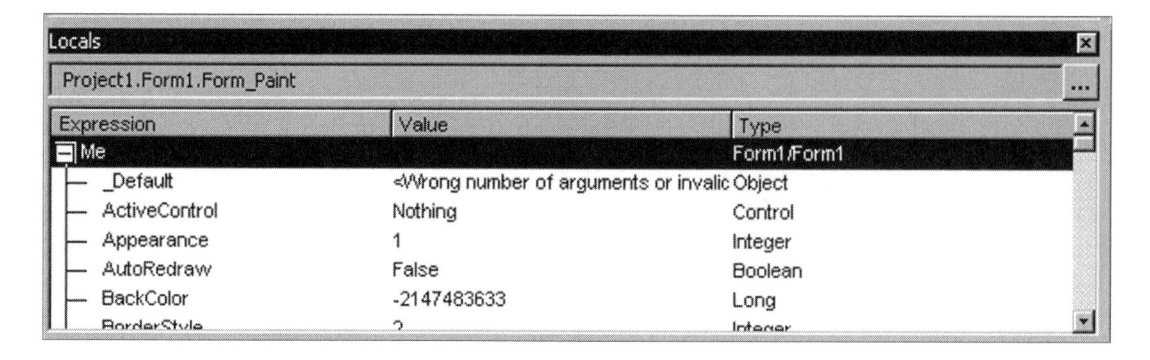

You can even change the value of any writeable properties or variables, should you wish to. This is a big step forward in Visual Basic 5, since in previous versions the only way to change property values at run time was to pop up the Immediate Window and type in some code to do it. Now, though, we can just click on the value in question, and type in the new one—it's as simple as that.

Summary

In this chapter I've tried to introduce some of the tools that can increase the chances of you ending up with a working program. There's no single solution to the age-old programming problem of bugs and errors creeping into your code. However, there are lots of things you can do that, together, help you get there in the end. Throughout the rest of this book, and through your own programming, you will get totally accustomed to, and to a certain extent reliant upon, the debugging tools and error handling facilities in Visual Basic.

The steps to producing programs that work are, in summary:

- Break your programs into parts that have a single purpose
- Use tried and tested code when you can, and build a library of routines to do that
- Put error trapping code into your program to allow it to survive in real world environments
- Be prepared to debug your code and make full use of the tools that Visual Basic provides

Why Not Try...

1. Long before debug windows and watch expressions, programmers used this technique to see what was going on behind the scenes of their program. Create an application with a form, two command buttons and a two labels. In the `Click` event of `Command1`, use a loop to count from 1 to 1000, and display the counter as the caption for `Label1`. In the `Click` event of `Command2`, use a loop to count backwards from 1000 to 1, and display the counter as the caption for label2. *Hint:* Be sure to include `DoEvents` in the loop, so that the label displays a running total of the loop.

2. Use a watch expression to view the loop variable for `Command1`.

3. Set a watch expression that pauses the program when `Command2`'s loop counter reaches a value of 383.

4. Use the immediate window and `Debug.Print` to display the value of `Command1`'s loop counter.

5. Add a text box to the form. Use the text box to display the value of `Command2`'s loop counter. *Hint:* Remove the watch expression for the `Counter` variable before trying this.

asic Visual Basic Visual Ba
al Basic Visual Basic Visual
Basic Visual Basic Visual Ba
ual Basic Vi
Basic Visu
ual Basic V
l Basic Vis
sual Basic Visual Basic
al Basic Visual Basic Visua
Visual Basic Visual Basic Visu
l Basic Visual Ba
l Basic Visual
ic Visual Basi
Basic Visual B
ic Visual Basi
l Basic Visual
ual Basic Visual Basic Visual Ba
Visual Basic Visual Basic Visu
sual Basic Visual Basic Visu
Visual Basic Visual Ba

Working With Menus

Menus are an integral part of any Windows application. Visual Basic makes the process of creating and modifying menus a breeze when compared to old-style Windows programming. However, there's still a big difference between a good and a bad menu structure, as any frustrated Windows user will tell you.

In this chapter you will learn all about:

- What a good Windows menu should look like
- How to create simple menus using the menu editor
- Adding options to drop-down menus
- Using shortcut and access keys
- Cascading menus
- Creating dynamic menus
- How to add code to menu events

You Already Know Menus

If you've used PCs for any length of time, then you should be familiar with what a menu is. In this world of graphical user interfaces, point and click, icons and highly intuitive mouse-driven programs, you still can't beat a good, text-based list of options, that opens up the power and features of your application to your users.

A Great Windows Menu

This book was written using Word which, in many ways is an archetypal Windows application. You just need to look at how the Microsoft application programmers have implemented this excellent product to learn a lot about creating well-crafted Windows applications.

Consider the Word menu bar:

Each word you see on the menu represents a group of functions. For example, click on the File option and a list of **menu items** appears. These relate to things you can do with files in a *virtual* sense!

In this chapter we'll explore the two types of menu that Visual Basic provides: **drop-down menus** and **pop-up menus**. We'll find out how to create them, control them, and make use of them in our applications. There is one control that all Windows applications seem to have and that's the menu bar. Ignore it at your peril, but use it well and your users will love you forever!

Drop-Down Menus

The standard type of menu (and the easiest to develop) is the drop-down menu. In its simplest form, you pick some categories for your program functions, such as file handling, editing and program options, and place these category names onto a menu bar. Then, all you need to do is add functions to each category that may be 'clicked on' as menu items.

Let's look what you have to do to achieve an end product like this:

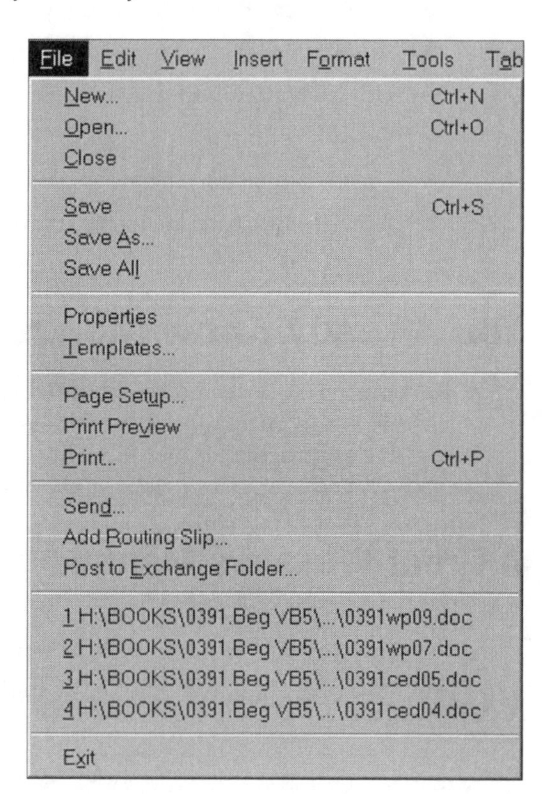

Don't panic! We're going to work through each stage step by step.

How Drop-Down Menus Work

If you're a programmer who has come to Visual Basic from some other language, you may be a little daunted at the prospect of having to provide such menus in your programs. Questions like 'How do I know if the mouse is over a menu heading?' or 'How do I place a menu list over the form and redraw the form when the menu goes?' are probably making you break out in a cold sweat already. Worry not—Visual Basic (or more to the point Windows) does it all for you.

Menus, just like command buttons or list boxes, are controls. Once you've set up the menu control, you only have to worry about handling the events that each menu item can trigger—in the same way as if you were using a command button. Windows automatically takes care of drawing the menu, redrawing the covered parts of the form when the menu vanishes, displaying and positioning submenus, and so on. In fact, menus are one of the easiest controls you'll come across in Visual Basic; the most time-consuming part is typing all the text that forms the menus themselves.

Creating Menus Using Menu Editor

Unlike other controls, the menu control isn't found in the standard Windows toolbox. Instead, Microsoft (in their wisdom) chose to place it as an icon on the main Visual Basic toolbar.

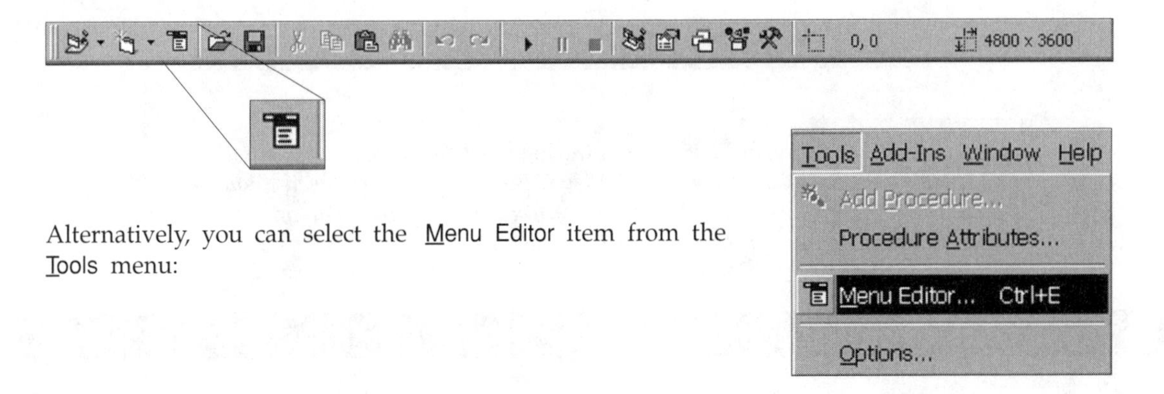

Alternatively, you can select the Menu Editor item from the Tools menu:

The Visual Basic Menu Editor

Setting up a menu is done via a fairly complex dialog box called the **menu editor**. If you have a form visible, click the menu icon and you'll be launched into the menu editor.

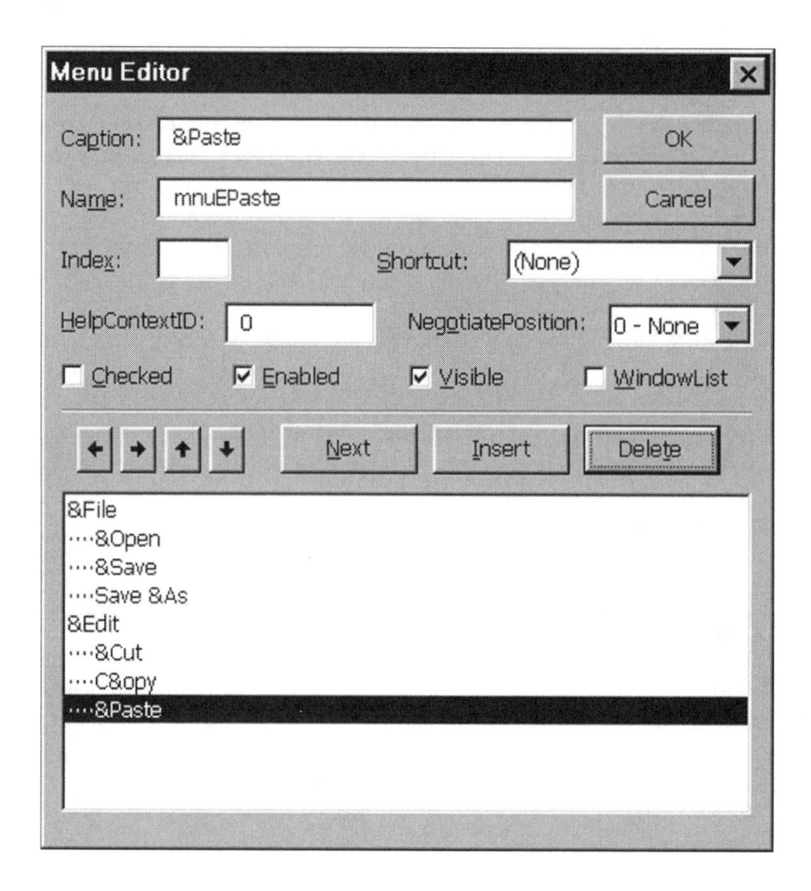

> *If you don't have a form visible, then the menu editor icon is actually disabled, so there's no way that either you or Visual Basic can get confused about what's actually going on in the development environment. Visual Basic adds the menu you create to the form that is currently selected.*

Try It Out - Creating a Simple Menu

Most Windows applications have a File menu that allows your users to open and save data, exit the application, and so on. Actually creating the menu with the Visual Basic menu editor is a simple task:

1. Start up a new, Standard EXE project in Visual Basic and make sure that the form is visible.

2. Click on the menu editor icon on the Visual Basic toolbar. 

3 When the menu editor dialog appears, enter &File in the Caption property, and mnuFile as the Name property.

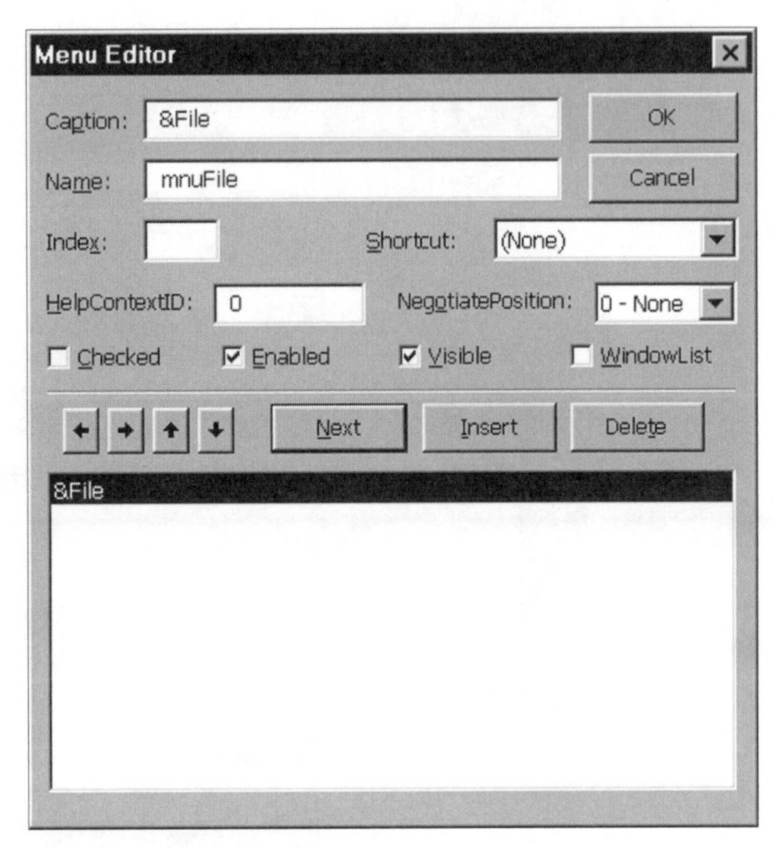

As with any other control's caption, putting & before a letter in the caption makes that letter a hot key for that menu item. You can use any letter in the word, not just the first one. Going back to the File example, you can usually select a ***File*** *menu by pressing* Alt *and* F *together. The user knows this because what they actually see on screen is the word* ***File****, with the F underlined. To set this up in the caption is to simply say that this item's caption is* ***&File****.*

4 Now click Next or press *Enter*. Visual Basic will store the menu item in the list area at the bottom of the dialog and move the highlight down to the next line.

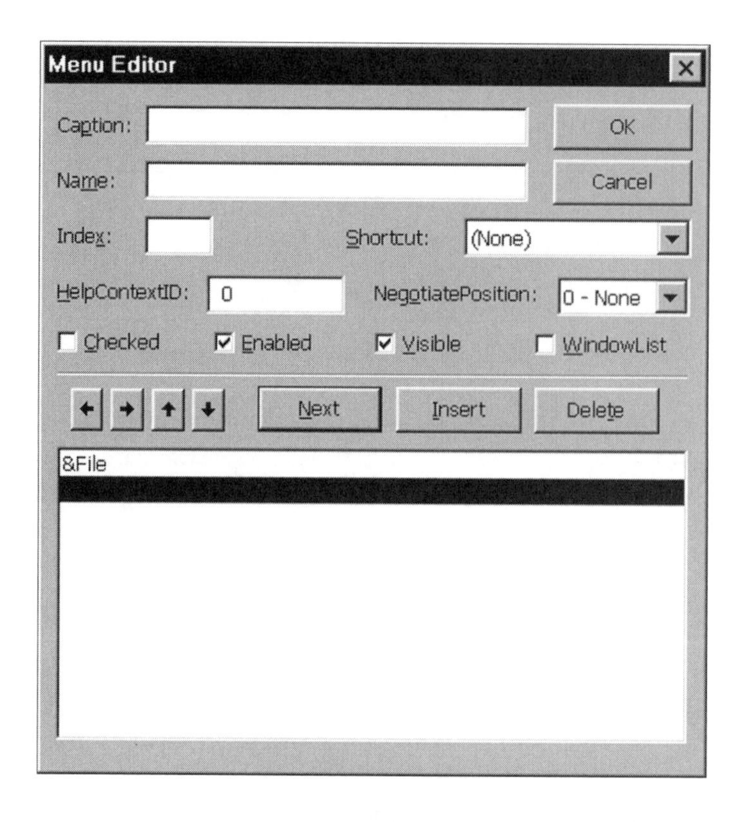

5 Use the same process to enter the Open and Save As menu items. First enter &Open for the Caption, mnuOpen as the Name. Then enter Save &As (note the space!) as the Caption, and finally mnuSaveAs as the Name property. The Name and Caption properties are the bare minimum you can specify when creating a menu. We'll look at the other optional properties in a moment.

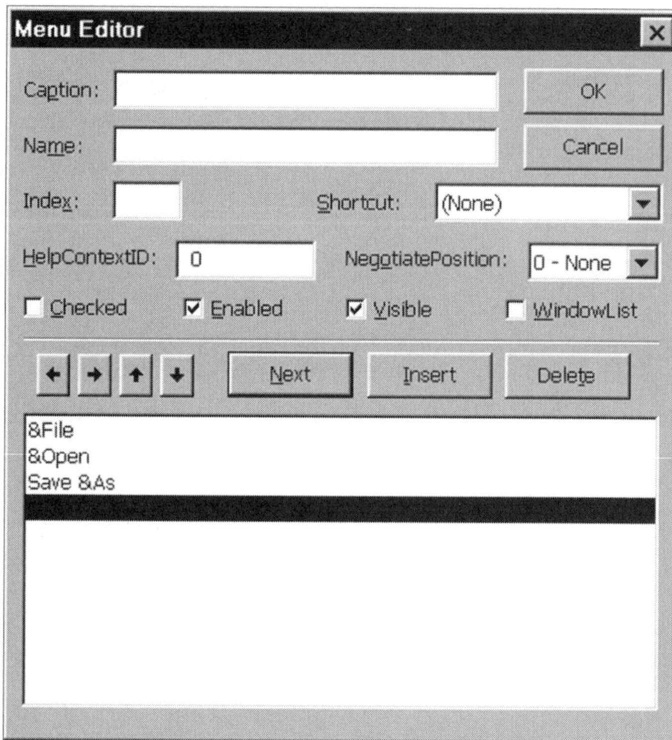

6 If you now hit the OK button, Visual Basic checks the dialog to make sure you don't have any errors in the properties. When it's satisfied that everything's OK, it will create your new menu structure on the visible form, in this case Form1.

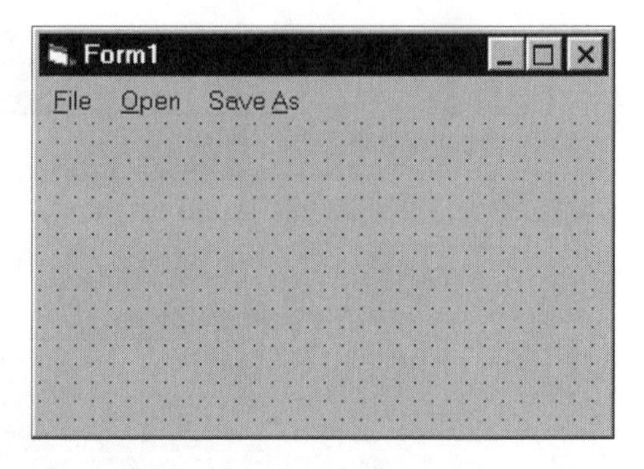

Well done, you've just created your first Visual Basic menu!

> *If you try to press **OK** without adding an item **Name**, you will have created a blank menu item and Visual Basic will respond with an error message: **Menu control must have a name.***

Try It Out - Creating a Drop-Down Menu

OK, let's admit it. The menu we've just created isn't exactly a classic piece of Windows design. Ideally the Open and Save As options shouldn't actually be visible at this point. Instead they should be drop-down items that become visible when you click on the word File.

Let's fix it by creating a proper drop-down list of options from a single menu header.

1 Click on the menu editor icon again to reload the menu dialog and display the list of menu items you've created. Click on the &Open menu item and then on the right arrow in the small toolbar

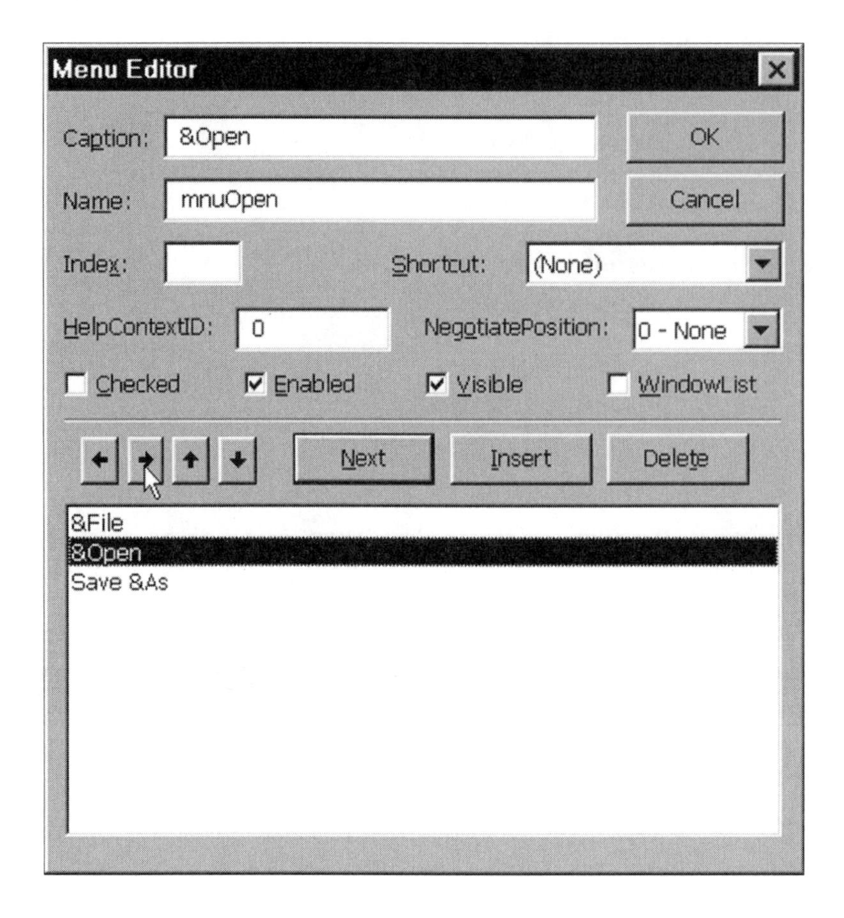

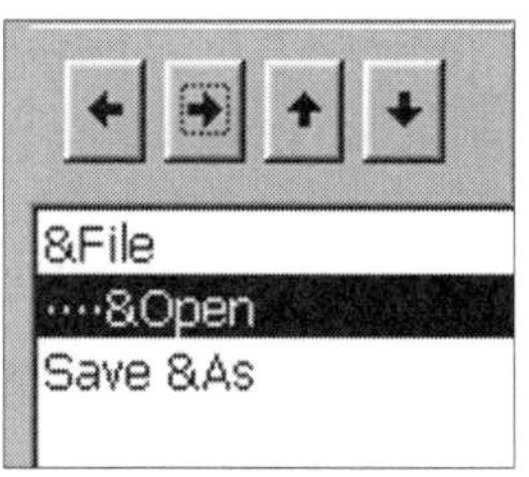

2 The &Open option will shift to the right. This indicates that it's now an option from the &File option.

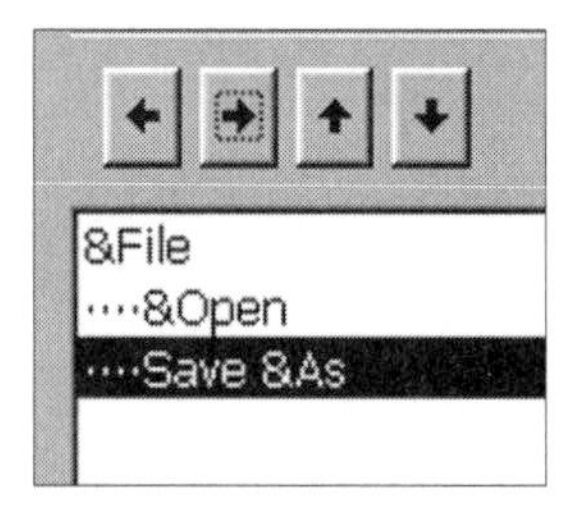

3 Do the same for the Save &As item.

4 To view your finished menu structure, click OK.

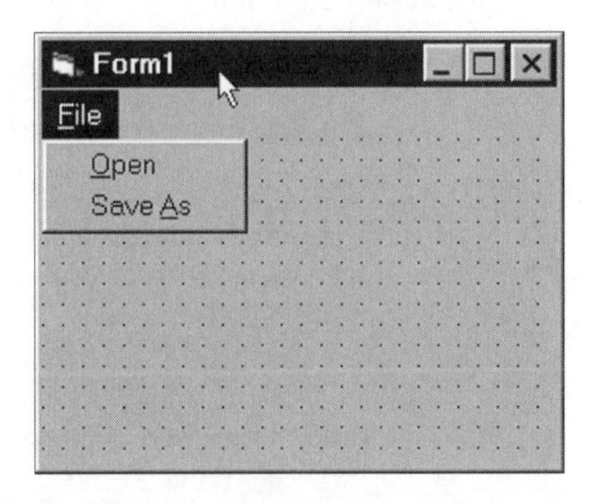

5 The form will now only show one menu item on its menu bar—the &File option. Click once on this heading to see the menu underneath it.

The process of aligning the menu items to create the right structure is called ***outlining****.*

Try It Out - Editing Your Menu Structure

Of course, when you come to write your own applications, it's rare to find all parts of the development process whiz by as smoothly as following a Try It Out section. It's easy to miss menu items off or get them in the wrong order. Thankfully, Visual Basic's menu editor lets you go back and make changes.

1 Click on the menu editor icon again. The menu edit form appears, showing the menu we just created.

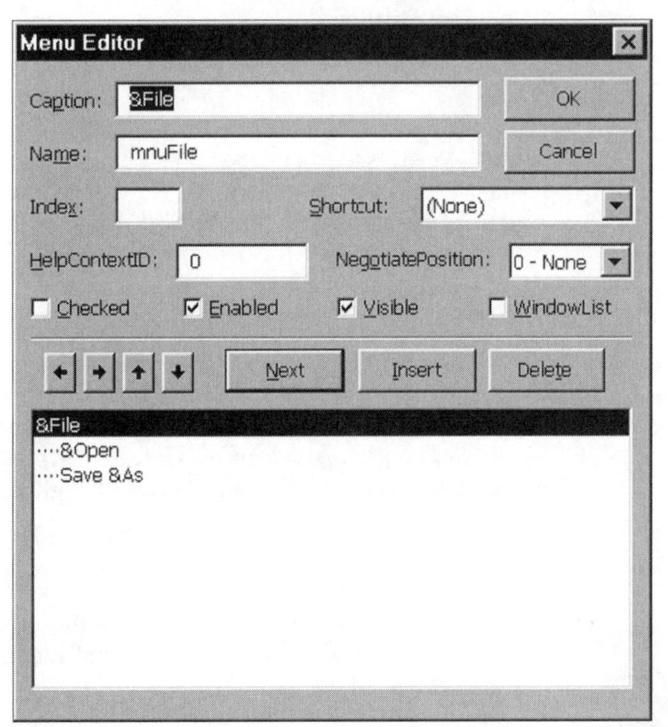

2 To the right of the four arrows in the menu editor there are three more command buttons; Next, Insert and Delete. Let's see what they do:

3 Click on the top item in the list, the &File item, to highlight it. Click on the Next button and the highlight moves down to the next item in the list, &Open. When you reach the bottom of the menu, Next creates a new blank item ready for you to add a new menu option.

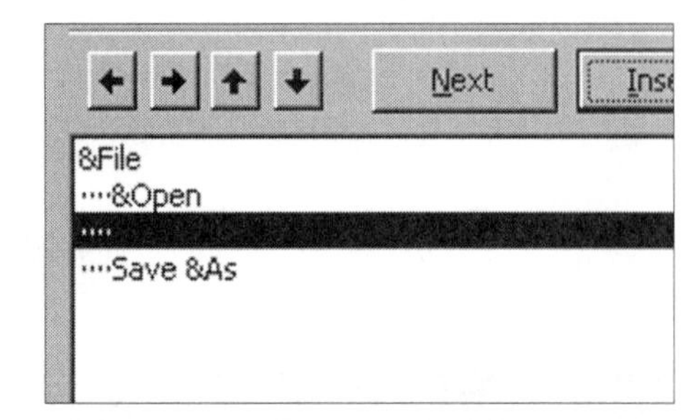

4 Now click on the Save &As item. If you click the Insert button, the Save &As option drops down a line and a new item is added immediately above it. Do it now. Notice how it automatically indents it for you as well.

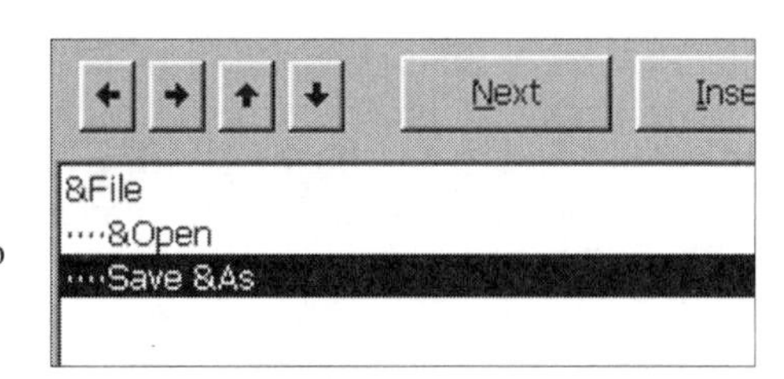

5 The Delete button does just the opposite of Insert, removing the currently selected item from the list. Click it now—the new blank item vanishes and Save &As moves back up to its original position.

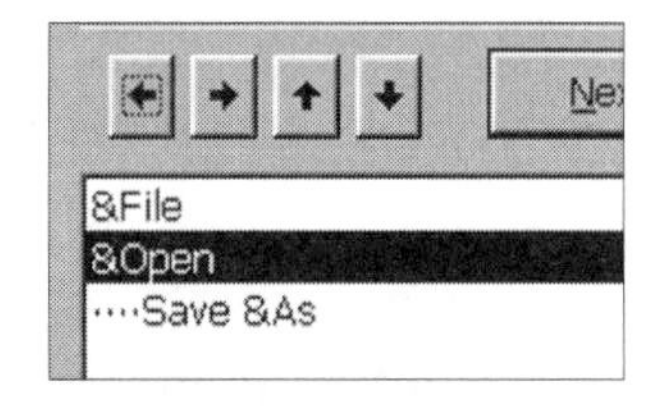

6 You've already seen how the right pointing arrow can shift menu items across the menu structure. The left, up, and down arrows work in a similar way. Click on the &Open menu item, then click the left arrow.

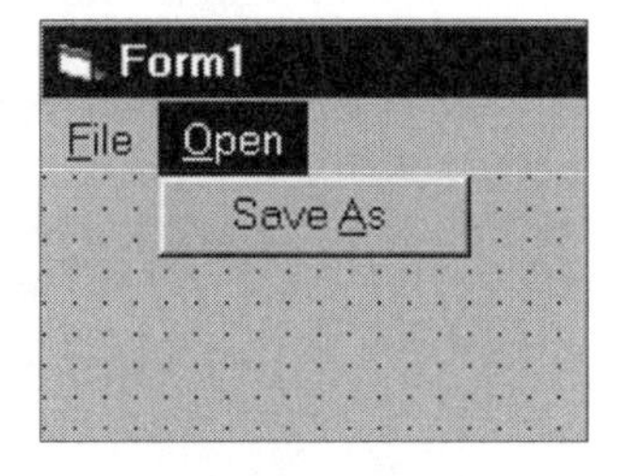

7 The item shifts to the left, so that if you pressed OK now you'd have a File and Open menu with Save &As underneath Open. Don't press OK yet though.

8 With the &Open item still selected, click the up arrow and it will move up to the top of the list. The effect this has on the final menu is that &Open now appears on the title bar before &File.

9 To put the menu back to normal, click on the right arrow, then click on the down arrow.

Nested Menus and Menu Items

At last our menus are starting to look the way they're supposed to. One further layout option is to place menu items in lists—branching off from another menu item. This is called **menu nesting**. Take a look at this menu:

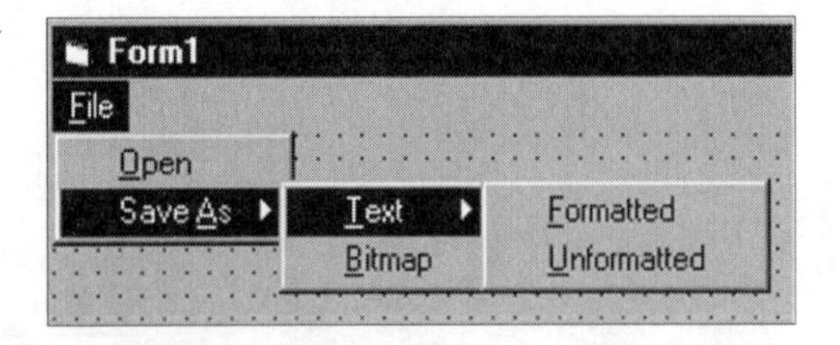

You can create up to five levels of indentation, though most experts recommend that you don't use more than two. You should also avoid putting frequently used commands in the cascaded menus, as this can really annoy your users. Let's have a go at creating a nested menu.

Try It Out - Nested Menus

You can create nested menus in the same way that you create normal menus—you simply add new items to the list and shift them to the right of the one you want them to be nested under.

1 With the menu editor still visible, click on the Save &As item and press the Next button to create a new menu item.

2 Set the caption of this new item to &Text and the name of the menu to mnuText.

3 Repeat this process to create three more items with their captions and names set like this:

&Bitmap	mnuBitmap
&Formatted	mnuFormatted
&Unformatted	mnuUnformatted

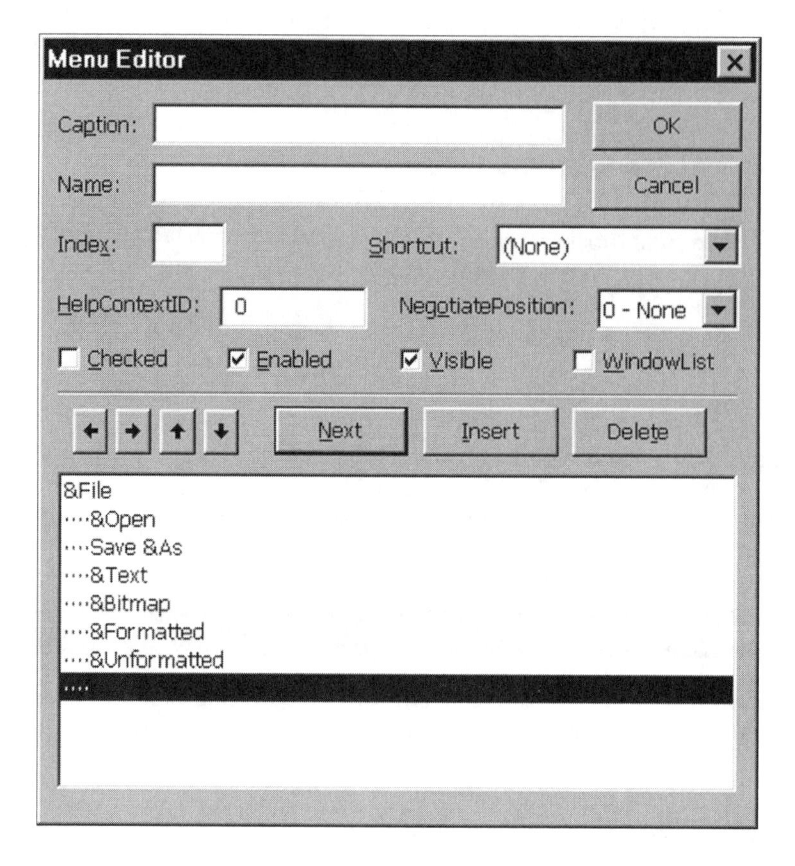

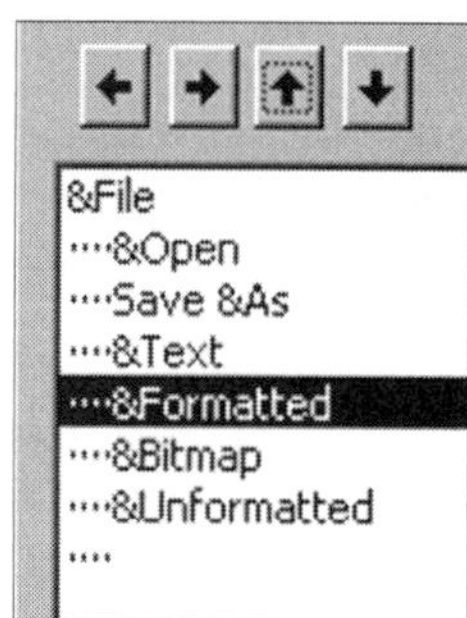

4 The order of these items is wrong. We want Formatted and Unformatted to appear underneath the Text item. Click the &Formatted item and press the up arrow once.

5 Now do the same for the Unformatted item.

6 We need to indent our new menu items to make them appear as nested submenus of other menu items. Click on each of the four new items and press the right arrow.

7 This makes all the four new menu items appear as a submenu of the Save &As item. The next step is to make the Formatted and Unformatted items appear as submenus of the &Text item.

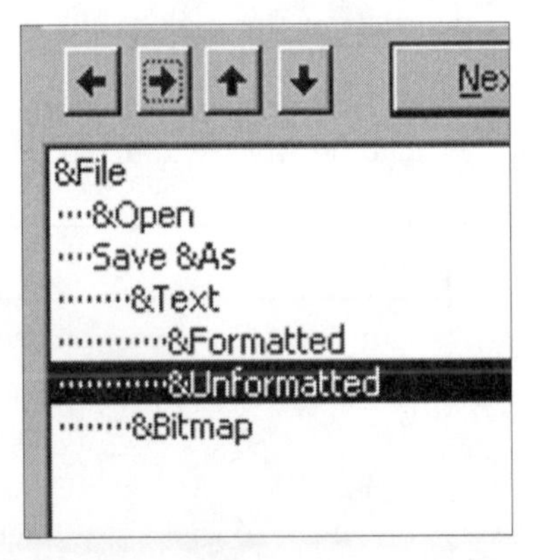

8 Indent the Formatted and Unformatted items to the right again.

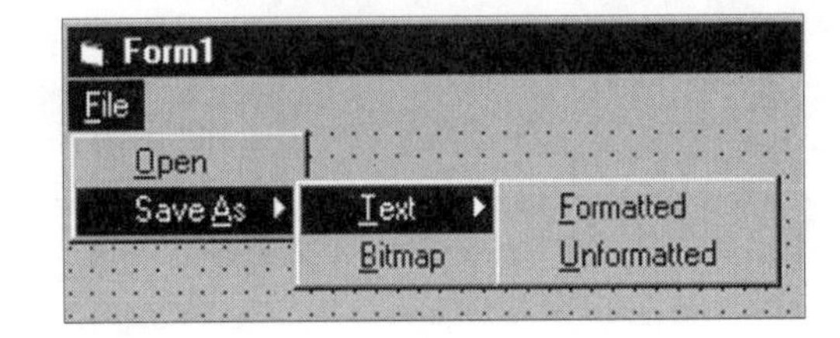

9 If you now press OK, you'll find that the menu structure is how we want it.

Menu Properties

We said earlier that a menu is a control, and like other Visual Basic controls you can change its appearance and behavior by manipulating its properties.

Just as the menu control isn't accessed in the normal way (by clicking on an icon from the toolbox), its properties aren't accessed through the Properties window either. Instead, the properties are all constantly displayed in the menu editor window itself.

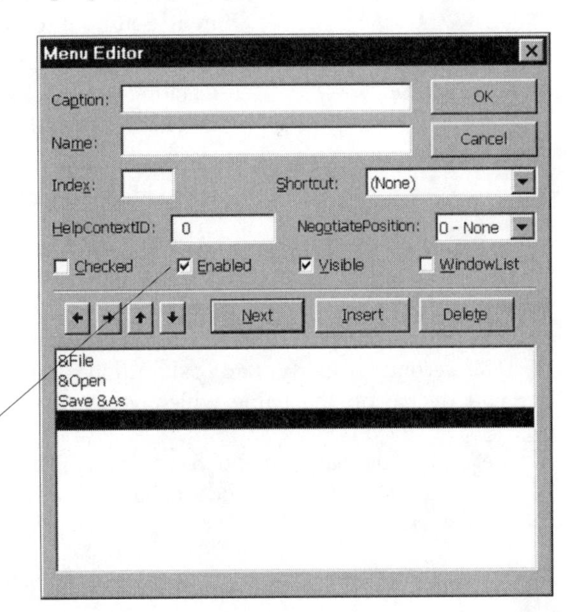

Here are the menu properties.

The normal flow of work when designing menus is to first create a menu item, then set its properties, then move onto the next item. So far, we've only dealt with the Caption and Name properties, which are mandatory. In the interests of speed we've ignored the middle section of the dialog, but now it's time to go back and see what we can do with properties.

The following properties can be set at design time using the Menu Editor dialog box, or at run time from within your code.

Name	Description
`Caption`	The text of the menu that the user will see.
`Name`	The name that you'll use in your code to address this menu and to identify the event code for each menu item.
`Index`	Used to form menu control arrays. This is where more than one menu item has the same name property, so a number in the **`Index`** property is used to address each item individually.
`Shortcut`	The menu can be invoked either by clicking it with the mouse in the normal way, or by pressing the shortcut key; for example, *Ctrl-C* is usually the same as a Copy menu item.
`WindowList`	This is used in Multiple Document Interface (MDI) applications. These are applications that have one main form, with smaller subforms contained with it (like Excel and Word). The **`WindowList`** property tells Visual Basic to display the captions of the child windows in this menu item.
`Checked`	Clicking on this property, or setting it to **`True`** in code, causes a tick, or **check mark**, to appear beside the menu item. This is great for lists of options.
`Enabled`	If this is clicked or set to **`True`**, then the user can select the menu item. Setting it to **`False`** by clearing the check box causes the menu item to appear **grayed out**, meaning the user can't select it.
`Visible`	Clicking the check box to set this to **`True`** causes the menu item to be visible at run time. Clearing the check box makes it invisible.
`NegotiatePosition`	Controls where, if at all, the menu appears when dealing with embedded ActiveX objects. More on this in the OLE chapter later in the book.

Menu Name Properties

The second property, **`Name`**, should be fairly straightforward by now. It's the property where you decide on the name which you will use in your code to refer to a menu item.

Let's say you had a menu heading of File. If you gave this the name **`mnuFile`**, you could then use the following code to change any other property of that menu item:

```
mnuFile.<property name> = <value>
```

One of the greatest hassles when dealing with menus is deciding what to call them. Each menu item is a control and needs to have its own caption and name. With a big menu structure, such as the one in Word 97 or even Visual Basic, deciding on unique names for each control can become a real problem.

There are two ways to approach this problem. The first solution, and the one that the Visual Basic Programmer's Guide advocates, is to create **control arrays** of menu items. Here each item under a certain heading has the same name, and is part of a commonly named control array.

The other approach, and the one I prefer, is to give each menu heading a name starting with **`mnu`** and ending in the name of the menu heading. For example, if you had a File heading, then its name would be **`mnuFile`**. Each item of the menu is then named with the heading name (or an abbreviated version of it) followed by a cut-down version of the caption. So, if under your File heading you have a Save As option, it would be named **`mnuFileSaveAs`**. This is simple, easy to understand, and a whole lot less likely to melt your brain!

The Menu Index Property

`Index` is another familiar property and is used to identify a menu item that is part of a control array. Using the **`Index`** property, it's possible to set up a number of menu items all with the same name. You'll see this in action later in Chapter 14: *Object Variables*, where the property is used to create menus that are built up with code. Much like the list of recently opened projects that Visual Basic shows you in its File menu:

1 D:\PSYNET\BOOKS\BG2VB4\CHAP06\CHAP06.DOC
2 D:\PSYNET\BOOKS\BG2VB4\CHAP06\192_06.LAY
3 D:\PSYNET\BOOKS\BG2VB4\CHAP08\CHAP08.DOC
4 D:\PSYNET\DOCS\LETTERS\DANIELS1.DOC
Exit

Enabling Menu Items

The **`Enabled`** property determines whether or not the menu option is actually available for use. It appears grayed out if the **`Enabled`** property is set to **`False`**. The **`Visible`** property indicates whether this particular menu item should appear on the menu at all.

Take a look at this screenshot:

These items have their **`Enabled`** *properties set to* **`False`**.

Menu items that are disabled, and menu items that are invisible. OK, you can't actually see the invisible ones, but that just shows how effective it can be!

Later in this chapter you'll see how to create pop-up menus. By creating an invisible menu, you can create menus that the user can't see until you decide to pop them up onto the screen using some code. You can also use the **`Enabled`** and **`Visible`** properties when you need to build some kind of access security into your programs. Menu items that you don't want certain users to be able to use can be either disabled or made invisible.

Assigning Shortcut Keys

The **`Shortcut`** property is rather novel. Hot keys created with & in their caption only work if that particular menu item is visible when *Alt* and the appropriate letter are pressed. Think back to the menus we created earlier.

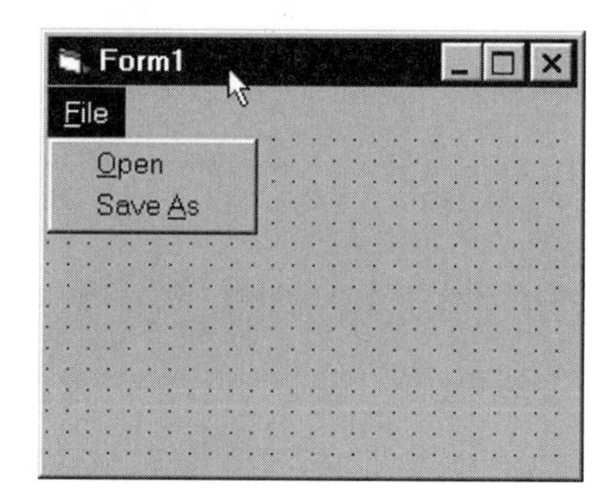

The Open item was created with a text property of &Open. The O of Open is underlined in the menu, meaning that we can access it by pressing *Alt* and *O* together. This only works, however, when the File menu is actually dropped down and visible. The **`Shortcut`** property allows you to do this even when the menu isn't visible.

By assigning a key combination to **`Shortcut`**, you can actually call the menu option from any point in the program by simply pressing the shortcut keys. You may have come across some of the more standard shortcuts in Visual Basic: *Ctrl-X* to cut something, *Ctrl-V* to paste it, and so on. It's a good idea to try and stick to standard shortcuts. Remember that they'll work when the relevant menu item isn't open. Your code could run when the user is least expecting it.

Try It Out - Assigning a Shortcut Key

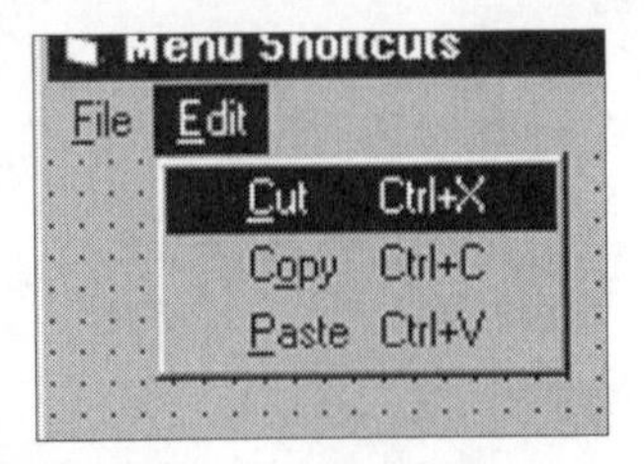

Assigning a shortcut to a menu item is as simple as point and click—point at the arrow to the right of the Shortcut combo box and click on one of the key combinations listed. Let's try it. We'll create an edit menu and assign all the usual edit shortcut keys so that the items appear like this:

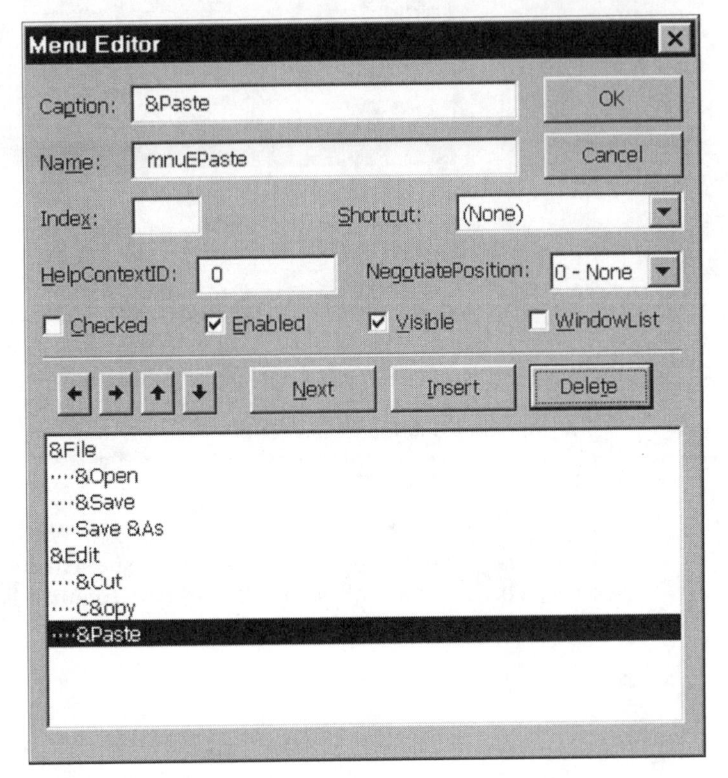

1 Edit the menu you created earlier, or start again and create the menu arrangement shown here:

2 We need to add shortcuts to the Cut, Copy and Paste items. Cut will be *Ctrl-X*, Copy will be *Ctrl-C* and Paste will be *Ctrl-V*.

3 Click on the Cut item, and click on the down arrow beside the Shortcut combo box. Then scroll down the list until you find *Ctrl-X* and select it by clicking it with the mouse.

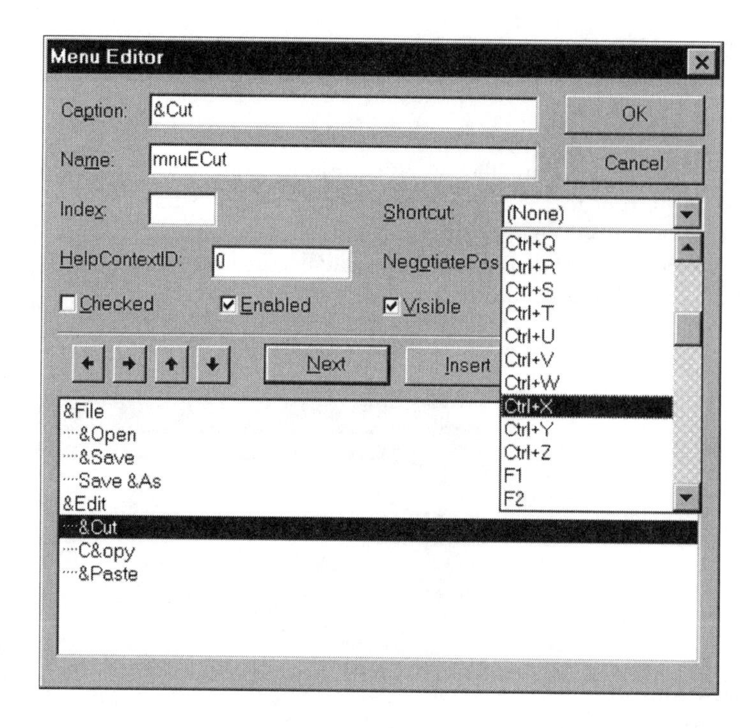

4 The menu editor dialog will now change to show you that the Shortcut selected is *Ctrl-X*.

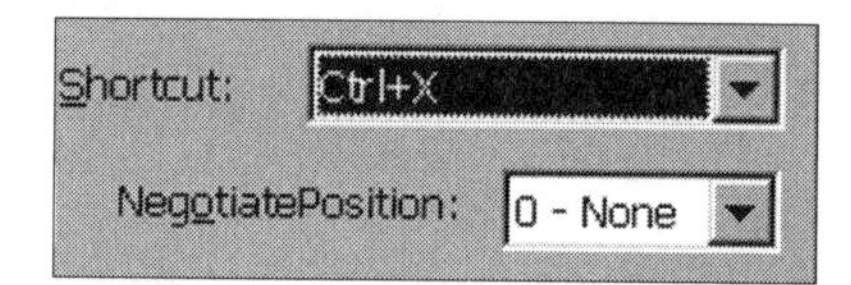

5 Using the same process select the *Ctrl-C* shortcut for the Copy menu item, and *Ctrl-V* for Paste. These are all standard shortcut commands that Microsoft recommends for the Edit menu items.

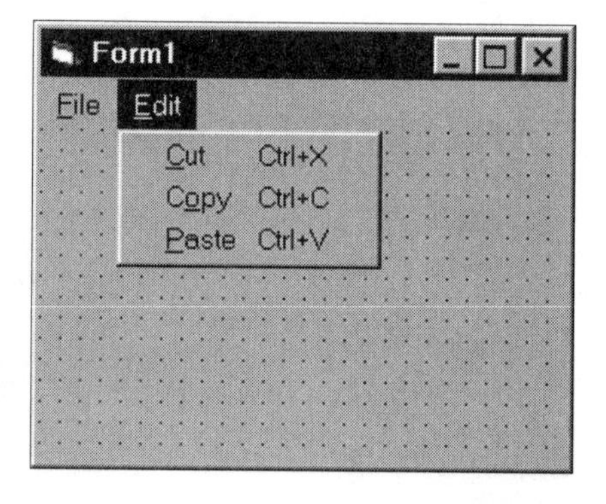

6 When all the shortcuts are set, click on the OK button on the menu editor and take a look at your new edit menu.

7 Now save the project as `Menu.vbp`. We'll come back to it later and add some code to show just how these shortcuts work.

You can't add a shortcut key to a menu item that isn't indented.

Menu Separators

The final menu design feature we need to look at is **separators**. If you have a drop-down menu that has a large number of items on it, it makes sense to break up the items into logical groups. For example, on the Visual Basic File menu, the options are grouped according to whether they apply to projects or files.

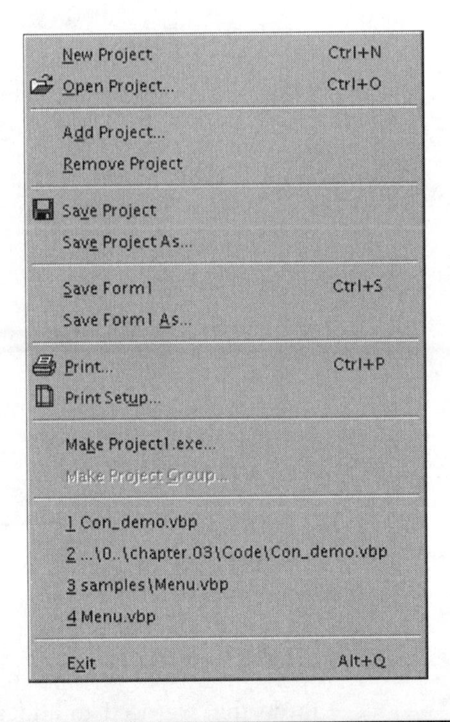

Try It Out - Adding Separators

Separators are just as easy to create as any other menu item. Simply enter a dash for the item Caption, and a dummy name such as mnuDash1 as the Name property. Visual Basic automatically interprets a menu item with a **dash** for a Caption as being a separator line.

1 If you've still got the last project open, click on the menu editor icon on the toolbar. If not, open up the **`Menu.vbp`** project in Visual Basic and, when the main form appears, click on the menu editor icon.

2 Add an Exit option to the bottom of the File menu as shown. Do this by selecting the existing &Edit item, and then clicking the Insert button. Don't forget to indent the new menu item.

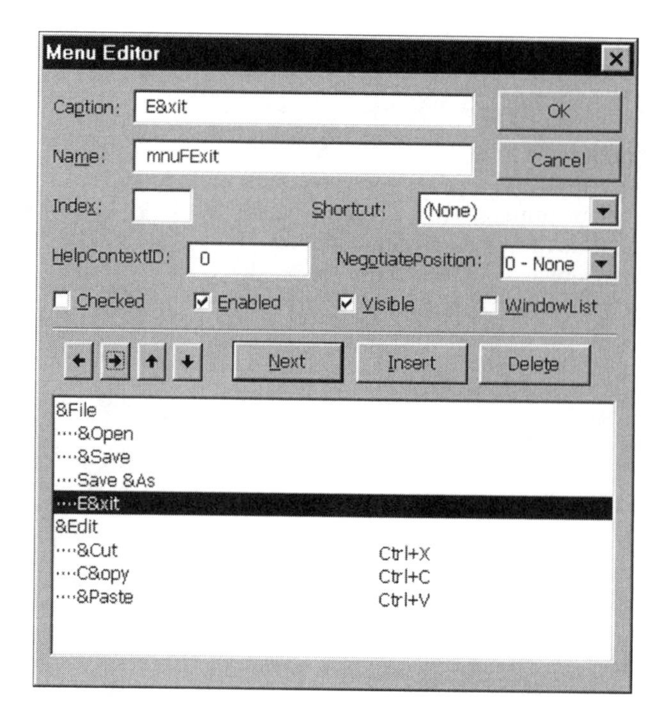

3 It would make sense if, at run time, that Exit option were split off into its own little area. To do this we need to add a separator bar above the Exit option, so click on the &Exit entry in the list and then click the Insert button (or press *Alt-I*).

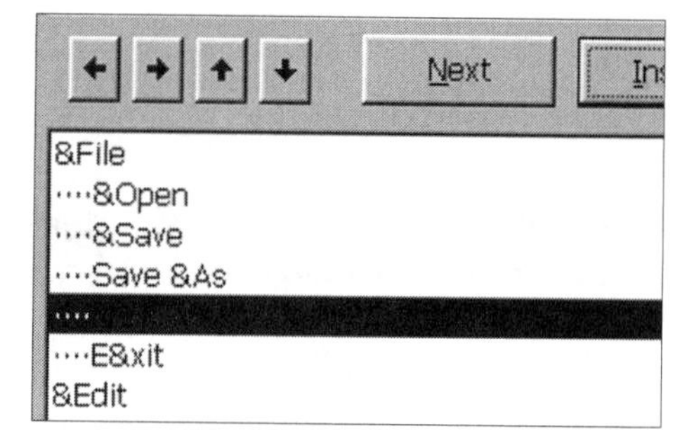

4 For the Caption of the separator bar just enter a dash. The only gripe I have with the way Visual Basic handles separator bars is that you still need to give each one a unique name. In the Name property enter mnuFDash1 to show that this is the first dash on the File menu.

5 Press OK to finish editing, save your work, and then—on the form—take a look at the File menu.

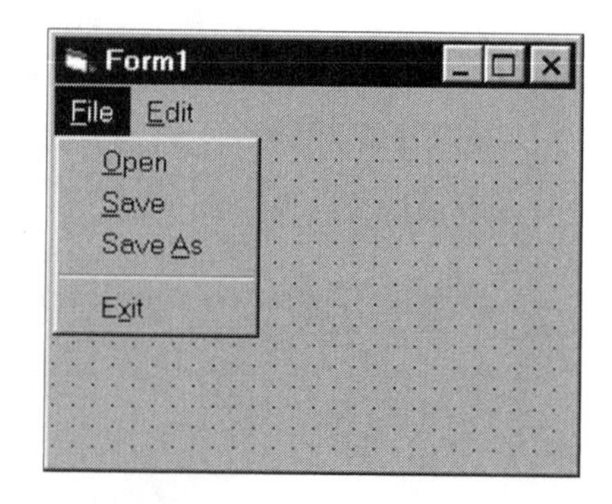

Adding Code to Menu Items

Unfortunately, up to now, our new menus don't actually do anything. To bring them to life we have to write some code. Selecting a menu item triggers a **`Click`** event. To bring up the Code window for a particular menu item, single-click on the relevant menu item, on the form, at design time.

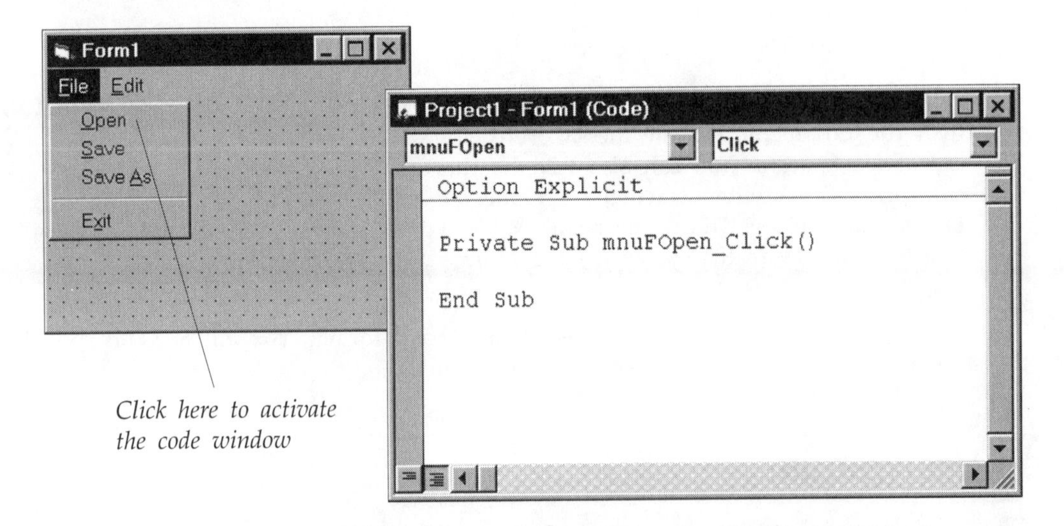

Try It Out - Adding Code to Menu Items

Adding event code to a menu item is as easy as adding code to a normal control.

1 Open up the **`Menu.vbp`** project that we've been working on. Earlier we created shortcuts for the entries on the Edit menu. Let's now prove they work.

2 Select the Cut item from the Edit menu. You should see the Code window appear with Visual Basic waiting for you to key in some code to respond to that menu item's **`Click`** event.

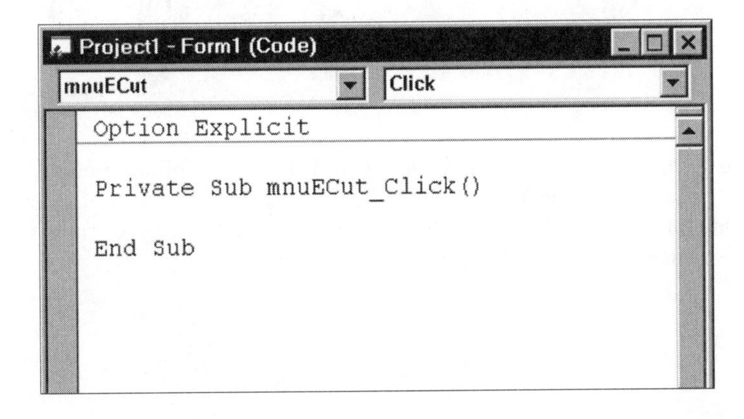

3 Let's add some code to make this menu item pop up a message box. Change the **mnuECut_Click()** event so that it looks like this:

```
Private Sub mnuECut_Click()

    MsgBox "You selected Cut from the Edit menu"

End Sub
```

4 Once this is done, run the program. Select Cut from the Edit menu and the message box you've just added appears. You can also test the short cut—press *Ctrl-X* without actually opening the Edit menu, and you'll get the same result. When you finished, make sure that you save the project.

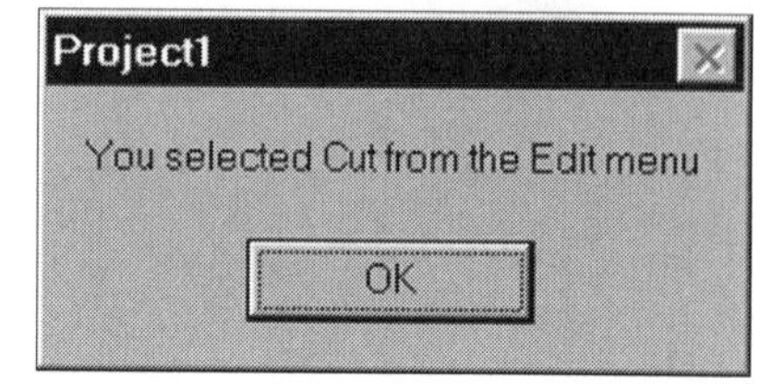

That just about covers drop-down menus in their basic format. We still need to consider the second type of menu though—the pop-up menu.

Pop-Up Menus

Once you've created your menu structure, you aren't limited to simply displaying drop-down menus. Visual Basic provides a command you can use, which displays a menu anywhere on the screen—whenever you want.

What's a Pop-Up Menu?

Although it can sound a little daunting at first, a pop-up menu is really exactly the same as a normal menu. The only obvious difference is that it can pop up almost anywhere on the screen that you choose. Take a look at this example.

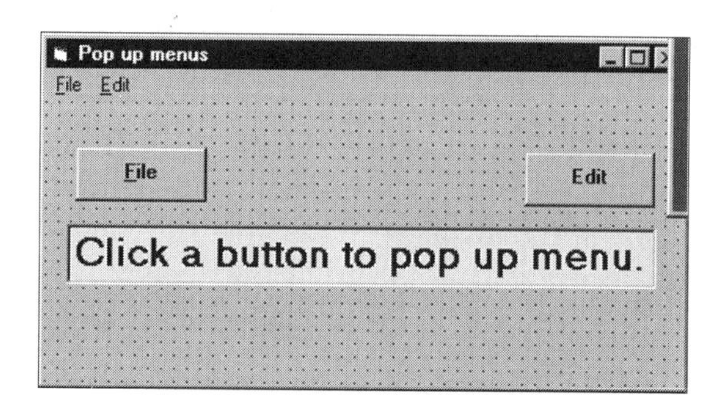

Here we have a program with a single form and a very familiar menu layout. There are also command buttons on the form, which have similar captions to the menu headings. Clicking on one of these command buttons will pop up the appropriate menu underneath the command button.

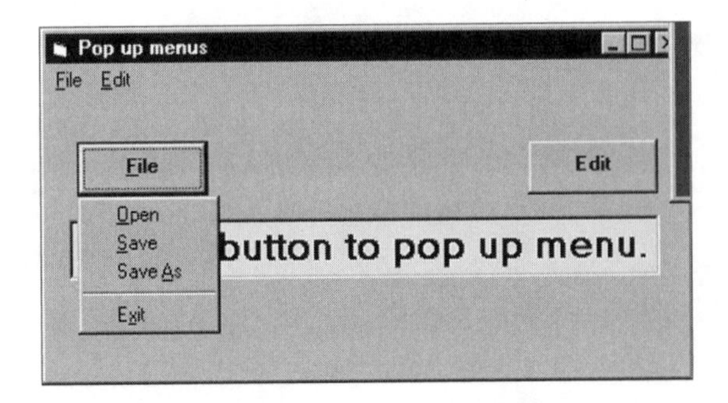

Try It Out - Creating Pop-Up Menus

The command that implements this kind of menu is the ingeniously named **PopUpMenu** (and you thought learning Visual Basic would be tough!).

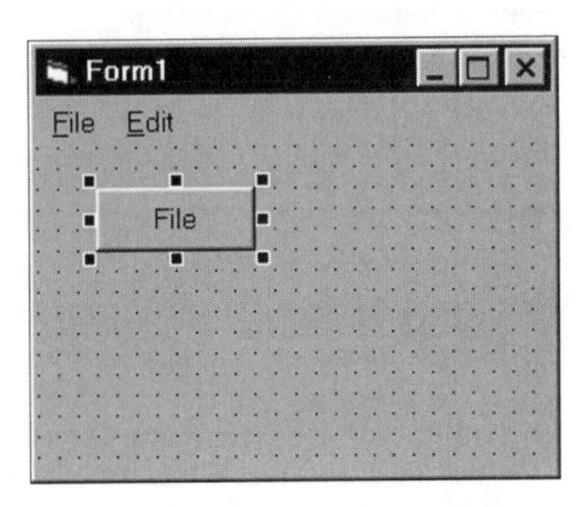

1 Drop a command button onto the form we've been working with, and change its caption property to File.

2 Double click on the button on the form to bring up the code window, and type in this line of code:

```
Private Sub Command1_Click()

PopupMenu mnuFile, vbPopupMenuLeftAlign

End Sub
```

3 Now run the application and click on the button you created. You'll see the File menu, which is normally attached to the menu bar, appear near your mouse pointer. Easy!

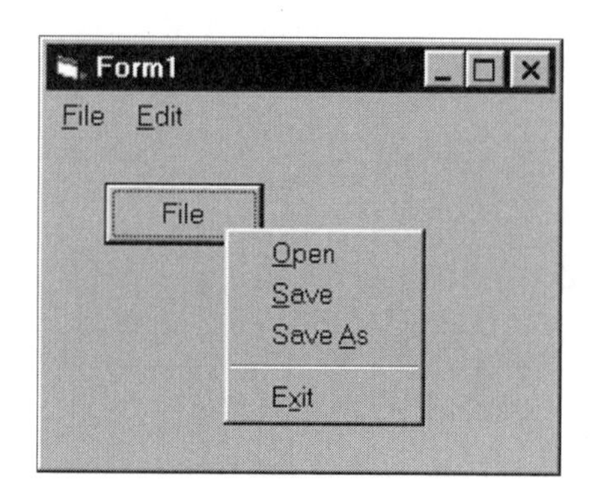

Don't worry about saving the project this time as we're going to improve upon this example shortly.

While we wrote some code in this application to pop up the menu when a button on the form was clicked, you have to bear in mind that it would have been just as easy to pop up the menu with a right mouse button click. At this point you're approaching the world of context sensitive menus—a very big thing in Windows 95 and later as I am sure you're aware.

Let's take a look, though, at exactly what the code does and how it does it.

How It Works

All the code does is call the **PopupMenu** command in Visual Basic, telling it the name of the menu that you want to pop up. The name we set in the menu editor for the File menu, **mnuFile**, is the name that we pass to the **PopupMenu** command.

Immediately following the name of the menu, you need to supply Visual Basic with a number (known as a **flag**) that it then uses to determine how you want the menu displayed. Instead of using straight numbers, you can make use of VB5's intrinsic constants, **vbPopupMenuLeftAlign**, **vbPopupMenuRightAlign** and **vbPopupMenuCenterAlign**.

In this case, **vbPopupMenuLeftAlign** indicates that we want the left-hand edge of the menu to appear at the current mouse coordinates. We could have said **vbPopupMenuCenterAlign**, or **vbPopupMenuRightAlign** to have the menu centered or right aligned with the current mouse pointer position. It's really just a question of personal taste, and how much screen space you have to display the menu.

That's really all there is to it. You click the button, and the menu appears wherever the mouse pointer is at that point in time. However, you aren't limited to displaying the pop-up menu at the position of the mouse pointer. You could have told Visual Basic exactly where to put the menu on the form by sending X and Y coordinates to the **PopupMenu** command. For example, if you had wanted the menu to appear exactly aligned with the button on the form then you could have entered this as the command:

```
PopupMenu mnuFile, vbPopupMenuLeftAlign, Command1.Top, Command1.Left
```

Here we're telling Visual Basic the top and left coordinates to display the menu at, which just happen to be the same values that are already in the command button's **Top** and **Left** properties. If you actually were to type this in and run the program then the menu would pop up perfectly aligned with the upper left corner of the button on the form.

Try It Out - A Floating Pop-Up Menu

This first pop-up menu is a bit poor. I mean, who has control buttons drifting around in the middle of a form? Let's make it into one of those nice floaty menus that appear with a click of the right mouse button.

1 Start by deleting the command button that you just added to **Menu.vbp**. You should also delete the line of code you added in the code window.

2 In the code window, drop down the list of events and find the form's **MouseUp** event. In order for us to pop the menu up on to the screen at run time, when the user clicks the right mouse button, we need to add some code to this event.

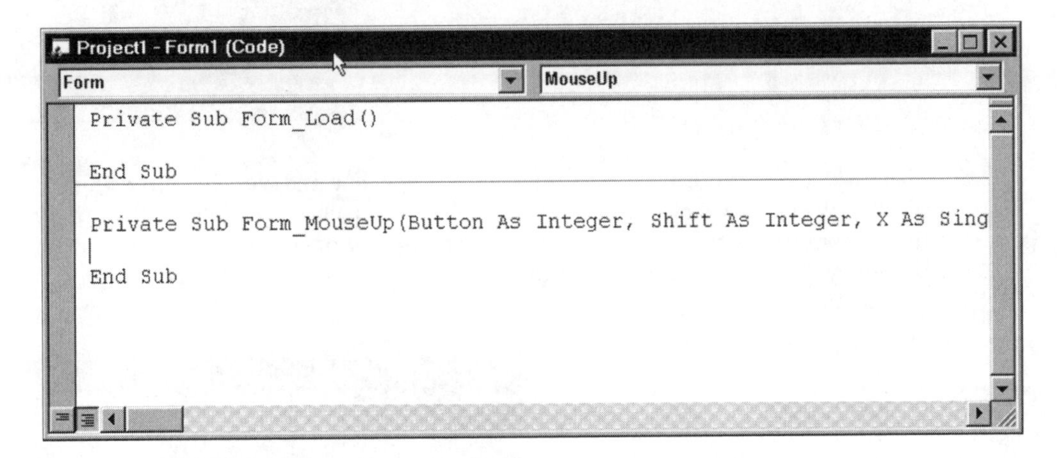

3 The **MouseUp** event is triggered whenever the user releases a mouse button—any mouse button—over the form. We still need to check which button they pressed though. As you may remember from Chapter 6, a **Button** parameter is passed to the **MouseUp** event. This is set to **vbLeftButton** (**1**) if the button that got released was the left one, and **vbRightButton** (**2**) if it was the right one. A simple **If** statement is needed I think. Add the following line:

```
Private Sub Form_MouseUp(Button As Integer, Shift As Integer, X As
  ↳ Single, Y As Single)

    If Button = vbRightButton Then

End Sub
```

4 All that remains now is to call the **PopupMenu** command, as before, to bring the menu we want into view:

```
Private Sub Form_MouseUp(Button As Integer, Shift As Integer, X As
  ↳ Single, Y As Single)

    If Button = vbRightButton Then
```

```
    If Button = vbRightButton Then
        PopupMenu mnuFile, vbPopupMenuLeftAlign
    End If

End Sub
```

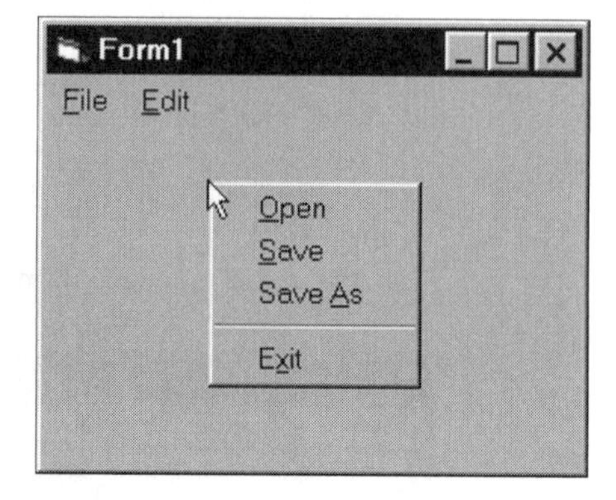

5 Now run the application and right click on the form. Your pop-up menu will appear.

6 There's just one more little trick that we haven't covered yet. In our application, the menu heading is visible even before the user right clicks. However, it's quite rare to find a context sensitive menu in any other application standing proudly on the menu bar—they normally live out of sight until you hit that right mouse button on a certain part of the form.

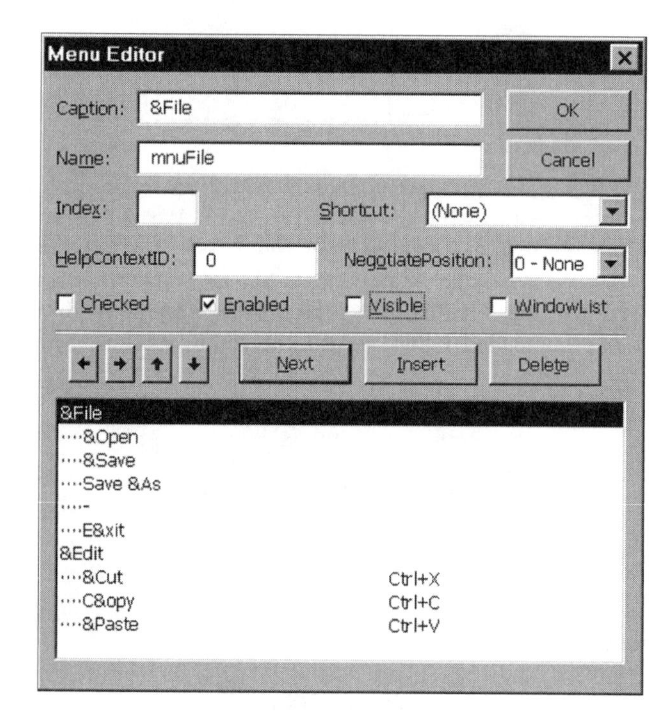

If the application is still running stop it, bring up the menu editor, select the &File menu item and turn the **Visible** property off.

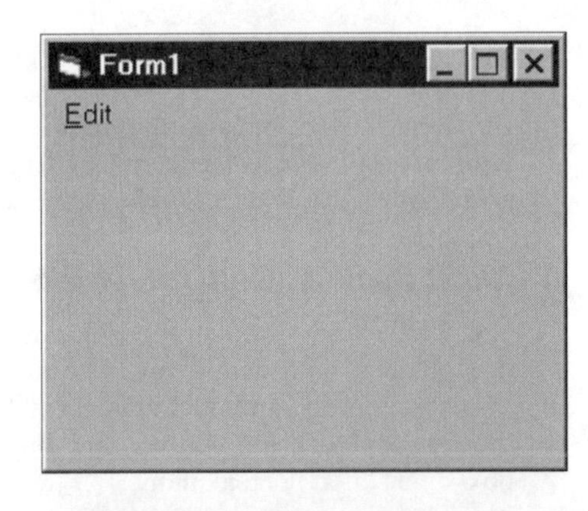

7 Then run the application again.

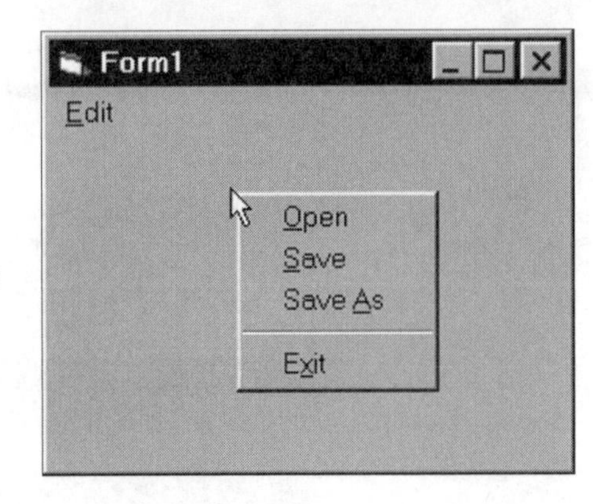

8 When the program runs, the File menu is nowhere in sight (it's actually nowhere in sight now in design mode as well). However, if you click the right mouse button, you'll see that it appears where the mouse is, just as you would have expected.

Dynamic Menus

As well as using the design-time menu editor to create and change your menu structure, it's also possible to create new menu items at run time. This is great for creating dynamic menus, such as the Visual Basic File menu which automatically shows you the last four Visual Basic projects you worked on, cutting out the need for you to traverse your hard disk.

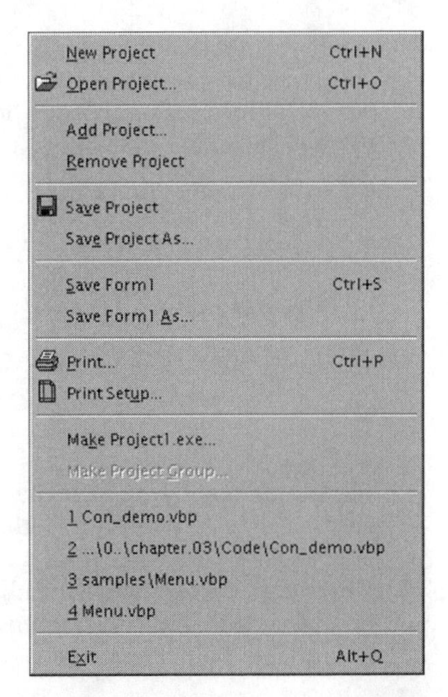

Adding Menu Items at Run Time

Dynamic menus such as this all revolve around control arrays. A control array is like a regular array that we covered in Chapter 5 apart from the fact that the elements in the array aren't numbers or strings, but controls.

A Quick Look at Control Arrays

One of the great things about VB is that you can assign whole controls to variables as though they were just a lowly number. This stores everything about the control, including all its properties and methods, in a little box called an **object variable**. You can open up the box and use the control any time you like, but like all variables you can call it by the box name, not its real name.

*In actual fact, what we store in the object variable is a **pointer** to the object itself. But you don't need to worry about that. Visual Basic looks after all the background stuff for us automatically.*

The first time you meet control arrays is when you try and copy controls on a form. If you already have a control on the form called Command1 and you copy and paste it onto the same form using the right mouse menu, VB will ask you this:

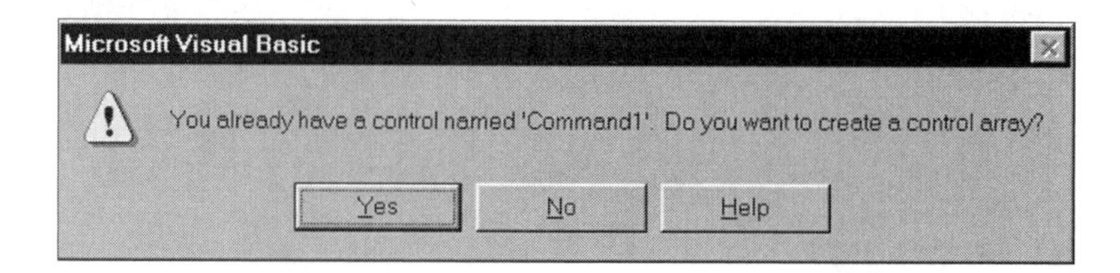

If you try to paste a control with an identical name to one that already exists, VB assumes you want to start a control array. If you click Yes VB will name both buttons Command1, but set their **Index** properties to **0** and **1** respectively. If you add more Command1 buttons, VB will increment the index accordingly. It won't prompt you again, because you've already got a control array.

If you now wanted to set the captions of, say, 5 buttons in code, you could do it like this:

```
Dim nIndex As Integer

For nIndex = 0 To 4
    Command1(nIndex).Caption = "Number " & nIndex
Next nIndex
```

All the buttons have the name **Command1**, but you can identify each of them by their position in the control array that VB created for you.

This sounds tricky and in truth it requires a slight leap of the imagination. We'll see object variables more and more throughout the course of the book, so you'll gradually get comfortable with them. For now, just think of them as containers for controls.

You can do the same thing with menu items at run time. You will see in the next chapter, when we deal with file dialogs, that these arrays can be very useful for building up something like a recently used files list on the File menu.

Let's see this dynamic menu creation in action though.

Try It Out - Creating Dynamic Menu Items

1 Start up another new VB project and create a simple menu like the one shown below.

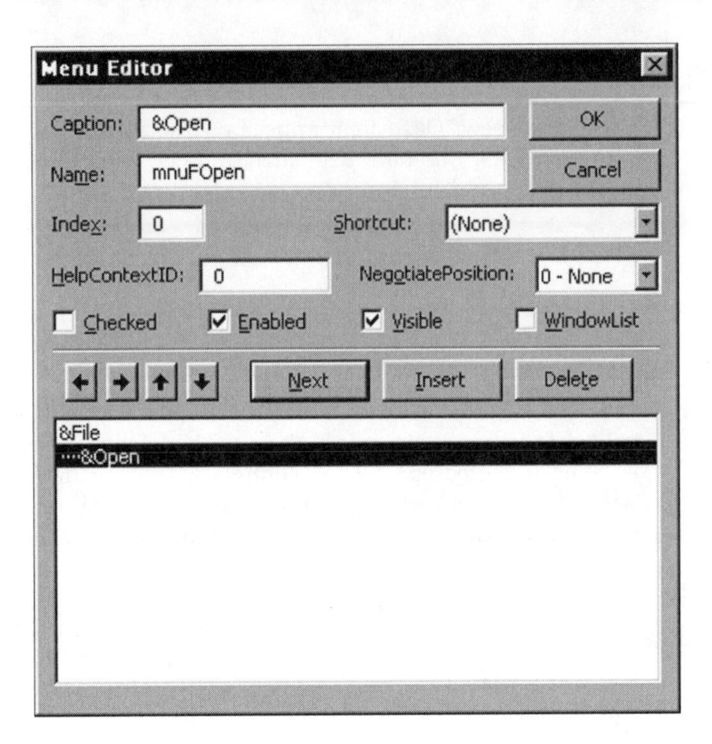

Notice how I have set the **Index** property to **0** for the Open item. This makes it a control array. Do the same on your menu and then close the menu editor down.

2 Click on the Open item on the File menu of your form to bring the code window into view.

3 When I was talking about command buttons a little while ago, I was assuming that you wanted to create a set of buttons on a form at design time, all with the same name, but each distinguished from the other by a unique number in the **Index** property. With this menu, though, we need to create the new menu items at run time, not design time... how?

Well, it's actually quite simple. We use the **Load** command, which just loads another instance, or copy, of the item into memory and makes it part of a control array. If you try to load in a new menu with an index number that hasn't already been used, then you'll create a new menu item. Try it—change the code in the Open item's **Click** event so that it looks like this.

```
Private Sub mnuFOpen_Click(Index As Integer)

    Load mnuFOpen (Index + 1)

End Sub
```

4 If you run the program now and click on the Open item on the File menu then you'll see a brand new Open item appear on the menu. If you click this new item then another will appear and so on.

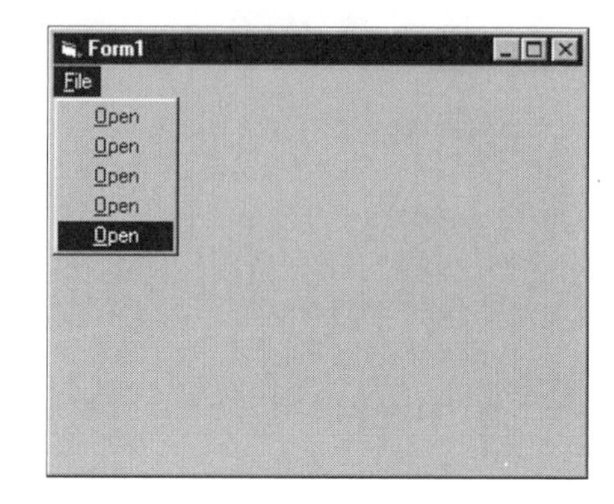

How It Works

When the index value for a control or menu item is set, you'll find a new parameter passed to your events called **Index**. This is the index number of the control that the event is being triggered on. All the controls will share the same event handler, so it's possible to write code to look at this index property and figure out exactly which control we're dealing with. In our case though, we just add one to it and call the **Load** command to load a new element to the control array.

This means you have to keep on selecting the last Open item on the menu, otherwise the code will try to load a menu item with an index that already exists. This results in a run-time error unless you have some error handling to cope with it.

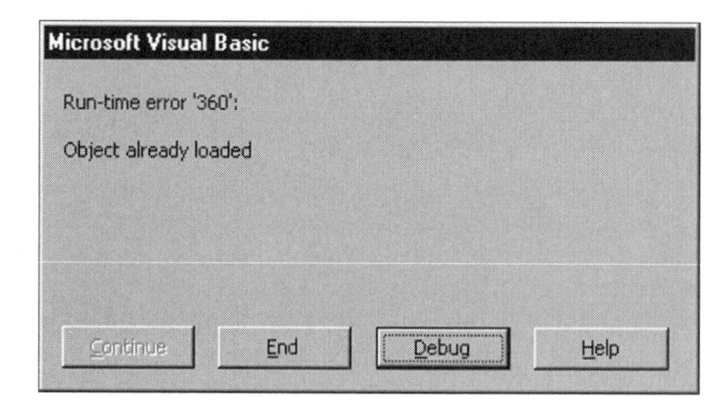

Later on in the book we'll look at something known as a **collection**, which can be an absolute gift if you need to produce code that intelligently handles just this kind of situation.

A Note on Good Design

Whatever your personal view on Windows (and I'm assuming that you don't actually *hate* it), it's hard to disagree with the notion that keeping the design of the user interface as standard as possible across various applications is a worthwhile objective.

Microsoft has issued guidelines for how Windows applications should look. There are lots of changes in the Windows 95 version that you would do well to emulate. The best source of help is *The Windows Interface Guidelines for Software Design (Microsoft Press, 1995 ISBN 1-55615-679-0).*

The bottom line on menus is: the more they resemble the applications your users are familiar with, the easier they'll find their way round your program.

Summary

Menus are very useful tools for both you as a developer and for the users of your applications. In this chapter you learned how to:

- Create new menus from scratch
- Nest and subnest menus
- Change the order of menu items
- Add separator bars to menus
- Add code to menus
- Turn a standard menu into a pop-up one
- Name menus in a standard way

In the next chapter we'll take a look at dialogs. These are pop-up information windows that perform a variety of functions. Some of them, like the common dialogs we used to save and load files, come up as a result of menu selections.

Why Not Try...

1. How many shortcut keys are available within the menu editor?

2. Try to assign the same shortcut key to more than 1 menu option. What happens?

3. Create a form with a menu structure containing a control array. Place a command button on the form which when clicked creates another member of the menu control array.

4. Modify the last exercise by creating another command button. Have this button remove the members of the menu control array dynamically.

5. Create a form that displays a pop-up menu when the right mouse button is clicked anywhere over the form.

asic Visual Basic Visual Ba

al Basic Visual Basic Visual

Basic Visual Basic Visual Ba

ual Basic Vi

Basic Visu

ual Basic V

l Basic Visu

isual Basic Visual Basic

al Basic Visual Basic Visua

Visual Basic Visual Basic Visu

l Basic Visual Ba

l Basic Visual

ic Visual Basi

Basic Visual B

ic Visual Basi

l Basic Visual

ual Basic Visual Basic Visual Ba

Visual Basic Visual Basic Visu

sual Basic Visual Basic Visu

Visual Basic Visual Ba

Dialogs

Dialogs are a useful way of getting specific bits of information to and from your users. They serve to focus the user's attention on the job at hand and are, therefore, extremely useful in Windows applications.

Dialogs come in a variety of forms, each adapted to a particular purpose. In this chapter we'll look at each of the four main types of dialog and examine how and when to use them.

In this chapter you'll learn about:

- What dialog boxes are
- When to use them
- Modality
- Message boxes
- Input boxes
- Common dialogs
- Custom dialogs

Introducing Dialog Boxes

If you're in the company of Windows developers or flicking through a Windows magazine it won't be long before you come across the term **dialog**. Dialog boxes are the small windows that pop up now and again in Visual Basic and Windows to give you an error message or to ask for further information to complete a certain operation.

For example, if you try and leave Word without having saved your file, you'll see something like this:

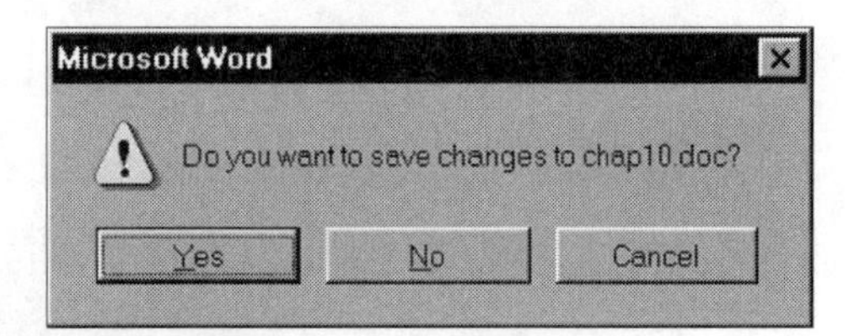

We've used message boxes, input boxes and common dialogs very briefly in earlier chapters. I said I'd explain it all later, and sure enough, here I go!

Although dialog boxes are common, their appearance can differ dramatically depending on the type. All of them, however, are just variations on four basic types.

Message Boxes

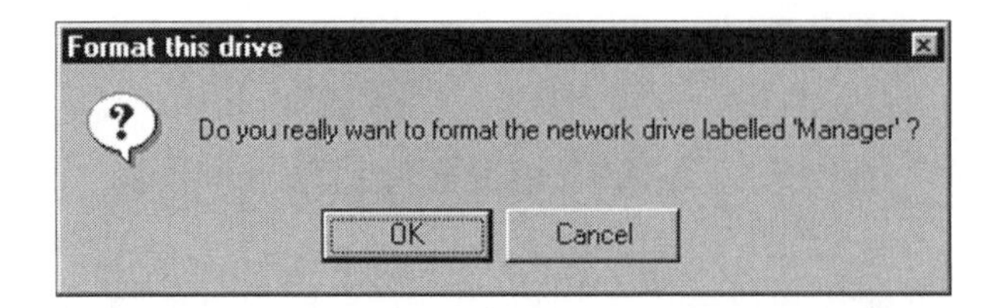

These are invoked by **`MsgBox`**. As a **statement**, they show text which the user must acknowledge by clicking one of the buttons also displayed. As a **function**, they return the ID of the button that the user presses. Therefore, when using **`MsgBox`** as a function you must use the syntax **`Returnval = MsgBox("Hello ", vbYesNo)`**.

Input Boxes

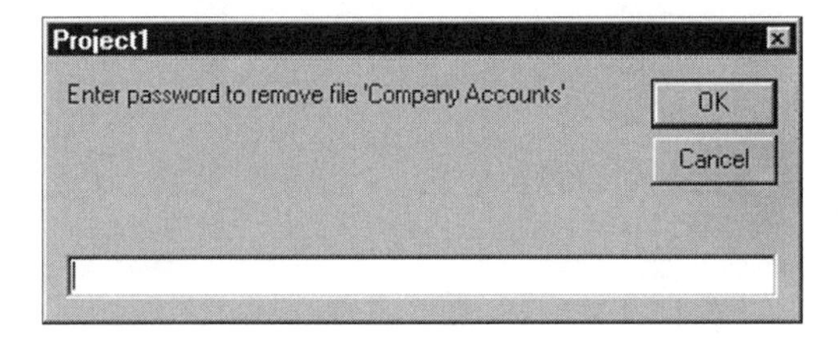

These are invoked by **`InputBox`**. An input box is a box with a message that allows the user to enter a line of text.

Common Dialogs

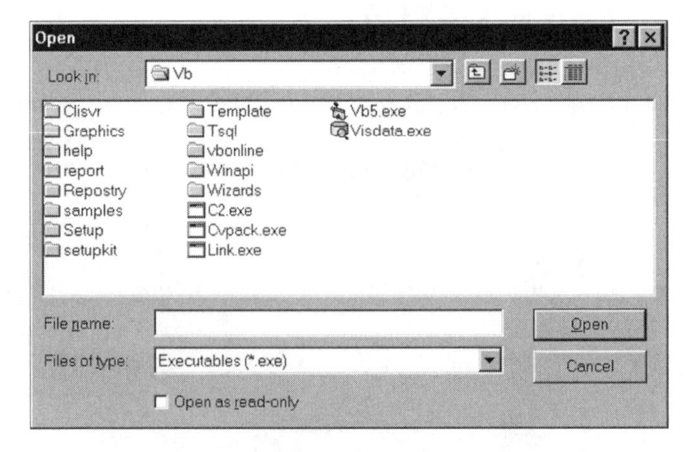

These include a variety of standard Windows dialogs for system settings. They can be invoked once the common dialog control has been added to a form by using the **`CommonDialog1.Showxxxxx`** command. The **`xxxxx`** determines what type of common dialog is displayed. You can use common dialogs for a variety of purposes, including printing, saving a file, opening a file, changing the color or font, etc.

Custom Dialogs

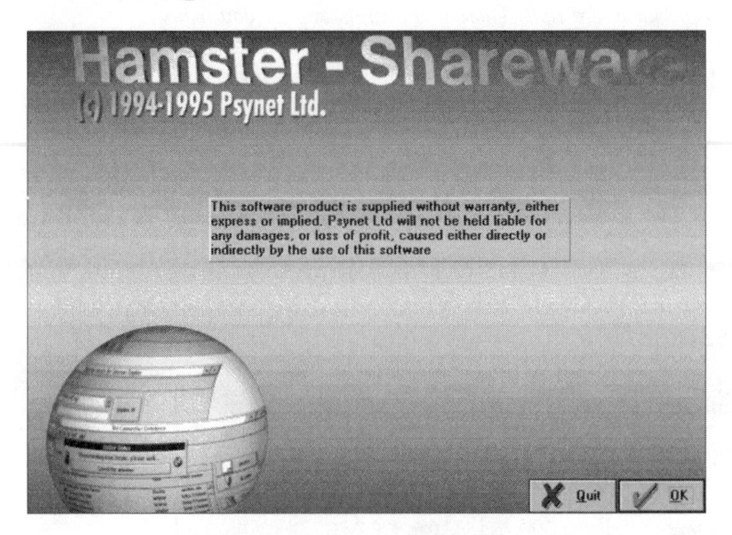

These are standard Visual Basic forms dedicated to a single message or function and made to look like a message box. In code they are referred to as **`frmYourName`**.

Over the course of this chapter we'll look at each type of dialog and learn how to use them in applications.

When to Use Dialog Boxes

Although dialogs are an important part of a programmer's toolkit, they are very different from the forms and windows that you're used to.

As a rule, forms are used to handle data that's fundamental to your application, that is, the data that your program was actually written to deal with. In a customer database, for example, your forms display a customer's details or get those details from the user. Dialog boxes, on the other hand, are used for information about the operation of the program itself, and not necessarily the data that the program deals with.

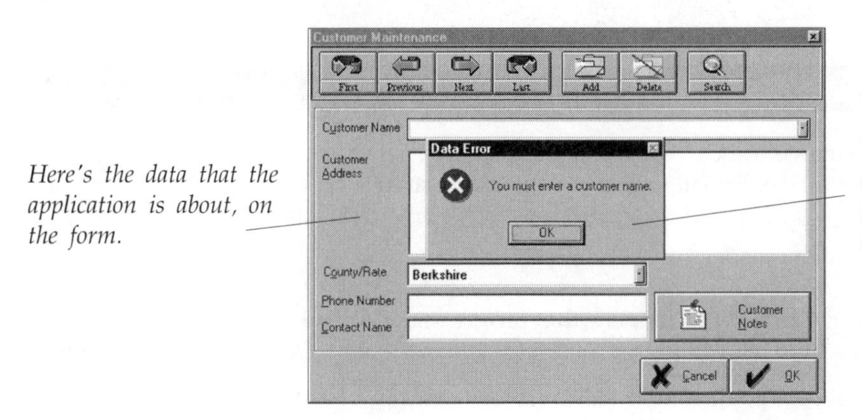

Here's the data that the application is about, on the form.

This is information that deals with how the program executes, on a dialog box.

For example, if your user decided that the font used in your application needed changing, then you'd display a font dialog box. This has no relationship to what your program actually does—it controls the way the program itself works.

Dialog boxes allow you to display and obtain information about what your program is doing, display error messages or warn the user if they do something potentially dangerous. It's bad practice to use them to actually get information about the program data; users expect to see proper forms for that. There's nothing stopping you using dialogs to obtain data, but the idea behind Windows is to keep everything standard. Therefore, the very general rule is: use dialogs for program and system information and forms for program data.

Message Boxes

The simplest form of dialog in Visual Basic is called a **message box**.

The Components of a Message Box

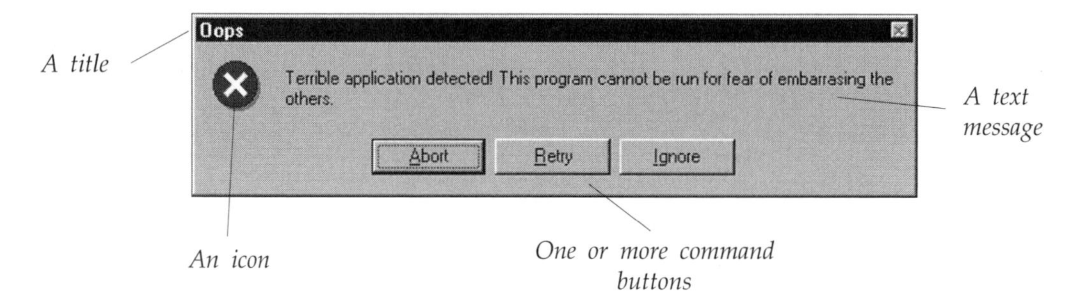

All these features of the message box can be set up with just one small line of code, using the **`MsgBox`** command.

Message boxes come into their own when you need to give the user a simple message, such as an error message or a warning. When you close a file in Word, for example, a message box appears with a Yes, No and Cancel button asking if you want to save changes to the file.

Try It Out - A Simple Message Box

Let's create a simple message box that could be displayed when the user clicks Exit in your application, and asks for confirmation that the program should be closed down.

1 Load up Visual Basic and create a new project.

2 We're going to get rid of the form in this project and just use a message box instead. Delete the form from the project by selecting Remove Form1 from the Project menu.

3 Next add a new module by selecting Project then Add Module and type the following code into the code window:

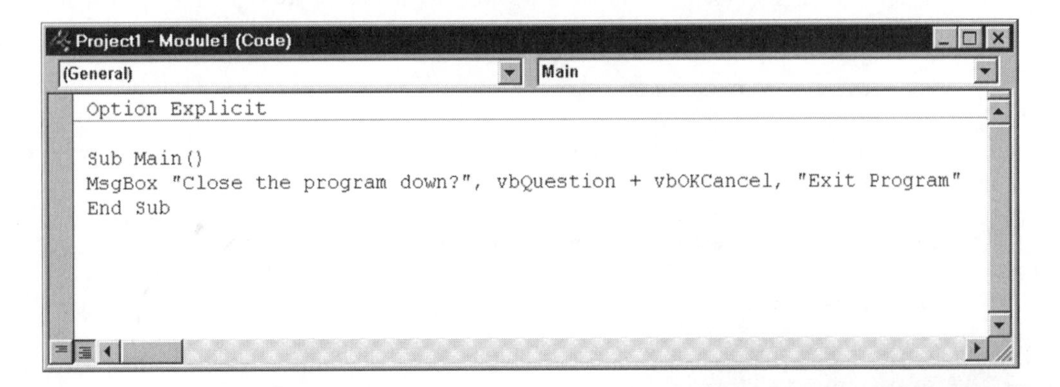
Project1 - Module1 (Code)
(General)
Main
Option Explicit
Sub Main()
MsgBox "Close the program down?", vbQuestion + vbOKCancel, "Exit Program"
End Sub

4 Now run the program. You'll see a message box appear asking you if you want to close the program down. At the moment, though, clicking either OK or Cancel has the same effect—they both stop the program. You'll see how to fix this in a little while.

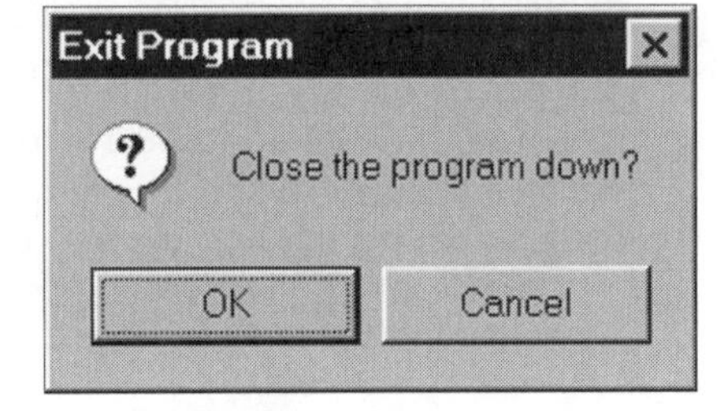
Exit Program
Close the program down?
OK
Cancel

How It Works

The message box you've just created is the most straightforward type—created from a **MsgBox** subroutine. As it stands, the program has no way of knowing which button was pressed—the message box simply takes the button click in its stride, closes down and, since there are no forms and no other code in the project, takes the program with it.

When a message box is open, your program stops running and waits for you to respond to it. Once you've clicked one of the boxes, execution returns to the line in your code after the **MsgBox** command. In our case, there's nothing else here, so the program ends.

Let's take a look at the code you just entered. **MsgBox** is the Visual Basic command which displays a message box (no surprises there!). There are actually two **MsgBox** commands in Visual Basic. One is a subroutine (the one we used here) and the other is a function. They look identical, but the difference between them is that the function returns a number which allows you to see which button was pressed. We'll look at the **MsgBox** function a little later—don't worry about it for the moment.

Immediately following the **MsgBox** command there's a text string:

```
"Close the program down?"
```

This is the message we want displayed in the box.

After the message there are two Visual Basic message box constants which are used to define which icon appears in the box, and which buttons are available to the user. There are quite a few of these constants available to you; we'll take a look at the full list in a moment.

```
vbQuestion + vbOKCancel
```

In this particular example, we're telling Visual Basic to display a message box with a question mark icon, along with an OK and Cancel button.

The final part of the message box command is another text string:

```
"Exit Program"
```

Take a look at the screenshot again and you'll notice that this piece of text is used for the message box title bar.

Message Length in Message Boxes

If you place a long message into a message box, Windows will automatically split it over a number of rows. While this is quite a handy feature, the result can look a real mess. If you want to define the line breaks yourself, you can insert a **CHR$(10)** character, like this:

```
MsgBox "This is a multi-line " & chr$(10) & "message."
```

The resulting message box is then:

The **CHR$()** function returns the character associated with the number in brackets (we mentioned ASCII codes back in Chapter 3). **CHR$(10)** returns a linefeed character which causes a new line to be started.

> *As with many things in Visual Basic, there's actually a predefined constant to save you the drudgery of typing in all those cumbersome **Chr$()** statements. It's called **vbCrLf** and does exactly the same for you as typing **Chr$(10) & Chr$(13)**, but without the risk of getting them the wrong way round and having strange results in your program.*

Selecting the MsgBox Type

A couple of pages back, I mentioned Visual Basic's message box constants. There are a number of constants built into Visual Basic which you can use to determine which icon and which buttons appear on the message box. Simply find the icon constant you want and, in your code, add it to the button constant you want.

Message Box Button Options

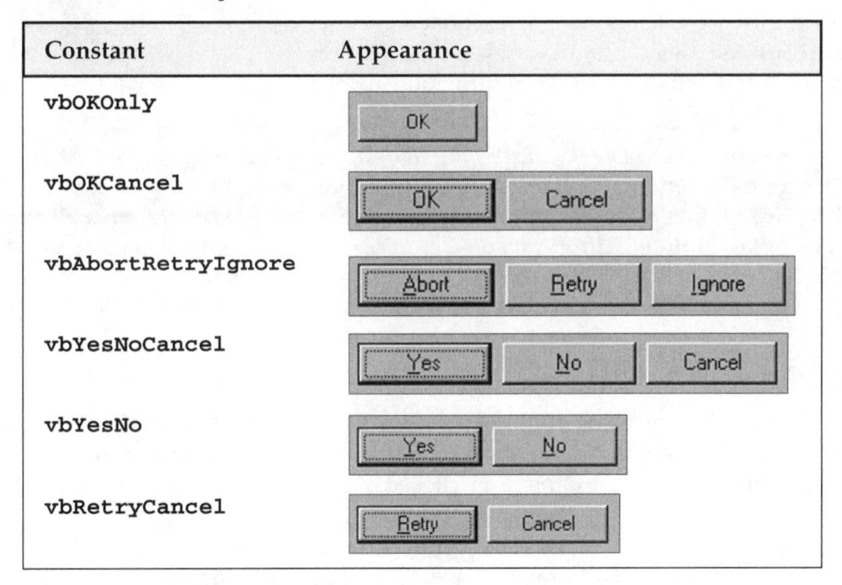

Constant	Appearance
`vbOKOnly`	OK
`vbOKCancel`	OK, Cancel
`vbAbortRetryIgnore`	Abort, Retry, Ignore
`vbYesNoCancel`	Yes, No, Cancel
`vbYesNo`	Yes, No
`vbRetryCancel`	Retry, Cancel

Message Box Icon Options

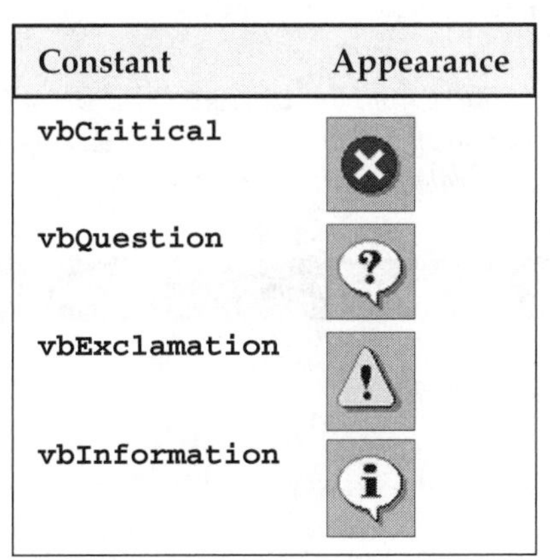

Constant	Appearance
`vbCritical`	
`vbQuestion`	
`vbExclamation`	
`vbInformation`	

Building the MsgBox Parameter

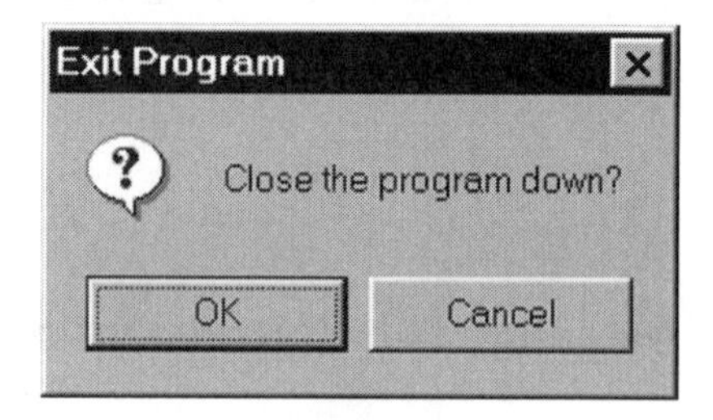

To display a particular message box, first look at the button options table and decide which you want. For our example we wanted an OK and a Cancel button. Therefore the constant we needed to use was **vbOKCancel**. Next, pick the icon you want from the icon options table. We wanted the information icon and so we used the constant **vbInformation**. All you do then is add the two constants together (**vbOKCancel + vbInformation**) and there you have it—a message box with OK and Cancel buttons and an information icon!

> *As you've seen there are quite a lot of different options and parameters that you can use with the **Msgbox** method. Thankfully though, with VB5 the days of looking these things up in the online help system every five minutes are well and truly over. Just turn the Autofill wizard, that we saw in Chapter 6, on and VB will list all the options open to you as you type in the method.*

MsgBox as a Function

I mentioned earlier that by using the **MsgBox** function, it's possible to find out which button was pressed. You can use this information to perform the appropriate action in your program depending on which button was clicked.

The form **QueryUnload** event occurs just before a form unloads, so we could use the message box function here. For example, we could put a message box up with a Yes and No button, and then respond according to which button the user presses. Because this time we're using a function rather than a subroutine, the syntax for **MsgBox** is slightly different and we now need to place parameters in parentheses.

*The **QueryUnload** event differs from the **Unload** event in that it takes place before the form unloads, as opposed to after. This may seem nit-picking, but it can mean the difference between saving your data and losing it forever.*

Try It Out - The MsgBox Function

1. Create a new Visual Basic project.

2. As before, delete the form and create a module instead.

3. Enter this code in the code window that appears for the module:

```
Public Sub Main()

  Dim iResponse As Integer
```

```
    iResponse = MsgBox("Hit one of the buttons",
        ↳vbAbortRetryIgnore + vbInformation, "Hit me")
    MsgBox "You pressed button code " & iResponse

End Sub
```

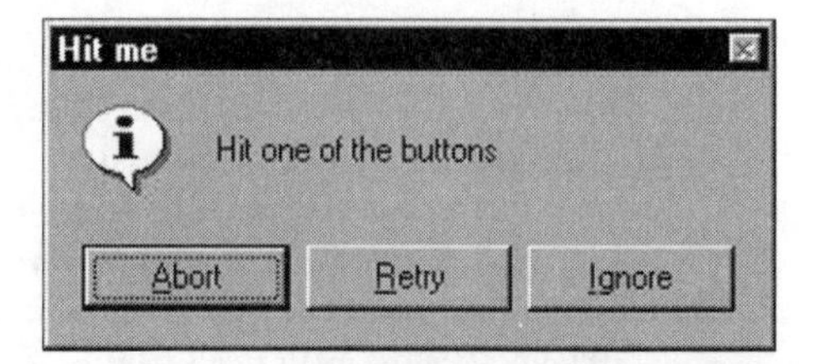

4 Now run the program. The first message is a function that asks you to press one of the buttons.

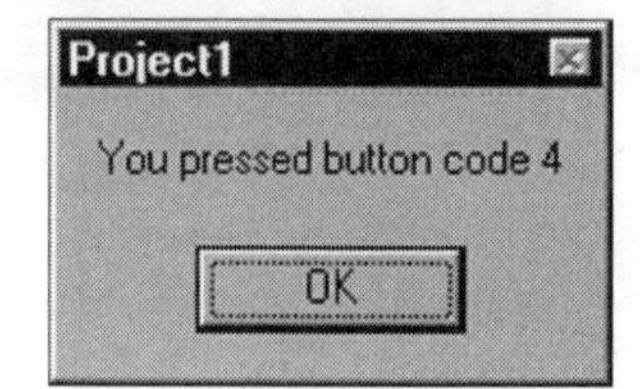

5 The value of the button you press is then assigned to the **iResponse** variable. This is then printed out as part of the **MsgBox** statement at the end.

How It Works

The number of the button pressed corresponds to one of yet more of Visual Basic's intrinsic constants:

Value	Name	Constants
1	OK	vbOK
2	Cancel	vbCANCEL
3	Abort	vbABORT
4	Retry	vbRETRY
5	Ignore	vbIGNORE
6	Yes	vbYES
7	No	vbNO

As you can probably guess from this lot, you can check the return value using either the numbers shown or the built-in Visual Basic constants. The latter is obviously a much better idea since it makes your message box code instantly understandable to any other programmer that may come along, as well as to you when you return to your code in three months time in order to fix it.

If you find yourself frequently typing **MsgBox** *statements with identical icons and buttons but different text, why not define a global subroutine to deal with them? A common use for this is in a global error routine, like the one shown here:*

```
Public Sub ErrorMessage (ByVal sError as String)

 MsgBox sError, vbCritical, "Error"

End Sub
```

*This way, all your error message code is kept in one place, and you don't have to worry about getting the **MsgBox** type number wrong, or about keeping the message box title the same from one message to another. It also makes your code much more maintainable. Changes to the error handler need only be made to one single module rather than to separate error handlers in all the individual modules. If a user then asks you to dump all the error messages to a text file on the disk, you only need to add a couple of lines of code to a single routine, rather than to a hundred (or more) routines. You need to put this kind of global routine in its own **.BAS** module.*

Modality

By default, all message boxes are **application modal**. This means that whilst a message box is visible, no other windows in your application can get the focus. The user must respond to the message before they are able do anything else in that application. However, they can still switch to other applications by clicking on the taskbar or using *Alt-Tab*.

If you have a very serious message box that you wish to take precedence over everything else (including other Windows programs), what you really want is a **system modal** dialog box. This is a message box that will remain visible, even if the user switches to another application.

System modality is selected by adding yet another Visual Basic constant to the parameter. In this case, the constant is **vbSystemModal**.

Try It Out - Creating a System Message Box

1 Start up a new project in Visual Basic.

2 Double-click on the default form to display the code window with the **Form_Load** event displayed.

3 Add the following line of code to the **Load** event:

```
Private Sub Form_Load()

   Msgbox "This is a system modal box. Try clicking on any other form",
         ↳vbSystemModal

End Sub
```

4 Now run the program. Just before the default form appears, a message box pops up. This is a system modal dialog box and not only means that you can't do anything else anywhere in the application until you click the OK button, but also stays in your face even when you switch to other applications.

This is great for really serious error messages in your program, since no matter where the user is in Windows, they won't be able to get away from the dialog box.

In Windows 3.x, system modal dialogs prevented you from switching applications altogether. You had no choice but to acknowledge the message box. Windows 95, however, runs each application in its own protected memory space, effectively insulating it from other applications that you're running. You can't interfere with the system to stop other apps like you could in earlier versions of Windows. This is good news for those of us who have seen a duff app bring the whole system down.

Input Boxes

Message boxes are great for relaying information to the user and getting them to press a single button, but what about when you need to get more information from the user? Well, that's where the input box comes into its own.

Input boxes are closely related to message boxes in that they are simple in both appearance and use, and are able to display a message to the user. The difference between the two is that an input box can accept data from the user.

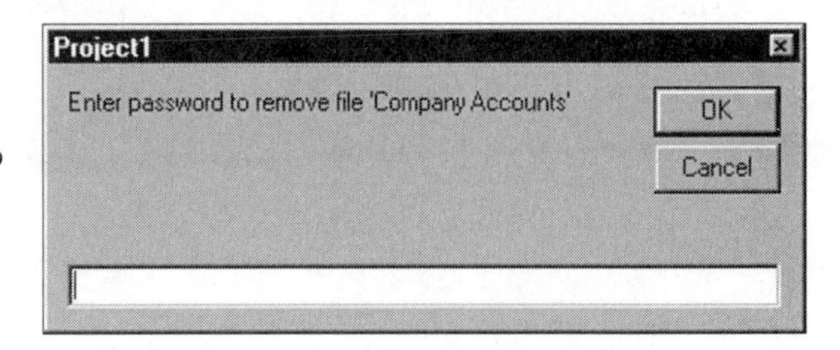

When to Use Input Boxes

Despite their apparent ease of use both for you and your users, input boxes are very rarely used in state-of-the-art applications. The main reasons for this are simple:

- Input boxes can't be programmed, so there's no way you can validate the data a user enters until *after* they've entered it. For example, if you were using a standard form, you could place a text box on to it and add code to either the **`KeyPress`** or **`Change`** events to check that the user is behaving. With an input box, you can't do that.
- They only allow the user to enter one piece of information. Programmers usually need more than this, and so use a custom form instead.
- Finally, they don't look great. Developing for Windows is like buying fashionable clothing—you don't want to be wearing the same old junk as everyone else. Custom dialogs are a cut above the built-in variety.

Despite these drawbacks, input boxes are a quick and easy way of getting a single piece of information from your user, so let's take a look.

Try It Out - An Input Box

1 Start a new project in Visual Basic and delete the form and create a module.

2 Type the following into the code window:

```
Public Sub Main ()

  Dim sReturnString As String
  sReturnString = InputBox$("Enter your name", "Name Please", "Fred")
  MsgBox "Hi there " & sReturnString, vbOK, "Hello"

End Sub
```

3 Run the program and you should see the input box appear exactly like this:

4 The default name, Fred, is highlighted in the input box. If you don't want to change the name, just press OK and see what happens.

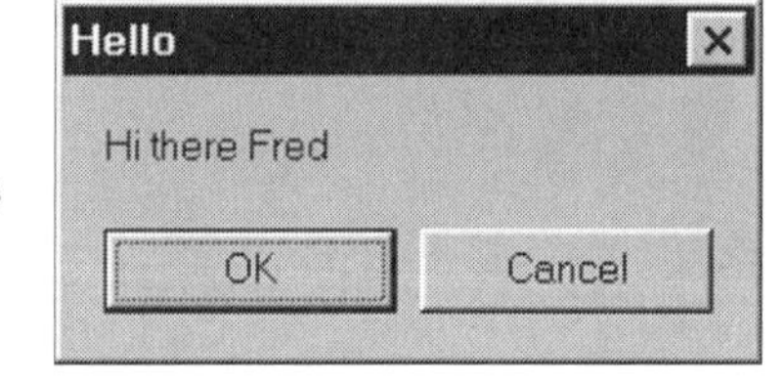

How It Works

Now for the first shock. Although the input box and message box both come from the same family of commands, you can't tell Visual Basic to display an icon, or tell it which buttons to display.

The parameters you can enter are fairly straightforward. This is the above example:

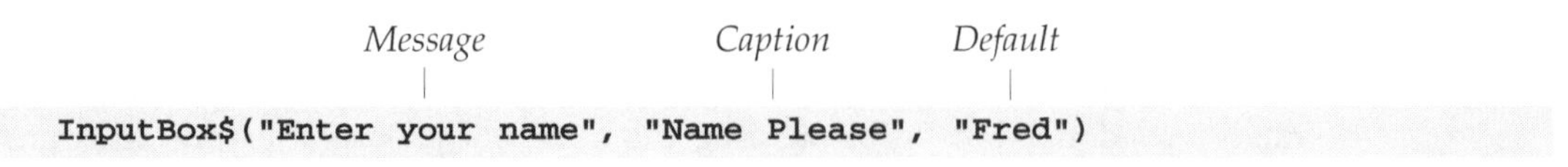


```
InputBox$("Enter your name", "Name Please", "Fred")
```

The first block of text is the prompt, in this case **"Enter your name"**. In message box speak this is the same as the message. Next comes the title, which is the same as the title on a message box. Finally, the third parameter is known as default. This is the value that is automatically displayed in the input box when it loads up.

Positioning Your Input Box

There are two other parameters which we didn't use in the above example: X and Y. These are the coordinates at which you want the input box to appear. For the sake of completeness I should say that the X and Y coordinates are measured in twips, but that is a topic we cover in more detail in the next chapter.

> *If you have* Autofill *turned on, then you will have noticed that there are two additional parameters, called* **Helpfile** *and* **Context**. *These are for use with help files in your application, and are a little bit beyond the scope of a mere beginner's guide. Just ignore them for the moment.*

For now, all you need to know is that X is a number beginning at 0, increasing as the coordinates move towards the right-hand edge of the screen. The maximum value depends on the resolution of the screen. The Y coordinate begins at 0 for the top of the screen and increases as it moves towards the bottom.

Try It Out - Placing the Input Box

1 Try adding **0,0** after the third parameter in the input box command above.

```
InputBox$("Enter your name", "Name Please", "Fred",0,0 )
```

2 Rerun the program to see the effect. The input box now appears at the top left corner of the screen.

Data Types and Input Boxes

As with the message box, there are two input box commands, but this time both are functions—one returns a string value ready to go straight into a string variable, whilst the other returns a variant. As we learned back in Chapter 5, Visual Basic deals with variants a lot slower than it deals with explicit data types such as strings or integers.

InputBox$** returns a proper string to your code, **InputBox$ returns a string type variant. If you needed to get numbers or dates from the user, you would use **InputBox**. For instance:

```
Private Sub Form_Load ()

        Dim varValue As Variant
        Dim nAge As Integer
```

```
        varValue = InputBox("Please type your age", "Age", "23")
        If IsNumeric(varValue) Then
             nAge = Val(varValue)
        Else
            MsgBox "No, no, no - enter your age as a number!", ,
               ↳"User Error"

        End If

End Sub
```

Common Dialogs

Have you ever noticed how all Windows programs have the same dialog box pop up when you try to load or save something? Have you also noticed that most of the programs have identical font, color and printer dialogs too?

The reason for this is the common dialog library. All the functions in Windows which allow programs such as Visual Basic to create windows, move graphics, change colors and so on, are held in files known as dynamic link libraries, or **DLLs**. One such file is the common dialog DLL. Visual Basic 5 comes with a special OLE custom control, **Comdlg32.ocx**, which makes using the functions in this DLL easy to master.

A DLL is a collection of functions and procedures, usually written in C or C++, which you can use in your programs to get at features of Windows which aren't normally available. Actually using DLLs isn't entirely straightforward, so Visual Basic encompasses most of the functions of the DLLs in OCXs. **Comdlg32.ocx** *provides you with an easy way to use the functions in the* **Comdlg32.dll**. *Instead of using some weird declaration statements and a lot of code, you can now call the DLL functions simply by changing properties. We'll look at how to use DLLs that don't have their own OCX later when we delve into the world of the Windows API.*

Using Common Dialogs

The common dialog control provides a set of five common dialog boxes for opening files, saving files, printing, setting colors and choosing fonts. There is also a sixth function of the control that doesn't actually show a dialog, but starts the Windows online help engine. I don't count it as a common dialog as such, although it is a function of the control.

The dialogs don't actually do anything to your application or its data. They simply receive the user's choices and return the values of these choices to your program through the properties of the common dialog control.

Actually programming the common dialogs is a bit of an esoteric exercise. Although there are five manifestations of the common dialog, there's only one common dialog control. This single control has various **Show** methods that invoke each of the dialogs.

Name	Method
Open File	`ShowOpen`
Save File	`ShowSave`
Color	`ShowColor`
Font	`ShowFont`
Print	`ShowPrinter`
Help	`ShowHelp`

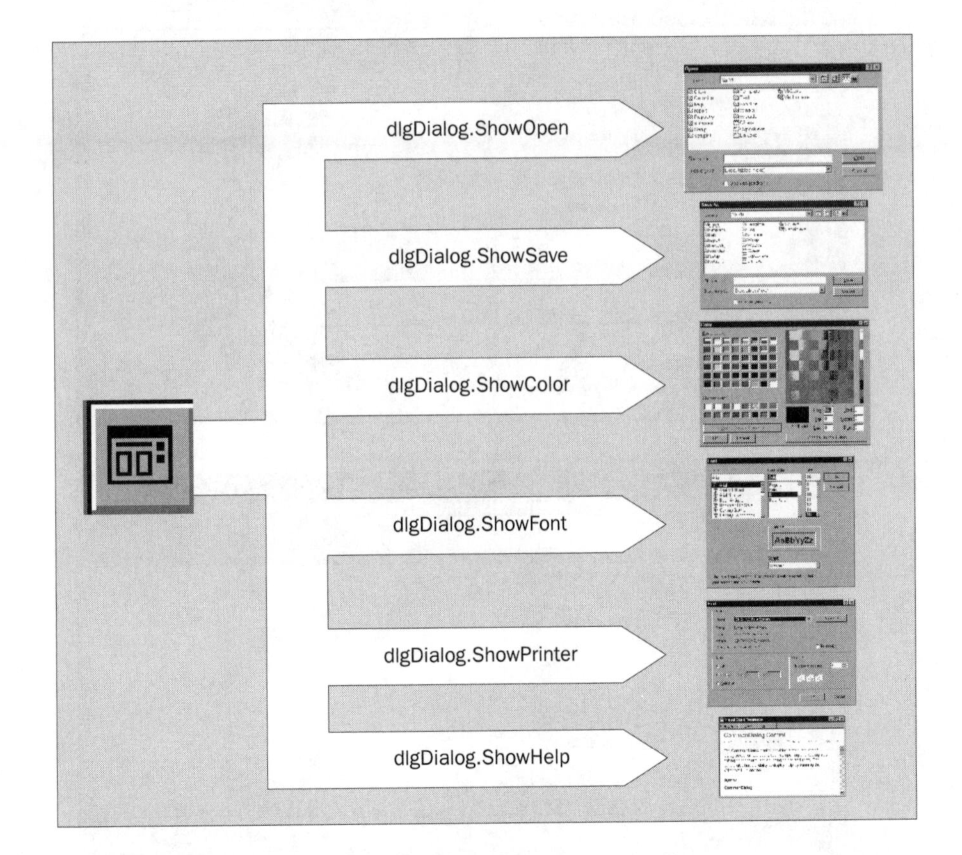

At a first glance a common dialog may appear a little daunting. There are so many controls to think about, surely there must be a lot of code involved? That's the real beauty of common dialogs—they can provide a vast amount of information and functionality to your users, but only require a tiny amount of code from you.

The Open and Save File Dialogs

The open and save file common dialogs are similar in both looks and function. Both display drive, directory and file lists, and enable the user to move around the hard disk in search of a file name. There's also a text entry area where the selected file name is displayed or into which a new file name can be entered. Finally, to the right of the dialog there are OK and Cancel buttons allowing the user to accept or discard their choice.

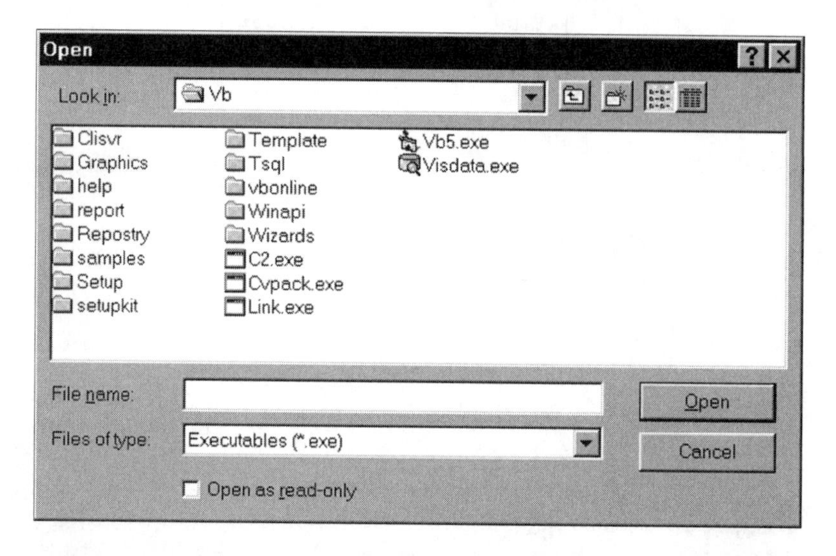

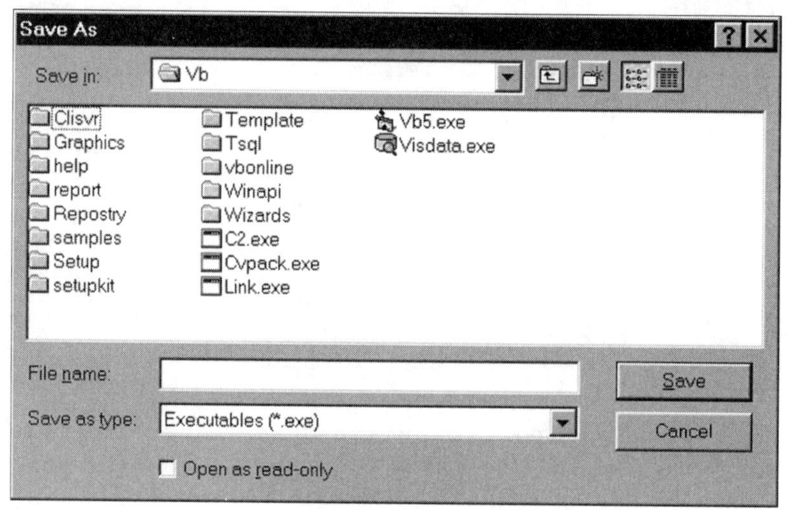

Let's see these dialogs in action with a program that displays an open file dialog box.

Try It Out - An Open File Dialog

1 Create a new project.

2 Make sure you have the common dialog control in the project.

If you don't see the icon for it in the toolbox, you can add it by selecting Components... from the Project menu, and checking the Microsoft Common Dialog Control option

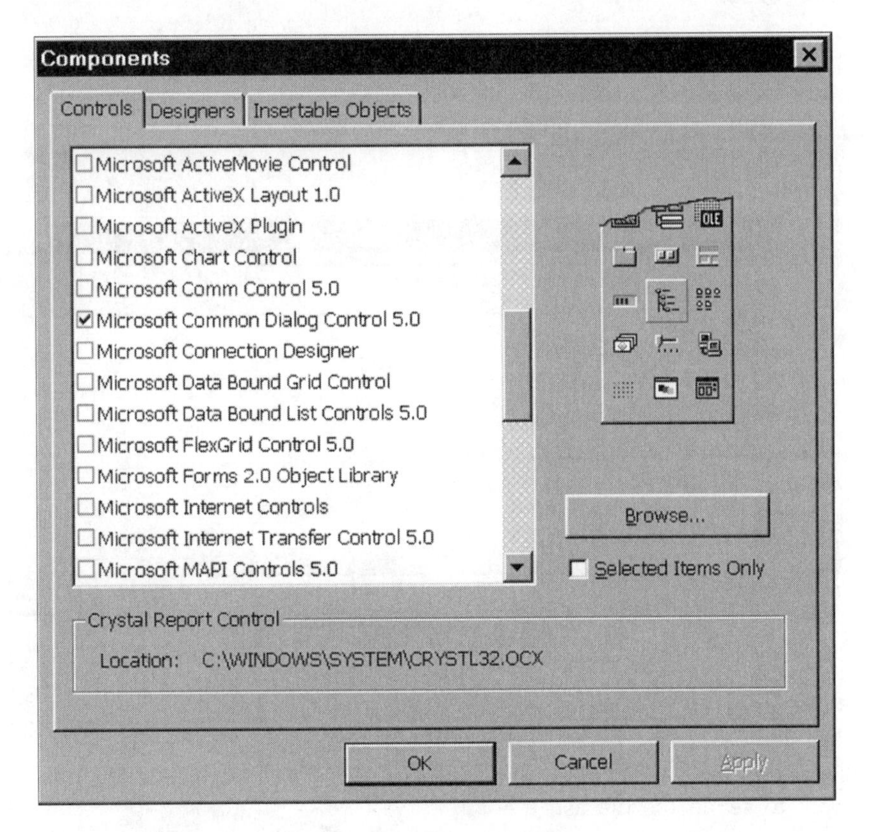

3 Place the common dialog icon on to the form. This is like the timer control in that it just sits on the form and can't be resized. It also doesn't show on the form at run time, so it doesn't matter where you place it.

4 Bring up the form's code window and type the following code into the **Load** event:

```
Private Sub Form_Load()

    On Error GoTo DialogError

    With CommonDialog1
```

```
            .CancelError = True
            .Filter = "Executables (*.exe)|*.exe|Com Files
             ↳ (*.com)|*.com|Batch Files (*.bat)|*.bat"
            .FilterIndex = 1
            .DialogTitle = "Select a program to open"
            .ShowOpen

            MsgBox "You selected " & .filename

        End With

    DialogError:

    End Sub
```

5 If you run the program now, an open file dialog appears asking you to select the name of a file.

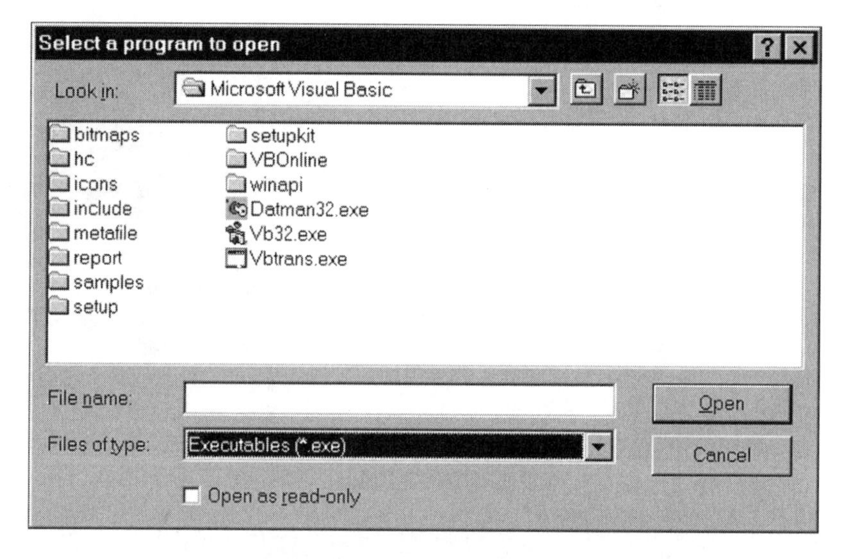

6 The drop-down list at the bottom of the dialog lets you select the types of file you want to see in the file list.

How It Works

In order to decide which of the six common dialogs to select, and how it should work, before you launch the dialog you must cycle through the properties of the control and set them appropriately.

In the next few pages we'll cover each of these properties in depth, but for now there's one part of this code that warrants attention. That's the **`With...End With`** block that we use to cycle through the properties.

```
    With CommonDialog1

        .CancelError = True
        .Filter = "Executables (*.exe)|*.exe|Com Files
         ↳ (*.com)|*.com|Batch Files (*.bat)|*.bat"
        .FilterIndex = 1
        .DialogTitle = "Select a program to open"
        .ShowOpen

        MsgBox "You selected " & .filename

    End With
```

This is an advantage as by saying that we're going to be doing whatever is inside the block **`With CommonDialog1`**, we don't need to retype this before each of the properties we set. Visual Basic assumes we mean the property belongs to **`CommonDialog1`**.

Using **`With...`** **`End With`** not only saves you a lot of typing but, by indenting the code inside the block, you can make your code much more readable, and faster too (since VB no longer has to figure out which object each and every line of code is dealing with—you've already told it). There's nothing worse and more tiring than reading line after line of

```
dlgDialog.Property =
dlgDialog.Property =
dlgDialog.Property =
dlgDialog.Property =
```

Setting Up the Open File Dialog

The common dialog control is unlike other Visual Basic controls in that it doesn't have any events. Instead, you interact with it by setting various properties and by using its **`Show`** methods. As with most controls, you can set the properties at design time, run time or a combination of both.

Setting Properties at Design Time

At design time you have the luxury of a choice of two options for setting properties. You can hit *F4* and bring up the usual properties window.

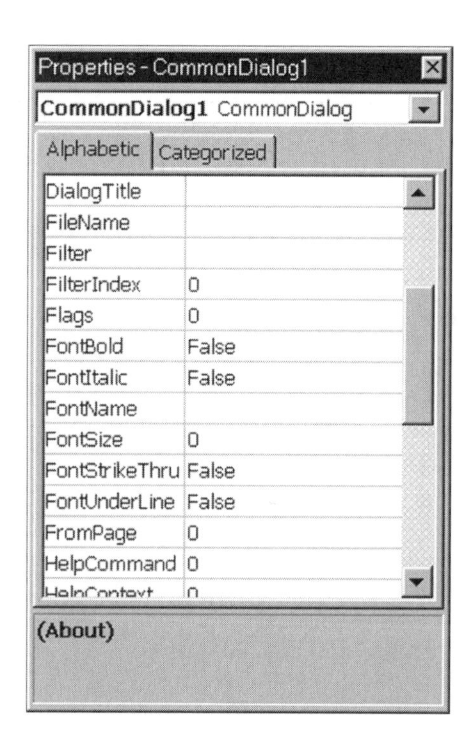

This window is a bit unhelpful in that it lumps all the properties for all the common dialogs together, when in reality some properties are only relevant to certain dialogs, while others fall into to the 'err, what's that for then...' category.

To make life easier, Visual Basic provides a nice little tabbed dialog that organizes the key properties by dialog. You get to the dialog by double-clicking on the (Custom) property in the property window or by right clicking on the control itself and selecting Properties.

The dialog looks like this:

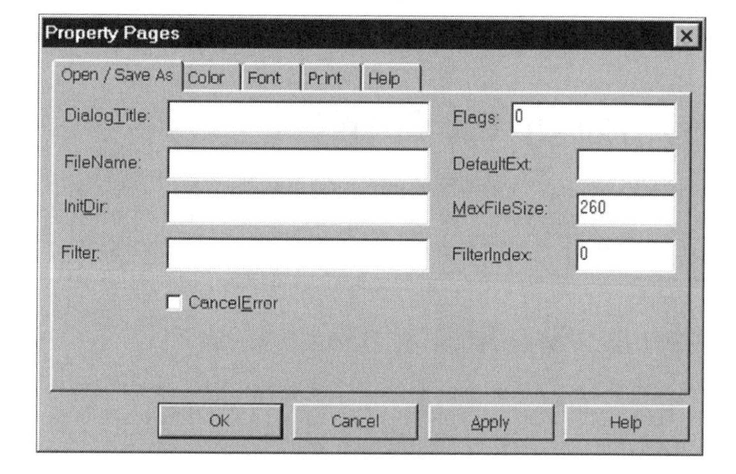

However, the problem with setting properties for the common dialog at design time is that this then locks into one dialog. The whole point of the common dialog control is that is gives you six controls for the price of one, so it makes sense to keep your options open by not committing the control to one type of dialog at design time and instead, making your choices in code.

Setting Properties from Code

Before we look at implementing the dialog setup code, let's see which properties need setting for the open and save common dialogs:

Property	Description
`FileName`	The full file name of the selected file, e.g. `C:\Temp\ReadMe.Doc.` This property is what you see when the file has been selected for opening. You rarely set this in code directly.
`FileTitle`	The file name of the selected file, but without the path, e.g. `ReadMe.Doc`
`Filter`	Defines the types of file that the dialog will show. Basically, you need to enter wildcards here, with a description of each. For instance `dlg.Filter = "Text	*.txt	Icons	*.ico"`. This selects which types of file to display in the combo box at the foot of the file dialog. To keep the user focused, set this before you call the dialog.
`FilterIndex`	Defines the initial filter to use. Earlier we set up three filter values—for `.exe`, `.com` and `.bat` files. We then set `FilterIndex` to 1 before displaying the dialog box, causing it to display only files matching the first filter, that is, `*.exe` files, i.e. executables. Setting it to 2 would display only `.com` files in the file list, and so on.
`Flags`	Governs the way the dialog actually works—we'll look at this later in the chapter.
`InitDir`	Specifies the initial directory to list in the dialog. This suggests to your user where the files should go/come from.
`MaxFileSize`	Allows you to tell the dialog the maximum number of characters you want to see displayed for a file name.
`DialogTitle`	Effectively the same as the `Caption` property on a form.
`CancelError`	Set this to true to trigger a run-time error if the user presses the Cancel button. We can catch this error in our code if we use the `On Error` statement, and then take the necessary action.

Selecting the Correct Files

In our earlier sample program, we set the **Filter** and **FilterIndex** properties of the open dialog to control the types of file listed in the dialog:

```
.Filter = "Executables (*.exe)|*.exe|Com Files
  ↳ (*.com)|*.com|Batch Files (*.bat)|*.bat"
.FilterIndex = 1
```

Filter contains a string where each element of the string is separated by a | sign.

On most keyboards the | symbol is two vertical dashes, one on top of the other. If you come from a UNIX background then you'll know this old friend as the Pipe symbol.

First, you enter a description for the type of file, for example: **Com Files (*.com)**. These descriptions are what appear in the drop-down list box at the bottom of the dialog. After each description you must then enter the wildcard for the files which match that description. In this case it's simply `*.com`. As you select descriptions from the drop-down at the bottom of the dialog, the file list changes to show only those files which match your wildcard.

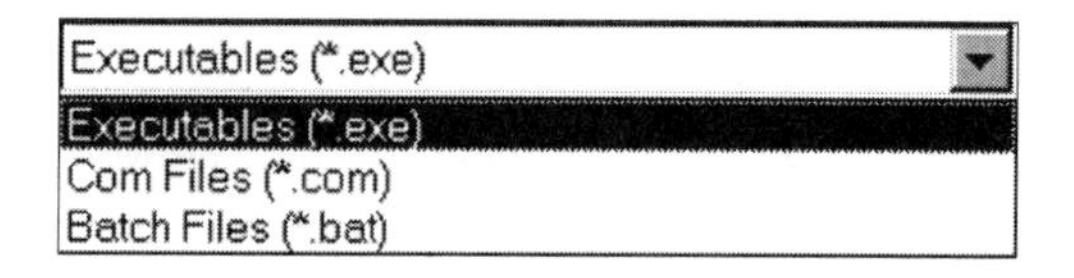

The **FilterIndex** property is a number between **1** and the number of elements in the filter. It defines the default or start-up filter that should be used. In the example, I say **FilterIndex = 1**. Therefore, the default filter to use will be the first one, which is **Executables (*.exe).**

Naming the Dialog

Instead of the normal **Caption** property, common dialogs use the **DialogTitle** property to set the message displayed on the title bar of the common dialog. The following line sets this up:

```
.DialogTitle = "Select Program To Open"
```

If you don't set this property of the dialog, Visual Basic will automatically display an appropriate title of its own.

Selecting and Launching the Dialog

Finally, the dialog is brought into view by using the appropriate **Show** method. For example, **.ShowOpen** shows the open dialog, **.ShowSave** shows the save dialog, and so on. A complete list of these **Show** methods was given earlier.

When the user has selected a file name, it's returned in the common dialog **FileName** property.

Error Handling with Common Dialogs

We set the **CancelError** property to true at the start of the code:

```
On Error GoTo DialogError

With CommonDialog1

.CancelError = True
```

This means that if Cancel is clicked, it triggers a Visual Basic error.

> *This only applies to the **Cancel** buttons you'll find in the common dialogs. It doesn't apply to the **Cancel** buttons on message boxes or input boxes.*

The last lines of code in the example are designed to trap any errors:

```
DialogError:

End Sub
```

Why do we need to do this? Well, it means that when the user presses Cancel on the common dialog, an error event is triggered, causing the **DialogError** code to take control out of the main procedure and exit. If we didn't set **CancelError** to True and then put an error handler in place, if the user canceled the dialog then we would have no way of knowing which button the user hit to get rid of it. At that point we would need a condition or two to check whether or not the returned value is valid. Using error handlers in this way simplifies the flow of code, making it a lot easier to read and maintain, and see at a glance everything that is going on.

The Color Dialog

The color dialog is even easier to set up than the file dialogs. Its purpose is to allow the user to select and display colors from the palette of colors currently available on that particular computer.

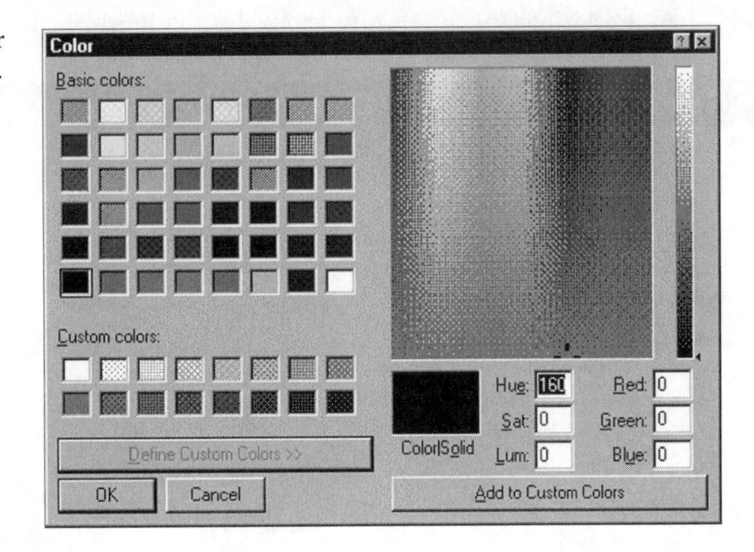

Properties of the Color Dialog

Property	Description
`Color`	Holds the long integer value of the color the user selected.
`Flags`	See the section later in this chapter for details of the most common flag values.
`CancelError`	Set **CancelError** to true to trigger a run-time error if the user clicks on the Cancel button on the dialog box.

To bring the color dialog into view, use the **ShowColor** method on the common dialog control on your form.

The actual color selected is returned in the dialog's **`Color`** property. You can move it directly from there to the color properties of any controls whose color you wish to change.

In terms of functionality, the color dialog is actually a little more powerful than the others. The Add to Custom Colors button, for example, lets you create your own colors and add them to the Windows palette.

Invoking the Color Dialog in Your Code

When using the color dialog, you should first place the number 1 into the **`Flags`** property to initialize it and then use the **`ShowColor`** method on the control itself. We take a look at the **`Flags`** property in more detail a little later on in the chapter. However, in a nutshell, you can feed values into the **`Flags`** property to change the default appearance and behavior of any of the common dialogs. For example in the Font dialog, you can use the **`Flags`** property to force it to only show you fonts for the screen, or only show you printer fonts. As I said though, don't worry about this too much right now. We do look at it later on.

Try It Out - Using the Color Dialog

OK—time to take a little peek into exactly how the color dialog works in the real world.

1 Start up a new project in VB and drop a picture box and common dialog control on to the form so that it looks like this

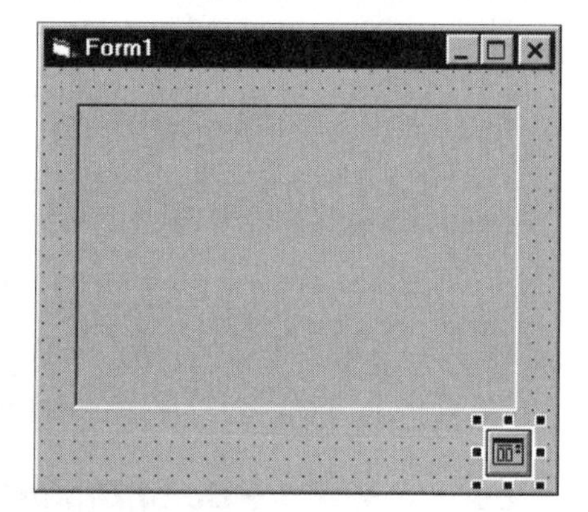

Remember that there's a chance, depending on which version of Visual Basic you're using and how you have it configured, that you may not have a common dialog control on your toolbar. To get around this, use the **Components** *and* **References** *items on the* **Project** *menu to ensure that you have set up full support for dealing with the common dialog controls in this project.*

2 What we want to do here is when the user clicks on the picture box at run time, the color dialog should pop up and allow the user to choose the color to use for the background of the picture box. So then, now would obviously be a good time to open the code window and find the picture box's **`Click`** event.

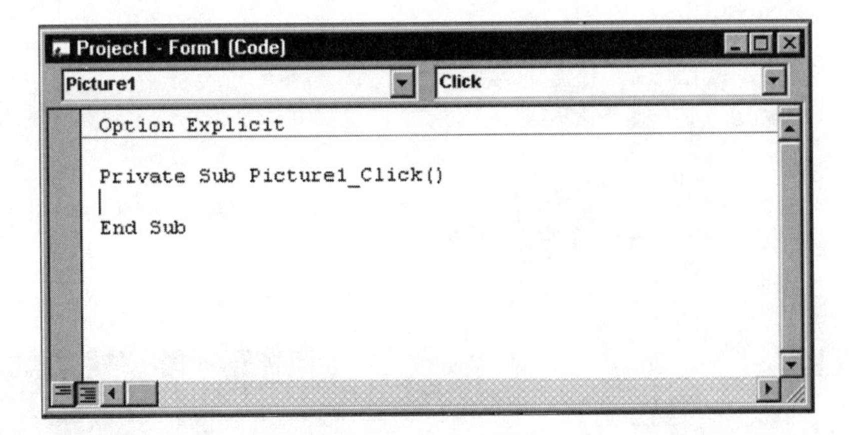

3 The first thing we need to do is tell the common dialog what to do when the Cancel button is clicked. Ideally it would be nice to have it trigger a trappable error and then put an error handler in our code to deal with this nicely. As you've already seen, this is pretty simple to do. Change the **Click** event so that it now looks like this.

```
Private Sub Picture1_Click()

    CommonDialog1.CancelError = True
    On Error GoTo No_Color_Chosen

'Stop error trapping
    On  Error GoTo 0

'More code
    Exit Sub
No_Color_Chosen:
    MsgBox "No color selected - just thought you should know",
      ↳ vbInformation, "Cancelled"

End Sub
```

4 All that remains then is to get the dialog to appear, and then dump the chosen color into the picture box on the form. Don't panic—as always VB makes something like this a lot easier than it sounds.

Add some more code to the event so that it now looks like this

```
Private Sub Picture1_Click()
    CommonDialog1.CancelError = True
    On Error GoTo No_Color_Chosen

    CommonDialog1.Flags = cdlCCFullOpen
    CommonDialog1.ShowColor

    Picture1.BackColor = CommonDialog1.Color
```

```
' Stop error trapping
    On Error GoTo 0

'More Code
    Exit Sub
No_Color_Chosen:
   MsgBox "No color selected - just thought you should know",
   ↳ vbInformation, "Cancelled"

End Sub
```

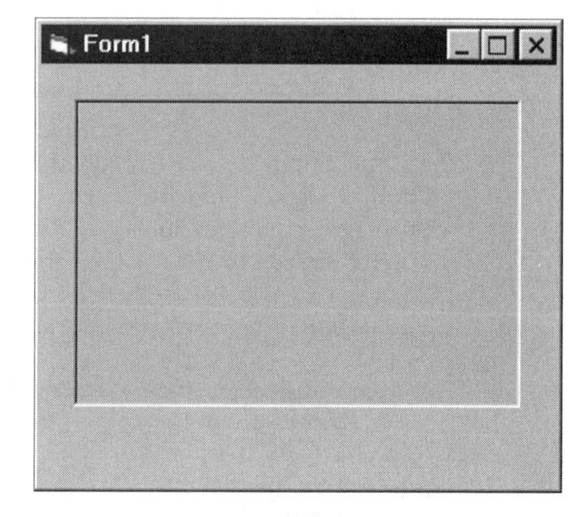

5 Now try it. Run the program and see what happens when you click on the picture box.

6 Finally, before we move on, save your application as **`Color.vbp`**. We will build on this in the next example.

> *It's worth noting at this point, that colors are one of the things that would make it real easy to turn users off your application. Windows 95 gives the user a lot of control over the colors that they want to see in use throughout their desktop and the applications they run. Jumping in and changing them totally can be extremely annoying.*
>
> *For this reason, it's best to limit the use of the color dialog in your application to providing users with a way to change the colors of various parts of the data they are dealing with, rather than using it to change the look and feel of the application as a whole. VB provides a great many color constants, which you'll see in the graphics chapter, to enable you to use the currently set system colors for your controls, forms and so on.*

How It Works

The code for this example is really very simple.

```
CommonDialog1.CancelError = True
    On Error GoTo No_Color_Chosen
```

We started by adding some error handling—we told the common dialog control that if the user cancels it, the dialog should trigger a trappable error, i.e. one which gets routed to a local error handler on the next line of code.

In the event that the user does cancel the dialog then the error handler at the bottom of the **Click** event does nothing more than display a message to the user telling them what is taking place behind the scenes. Whether they cancel or not though, the **On Error GoTo 0** lines turn off error handling in the normal way before the subroutine is done.

We then added functionality to the program.

```
CommonDialog1.Flags = cdlCCFullOpen
    CommonDialog1.ShowColor
```

We set the **Flags** property of the dialog so that when it appears at run time, what the user sees is a full dialog, rather than the more customary reduced one. Then, we invoked the **ShowColor** method in order to bring the dialog into view.

```
Picture1.BackColor = CommonDialog1.Color
```

Assuming the user doesn't cancel the dialog, then the next line of code to run will set up the picture box's **BackColor**, using the value in the **Color** property of the common dialog, which is the color that the user has chosen.

The Font Dialog

The font dialog enables the user to select fonts from the printer's font list, from the screen font list or from both together. You can also use the **Flags** property of the dialog to limit exactly which types of fonts to display in this dialog, for example make it display printer fonts only, or screen fonts only.

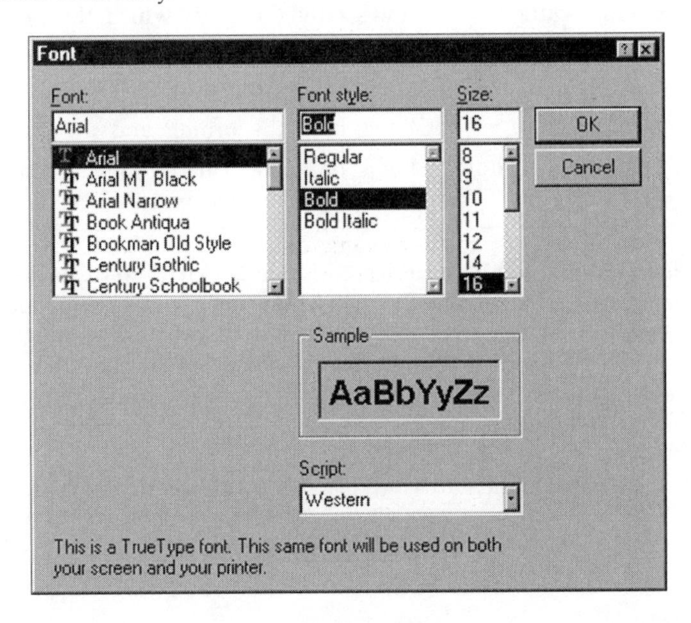

Properties of the Font Dialog

Property	Description
`Color`	Holds the long integer value of the color that the user selected in the dialog.
`FontBold`	True if the user selected Bold in the dialog, false if not.
`FontItalic`	True if the user selected Italic in the dialog.
`FontStrikeThru`	True if the user selected StrikeThru in the dialog.
`FontUnderLine`	True if the user selected Underline in the dialog.
`FontName`	Use your imagination!
`Max`	Specifies the size, in points, of the largest fonts to be displayed.
`Min`	Specifies the size, in points, of the smallest fonts to be displayed.
`FontSize`	Holds the size of the selected font.
`Flags`	See the section later in this chapter for some useful values for the **`Flags`** property.
`CancelError`	Set this to true to cause a run-time error whenever the user clicks on the Cancel button in the common dialog. This can be trapped in code with the **`On Error`** statement.

You can determine which font list will be displayed by loading either a number or a built in VB constant into the **`Flags`** property. The numbers you need to place in the **`Flags`** property are:

Constant	Value	Effect
`cdlCFPrinterFonts`	`&H2`	Shows only the fonts which the printer is capable of.
`cdlCFScreenFonts`	`&H1`	Shows only the screen based fonts, which may not be supported by the printer.
`cdlCFBoth`	`&H3`	Shows both the printer and the screen fonts.
`cdlCFScalableOnly`	`&H20000`	Shows only the scalable fonts, such as the TrueType fonts that you have installed on the computer.

In this age of laser printers and true What You See Is What You Get editing, it's quite important to note that not all of these options may have a noticeable effect. For example, the difference between a screen font and a printer font becomes somewhat blurred when you have a printer beside your computer capable of producing anything you like. However, this may not be the case on your users' machines, some of which may still be using aging Dot Matrix printers. Bear this in mind.

The dialog can then be brought into view using the **`ShowFont`** method.

> *If you don't set the **`Flags`** property to one of these values before displaying the fonts dialog, then you'll get an error—**No Fonts Exist**.*

If you want to be able to select a font color, you should add 256 to the value in the **`Flags`** property. If you don't do this, you won't be able to select colors, only font names, styles and sizes.

When the user exits the dialog, your code can check the **`Color`** property and the values of the **`Font`** properties to find out what the user actually chose.

Try It Out – Using the Font Dialog

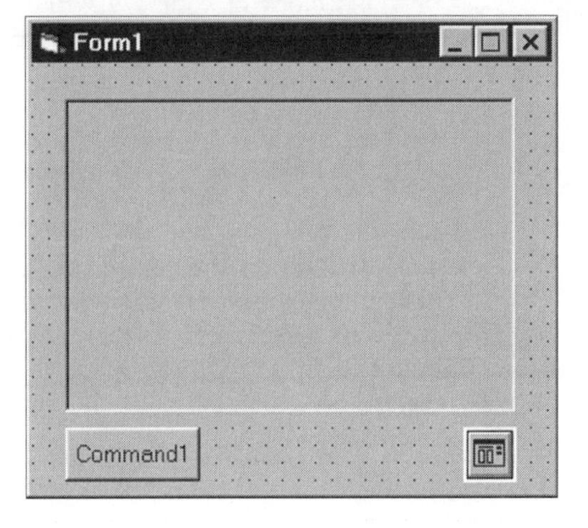

1 Open up the project **`color.vbp`**, if it's not still open and start by dropping a button on to the form.

2 This time around we're going to deal with the command button's **`Click`** event. There's a bit more code than last time, but it's just as simple. Add code so that the button's **`Click`** event looks like this:

```
Private Sub Command1_Click()

    CommonDialog1.CancelError = True
    On Error GoTo No_Font_Chosen

    CommonDialog1.Flags = 1
    CommonDialog1.ShowFont


    With Picture1.Font

        .Bold = CommonDialog1.FontBold
        .Italic = CommonDialog1.FontItalic
        .Name = CommonDialog1.FontName
        .Size = CommonDialog1.FontSize
```

```
            .Strikethrough = CommonDialog1.FontStrikethru
            .Underline = CommonDialog1.FontUnderline

        End With
        Picture1.Print "This is a sample"

        On Error GoTo 0
        Exit Sub

    No_Font_Chosen:
        MsgBox "No font was chosen", vbInformation, "Cancelled"

    End Sub
```

Don't be daunted by the sheer volume of code here—it really is the same as the previous block of code we wrote. In fact the only difference (aside from the fact that this one shows a font dialog instead of a color dialog) is that it deals with more properties.

3 Run the program and see how it works... after clicking on the command button the font dialog comes into view. If you select a font, style and size and then click on the OK button then text will be displayed in the picture box containing all the attributes you selected.

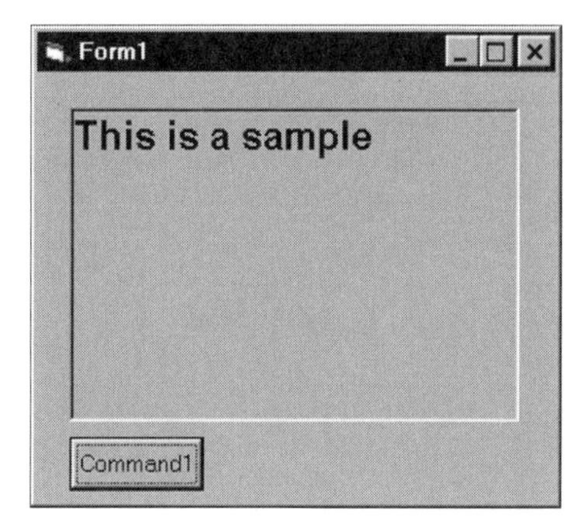

The code here just feeds the values in the **`FontBold`**, **`FontItalic`**, **`FontName`**, **`FontSize`**, **`FontStrikeThru`** and **`FontUnderline`** properties of the common dialog into the corresponding properties of the font object attached to the picture box. Simple as that.

The Print Dialog

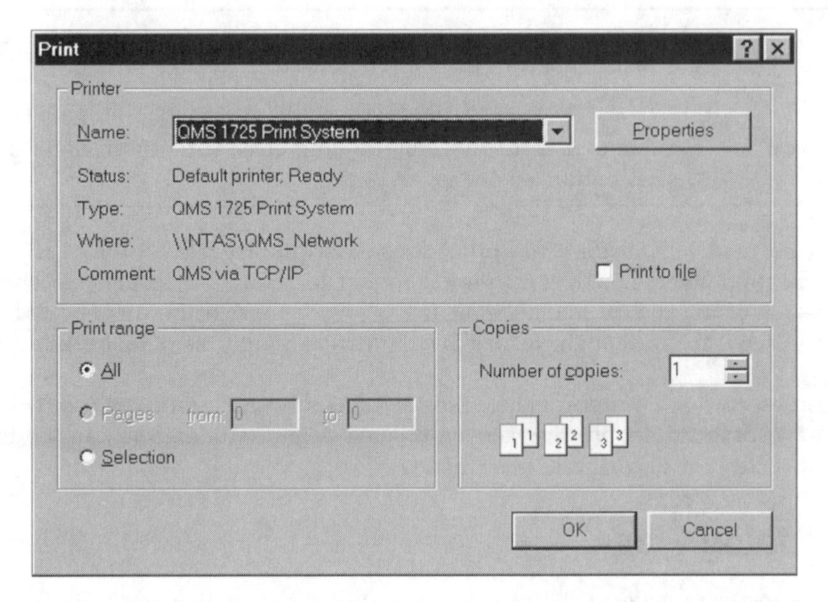

The print dialog allows the user to not only determine how much data they want to print, but also how the printer itself should work. This includes at which resolution and speed the printer should print, which printer or printer driver to use, and even whether or not to ignore the printer totally and print direct to a disk file. Just to really confuse your application, the dialog even allows the user to specify the number of copies to print and whether these copies should be collated. This last option is only available on some printers. Another important point to note is that if you use this dialog to select a new printer, then the default printer setting throughout Windows will change. Without delving into the API and producing your own special format print dialog, there really is no way around this.

Properties of the Print Dialog

Property	Description
`Copies`	Holds both the initial value and the value entered by the user for the number of copies to print.
`FromPage`	Holds the number of the first page to print. Can be set by code before the dialog is displayed, or by the user keying in a number.
`Max`	Holds the maximum number of copies the user can select.
`Min`	Holds the minimum number of copies the user can select.
`PrinterDefault`	If you set this to true, then any changes the user makes in the Printer Setup dialog are saved as permanent changes to your system. They will also affect any programs running which you may want to make use of the printer.

Table Continued on Following Page

Property	Description
`ToPage`	Holds the number of the last page to print. You can also set it before the dialog appears to give your users a default setting.
`Flags`	See later for some of the more useful flag values for this property.
`CancelError`	Set this to true to cause a run-time error if the user clicks on the Cancel button on the print dialog.

Unlike the color and font dialogs, the print dialog box doesn't need to have anything placed into its **`Flags`** property, although it is quite common to set values in there to change the default behavior of the dialog, and to limit the user's options to those supported by your code. All you need to do, though, to display the dialog is run the **`ShowPrinter`** method.

Three properties are used to return the user's selections to your program: **`Copies`**, **`FromPage`** and **`ToPage`**. In order to supply the user with some default values, you can set these properties up before displaying the print dialog.

Common Dialog Flags

The **`Flags`** property provides a useful way to control the operation of the common dialogs and the information they present to your users. In all, there are 48 different values you can use for the **`Flags`** property, and these can be combined to give you some really weird custom effects. However, of those 48, only a handful are really common.

The table below shows you the most useful flags and the VB constants you can use for them. I guess you'd call it *'My Favorite Flags'*.

Name	Dialog	Description
`cdlPDPrintSetup`	Print	Displays the printer setup dialog instead of the print options dialog.
`cdlPDNoSelection`	Print	Stops your users from choosing to print only the current selection of text. This feature involves a lot more code, which you may not be keen to write.
`cdlPDHidePrintToFile`	Print	Hides the print to file option on the dialog, for the same reasons as above.
`cdlCCPreventFullOpen`	Color	Stops the user from defining their own custom colors.
`cdCClFullOpen`	Color	Starts the dialog up with the custom color window already open.
`cdlCFWYSIWYG`	Font	Shows only those fonts that are available on both the printer and the screen. You also need to add it to **`cdlCF_BOTH`** and **`cdlCFScalableOnly`**.
`cdlCFBoth`	Font	Lists all the printer fonts and all the screen fonts.

Name	Dialog	Description
`cdlCFScalableOnly`	Font	Only shows you fonts which can be resized—normally Truetype fonts.
`cdlCFPrinterFonts`	Font	Lists only the printer fonts.
`cdlCFScreenFonts`	Font	Lists only fonts which can be displayed on screen.
`cdlOFNAllowMultiselect`	File	Allows the user to select more than one file from the file dialog boxes.
`cdlOFNFileMustExist`	File	The user can only type in the name of a file that exists.
`cdlOFNOverwritePrompt`	File	In the save as dialog box, if the user selects a file that already exists, then the dialog will ask the user if they really want to overwrite that file.

Custom Dialogs

The alternative to message boxes, input boxes and common dialogs is the do-it-yourself approach, where you create your dialogs in exactly the same way as you would create any form in your application. This approach has both benefits and drawbacks.

On the benefits side, because you design the form you'll use as a dialog, you can ensure that it keeps the same colors and interface standards as the other forms in your application. Since it is 100% homemade, you're free to put whatever icons, controls, text or graphics you want on it. The only limit is your imagination.

The drawbacks, on the other hand, are substantial. Each form in your application uses system resources, such as memory and processor time, when your program is running. It doesn't take that many custom dialogs in your application before something as simple as trying to run the application could cause a lesser-powered machine to grind to a halt.

Try It Out – Creating a Custom Dialog

Thanks to the object-oriented nature of Visual Basic, it's easy to create a re-useable dialog of our own, in just the same way that Microsoft provided the standard message box as a pre-built, reuseable dialog.

What we're actually going to do here is write a very simple login dialog. I say simple because it won't actually check whether the user can log in or not, it'll just grab their user name and password and return them to the calling code. This way, the login dialog is reuseable, and that's just what we want from a dialog. If we were to put in some database code then we would tie the dialog to one particular database, or at least database structure—and that ruins the whole idea of code reuse.

Let's take a look.

1 Start up a new project in Visual Basic. The default form that appears is going to be our dialog. Add some buttons, labels and text boxes to your form, remembering to set the captions and clear the text properties, so that it looks like this:

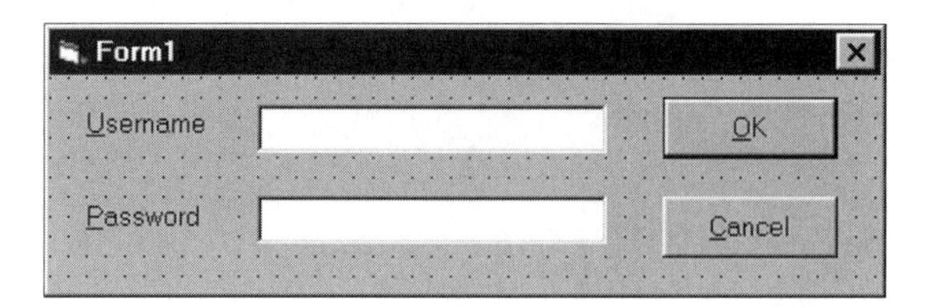

2 Set the **PasswordChar** property of the password text box to *, otherwise your login dialog will be useless since it will show anyone watching what your user's password is. Also, set the **BorderStyle** of the form to 3 so that the form appears as a dialog. Finally, set the **StartupPosition** of the form so that the dialog always appears center of the screen at run time.

3 When the dialog runs, your users will almost certainly expect to be able to press the *Return* key to do the same thing as clicking on the OK button, and the *Escape* key to do the same as clicking on the Cancel button. Remember when we looked at command buttons way back? You need to set the **Default** property of the OK button to True in order to get it to work as expected, and the **Cancel** property of the Cancel button to True, in order to get that one to work.

4 It's almost time to write some code now to bring the dialog to life. In order that my code works on your dialog though, make sure you have set the name of the form to **frmLogin**, the name of the user name text box to **txtUsername** and the name of the password text box to **txtPassword**. I have set my OK buttons name up as **cmdOK** and the Cancel button to **cmdCancel**, which may also help you avoid some confusion. Other than that though, it's also darn good programming practice.

5 The bulk of the code that we'll write will be in the method that we can use to invoke the dialog and return the details of the values entered. However, we still need to add a little code to the components on the dialog itself to make the form work. Most importantly, we need to get those buttons working.

Double click on the OK button to bring up its **Click** event, and add just one line of code, so that it looks like this.

```
Private Sub cmdOK_Click()

    frmLogin.Hide

End Sub
```

Don't be shocked—that really is all that we need the OK button to do.

6 The Cancel button has two additional lines of code. Edit its **Click** event to look like this.

```
Private Sub cmdCancel_Click()

    txtUsername = ""
    txtPassword = ""
    frmLogin.Hide

End Sub
```

This time, we have two lines of code in there to clear out the text boxes. Think about it. This is a login dialog and so there are really two instances where you would expect the user to not want to go any further: when they enter no information, or when they click OK. Of course you could add code in later on to verify whether they have access to your system and deny them access if necessary, but as far as we're concerned in this simple example, clicking Cancel is as good as declining to give a user name and password.

7 Time to write that magic method that will make the dialog act as a standalone entity. In the form's code window, type in the following routine. Remember, this is not an event of the form, so you will have to type in ALL the lines

```
Public Sub GetUserInfo(sUsername As String, sPassword As String)

    frmLogin.Show vbModal

    sUsername = txtUsername
    sPassword = txtPassword
    Unload frmLogin

End Sub
```

Pretty simple, huh? This code works just fine and does everything we want it to do, as you'll see in a moment.

8 Add a module using the Project menu. When the code window appears, type this lot in:

```
Sub Main()

    Dim sUsername As String
    Dim sPassword As String

    frmLogin.GetUserInfo sUsername, sPassword

    If sUsername = "" Then
        MsgBox "The user cancelled,or failed to log in", vbInformation,
          ↳ "Login aborted"
```

```
    Else
        MsgBox "User " & sUsername & " logged in with password " &
          ↳ sPassword, vbInformation, "Login accepted"
    End If

End Sub
```

9 One more thing remains before we can run the program. Select Project1 Properties from the Project menu and set the startup object to Sub Main, so that this subroutine will be the first thing to run when you hit Start.

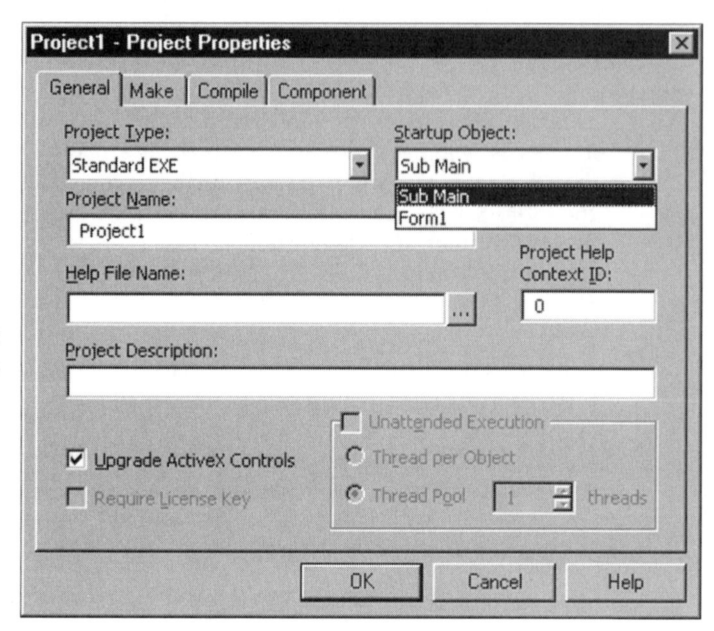

10 When you've done that click on the OK button and then run your project. The login dialog will appear as expected, waiting for you to enter your username and password.

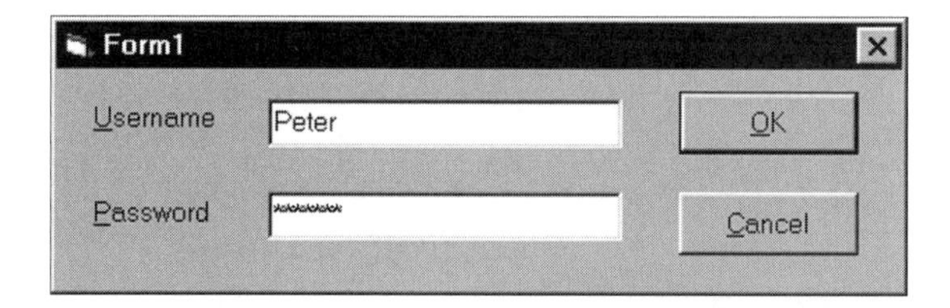

11 Hit the OK button, or the Cancel button and the form will vanish and the code that you wrote into the **`Main`** subroutine will display a message box telling you exactly what you did.

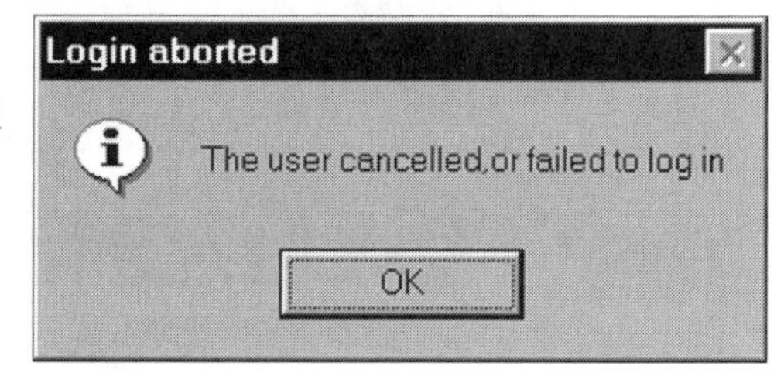

How It Works

The code for the OK and Cancel buttons is self-explanatory so we'll start by looking at the routine that retrieves the user name and password.

```
Public Sub GetUserInfo(sUsername As String, sPassword As String)

    frmLogin.Show vbModal

    sUsername = txtUsername
    sPassword = txtPassword
    Unload frmLogin

End Sub
```

The first line, **frmLogin.Show vbModal**, shows the form as a modal form. This is the feature that we exploit to our advantage. If you show a modal form in your code like this, then the routine which showed it will stop in its tracks. The next line of code will only run when the form is hidden from sight (remember those **Hide** statements in the OK and Cancel button **Click** events?).

So, once the user clicks on a button on the form and the form is hidden, then the code here can continue. The **sUsername** and **sPassword** parameters are passed to the routine by reference which means that we're quite within our rights to go and change them to whatever values we want and the calling code will see the changes too. In this case all we do is copy whatever is in the text boxes on the login form into the two parameters and then unload the form.

The main subprocedure takes the user input and checks to see if the user did type anything into the dialog and accepts it if they did.

```
Sub Main()

    Dim sUsername As String
    Dim sPassword As String

    frmLogin.GetUserInfo sUsername, sPassword

    If sUsername = "" Then
        MsgBox "The user cancelled,or failed to log in", vbInformation,
         ↳ "Login aborted"
    Else
        MsgBox "User " & sUsername & " logged in with password " &
         ↳ sPassword, vbInformation, "Login accepted"
    End If

End Sub
```

The code itself should be quite self-explanatory to you by now. It first sets up a couple of variables to hold the user name and password and then goes on to call our **GetUserInfo** method that we added to the form, passing the new user name and password variables across as parameters. Remember how the method defines these parameters as being passed across by reference. As far as the routine you see here is concerned that means that when the method is finished, **`sUsername`** and **`sPassword`** will contain the name and password that the user used to log in. Alternatively, if they canceled, then they will both be blank.

The rest of the code just checks to see whether the user did actually add a name and password, or whether they canceled, and displays the appropriate message.

One final point, did you notice how bad the caption on the login form looked? For a little exercise why not go and add another parameter to the **`GetUserInfo`** routine which specifies the caption to show on the login dialog, and then write a little bit more code into the **`GetUserInfo`** routine to actually set the caption of the form up—it's easy, why not give it a go?

Writing Your Own Word Processor

Now's a good time to pull together a few of the things we've covered recently into one project. The project is a very rudimentary notepad. The techniques we'll cover are menus, string functions and custom dialogs, along with something new—file handling.

I will be honest with you—I hate disk files. They are clunky, awkward and require you to remember a lot of arcane command syntax. Basically, they encompass all the things you came to Visual Basic to avoid.

The good news is that with the advent of database controls and bound controls, which we'll cover shortly, you need to work with raw disk files less and less. It makes sense to let Visual Basic or Access do the hard work for you. However, there are times, I admit, where you have to roll up your sleeves and open up those itsy-bitsy disk files yourself. In the next section we'll have a brief look at how disk files work. We'll just use the simplest type in our project and hopefully come away unscathed.

File Handling

Disk files come in three types:

- **Sequential files** store a long chunk of data as a stream of ANSI characters. These are your basic text files that have the extension **`.txt`**. There's almost no formatting information contained in the file, just letters. These kind of files are useful when the application using them works with the contents as a dumb block, without having to interpret the contents.
- **Random Access files** again contain only text, but they have some structure to them. You can define the structure which then tells you what the stream of characters mean. A good example is a name and address file. You create a set of fixed length fields for names and addresses, and providing you follow your own pattern to the exact letter, you can fish data in and out of the file without having to grab the whole lot and work out what it all means. The emphasis here is on your ability to organize. Happily, though, database controls exist that ease the organizational burden.

- **Binary files** are files where the records don't have a fixed length—so they are random access files without the structured field system that allows you to know what's going on. This sounds tragic, and it is. You have to read through all the records and find the one you want by hand. The benefit over random access files is that binary files are smaller.

You will be pleased to learn that we're only going to look in detail at sequential files. The process of opening and closing a file is similar in all three cases and, in my opinion, if you start playing around with random and binary files, then you'll get what you deserve!

Opening Sequential Files

A disk file exists in its own right, independent of your application. In order to read from or write to files, you have to make a connection between your code and the file on the disk, and give the operating system the chance to physically locate the file. In order to get the file ready for business, you have to open it up by using the `Open` command with the correct parameters.

The `Open` command needs to know which file you want to open, what you're going to do with it, and what reference number you want to give it when you're dealing with it. So, typically, you might say:

```
Open Textfile.txt For Input As #intRefFileNumber
```

In Visual Basic they call the number the file number, but any programmer worth their salt calls it by its real name—the **file handle**. The file handle is what Windows uses to talk to the file for all the time it's open. It's the name you and Windows have agreed between you to use to refer to the file. The handle is a unique label that points to where the file actually is on the disk and allows the operating system to work with files efficiently and safely. If it makes it easier to understand, you can put a # in front of the number when using file handles in Visual Basic. You can use a hard coded number, such as 1, in your code, but you then have to be careful not to use it again while it's in use. It's better practice to use a variable and assign an available file handle with the `FreeFile` function. This function just returns the next file number that isn't currently in use. Its use is very simple.

```
Dim intFileNumber as Integer
intFileNumber = FreeFile
Open Textfile.txt For Input As #intRefFileNumber
```

In the `Open` statement above, we told Visual Basic that we want to open the file for `Input`. This means we want to input from the file into our program, not the other way round. If we had wanted to write data from our program into the file, we would have said `for Output` here. You can also add stuff on to an existing file by using `for Append`.

Input from the File

There are three flavors of the **Input** function.

- **Input (number, filenumber)** where **number** is the number of characters you want. You can stick these straight into a variant:

```
varInputFromFile = Input (100, #intFile)
```

A good way to grab the whole file and drop it into a variable is to use the **LOF()** function. If you pass the file handle to this function, it returns the length of the file. If you then put this into the **Input** command, you get the whole banana:

```
varTheWholeBanana = Input (LOF(#intFile), #intFile)
```

- **Input #** followed by the file handle and a list of the variable names you want to put the data into. This function assumes that the data is separated by commas, allowing Visual Basic to tell where each variable begins and ends. You can have a long list of variables if you want, but this method is prone to all the problems inherent in trying to make sense of masses of file data.

```
Input #intFile, sName, nPhoneNumber
```

- **Line Input** reads in a line of text at a time and puts into a variable. A line means a chunk of text ending with a carriage return and line feed character combination (**Chr(13) + Chr(10)**). Again, this relies on you knowing what it is you're reading before you read it. The function is a throwback to the days when old terminals used to put a CR and LF and the end of every line. Nowadays these only come at the end of a paragraph, so you can get a lot more data than you bargained for.

Writing Data to a File

In order to write data to a file, you have to first make sure that the file is opened in **Output** or **Append** mode, depending on whether you want to overwrite the existing data or to add things on to the end of it. Once you've set this up and have the handle there waiting, you have two methods available.

- The **Print** statement just unloads all the data from the variable into the file like this:

```
Print #intFileNumber, Text1.Text
```

- This writes the contents to the **Text1** control into the file with handle **#intFileNumber**. If you want to mess around and put the data into specific parts of the file, perhaps in anticipation of using the **Input #** command later, then you can use the **Write** command.

```
Write #intFileNumber sName, nAddress
```

This code puts the name and address fields into the file separately. You would tend to use it inside a loop.

Closing it all Down

Once you have finished doing your stuff with the file, you mustn't forget to close it down again. Visual Basic will actually do this for you when your program stops executing, but that's BAAAD programming. It leaves your valuable data drifting around with no protection and uses up your system resources, to mention just two reasons for avoiding it. There is no excuse for not closing files down, as a simple

```
Close
```

will close all open files. If you don't want to close them all down, you can name the specific files:

```
Close #intFile1, #intFile4, #intFile7
```

Having got all the background out of the way, let's get on and see how it all works in practice.

Try It Out - Your Own Word Processor

We are going to create a simple notepad that can read text files from disk.

1 Create a new project in VB and drop a text box on to the default form. Set the form's caption to NoteBook and name the form **frmNoteBook**. You'll also need to change the following properties of the text box to make it behave as you would expect it to in a simple word processor or text editor.

Property Name	Value
Text	<Clear out all the text in this property>
Multiline	True
Scrollbars	Both
Name	**txtNoteBook**

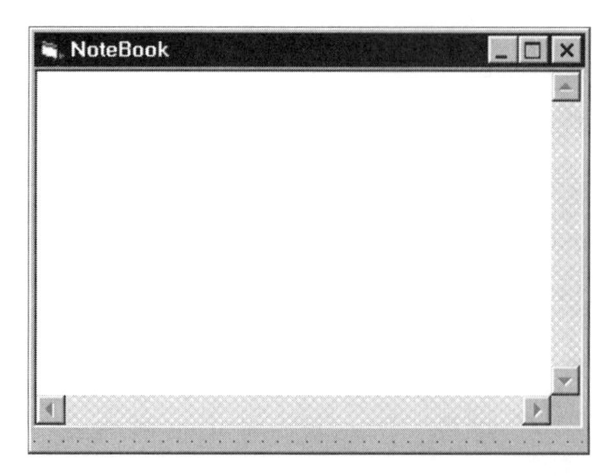

2 Next we need to build up the menu structure. Load up the menu editor and create a menu that looks like this.

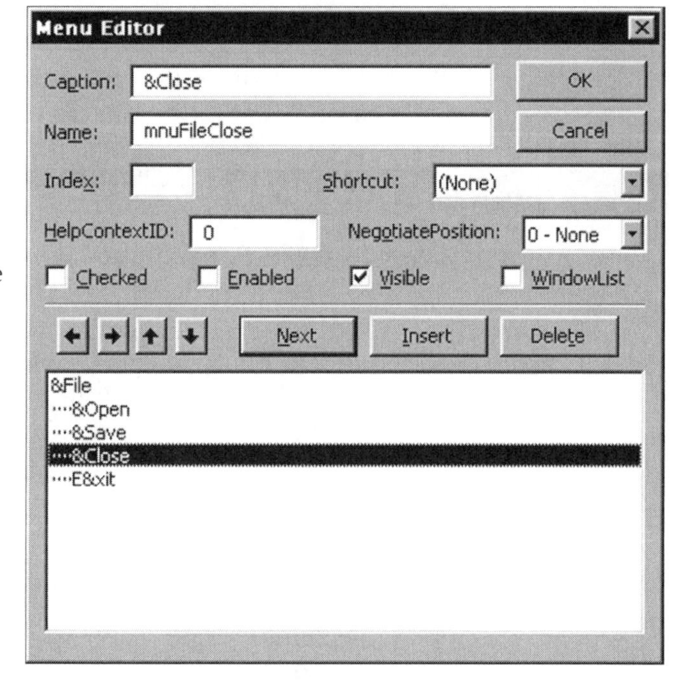

Clear the enabled check box for the Save and Close options. We will use code to enable these commands once a file has been loaded in. Name the menu items according to their function and the menu they appear on e.g. **`mnuFileOpen`**.

3 Before we can add code to these menu items, we need to add a common dialog control to the form. Drop it on the form and name it **`cmOpenFile`**.

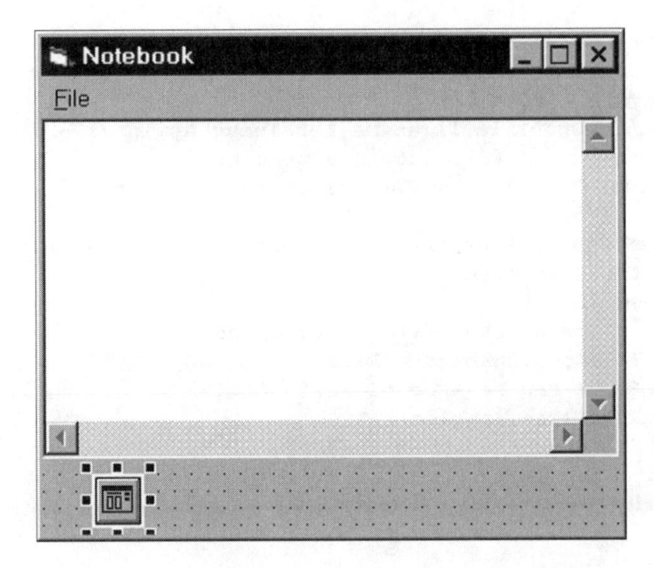

4 In order for the dialog to be useful, we need to set up its parameters in the **Form_Load** event. Open the code window and type this code in:

```
Private Sub Form_Load()

' Set up the common dialog control to open a text file
    With cmOpenFile
        .CancelError = True
        .Filter = "Text Files (*.txt)|*.txt"
        .FilterIndex = 1
        .DialogTitle = "Select a Text File"
    End With

End Sub
```

5 Now let's add the code we need to the various menu options.This code opens up the common dialog and reads a text file off the disk into the text box.

```
Private Sub mnuFileOpen_Click()

    On Error GoTo er_FileOpen
        Dim intFile As Integer
        Dim intMessageResult As Integer
        If blnIsDirty = True Then
          intMessageResult = MsgBox("Do you want to save changes?", _
                     vbQuestion + vbYesNo, "File Changed")
          If intMessageResult = vbYes Then
            Call mnuFileSave_Click 'Save the file
          End If
        End If
    ' Common dialog has been set up in form load event
```

```
        cmOpenFile.ShowOpen
    ' take filename selected by user and open it up
        intFile = FreeFile
        Open cmOpenFile.filename For Input As intFile
    ' read the whole file into the text box
        txtNoteBook.Text = Input(LOF(intFile), intFile)

        frmNoteBook.Caption = "NoteBook " + cmOpenFile.filename
    ' Now close the file
        Close #intFile
    ' don't allow another file to be opened
        mnuFileOpen.Enabled = False
    ' however we can save or close the file
        mnuFileClose.Enabled = True
        mnuFileSave.Enabled = True
        Exit Sub
er_FileOpen:

End Sub
```

6 Next we need to be able to save the file. To do this, we open up the **cmOpenFile** common dialog that we set up at the start. The only difference, besides using the **ShowSave** method, is to change the dialog title to reflect its new purpose. Easy. Be careful though—once you change that dialog title then the change remains in effect for the rest of your program. When the user next goes to load up a file then you'll need to set the dialog title there as well. I'll show you how to do it, and then you should have no problem making the change to the original Open code yourself.

```
Private Sub mnuFileSave_Click()

    On Error GoTo er_FileSave
        Dim intFile As Integer
    'Open up a save file dialog using the previous properties, except
'title

        cmOpenFile.DialogTitle = "Save Your Text File"
        cmOpenFile.ShowSave
        intFile = FreeFile
    'Open will overwrite an existing file when for OUTPUT
        Open cmOpenFile.filename For Output As intFile
    ' put the whole text box into the file
        Print #intFile, txtNoteBook.Text
    ' now update the filename on the caption
        frmNoteBook.Caption = "NoteBook " + cmOpenFile.filename
        mnuFileClose.Enabled = True
        Close #intFile
        blnIsDirty = False 'Let the program know the file has been saved
        Exit Sub
er_FileSave:

End Sub
```

7 If the user tries to close without saving, then a dialog is displayed asking them if they are sure. Note that we have to clear the text box afterwards.

```
Private Sub mnuFileClose_Click()

        Dim intMessageResult As Integer
' If the text has changed we need to prompt the user
' to save the file
        If blnIsDirty = True Then
          intMessageResult = MsgBox("Do you want to save changes?", _
                    vbQuestion + vbYesNo, "File Changed")
          If intMessageResult = vbYes Then
            Call mnuFileSave_Click 'Save the file
          End If
        End If

' reset the menus, text and the caption bar

        mnuFileOpen.Enabled = True
        txtNoteBook.Text = ""
        frmNoteBook.Caption = "NoteBook"
        mnuFileClose.Enabled = False
        mnuFileSave.Enabled = False

End Sub
```

8 We have to add a couple of lines of code to the Notebook change event so that when the text box has been amended/updated, the menu save button is enabled again so that you can save your work.

```
Private Sub txtNoteBook_Change()

   blnIsDirty = True
   mnuFileSave = True

End Sub
```

9 This menu tree is completed by putting **`End`** into the **`mnuFileExit Click`** event.

10 Now we just need to add a variable which checks to see if the document has been changed before we open, save or close a document and we have arranged to prompt the user accordingly with a suitable dialog.

We'll use the variable **`blnIsDirty`** and set it to true if the document has been altered (is 'dirty'). As this variable applies to the Open, Save and Close routines, it needs to be accessed by all of the routines and not just local to one of them, so we'll declare it in the General Declarations section after Option Explicit. All you need to do is add this line of code:

```
Private blnIsDirty As Boolean
```

11 After all that hard work, run the program as it stands. It's not MS Word, but it's a start.

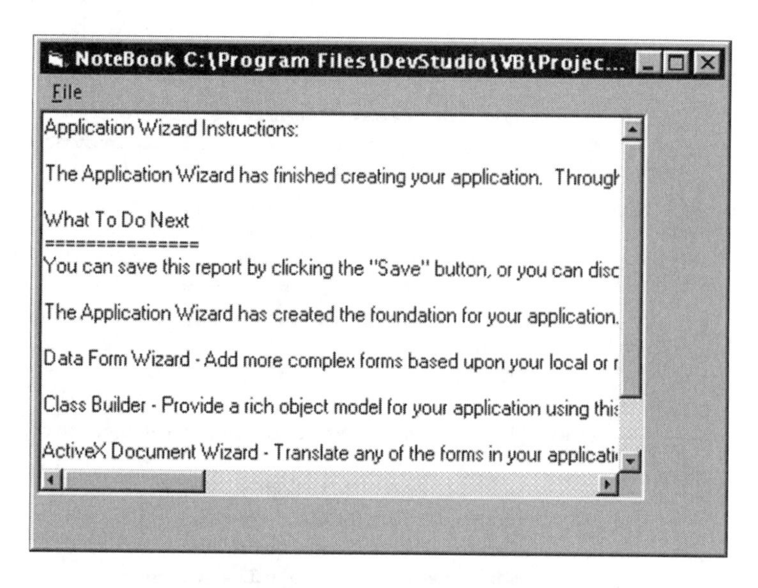

This is a pretty good, simple shell program from which to strike out and start to experiment with new features, so save it now. Why not try some things on your own. For example you could add color support and, based on a menu selection, get the user to choose the colors to use in the text box. Alternatively, you could add a font dialog to the program to let the user choose which font to use. If you're feeling really brave, why not use what we learned earlier about building dialogs to add a simple search dialog to the system which displays a message box showing where in the text box a certain string occurs, if at all (hint: you can use the `Instr` function to find one string inside another one—take a look at the online help for more info on this).

Summary

By now you should be well acquainted with dialog boxes. You've learnt how to create your own and how to use the built-in ones in your own applications. We have covered:

- Using the `MsgBox` function and procedure to display a message box
- Using the `InputBox` and `InputBox$` functions to get user input
- Application and system modal dialog boxes
- Using common dialogs to add functionality and professionalism to your programs
- Creating your own custom dialogs

In the next chapter, we start to bring all the things we've learned so far into more substantial and challenging programs.

Why Not Try...

1. Create a project with a single form. In the **Form_Load** event, create nested **For...Next** loops which display the 24 combinations of message boxes. If you are not sure of the **Msgbox** values, check on-line help by searching for "Msgbox Constants". Ignore the modal argument (for now).

2. Our reader is up early. Use the **Inputbox** function to ask them if they would care for a cup of coffee or tea? Set a default value of "Coffee", and position the **InputBox** in the upper left hand corner of the screen. What is it about the **InputBox** that makes it not the ideal method to solicit input from the user?

3. Modify exercise 1 to make the message boxes display as system modal boxes. How does the behavior of the message box change?

4. Create a project with a single form and a command button. When the command button is clicked, invoke a common dialog box to change the background color of the form.

5. Create a project with a single form and a label. Use a common dialog box to change the font size of the label.

   Hint: *Take note of this warning from Visual Basic's on-line help. Before you use the* **ShowFont** *method, you must set the* **Flags** *property of the common dialog control to one of three constants or values:* **cdlCFBoth** *or* **&H3**, **cdlCFPrinterFonts** *or* **&H2**, *or* **cdlCFScreenFonts** *or* **&H1**. *If you don't set* **Flags**, *a message box is displayed advising you that "There are no fonts installed.", and a run-time error occurs.*

asic Visual Basic Visual Ba
al Basic Visual Basic Visual
Basic Visual Basic Visual Ba
ual Basic Vi
Basic Visu
ual Basic V
l Basic Visu
isual Basic Visual Basic
al Basic Visual Basic Visua
Visual Basic Visual Basic Visu
l Basic Visual Ba
l Basic Visual
ic Visual Basi
Basic Visual B
ic Visual Basi
l Basic Visual
ual Basic Visual Basic Visual Ba
Visual Basic Visual Basic Visu
sual Basic Visual Basic Visu
Visual Basic Visual Ba

Graphics

Graphics sell software. Think about what people look for when they buy computer magazines. Sure, there are reviews of hot new programs, be they for a spreadsheet or a game. The copy might be interesting, but what are the first things you look at? The screenshots of course. Graphics catch people's attention and make them dig deep for your program, so they are well worth taking some time over. However, it's not just as simple as waving a wand and making them appear. You need to know about the workings behind their display and positioning, as this can help a great deal in other areas of Visual Basic, such as when printing, or when moving controls around through code (since you need to know about how the screen is organized).

So, in this chapter you'll learn about:

- The simple `Print` command
- How Visual Basic handles color
- How Visual Basic screen coordinates work
- The four Visual Basic graphics controls
- The graphics methods and when to use them
- Some tips on how to create really great graphics

What You Need to Know About Graphics

Visual Basic allows you to create graphics in two ways:

- Using the graphics **controls.** These are pre-defined shapes and symbols that are drawn on forms in the same way as any other control.
- Creating graphics on the fly using the built-in graphics **methods**.

We're going to discuss both of these processes in this chapter. In addition, you'll find out about the different coordinate systems that Visual Basic uses. We'll also look at some technical stuff, like how to create your own colors, what a brush is in Windows speak, and how to create all manner of lines and shapes!

Graphics is a big area, and Visual Basic provides lots of graphics facilities. However, we're only going to look briefly at each of the sections. There are two reasons for this:

- Graphics in Visual Basic are fairly straightforward and intuitive. Once you understand the basic concepts and the tools at your disposal, the best way to learn will be to experiment. Apart from a few simple ground rules, there are no right or wrong ways to do things—what matters is the effect you want to create.
- Compared to certain other development tools, Visual Basic really isn't the fastest tool for throwing graphics around the screen. For that reason, most of you corporate VB programmer types have your salaries paid for developing more mundane applications. That's not to say, though, that you can't have a little fun now and then....

Of course, even the most straight-laced application can benefit from a bit of flair and excitement, so let's get to it.

Printing on the Screen

If your experience with BASIC harks back to the heady days of the TRS-80 and Commodore's ubiquitous PET, then you'll be familiar with the good old **`Print`** command. For the less wizened among you, **`Print`** was (and still is) a simple command which can be used to display a string of text directly on to the output device, be that a screen or printer. For many newcomers to BASIC, **`Print`** was the first command they ever learned.

Not only has Microsoft kept the **`Print`** command in Visual Basic, they've also extended its usefulness somewhat. Older computers displayed information in two modes: text and graphics. It was rare if you found a BASIC system that could print in graphics mode or draw in text mode.

With Visual Basic you're always working in what would traditionally be called graphics mode. This in turn means that the usefulness of the **`Print`** command has been extended. You can now animate by doing nothing more than changing some properties and then printing some text. Text can also be printed in a variety of fonts, font styles, colors and font sizes, again just by changing or setting some properties and then printing. The **`Print`** command can also be used within Visual Basic as an aid to debugging, as you saw in Chapter 8.

Let's write some code to see how **`Print`** works.

Try It Out - Using the Print Method

Let's create a simple program that prints directly on to a form.

1 Start up a new Visual Basic project.

2 When the form appears, double-click on it to bring up the code window with the **Form_Load** event.

3 Type in the following lines of code:

```
Private Sub Form_Load ()

    Dim nLineNumber as Integer
    Form1.Show

    For nLineNumber = 1 to 10
       Form1.Print "This is line " & nLineNumber
    Next

End Sub
```

4 Run the program and you'll see the loop and **Print** command in action. However, there's a very subtle bug in the program in its current state—try minimizing the window, then maximizing it. Notice that when the form comes back into view, the text you printed has gone. Let's fix this.

5 Stop the program running and bring up the properties for the form. Find the **AutoRedraw** property and set it to true. Now if you run the program again and try minimizing and maximizing the form, the text will not vanish. This is known as **graphic persistence** and is a very important topic when it comes to dealing with graphics in Visual Basic and keeping your applications up to speed. We'll look at it in more detail a little later.

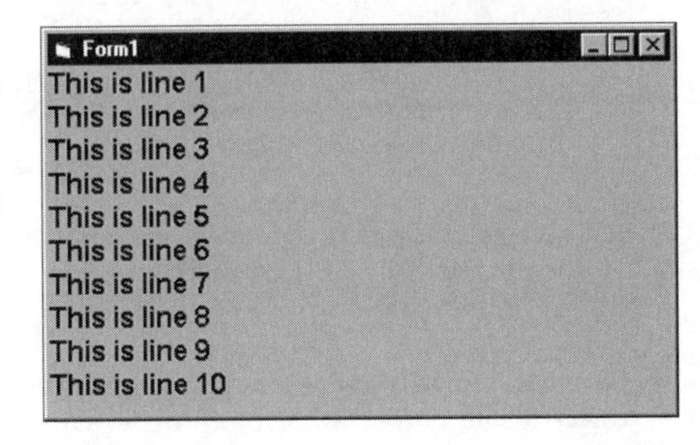

How It Works

The program runs a **For...Next** loop 10 times, each time using the **Print** command to display a line of text. This line is followed by the line number. Notice how each line of text automatically appears beneath the previous one. This is something that **Print** does for you automatically, but you *can* stop it happening, as you'll see in a moment.

The **Print** method can only be used with forms and picture boxes, not with any other controls. For example, add a picture box to your form and change the following line of code to read:

```
Picture1.Print "This is line " & nLineNumber
```

If you run the program now, the text appears inside the picture box rather than on the form. **`Print`** always needs to know the object that you want to print onto.

Introducing AutoRedraw

Visual Basic does a very good job of isolating its developers from the mundane tasks that the C/C++ propeller heads live for. One of these tasks is redrawing the form—for example, when the form has been minimized and then maximized. Visual Basic maintains an internal list of controls that are on the form, and a list of all the properties that are needed to return the window to its original state. Normally, when the form comes back into view, Windows sends your program a message indicating that the form needs to be redrawn. This manifests itself in Visual Basic as a **`Paint`** event. The only snag is that when you print on the form using the **`Print`** method, you're creating a local graphical image that's not registered by Visual Basic as a component of the overall form. So it disappears.

Luckily Microsoft realizes this and has given Visual Basic developers the **`AutoRedraw`** property. Set this to true and Visual Basic will store a copy of everything you draw on the form so that it can redraw the form itself without burdening you with extra code.
While this is a useful procedure, it does result in your program running a little slower and using a little more memory than normal. This leaves you with the task of choosing a compromise: do you sacrifice speed and memory for less code, or code the **`Paint`** event by hand to keep the 'footprint' of your application as small as possible?

> *The footprint of an application is how much space it takes up, both on the users hard disk, and in terms of memory and processor time when its running. In general the smaller the footprint, the happier the user—providing, of course, that the application does everything else its supposed to.*

It's a choice only you can make, depending on the kind of application you're writing. However, since all the apps in this chapter are really quite small, we'll set **`AutoRedraw`** to true from here on in.

So what's actually going on behind the scenes? Well, no Windows program ever draws direct to the output. Instead, an area of memory is allocated and attached to a block of data called a **device context**. The device context tells Windows how to display the information held in memory, which window to display it in, what portion of memory to display, and so on.

> *When **`AutoRedraw`** is set to false, the image in memory is the clean window—it's the window and whatever graphical controls (not normal controls, like text boxes, but graphical controls such as labels, lines, etc.) that you drew on at design time. Here 'graphical' means that they don't accept data input at run time.*
>
> *When you draw into the window at run time, Visual Basic doesn't bother to update the image of the form in memory. With **`AutoRedraw`** set to true, though, Visual Basic stores two copies of the form in memory. One is the one that's on display, the other is a back-up image with any changes your code has made.*

When you print to the form, you actually draw on the back-up image and Visual Basic automatically copies the changes to the visible image. The net result, as you can probably see, is more memory in use and a slightly slower refresh rate. You're working with two copies of the form instead of one.

Printing Fonts

The way in which text appears in your application is controlled by the font object which is attached to most visual controls and to the form itself. To change the style of the text, simply change the font object's properties. For example, if you want to change the size of the text, change the **`Font.Size`** property. Let's give it a go....

*If you're used to the Visual Basic 3 way of working (where you change the **`FontSize`**, **`FontBold`**, etc. properties), don't panic. You can still do that. However, it really is a good idea to get into the spirit of things and use the VB5 font object and its properties for playing around—your app will run slightly faster too.*

Try It Out - Changing the Font and Color Properties

1 If the last program is still running, stop it. Remove the picture box you drew.

2 Bring up the code window again to view the **`Form_Load()`** event.

3 Change the **`For...Next`** loop so it reads:

```
For nLineNumber = 1 To 10
   Form1.Font.Size = Form1.Font.Size + nLineNumber
   Form1.ForeColor = QBColor(nLineNumber)
   Form1.Print nLineNumber;
Next
```

Notice the semicolon at the end of the penultimate line.

4 Run the program again.

How It Works

This time there are three major differences from the previous example:

- The numbers are printed side by side, instead of on separate lines. The semicolon you placed at the end of the **`Print`** command tells Visual Basic that the next time you print, the text should be displayed on the same line as before.
- The text gets bigger with each successive number. The first line of the **`For...Next`** loop adds the value of the **`nLineNumber`** variable to the current **`Size`** property of the form's font object. The result is larger text.
- The color of each number is also changed. Visual Basic gives you a number of ways to select and change colors for graphics, controls and printed text. In our example, the **`QBColor`** function is used to load a color value into the **`ForeColor`** property of the form. The **`ForeColor`** property (same as the **`BackColor`** property) accepts a hexadecimal value to specify the color. You don't normally have to do this by hand—simply double-click on the appropriate entry in the properties box and the Visual Basic color palette, which we saw in Chapter 3, appears.

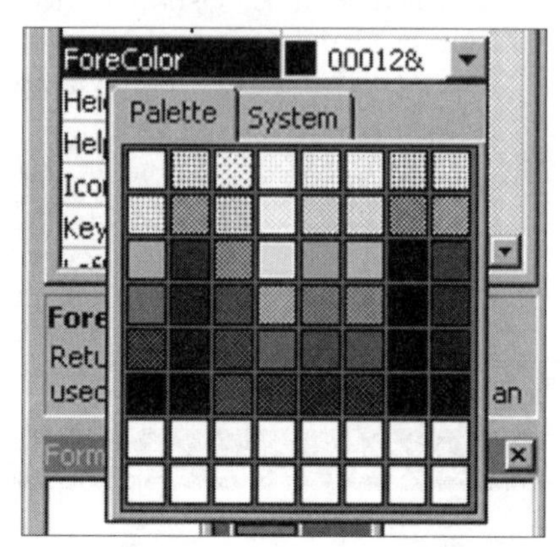

We'll learn more about this, and how it can be useful, a little later on. For now, though, let's look at how to deal with colors from code in a little more detail.

Specifying Screen Colors

Visual Basic assigns a number to each of the colors it can display, and lets you choose and specify the color number for objects like forms and text in four different ways.

- You can assign the number directly or choose the color from the palette on the properties menu. The problem here is that the color numbers are all hexadecimal (base 16, known as **hex**) so Visual Basic provides some simpler methods.
- The **`QBColor`** function selects one of 16 colors, that were supported by earlier editions of Basic.
- The **`RGB`** function produces a color by mixing red, green and blue.
- You can use one of Visual Basic's intrinsic color constants. You can find out what these are by selecting Color Constants from the online help system.

Before we dive into hexadecimal, let's first look at an easier method.

The QBColor Function

This function is primarily for those BASIC programmers who have come to Visual Basic from Microsoft's venerable QBasic environment. In QBasic, you specify colors as single digit numbers: color number 1 would be blue, 2 green, 3 cyan, and so on. The **QBColor** function allows you to use these QBasic color codes without having to worry about converting them into long integers by hand. You simply use:

```
Form.ForeColor = QBColor(<Color number>)
```

Value	Color	Value	Color
0	Black	8	Gray
1	Blue	9	Light Blue
2	Green	10	Light Green
3	Cyan	11	Light Cyan
4	Red	12	Light Red
5	Magenta	13	Light Magenta
6	Yellow	14	Light Yellow
7	White	15	Bright White

Try It Out - The QBColor Selection

We can adapt our last program to show the full range of colors for this function.

1. Change the **For...Next** loop in the form load event to run through all the colors from 0 to 15.

```
For nLineNumber = 0 To 15
   Form1.ForeColor = QBColor(nLineNumber)
   Print nLineNumber;
Next
```

2. Double-click the **Font** property in the properties window to display the font dialog box. Use this dialog to select a font size of 24. You can also change the font style in other ways if you want—it isn't going to damage the program.

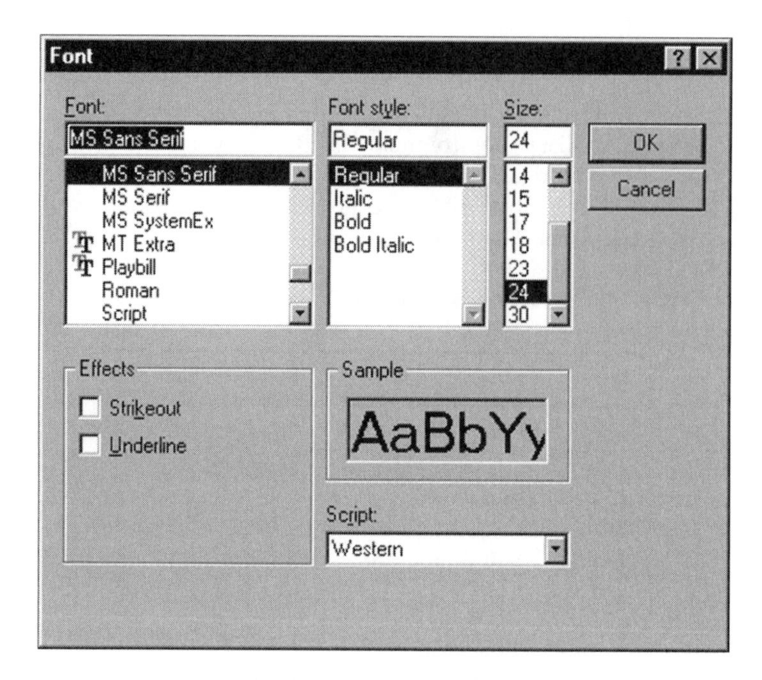

3 Run the program. You may need to resize the form at run time to bring all the text into view.

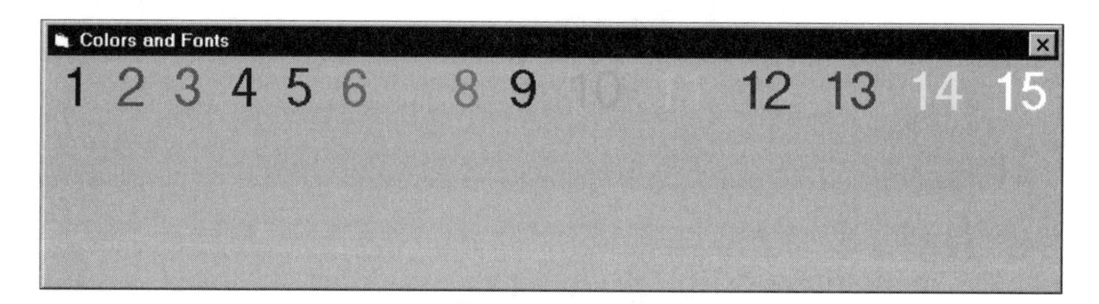

Hexadecimal Notation

A few lines back I confused the hell out of you by mentioning **hexadecimal notation**. You need to know hexadecimal to be able to specify color values in Visual Basic directly. It's not that difficult really, so let me explain.

We normally use decimal notation as our number system. In decimal notation, there are ten digits used to form our numbers: the digits 0 through 9.

In the hexadecimal system, there are 16 digits (if you studied Latin in school, you'll probably know that already!). Not only are there the numbers 0 through 9, but also the letters A – F.

Decimal	0	1	2	3	4	5	6	7	8	9	10	11	12	13	14	15
Hexadecimal	0	1	2	3	4	5	6	7	8	9	A	B	C	D	E	F

Our decimal numbers can be broken down into columns. The right-most column is units or ones, the next is tens, the next one hundreds, and so on. Therefore, the number 4524 is 4 thousands, plus 5 hundreds, plus 2 tens, plus 4, which equals four thousand, five hundred and twenty four.

Hex works in a similar way. The columns from right to left are units, sixteens, two-hundred-and-fifty-sixes, and so on. Therefore, the number 9CD is in reality (9 x 256) + (12 x 16) + 13, which equals 2509!

Why Put This Hex on Me?

Color values are held in long integers and the maximum number you can store in a long integer is FFFFFFFF written in hex, which is a lot more readable than its decimal equivalent. Three separate numbers are actually combined into one long integer, these three numbers being exactly how much red is in the color you want (between 0 and 255), how much green (same again) and how much blue.

Because each of these settings can be between 0 and 255, or between 0 and FF in hex, it's fairly easy to invent your own colors in hex. White, for example, has the maximum amount of red, green and blue, so the color value is hex FFFFFF. This is written in Visual Basic as &HFFFFFF&. The &H tells Visual Basic that we're now giving it hex numbers, the & at the end shows that the value is stored in a long integer. Red is the value &HFF&, blue is &HFF0000&, and green is &HFF00&. A bright red form would therefore be:

```
Form1.BackColor = &HFF
```

The RGB Function

However, you might not like the idea of hex; all those weird symbols and & signs everywhere—nasty business! Fear not, at the expense of a little speed at run time, there's a function called **RGB** which you can use to produce your hex number for you.

Try It Out - Hassle-Free Hex Using RGB

Time to write an application. Remember the scroll bar controls that we looked at way back in Chapter 5? They can be great for dealing with color values, and incredibly useful when it comes to the **RGB** command in Visual Basic. Let's take a peek.

1 Start up a new, Standard Exe project and drop a few scrollbar and label controls on to the form so that it looks like this:

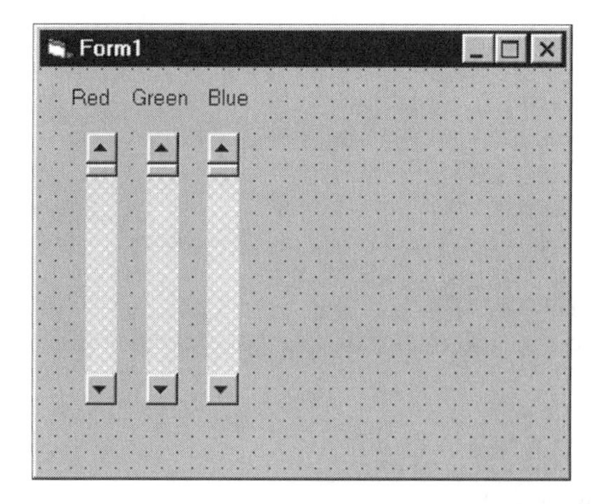

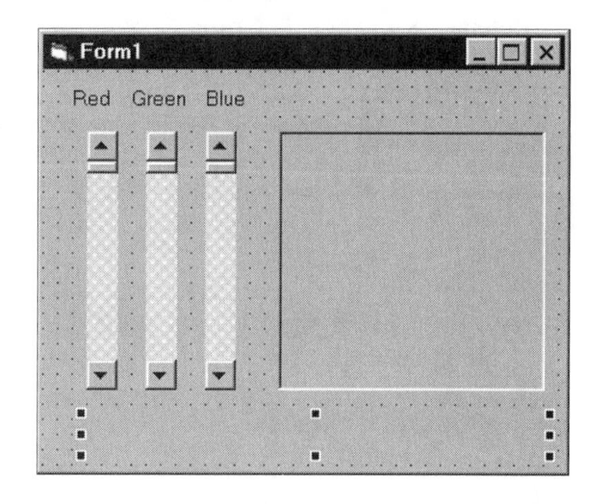

2 Now add a picture box to the right of the scrollbars and a label below them—remember to clear its caption. We're going to use the scrollbars to feed values to the **RGB** command so that we can change the color of the picture box at run time. The label will show the values selected.

3 Still with me? As you'll see a little later, the **RGB** command lets us tell Visual Basic to display a color by specifying how much of that color is made up of red, how much of it is made up of green and how much of it is made up of blue. In each case we need to supply a number to the function between 0 and 255. We can make sure that the scrollbars only supply values in this range by setting up their **Min** and **Max** properties. Use the properties window on each of the scrollbars to set the **Min** value of each to 0, and the **Max** value of each to 255.

HelpContextID	0
Index	
LargeChange	1
Left	240
Max	255
Min	0
MouseIcon	(None)
MousePointer	0 - Default
SmallChange	1
TabIndex	0

4 Almost there. The last thing that we need to do before we can write some code, is give those scrollbars a name. Now, think about this for a second. Whenever any of the sliders is moved, we want to trigger an event that will fire off the **RGB** function to specify the color of the picture box. There are a number of ways we could do this. We could write a routine to change the color of the picture box and get an event on each scrollbar to call it, or we could write the code out three times—once for each scrollbar. A much better route though is to use the control array facilities in Visual Basic. Think back to when we covered these things earlier in the book. To set up a control array, all we need to do is set up the **Index** property of each scrollbar and then give them all the same name. Set the index of the leftmost scrollbar to 0, the next to 1 and the last to 2, then, still using the properties window, set the name of all the scrollbars to **scrColor**.

5 Name the label at the bottom of the form **lblValue** and name the picture box **picColor**.

6 At last we can write some code. Double-click on any of the scrollbars to bring up the code window, and then use the Events drop-down to find the **Change** event. Since we have a control array, whenever the value of any of the sliders changes, they will all run the same **Change** event.

7 What we need to do in this event is pass the value of each slider across to the infamous **RGB** function. Change the code so that it looks like this.

```
Private Sub scrColor_Change(Index As Integer)

Dim sCode As String

    With picColor

        .BackColor = RGB(scrColor(0), scrColor(1), scrColor(2))

    End With

sCode = "picColor.BackColor = RGB(" & scrColor(0).Value & ", "
sCode = scode & scrColor(1).Value & ", " & scrColor(2).Value & ")"

lblValue.Caption = sCode

End Sub
```

8 Finally, run the program to see what it does.

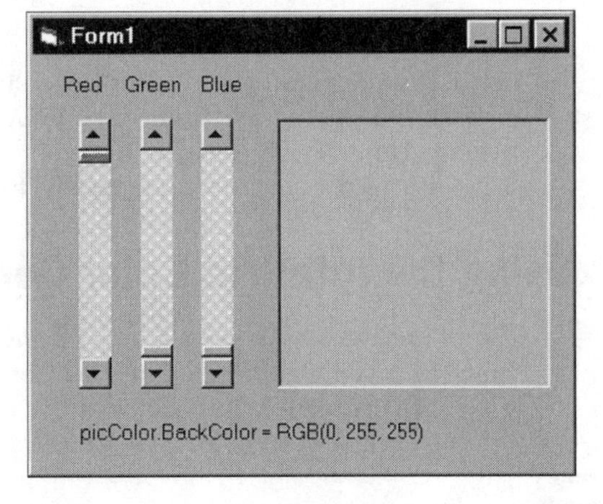

How It Works

In the **Change** event, the values of the three scroll bars are passed to the **RGB** function and the picture box color is built up.

```
With picColor

        .BackColor = RGB(scrColor(0), scrColor(1), scrColor(2))

End With
```

The three-part value is created by joining all three **scrColor** values together, separated by commas. The value returned by the function is placed into the picture box's **BackColor** property, the result being that the color changes to reflect the new color selected by the user.

Each color has a unique identifying hex value, built up from the required amount of each base color, and the rest of the code simply displays this in the label at the bottom of the form.

For certain values, the color in the box is not homogeneous, but appears to be made up of blobs of other colors. This effect is known as **color mapping**.

Color Mapping

Depending on your screen resolution, the actual color you see can vary. Most Video Graphics Adapter (VGA) systems can display a maximum of 256 colors on screen at once. This is due to a design limitation, although some would call it a feature! However, a little math will soon show you that the **RGB** function is capable of returning a value representing any one of 16,777,216 colors.

To be able to accommodate this, Windows does a thing called **color mapping.** The color you want to display is matched against the colors available. If an exact match is found, then the color is displayed. However, more often that not, Windows will combine two or more colors to create what is called a **custom** color. On screen, this appears as a dotty color, with dots of different hues and tints placed next to each other to give the illusion that you have a new color on screen. It's rather like a painting by Seurat, though it won't fetch half a million at auction!

You need to be aware of the differences between screens if you plan to distribute your Visual Basic applications to other users and computers. You may have designed the application using a state-of-the-art SVGA display. Your users, however, may be using systems that can only display 16 colors at a time. The way your forms and colors appear on your screen can differ dramatically from what they will see.

Using the Intrinsic Color Constants

One of the most admired features of any GUI, including Windows of course, is the user's ability to customize the look and feel of their desktop. In Windows 95 and above, as many of you will be aware, this includes the color scheme in use.

If you sit back and think about this for a second then you might start to get pretty worried. After all, if the user can choose their own color scheme then your application may look a little out of place on their system. Worse still, what if a user of yours has a genetic defect making them allergic to grey, and all your dialogs use just that color (unlikely I know, but you'll be amazed with the excuses users can produce to berate your application if they aren't happy with it)?

The solution is a set of miracles known as the intrinsic colors—I prefer to call them the built-ins.

With these little gems you no longer need to tell your application that a dialog should make use of grey for its background. Instead, you can tell VB to use whatever color is set up on the target system to hold the window color.

Confused? Take a look at the pop-up color dialog that appears when you click on the **`BackColor`** property, and then select the System tab:

By choosing one of these intrinsic colors you can make sure that your application remains consistent with whatever your users choose to set up for their system colors.

You can also specify these colors in code, using the intrinsic color constants, such as **`vbDesktop`**, **`vbActiveTitleBar`**, and so on. You can get a complete list of all the color constants in Visual Basic by simply looking up Color constants in the online help system.

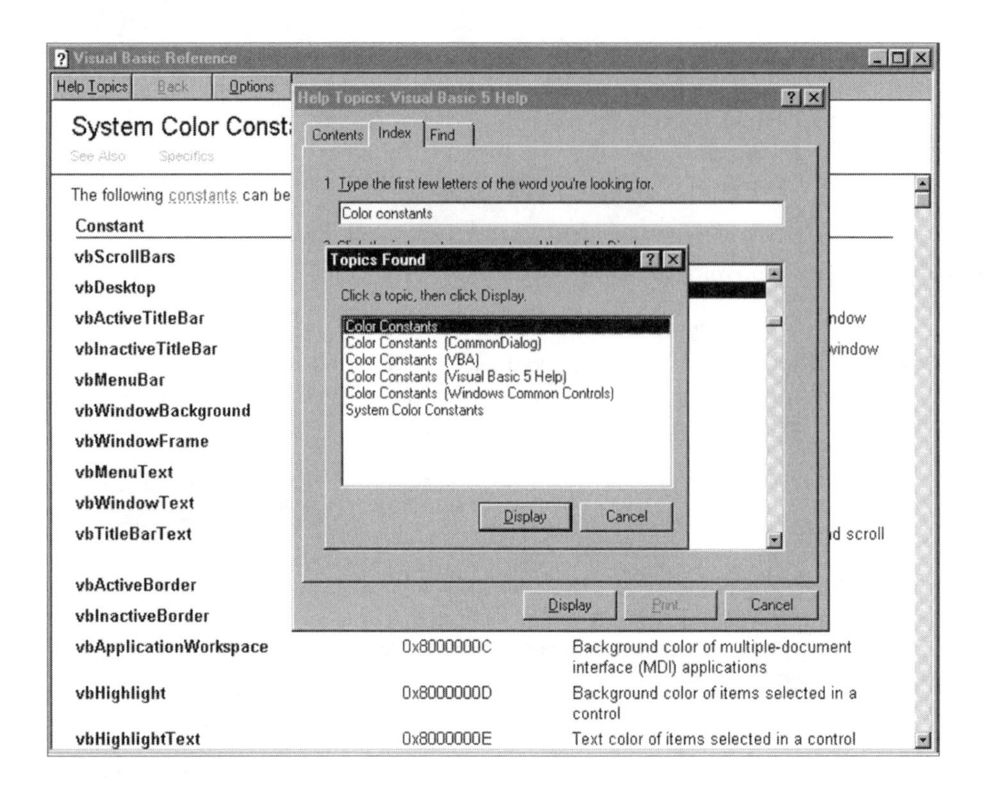

Coordinate Systems

The screen and the forms you display on it are divided up into tiny dots. When you start drawing things on your forms, you need to be able to specify at precisely which dot on the form or screen you want something to appear. This is where coordinates come in.

The top left corner of the screen is coordinate 0,0. Here X = 0 and Y = 0. As you move across the screen, the number of the X coordinate increases. As you move down the screen, the number of the Y coordinate increases.

I frequently mention screens, but in Visual Basic you can only draw on forms, picture boxes and image boxes. Each has its own coordinate system, and so (0,0) on a form is very different from (0,0) on the screen. Whenever you draw on an object, always use a coordinate system that relates to the top left corner of the object you're drawing on.

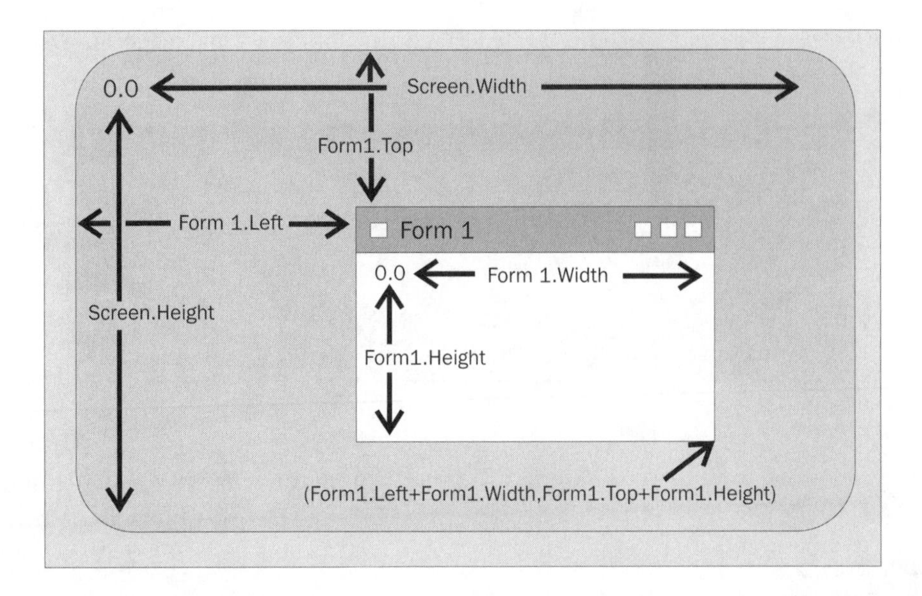

There are parts of an object that you can't draw on—for example, the title bar and borders of a form are strictly off-limits. Visual Basic only lets you draw in a form's **client** area. So how do you find out where the client area starts and ends? Objects you draw on have two properties: **`ScaleHeight`** and **`ScaleWidth`**. These tell you the maximum height and width of the object's client area.

Try It Out - Placing a Letter in the Center of a Form

1 Start a new project in Visual Basic, bring up the code window and select the **`Form_Resize`** event.

2 Type in code so that your code window looks like this.

```
Project1 - Form1 (Code)
Form                                Paint

Private Sub Form_Resize()

    With Form1

        .Cls
        .CurrentX = .ScaleWidth / 2
        .CurrentY = .ScaleHeight / 2
    End With

    Print "X"

End Sub
```

3 Run the program and see how the letter stays in the center of the form, even when you resize it.

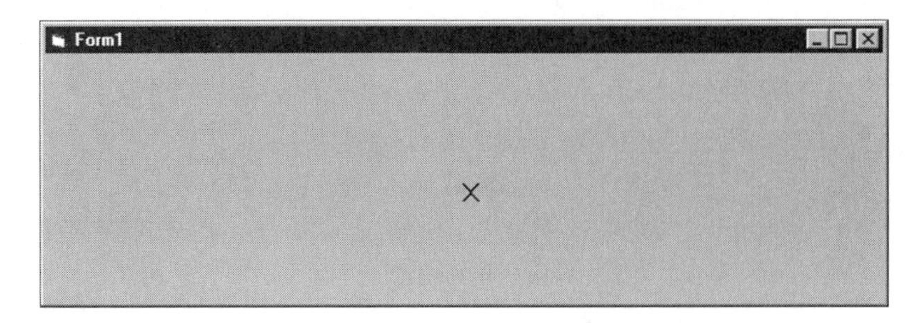

How It Works

Let's take a look at how the code works. The first line of real code uses the `Cls` method to clear `Form1`:

```
With Form1

    .Cls
```

Attached to each form is an invisible object known as a **cursor**. This is the point on the form at which subsequent `Print` statements will display text. Therefore, if you set the form's `CurrentX` and `CurrentY` properties, the cursor moves to the point you specify.

The `ScaleWidth` and `ScaleHeight` properties give us the dimensions of the client area. Therefore, if you set `CurrentX` and `CurrentY` to half the client area width and height, this has the effect of moving the cursor to the center of the screen.

Twips, Pixels, Inches and Centimeters

The default coordinate system used on a form is called **twips**. In twips, each point is roughly equal to 1/567 of a centimeter. So if you drew a line on your form that was 567 units long, it would appear a centimeter long if you actually printed it out on paper. This is known as a **device independent** coordinate system: it doesn't matter whether you're drawing a line on a standard VGA display, on a printer, or on the latest state-of-the-art high-res screen, if you were to print the results it would still appear a centimeter long. Twips are great if you're producing **what you see is what you get** applications, such as a desktop publishing package or a word processor.

In reality, however, a much more useful coordinate system is the **pixel** system. Here each unit on the X or Y axis of the screen equals exactly one dot, or pixel.

> *The pixel coordinate system also enables you to draw your graphics more speedily on screen. Windows knows that one pixel equals one dot and doesn't have to worry about converting your coordinates into something that can actually be drawn.*

You can change the coordinate system of a form by bringing up the properties window and double-clicking on the **`ScaleMode`** property.

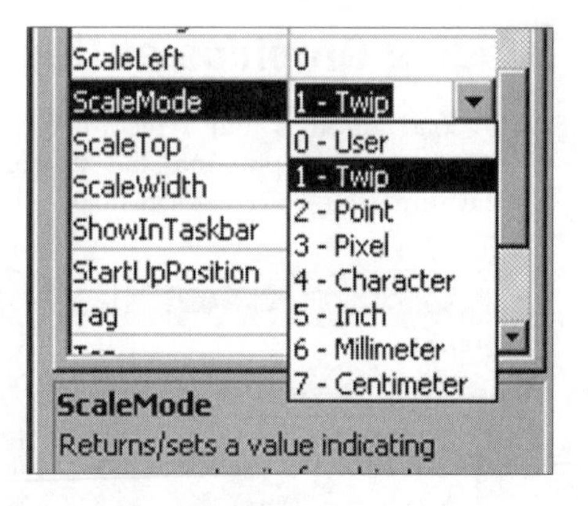

Changing the scale mode doesn't have any immediate visible effects on your application, but it is something that you need to take into account when dealing with coordinates in your code. A line that was previously drawn 100 twips long may actually be only 20 pixels long, thus having a completely different effect. Changing the coordinate system on a form only affects any subsequent changes to the form—it doesn't resize or redraw the controls and images already on the form. To accomplish that little feat you need to write some heavyweight code, which is beyond the scope of our brief look at graphics.

Using Graphics

Having understood some of the background to graphics in Visual Basic, we can now start putting graphics objects onto our form. There are two alternative ways to do this in Visual Basic:

- **Graphical controls** are like ordinary Visual Basic controls which are placed on your form and can be laid out interactively at design time. Two of the controls, the image box and picture box, allow you to work with various image files, while the **line** and **shape** controls draw lines and shapes on your form (what a surprise!).
- **Graphics methods** are commands that enable you to draw directly onto your form at run time. The commands available for this in Visual Basic are **`Cls`**, **`Pset`**, **`Point`**, **`Line`** and **`Circle`**.

For some jobs, controls and methods are interchangeable. We'll cover the pros and cons of each later, but first we'll take a look at the graphical controls.

Image and Picture Boxes

The most common graphical controls are the picture and image box controls. These let you load up images from the disk and display them on screen, either in design mode or at run time through your code, and provide you with an ideal way to spice up any dialog, or to provide animation to your users, perhaps for a game.

Loading Graphics at Design Time

To load graphics into a picture box or image box at design time you simply type the file name of the graphic into the `Picture` property of the appropriate object. You can also do the same thing for a form object. Take at look at the properties window for each object.

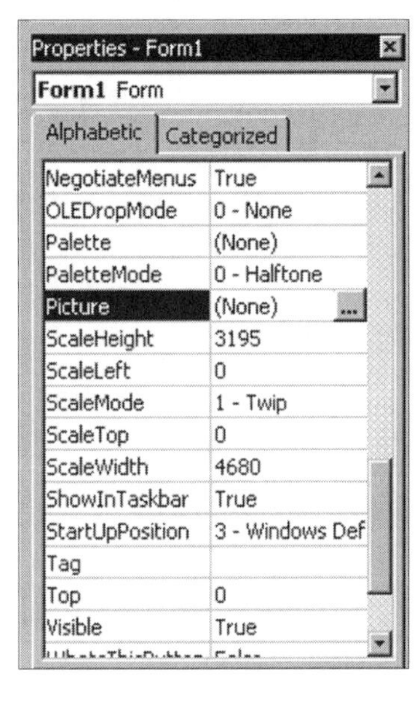

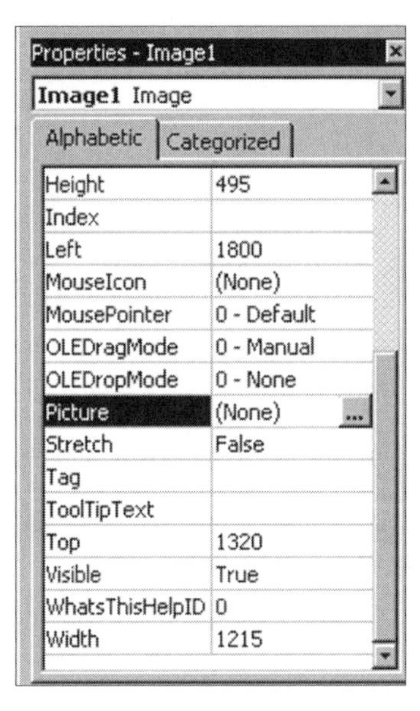

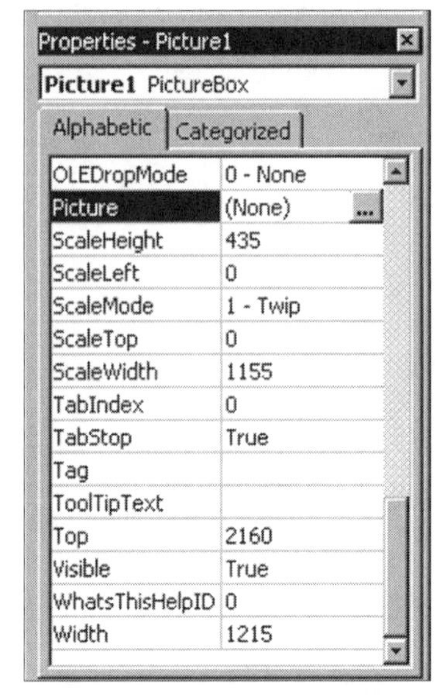

The action is fairly similar for each object, so let's look at one in particular. The image control is a good place to start because it has an extra property which allows you to stretch an image.

Try It Out - Loading and Resizing an Image Control

1 Start a new project and double-click the image control icon in the toolbox to draw an image control on the form.

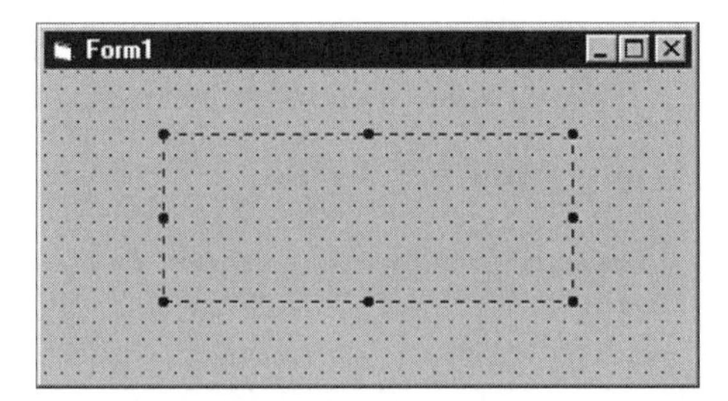

2 Select the image control and bring up its properties window using *F4*. Find the **`Stretch`** property and make sure it is set to true. The easiest way to do this is by double-clicking on it.

3 Now find the **`Picture`** property and double-click on it. A file dialog box appears asking you to select a graphics file. Point the file dialog to your **`Windows`** directory, or take a look at the Visual Basic CD-Rom and pretty soon your find yourself looking at a list of **`BMP`** graphic files… choose one and click on OK.

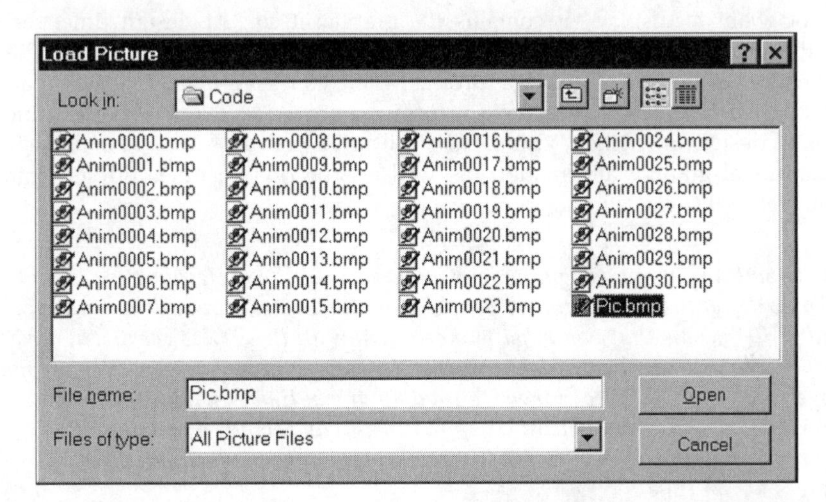

4 The bitmap appears on the form, inside the image control.

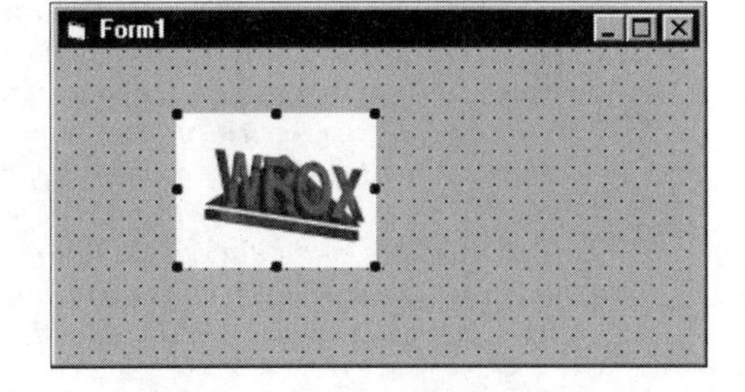

5 Resize the control by dragging its resize handles. Notice how the picture inside also changes.

Loading Images at Run Time

You'd be forgiven for thinking that adding the image to the object at run time must be as easy as assigning the right path and file name to the **`Picture`** property. Unfortunately, it isn't quite that easy: at run time you have to use the **`LoadPicture`** function.

The reason for this is that the **`Picture`** property doesn't really contain the file name of the graphic you want to display—it contains the graphic itself. At design time, though, to simplify the properties window, Visual Basic just shows you the file name. The actual binary file information is stored inside your project when you save it, in the files that end in `.frx` to be precise. For example if you save a form as `Form1.FRM` and include some graphics on that form at design time, then Visual Basic will give you a `Form1.FRX` file which includes all the additional graphic information (as well as one or two other tidbits of information, but for now let's keep it simple).

The good thing about assigning your images to the file at design-time is that they don't get lost. The alternative (pointing the control towards an external image file) means that you must make sure that all these files get distributed along with your application. The downside is clear: your program files are much larger, and thus take a lot longer to load up at run time.My advice is to include your images with your code at compile time if you intend to distribute the application. If you're only going to keep it on your own machine, then load the images at run time.

Alternatively, if you have access to a C development system such as Visual C++, or the Enterprise and Professional editions of Visual Basic, you can load the images into a resource file, using something known as a resource compiler. The resource compiler basically takes a small program known as a resource script which lists all the binary data that you want to compile with the application into the resulting EXE file to prevent you having to ship a lot of graphic files that the user's could play with. The resource compiler takes this script and produces a resource file, which you can then add to your VB project just like any other. At run time you can then use the **`LoadResPicture`** *method.*

As you can probably see, though, this is a little beyond the scope of a Beginning Guide.

Finding Your Images at Run Time

One of the problems of loading images in at run time is that you have to make sure that the files you want are where your program expects them to be. When you install your application, it's easiest to store your image files in a subdirectory off the main directory (in the place where the executable file is). Remember that the user may not install your application in exactly the same drive and directory that you used to create the program. If you store the graphics in a subdirectory of the directory where the executable is, you can then say this at run time:

```
Image1.Picture = LoadPicture (App.Path & "\graphics\<imagename>")
```

Here **<imagename>** is the name of the graphics file you want to load. The **App.Path** part returns the path along which the executable file is located. This function is always available anywhere in your program—you're actually examining the **Path** property of Visual Basic's built-in **App** object.

When using **App.Path**, you must remember that in some cases the path may end in a slash, and in others it may not. For example, if your VB program was running off the root directory of a hard disk, then **App.Path** may return **C:**. However, if it was in a directory called **My_APP**, then **App.Path** would be **C:\My_App**—without the trailing slash.

For this reason, it is always good to use the **Right$** function to check whether or not **App.Path** ends in a slash:

```
If Right$(App.Path ,1 ) = "\" then
    Image1.Picture = LoadPicture(App.Path & "File1.bmp")
Else
    Image1.Picture = LoadPicture (App.Path & "\File1.bmp")
End If
```

Comparing Image and Picture Controls

Having now used these two controls in both Chapter 3 and here, you should have an idea of their relative strengths and weaknesses. These can be summarized as follows:

- As they change shape, image controls stretch the image they contain. Picture boxes and forms don't do this.
- Picture boxes, on the other hand, can be used as container objects. I'll explain exactly what this means in a moment.
- Image controls are **lightweight** controls. This means that an image control consumes less of your PC's memory and is faster to deal with than a heavyweight control, such as a picture box.
- The image and picture controls are also **bound** controls. This means that they can be bound to certain data fields in a database. We'll examine databases and bound controls later in the book, but suffice to say it's an important feature.

- The other big difference between the two controls though is that the graphics methods, which allow you to draw graphics on the fly at run time, can't be used to draw over the image in an image control, but they can be used to draw over something displayed in a picture control.
- Let's take a look at the properties of both controls to get a good idea of the some of the main differences.

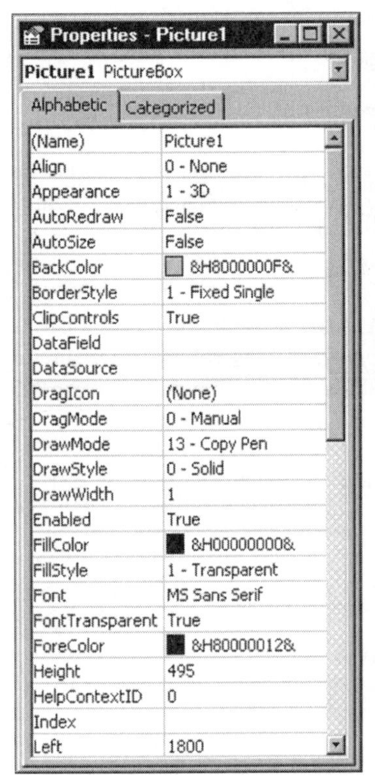

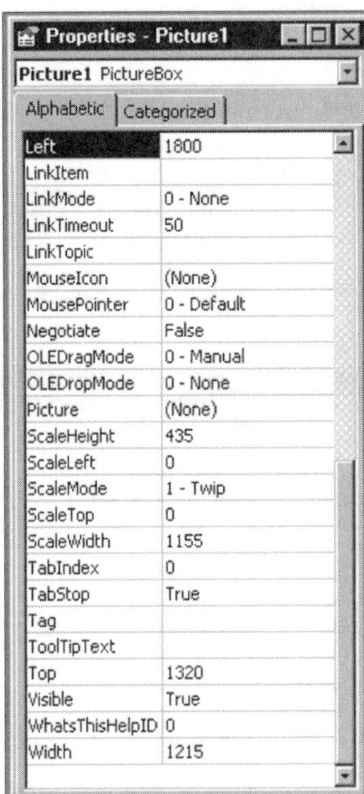

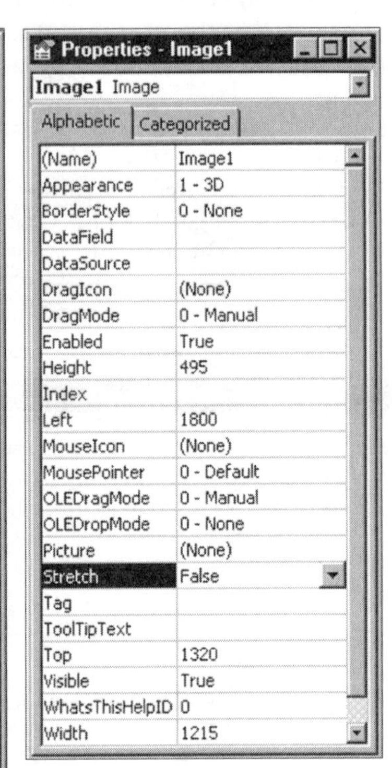

Picture Boxes as Containers

Unlike the image control, the picture box is a **container** control. A container control allows other controls to be drawn inside it. Anything you then do to the picture box also affects the controls contained within it. For example, if you make the picture box invisible, its controls also become invisible; if you move the picture box within the form, the controls go with it.

This is where picture boxes come in handy. By placing a picture box on a frame or form, and then placing controls inside the picture box, you can begin to break a large group of functions down into related chunks.

You could, for example, place a group of option buttons together in a picture box. If you change the `BorderStyle` property of the picture box to 0 - None, you can make the picture box seem to disappear. The option buttons will still be in view and they'll still be grouped in the picture box, separate from others on the form.

Picture boxes used in this way provide a way of removing a group of option buttons from view. If you change the **Visible** property to false, the picture box vanishes completely, taking everything drawn on it out of sight too.

Try It Out - Picture Boxes as Container Controls

1 Start a new Visual Basic project and place a picture box on the form.

2 Now draw a command button inside the picture box.

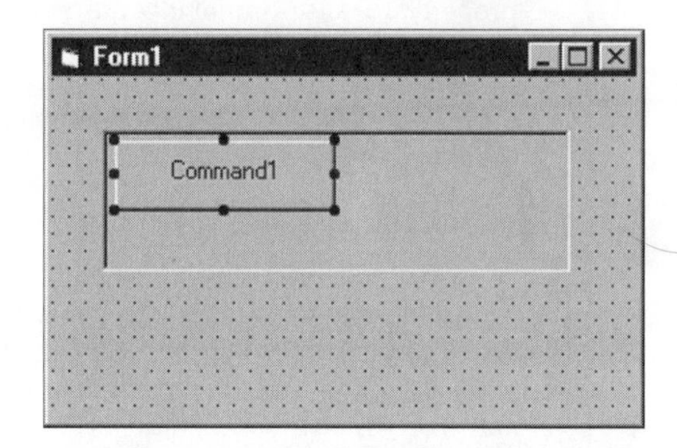

3 Select the picture box and move it to a different place on the form. Watch how the command button goes with it.

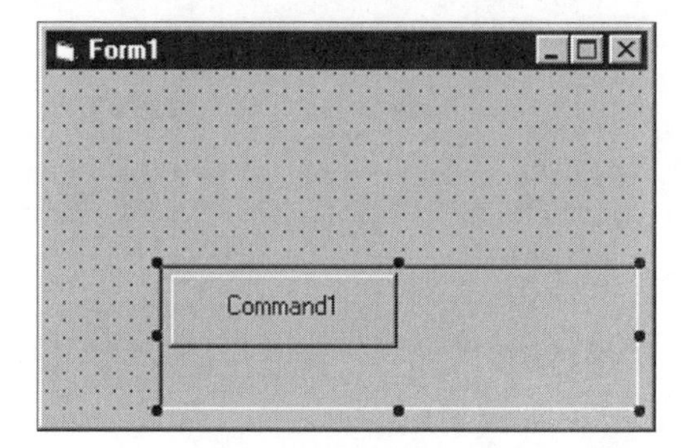

4 Select the command button and try to drag it off the picture box. Visual Basic won't let you do it as the command button belongs to the picture box.

5 Double-click the form to bring up the **Form_Load** code window. Type in the following line:

```
Private Sub Form_Load()

    Picture1.Visible = False

End Sub
```

6 Now run the program. When the form appears, you'll see that both the picture box and the command button have gone. Making the picture box invisible means that any objects contained within it also disappear.

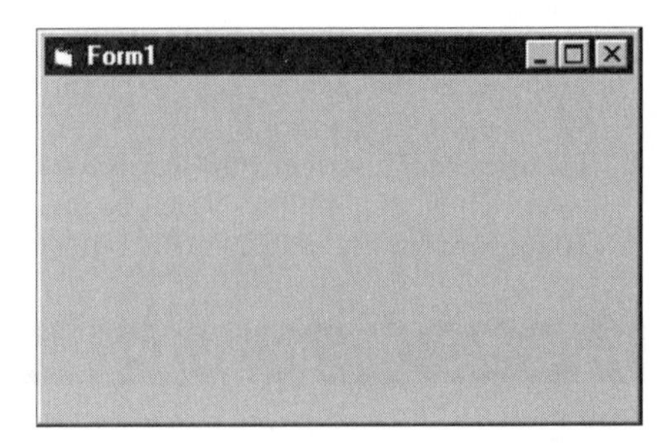

7 Stop the program and change the **Load** event so that it sets the picture box's **Enabled** property to false, removing the reference to the **Visible** property.

```
Sub Form_Load()

Picture1.Enabled = False

End Sub
```

8 Run the program again. This time, both the picture box and command button are visible, but neither can be selected. Try clicking the command button—nothing happens! Of course, the downside here is that the button control doesn't look disabled and inaccessible. You should bear this in mind; disabling a container control also prevents the user from using the controls it contains, but doesn't necessarily show this—something which can be very confusing for a user at run time.

Using picture boxes in this way can save you a lot of time and effort. If you need to hide a large number of controls, or make the controls pop up in response to the user doing something, just place those controls inside a picture box and flip the picture box's **Visible** property.

> *Incidentally, the picture box is really just one of two container controls in Visual Basic, the other being the slightly less versatile frame control. Whereas the picture box is really designed to show graphic images (as you will see later) but also does a darn good impersonation of a container control, a frame is nothing more than a container control. In fact the only advantage a frame has over a picture box is a slightly better look to it, and the fact that you can put a caption on its border—take a look for yourself. Incidentally, you can also turn off the border property of the control to get an invisible container, should you need to.*

The Shape Control

The shape control allows you to draw a simple geometric shape, such as a line, box or circle on to a form at design time. To use the shape control, you select the control from the palette and then drag a rectangle on the form in the same way as you draw any other type of control.

Try It Out - Using the Shape Control

1 Start a new Visual Basic project.

2 Double-click the shape control on the toolbox to place it onto the default form.

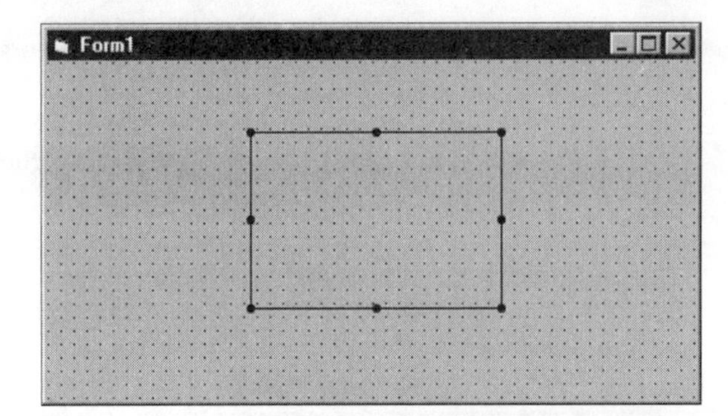

3 Resize the shape by clicking and dragging the resize handles in the usual manner.

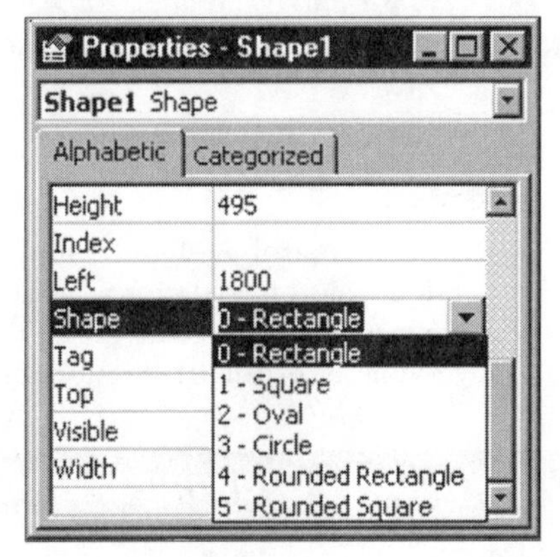

4 Bring up the properties window and find the **Shape** property. This allows you to change the shape that will be displayed. Double-click the **Shape** property to cycle through the available shapes.

5 You can change the style of the border around the shape from a solid line to various types of dashed line, using the **BorderStyle** property. Find it in the properties list and double-click it to cycle through all the available options.

6 The **BackStyle** property allows you to specify whether the shape should be filled or not.

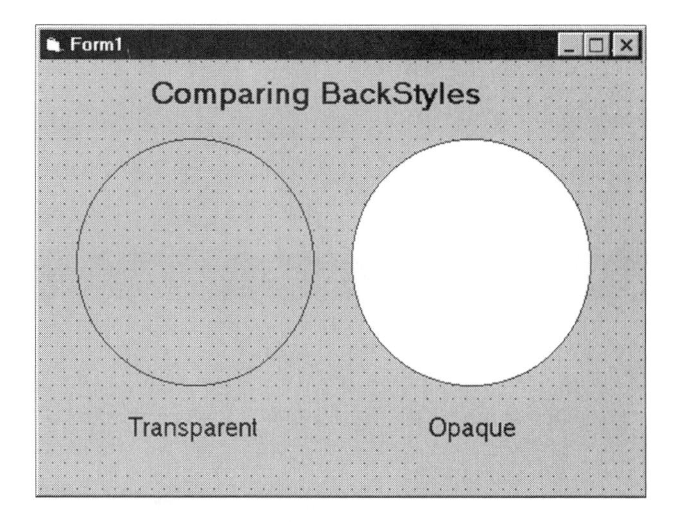

7 You can change the thickness of the border of the shape using the **`BorderWidth`** property. Find that property in the properties window and enter the number 10. The style of the border changes dramatically.

To be honest with you, I never use the shape control—it's too limiting to build up complex images at design time. If I need graphics at run time, then I use the graphics methods to create them. However, many people do *use the shape control for placing borders around items on forms, without the memory overhead that comes with a frame or a picture box. You also need to bear in mind that the Shape controls, because they are lightweight controls, cannot receive focus at run time. They are good for absolutely nothing other than jazzing up the appearance of your forms.*

The Line Control

The line control is slightly simpler to use than the shape control. It allows you to draw a straight line on your form. This is great for breaking up the controls on a form, or for underlining a particular area. It's something that interface designers call a feature, but everyone else calls it decoration.

Try It Out - Drawing a Line on a Form

1 Double-click the line control on the toolbox to place a line on the form.

2 The line control has two resize handles, one at each end, which you can drag around to change the size and slope of the line.

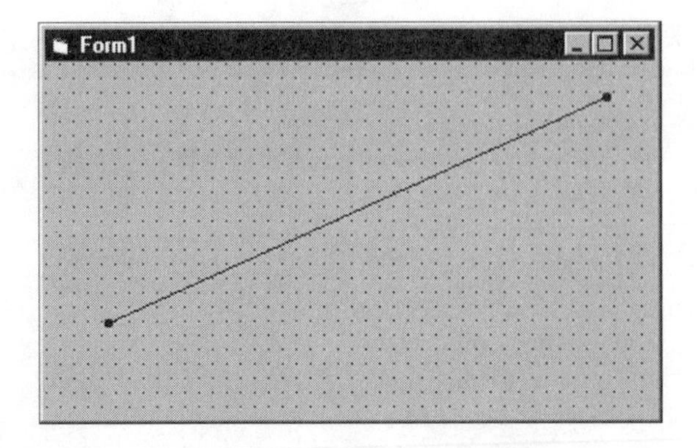

3 Just as with the shape control, you can change the thickness and type of line drawn using the **BorderStyle** and **BorderWidth** properties. Bring up the properties window and try double-clicking the **BorderStyle** property to cycle through the available line types. Next, enter a number into the **BorderWidth** property to change the thickness of the line. Other than that there isn't too much else that you can change.

The Graphics Methods

The graphics methods in Visual Basic provide a lot more flexibility when dealing with graphics. Unlike the controls (all of which need to be drawn on to a form at design time), the graphics methods allow you to create graphics on the fly. This includes drawing lines and shapes, setting individual pixels on the form, and so on. With a little thought, these methods can be taken beyond the obvious into the realms of games and animation programs. In fact, surprisingly little coding experience is needed to create some quite stunning effects, as you'll find out.

Yes, But is it Art?

If there is one area in Visual Basic that has always been sadly lacking, it has to be that of copying a mass of graphics from one area to another. Previously, if you wanted to accomplish such a feat, you would either have had to duplicate image or picture controls on the fly, or drop down to the rather frightening Windows API in order to use the **BitBlt** function.

Thankfully, Microsoft's R&D team don't just sit around drinking coffee and saying "Cool!" all day. In VB4 they introduced the amazing **PaintPicture** method. Despite its name, you don't simply say

```
Form1.PaintPicture "Something with a renaissance feel to it"
```

Instead, the **PaintPicture** method allows you to copy chunks of graphical data very rapidly from one area on a form, picture box or the printer to another—great for animation.

Try It Out - The PaintPicture Method

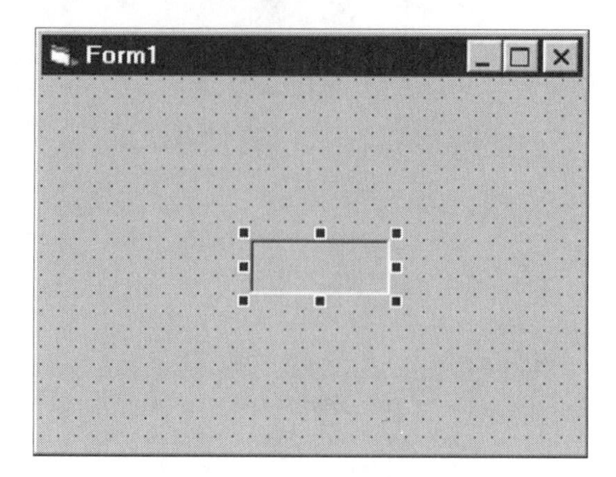

1 Start a new project and double click on the picture box icon in the toolbox to place a picture box on the form.

2 Name the picture box **picGraphic** and change its **Visible** property to false—we don't want this picture to be shown at run time.

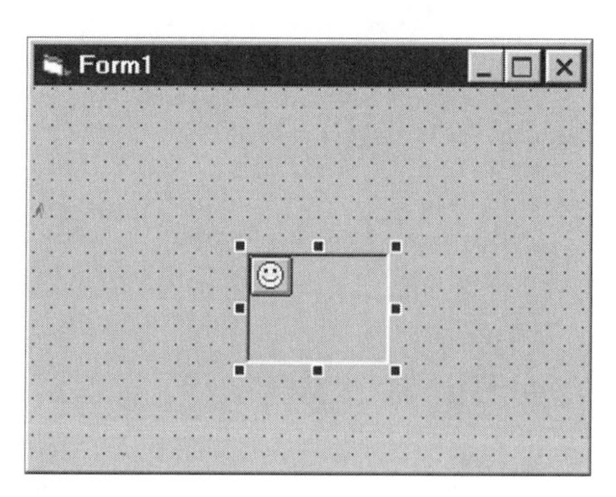

3 Double-click on the **Picture** property of the picture box to show the Load Picture dialog. Select an icon or small bitmap from anywhere on your system. (The **vb/Samples/Pguide/Controls** has some suitable playing card symbols).

4 Next we need to add some code. We're going to make the picture move round the screen when the user drags it with the mouse. To do this, we need to start by setting up a yes/no variable that will tell us when the mouse is being dragged round the screen. In the General Declarations section of the code window, type in

```
Dim lDragging As Boolean
```

5 We want **lDragging** to be set to true when the **MouseDown** event occurs and we want it to be false when the **MouseUp** event occurs. When the form loads, we want to start by assuming that the dragging hasn't yet begun. So, we need to set this variable in three different event handlers:

```
Private Sub Form_Load()

     lDragging = False

End Sub

Private Sub Form_MouseDown(Button As Integer, Shift As Integer, X As
Single, Y As Single)

     lDragging = True

End Sub

Private Sub Form_MouseUp(Button As Integer, Shift As Integer, X As
Single, Y As Single)

     lDragging = False

End Sub
```

6 Finally, we can use the **PaintPicture** method to add the action. This takes place in the **MouseMove** event. Add the following code:

```
Private Sub Form_MouseMove(Button As Integer, Shift As Integer, X As
Single, Y As Single)

     If lDragging Then
          Form1.PaintPicture picGraphic.Picture, X, Y, picGraphic.Width,
                 ↳    picGraphic.Height
     End If

End Sub
```

7 Now run the program. If you click and hold the mouse button down and then drag the mouse around, look what you get. Move it quickly and the images show up nicely.

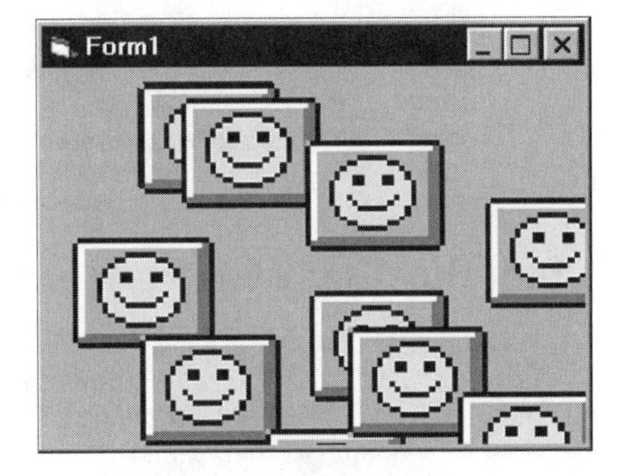

How It Works

The **PaintPicture** method works like this:

```
[object.]PaintPicture pic, destX, destY [,destWidth [,DestHeight [,srcX [,srcY
[,srcWidth [,srcHeight,[Op]]]]]]]
```

The first parameter in the method is the object parameter. You have to tell Visual Basic on which object you want the **PaintPicture** method to work. **PaintPicture** will quite happily work on forms, picture controls and, of course, the printer object.

The **pic** parameter is the picture that we're going to copy. Normally you'll pass the **Picture** property of a picture control or form here.

destX and **destY** are the coordinates on the target object where you want the picture to be displayed. The **DestWidth** and **DestHeight** properties specify the size of the resulting picture, and how much of the target object will be drawn on.

In the above example, we used **PaintPicture** on the form (**Form1**) and copied the image from the hidden picture box control called **picGraphic**. The X and Y coordinates were the same as the mouse X and Y coordinates and the width and height were taken from the width and height properties of the picture control:

```
If lDragging Then
 Form1.PaintPicture picGraphic.Picture, X, Y, picGraphic.Width,
       ↳    picGraphic.Height
End If
```

The remaining properties are, happily, optional. They allow you to specify a clipping region, which lets you copy only a portion of the source picture on to the target object. You do this by specifying the coordinates in the picture where the graphic you're after starts, and its width and height. The final parameter, **Op**, lets you specify something known as a raster operation, such as **And** and **Xor**. We'll look at these a little later.

> *Before we go on, there's a little quirk to* **PaintPicture** *that's worth knowing about. If you specify negative values for the* **Width** *and* **Height** *of the target image, the image appears flipped either horizontally or vertically, depending on which parameter you set to negative.*

Pixel Plotting with Pset

Having looked at the graphics controls, we'll now discuss the various graphics methods. The first one we'll look at is **Pset**. **Pset** actually means **point set** and allows you to set individual pixels (points) on a form. For instance, you could cover a form in multicolored dots to simulate splatter painting, or move dots around the screen in an orderly fashion to explore far off galaxies, to boldly go ...(you know the rest!).

Try It Out - Splatter Painting

1 The principles behind this are really simple, but the effect could quite well be used as a background for a title form in an application. Start up a new application and change the name of the default form to **frmMain**, and its **AutoRedraw** property to True.

2 Change the **BackColor** property of the form to black so that our painting will show up well.

3 Add the following code to the form's **Click** event so that it looks like this:

```
Private Sub Form_Click()

   Dim nIndex as Integer
   Dim nXCoord as Integer, nYCoord as Integer
   Dim nRed as Integer, nGreen as Integer, nBlue as Integer

   Randomize
   For nIndex = 1 To 2000
     nXCoord = Int(Rnd(1) * frmMain.ScaleWidth)
     nYCoord = Int(Rnd(1) * frmMain.ScaleHeight)
     nRed = Int(Rnd(1) * 255)
     nGreen = Int(Rnd(1) * 255)
     nBlue = Int(Rnd(1) * 255)

     PSet (nXCoord, nYCoord), RGB(nRed, nGreen, nBlue)
   Next
      Msgbox "All Done!"

End Sub
```

4 When you're done with typing in the code, run the application. When the form appears, click on it.

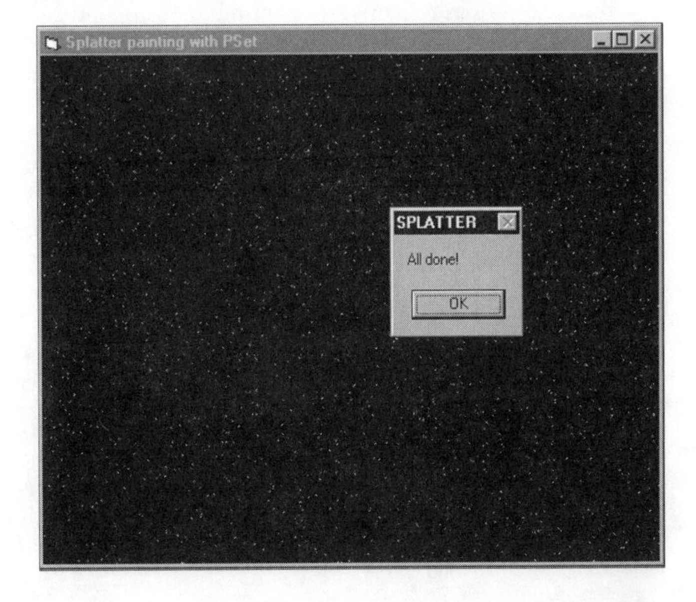

How It Works

First an overview. The **For...Next** loop runs 2000 times, each time deciding on some random coordinates at which to display a dot on the screen. This is what the **Rnd()** command does.

> *Visual Basic doesn't generate random numbers in the true sense. For example, you're not being asked to close your eyes and hit a key on the numeric keypad. Rather, it generates a sequence of seemingly random numbers which it stores in memory. That's the purpose of the* **Randomize** *command at the head of the code—***Randomize** *generates that sequence of numbers ready for you to pull them out with the* **Rnd()** *command. Philosophers among you will of course note that it is impossible to create a truly random number.*

If we use **Rnd(1)**, we tell Visual Basic to give us the next number in the random number sequence. The actual number we get is a decimal number somewhere between 0 and 1. Therefore, the line:

```
Rnd(1) * frmMain.ScaleWidth
```

gives us a random number between 0 and the width of the form client area. The client area of a form is the part on which you can draw or place controls. It's the bit in the middle, not including the borders and caption bar area.

So far so good! There's still some work to do on this random number before it can be used, though. Let's say the form width is something like 2437, and the random number that **Rnd(1)** gives us is 0.5412. Multiplying these two numbers together we get 1318.9044. Obviously that can't be used as the X coordinate—Visual Basic needs an integer number, not a decimal.

The **Int** statement converts a number to an integer value. In our example it would convert 1318.9044 to 1318 by just cutting the decimal part off. Now this is a number we can use. The same technique is applied to get the dot's Y coordinate, and the values of red, green and blue which will be used to produce our dot's color.

Finally, **PSet** is called to actually draw the dot. The format for the **PSet** method is:

```
Pset (<X coordinate>, <Y Coordinate>), <Color value>
```

Since our program has already decided on some coordinates for the dot, as well as the random values needed to use the **RGB** function, we have all the components we need to draw a dot somewhere on the screen, in a random color. If you run this 2000 times, lots of random multicolored dots appear, as in the example.

Drawing Lines

Dots are fine for learning about how graphics are drawn and about Visual Basic's rather eccentric coordinate system. However, for graphs and really impressive graphics you need to start thinking about drawing lines. Although this might be taken for granted, the ability to draw lines in your code opens up an infinite number of programming possibilities.

If you can draw lines, you can also draw graphs, three dimensional graphics and explore virtual reality. You could even simply mellow out with the computer equivalent of a psychedelic laser show!

Visual Basic has an extremely versatile command for drawing lines called the **`Line`** command. In its most basic form, you give the **`Line`** command two sets of coordinates—one stating where the line starts, the other where it ends. You can also supply a color value, just as you can with **`Pset`**. Visual Basic will then happily wander off for a few fractions of a second and draw the line for you.

Try It Out - Drawing Lines

1 Start a new project in Visual Basic and change the form's **`AutoRedraw`** property to true.

2 Run the program and then, when it's running, press *Ctrl-Break* to pause it or click the pause icon on the Visual Basic toolbar.

If the main form disappears when you do this, make it reappear by selecting from the Windows 95 toolbar. Indeed at any time during the following try it outs, just click on the Form icon on the toolbar to make it reappear.

3 Now that the program is paused, the Immediate window should be visible. Arrange the form and window so that you can see them both. As you'll remember from Chapter 8, the Immediate window allows you to enter most of the commands that you would normally type into the code window, the difference being that as soon as you hit *Enter* in the Immediate window, the command runs.

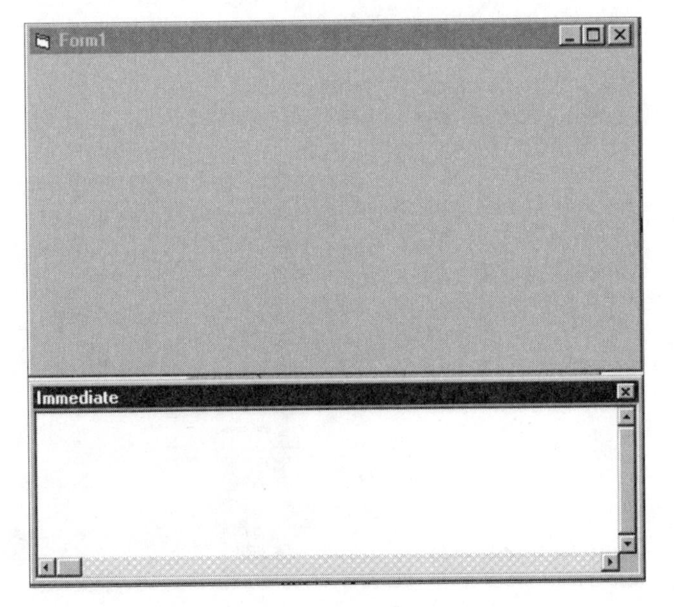

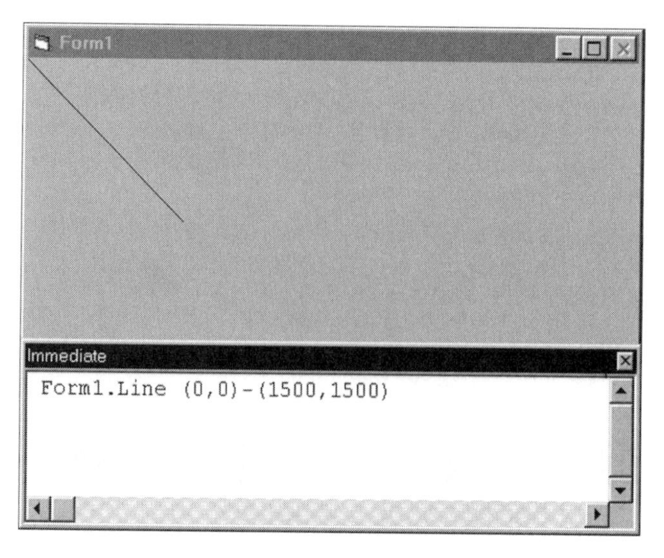

4 Let's draw some lines. In the immediate window, type **`Form1.Line (0,0)-(1500,1500)`** and press *Enter*. A line will appear on the form.

5 Unless you specify otherwise, Visual Basic draws a line in the color specified in the form's **`ForeColor`** property. You can also specify a color in the **`Line`** command itself. Type this into the immediate window and press *Enter*.

```
Form1.Line (0,0) - (2000,900), vbMagenta
```

This time the line is drawn in pink.

6 You can also tell Visual Basic to draw a line from the point at which the previous line ended. Type these two commands in and press *Enter* after each.

```
Form1.Line -(3000,3000)
Form1.Line -(0,0)
```

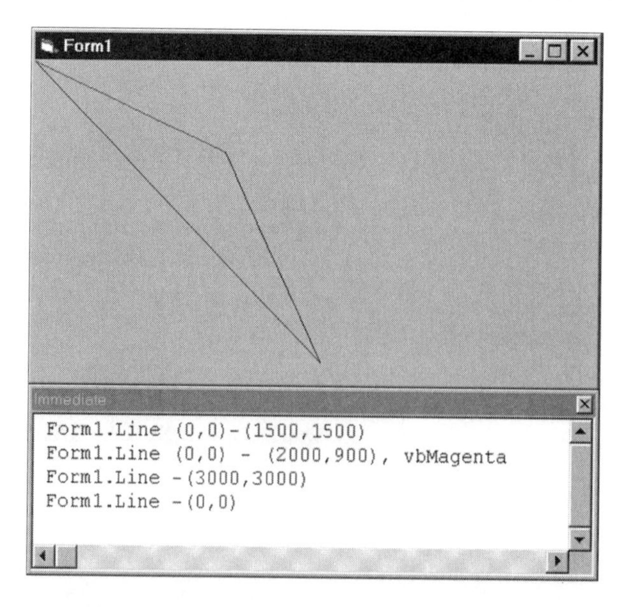

7 Finally, the **Line** command can also be used without specifying exact coordinates, but instead by using **offsets**. Try typing these lines in:

```
Form1.Line  (0,0)-Step(2000,400)
Form1.Line  Step(1000,1000)-Step(500,500)
Form1.Line  -Step(2000,-800)
```

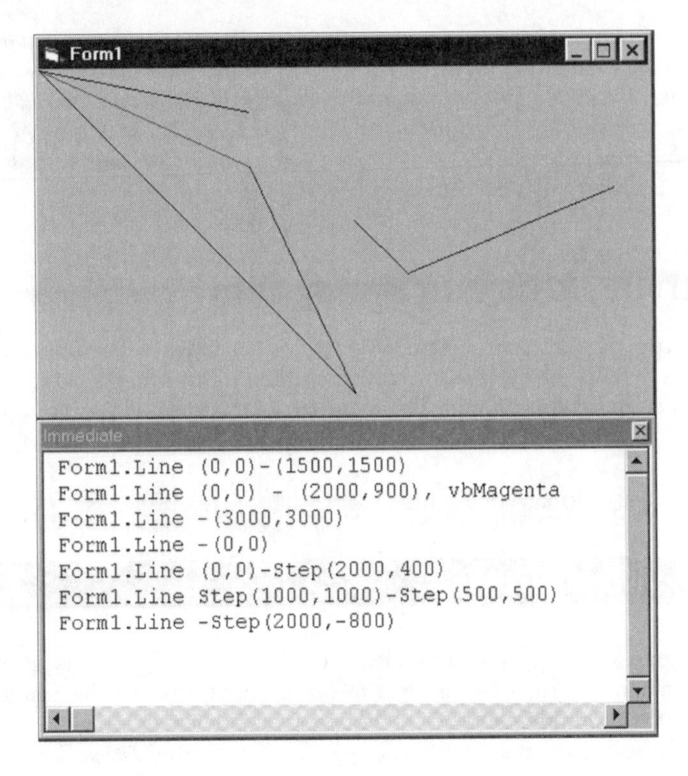

8 You get some pretty weird results with these. The **Step** keyword tells Visual Basic that the coordinates after the word **Step** should be added on to the last coordinates drawn. So **Form1.Line(0,0)-Step(1000,400)** starts the line at **0,0** and ends it at **(0+1000, 0+400)**.

9 Click on the End button, but keep the form open as the next few examples all require the same set up of form and Immediate window.

> *Although we've only really looked at the* **Line** *and* **Pset** *methods as a means of drawing static images, it's worth noting that it really doesn't take that much effort to get animation out of them. It is in fact a neat exercise if you want to try it yourself.*

> *Animation at the simplest level can be achieved by doing nothing more than drawing an image, then erasing it and drawing it again, either in a new position on the screen or in a new shape. Since both the* **`Pset`** *and* **`Line`** *commands let you specify a color to use when drawing, they are ideally suited to simple animation. First draw your image using a visible color, then erase it by drawing exactly the same image again, but in the background color.*
>
> *OK—so this isn't going to get you an award at the next leisure software industry convention, but it really is a good start on the road to really cool stuff with Visual Basic. If you want to find out more, then you can find two example programs that show this technique on the Wrox web site, at* **`http://www.wrox.com`**. *Alternatively, why not take a look at Instant Visual Basic Animation also from Wrox Press.*

Circles, Curves, Arcs and Bendy Bits

An extremely complex area of computer graphics has always been that of drawing curves and circles. Thankfully, Visual Basic greatly simplifies the process with its **`Circle`** command. Despite its rather misleading name, the **`Circle`** method can draw curves, circles, ellipses and segments of circles—which is excellent for pie-charts!

Let's take a look at normal circles first.

Try It Out - Drawing Circles

1 Stop the previous program (this clears the form of its previous graphics) and run the program again, pause it by using *Ctrl-Break* and bring up the immediate window with *Ctrl-G*. Catch your breath and pat yourself on the back for getting this far with no hassle. You can clear the immediate window using the *Delete* key if you're a neatness fetishist.

2 Arrange the two windows as before and type the following in the immediate window (don't forget to press *Enter* at the end of the command):

```
Form1.Circle (2000,1500), 1000
```

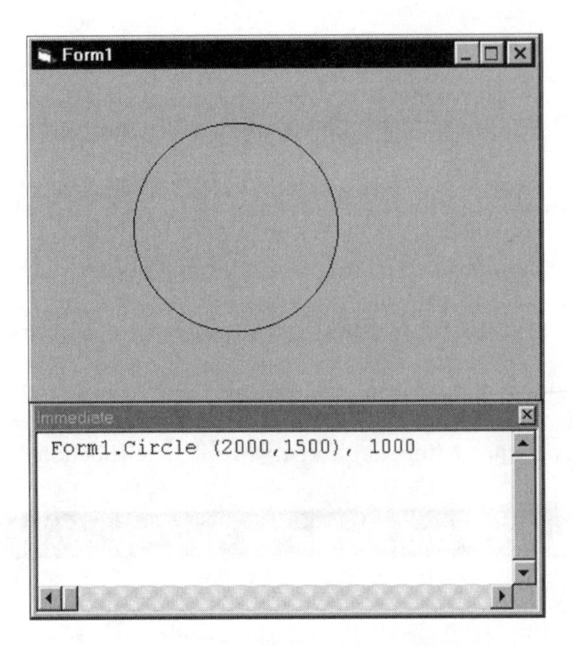

3 A circle appears. The coordinates which you specify in the brackets are the center of the circle, in this case 2000,1500. The number outside the brackets is the radius of the circle, here 1000. To make this clearer, draw two lines on the circle to show the center and the radius:

```
Line (2000,1500)-Step(0,1000)
Line (2000,1500)-Step(1000,0)
```

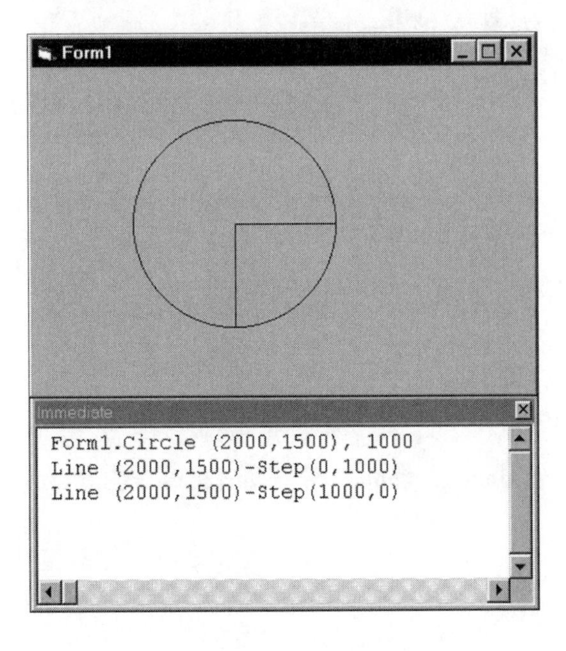

Drawing Arcs

Arcs require a little more effort. The **Circle** method you've used so far is a cut-down version of what it can actually do. The actual syntax for **Circle** is:

```
Circle (x,y), <radius>, <color>, <start angle>, <end angle>, <aspect>
```

Just to be awkward, most computers calculate angles and related stuff in terms of radians rather than degrees. I won't go into the logic of it all, nor give an explanation of what radians are—you don't need to know, and I failed pure math in college!

All you *do* need to know is that to convert a number in degrees to its equivalent in radians, you multiply the angle by Pi (3.142 roughly) and divide the result by 180. It's probably simplest to put this code into a function and then call that function—let's take a look.

Try It Out - Drawing Arcs and Slices

1 Stop the last program running.

2 Add a new code module to the project. Before we can go any further we need to create that function that converts degrees into radians. Type this function into the code window:

```
Function Rads ( ByVal nDegrees As Double ) As Double

    Dim nRadians As Double

    nRadians = (22 / 7) * nDegrees

    Rads = nRadians / 180

End Function
```

All the code does is take a number representing an angle in degrees, and then kick out a result in the radian equivalent.

3 Run the program, then pause it in the normal way. Hit *Ctrl-G* to bring up the immediate window.

4 Type the following into the immediate window to draw an arc which goes from 45 degrees of a circle to 230 degrees:

```
Form1.Circle (2000,2000), 1000,  , Rads(45), Rads(230)
```

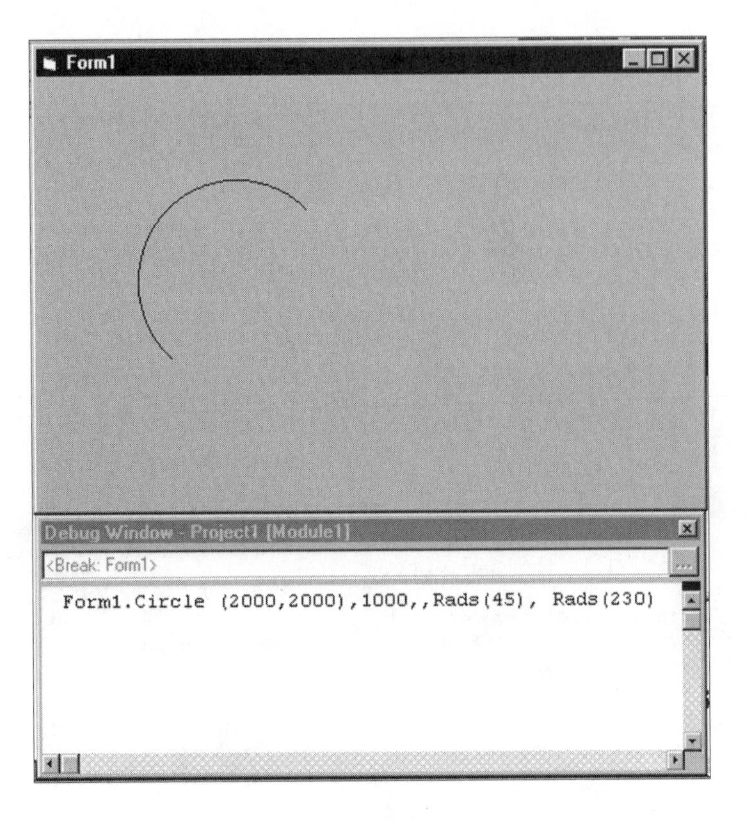

Note that the arc is drawn counterclockwise.

5 Previously we drew lines onto the circle with the **`Line`** command to mark out the radius and center. **`Circle`** can do that for you itself. Type in the following lines:

```
Form1.Cls
Form1.FillStyle = 0
Form1.FillColor = QbColor(14)
Form1.Circle (2000,2000),1000, , -Rads(90), -Rads(45)
Form1.FillColor = QbColor(1)
Form1.Circle (2050,1900),1000, , -Rads(45), -Rads(90)
Form1.FillStyle = 1
```

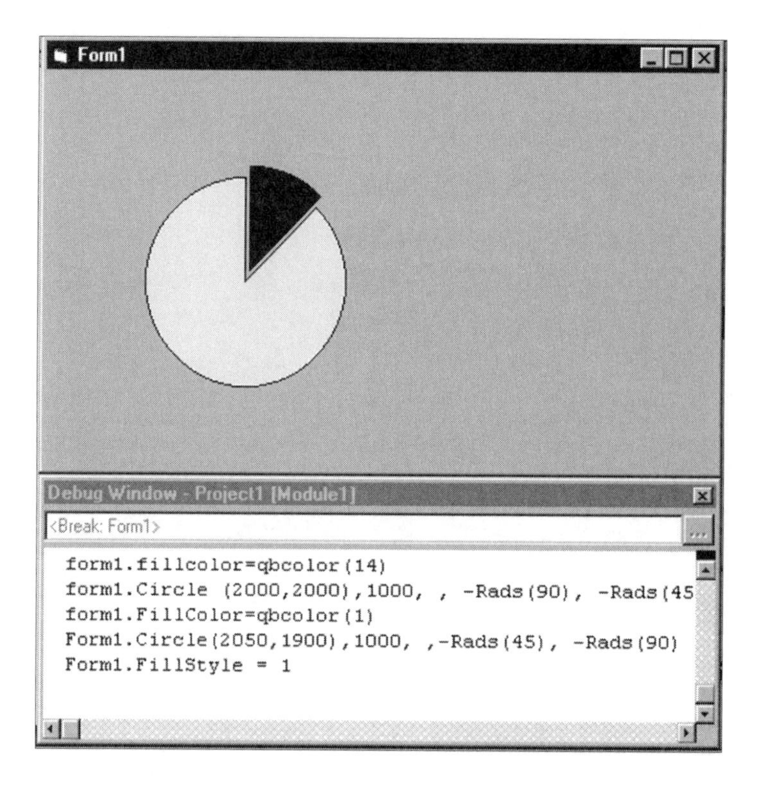

How It Works

There are some other interesting lines of code in what you've just typed. The **Cls** method actually stands for clear screen, but in Visual Basic it merely clears the form. After clearing the form with the **Cls** command, we set the form **FillStyle** property to 0. This tells Visual Basic to fill in any graphics it draws with the color in the **FillColor** property of the form. The next line sets the color to 14 (yellow) with the **QBColor** method.

In the two **Circle** commands, we pass negative start and end angles. This tells the **Circle** command to draw connecting lines from the start and end to the center of the circle. The last **FillStyle** line turns off the autofilling.

Before we go any further, save the module that we added the **Rads** function to as **Radians.Bas**—it might come in handy in your own code.

Drawing Ellipses

The final use of the **Circle** command is to draw ellipses. To draw an ellipse, all you need do is draw a circle in the normal way, then give Visual Basic a number for its **Aspect** parameter.

Before we go any further I'd better explain what aspect is. The aspect is the relationship between the horizontal radius and the vertical radius. For instance, an aspect of 2 would mean that the horizontal radius is twice as large as the vertical radius. Conversely, an aspect of 0.5 would display an ellipse which is twice as high as it is wide.

Try It Out - Ellipses

1 Stop the last program running and then run the program again, pause it (*Ctrl-Break*) and bring up the immediate window (*Ctrl-G*).

2 In the immediate window, type in the following lines and press *Enter*.

```
Form1.circle(2000,2000),1000,,,,3
Form1.circle(2000,2000),1000,,,,.5
Form1.circle(2000,2000),1000,,,,2
```

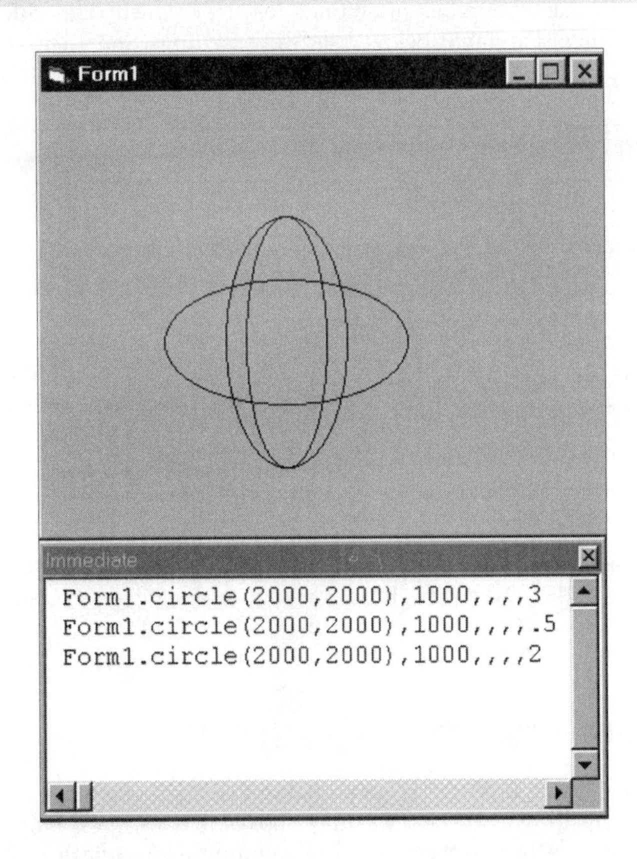

Even though I've called them commands and statements, and we've used them interactively in the debug environment, you must remember that these are graphics methods. When used in code, they must *apply to an object, which often defaults to the current form.*

Drawing Properties - Weird and Wonderful Effects

There are many different properties of graphics objects which you can use to create various effects.

The FillStyle Property

We saw that setting the **FillStyle** property of a form to 0 fills the circle with a solid color. Setting it to 1 (the default) leaves the circle's contents transparent.

FillStyle actually has a number of settings, each of which does different things to the shape you're drawing. The table below lists these settings and their effects on your works of art.

Value	Effect
0	Solid—fills the object.
1	Transparent—doesn't fill the object with anything.
2	Fills the object with horizontal lines.
3	Fills the object with vertical lines.
4	Fills the object with diagonal lines from the bottom left to the top right.
5	Fills with diagonal lines from the top left to the bottom right.
6	Draws a crosshatch pattern over the object.
7	Draws a diagonal crosshatch pattern over the object.

You can try out all these settings to your heart's content using the immediate window, as we've done for the other examples. Just run your project, pause it, go to the immediate window, set the **Fillstyle** property and draw away. Don't forget that changing the property doesn't do anything until you actually draw something.

The DrawWidth Property

Another interesting form property is **DrawWidth**. This specifies the thickness of the lines that your objects are drawn in, be they lines, boxes, circles, arcs, ellipses or whatever. The larger this number, the thicker the lines. The minimum line width is one pixel thick.

The DrawStyle Property

The **DrawStyle** property is another good one to play with. This lets you flip between drawing solid lines to dashed ones of varying types, such as .... or . -- . -- . -- .—, and so on. The best way to learn about these styles is to play with them using the immediate window.

The DrawMode Property

By far the most interesting property is the **DrawMode** property. This has 16 possible settings which govern how Visual Basic goes about drawing things. Four of the most useful are:

Value	Effect
4	Inverts the current pattern when drawing. The current pattern is that specified in the **FillStyle** property.
7	XOR Pen. Lets you draw an object, then when you redraw it, restores what was previously drawn.
11	Does nothing. It's like saying don't draw anything. Use it to in effect switch the drawing off.
13	Copy pen. This is the default **DrawMode** that we've been using so far.

XOR Mode

The **XOR** mode needs a bit more explanation. It's mainly used for games and the like. You may want to have a background graphic drawn on a form, and then move objects over the top of it. **XOR** mode lets you do this. When you first draw something on to the form it appears exactly as you'd expect. However, if you redraw the same object, in the same place, it vanishes, and the background that was there previously reappears.

This is achieved by performing an exclusive **OR** operation on the color values of the individual pixels on the screen. While we're not going to actually use this technique, it's interesting to understand.

Each pixel on your screen has a number assigned to it that determines its current color. This value is stored in your computer as a block of 1s and 0s (as are all numbers in computers). Each sequence of 1s and 0s corresponds to a certain color. A sequence of these bits (a bit is a 1 or a 0) is called a byte. When our new object swoops across the screen, it has its own set of pixel color values held in byte values.

When a pixel from the object comes over a pixel on the screen, an **XOR** operation is performed. This means that each bit in the screen byte is compared with each bit in the object byte. Exclusive **OR** means that if either both or neither of the values are true, then the result is false. If just one them is true, then the result is true. True here means of course a 1, while false means a 0.

The resulting color on the screen is determined by the outcome of the operation. This isn't the interesting part however. What's cool is that if you then repeat the **XOR** operation with the object and the changed screen color, you get back to the original screen color.

This is a really efficient way of making an alien glide across a lunar landscape without leaving a nasty trail behind it.

Repainting Forms Efficiently

I love Visual Basic. It's without doubt the best thing to happen to Windows programming. But even I have to admit that Visual Basic is a bit of a slouch when it comes to complex graphics. The problem is partly Visual Basic and partly Windows, but whatever the cause, there are some things you *can* do to make your Visual Basic graphics programs slicker and more efficient.

ClipControls

Let's start with **ClipControls**. Before we go any further it's worth noting that this can be a little confusing, and it's not absolutely necessary to use this thing. If you want to forgo all the hassle here, then its useful to know that most programmers are happy setting this property to false.

Whenever you draw something on a form and move an icon or the mouse across it, Visual Basic and Windows decide which areas of the form need to be repainted. For example, you wouldn't want to see the mouse trail left on the form indefinitely.

This is what **ClipControls** does. With the **AutoRedraw** property set to false, your program will receive **Paint** events whenever part of the form needs to be redrawn. The **ClipControls** property governs where you can draw. When it's set to true, you can redraw any part of the form you want to in the **Paint** event. Something called a **clipping region** is created around the controls on the form to make sure you don't draw over them. It basically establishes the 'blank' region behind the controls as the drawing area, while leaving the controls protected.

With **ClipControls** set to false, no matter where you try to draw on a form, Visual Basic will only change the areas of the form it thinks need repainting.

ClipControls also affects the way Visual Basic handles redrawing when the **AutoRedraw** property is set to True. When **AutoRedraw** is set to True, Visual Basic handles the redrawing of the graphics on the form, should the form get resized, moved or overlaid with another. The setting of **ClipControls** tells Visual Basic whether or not it needs to redraw the whole form, or just the affected parts of it.

To get your forms displaying and redrawing quickly, you need to have **ClipControls** set to false. This way, only the affected areas of the form are redrawn and Visual Basic and Windows don't have so much graphical data to deal with. You should only have **ClipControls** set to true if you're changing all the graphics on a form every time you redraw, such as in an action game where you might need to redraw the whole playing area a number of times every second.

AutoRedraw

Much more useful is the **`AutoRedraw`** property itself. By default this is set to false. This means that if another window appears on top of the one you're drawing, Visual Basic thinks you will look after redrawing the first form if the need arises. The net result of this is that, because Visual Basic assumes you can redraw your own graphics, everything runs that much faster.

Setting the property to true, however, tells Visual Basic that it should take care of your graphics for you. Each time you draw something, Visual Basic makes a mental note of what you did. Should parts of the form get covered by another object, Visual Basic automatically knows what to do to redisplay your graphics. This also works if your user switches to another application. When your form comes back into view, it's restored to its former glory. The downside is that your graphics run quite a lot slower.

> *If you want fast graphics, set* **`AutoRedraw`** *to false. If you don't want the hassle of the users mucking up your displays by dragging windows around indiscriminately, then you'd better set* **`AutoRedraw`** *to true, and live with the consequences.*

Summary

This has been a lightning tour of graphics with Visual Basic. I don't claim to have told you everything, but as we said at the beginning, graphics are nice, but they're often the icing on the cake. However, we did get a quick tour of the highlights, namely:

- How color works in Visual Basic
- The coordinate system
- Graphics controls, with image and picture boxes, and the shape and line controls
- Graphics methods

Along the way you learned how to choose between the image and picture controls, and the difference between graphics controls and methods. You learned how to create simple animation, and finally how to get the best performance from Visual Basic.

Why Not Try...

1 Use the line control to draw a "tic-tac-toe" board game.

2 Use the graphics line method to draw a tic-tac-toe board game.

3 Produce an animated tic-tac-toe game for a visiting alien. The game should appear to play itself, i.e. a "X" will appear followed by a "O", followed by another "X". You should decide how the game should be played and if there's to be a winner or if it is to be tied. If there's a winner then you should draw a line which connects the three winning entries. Include the graphics **`Circle`** method to produce the "O". Create the "X" any way you wish.

4 It's been a late night working on Visual Basic. You and a friend are hungry and decide to order a pizza. Your local pizza joint has two sizes of pizza. One is a 1000 twip diameter pie, and the other is a 1400 twip diameter pie. The price of the 1400 twip radius pie is 1/3 more than the 1000 twip pie. You argue that it makes more sense to splurge for the larger pie because a 1400 twip diameter pie has almost twice the surface (and therefore eating) area as a 1000 twip diameter pie. Your friend doesn't believe you. Armed with the knowledge that the area of a circle is equal to PI multiplied by the radius squared, develop a project which uses the graphics **`Circle`** method to draw the two pies, calculate their area, and display the calculated area on a form.

5 Be a sore loser, and obliterate the tic-tac-toe board and game you created in Exercise 3. You should do this by adding a command button to the form and when this button is pressed, the screen should be filled by random lines of random colors which completely cover the screen. This should be done by using a combination of a random number generator and the graphics **`Line`** method.

asic Visual Basic Visual Ba
al Basic Visual Basic Visual
asic Visual Basic Visual Ba
ual Basic Vi
Basic Visu
ual Basic V
l Basic Vis
isual Basic Visual Basi
al Basic Visual Basic Visua
Visual Basic Visual Basic Visu
l Basic Visual Ba
l Basic Visual
ic Visual Basi
Basic Visual B
ic Visual Basi
l Basic Visual
ual Basic Visual Basic Visual Ba
Visual Basic Visual Basic Visu
sual Basic Visual Basic Visu
Visual Basic Visual Ba

Using Database Controls

Welcome to the information revolution! By far the most popular application for computers in the 90s is the management of information: customer lists, accounts records, stock records in a warehouse, personnel information and so on. The ideal tool to manage all this information is a good database system. Visual Basic 3 was one of the market leaders as a cheap, powerful Windows database development tool. Visual Basic 4 introduced the VB community to the world of objects and classes and also managed to simplify database access a great deal. Visual Basic 5 looks set to hold on to this crown, with a faster database engine, faster execution times, and a wealth of new features designed to get you working with databases as quickly and painlessly as possible.

In this chapter you'll learn:

- How databases work
- Why Visual Basic is a good choice for database developers
- How to access existing databases using controls and properties
- How to use Data Manager to create new database

What is a Database?

The easiest way to understand how databases work is to consider how people organize their information in real life. The objective of any database is to make life easier. This implies that you know exactly what information you have to organize, and what people want to use it for. This sounds trivial, but it's at this stage that most databases start to go wrong. A useful database needs careful planning and design.

We'll start at the very beginning by seeing how computer databases are a logical evolution of the ways we organize information in real life. Then, once you have the general concepts under your belt, we can move on to look at how you build your own Visual Basic databases.

A Living Database

Imagine an office filing cabinet with three drawers:

- The top drawer contains information about each customer, such as their name and address
- The second drawer holds information about the stock of the business—perhaps the goods it sells, or the raw materials it holds in order to produce goods in the first place
- The third drawer contains invoices that the business has sent out to its customers

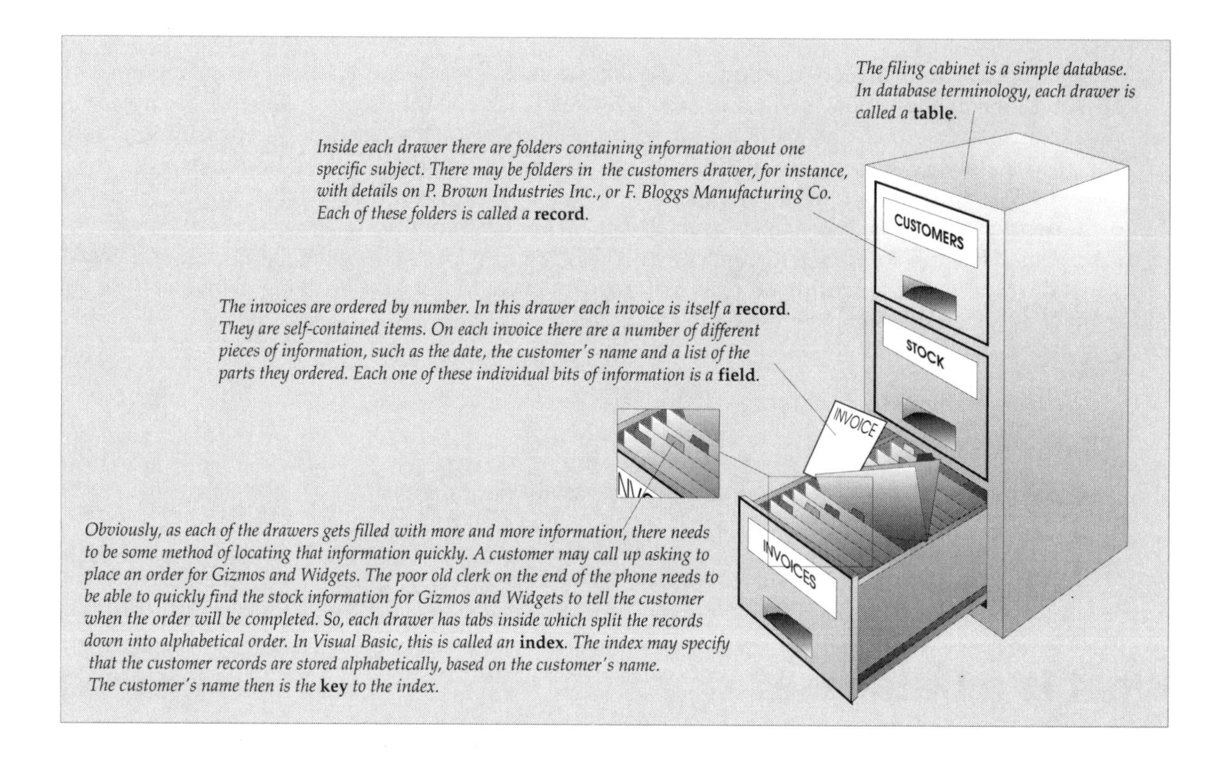

The filing cabinet is a simple database. In database terminology, each drawer is called a **table**.
Inside each drawer there are folders containing information about one specific subject. There may be folders in the customers drawer, for instance, with details on P. Brown Industries Inc., or F. Bloggs Manufacturing Co. Each of these folders is called a **record**.
The invoices are ordered by number. In this drawer each invoice is itself a **record**. They are self-contained items. On each invoice there are a number of different pieces of information, such as the date, the customer's name and a list of the parts they ordered. Each one of these individual bits of information is a **field**.
Obviously, as each of the drawers gets filled with more and more information, there needs to be some method of locating that information quickly. A customer may call up asking to place an order for Gizmos and Widgets. The poor old clerk on the end of the phone needs to be able to quickly find the stock information for Gizmos and Widgets to tell the customer when the order will be completed. So, each drawer has tabs inside which split the records down into alphabetical order. In Visual Basic, this is called an **index**. The index may specify that the customer records are stored alphabetically, based on the customer's name. The customer's name then is the **key** to the index.
CUSTOMERS
STOCK
INVOICE
INVOICES

Getting Information Out of a Real Database

Continuing the example, let's say that, a few days after placing his order for Gizmos, the customer still hasn't received his delivery. So he phones you, the clerk at J. Smith Inc., and asks when the order was dispatched. This sounds like a simple request, but think about it. It's actually quite tricky. Think about the information that each of the three drawers contains:

- The customer drawer has a separate file for each customer that contains their name and address, and a list of all the invoices that J. Smith has raised for this customer. Take a look at that customer's file. There's a list of invoice numbers and amounts, but that's it. How can you tell which order was for the Gizmos?
- The obvious thing to do is to make a note of the last invoice number in the customer's file, and then look in the invoices drawer. This drawer is ordered by invoice number, in database-speak it is **indexed** on invoice number. So, you can now pull out the invoice you want. There it is, the invoice to the customer who called in. Bad news! The invoice shows that you back-ordered the Gizmos because you were out of stock. Oh no—angry customer! Therefore, you decide to take a look in the stock drawer to see when a new delivery is due to come in.
- Luckily, the stock drawer is indexed in alphabetical order, like the customer drawer, so it's easy to pull out the Gizmos file and look at when the next delivery is due to arrive—next Friday. You call up the customer and he's cool about it.

You've probably done something like this yourself many times. In fact, what you've just done is a **multitable relational query**. It's **multitable** because you had to use three filing drawers (or **tables**) to get all the information you need. It's **relational** because you had to find a piece of information from one table (the invoice number from the customer drawer) and relate it to another table (the invoice drawer), in order to find the right file.

Flat-File vs. Relational Databases

Databases on computers are broken down into two camps: **flat-file** databases and **relational** databases

With flat-file databases, you tend to have a separate file on the disk for each table, and separate files for each index to a table. With flat-file databases, actually relating information from one table to another can be pretty tricky, since each table is really a totally independent entity.

Relational databases are a more elegant solution. With a relational database, most of the tables that hold the data are held in one large central database file, like our filing drawers are all in the same cabinet. Organizing and accessing the information in these tables is usually done for you by something called a **database engine.** The clerk who searches through the files at J. Smith Inc. is, in fact, a database engine.

What the Database Engine Does

As well as managing access to the database, the database engine also does a lot of housekeeping to keep the relational database nice and tidy. The clerk at J. Smith Inc. not only gets information out of the database, but also has to file new invoices in the right place and keep the stock and customer files up to date.

He also has to check that what's going into the database is not rubbish. To do that he has some simple rules. For example, if he gets an invoice through with a customer name that isn't already in his customer drawer, then he won't file it away until that customer is set up properly. Otherwise, the invoice would disappear into the drawer and not be related to anything. As invoice numbers don't mean anything on their own, it would probably just sink without trace. A database engine does this kind of checking in a computer database.

Relational databases are also rather special, in that the information held in the tables of the database is rarely duplicated. The database engine makes it easy to pull information out of more than one table at once, so duplication of information can be kept to a minimum.

In our customer and invoice example, for instance, when the time comes to print the invoice, your application would need to get the customer's name and address from somewhere to print on the invoice. All you'd need to store on each invoice record is some kind of unique customer identification number, like an account number, so that you could tell the engine to get the name and address of the customer from the customer table automatically. From a maintenance point of view this is great. If a customer rings you up to change their address, you don't need to trot through the database changing hundreds of old invoices. You only need to change the relevant records in the customer file, since that will be the only place where this information is held.

In this example, the customer account number that is used to find the right file in both the customer file and the invoice file is called the **primary key**. This is the item that **relates** the two tables together and each value of the primary key must be unique.

The Important Jargon

Now you have an idea about what databases really are, let's review the words that cropped up:

- **Tables** are collections of information that have some logical reason to fit together, like all the names and addresses of customers. In our example, this is a drawer in the filing cabinet.
- **Records** are the individual entries in a table, like all the details for one particular customer. These are also known as rows.
- **Fields** are the items that make up a complete record, like the street name of the customer's address. These are also known as columns.
- An **index** is a field or collection of fields that is used to sort the contents of a table into a logical order. In the customer table, the best choice is the customer's name. That way, the table is in alphabetical order.
- A **primary key** is a field in a table that identifies each record uniquely. The same field also appears in another table, allowing the data in each to be related. In our example, the customer account number appears in both the customer table and on all the invoices. Often, the index field and the primary key are the same thing.
- The **database engine** is the program that files, organizes and retrieves all the data from our tables. The great strength of relational databases is that the database manager is separate from the data itself. This means we can use Visual Basic to read Paradox databases and other types of data.

- A **query** is the process of sending the database manager away to find the information we want from the database.

These are the components of a relational database that you will find in any relational database development system. However, Visual Basic expands on these through the use of a new kind of object, known as the **recordset**.

Recordsets

In a nutshell, a recordset is, as the name implies, a set of related records. It doesn't matter whether the recordset is derived from a single table or from a collection of tables. When you look at the contents of a table, you're looking at a recordset. When you look at one line of data, that too is a recordset. In Visual Basic, you will come across three different kinds of recordset:

- A **table** type recordset is just what the name suggests. It is simply a recordset consisting of all the data from a single table. In VB, table type recordsets are the easiest to deal with, the least memory-hungry and also the fastest when it comes to accessing and retrieving data, since the recordset relates directly to a single table.
- A **dynaset** type recordset is one in which the records are built up from a number of different tables. For example, if you wanted to look up an invoice, you would use a dynaset to pull together the customer's name and address from one table, and the invoice details from another. Using a dynaset means you retain the editing and updating facilities available with the tables themselves.
- Finally, a **snapshot** type recordset works in the same way as a dynaset, but is read-only. You can still pull in data from multiple sources, but your users will be unable to add to or update the data. Snapshots are faster than dynasets since Visual Basic doesn't have to worry about updating the information. However, they are still slower than tables.

One way to think about a relational database is as a collection of components that work together. Your job is to define what those components are and how they fit together. You can dice the data in any number of different ways—there is no real right or wrong way. What matters is that it's easy to understand, safe and efficient. Database design is an art and we can't hope to cover such a massive and open-ended subject here. However, if you stick to simple rules, and always try and relate it back to a clerk sorting through a filing cabinet, you'll be fine.

Databases and Visual Basic

Visual Basic comes with the **Jet** database engine built in. This is one of Visual Basic's main selling points. Jet is the set of control software used in Microsoft's Access database system. You are practically getting Access for free.

The Jet engine can create and manage information in a wide variety of database formats. Using Jet you can deal with Access, Foxpro, dBase, Paradox, Oracle, SQL Server and Btrieve databases right from the word go. These comprise the bestselling databases available for PCs today. Being able to connect to them, and read and write the information they hold, can make you a very valuable commodity to many businesses. This has made Visual Basic the leading tool for Windows database development.

What does database development really mean? For VB programmers, it means writing what are called front-ends. While you can write a perfectly good application that takes data from a built-in database, the real action is in VB programs that take data from one or more so called back-end databases. The VB front-end then presents this information to the user in a way that works for them, and lets them do what they want with it. Another user with a different task may require a completely different set of views of essentially the same data. Visual Basic is great for knocking up a lot of different front-ends for the diverse needs of business users.

In the Learning edition of Visual Basic, you access and manipulate databases through the **data control**. The data control lets you view and modify records in a database with no code at all. With just a little code, you can let your users add and delete information, and your programs can also cope with wonderful things like indexed searching, transaction processing, and much, much more.

In the bigger (and more expensive) versions of VB, the Pro and Enterprise editions, you can talk to the Jet database engine directly, rather than using the data control as the glue to attach your program to the database. You do this by using a set of classes to create data access objects in your code. This is a very powerful way to manipulate databases, but requires a lot of code, a lot of skill, and a lot of cash to buy the bigger versions of VB. However, even at this level, it makes sense to use a mixture of the data control and data access objects, as the data control is so darn good—as we shall soon discover!

Building Visual Basic Databases

What is slightly harder in Visual Basic on its own is to build databases from scratch. You can create your own database using an add-on tool supplied with Visual Basic called **Visual Data Manager**. The Learning Edition of Visual Basic won't let you define or amend the structure of a database from within your code, you can only do that at design time. This means you couldn't have an option in your program to add new types of field to the database should you need them. You can only do this by stopping the program and redefining the database at design time. You can, of course, create new records and add data to predefined fields as much as you like.

How This Section Is Organized

I have taken the liberty of stretching our coverage of databases over 2 chapters. This recognizes both the importance of VB database programming and its depth and power, even with the Learning Edition.

So, what exactly are we going to do? First in this chapter, I will introduce the **data control**—which is the link between your code, its visual interface and any underlying database. Armed with this knowledge, we will then move on to **bound controls**—controls which allow you to display and change data on screen with little or no code.

In the next chapter, we'll look at how you can control the data control from code, giving you more flexibility and some powerful built-in methods.

First of all, though, let's look at the root of all data access in the Learning Edition of VB—the data control.

Using the Data Control

The data control is one of the most powerful controls in the Learning Edition of Visual Basic. For example, you can use it to create an application to browse records in a database without writing any code. But the data control's usefulness goes way beyond just browsing—its properties and methods give you complete access to the facilities of the underlying Jet database engine. This allows you to write code to search for individual records, add new records and delete existing ones.

The Data Control Itself 

On its own, the data control is pretty useless. On the screen it looks like this:

It provides you with a set of buttons that look very much like VCR buttons. These allow you to move through the records in your database. However, the data control itself provides no way of actually viewing the data in the current record. What it does provide is the glue that connects the database to other controls on the form, which you can then use to display the data you want.

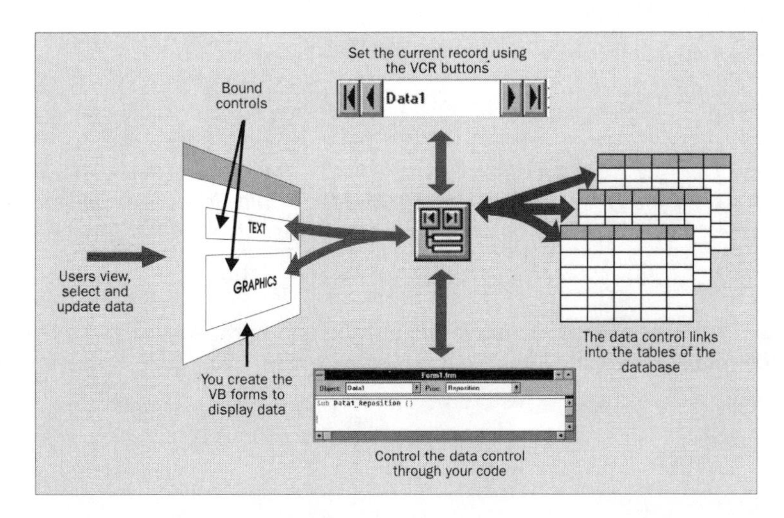

To get anything tangible out of the data control then, you have to add some controls to the form into which the data can be piped. These are called **bound controls**.

Bound Controls

Bound controls are controls which can be linked to a data control at design time, and made to display the data in the current record. All these complicated terms can be more than a little daunting at first, but don't panic—you've already used bound controls! Text boxes, check boxes, image controls, labels and picture boxes are all bound controls. They're all able to take information from certain fields in the current record of the current database, and display that data on a form.

There are two types of bound control available in the Learning Edition of VB. The controls we have already come across that also do double time as bound controls are called the **intrinsic** controls. All this means is that they are in your toolbox all the time and you can't get rid of them.

- Label
- Image
- Text box
- Check box
- Picture box
- List box
- Combo box
- OLE container

There are also three bound custom controls. You have to add these to your project using the Components menu option from the Project menu, as we did with the Common Dialog control earlier in the book. The three custom controls in question are as follows:

- Data bound list box
- Data bound combo box
- Data bound grid

When you add these bound custom controls from the Components dialog, the list box and combo box are grouped together under Microsoft Data Bound List Controls 5.0. *Check this option and* Microsoft Data Bound Grid Control *to add the three custom controls to your toolbox.*

These controls have been written from the ground up with data access in mind, and support a lot more data-related methods and properties than their intrinsic counterparts.

The BIBLIO.MDB Database

On the Visual Basic CD there's a Microsoft Access database called `Biblio.mdb`. The `.mdb` extension is standard for all Access databases. Before you start tooling around with a database, it's a good idea to know what's going on inside it. Until we get a bit more proficient with databases in general, though, you're going to have to rely on me to give you the lowdown.

The `Biblio.mdb` database is a listing of some database-related books. However, the data in the database isn't all lumped together in one big table, as it might be in a spreadsheet. Instead, similar types of information are grouped together into tables, which are then linked by common fields, or **keys** as they are known in database-speak. This process of breaking the data down into related groups is known as **normalization**, and has a lot benefits in terms of avoiding repeated data.

For example, most publishers in the table own more than one book. If there was only one table, with every piece of data relating to that title contained in a single row, then a big publisher would have their name entered over and over again. A better idea is to have a table that lists all the publishers once, and give them all a unique ID number which can then be used to link the publisher to the title. The `Biblio` database does just that and repeats it for authors as well.

Let's take a quick look at the tables in `Biblio`. I cheated and opened these in Access.

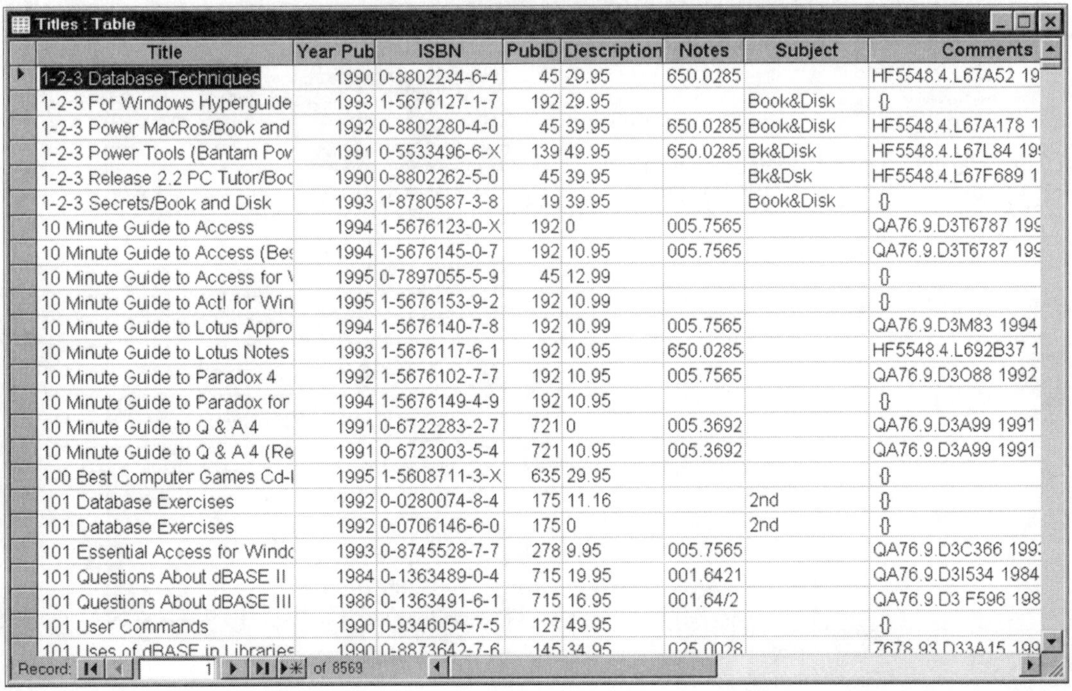

Titles : Table

Title	Year Pub	ISBN	PubID	Description	Notes	Subject	Comments
1-2-3 Database Techniques	1990	0-8802234-6-4	45	29.95	650.0285		HF5548.4.L67A52 19
1-2-3 For Windows Hyperguide	1993	1-5676127-1-7	192	29.95		Book&Disk	{}
1-2-3 Power MacRos/Book and	1992	0-8802280-4-0	45	39.95	650.0285	Book&Disk	HF5548.4.L67A178 1
1-2-3 Power Tools (Bantam Pov	1991	0-5533496-6-X	139	49.95	650.0285	Bk&Disk	HF5548.4.L67L84 19
1-2-3 Release 2.2 PC Tutor/Boc	1990	0-8802262-5-0	45	39.95		Bk&Dsk	HF5548.4.L67F689 1
1-2-3 Secrets/Book and Disk	1993	1-8780587-3-8	19	39.95		Book&Disk	{}
10 Minute Guide to Access	1994	1-5676123-0-X	192	0	005.7565		QA76.9.D3T6787 199
10 Minute Guide to Access (Be	1994	1-5676145-0-7	192	10.95	005.7565		QA76.9.D3T6787 199
10 Minute Guide to Access for \	1995	0-7897055-5-9	45	12.99			{}
10 Minute Guide to Act! for Win	1995	1-5676153-9-2	192	10.99			{}
10 Minute Guide to Lotus Appro	1994	1-5676140-7-8	192	10.99	005.7565		QA76.9.D3M83 1994
10 Minute Guide to Lotus Notes	1993	1-5676117-6-1	192	10.95	650.0285		HF5548.4.L692B37 1
10 Minute Guide to Paradox 4	1992	1-5676102-7-7	192	10.95	005.7565		QA76.9.D3O88 1992
10 Minute Guide to Paradox for	1994	1-5676149-4-9	192	10.95			{}
10 Minute Guide to Q & A 4	1991	0-6722283-2-7	721	0	005.3692		QA76.9.D3A99 1991
10 Minute Guide to Q & A 4 (Re	1991	0-6723003-5-4	721	10.95	005.3692		QA76.9.D3A99 1991
100 Best Computer Games Cd-I	1995	1-5608711-3-X	635	29.95			{}
101 Database Exercises	1992	0-0280074-8-4	175	11.16		2nd	{}
101 Database Exercises	1992	0-0706146-6-0	175	0		2nd	{}
101 Essential Access for Windc	1993	0-8745528-7-7	278	9.95	005.7565		QA76.9.D3C366 199
101 Questions About dBASE II	1984	0-1363489-0-4	715	19.95	001.6421		QA76.9.D3I534 1984
101 Questions About dBASE III	1986	0-1363491-6-1	715	16.95	001.64/2		QA76.9.D3 F596 198
101 User Commands	1990	0-9346054-7-5	127	49.95			{}
101 Uses of dBASE in Libraries	1990	0-8873642-7-6	145	34.95	025.0028		Z678.93.D33A15 199

Record: 1 of 8569

The Pub_ID field in the above Titles table is the same as in the Publishers table:

Publishers : Table

PubID	Name	Company Name	Address	City	State	Zip
624	A K PETERS	A K PETERS LTD				
518	A SYSTEM PUBNS	A SYSTEM PUBNS				
499	A-R EDITIONS	A-R EDITIONS				
116	AA BALKEMA	AA BALKEMA				
242	AARP	AMER ASSN OF RETIRED PERSONS				
97	ABACUS	ABACUS SOFTWARE				
616	ABC TELETRAINING	ABC TELETRAINING				
214	ABC-CLIO	ABC-CLIO				
102	ABLEX	ABLEX PUB CORP				
229	Ablex Pub	Ablex Pub				
99	ACADEMIC	ACADEMIC PR				
362	ACCESS	ACCESS PUB				
455	ACR	AMER COLLEGE OF RADIOLOGY				
530	ACS	AMER CHEMICAL SOCIETY				
526	ADAM HILGER	ADAM HILGER				
582	ADAMS HALL PUB	ADAMS HALL PUB				
369	ADARE PUB	ADARE PUB				
49	Addison-Wesley	Addison-Wesley	Rte 128	Reading	MA	01867
9	ADDISON-WESLEY	ADDISON-WESLEY PUB CO	Rte 128	Reading	MA	01867
710	Addison-Wesley	Addison-Wesley Publishing Co Inc.	Rte 128	Reading	MA	01867
628	ADVANCED MICRO SUPPLIE	ADVANCED MICRO SUPPLIES INC				
500	ADVANSTAR COMMUNICATI(	ADVANSTAR COMMUNICATIONS				
708	AFH SOFTECH	AFH SOFTECH				
419	AFIPS PR	AFIPS PR				

Record: 719 of 727

Then there is a table to link the title to the author. As each book has its own unique ISBN, we can use this as the identifier.

Title Author : Table

ISBN	Au_ID
0-0038307-6-4	7576
0-0038326-7-8	7576
0-0038337-8-X	7661
0-0131985-2-1	5681
0-0131985-2-1	5684
0-0133656-1-4	1454
0-0134436-3-1	128
0-0134436-3-1	132
0-0230081-2-1	203
0-0230081-2-1	659
0-0230081-2-1	1304
0-0230081-2-1	1306
0-0230362-0-6	203
0-0230362-0-6	1273
0-0230650-8-7	973

Record: 1

The Au_ID field points to the author record in the Authors table

Authors : Table

Au_ID	Author	Year Born
1	Jacobs, Russell	
2	Metzger, Philip W.	
3	Boddie, John	
4	Sydow, Dan Parks	
6	Lloyd, John	
8	Thiel, James R.	
10	Ingham, Kenneth	
12	Wellin, Paul	
13	Kamin, Sam	
14	Gaylord, Richard	
15	Curry, Dave	
17	Gardner, Juanita Mercado	
19	Knuth, Donald E.	
21	Hakim, Jack	
22	Winchell, Jeff	
24	Clark, Claudia	
25	Scott, Jack	
27	Coolbaugh, James	

Record: 1 of 6246

Connecting the Data Control to a Data Source

Before you can start to display information and use the data control to walk through the records in a database, you need to connect to the database in question. This is as simple as placing the name of the database in the data control's **`DatabaseName`** property.

Try It Out - Connecting to a Database

1 Start a new project in Visual Basic. Draw a data control on the form so that it looks like this. Before we go any further, select References from the Project menu and make sure that you have the DAO 3.5 Object Library selected. You'll see exactly what this dialog does a little later in the book, but for now all you really need to know is that since the database functionality is actually held in objects outside of Visual Basic, we need to make sure that Visual Basic is aware we are going to use them.

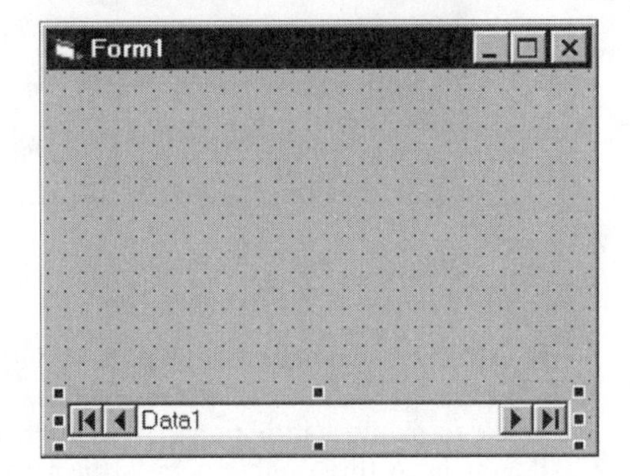

*An easy way to position the data control on your form is to select an option in the **Align** property drop-down list box.*

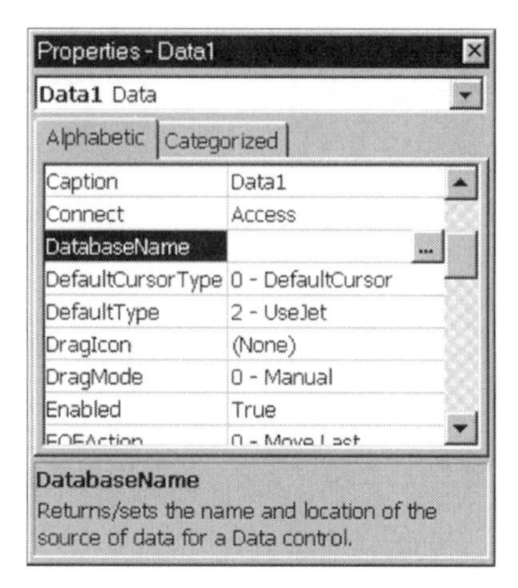

2 Bring up the properties window of the data control by pressing *F4*. When it appears, find the **DatabaseName** property and double-click it.

3 A dialog box appears. Use the dialog box to find the `Biblio.mdb` database. This will have been installed by your original VB installation program in the **vb** directory. When you have found the database, double-click it to select it.

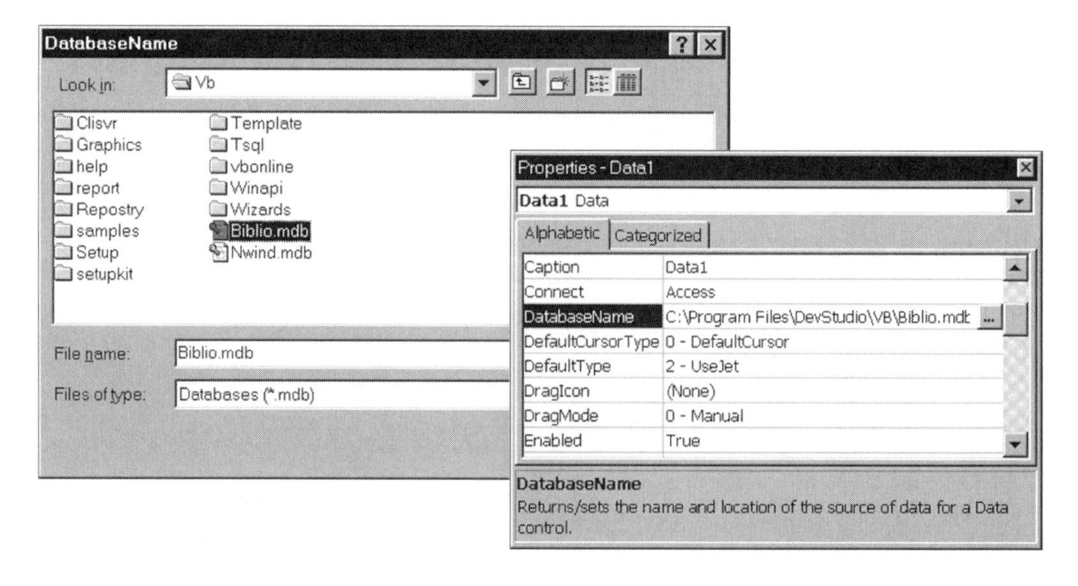

By selecting a database and putting its name and path into the **DatabaseName** property, you are telling Visual Basic which database to use for this data control. You can have more than one data control in a project, but each control can only connect to one database. Obviously, if you have three data controls on a form, you can connect to three databases at once. We'll see why you might want to connect to more than one database when we look at list and combo boxes.

At the moment, not much has happened to our form. The next step is to select a table from the database whose records we want to look at. This involves setting the **RecordsetType** and the **RecordSource** properties of the data control.

Choosing Tables from the Database

We saw in our introduction how a database can be made up of different tables. The tables correspond to the drawers in our filing cabinet. When deciding which tables you need, think about what information you want to display. In this project, we want to produce a single form that shows the details of an individual book title.

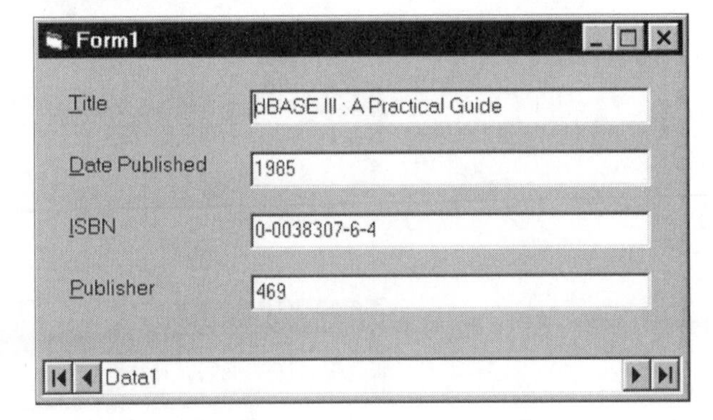

So that's where we're going. Now, how do we get there?

Try It Out - Selecting Tables from the Database

1 In the data control properties window, find the **RecordSource** property.

2 If you double-click on the **RecordSource** property itself, you can cycle through each of the tables in the database. Alternatively, you can click on the down arrow to the right of the property to drop down a list of options.

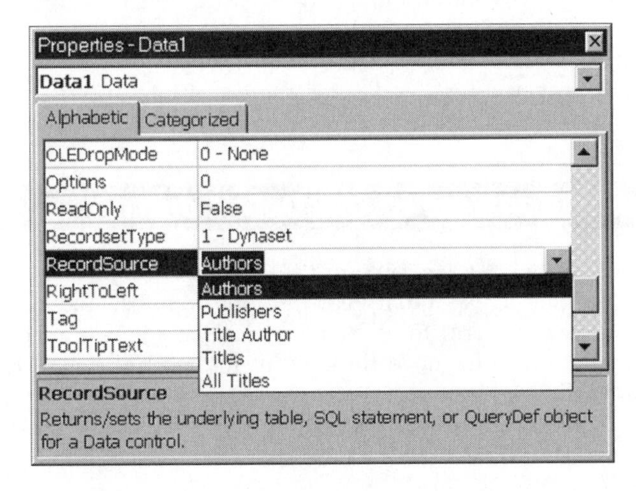

3 Select the **Titles** table.

4 Next you need to set the **RecordsetType** property. As we only want to access data held in a single table, the **Titles** table, it makes sense to set the **RecordsetType** property to **Table**. In our case, the whole table is going to be our designated set of records, but as we will see later, it could be a set of records that we select and define ourselves. You would then choose **Dynaset** or **Snapshot** as your **RecordsetType**. You don't have to choose **Table** here, but if you do, it makes the data control work a lot faster.

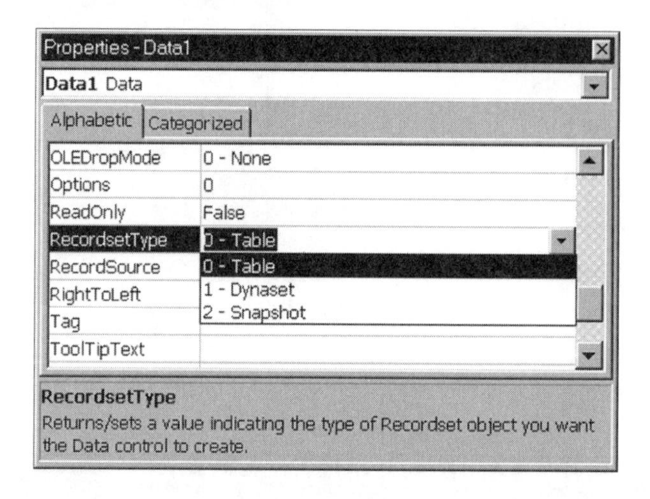

That's all there is to it. You have now selected a database and a table from that database. The next stage is to start using the bound controls to actually view the data in the table.

Using Bound Controls

Bound controls are data-aware. This means they can be linked to a data control and will then display data from that control automatically. Once you have drawn a data control on to a form, connected it to a database and selected a **RecordSource**, you can link the bound controls to the data control, via their **DataSource** property, and to a specific field in a table, via their **DataField** property. Let's add some more controls to our form to see how this works.

Try It Out - Binding Controls to the Data Control

There are four fields in the **Titles** table in the `Biblio.mdb` database that we are interested in: the book title, the date it was published, the ISBN number and the publisher. We'll draw text boxes and labels on the form to allow us to see the contents of these fields. By the end of the example you'll be able to move through all the records in the **Titles** table, still without any code at all.

1 Draw four labels on to the form and set their **`Caption`** properties so that the form looks like this:

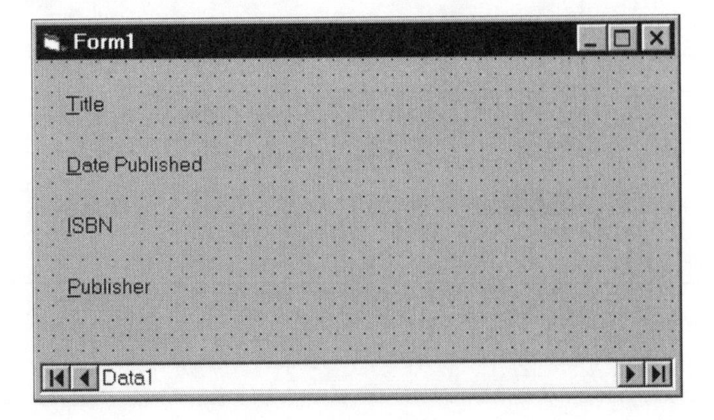

2 Draw the four text boxes that will actually hold the data from the database on to the form to the right of the labels.

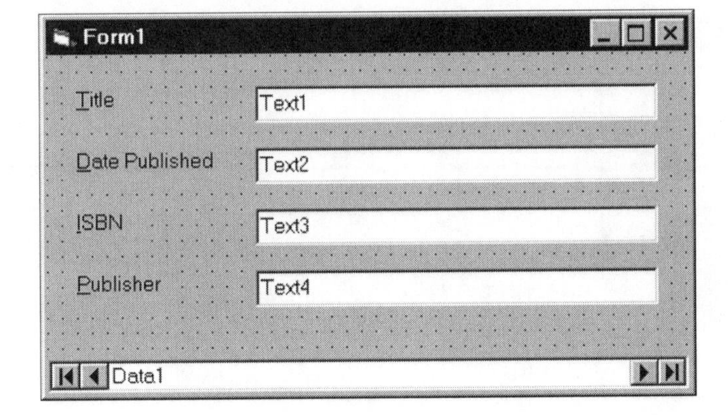

3 Clear the **`Text`** property of all the text boxes. Unfortunately, there's no quick way to do this—you have to select each text box and clear its property in turn.

4 You can, however, change the **`DataSource`** properties for all the text boxes in one go. Select all the text boxes by holding down the *Ctrl* key and clicking on each text box or by dragging the mouse over them all. Find the **`DataSource`** property in the properties window and double-click it—the name of the data control on the form will appear. You have now bound all the text boxes to the data control.

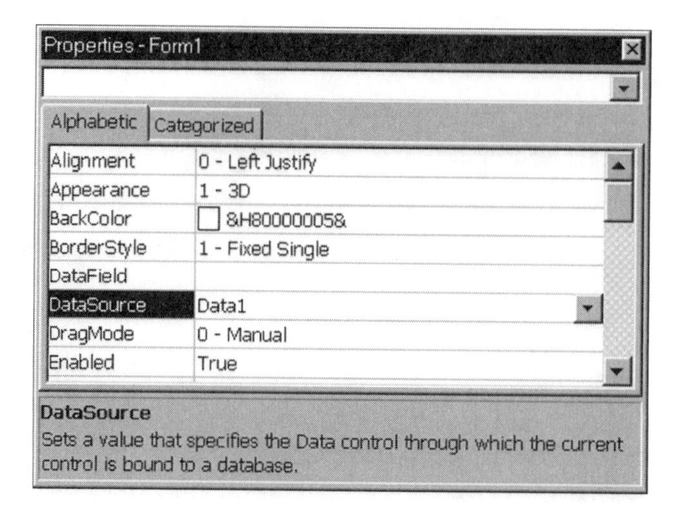

5 Click anywhere on the form to deselect all the text boxes. Then select each text box in turn, and using the properties window, set the **DataField** property to the values shown below.

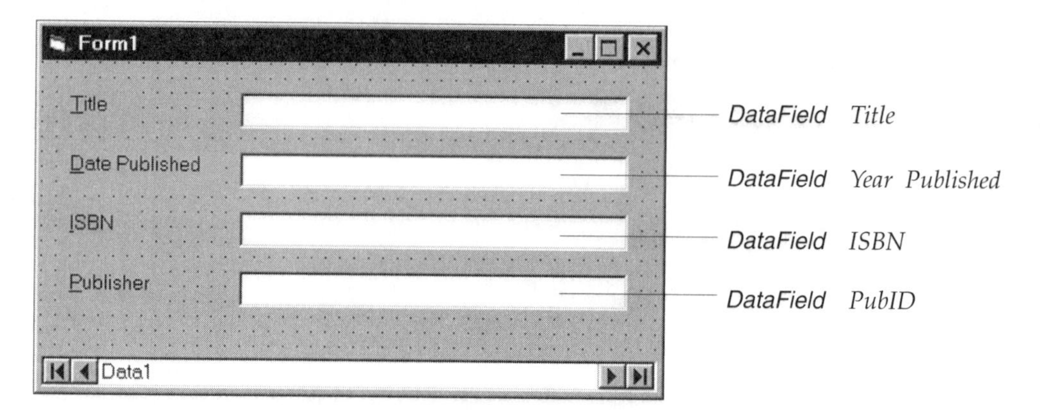

The field names we've used here were all set up when `Biblio.mdb` *was created.*

6 Before we go any further, save the project as it stands on your hard disk and name it **Bib_View**. We'll be coming back to this in the next chapter, as well as later in this one.

7 Finally, run the program. You have bound all the text boxes to the data control and, using the **DataField** property, you have told Visual Basic which fields to display in which text boxes. The result should be a form with which you can browse the **Biblio** database.

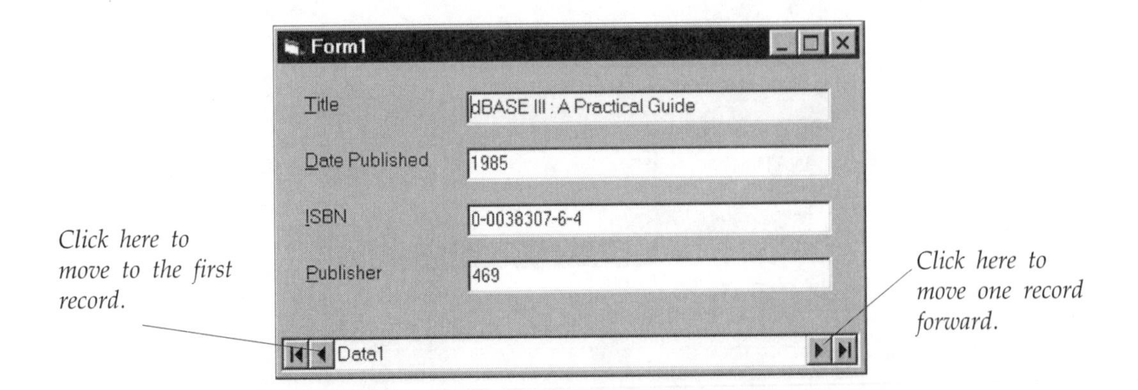

How It Works

Just by setting properties on the data control and the text boxes, you now have a complete database application. You can move through the records of the table by clicking on the data control arrows. You can even change the records displayed just by clicking in the text boxes and then typing in the new information. However, you might not want to do this to the `Biblio.mdb` database, as once you have made a change and clicked on the data control icons to move to a new record, Visual Basic automatically writes the changed records to the database. If you have an uncontrollable urge to make your mark, then I suggest you make a copy of the database first.

Once you bind controls to a database, you are no longer dealing with those controls in the traditional way. Normally, if you make a change to the contents of a text box, it doesn't matter unless you have code which stores that value somewhere. If you make changes to a bound control, though, you are directly changing the data in the database.

You can bind labels as well as text boxes to a database to display the contents of a field. This is great for displaying fields on the screen which you don't want the user to be able to change. Just because the control in question is a label control, though, don't expect the label to display the field names; it will only ever display the contents of a field, the same as any bound control.

Locking Bound Controls

As we have just said, thanks to the functionality that the data control offers, it's possible to edit information on screen. As soon as you move from the record you are editing to a new one in the recordset, the changes you make are saved permanently to the database.

However, it's possible to prevent users from making any changes to the underlying database. The answer to our prayers is the **`Locked`** property.

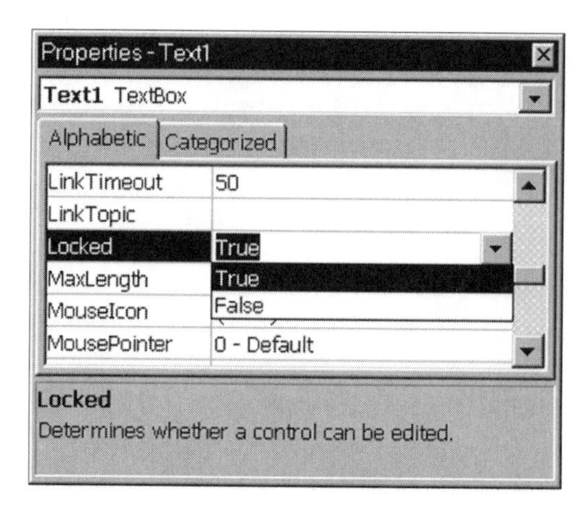

By setting this property to true on any or all of the text boxes, you're preventing the user from editing the information they see. They're still able to select the information, and cut and paste to the clipboard if they so desire. However, if a control is locked, they won't be able to make any changes to the data on display.

You could, of course, use a label control instead of locking a text box, but if you do, you aren't giving yourself the chance to later unlock the control.

Selecting the Data You Want

Although we've come a long way here, we're still very much constrained by the structure of the database we are given. So far, you've seen how to use bound controls to display information from just one table. The Access database is a relational database and lets you take information from more than one table as easily as from one, using two or more data controls to get at the information, or combining the information into one data control as a dynaset or snapshot type recordset.

In order to combine data from more than one table and then select the records we need, we use a set of data handling commands from a language called **SQL**. SQL, which is commonly pronounced 'sequel', is an acronym for Structured Query Language.

What Is SQL?

When the idea of the relational database evolved, SQL was created to provide a common language for defining and extracting data from databases. SQL began as an interactive language: you typed in the command and waited for the answer to pop out. Although there is now such a thing as embedded SQL which becomes part of your own code, all SQL 'programs' are really just one massive statement.

SQL is called a declarative language. You declare everything you want to do up front and then wait for it to happen.

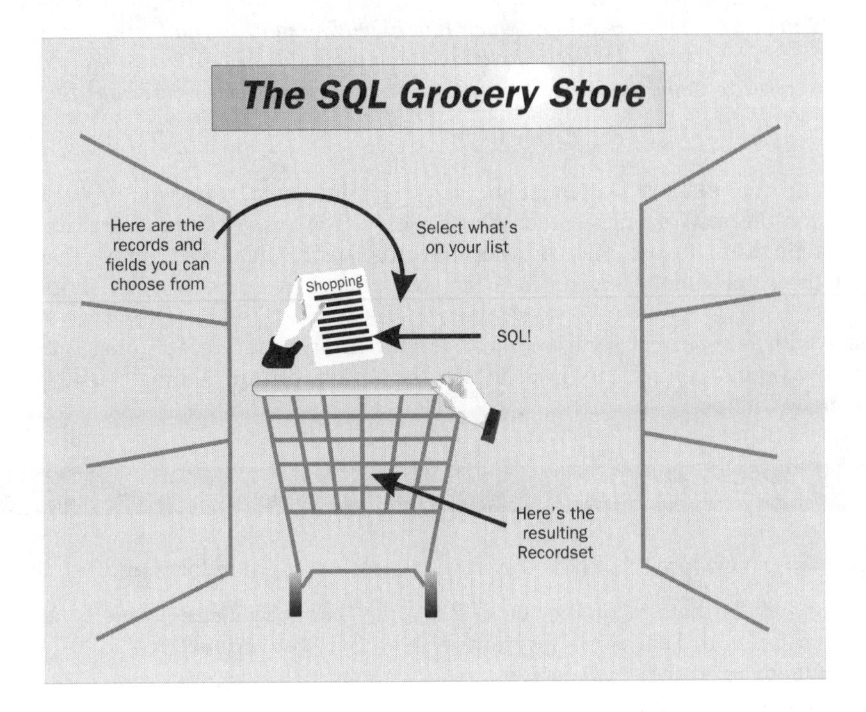

The reason that you, as a VB programmer, need to know some SQL, is that SQL commands provide a convenient and powerful way to talk to the Jet engine and manipulate the data it is working with. SQL gurus can do practically anything with SQL, but for us, its application will be limited to simple commands that tell the Jet engine which part of the database we want to deal with. These commands are all based around the **SELECT** statement.

> *If you have used SQL before, then it's worth noting that the version of SQL included with VB is a little different to most. The access differences of course depend on which database you are used to using. VB also lets you talk to other types of database, something which is a little beyond the scope of this book. However, if you are planning to do that, then in each case the SQL statements you enter have to conform to the standard of SQL expected by the database you are connecting to.*

The SELECT Statement

So far in this chapter, we've just taken what we've been given. We only had access to the records from one table, and even then we had to take the complete set of records and fields, regardless of whether we wanted them all or just a selection. That's the key here—selection. What we want to be able to do is choose which records or fields we want. To do that we use the SQL **SELECT** statement.

SQL uses some weird styles, the first of which is that all SQL commands are in capital letters—this isn't so much something forced on you, more of a standard which most programmers adopt, much like indenting your normal VB code. It also uses brackets and dots everywhere, which may not mean a lot to you now, but are vital to understanding SQL spaghetti. You can get away without them, but be careful.

If you look up the **SELECT** statement in the VB on-line help, you will probably be put off using SQL for the rest of your career. Don't worry. The explanations there are for database codeheads who want to use SQL to select records, define databases, grow flowers and wash cars all at the same time. Mere mortals like us can get away with a far simpler version.

In keeping with our normal style, let's go straight in and see what's going on. We're going to use a new bound control, the **grid**, to see the results of our SQLing. First, let's get comfy with this new control.

Try It Out - The Bound Grid

1. Open up a new project. Place the data control on to your form and set the **Align** property to the bottom of the form. Point the **DatabaseName** property at wherever the `Biblio.mdb` database is on your system. Set **RecordsetType** to 0-Table, and **RecordSource** to the **Titles** table.

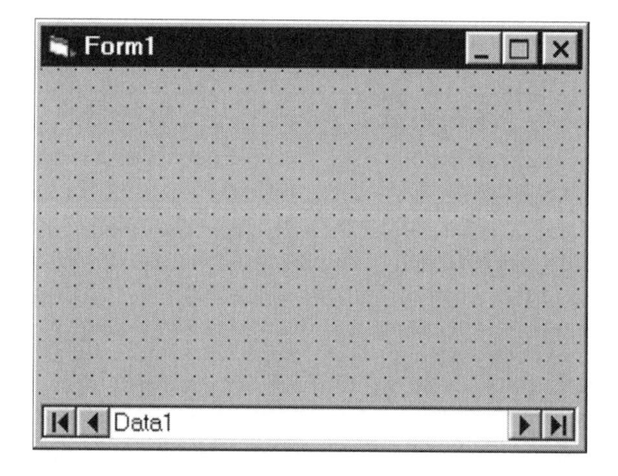

If you don't specify a **RecordsetType**, *then VB assumes you want a dynaset. We'll talk more about these in the next chapter.*

2 Now place a DBGrid control on to the form and resize it as shown below. Remember, if it's not already in your toolbox, you can add it by selecting Component... from the Project menu and then checking Microsoft Data Bound Grid Control.

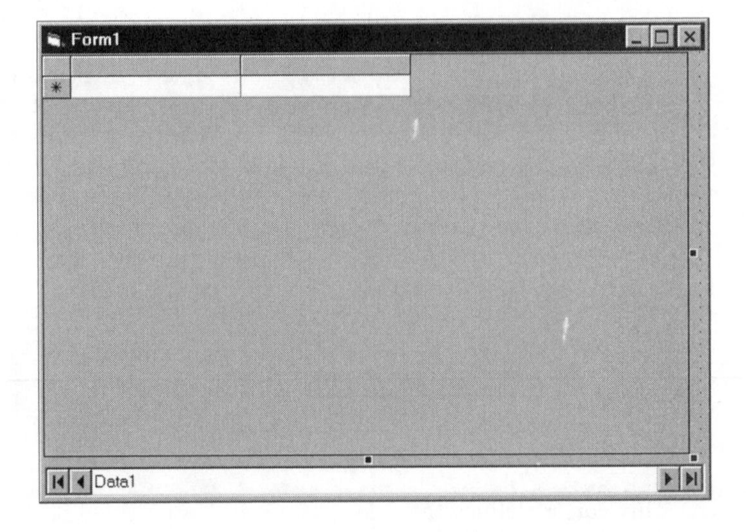

3 Point the **`DataSource`** property of the grid to the data control **`Data1`**.

4 Finally, run the program. Up comes the grid with the complete **`Titles`** table displayed in it. The grid control also gives us some nice little scroll bars to move the viewing window around if the underlying grid is too big—as this one is.

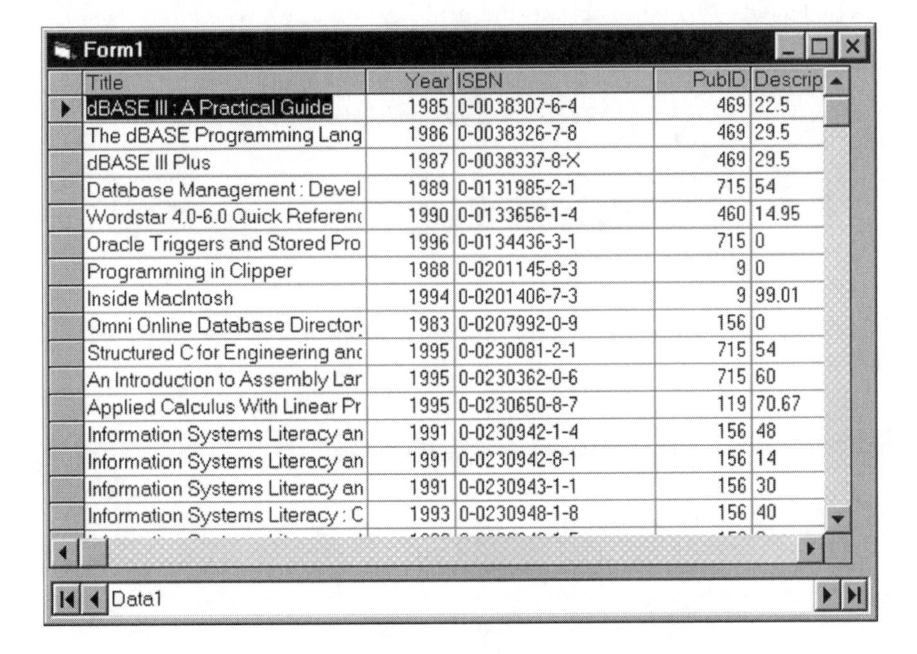

Title	Year	ISBN	PubID	Descrip
dBASE III : A Practical Guide	1985	0-0038307-6-4	469	22.5
The dBASE Programming Lang	1986	0-0038326-7-8	469	29.5
dBASE III Plus	1987	0-0038337-8-X	469	29.5
Database Management : Devel	1989	0-0131985-2-1	715	54
Wordstar 4.0-6.0 Quick Referen	1990	0-0133656-1-4	460	14.95
Oracle Triggers and Stored Pro	1996	0-0134436-3-1	715	0
Programming in Clipper	1988	0-0201145-8-3	9	0
Inside MacIntosh	1994	0-0201406-7-3	9	99.01
Omni Online Database Director	1983	0-0207992-0-9	156	0
Structured C for Engineering an	1995	0-0230081-2-1	715	54
An Introduction to Assembly Lar	1995	0-0230362-0-6	715	60
Applied Calculus With Linear Pr	1995	0-0230650-8-7	119	70.67
Information Systems Literacy an	1991	0-0230942-1-4	156	48
Information Systems Literacy an	1991	0-0230942-8-1	156	14
Information Systems Literacy an	1991	0-0230943-1-1	156	30
Information Systems Literacy : C	1993	0-0230948-1-8	156	40

How It Works

Setting up the data control here is the same as it has been before. Setting up the grid is, if anything, easier. The grid control is two dimensional: it can display all the records (rows) in a table and all the fields (columns) in each record. You don't have to choose a certain field to display, as you do with a single field control like the text box.

Also, look what happens when you hit the buttons on the data control. Because you have all the records in there already, it doesn't put new data into the grid, instead it moves a little cursor up and down the left side of the grid.

	dBASE III Plus	1987	0-0038337-8-X	469	29.5
▶	Database Managemen	1989	0-0131985-2-1	715	54
	Wordstar 4.0-6.0 Quick I	1990	0-0133656-1-4	460	14.95

This cursor defines the selected record. Visual Basic itself uses this cursor to tell it which records to load into the bound controls when you move around a database. We'll use it in the next chapter when we write our own code to work on the database.

Try It Out - Selecting Fields to View

Now let's get down to some SQL. We are going to use SQL to tell the data control to only pass selected fields from the table to the grid.

1 Back in design view, bring up the properties window for the data control. First of all we need to change the **RecordsetType** property to **Dynaset**.

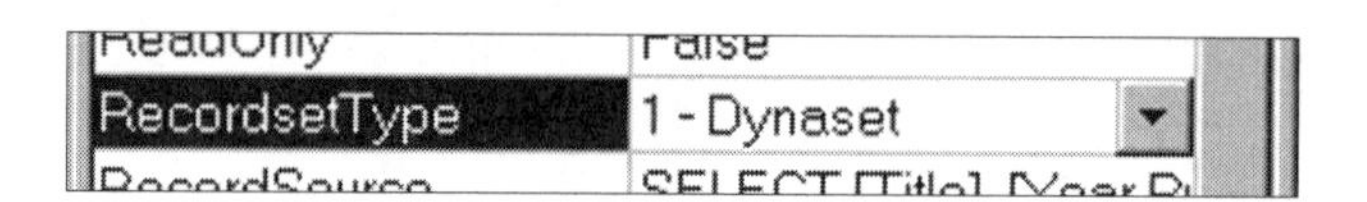

2 Now, put the cursor in the **RecordSource** property box and delete **Titles**. Enter the following SQL statement directly into the box:

```
SELECT [Title], [Year Published], [ISBN] FROM Titles
```

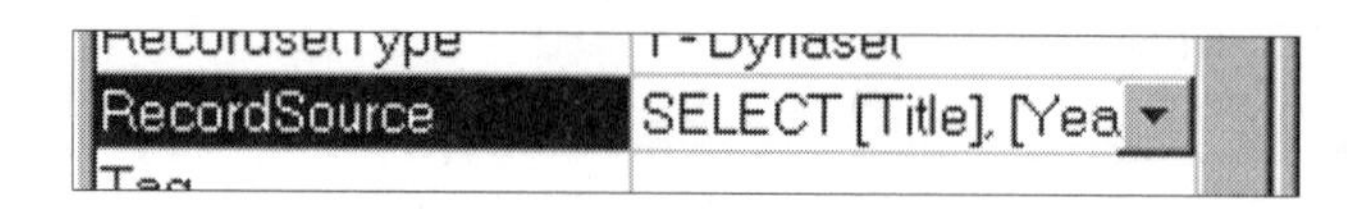

3 Hit run and see what we've got. There are only the fields we requested.

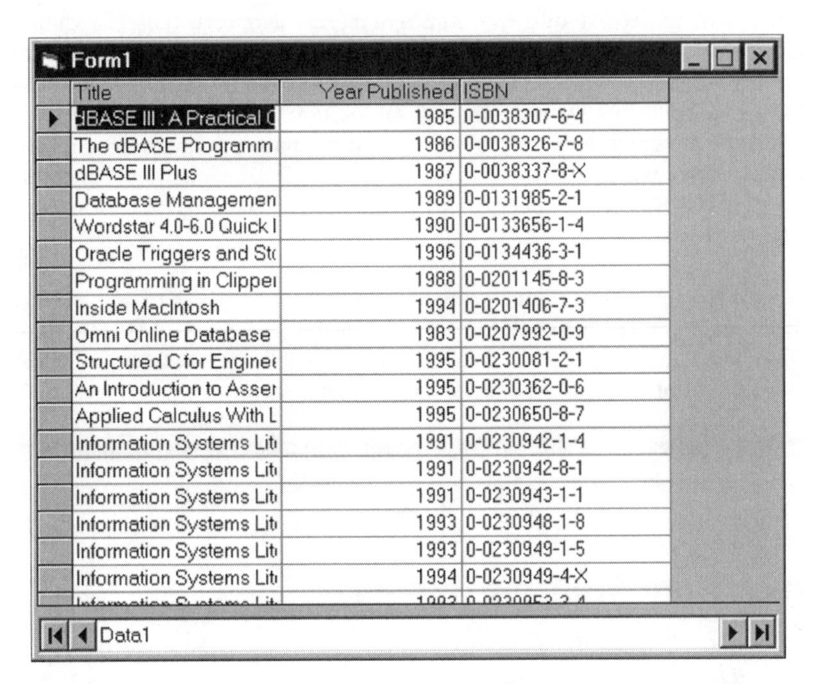

Form1

Title	Year Published	ISBN
dBASE III : A Practical C	1985	0-0038307-6-4
The dBASE Programm	1986	0-0038326-7-8
dBASE III Plus	1987	0-0038337-8-X
Database Managemen	1989	0-0131985-2-1
Wordstar 4.0-6.0 Quick I	1990	0-0133656-1-4
Oracle Triggers and St	1996	0-0134436-3-1
Programming in Clippe	1988	0-0201145-8-3
Inside MacIntosh	1994	0-0201406-7-3
Omni Online Database	1983	0-0207992-0-9
Structured C for Engine	1995	0-0230081-2-1
An Introduction to Asser	1995	0-0230362-0-6
Applied Calculus With L	1995	0-0230650-8-7
Information Systems Lit	1991	0-0230942-1-4
Information Systems Lit	1991	0-0230942-8-1
Information Systems Lit	1991	0-0230943-1-1
Information Systems Lit	1993	0-0230948-1-8
Information Systems Lit	1993	0-0230949-1-5
Information Systems Lit	1994	0-0230949-4-X

Data1

4 You can resize the columns of the grid control at run time by dragging them with the mouse.

Click and drag here to resize the columns at run time.

Form1

Title	Year	ISBN
dBASE III : A Practical Guide	1985	0-0038307-6-4
The dBASE Programming Language	1986	0-0038326-7-8
dBASE III Plus	1987	0-0038337-8-X
Database Management : Developing Application Systems	1989	0-0131985-2-1
Wordstar 4.0-6.0 Quick Reference Guide	1990	0-0133656-1-4
Oracle Triggers and Stored Procedure Programming	1996	0-0134436-3-1
Programming in Clipper	1988	0-0201145-8-3
Inside MacIntosh	1994	0-0201406-7-3
Omni Online Database Directory	1983	0-0207992-0-9
Structured C for Engineering and Technology/Book and Di	1995	0-0230081-2-1
An Introduction to Assembly Language Programming for the	1995	0-0230362-0-6
Applied Calculus With Linear Programming : For Business,	1995	0-0230650-8-7
Information Systems Literacy and Software Productivity Toc	1991	0-0230942-1-4
Information Systems Literacy and Software Productivity Toc	1991	0-0230942-8-1
Information Systems Literacy and Software Productivity Toc	1991	0-0230943-1-1
Information Systems Literacy : Concepts, DOS 5.0, Wordpe	1993	0-0230948-1-8
Information Systems Literacy : dBASE IV Release 1.1 and 1	1993	0-0230949-1-5

Data1

How It Works

The SQL statement we typed into the **RecordSource** property tells the data control which fields it should ask the Jet engine to retrieve from the underlying `Biblio` database. What the Jet engine then passes back to the data control is not the whole table as before, but a dynaset. This is a collection of records and tables that is derived from the underlying tables in the database, but which exists only for our immediate purposes. It's a kind of virtual thing that dies when you stop running the program. Both tables and dynasets are types of recordset, which is Microsoft's generic name for a set of records that you have got hold of and want to work on.

The SQL statement itself consists of two parts. The first is a list of the fields we want to retrieve: **[Title], [Year Published]** and **[ISBN]**. These are in square brackets to tell SQL that they are names of fields. Then we have to tell the **SELECT** statement which table to take this data from—in our case it is the **Titles** table.

That's it. This is, of course, a simple incarnation of the **SELECT** statement. Things get more complicated later on. However, the basic premise is the same. Tell the database what you want and where to get it from and off it goes.

Taking Data from Multiple Tables

Relational databases reduce the amount of information in a database by relating tables to each other. In the `Biblio` database, for example, the **PubID** field relates the **Titles** and **Publishers** table and saves the user having to type in the same publisher name over and over again in the **Titles** table.

You can actually tell the data control to take these links into account when you use it. For example, in the previous Try It Out, what would be really nice is to display the publisher's name and the author's name from the Publishers and Authors tables. You can do this using the **SELECT** command, and a dynaset type recordset.

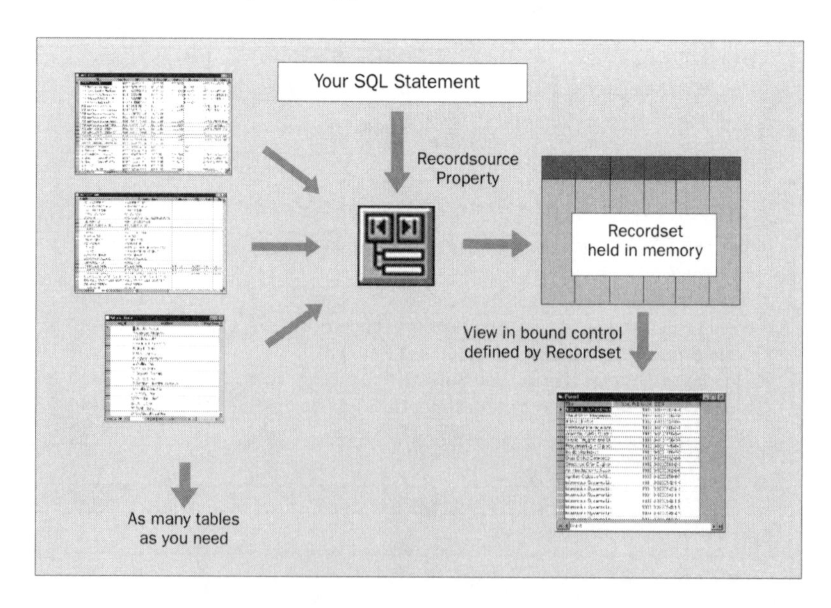

Selecting from Multiple Tables

With **SELECT**, you tell the data control which fields you want to display and which tables these fields come from. In our case, we'd use it like this:

```
SELECT [Title], [Year Published], [ISBN], [Name] FROM Titles, Publishers
```

This is actually the shorthand way of doing it. All the above field names are unique. For instance, you can't find an **ISBN** field in the **Publishers** table. If that wasn't the case, we'd have to specify the tables and the fields together like this:

```
SELECT Titles.[Title], Titles.[Year Published], Titles.[ISBN],
↳ Publishers.[Name] FROM Titles, Publishers
```

This way there's no doubt as to where each field comes from. Each field is prefixed by the actual table name in the same way as you'd prefix a property name with the name of its control. The field names are still enclosed in square brackets.

Visual Basic still has no way of knowing how to relate records in the **Publishers** table to records in the **Titles** table for example. Although we know that the designer of the `Biblio` database put a **PubID** in both tables, the Jet engine needs to be told that you would like it to use this as the link between the two tables. In database-speak this is called the **key**.

To tell the Jet engine that we want it to link the two tables together, using the **PubID** field as a key, we need to create a **JOIN** between the two tables. There are in fact several different kinds of **JOIN**, depending on how you want to compare the two sets of keys. The simplest type is the **INNER JOIN** which just connects records from the different tables that share the same **PubID** fields. The resulting dynaset will only contain records that match these conditions.

> *Although **JOIN** is a really useful command, it is quite specific to VB's Jet engine. If you are developing applications which are ultimately be ported to other database engines then you really should avoid it and stick with using nice long **WHERE** clauses, which any SQL database can support.*

```
SELECT Titles.[Title], Titles.[Year Published], Titles.[ISBN],
↳Publishers.[Name] FROM Titles INNER JOIN Publishers ON
↳Publishers.[PubID] = Titles.[PubID]
```

What the **INNER JOIN** operation does here is to say to SQL:

'Hey, give me the fields I want, some of which come from the Publisher table. I'll tell you that the main table is Titles, but that you want to also get hold of all the records in Publisher (INNER JOIN) that have the same PubIDs (ON clause)'

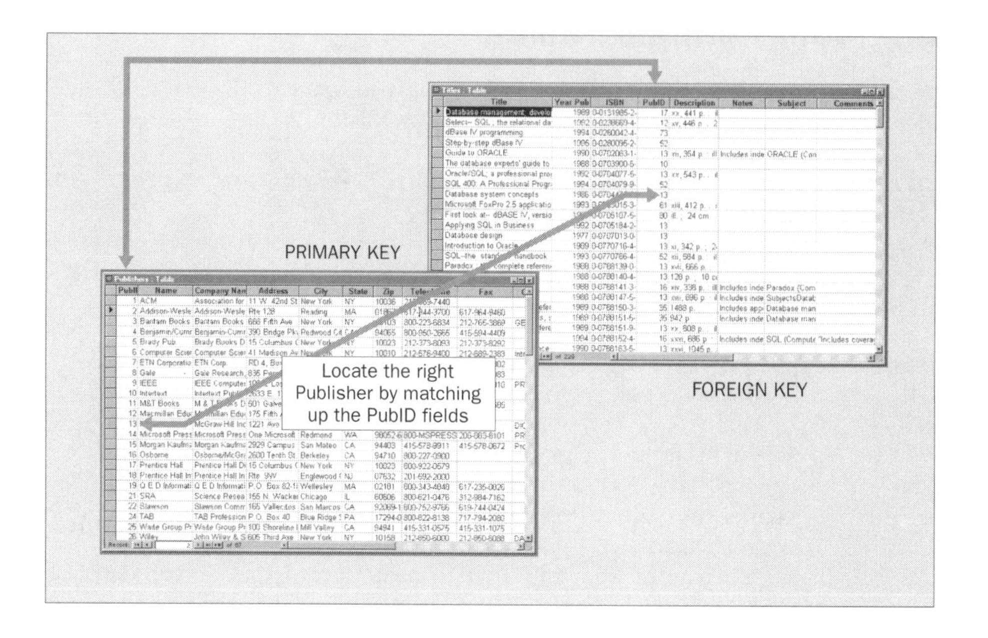

SQL is a bit tricky, so in the next chapter we will be developing a little project to let you play around with SQL statements interactively. In the meantime, let's try this out.

Try It Out - Selecting Information from Related Tables

1 Load up the **`Bib_View`** project that we created earlier.

2 Bring up the form with the bound controls on it. Display the properties window for the data control and change the **`RecordSetType`** property to **`Dynaset`**.

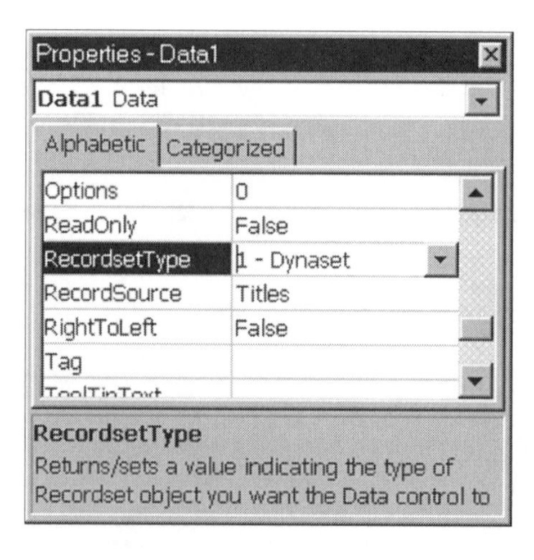

3 Then type this **SELECT** statement into the **RecordSource** property. There's a lot of it, so be very careful. Visual Basic doesn't check what you key into the **RecordSource** property until you run the program, unlike the code you might key into a code window.

```
SELECT Titles.[Title], Titles.[Year Published], Titles.[ISBN],
↳Publishers.[Name] FROM Titles INNER JOIN Publishers ON
↳Publishers.[PubID] = Titles.[PubID]
```

4 Press *Enter* after keying in the new **RecordSource** to accept it.

5 Select the text box set up to display the publisher information. Bring up its properties window and set the **DataField** property to Name by selecting it from the drop down a list of field names.

6 Run the program now. Instead of meaningless ID numbers for the publisher, you now see the publisher's full name. In the words of a certain Mr. Gates... 'Cool!'

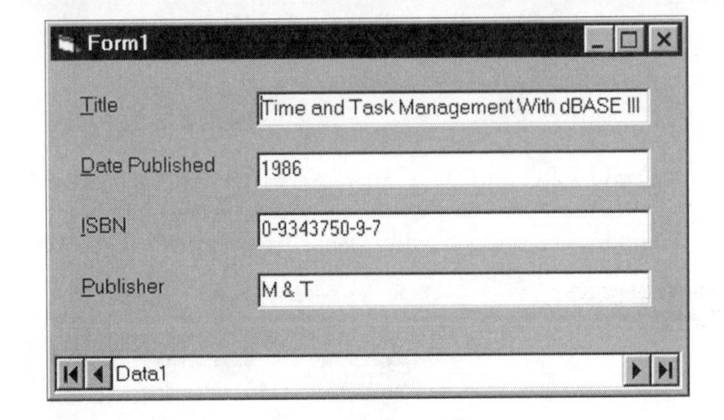

7 Finally, save the program. We'll be using it again in the next chapter.

Using VisData

Writing all this neat database code and doing cool things with bound controls is really only half the story when it comes to developing a database application. The best coding style in the world, and a full suite of the most powerful data controls are really going to do you no good at all if you don't have any data to deal with in your application.

In terms of creating a database for your application, creating the tables, fields and indexes inside it, and producing reliable SQL queries, there are really only two options open to you: the full featured, but expensive, Access database system from Microsoft, or the VisData add-in included with Visual Basic.

There are books and books on the subject of Access, and VisData could likewise easily warrant a small tome itself. However, just for you, I'll try to condense the power and features of the latter into a couple of pages.

Introducing VisData

Microsoft Access is a supremely powerful product, powerful enough even to produce full blown stand alone database applications, but VisData easily provides most Visual Basic developers with all the tools they need to develop and deliver effective, durable database applications.

VisData supports a wealth of functions, including the ability to graphically develop SQL queries for use in your applications, a table designer, and of course a data browser. As such, it represents the ideal platform for both developing your database and testing out the queries—and thus a great deal of the functionality that you'll use in your application.

VisData is a Visual Basic add-in,an application that quite literally bolts on to the Visual Basic development environment. If you take a look at the VB menu bar, you will see that there is an item called Add-Ins. Click on this to drop down the menu, and there, sitting at the top is VisData.

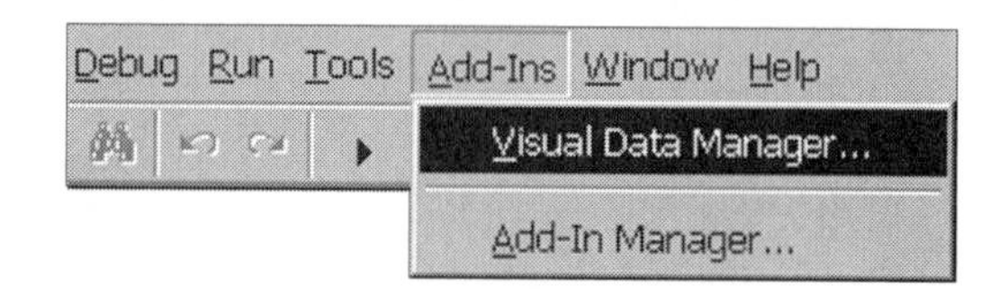

If you select this item, after a short pause VisData will magically appear. It's important to note, that since VisData is an addin (in previous versions it existed as a stand alone application shipped with Visual Basic)—you can't continue to use Visual Basic while it is loaded and running.

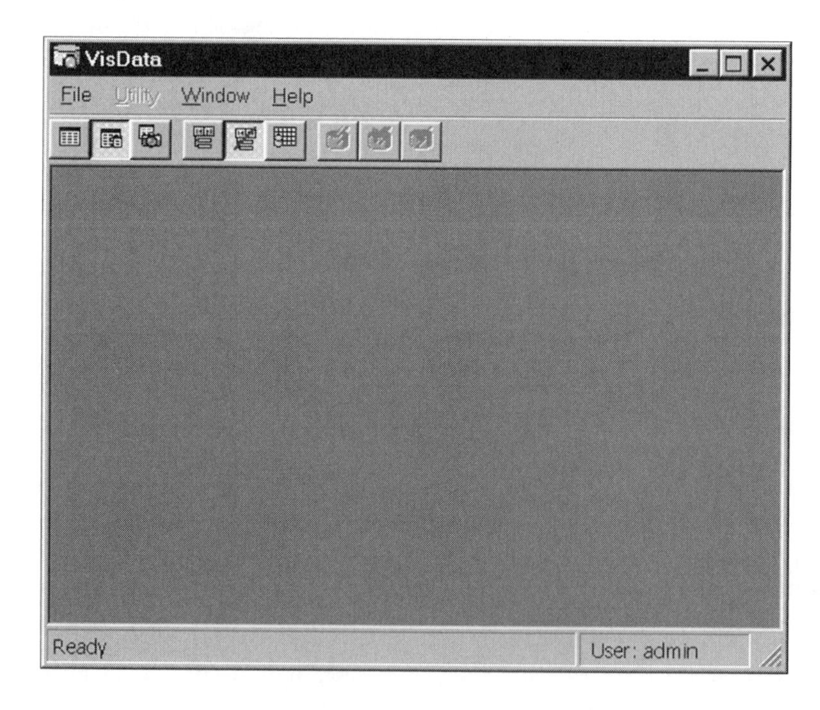

> *The very first time you run VisData you may be asked 'Do you want to add the System.md?'. We can ignore this since it is really only something that applies to very secure databases, and you really do need Access to set it up properly. If VB asks you the question then just answer No.*

It looks much like any other MDI application, with a status bar at the bottom of the main form that VisData uses to give you information and system messages as you work within the product, a menu bar at the top to provide you with access to the areas of functionality in the project, and a toolbar underneath this to provide you with one-click access to the most commonly used menu items.

Let's take a brief stroll around the menu bar:

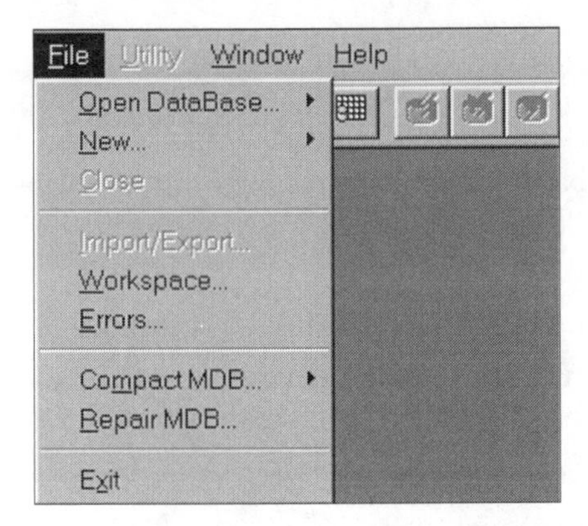

The File menu lets you deal with database files themselves, and should on the whole be pretty self-explanatory. The first item lets you open a database—a submenu appears asking you to specify what format of database you want to open (such as Access, Dbase, Paradox and so on). Likewise, the New item lets you create a brand new database for your application, and once again asks you through a submenu what kind of database you would like to create. Once you have a database open, the Close item simply lets you shut it down.

The next section on the File menu contains a number of utility items to help you in your work with the opened database. Import/Export allows you to quickly and painlessly import a lot of data into a table or dump it out to a file. Workspace, on the other hand, enables the security features on the database and allows you to relog into the database as a different user. Errors provides you with a dialog listing the most recent errors that occurred within the database engine, usually as a result of you doing something like creating an invalid field, or trying to run a buggy SQL query.

Finally, Compact and Repair provide you with the means to remove redundant space in the database file, and repair corrupt databases should the need ever arise (and if you have backups, then it really shouldn't).

The only other menu of any real interest is the Utility menu (since the Window and Help menus are nothing more than the standard Window and Help menus you would expect to find in an MDI application).

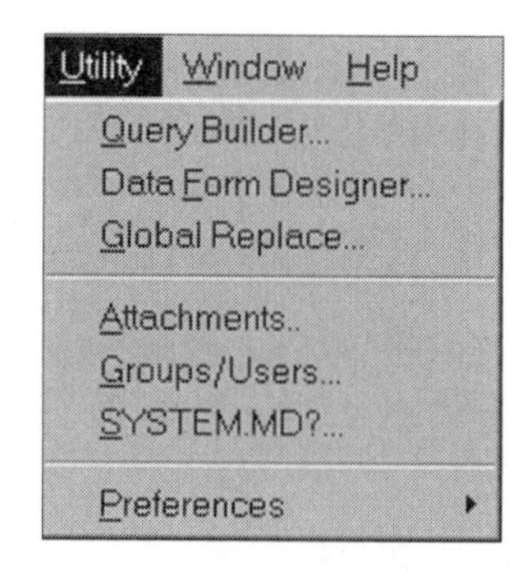

The utility menu (which only works when you actually have a database open) provides you with various gems to help you in the application build process, and in terms of configuring the way in which your database works.

The Query Builder helps you to build the SQL queries that you will use in Visual Basic to set up your dynasets, letting you drag and drop the fields to use in the query, and drag and drop to form the links between fields in a much more civilized fashion than having to code up inner joins and the like by hand.

The Data Form Designer, like its name suggests, provides you with a very quick and simple way to build up data bound forms in your VB application, again by doing very little more than dragging and dropping the fields that you want to see on the form.
Global Replace on the other hand is much simpler, and lets you replace occurrences of text in selected fields and tables in your database.

With the exception of Preferences, the remaining items all let you configure the way in which the database works. With the Attachments item you can attach tables from a remote server, such as a SQL server database, to your local Access database.

Groups/Users, and SYSTEM.MD? Both let you fully enable the security features of the database you are working on, adding users to the System table and grouping them by their access level and rights. Both of these topics though are a little beyond the scope of this book and are explained in a lot more detail in the follow on to this book: Beginning Application Development with Visual Basic 5. See the Wrox web site **http://www.wrox.com** for more details about the release and availability of this title.

Let's take a quick look at some of these items though in a little more detail. The easiest way to get to grips with many of them is to open up an existing Access database and start exploring. That's exactly what we are going to do now.

Delving Deeper in VisData

Open up the **Biblio** database by selecting Open DataBase from the File menu. A submenu will pop open asking you what kind of database you want to open—choose Microsoft Access.

Once the database is open, two windows will appear within VisData. The first is the database window itself, showing you the tables in the database. Next to this is the SQL window, waiting for you to enter a SQL query to test out and run.

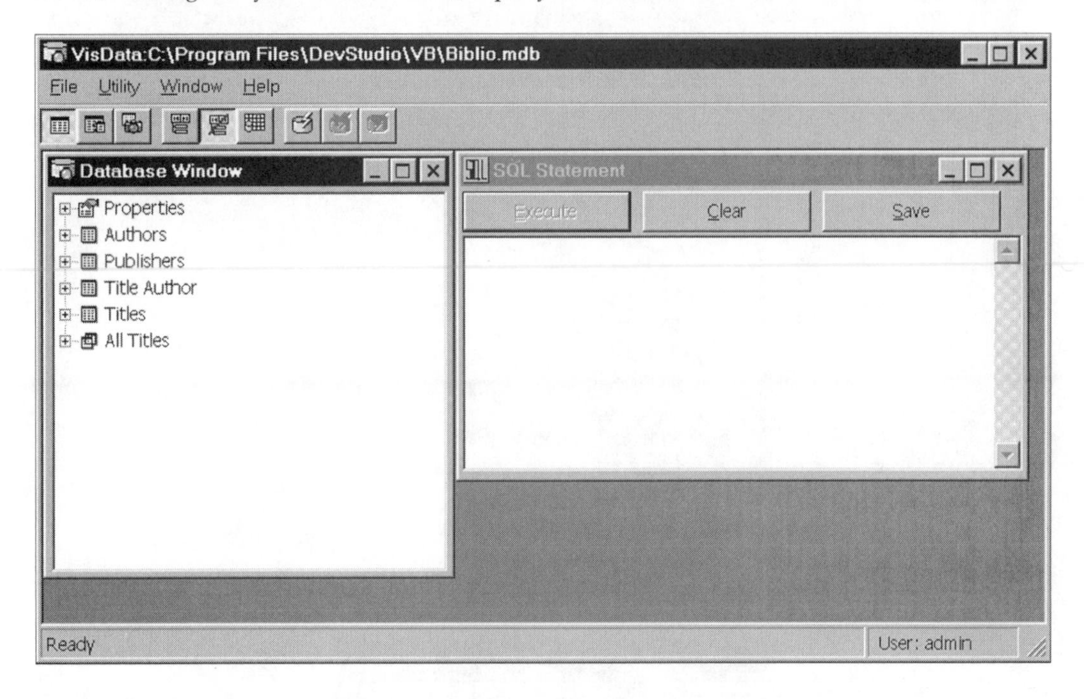

Notice how all the tables have a plus sign next to them indicating that the list has scope for expansion. Try clicking on the plus sign to the left of the `Titles` table to see what happens.

The list expands to show you Fields, Indexes and Properties items, each of which can be expanded yet further to reveal more information about your database. For example, expand the Fields item by clicking it and a list of fields appear.

Double-click on a field in the list, and the list expands yet further to reveal all the properties of the field in question.

What more could you want? Well, some way to add your own tables and fields would be nice. Right-click in the database window and select New Table from the pop up menu and that's just what you get—in the form of the Table Structure dialog.

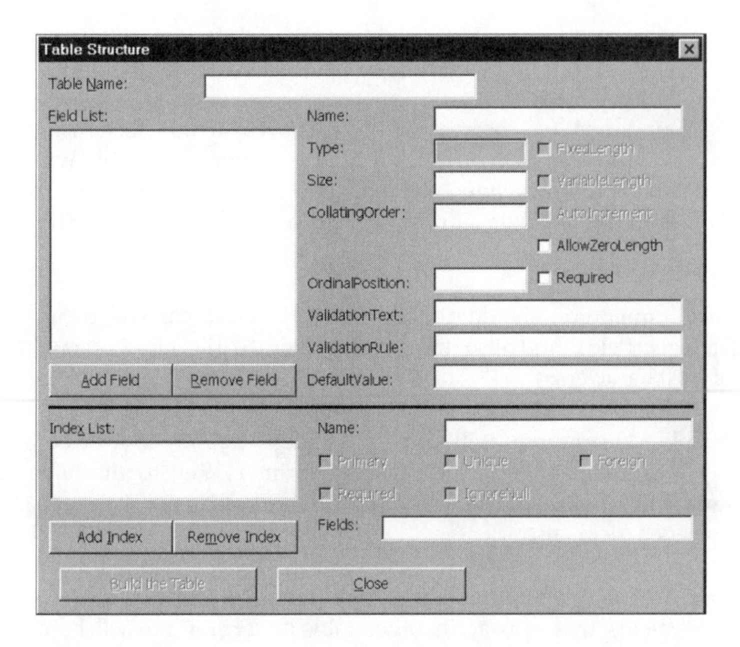

On the whole, it's pretty self-explanatory—click on Add Field to add a new field to a table, and then fill in the boxes on the dialog to specify the field name, its data type, validation rule and so on.

Try it—have a play. If you select New from the File menu then you can create a new database and try VisData out without risking anything on live data.

Summary

A large part of Visual Basic's popularity is due to its ability to handle databases. The Learning Edition of Visual Basic doesn't have all the database power of the Professional or Enterprise Editions, but it is, nonetheless, an excellent tool. It can browse through data in a number of different ways, and then present the data easily to the user using bound controls.

In this chapter we covered:

- What a database is
- How the data control links a program to a database
- What SQL is and how to use it
- How to set up the data control and bound controls interactively
- How to build your own databases using VisData

We've covered a lot in this chapter, and introduced you to a few new concepts, but all along we've been using the data control properties. You can, however, manipulate this control using code, which is what we'll do next.

Why Not Try...

1 Let's build a foundation for the rest of the exercises in this section. Having seen the profitability of a pizza parlor, you decide to open your own. You will need to design a relational database to track how you are doing. Using your choice of either Microsoft Access or the Visdata add-in, design a database called "Pizza" that contains three tables.

The first table, **`Customer`**, should contain 2 fields. **`Cust_ID`** will be an Access counter type (long integer field), and also the primary key to the table. **`Cust_Name`** will be a text field of 50 characters.

The second table, **`Inventory`**, will contain 4 fields. **`Stock_ID`** will be an Access counter type (long integer field), and also the primary key to the table. **`Description`** will be a text field of 50 characters. **`Cost`** will be a currency field. **`Selling_Price`** will be a currency field also.

The third and final table, **`Transaction`**, will contain 6 fields and two of them will be "foreign keys" (fields that appear in other tables). **`Trans_ID`** will be an Access counter type (long integer field), and also the primary key to the table. **`Date`** is a Date/Time field. **`Cust_ID`** will be a long integer field. **`Stock_ID`** will be a long integer field. **`Quantity`** is an integer field. And **`Total_Price`** will be a currency field. When we get a bit more advanced, we'll see that we'll calculate the **`Total_Price`** field ourselves. For now, however, we'll need to enter it ourselves. Please note that because we have defined the primary key fields as "counter" or "auto increment" fields, you cannot assign a number yourself. When you add data to the tables either through Access or Visdata, the counter field will be incremented for you automatically.

Populate the tables with the following data:

Customer Table:

Cust ID	Customer
1	Alice Jones
2	Mary Smith
3	John Doe
4	James Jackson

Inventory Table:

Stock_ID	Description	Cost	Selling_Price
1	Cheesesteak	$1.00	$3.75
2	Pizza Steak	$1.25	$4.25
3	Small Pizza	$2.00	$6.00
4	Medium Pizza	$3.00	$7.25
5	Large Pizza	$4.00	$8.50

Transaction Table:

Trans_ID	Date	Cust_ID	Stock_ID	Quantity	Price
1	01/01/97	1	1	1	$ 3.75
2	01/03/97	1	2	1	$ 4.25
3	01/04/97	1	3	2	$12.00
4	01/06/97	1	1	1	$ 3.75
5	01/04/97	2	4	2	$15.50
6	01/01/97	3	3	1	$ 6.00
7	01/06/97	3	4	2	$15.50
8	01/07/97	3	5	1	$ 8.50
9	01/07/97	4	1	3	$11.25

2 Design a form that displays the **Date**, **Cust_ID**, **Stock_ID**, **Quantity** and **Total_Price** fields of the **Transaction** table. Use a data control and 5 text boxes. Save the project separately after completing it.

3 One problem with the exercise we just completed is that the casual user is not going to know that on January 3, 1997, Alice Smith purchased a pizza steak. That is because Alice Smith is represented by a customer id of 1 in the **Transaction** table, and the pizza steak is represented by stock id 2. A data entry clerk would probably recognize customer id's and stock id's, but not the casual user. Enhance this project so that it displays the corresponding customer name for **Cust_ID** and the corresponding inventory **Description** for **Stock_ID**. Display this information in either two additional text boxes or two additional labels.

Hint: *You'll need to use two additional data controls and issue a SQL statement from within your code.*

4 Modify Exercise 2 to use the data grid instead of bound text boxes. Use a SQL statement to retrieve the data instead of using the **RecordSource** property at design time.

5 Modify Exercise 4 to display the associated customer name and inventory description. This sounds easy, but you'll need to generate a SQL statement to do this.

Hint: *Try building the query using either Microsoft Access or Visdata. Then copy and paste the resultant SQL statement into your application.*

asic Visual Basic Visual Ba
al Basic Visual Basic Visual
Basic Visual Basic Visual Ba
ual Basic Vi
Basic Visu
ual Basic V
l Basic Vis
isual Basic Visual Basic
al Basic Visual Basic Visua
Visual Basic Visual Basic Visu
al Basic Visual Ba
l Basic Visual
ic Visual Basi
Basic Visual B
ic Visual Basi
al Basic Visual
ual Basic Visual Basic Visual Ba
Visual Basic Visual Basic Visu
sual Basic Visual Basic Visu
Visual Basic Visual Ba

Programming Database Access

In the previous chapter, we used the data and bound controls pretty much interactively by setting their properties beforehand. However, like all other Visual Basic controls, what you can do at design time is just the tip of the iceberg. The real action comes when you work with the control as an object in your code.

In this chapter you'll learn:

- How to address the data control in code
- What a recordset really is
- How the data bound combo and list controls work
- How to use the data control methods to work with a recordset
- What events are interesting on the data control
- The limits of the data control

Programming the Data Control

The Learning Edition of Visual Basic lets you use the full potential of the data control in your code. However, it only allows you this one route to a database.

The data control has to be in your project, sitting between you and the Jet engine at all times. At our kind of level, though, this is perfectly adequate. The data control supports a lot of powerful methods and events, and enables you to create extensive database applications.

The alternative method of data access, which is not supported by the Learning Edition, is to bypass the data control altogether, and create objects from the underlying Jet engine and the database itself, which you can then manipulate using code. Using Data Access Objects (or DAO as they are known), as you might imagine, is more powerful than going through the data control. They give you direct access to all the objects in the database, as well as to a lot more of the Jet engine's functionality than is supported by the data control. However, they are also a lot harder to implement and require you to write a lot more code.

Given the power that's there in the data control, don't feel bad about not being able to tool around with DAO directly. You can do plenty of great things with the data control, and with a lot less hassle.

To really understand how to work with the data control, we have to understand the concept of a recordset. That's where we'll start.

The Recordset Object

In the previous chapter, we used the data control to select groups of records from single tables and multiple related tables. The recordset object, often called the **`RecordSet`** property of a data control, lets you access the selected records as if they were all in one table. It creates a temporary collection of the records you want for the time that your program is running.

For example, you may have a **`SELECT`** statement in a data control which pulls information from three tables. Rather than having to worry about all three tables in your code, you can deal with the recordset object instead, which brings the contents of all three tables together.

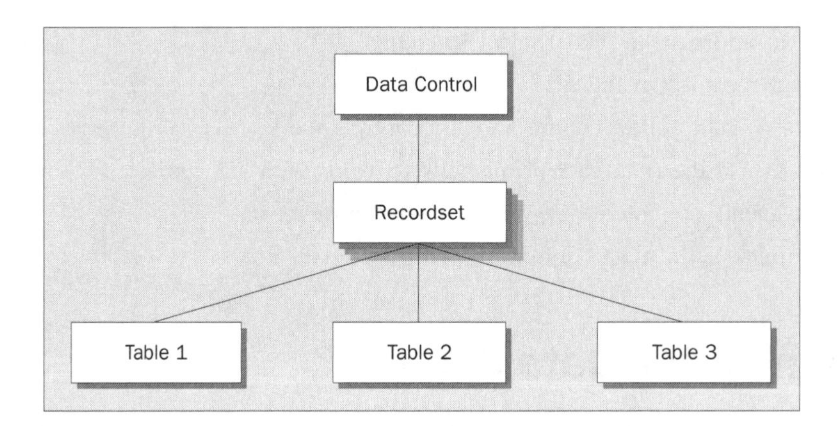

Types of Recordset

As you'll remember from the last chapter, the Jet engine supports three types of recordset that you choose between, depending on where the data comes from and what you want to do with it.

Table, Type vbRSTypeTable

This passes the complete table from the underlying database through to your program. You have to take the whole table, and any changes you make to the recordset are reflected in the original table. To all intents and purposes, you aren't looking at a recordset—you're looking directly at the underlying table.

Dynaset, Type vbRSTypeDynaset

This is created by filtering or combining records and fields from one or more underlying tables. You control its make-up using an SQL statement or other query. If you change any part of the resulting set of records, then the changes are also made in the corresponding tables.

Snapshot, Type vbRSTypeSnapshot

This is like a dynaset in origin, but it isn't updatable. The underlying tables are protected from any changes you make to the recordset.

We saw earlier that the default type is vbRSTypeDynaset, the dynaset. This is because, most of the time, you'll want to use something more complex than a table, and you'll want to update the database. Snapshots can be very useful for viewing data though, as they offer better performance than a dynaset in many cases.

Try It Out - Creating a Recordset with Code

Let's recreate the grid project from the previous chapter in code, so that we bind the controls to the data at run time, rather than at design time.

1 Start a new project and create a similar form to the one we used in the last chapter. Add a data control and a grid control as shown.

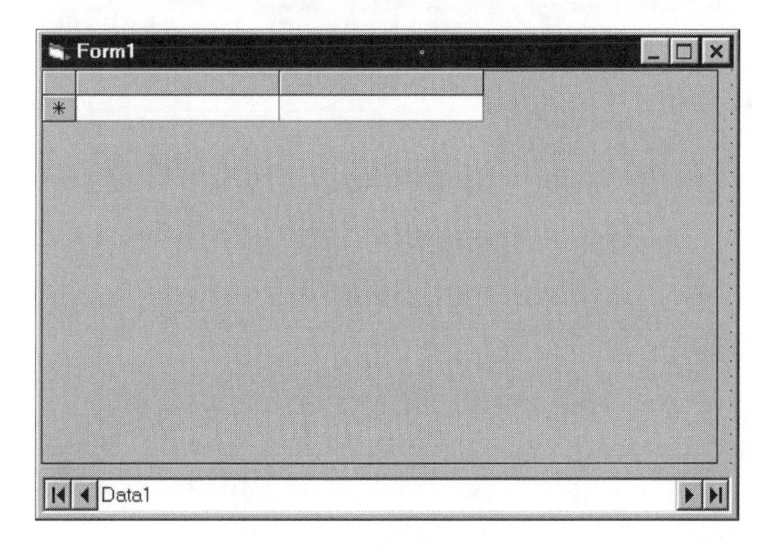

If the grid control is not in the toolbox, remember to select it from the **Components** *dialog on the* **Project** *menu.*

2 Set the **DataSource** property of the grid to Data1. We are going to set the **DatabaseName** and **RecordSource** properties of the data control at run time, but Visual Basic won't let you set the **DataSource** property from code.

3 Now let's add some code that will attach the database and feed the data into the grid. Type this code into the **Form_Load** event:

```
Private Sub Form_Load()

    Data1.DatabaseName = "C:\Program Files\DevStudio\Vb\Biblio.mdb"
    Data1.RecordsetType = vbRSTypeTable
    Data1.RecordSource = "Titles"

    Data1.Refresh

End Sub
```

> *Note that you may need to change the code above to reflect the correct pathname for your copy of* **Biblio.mdb***.*

4 Now hit run and there's the data.

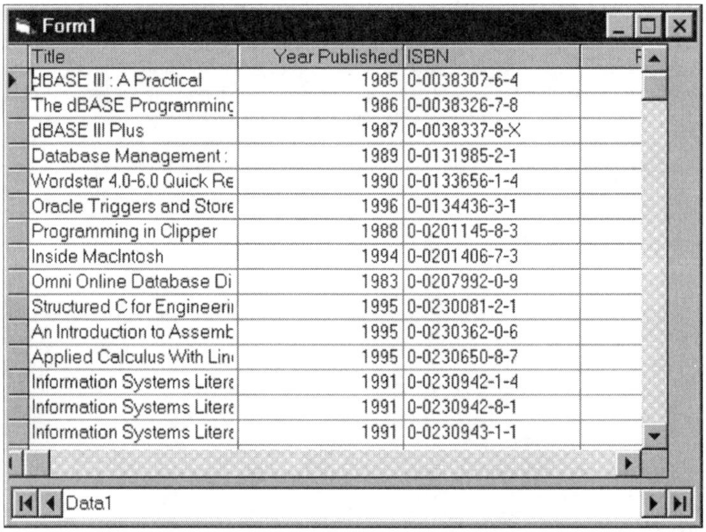

Form1

Title	Year Published	ISBN	P
dBASE III : A Practical	1985	0-0038307-6-4	
The dBASE Programminc	1986	0-0038326-7-8	
dBASE III Plus	1987	0-0038337-8-X	
Database Management :	1989	0-0131985-2-1	
Wordstar 4.0-6.0 Quick Re	1990	0-0133656-1-4	
Oracle Triggers and Store	1996	0-0134436-3-1	
Programming in Clipper	1988	0-0201145-8-3	
Inside MacIntosh	1994	0-0201406-7-3	
Omni Online Database Di	1983	0-0207992-0-9	
Structured C for Engineeri	1995	0-0230081-2-1	
An Introduction to Assemb	1995	0-0230362-0-6	
Applied Calculus With Lin	1995	0-0230650-8-7	
Information Systems Litera	1991	0-0230942-1-4	
Information Systems Litera	1991	0-0230942-8-1	
Information Systems Litera	1991	0-0230943-1-1	

Data1

5 Save this project as **BibGrid** as we'll come back to it in a moment.

How It Works

In this program we hardwired just one property at design time: the **DataSource** property of the grid. Apart from this, the data control is young, free and single, and looking to get bound to the next available data source so they can make little recordsets together.

In order to get the data control working, you have to first tell it the exact name and path of the target database. In our case this is:

```
Data1.DatabaseName = "C:\Program Files\DevStudio\Vb\Biblio.mdb"
```

There's actually a stage prior to this that we've skipped, which is to specify a **`Connect`** *property. This tells VB the type of database you are connecting to, for example ODBC, FoxPro etc. If you look at the properties window, you'll see that the default type is Access, so we didn't have to do anything here.*

You then have to specify the type of recordset you want to work with. We could have left this blank, defaulting to a dynaset, but instead we set it to table (type vbRSTypeTable). The type values, such as vbRSTypeTable, also equate to actual numbers, but it's a good habit to use the constants as they are more readable. However, here are the numeric values anyway:

Constant	Value	Meaning
`vbRSTypeTable`	0	Table
`vbRSTypeDynaset`	1	Dynaset
`vbRSTypeSnapshot`	2	Snapshot

After that, we have to tell the data control which table we are going to connect to.

```
Data1.RecordSource = "Titles"
```

Once it's all set up, you kick the data control into action using the **`Refresh`** method:

```
Data1.Refresh
```

In our particular case, you could leave this out as the **`Form_Load`** event itself causes the controls to be refreshed. However, it's good practice to get used to having it there, since you almost always need to refresh the data control if you change any of its properties.

Defining the Recordset

Having got to grips with the idea of attaching the data control to databases on the fly, we can now move on and see how to use the **`RecordSource`** property of the data control to determine what records and fields actually go into our recordset. In the previous example, we just lifted the whole **`Titles`** table into the grid. This time, let's control the **`RecordSource`** property of the data control directly to dictate what appears in the grid.

Try It Out - Playing with SQL

What we're going to do is add a window on to the grid form that lets you submit SQL statements to the data control at run time.

1 Let's try changing our previous example. Open up the form in design view, drag the bottom of the grid upwards and draw a big text box at the bottom. This is going to be the window into which we can enter SQL commands. Name the text box **txtSQLCode**, set its **Multiline** property to true to allow for extra long commands and clear its **Text** property.

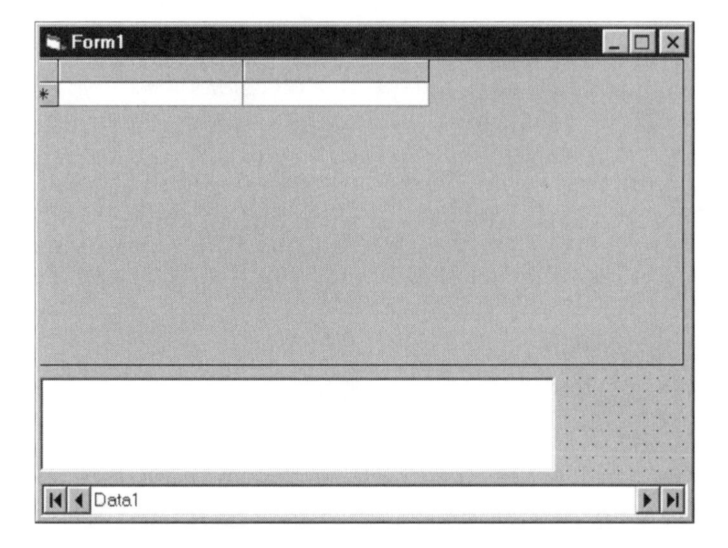

2 Now add two command buttons as shown. Call them **cmdExecute** and **cmdQuit** and set their captions accordingly. Set the **Enabled** property of the Execute button to false, but set its **Default** property to true.

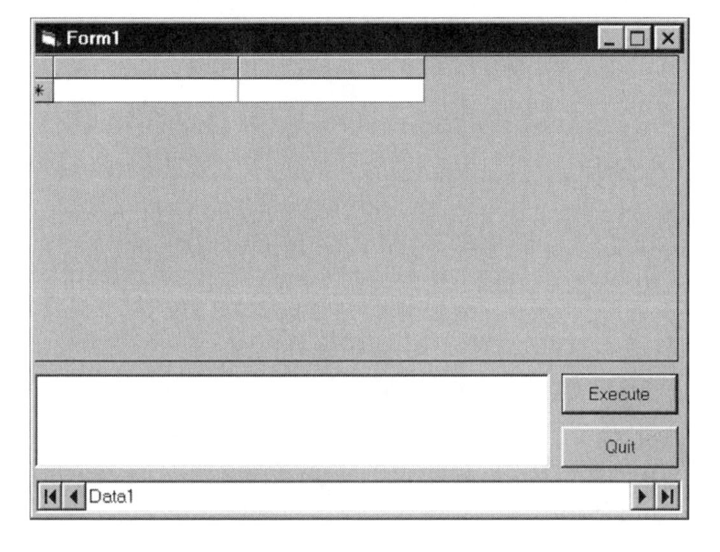

3 Open up the code window for the **cmdExecute_Click** event and add this code.

```
Private Sub cmdExecute_Click()

    Data1.RecordSource = txtSQLCode
    Data1.Refresh

End Sub
```

4 Add an **End** command to the **cmdQuit_Click** event.

5 Leave the code in the **Form_Load** event the same as before, except for changing the recordset type to dynaset.

```
Private Sub Form_Load()

    Data1.DatabaseName = "C:\Program Files\DevStudio\Vb\Biblio.mdb"
    Data1.RecordsetType = vbRSTypeDynaset
    Data1.RecordSource = "Titles"

    Data1.Refresh

End Sub
```

6 Add this code to enable the Execute button when there's something there to execute.

```
Private Sub txtSQLCode_Change()

    If Trim$(txtSQLCode) <> "" Then
        cmdExecute.Enabled = True
    Else
          cmdExecute.Enabled = False
    End If

End Sub
```

7 Now run the project. Enter the following SQL command into the text box and watch the grid change when you hit Execute.

```
SELECT Titles.[Title], Titles.[Year Published], Titles.[ISBN] FROM Titles
```

8 Finally, save the project.

How It Works

The main change from the grid project in the previous chapter is that here we built up the **RecordSource** property for the data control from a string taken from the text box. Assuming that the user types in a valid SQL statement, this is placed inside the required quote marks and assigned to the **RecordSource** property by the line:

```
Data1.RecordSource = txtSQLCode
```

The **Change** event for the text box looks to see if there's anything in the string before it enables the Execute button, thereby preventing empty statements being submitted.

This is a very simple program, but it's a great way to learn SQL. While we're here, let's take a look at some other useful SQL commands that you can use to create more complex recordsets.

Try It Out - Selecting Certain Records

So far, we've only used the `SELECT` statement to pick out certain named fields. What's more interesting, is to filter the recordset based on certain criteria.

1 Let's go back and change our previous example some more. Load it up, and type in this SQL code:

Form1

Title	Year Published	ISBN	PubID	D
dBASE III : A Practical (	1985	0-0038307-6-4	469	22
The dBASE Programm	1986	0-0038326-7-8	469	29
dBASE III Plus	1987	0-0038337-8-X	469	29
Database Managemen	1989	0-0131985-2-1	715	54
Wordstar 4.0-6.0 Quick I	1990	0-0133656-1-4	460	14
Oracle Triggers and St	1996	0-0134436-3-1	715	0
Programming in Clippe	1988	0-0201145-8-3	9	0
Inside MacIntosh	1994	0-0201406-7-3	9	99
Omni Online Database	1983	0-0207992-0-9	156	0
Structured C for Engine	1995	0-0230081-2-1	715	54
An Introduction to Asse	1995	0-0230362-0-6	715	60

SELECT Titles.* FROM [Titles] WHERE [Year Published] > 1994

Execute

Quit

Data1

2 Hit Execute and this is what you see. Only the titles published after 1994 are shown. Notice that all the columns in the whole `Titles` table are shown. This is because of the `Titles.*` in the SQL that you typed in. The asterisk is a special symbol in SQL that says to include all the fields in a table.

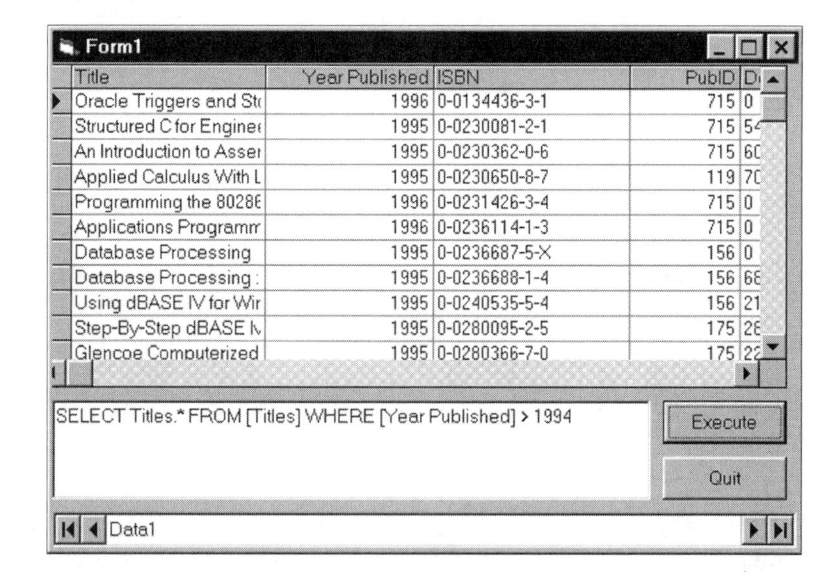

I know what you're thinking. It's so annoying if you get a statement wrong. Up pops the error window and you lose the lot. Well, wait your turn. Later in the chapter we'll discuss adding error handling to our database programs. In the meantime, copy the SQL statement in the window using the right mouse button before you execute. That way you can paste it in again if it fails.

3 Now change the statement to take data from the **`Publishers`** table.

Form1

Title	Year Published	Name
Oracle Triggers and Stored Procedure	1996	Prentice Hall
Structured C for Engineering and Technc	1995	Prentice Hall
An Introduction to Assembly Language F	1995	Prentice Hall
Applied Calculus With Linear Programm	1995	DELLEN
Programming the 80286, 80386, 80486, a	1996	Prentice Hall
Applications Programming in ANSI C	1996	Prentice Hall
Database Processing	1995	MACMILLAN
Database Processing : Fundamentals, [	1995	MACMILLAN
Using dBASE IV for Windows	1995	MACMILLAN
Step-By-Step dBASE Iv/Book and Stud	1995	GLENCOE
Glencoe Computerized Accounting : Wir	1995	GLENCOE
Using IBM Microcomputers in Business :	1996	HBJ COLLEGE

SELECT Titles.[Title], Titles.[Year Published], Publishers.[Name] FROM Titles INNER JOIN Publishers ON Titles.[PubID] = Publishers.[PubID] WHERE Titles.[Year Published] > 1994

Execute

Quit

Data1

4 Now add an **`ORDER BY`** clause to the end:

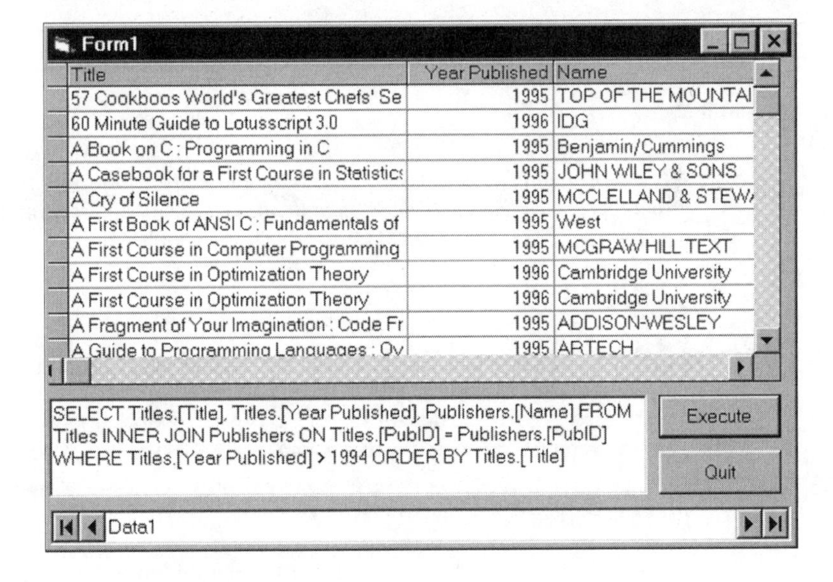

Title	Year Published	Name
57 Cookboos World's Greatest Chefs' Se	1995	TOP OF THE MOUNTAI
60 Minute Guide to Lotusscript 3.0	1996	IDG
A Book on C : Programming in C	1995	Benjamin/Cummings
A Casebook for a First Course in Statistic	1995	JOHN WILEY & SONS
A Cry of Silence	1995	MCCLELLAND & STEW
A First Book of ANSI C : Fundamentals of	1995	West
A First Course in Computer Programming	1995	MCGRAW HILL TEXT
A First Course in Optimization Theory	1996	Cambridge University
A First Course in Optimization Theory	1996	Cambridge University
A Fragment of Your Imagination : Code Fr	1995	ADDISON-WESLEY
A Guide to Programming Languages : Ov	1995	ARTECH

SELECT Titles.[Title], Titles.[Year Published], Publishers.[Name] FROM Titles INNER JOIN Publishers ON Titles.[PubID] = Publishers.[PubID] WHERE Titles.[Year Published] > 1994 ORDER BY Titles.[Title]

How It Works

Let's look at the mega-statement that we had at the end:

```
SELECT Titles.[Title], Titles.[Year Published], Publishers.[Name] FROM
Titles INNER JOIN Publishers ON Titles.[PubID] = Publishers.[PubID] WHERE
Titles.[Year Published] > 1994 ORDER BY Titles.[Title]
```

You can see how SQL has a habit of mushrooming into great wads of clauses. However, there's a simple enough logic to it all:

- Start with **SELECT** and tell the database which fields you want, preferably fully named:

```
SELECT Titles.[Title], Titles.[Year Published], Publishers.[Name]...
```

- Then tell the database where to get these records from, and if and how you want to combine records from more than one table:

```
...FROM Titles INNER JOIN Publishers ON Titles.[PubID] =
Publishers.[PubID]...
```

- Then tell it how to choose which titles to include in the dynaset:

```
...WHERE Titles.[Year Published] > 1994...
```

- Then, at the end, tell it how to sort them:

```
...ORDER BY Titles.[Title]
```

This is only touching the tip of the SQL iceberg, but now you've got the general idea, you can build the statements you need to get the data you want out of your underlying database.

There are a lot of good books on SQL. Take a look at Instant SQL from Wrox. It contains a complete guide to SQL, with all the code in Access format, as well as Oracle and Sybase. Its ISBN is 1-874416-50-8. Shameless plug.

Recordset Objects, Properties and Methods

In VB, the word recordset signifies both a property and an object at the same time. Although we haven't done it yet, you can assign a recordset to an object variable like this:

```
Set rsMyData = Data1.Recordset
```

You can then use the shorter variable **rsMyData** in your code to refer to the current recordset. In this case, we're using recordset as a property of the **Data1** object.

If you add another level of reference to this naming scheme, the recordset becomes part of the object name, to which you can apply a number of properties and methods. The most useful of these are geared to helping you navigate around the recordset using code, rather than the VCR buttons on the data control.

The methods and properties that are available for a recordset are dependent on what kind of recordset you have open. This is normally intuitive. For example, only the table type recordset supports the **DateCreated** property. After all, this would be meaningless for a dynaset or snapshot type recordset which is created afresh each time you run the program. The table is the only persistent recordset. Similarly intuitive criteria apply to whether a property is read/write or read-only in code. You would be right to assume that the **DateCreated** property is read-only: you don't want to be able to cheat the system and create your own date stamps.

We aren't going to cover every property and every method here. It would take too long, and a great many of them are beyond the scope of the techniques I want to highlight. If you're consumed with curiosity, search on Recordset Properties in the online help. We'll start off by looking at the recordset properties that tell you where you are in the data.

Recordset Properties

We'll take a look at these properties in more detail later, but for now, here's a quick rundown of the most useful recordset properties:

Property	Description
BOF	True if you are at the beginning of the recordset, before the first record.
EOF	True if you are positioned at the end of the recordset, after the last record.
BookMark	Reading this gives you the ID of the current record. Writing to this property jumps you immediately to the record with the **BookMark** value you write.
LastModified	The **BookMark** of the last changed record.
LastUpdated	The **BookMark** of the last updated record. There may not have been any actual changes to the record during the update.
NoMatch	Used when searching for records using the **Find** events you'll see later. If this property is true, then no match could be found.

Two of the most useful properties here are the **BOF** and **EOF** properties. These mark the beginning (**BOF**) and end (**EOF**) of the recordset. If both these properties are set to true, then you are at both the beginning and end of the **Recordset**—meaning the **Recordset** is empty.

There are also two data control properties that define how the recordset actually behaves:

Property	Description
`BOFAction`	Defines what happens when the user tries to move before the first record of the recordset. Can be used to automatically reposition on the first record, or on an invalid record with the Previous button disabled on the data control.
`EOFAction`	Defines what happens when the user tries to move beyond the last record of the recordset. Can be used to automatically reposition on the last record, on an invalid record with the Next button disabled, or to create a new record in the recordset.

Each of the above properties can take either a number or another of VB's inbuilt constants. **`BOFAction`** can be set to either **`vbBOFActionMoveFirst`** or **`vbBOFActionBOF`**. The first moves to the first record in the recordset if the user tries to move before the first record. The second moves to a non-existent record in the recordset and disables the previous button on the data control.

The **`EOFAction`** property can have similar values: **`vbEOFActionMoveLast`**, **`vbEOFActionEOF`** or **`vbEOFActionAddNew`**. The first two of these correspond to the **`vbBOFAction`** values. **`vbEOFActionAddNew`** lets the data control create a new record if the user tries to move beyond the last record in the recordset.

These properties mean that you can write an application that allows users to view, edit and update information without actually writing any code. For example, if you set the **`vbEOFActionAddNew`** flag, then once you reach the end of a recordset, the data control puts up a blank new record and you can type into it. Moving to another record updates the database with this new record.

However, it's far more common to handle record creation and deletion (something the data control can't do on its own) through code. Before we get our teeth into doing this, we need to know how to move about the recordset using code.

Recordset Methods

Simply using the data control to display records from a table in the existing order is rather limiting. One of the real powers of database applications is their ability to find individual pieces of data for you quickly and easily. In order to do anything more sophisticated, though, we need first to understand how the data control moves through the records.

To get a clear understanding of recordset methods, it helps to keep an image in your mind of what a recordset is. It's a *virtual* table which you have assembled in memory from the underlying tables in your database, and only includes the records and fields that you want to work with at the moment. Although it's a virtual table in the sense that it exists only as long as your application is running and you decide to keep it there, it does have a real structure as far as your code is concerned. The records are assembled in the order that you determined by your SQL **`RecordSource`** statement, which could of course be unspecified, in which case they are 'as found'.

Whatever the order of your records, they sit there as a block. In order that you and your code know which record you're dealing with at any one time, the Jet engine maintains a cursor that indicates the current record. We saw this as a little triangle on the bound grid. There's always a cursor there in your recordset; when you first open the recordset it points to the first record.

In this section, we are going to look at the **`Move`** methods which the data control calls with its VCR buttons, as well as the **`Find`** methods which you can use to locate individual records. Finally, we'll take a look at the **`Seek`** method for table type objects. These are all ways of moving the cursor through the records.

> *As before, with recordset properties, there are lot more methods than we are going to cover here, and some apply only to certain types of recordset. For example, the* **`AddNew`** *method isn't supported by the snapshot type object, for obvious reasons.*

Using the Move Methods

Visual Basic has five **`Move`** methods to let you move around a table record by record. These are:

Method	Description
`MoveFirst`	Moves to the first record in a table.
`MoveLast`	Moves to the last record in a table.
`MoveNext`	Moves to the next record in a table.
`MovePrevious`	Moves back one record.
`Move -n`	Moves backward n records.
`Move n`	Moves forward n records.
`Move 0`	Reloads the current record.

Four of the methods relate to the four icons you see on the data control when you draw it on a form.

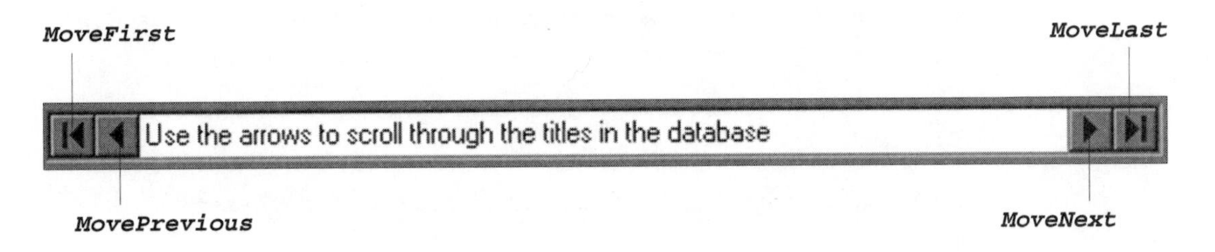

Try It Out - Moving Around the Database

1 Let's save ourselves a bit of time here and work with the example that we created in the last chapter. Load up the **Bib_View** project and drop four buttons on the form so that it looks like this. Don't forget to set up the captions as shown, and set the names up to be **cmdFirst**, **cmdPrevious**, **cmdNext** and **cmdLast**. Also, change the **Visible** property of the data control to false so that it doesn't appear at run time, and make sure the **RecordSetType** is set to Dynaset.

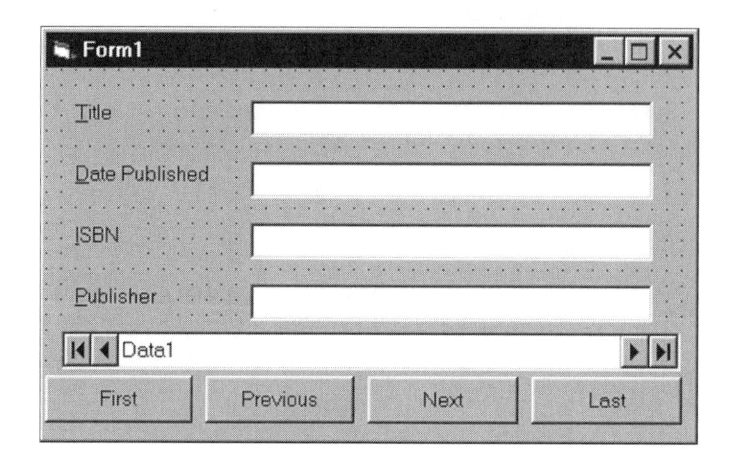

2 Ready for some typing? Bring up the code window and type these events in to deal with each command button's **Click** event.

```
Private Sub cmdFirst_Click()

  Data1.Recordset.MoveFirst

End Sub

Private Sub cmdPrevious_Click()

     If Not Data1.Recordset.BOF Then Data1.Recordset.MovePrevious

End Sub

Private Sub cmdNext_Click()

     If Not Data1.Recordset.EOF Then Data1.Recordset.MoveNext

End Sub

Private Sub cmdLast_Click()
```

```
    Data1.Recordset.MoveLast

End Sub
```

3 Run the program to get a feel for how it works.

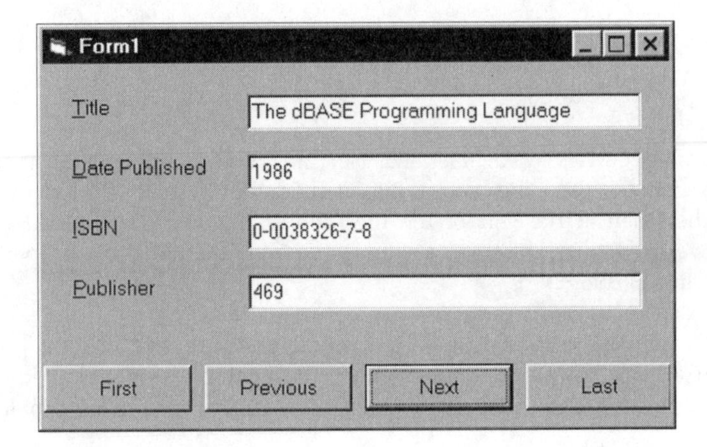

This time, in addition to the data control, there are four command buttons at the base of the form which allow you to move through the records using the **Move** methods

4 All appears to be OK, but go to the end of the recordset and hit the Next button. The screen goes blank. Obviously Visual Basic is letting us move past the end of the recordset. Let's find out what's going on.

How It Works

The code for the First command button moves to the first record of the **Titles** table, using the invisible data control:

```
Private Sub cmdFirst_Click()

    Data1.Recordset.MoveFirst

End Sub
```

The bound controls change as soon as the data control arrives at the new record. The Last command button works in a similar way to First, but uses the **MoveLast** method instead of **MoveFirst**. The Previous and Next buttons are a little more complex, and that's where the problem is.

There are only ever a finite number of records in a database. The **EOF** and **BOF** properties check whether or not the user has reached the beginning or end of the file:

```
Private Sub cmdNext_Click()

    If Not Data1.Recordset.EOF Then Data1.Recordset.MoveNext

End Sub
```

```
Private Sub cmdPrevious_Click()

    If Not Data1.Recordset.BOF Then Data1.Recordset.MovePrevious

End Sub
```

Back to our problem. We clicked Last and Next and ended up with a blank record. What happened was that we used the **MoveNext** method, but actually ended up at the next to last record rather than at the end of the file. The end of the file showed up as a blank record when we tried to move to it, as the **Data1.Recordset.EOF** property was still not true when we hit **cmdNext**.

The reason this happens is that Visual Basic doesn't set the **EOF** or **BOF** properties to true until after you attempt to move beyond either the beginning or end of the recordset. This works great for writing code to loop through records, but causes us problems in our case.

The way around this problem is to check the **EOF** property after the **MoveNext** event. If it is **True**, then we just need to back up one record using **MovePrevious**.

```
Private Sub cmdNext_Click()

    Data1.Recordset.MoveNext
    If Data1.Recordset.EOF Then Data1.Recordset.MovePrevious

End Sub
```

Finding Records

The **Find** methods provide the most powerful and versatile way of locating records in your data. Let's explore these methods interactively—it's a much easier way to get a feel for how they work. Time to enhance that project just one more time.

Try It Out - Finding Records

1 Start by correcting the code in the **cmdNext** and **cmdPrevious** events as shown on the opposite page.

```
Private Sub cmdNext_Click()

    If Not Data1.Recordset.EOF Then Data1.Recordset.MoveNext

End Sub
```

```
Private Sub cmdPrevious_Click()

    If Not Data1.Recordset.BOF Then Data1.Recordset.MovePrevious

End Sub
```

2 Save the program so we can come back to it later, and then run it. Press *Ctrl-Break* to pause it, and *Ctrl-G* to bring up the immediate window (if it's not already visible). Type the following in the immediate window, and press *Enter*.

```
    Data1.Recordset.FindFirst "[Year Published] = 1989"
```

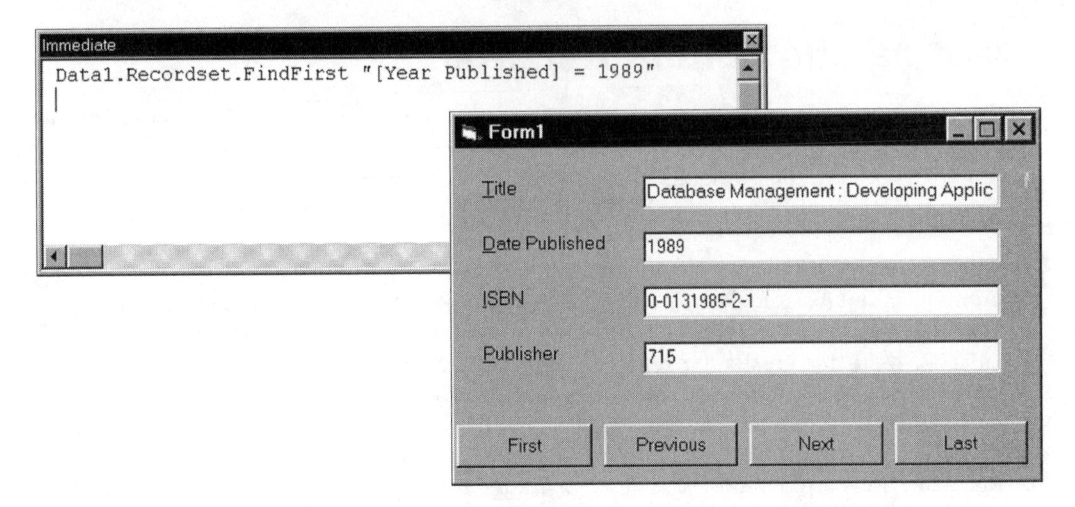

This finds the first record in the **Titles** table where the year published is 1989 (don't worry if the record displayed, when you run it, is not the same as in the screenshot). The syntax of all the **Find** commands is the same: after specifying which **Find** method you want to use—**FindFirst**, **FindNext**, **FindPrevious**, or **FindLast**—you put the criteria that you want to match inside quote marks.

How It Works

In the example above, the field we want to match is called **Year Published**. We'll look at how to find out what field names are available to match later.

Since this field name contains a space, I've put square brackets `[]` around the name. It's good practice to do this all the time, to prevent confusion between field names and the values you are searching for.

Straight after the field name, the phrase **`= 1989`** tells Visual Basic that we want to find the first record in the **`Titles`** table where the **`Year Published`** field is equal to **`1989`**. You could equally well have put **`>`** for greater than, **`<`** for less than or **`<>`** for not equal to, and so on.

The **`FindFirst`** method finds the first matching record in the table, regardless of which record you were looking at before you did the find. You could have had the last record in the table up on screen and Visual Basic would still move you back through the table to the first matching one.

*It is important to note that **`Find`** and its related methods will not work on a table type recordset, only dynasets and snapshots.*

Creating and Editing Records

Databases are only useful when the information contained in them is up-to-date and accurate. We're going to introduce two new concepts in the next example to help you do just that. Before you start panicking, these are both natural extensions of things you've looked at previously and shouldn't cause you too many problems.

The first concept is that of using the methods of bound controls to add and delete records from your database to keep it up to date. We've already used methods to find records and move to them, and adding and deleting is done in much the same way. However, as we're offering users far greater power, we therefore need to take extra steps to help protect the information being stored in the database. So we'll introduce the bound combo control, which helps protect the information in your database by forcing the user to select from a finite list of choices. We've already looked at list controls and combo boxes, so this shouldn't prove too much of a leap in understanding. Before we launch headlong into our example, we'll take a brief glance at how bound list and combo controls work.

Bound List and Combo Controls

Control of incoming data is fundamental to working databases. Bound list and combo controls are truly useful when it comes to giving the user a limited range of options for data entry. For example, imagine if you let users type their own version of the country field in an address database. You might want them to enter UK, but left to their own devices, they could enter England, GB or Britain. A better option would be to list the options in a combo box and let the user select one that you've already entered. In database-speak this is called a **look-up table**.

Although the bound versions of the combo and list boxes are there to make your life easier (and they do!), they are initially very confusing. When dealing with bound combo boxes, you will generally have two data controls.

> *Remember that one data control can only manage one recordset. If you want to relate two tables or recordsets together on the fly in your code, you need a data control for each one.*

Because of this, a bound combo box has two properties for linking to tables or recordsets. The **`DataSource`** property links to the first data control; **`RowSource`** links to the second. Don't worry all will become clear very soon.

Try It Out - An Improved Database Viewer

Now check you're sitting comfortably, put the cat out if necessary and get yourself a cup of tea; it's time to write a decent sized application—I hope you're ready for some typing. We're going to write another database viewer that will allow you to browse the records of the **`Biblio`** database. However, this one will provide a combo box for the publisher, instead of confusing numbers and, at the same time, will let you add and delete records.

1 Start a new project and drop some controls on to the form so that it looks like this. Remember to clear out the **`Text`** properties of the text boxes and to set up the captions on the labels and the buttons.

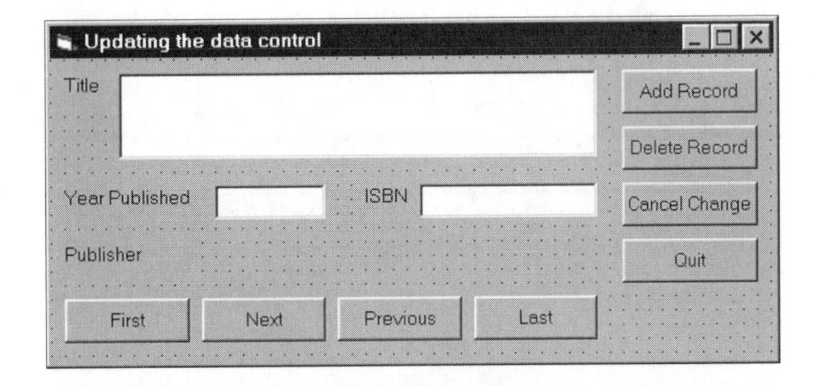

2 Next, add two data controls to the form and set their **`Visible`** properties to false. We need two data controls because we're going to supply the publisher's name rather than just a number.

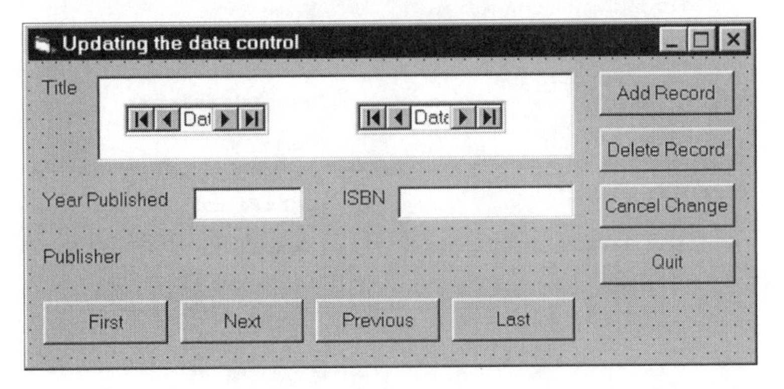

3 Add a dbCombo box as shown. Remember, you may have to load this control into your toolbox using the Project | Components... menu item for data bound list controls. Don't worry too much about the specifics of this control just yet, as we'll cover the dbCombo and dbList controls in more detail later in the chapter.

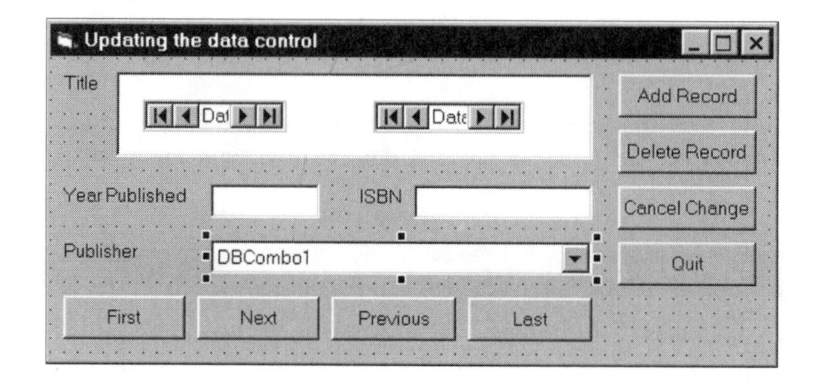

4 Now save the application to your hard disk as **`Bib_Edit.vbp`**. We're going to use code to open the **`Biblio.mdb`** database, so to make things easier, copy the database into the same directory as your application, using Explorer. This means we can use code that will assume that the database is in the same directory as the application. Copying the database will also mean that you can avoid permanent changes to the database when we edit the records.

5 Set up the other properties of the controls as shown in this table:

Control	Property	Value
First data control	**`Name`**	**`datPublishers`**
	`DatabaseName`	**`Biblio.mdb`**
	`Recordsource`	**`Publishers`**
	`RecordsetType`	**`2 - Snapshot`**
Second data control	**`Name`**	**`datTitles`**
	`DatabaseName`	**`Biblio.mdb`**
	`Recordsource`	**`Titles`**
	`RecordsetType`	**`1 - Dynaset`**
Titles text box	**`Name`**	**`txtTitle`**
	`DataSource`	**`datTitles`**
	`DataField`	**`Title`**
Year Published text box	**`Name`**	**`txtYear`**
	`DataSource`	**`datTitles`**
	`DataField`	**`Year Published`**

Table Continued on Following Page

Control	Property	Value
ISBN Text box	Name	txtISBN
	DataSource	datTitles
	DataField	ISBN
Publisher data combo	Name	dbcPublisher
	DataSource	datTitles
	RowSource	datPublishers
	BoundColumn	PubID
	DataField	PubID
	ListField	Name
Add command button	Name	cmdAdd
Delete command button	Name	cmdDelete
Cancel command button	Name	cmdCancel
Quit command button	Name	cmdQuit
First command button	Name	cmdFirst
Next command button	Name	cmdNext
Previous command button	Name	cmdPrevious
Last command button	Name	cmdLast

6 When you've done that little lot, bring up the code window and click on the button in its lower left corner to select Full Module view. When you've done this, type in the following declarations in the General Declarations section.

```
Option Explicit

Private m_bAdding As Boolean
Private m_bCancel As Boolean

Private sPreviousRecord As String
```

7 Then add the event handlers. Remember, VB will highlight the line in red if you get it wrong, so keep an eye on what VB is telling you. The code looks daunting at first, but just type it in for now, trying to keep track as you go, then we'll step through it section by section in a moment. This is the code for the Add button:

```
Private Sub cmdAdd_Click()

Dim bOK As Boolean
bOK = Check
If Not bOK Then Exit Sub
If m_bAdding Then
    If bOK Then
        datTitles.Recordset.Update
        datTitles.Recordset.AddNew
```

```
        Else
            Exit Sub
        End If
    Else
        sPreviousRecord = datTitles.Recordset.Bookmark
        datTitles.Recordset.AddNew
        m_bAdding = True
    End If

End Sub
```

This is the code for the Cancel button:

```
Private Sub cmdCancel_Click()

    If m_bAdding Then
        m_bCancel = True
        m_bAdding = False
    End If

        datTitles.UpdateControls
        datTitles.Recordset.Bookmark = sPreviousRecord

End Sub
```

This is the code for the Delete button:

```
Private Sub cmdDelete_Click()

    Dim nResponse

    If m_bAdding Then
        cmdCancel_Click
    Else

       If datTitles.Recordset.EOF Or datTitles.Recordset.BOF Then Exit
        ↳ Sub

        nResponse = MsgBox("Do you really want to delete this record?",
        ↳ 20, "Delete Record")

       If nResponse = 6 Then
           datTitles.Recordset.Delete
           datTitles.Recordset.MoveFirst
       End If

    End If

End Sub
```

This is the code for the First button:

```
Private Sub cmdFirst_Click()

If Check = False Then Exit Sub
    If m_bAdding = True Then
        datTitles.Recordset.Update
        m_bAdding = False
    Else
        datTitles.UpdateControls
    End If

    datTitles.Recordset.MoveFirst

End Sub
```

This is the code for the Last button:

```
Private Sub cmdLast_Click()

If Check = False Then Exit Sub
    If m_bAdding = True Then
        datTitles.Recordset.Update
        m_bAdding = False
    Else
        datTitles.UpdateControls
    End If

    datTitles.Recordset.MoveLast

End Sub
```

This is the code for the Next button:

```
Private Sub cmdNext_Click()

If Check = False Then Exit Sub
    If m_bAdding = True Then
        datTitles.Recordset.Update
        m_bAdding = False
    Else
        datTitles.UpdateControls
    End If

    datTitles.Recordset.MoveNext
    If datTitles.Recordset.EOF Then datTitles.Recordset.MovePrevious

End Sub
```

This is the code for the Previous button:

```
Private Sub cmdPrevious_Click()

  If Check = False Then Exit Sub
    If m_bAdding = True Then
        datTitles.Recordset.Update
        m_bAdding = False
    Else
        datTitles.UpdateControls
    End If

    datTitles.Recordset.MovePrevious
    If datTitles.Recordset.BOF Then datTitles.Recordset.MoveNext

End Sub
```

This is the code for the Quit button:

```
Private Sub cmdQuit_Click()

    End

End Sub
```

And this is the code that executes when the program first executes:

```
Private Sub Form_Load()

    Dim sDatabasename As String

    sDatabasename = App.Path & "\" & "biblio.mdb"

    If Dir$(sDatabasename) = "" Then
        MsgBox "Database could not be found, please make sure that
          ↳ Biblio.mdb " & Chr$(10) & "is in the same location as this
          ↳ program", , "Database Error"
        End
    End If

    datTitles.DatabaseName = sDatabasename
    datPublishers.DatabaseName = sDatabasename

    m_bAdding = False
    m_bCancel = False

End Sub
```

8 You'll also need to add a function that checks to see whether you have filled all of the fields, as if you add a record with an empty field to the database, it will cause an error. To stop this unpleasantness from ever rearing its ugly head, you need add this code underneath the General Declarations section:

```
Function Check() As Boolean
If txtTitle = "" Or txtYear = "0" Or txtISBN = "" Or dbcPublisher = ""
Then
    MsgBox "This record is incomplete. You cannot update the database!"
    m_bAdding = False
    Check = False
Else
    Check = True
End If
End Function
```

9 Now hit the save button to preserve all your hard work.

OK—now the code's all there, let's explore the application a little.

Try It Out - Viewing the Records

1 Start up the project. There's the data:

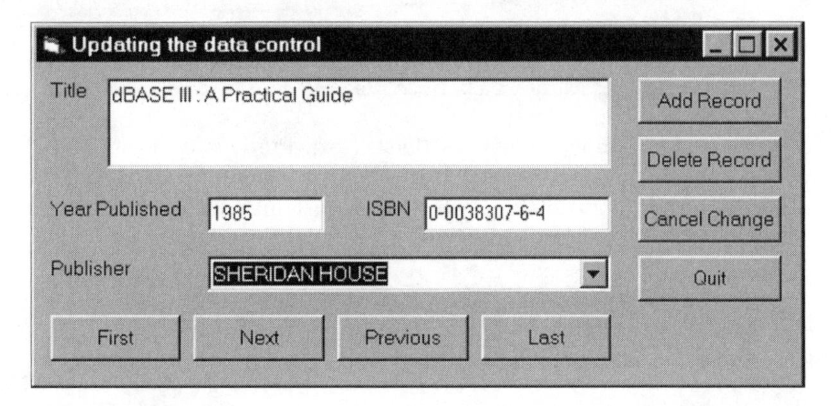

2 Click on the Add Record button. Up pops a blank record, ready and willing. Numeric fields are automatically defaulted to 0, that's why the Year Published field starts out displaying a 0.

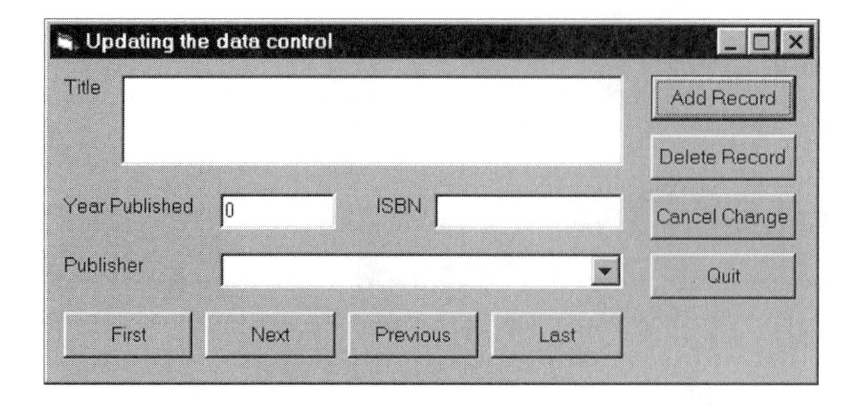

3 Let's add a phantom bestseller. Type one in, making sure that you choose the publisher from the list in the combo box rather than making your own up.

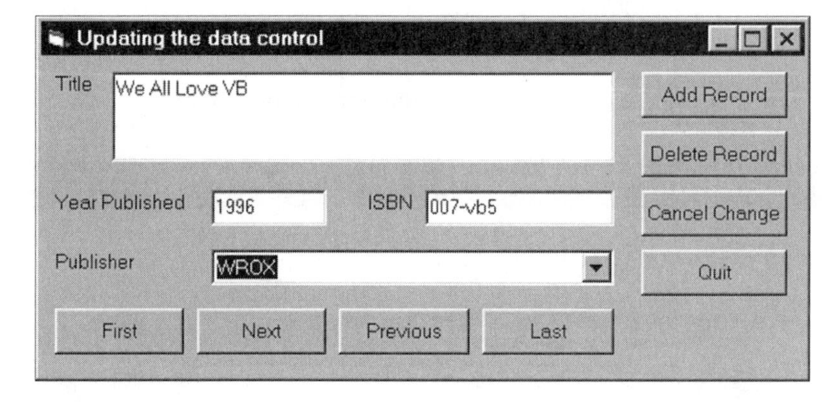

4 Hitting one of the movement keys (First, Next, Previous or Last) saves the new record. Move to the previous record and then hit Last. There's your record. To avoid debris in the file, I suggest you delete it afterwards. Just hit the delete button, confirm that you really want to delete it and it's gone.

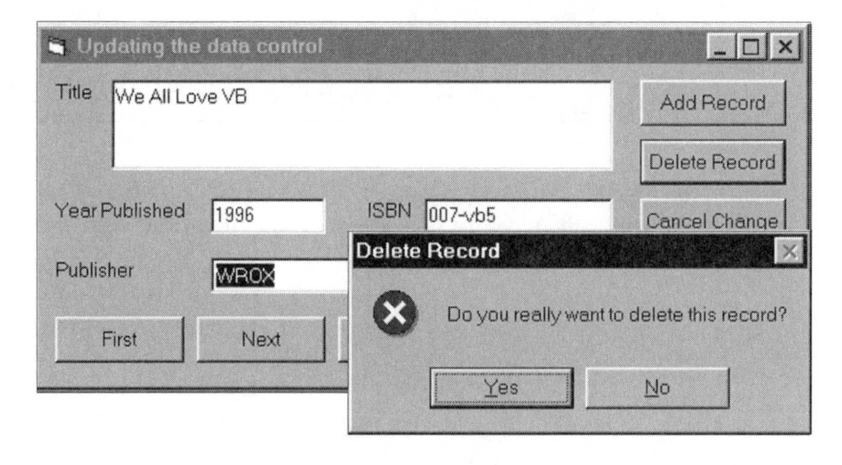

5 You can also cancel adding a new record in mid-flow. Start to type in a new record and then hit Cancel change. You're returned to the previous record again.

There is obviously a lot going on here, so I'm going to explain how each section works individually.

How It Works - Opening the Database

I've used code to set the database to open up, as we did earlier on. However, I've added a tricky little line of code that looks for **Biblio** in your current directory:

```
Private Sub Form_Load()

    Dim sDatabasename As String

    sDatabasename = App.Path & "\" & "biblio.mdb"

    If Dir$(sDatabasename) = "" Then
        MsgBox "Database could not be found, please make sure that
          ↳ Biblio.mdb " & Chr$(10) & "is in the same location as
          ↳ this program", , "Database Error"
        End
    End If

    datTitles.DatabaseName = sDatabasename
    datPublishers.DatabaseName = sDatabasename

    m_bAdding = False
    m_bCancel = False

End Sub
```

The **sDatabaseName** string is built up from the database name, **Biblio.mdb** and the path of the application, **App.Path**. This is why you needed to copy the **Biblio** database into the same directory as your application.

Once **sDatabaseName** is sorted out, we can assign it to the two data controls on the form. We need two data controls as the combo list box that shows the list of publishers' names has to connect directly to the **Publishers** table through its own data control.

Finally, we set two module-level variables—**m_bAdding** and **m_bCancel**—as false. These are two Boolean (i.e. on/off) values that keep track of whether we are in the middle of adding a new record or if we've hit the Cancel button. You'll see exactly what these do in a minute.

How It Works - Moving Around the Database

Rather than use the mundane-looking data control, which is believed to be the height of unhipness for Visual Basic programmers, we put navigation buttons on to the form and made both data controls invisible. The code for each button is pretty much the same. This is the Next button.

```
Private Sub cmdNext_Click()

If Check = False Then Exit Sub
     If m_bAdding = True Then
          datTitles.Recordset.Update
          m_bAdding = False
     Else
          datTitles.UpdateControls
     End If

     datTitles.Recordset.MoveNext
     If datTitles.Recordset.EOF Then datTitles.Recordset.MovePrevious

End Sub
```

- The last two code lines here are familiar. We use the **MoveNext** method and then check to see if we've dropped off the end of the recordset. However, before we can go zooming about, we have to check whether we are in the middle of adding a new record, so that we can save any additions.

We saw how, when the user clicks the Add Record button, the bound controls all clear and wait for input. In an event-driven world, we wait for the user to type in what they want. The navigation event code must cover three conditions:

- The user has just completed a new record and has typed everything in correctly. At this point, what's in the bound controls is a new record. However, that new record is only in those controls. It's not yet been passed to the Jet engine so that it can update the underlying database. To do this we have to issue an **Update** command. This confirms that we want to write the new record into the database.

  We therefore assume that if the user clicks one of the navigation buttons after having entered a new record, they want us to keep it. As we'll see in a minute, the Add Record button event code sets **m_bAdding** to true, and providing the Cancel button event code didn't change it to false, it will still be true when and if the user hits a navigation button. If it's true, then we issue an **Update** method and change it back to false, indicating that we've added any outstanding records.

- The user has started entering a new record, but not completed the information on the form and has left at least one blank field when he/she tries to update the record. What happens is that when any movement key is pressed, function **Check** is automatically called and it cycles through each field to see if the field is blank. If it finds a blank field, it informs the user of the problem and returns the user to that record.
- There's no new record waiting to be passed to the database. This could either be because the user didn't enter one, or because they did but they then canceled it. Either way, **m_bAdding** is set to false. In case the bound controls contain a rejected record that we want to discard, we issue the opposite of an **Update** method—**UpdateControls**. This takes a new version of the recordset from the underlying database and uses it to refresh the bound controls, effectively overwriting any discarded records.

How It Works - Adding a New Record

Now for the meat in the sandwich, so to speak. You can add and delete records easily using the data and bound controls. To add a new record we'll use the **AddNew** method on the **RecordSet** object:

```
DataControl.RecordSet.AddNew
```

*Having seen this format, you will understand why **RecordSet** is an object rather than a property. It can have properties and methods of its own. It's basically an object within the data control object. More on this later.*

The above line tells the database to find a space in the current table where it can add a new record. The database dutifully does this, clears out all the fields for you and blanks out all of your bound controls. You can then set about putting values into the fields of the table, with the bound controls. Hopefully this illuminates now how the following code works:

```
Private Sub cmdAdd_Click()

Dim bOK As Boolean
bOK = Check
If Not bOK Then Exit Sub
If m_bAdding Then
    If bOK Then
        datTitles.Recordset.Update
        datTitles.Recordset.AddNew
    Else
        Exit Sub
    End If
Else
    sPreviousRecord = datTitles.Recordset.Bookmark
    datTitles.Recordset.AddNew
```

```
        m_bAdding = True
    End If

    End Sub
```

First of all, we define a check variable **bOK**. This is used to check that the user hasn't started to add information and then tried to add a new record, leaving blank fields in the old record. Function **Check** is called to examine each of the fields on the form and prevents the user from adding another record until all of the fields on the form have been filled.

Next, we store the location of the current record in a **bookmark**. A bookmark is a label that the database uses to identify the current record, so putting its current value into **sPreviousRecord** will mean that if the user presses Cancel, we can get back to where we were before we started adding the new record. We need to do this because the recordset we're using here is unordered, so the Jet engine orders them by age, with the last record to be added coming at the end. That's why when we do add the record it disappears to the end of the recordset.

Many other applications use bookmarks as a way of allowing the user to set bookmarks of their own, which they can jump to whenever they want. Imagine a user is working on a table when the phone rings. You could allow the user to store the bookmark of the current record in order to return to it later. Be careful though! You can only store bookmarks in variables. There's little point in saving them in files or even in the database since they can change each time the database is used. You can only set a bookmark for as long as your data control is active.

Then we issue the **AddNew** method. This gets the Jet engine to do all the hard work for us. The bound controls are cleared and wait for input. We also then set **m_bAdding** to true so that we know there's a new record waiting in the bound controls.

How It Works - Canceling an Entry

If we are adding a new record but then decide that we don't wish to complete it, we need to have the option of hitting the Cancel button. The code in the button has to get rid of the current record and return the database to the state it was in before we started messing around.

```
Private Sub cmdCancel_Click()

    If m_bAdding Then
       m_bCancel = True
       m_bAdding = False
    End If

       datTitles.UpdateControls
       datTitles.Recordset.Bookmark = sPreviousRecord

End Sub
```

First of all, we check whether we are actually in the middle of a new record. If so, we can set **m_bAdding** to false again, as we are about to take care of it all. Then we issue an **UpdateControls** method. This brings the database from the underlying engine to update the controls, so discarding whatever is in them. We then reassign **sPreviousRecord** as the current record.

How It Works - Deleting a Record

The final button pressing bit of the program is the Delete Record event handler:

```
Private Sub cmdDelete_Click()

    Dim nResponse

    If m_bAdding Then
        cmdCancel_Click
      Else

       If datTitles.Recordset.EOF Or datTitles.Recordset.BOF Then Exit Sub

        nResponse = MsgBox("Do you really want to delete this record?",
         ↳ 20, "Delete Record")

        If nResponse = 6 Then
           datTitles.Recordset.Delete
           datTitles.Recordset.MoveFirst
        End If

    End If

End Sub
```

If the user hits the Delete key whilst in the middle of creating a new record, i.e. when **m_bAdding** is true, then we want to handle it in the same way as a **Cancel** event. This code checks whether that's the case and if so, runs the cancel button event instead:

```
If m_bAdding Then
        cmdCancel_Click
    Else
```

Otherwise, we want to use the **Delete** method to remove the current record. It's good manners to check whether the user really meant to hit the Delete button—which we do with the message box. It's also sensible to check whether we're at a valid record:

```
If datTitles.Recordset.EOF Or datTitles.Recordset.BOF Then Exit Sub
```

If the **BOF** property is true, it means that the data control is currently looking at the record in front of the very first one in the recordset. Think of the recordset as a book. All the interesting information is contained on the pages inside, not on the front or back covers. **BOF** essentially tells you that the data control is looking at the front cover of the book, rather than at a meaningful page of information.

EOF does a similar thing, telling you when the data control has moved beyond the end of the recordset, in other words looking at the back cover of the book. If either of these properties are set, there is currently no valid record. If both **EOF** and **BOF** are true, then that tells us that there are no records in the recordset at all.

In the code, if either of these properties is set, then the subroutine is exited using **Exit Sub**, thus preventing the delete from taking place and avoiding embarrassing run time errors.

If everything's OK, issue the method and then move to beginning of the recordset:

```
            datTitles.Recordset.delete
            datTitles.Recordset.MoveFirst
```

How It Works - The Bound Combo Box

The essence of what's going on here is that we're using the combo box control to relate the **Titles** and **Publishers** tables together using the **PubID** field as the key, or common field. This is much the same as we did with the SQL **INNER JOIN...ON** statement. The difference is that instead of showing a single publisher's name, we make them all available in the combo box.

The dbCombo control has a lot of work to do.

- It has to put a list of all the available publishers into its item list. It takes the information from the data control named in its **RowSource** property. You tell DBCombo that you want to display the publisher names from the table, by specifying the field name in the **ListField** property.
- DBCombo then has to make sure that the publisher name that's displayed corresponds to the title that's been selected using the **datTitles** control. I have already mentioned that the combo box control has two properties that link to different tables: **DataSource** and **RowSource**. The properties that specify the field we are interested in from each table are **DataField** and **ListField** respectively. We want to relate the two tables using **PubID** as the common field. Therefore, to join them, we place the common field (**PubID**) in the **BoundColumn** and the **DataField** properties.

In order that the right fields are available to the combo box control via the ***datPublishers*** *control, the* ***RecordSource*** *property of* ***datPublishers*** *must be pointing at the* ***Publishers*** *table. While it can be any type of recordset, a snapshot is preferable to prevent any changes to the underlying data.*

- All that's left is to pass the **PubID** field back to be entered in to the **Titles** table for any new records, when a publisher name is selected in the combo box. You can't pass the **Text** property of DBCombo back, as that contains the name of the publisher and there's no field for this in the **Titles** table. DBCombo looks up the **PubID** of the selected publisher in the **Publishers** table and places it into its **BoundText** property.

*If you want to see the value of the **`BoundText`** property, add a little text box to the form and copy the **`BoundText`** property to it from the DBCombo **`Change`** event by setting the new text box property to the **`BoundText`** property as it changes.*

See if this diagram helps.

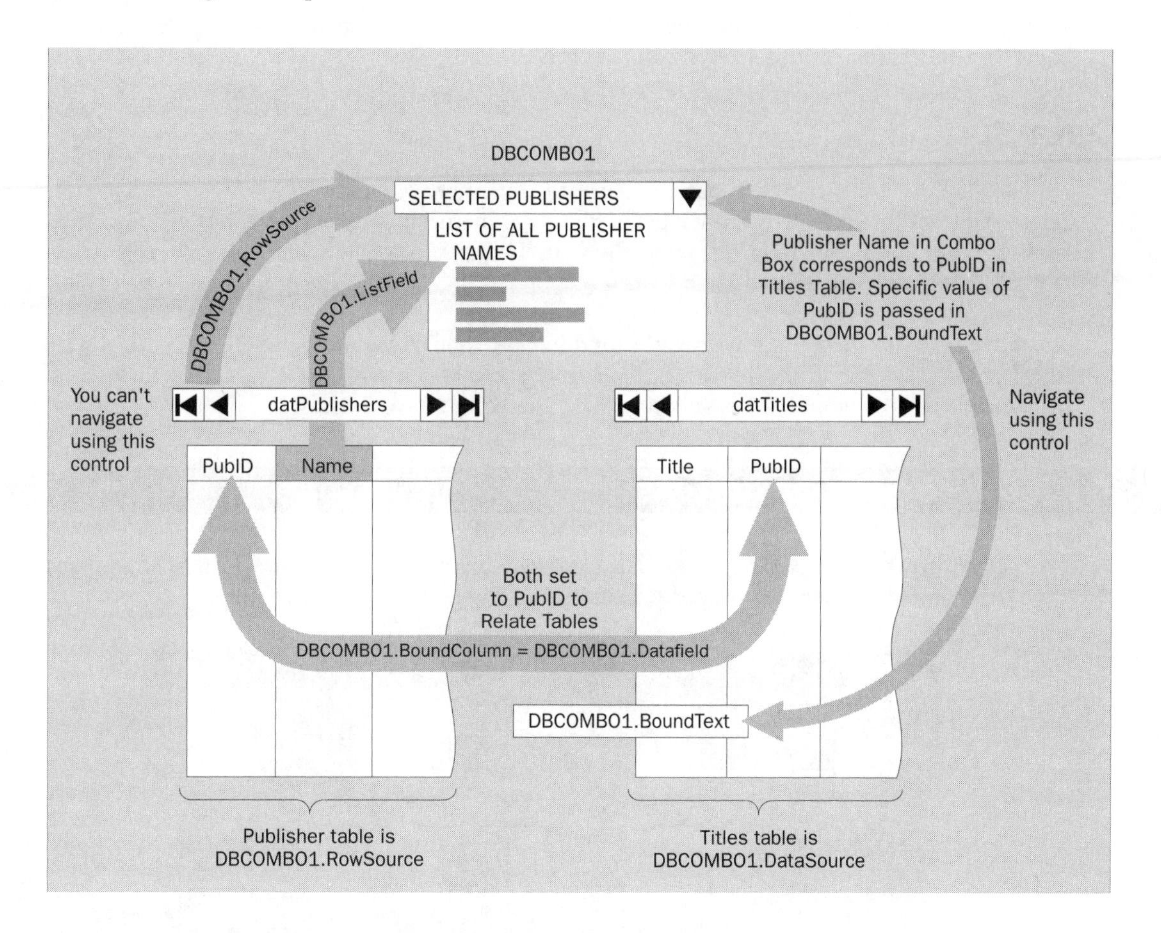

The bound list control is very similar in operation to the bound combo box, with the differences being intuitive if you've understood how the unbound versions differ. From a database handling point of view they are the same.

Working with Records in Code

There's actually a second way of working with records and that involves manipulating the records directly in your code. This isn't actually the exclusive preserve of masochistic programmers for whom bound controls are morally decrepit; there are two very good reasons for using code instead of bound controls:

- Not all controls are bound, so in those cases you have to write the code to load and edit the data yourself.
- Bound controls can be slow. This may not seem a problem to you now, but for VB programmers working with a massive database, possibly across a network, speed can be a large headache.

We'll look at how to work with the fields and records in a database using code when we cover list and grid controls later in the chapter.

Data Surfing

One of the annoying things about our supposedly improved database viewer is that you can't scroll easily through the data by holding down the movement buttons. Adding this facility is not hard, but requires some thought. In the process we'll discover some interesting features of Visual Basic—so let's have a go.

What we want is to be able to press a button and then have the action that button invokes repeated for as long as the button is held down. However, we don't want this to kick in too fast, otherwise we would keep shooting past the records we wanted.

Try It Out - Repeating Buttons

1 Open up the **Bib_Edit** project. Add a timer to the main form and set its **Interval** to 1000 and the **Enabled** property to false. I'll explain why in a minute.

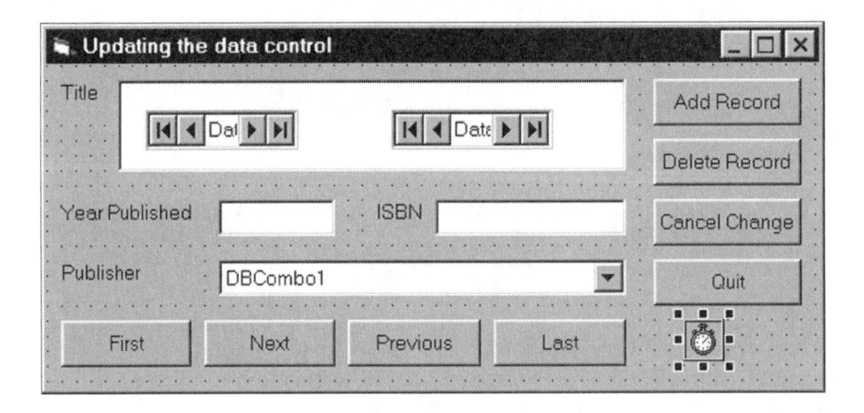

2 Now double-click on the Next button. This is the code we have currently:

```
Private Sub cmdNext_Click()

    If m_bAdding = True Then
        datTitles.Recordset.Update
```

```
        m_bAdding = False
    Else
        datTitles.UpdateControls
    End If

    datTitles.Recordset.MoveNext
    If datTitles.Recordset.EOF Then datTitles.Recordset.MovePrevious

End Sub
```

3 However, this is no good to us as it's only executed after the **Click** event, i.e. after the button has gone down and up. We need to do things while the button is held down. Select the body of the event code and cut and paste it to the **cmdNext_MouseDown()** event.

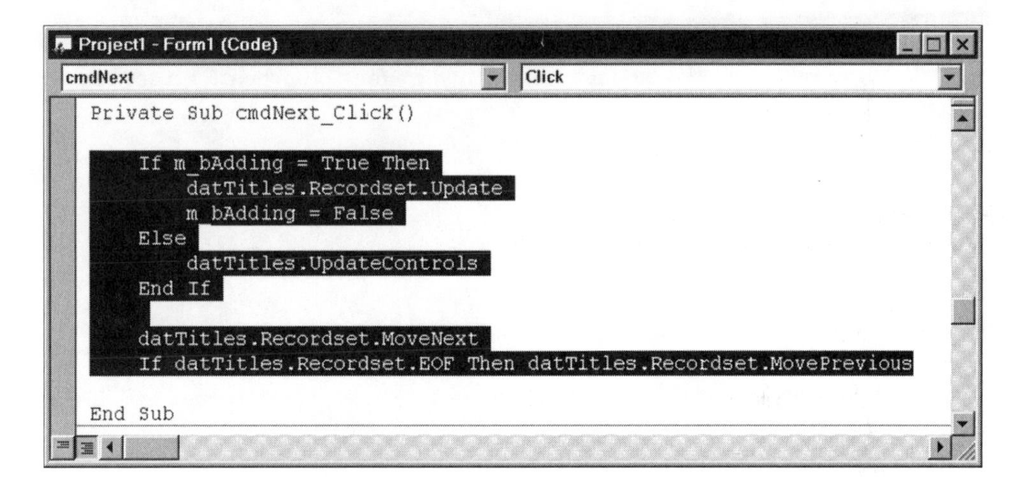

4 Now we need to add some code to the event. The code to add is shaded:

```
Private Sub cmdNext_MouseDown(Button As Integer, Shift As Integer, X As
Single, Y As Single)

    If m_bAdding = True Then
        datTitles.Recordset.Update
        m_bAdding = False
    Else
        datTitles.UpdateControls
    End If

    datTitles.Recordset.MoveNext
    If datTitles.Recordset.EOF Then datTitles.Recordset.MovePrevious
```

```
    m_bKeepMoving = False
    m_bButtonDown = True
    Timer1.Enabled = True

    Do While m_bButtonDown = True
        DoEvents
        If m_bKeepMoving = True Then
            datTitles.Recordset.MoveNext
         If datTitles.Recordset.EOF Then datTitles.Recordset.MovePrevious
        End If
    Loop

    Timer1.Enabled = False

End Sub
```

5 In order to switch the scrolling off when the user stops holding the mouse button down, put this into the **MouseUp** event, which fires off when the user releases the mouse.

```
Private Sub cmdNext_MouseUp(Button As Integer, Shift As Integer, X As
Single, Y As Single)

    m_bButtonDown = False

End Sub
```

6 Now add this code to **Timer** event.

```
Private Sub Timer1_Timer()

    m_bKeepMoving = True

End Sub
```

7 Now we need to declare the two variables as form level, so add these two lines near the top of the general declarations section.

```
Dim m_bKeepMoving As Boolean
Dim m_bButtonDown As Boolean
```

8 Now run it. Hold the button down and wait for a few seconds—you'll then scroll forwards. You can change the waiting period by adjusting the interval on the timer in its properties window.

How It Works

At the heart of the new bit of code is a loop that keeps running as long as the Next button is depressed. We use the Boolean form level variable **m_bButtonDown** to keep track of whether the button is still depressed. This is reset by the **MouseUp** event that occurs as you let the button come up. The question, of course, is how VB executes the **MouseUp** event code while apparently being locked in this loop.

```
Do While m_bButtonDown = True
    DoEvents
    If m_bKeepMoving = True Then
        datTitles.Recordset.MoveNext
     If datTitles.Recordset.EOF Then datTitles.Recordset.MovePrevious
    End If
Loop
```

The answer lies in the **DoEvents** command. We've come across this before. Windows is a multitasking system, which means that more than one program can be executing at one time. They don't actually execute at exactly the same time (as a parallel processing machine would) but Windows swaps between the active jobs quickly to give the appearance of doing several things at once.

To some extent, a Visual Basic program looks like more than one program to Windows, in the sense that you can trigger events while code is still running. The problem is that Visual Basic won't check for those events unless you allow it to take its eye off the job in hand for a second.

That's what **DoEvents** allows Windows to do: see if there is anything else waiting to happen. In our case there are two events we're waiting for: a **MouseUp** event or a **Timer** event. We'll come back to the **Timer** event shortly. Without the **DoEvents** line in here, VB wouldn't check to see if the user had taken their finger off the mouse button, so the loop would run forever. Try it if you like, but be prepared to use *Ctrl-Break* to stop the program.

As for the timer, well that's there to create a delay between the user first pressing the mouse button and the repeat scrolling. It is first enabled in the **MouseDown** event. The timer is set to go off a certain period ahead determined by the value of **Interval**. Up until the timer goes off, another form level variable, **m_bKeepMoving**, is false. Once the **Timer** event triggers, this is set to true:

```
Private Sub Timer1_Timer()

    m_bKeepMoving = True

End Sub
```

This remains true and we keep moving until the **cmdNext_MouseUp** event stops it all. All the timer event does is to create a delay between when you press the button and when you start scrolling. This stops the database racing away at the first press.

```
Private Sub cmdNext_MouseUp(Button As Integer, Shift As Integer, X As
Single, Y As Single)

    m_bButtonDown = False

End Sub
```

The Database to Data Connection

At various points so far we've had to take an interest in how the various actors on the database stage interact to get the job done. In order to get exactly what you want, you have to take the connection between your bound controls, the Jet engine and the underlying database into account. Let's take a look at how they all fit together.

The Validate Event

The most useful event available to monitor the activity of the data control is its **Validate** event. As far as events go, **Validate** is a very flexible tool. Everything that happens to the data control and, more importantly, to the data it provides access to, can be caught, monitored and even canceled through the **Validate** event. In fact, you can even use the **Validate** event to tell the data control to do something totally different to what it was originally hoping to do. Before we start to look at some code, though, you need to know a little more about how bound controls work.

How Bound Controls Work

Database information is held in three places while your program is running:

- The data you see on screen in the bound control is held in a part of memory specifically reserved for this purpose. Once a bound control has pulled data from the database, it stores its own copy of this information somewhere in memory.
- The database itself has a copy buffer in memory. This is where information that has just been read from, or is about to be written back to the database, is held. As you change information in the bound controls, Visual Basic copies the new data from the control to the copy buffer.
- Then, when all the changes have been made, the **Update** method updates the actual database record with information from the copy buffer. The point here is that the database records on disk are only physically changed after this method is invoked.

The **Validate** event is the last stop for everything that affects the data control. Everything you do to the records in a data control triggers the **Validate** event: moving to a new record, moving to the first or last record, writing a record to the database, and so on. You can use the **Action** parameter that's passed to the **Validate** event to find out exactly what is about to happen—the **Validate** event always occurs before something happens, not after. This makes the **Validate** event the ideal place to catch changes to the data and prevent them from happening.

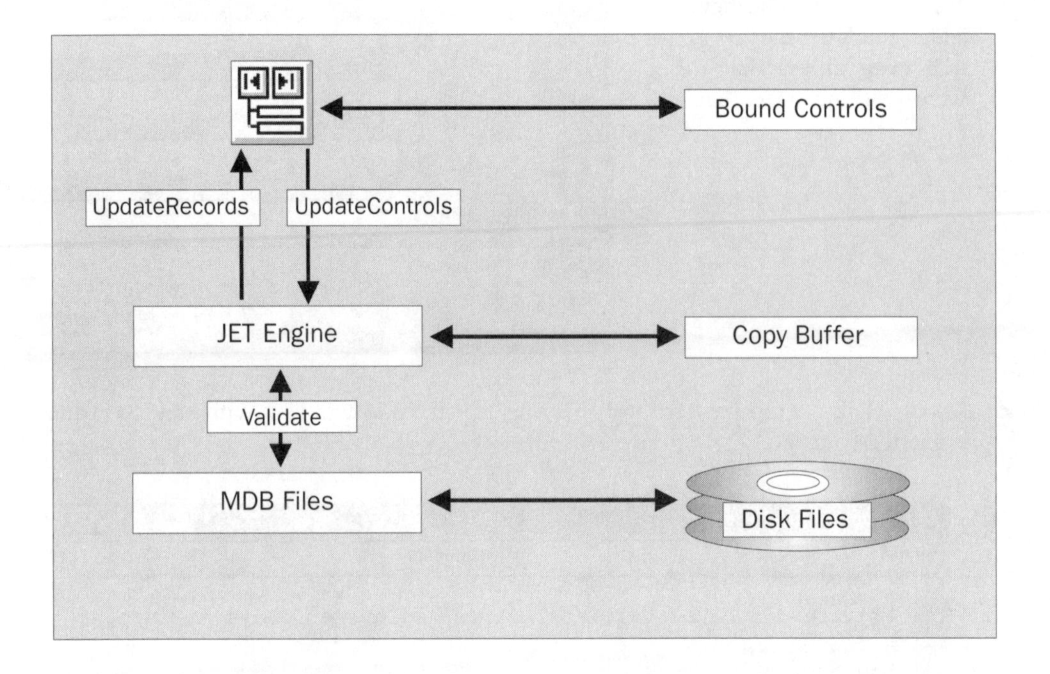

*There is also a **Reposition** event which occurs after a different record is loaded into the data control. We'll discuss this later in the chapter in more detail.*

One of the most common uses of the data control **Validate** event is to catch the times when the data control is about to move information from the copy buffer to the physical database. If you don't want the update to take place, or you only want part of the data to move from the copy buffer to the database, then you can use code in the **Validate** event to handle it.

Using the Validate Event to Prevent Changes to Data

In our last example, we had to write a separate function which handled the checking to see whether or not a record was updated. However, it's much easier to use the **Validate** event. We'll now look at the **Bib_View** project and add some code to the **Validate** event so that updates to the **Titles** table can't take place under any circumstances.

Try It Out - Coding the Validate Event

1 Time to write some new code. Load up the **Bib_View** project that we were working on earlier.

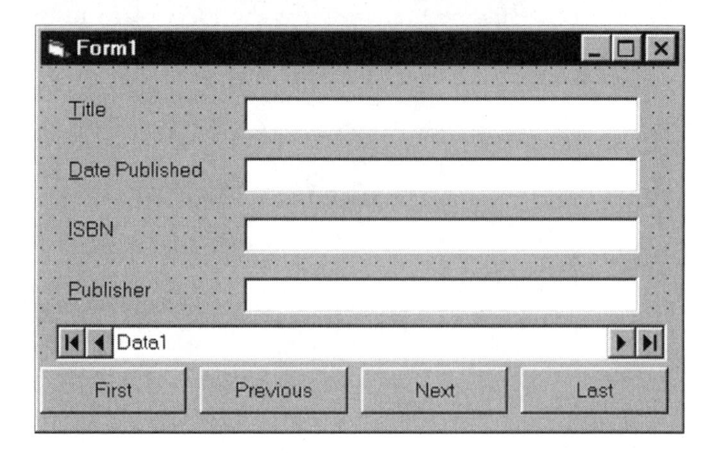

2 Double-click on the data control to bring up its code window with the **Validate** event ready to go.

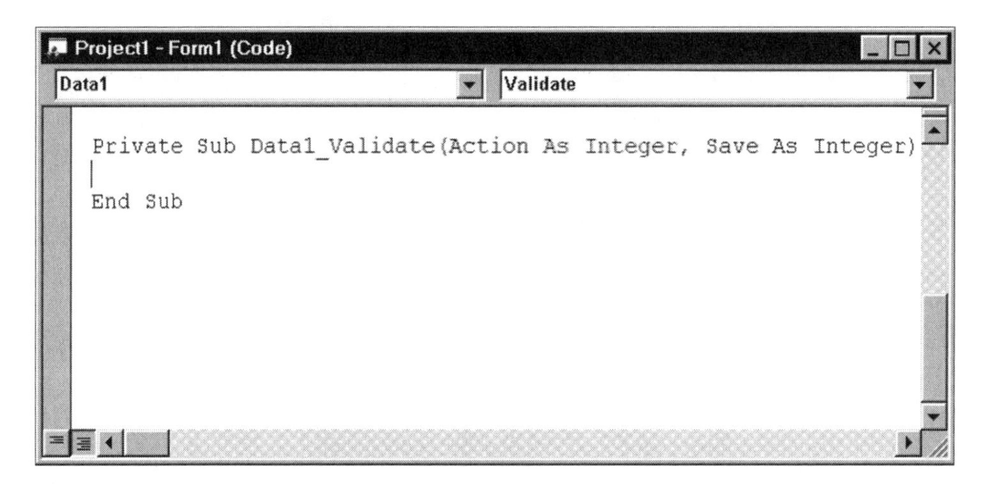

3 Type in code so that the event looks like this:

```
Private Sub Data1_Validate (Action As Integer, Save As Integer)

    If Save = True Then
        MsgBox "You cannot edit data in this database." & Chr$(10) &
         ↳ "Changes have been abandoned"
        Save = False
    End If

End Sub
```

4 Try running the program now and changing the data you see on screen.

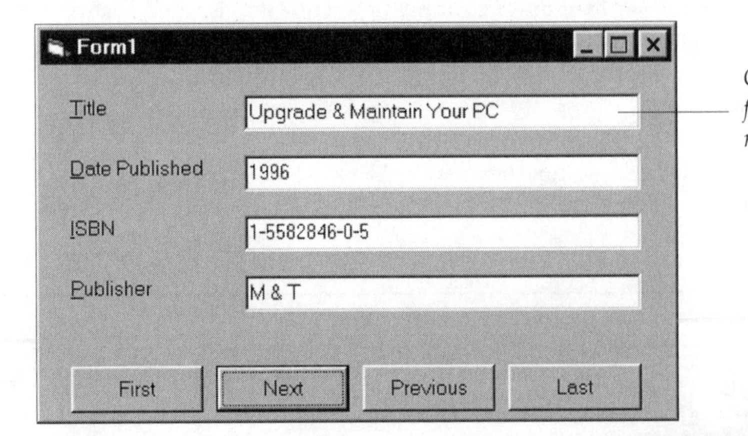

Change one of the fields, then try and move to another record.

5 As soon as you try to move to a different record, a message box appears. If you move back to the record you tried to change, you'll see that it is reset to its previous value.

How It Works

The `Validate` event gets two parameters which we can use at run time to check what's going on.

```
Private Sub Data1_Validate (Action As Integer, Save As Integer)
```

Here, the `Save` parameter is the most important of the two. `Save` is actually a logical value, either true or false.

> *The `Save` parameter is a boolean. In VB3, however, it used to be an integer and, for compatibility, is still declared as integer. Booleans were new with VB4.*

It does nothing to your event code, but has an effect when the event exits. `Save` tells your code whether or not any of the information in the bound controls has been changed since it was loaded in.

- If the `Validate` event finishes and `Save` is set to true, Visual Basic automatically fires off the `UpdateRecord` method to write information from the bound controls to the copy buffer, and then right out to the current record of the database.
- If the `Validate` event finishes and `Save` is set to false, then the changes made to the bound controls on screen are lost forever and aren't copied back into the database table itself.

The **Action** parameter can be used to check exactly what is going to happen when the **Validate** event finishes. The **Validate** event always occurs immediately before something happens, and that something is held in the **Action** parameter.

The Action Parameter

The **Action** parameter is actually a number that tells us what triggered the **Validate** event. Thankfully, you can make use of Visual Basic's intrinsic constants to get a clearer picture:

VB Constant	Action to be Performed
VbDataActionCancel	Cancels any operation that is about to happen.
VbDataActionMoveFirst	Moving to the first record.
VbDataActionMovePrevious	Moving to the previous record.
VbDataActionMoveNext	Moving to the next record.
VbDataActionMoveLast	Moving to the last record.
VbDataActionAddNew	A new record is about to be added.
VbDataActionUpdate	The copy buffer (not the bound control) is about to be written to the database.
VbDataActionDelete	The current record is about to be deleted.
VbDataActionFind	The **Find** method was called to find a record.
VbDataActionBookmark	The **BookMark** property was set.
VbDataActionClose	The data control is about to disconnect from the database.
VbDataActionUnload	The form is about to unload.

You can check the **Action** parameter against any of these values to determine what's about to happen. To stop something from happening, just set the **Action** parameter to **vbDataActionCancel**. For example, to stop the user moving to the next record, you could set **Action** to **vbDataActionCancel** whenever an event occurs with **Action** set to **vbDataActionMoveNext.**

The Save Parameter

Having said all that, you need to be careful with the **Validate** event. Just because you're canceling the current action doesn't mean that you'll cancel any updating of the records that may take place. If the **Save** property is true when the event finishes, the data in the bound controls will be written to the database, regardless of what you did to the **Action** parameter.

To stop any data being written back to the underlying database, set the **Save** parameter to false like we did in the earlier example. Remember—the **Validate** event occurs before anything ugly happens. In fact, it exists for the sole purpose of protecting your data.

There are an untold number of uses for the event, depending on what kind of data you are using. The general principle is to use **Validate** as a final gatekeeper for your database to make sure that users only get to do what you want them to do to your valuable data.

The Update Methods

Visual Basic provides you with three ways of updating information in your tables and on screen. These are known as the **Update** methods.

Update

The first and simplest is **Update** on its own. For example, if you directly code a change to the value of the **PubID** field selected from a data control named **Data1**, you can write this change to the database using the **Update** method.

```
Data1.Recordset.Fields("PubID") = 12
Data1.Recordset.Update
```

Beware though. To use **Update** in code you must first use **Edit**. The **Edit** method tells Visual Basic that you're about to make changes to the fields in a database, then **Update** tells it to actually save those changes.

```
Data1.Recordset.Edit
Data1.Recordset.Fields("PubID") = 12
Data1.Recordset.Fields("Title")  = "Beginning Visual Basic 5"
Data1.Recordset.Update
```

Normally, the data control does all this for you. If you change the values in a bound control, such as a text box, at run time, and then move to a new record, Visual Basic automatically does an **Edit** for you.

UpdateRecord

To do what the data control does yourself could require a lot of code. If you have a form with fifteen bound controls on it, it can take a lot of typing to copy the contents of these controls to the fields one by one and then do an **Update**. The **UpdateRecord** method provides an easy way round this:

```
Data1.UpdateRecord
```

This does the **Edit** for you, copies the bound control contents to the database, and then does an **Update**—all in one swoop.

UpdateControls

The inverse of this is the **UpdateControls** method, which copies the data from the table to the bound controls. For example, if your users change data in the bound controls and then decide they want to cancel the operation, you can use **UpdateControls** to restore the values that were in the controls before the user confused the issue:

```
Data1.UpdateControls
```

To summarize the update methods:

Method	Description
`Update`	Used after an `Edit`, and after you change the fields in the data control with code. `Update` permanently saves the changes you make to the fields in the database.
`UpdateRecord`	Stores the values of the bound controls in the underlying tables.
`UpdateControls`	Copies information from the fields selected with the data control into the bound controls. Great for canceling changes that the user has made and restoring the bound controls to their initial value.

The Limits of the Data Control

To wrap up our extended look at using Visual Basic with databases, I thought it would be useful to explore the limits of the data control. We've accomplished a lot with the much derided data control in this chapter, but there's no getting away from its limitations. Let's face it—from Microsoft's point of view, you have to have a good reason to upgrade to the Pro and Enterprise editions of Visual Basic, and that reason is being able to use Data Access Objects instead of the data control to access databases.

Data Access Objects are, as the name suggests, a way of representing the complete database with all its associated tables, fields and queries as a big collection of objects. We'll be looking at objects in the next chapter, but suffice to say that once you've got the object, you've got the lot. You can pretty much do anything you like with any part of the database. This power comes at the price of complexity (and about three hundred bucks!). The data control is just a window on to the underlying database, and although we can represent it as an object, we're always limited by what the data control, rather than the database, could do given the chance.

For a really good example of where the data control falls down, we just need to look at how it makes information about the structure of the underlying database available to us, both to read information about which fields and tables are present, and then to make changes to that structure. We'll take a look at a simple database browser that lets us see which tables and fields are in the database—but does so by working around the limitations of the data control.

Try It Out - A Database Browser

When you walk into Big Cheese Industrial on your first day as a database developer, you'll probably be presented with a pile of company databases and asked to create some funky windows front-end using Visual Basic. The first thing you'll want to do is check out these databases and get a good idea of what's in them. We're going to create a simple viewer that you can use to do this.

1. Open up a blank form and put a bound grid control on to it (not forgetting to add it from the Project menu). Change the caption to something more interesting like Table Analyzer. Call the grid control **`dbgDisplay`** and the form **`frmSQL`**.

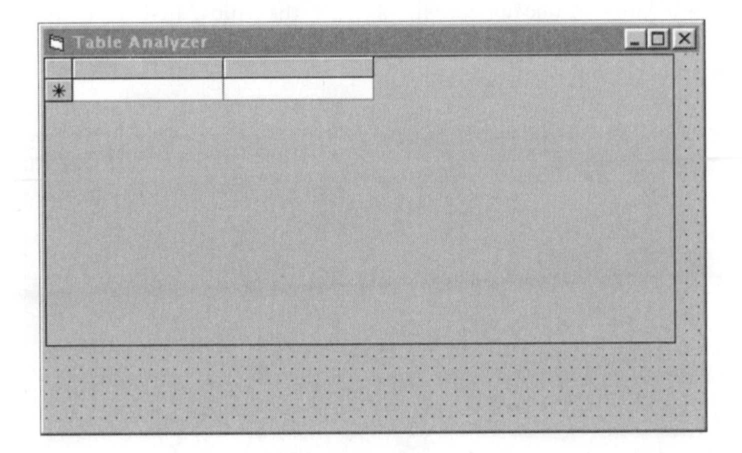

2. Now add a data control to the form to populate this grid. Call it **`datTable`** and set its **`Visible`** property to False—we aren't going to use it for navigation. We'll set the rest of the properties from code. Don't forget to go set the **`DataSource`** property of the grid to **`datTable`**.

3. Place a frame below the grid. This will hold all our controls in the interests of neatness. Erase its **`Caption`** in the properties window and leave the name as **`Frame1`**. We aren't going to be using its name, so it doesn't matter what it's called.

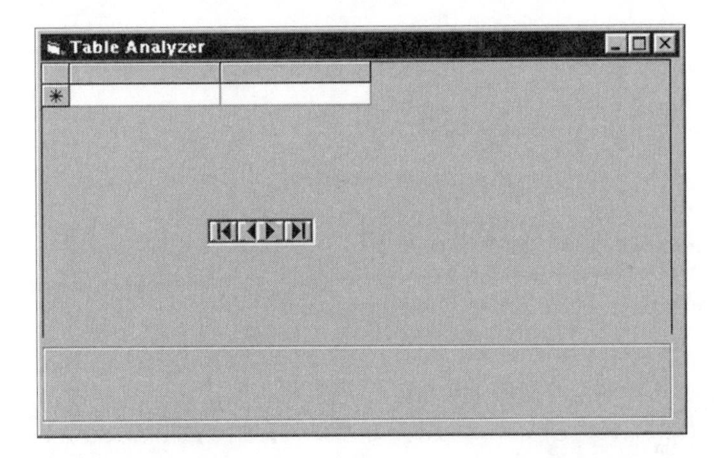

4 Now we want to add some information controls inside the frame.

- First add a text box that we'll use to display the name of the current database. Call it **txtDatabaseName** (we're naming properly boys and girls, so be good) and add a label to it as well.
- Next add two combo boxes, and call them **cmbTables** and **cmbFields** and again, let's have a label to show we can play by the rules. Just keep all the properties for these as the defaults, except make the **Text** property the same as the name, so you can remember what they are called.

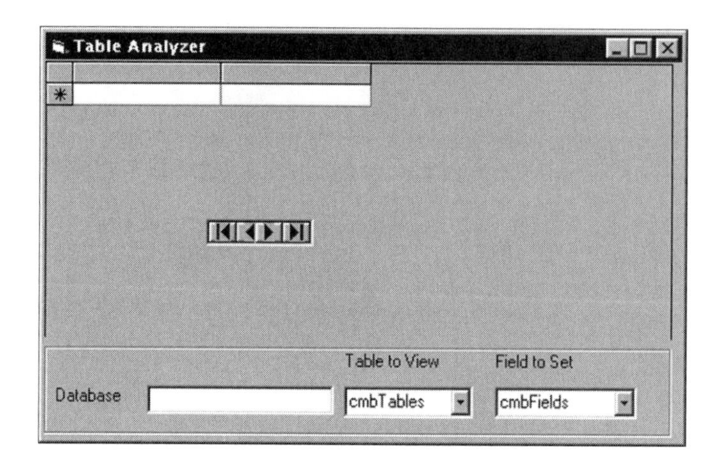

5 Now it's code time kids. First of all, declare the variables in the General Declarations section.

```
Option Explicit

Dim sCurrentDatabase As String
Dim DB As Control
```

6 Then let's sort out the **Form_Load** event

```
Private Sub Form_Load()

Dim objCurrentColumn As Column

frmSQL.Show
DoEvents
Set DB = datTable

With cmbTables
     .AddItem "Titles"
     .AddItem "Publishers"
     .AddItem "Authors"
```

```
End With

cmbTables.Text = "Titles"
cmbFields.Text = "Title"

sCurrentDatabase = App.Path & "\Biblio.MDB"
DB.DatabaseName = (sCurrentDatabase)
DB.RecordsetType = 1
DB.RecordSource = cmbTables.Text

DB.Refresh
DB.UpdateControls

For Each objCurrentColumn In dbgDisplay.Columns
   cmbFields.AddItem objCurrentColumn.DataField
Next

txtDatabaseName = sCurrentDatabase

End Sub
```

7 Now we need to add code to change the grid and the field list in the combo box whenever we change the selected table. Add this to the **Click** event for the combo box.

```
Private Sub cmbTables_Click()

Dim objCurrentColumn As Column

cmbFields.Clear

DB.RecordSource = cmbTables.Text
DB.Refresh

For Each objCurrentColumn In dbgDisplay.Columns
   cmbFields.AddItem objCurrentColumn.DataField
Next

cmbFields.Text = cmbFields.List(0)
cmbFields_Click

End Sub
```

8 Now let's add code to sort the grid based on the field selected.

```
Private Sub cmbFields_Click()

On Error GoTo SortError

   DB.RecordSource = "SELECT " & cmbTables.Text & ".* FROM " &
```

```
cmbTables.Text & " ORDER BY [" & cmbFields.Text & "]"
   DB.Refresh

On Error GoTo 0
Exit Sub

SortError:
    If Err = 3117 Then
        MsgBox "Can't sort on a memo field"
       cmbFields.ListIndex = cmbFields.ListIndex + 1

       Resume
       End If

End Sub
```

9 The last thing to do is make sure that you've got **Biblio.MDB** in the same path as the program, then run it. Up comes the form.

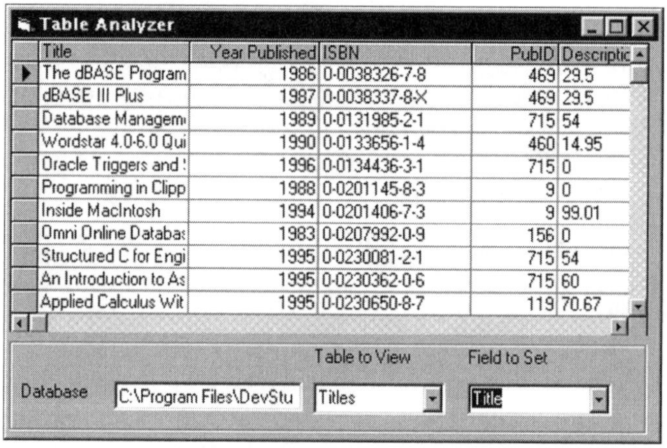

Table Analyzer

	Title	Year Published	ISBN	PubID	Descriptic
▶	The dBASE Program	1986	0-0038326-7-8	469	29.5
	dBASE III Plus	1987	0-0038337-8-X	469	29.5
	Database Managem	1989	0-0131985-2-1	715	54
	Wordstar 4.0-6.0 Qui	1990	0-0133656-1-4	460	14.95
	Oracle Triggers and !	1996	0-0134436-3-1	715	0
	Programming in Clipp	1988	0-0201145-8-3	9	0
	Inside MacIntosh	1994	0-0201406-7-3	9	99.01
	Omni Online Databa:	1983	0-0207992-0-9	156	0
	Structured C for Engi	1995	0-0230081-2-1	715	54
	An Introduction to As	1995	0-0230362-0-6	715	60
	Applied Calculus Wit	1995	0-0230650-8-7	119	70.67

Table to View   Field to Set

Database C:\Program Files\DevStu   Titles   Title

10 Click on the Table combo box and the new table is loaded into the grid, and at the same time the Fields combo box is filled with the field names from that Table.

Make sure that you save your finished program into the same folder as the **Biblio** *database before you run it, so that* **App.Path** *returns the right path to the database.*

How It Works

As you probably noticed, there's a bit of jumping through hoops going on here. The core of the problem is that all the interesting properties of the data control, like the **RecordSource** and **DatabaseName** properties, can't be read at run time. Therefore, it's impossible to find out what the name of the current database is, and which tables are available in it. This makes our database browser somewhat hard to implement.

I've dealt with the problem in two ways.

- For the table names, I've just hardcoded the names into the program. There is just no way around this with the Standard Edition of Visual Basic. The code that does it is in the **`Form-Load`** event.

```
With cmbTables
    .AddItem "Titles"
    .AddItem "Publishers"
    .AddItem "Authors"
End With

cmbTables.Text = "Titles"
```

  This makes the browser useless in the sense that you have to rewrite the code for each database. Ugly.

- The way around not being able to read the field names from anywhere is to use the data bound grid to do the work for you. The grid automatically binds to each field in the specified table, and assigns the field names to its **`Column.DataField`** properties. By cycling through the columns collection of the grid we can pick up all these names and put them into the list box.

```
For Each objCurrentColumn In dbgDisplay.Columns
   cmbFields.AddItem objCurrentColumn.DataField
Next

cmbFields.TEXT = cmbFields.List(0)
```

We've used some tricky code here, and dived into object variables which we cover in the next chapter. However, the way the code is written makes it easy to see what's happening. We go through each of the column objects in the collections of columns that belong to the grid, and place its data field into the Fields combo box. At the end, we set the selected field to the first one in the list.

Changing the entry in the Fields list box causes the grid to be re-sorted on the selected field. The only snag is that you can't sort on memo fields in Jet, since they're designed to hold free-form information. So we intercept the resulting error and move on the next field.

```
Private Sub cmbFields_Click()

On Error GoTo SortError

    DB.RecordSource = "SELECT " & cmbTables.Text & ".* FROM " &
        ↳cmbTables.Text & " ORDER BY [" & cmbFields.Text & "]"
    DB.Refresh

On Error GoTo 0
Exit Sub
```

```
SortError:
    If Err = 3117 Then
        MsgBox "Can't sort on a memo field"
       cmbFields.ListIndex = cmbFields.ListIndex + 1

       Resume
       End If
End Sub
```

The only other interesting part of the code is that we chose to use the **Click** event for each of the combo boxes. Intuitively, you would expect to use the **Change** event to do something when a new item from the list is selected. However, the combo box **Change** event is only activated when you add or delete an item from the list. The **Click** event traps the new selection.

So, by going via the grid, we've at least found a way round the lack of listing fields when using the data control. You could add the grid to the projects where you need a field list and make it invisible, keeping the field name list available for your code. However, the bound grid is a heavy control that uses a lot of memory and resources. I'm afraid the real answer is an upgrade to the Pro Edition if you're serious about database work.

Summary

We've covered a lot of ground in this chapter. We've seen how powerful the data control is and yet how simple most of its actions are. You have learnt:

- What kind of recordsets you can create
- How to use SQL statements to filter and sort your recordset
- How to program the data control using its methods
- How to use the data bound controls supplied with Visual Basic
- How to add and delete records in a database
- How the data buffers fit together
- How to control what happens to the underlying database
- The limits of the data control

Why Not Try...

1. Modify the project from Exercise 12-2. Make the data control "invisible" and replace its functionality with command buttons.

2. Enhance the above project by creating a Find button. When clicked, this button should provide a way for the user to find a particular **`Cust_ID`**.

3. Continue to enhance the project by providing Add , Delete, and Cancel buttons.

4. Satisfy yourself that you understand how and when user actions trigger the data control's **`Validate`** event. Place code in the **`Validate`** event that displays a message box for every action that the user can take which triggers an event.

5. Modify the project from Exercise 12-4 by providing a list box that displays customer id's. When the user makes a selection, display only matching records in the database grid.

asic Visual Basic Visual Ba
al Basic Visual Basic Visual
Basic Visual Basic Visual Ba
al Basic Vi
Basic Visu
ual Basic V
l Basic Vis
isual Basic Visual Basic
l Basic Visual Basic Visua
Visual Basic Visual Basic Visu
l Basic Visual Ba
l Basic Visual
ic Visual Basi
Basic Visual B
ic Visual Basi
l Basic Visual
ual Basic Visual Basic Visual Ba
Visual Basic Visual Basic Visu
sual Basic Visual Basic Visu
Visual Basic Visual Ba

Object Variables

Almost all the objects you've come across so far that make up the components of Visual Basic, such as controls and forms, can themselves be used as object variables. This means you can write code that manipulates objects as well as data and, therefore, change the appearance and operation of your program as easily as changing a variable value.

It also allows you to write generic pieces of code that accept objects as parameters in the same way they would accept regular variables. This makes for powerful programs.

In this chapter, you'll learn:

- How to manipulate controls as you do variables
- What kind of object variables are available
- How you create arrays of objects
- What an MDI application is
- How to work with multiple forms in your applications

Visual Basic and Objects

Really, everything you deal with in Visual Basic is an object. A form is an object, the screen is an object, there are even invisible objects such as the printer and application objects. We've already seen a little object theory when we covered class modules back in Chapter 7. What we've previously covered are objects from an object developer's point of view. In this chapter, we're going to look at objects from an object user's standpoint.

An object is like a 'black box' that contains code that someone else has written. You can use this object in your own applications. The good thing is that you don't have to know what's going on inside the box to be able to use it—you just set the properties of the control and use its methods to make things happen. It's useful to think of these objects as building blocks to construct your program. Programming Visual Basic is a process of choosing the right combination of these objects (forms, controls, etc.) and linking them together with code and your own object templates (classes) to make a project.

So far, when we have written code, we've generally just referred to controls and forms by the names we gave them at design time. This is fine for simple programs, but it limits what you can do. You've seen how being able to refer to your data indirectly through variables makes your programs more flexible and adaptable. The same applies for objects. You can put an object (such as a form or a control) inside a variable and refer to it by the name of the variable rather than the object. This approach allows you to use one piece of code for a number of different instances of a certain object type.

In this chapter we're going to look at how to create arrays of objects, how to copy objects into variables, and how to pass objects as parameters to subroutines and functions. We're also going to take a look at something Visual Basic calls **collections**, which are basically special arrays of objects.

Introducing Object Variables

Visual Basic lets you take control of objects in your code through special variables known as **object variables**. Using these you can:

- Create new controls at run time
- Copy controls to produce new **instances** of existing ones
- Create duplicate forms, all with identical names, controls and code, but each containing and dealing with different data—much like the different documents you might have loaded in a Word session or multiple worksheets within an Excel Workbook

Object variables provide a way to write general routines that deal with specific controls. For example, you may have a text box validation routine that can only be used if you explicitly specify the name of the control in the code. However, if you want to make the routine independent so that it can be used with any control, you can treat the control as an object variable. This makes your code much more transportable and, ultimately, more useful.

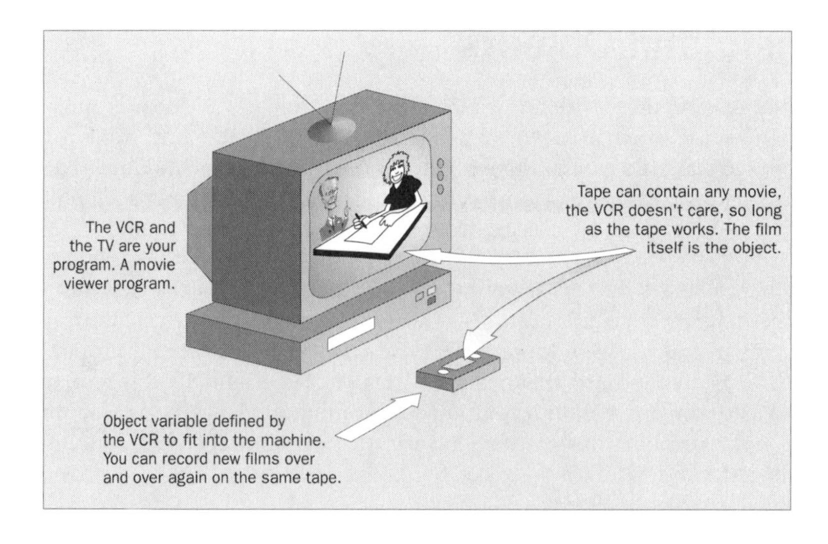
The VCR and
the TV are your
program. A movie
viewer program.
Tape can contain any movie,
the VCR doesn't care, so long
as the tape works. The film
itself is the object.
Object variable defined by
the VCR to fit into the machine.
You can record new films over
and over again on the same tape.

This isn't really as scary as it sounds. Think back to class modules for a moment. Remember how we can **Dim** a variable as the name of a class module to bring it to life.

```
Dim NewEmployee As New cEmployee
```

Here, we've just created a new instance (object) of our class **cEmployee** and assigned it to the variable **NewEmployee**. That's the essence of object variables.

Controls as Object Variables

In the Menus chapter (Chapter 9), one of the things we did was create a dynamic menu—a menu where the number of items grew each time we selected a file name. Menu items are controls, just like text boxes, command buttons, and so on. What we were actually doing was creating dynamic controls, i.e. controls that only exist at run time, not at design time. The more files we opened, the bigger the array of objects became in the menu list. We were, in effect, creating instances of objects in the same way that we do with variables.

The ability to create controls dynamically can be extremely useful for applications where you need to create a great many controls of a similar type—for example, for a toolbar—but don't want the hassle of drawing them all by hand. Using object variables, you can even let your users create their own custom toolbars.

Creating Controls at Run Time

The principles of creating controls on the fly are easy to follow. The simplest method is to create a control array at design time, then extend that array with code at run time. If you set the **Index** property of the first control to 0 at design time, you can add additional controls (of the same type) as needed at run time. Controls created at run time share the same name, type, and event procedures as the control they are created from.

In the same way that you can alter the size of a normal variable array, you can extend and shrink control arrays. The difference is that you don't **Redim** a control array like you do a variable array. Instead, you have to **Load** new instances of the controls into the array. When you want to remove controls, you **Unload** them.

Try It Out - Creating Controls at Run Time

Let's put this into practice by creating a row of command buttons on a form. We'll just draw one command button at design time and create the rest through code.

1 Start a new project and draw a small command button on the form.

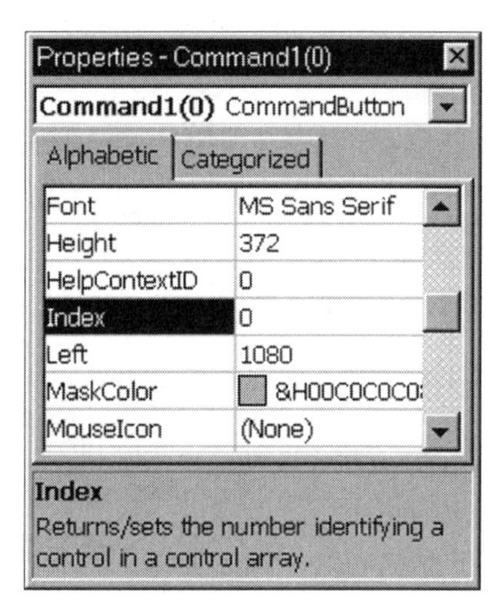

2 When you have created the command button, place 0 into its **`Index`** property. This creates a control array with just one control in it.

3 Type the following code into the **`Click`** event for the command button:

```
Private Sub Command1_Click (Index As Integer)

   Static sNextOperation As String
   Dim nIndex As Integer

   For nIndex = 1 To 5

     If sNextOperation = "UNLOAD" Then
       Unload Command1(nIndex)
     Else
       Load Command1(nIndex)
       With Command1(nIndex)
           .Top = Command1(nIndex - 1).Top + Command1(nIndex - 1).Height
           .Caption = nIndex
```

```
        .Visible = True
      End With
    End If

  Next

  If sNextOperation = "UNLOAD" Then
    sNextOperation = "LOAD"
  Else
    sNextOperation = "UNLOAD"
  End If

End Sub
```

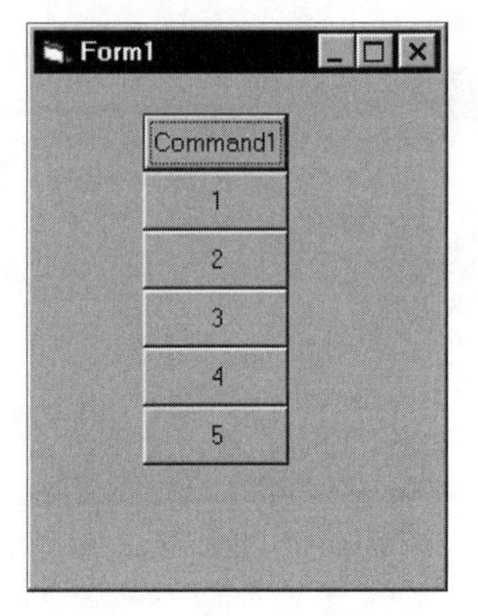

4 Run the code and click on the command button several times. Each time you click, five new buttons are either created or deleted.

5 Save the code on your hard disk and call it **NewCtrl.vbp**—we'll be coming back to it a little later in the chapter.

How It Works

The most important part of this code is the **For...Next** loop which actually creates or deletes the new command buttons, depending on the contents of the **sNextOperation** variable.

```
For nIndex = 1 To 5

    If sNextOperation = "UNLOAD" Then
      Unload Command1(nIndex)
    Else
      Load Command1(nIndex)
      With Command1(nIndex)
        .Top = Command1(nIndex - 1).Top + Command1(nIndex - 1).Height
        .Caption = nIndex
        .Visible = True
      End With
```

```
        End If

    Next
```

First, the contents of the variable **sNextOperation** are checked to see whether we need to **Unload** or **Load** elements. The first time you press the command button, **sNextOperation** isn't set, and so it defaults to the **Else**, or **LOAD**, portion of the code. The array is then extended using **Load**. This takes the name of the initial command button as an argument, followed by the new index number in brackets. In our case, the index variable is **nIndex**, which is used for the loop counter:

```
        Load Command1(nIndex)
```

*Note that here we've called our index **nIndex**. You can call it whatever you like*

The **Top** property is set to position the new button directly below the previous one. Once each new button has been created, its **Visible** property is set to true to make the button appear:

```
            With Command1(nIndex)
                .Top = Command1(nIndex - 1).Top + Command1(nIndex - 1).Height
                .Caption = nIndex
                .Visible = True
            End With
```

By default, new controls created at run time appear in exactly the same position as the original control, and are invisible. Since they're invisible at the start, you can position and resize them without the user seeing what's happening. It also stops Windows from having to redraw a load of controls, which will not only slow your program but make the display appear quite disordered while you're moving them about. We only make the control visible after we have moved it and set the caption.

The last instruction in the loop puts a caption on the new command button showing its index number:

```
    .Caption = nIndex
```

Once the loop has run five times and created the complete array, the **sNextOperation** variable is set to the opposite action. The first time round this means setting it to **UNLOAD**, so that the next time you press a command button, the array is unloaded.

```
    If sNextOperation = "UNLOAD" Then
        sNextOperation = "LOAD"
      Else
        sNextOperation = "UNLOAD"
    End If
```

Control Array Events

The problem with the **Command1** control array that we just created is that, no matter which button you press, the same thing happens. We now have 6 controls in our array—the original and 5 copies. Each has its own properties, such as **.Caption**, that can be set individually. However, each of our 6 controls share the same events. For example, when any of our 6 buttons are clicked, the same click event is triggered. From an event point of view, it appears that the control array is behaving as one big control. Of course, control arrays would be of limited value if this was the end of the story. It isn't, though. Your code can tell which button in the control array was pressed, allowing you to respond in different ways for different buttons.

The key lies in the declaration for the **Click** event:

```
Private Sub Command1_Click (Index As Integer)
```

The parameter for the **Click** event on a control array is the index of the control that was clicked. Notice that Visual Basic automatically added the **Index** parameter for us when we created the control array by setting the index property to 0. VB now knows you wish to create a control array.

We've already come across the index—we set it to 0 at design time to create the original control array. We then referred to the individual command buttons using their position in the control array:

```
With Command1(nIndex)
```

The index of a control array works just as it does in a regular array, and again begins with zero for the first element.

Armed with this knowledge, we can now rewrite the **Command1_Click** event and make it more useful.

Try It Out - Handling Events for Control Array Members

1 Load up the **NewCtrl.vbp** project that we just created and bring up the command button **Click** event.

2 Add the highlighted code to the event handler.

```
Private Sub Command1_Click(Index As Integer)

  Static sNextOperation As String
  Dim nIndex As Integer

  Select Case Index
    Case 0
       For nIndex = 1 To 5
```

```
            If sNextOperation = "UNLOAD" Then
               Unload Command1(nIndex)
            Else
               Load Command1(nIndex)
               With Command1(nIndex)
                  .Top = Command1(nIndex - 1).Top + Command1(nIndex - 1).Height
                  .Caption = nIndex
                  .Visible = True
               End With
            End If

         Next

            If sNextOperation = "UNLOAD" Then
               sNextOperation = "LOAD"
            Else
               sNextOperation = "UNLOAD"
            End If
      Case 1, 2, 3, 4, 5
          MsgBox "You pressed Button " & Index
      End Select

   End Sub
```

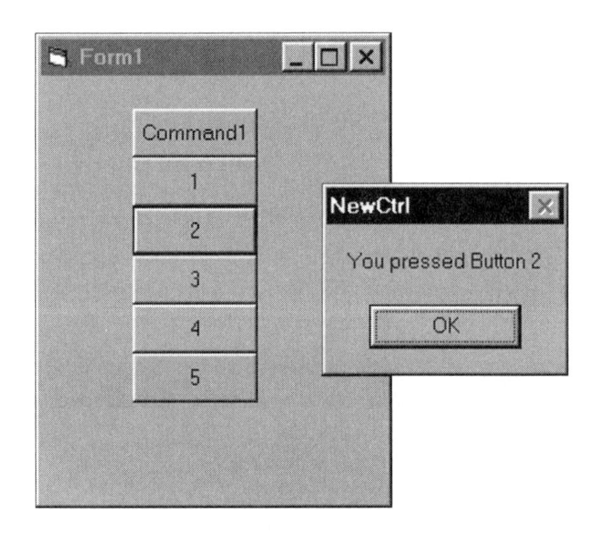

3 Now run the program. If you press the first command button, the rest are created. If you click a newly created copy, a message box pops up telling you which button you clicked.

*Note that you can use the **`Unload`** statement to remove any control in the array created with the **`Load`** command. However, you can't **`Unload`** any controls created at design time, regardless of whether or not they are part of a control array. This will cause VB to generate an error.*

How It Works

This is really simple. All we did was to add a **Select Case** statement that looks at the value of the index number that was passed to the **Click** event handler. The index tells us which key was pressed. All the buttons, except the original one, are put into a handler that pops up the message box. **Select Case** is so handy it seems like it was just made for control arrays, believe me.

When you think about it, really, it's obvious that the elements in a control array 'inherit' common event procedures. You can't create new code at run time as you create new controls, so if they didn't inherit event procedures, you would end up with objects that don't have any events. Each new member of the control array uses the same event code as the founder member.

Managing Controls as Object Variables

Not only can you use objects as variables in control arrays, you can also pass both object variables and object arrays to procedures as parameters to subroutines. You may wonder why such an arcane sounding activity could be useful, but in fact you'll see that it's a really powerful and useful feature of Visual Basic.

Picture the scene: you have a form with thirty text boxes on it, each requiring a specific type of validation. Some must only accept numeric information, others only alphabetic information. Still others must be able to accept both, but also need to check that a certain number of characters is not exceeded.

Normally, this would mean three separate routines, one for each eventuality. There would be a line of code in each control's **KeyPress** event to pass the contents of the text box to a subroutine for checking. The subroutine, after performing the validation, would then need to pass the information back to the **KeyPress** event. If the keystroke passed the validation routine it would then need to be written into the **Text** property of the control. This can soon add up to a lot of code. The solution is to treat each text box as an object in itself, and pass it to a central, generalized procedure. The easiest way to understand this is to see it action.

A Text Box Validation Routine

Wouldn't it be great to have just one routine that you could call to do all your text box validation? Such a routine would automatically know what kind of data each text box needed and what the maximum length the data should be. It could then automatically abandon key presses that break the rules. Object variables mean that all this is possible, and with surprisingly little code.

Try It Out - Text Box Validation

1 OK, time to write a little code to deal with this whole thing. Create a new project and drop some controls on to the form so that it looks something like this.

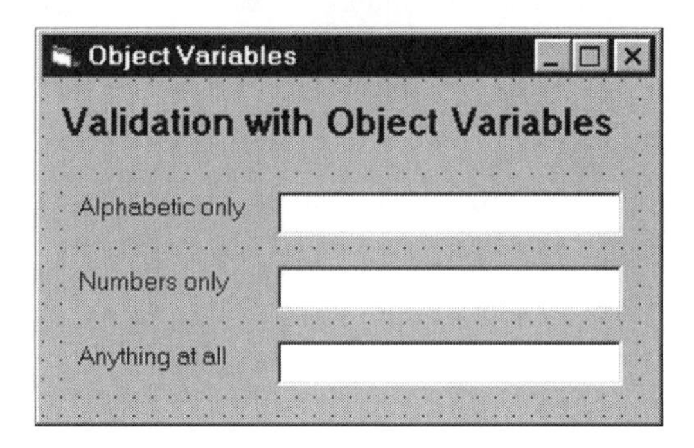

2 Set up the properties of the text boxes to these values:

Description	Property	Value
Alphabetic only text box	`Tag`	A12
	`Name`	`TxtValidate`
	`Index`	0
Numbers only text box	`Tag`	N5
	`Name`	`TxtValidate`
	`Index`	1
Anything text box	`Tag`	*4
	`Name`	`TxtValidate`
	`Index`	2

You must ensure that the letters in the Tag entry in the properties dialog are in upper case, otherwise the example won't work.

3 Now all that remains is to actually enter the code to make the application work—and then we can start exploring. Open the code window and enter the following subroutines:

```
Option Explicit

Private Sub ValidateKeyPress(txtControl As TextBox, nKeyAscii As Integer)

    Dim sMaxLength As String
    Dim sKey As String * 1

    If nKeyAscii < 32 Or nKeyAscii > 126 Then Exit Sub
```

```
    sMaxLength = Right$(txtControl.Tag, Len(txtControl.Tag) - 1)

    If Len(txtControl.Text) > Val(sMaxLength) Then
        Beep
        nKeyAscii = 0
        Exit Sub
    End If

    Select Case Left$ (txtControl.Tag, 1)

        Case "A"
            sKey = UCase(Chr$(nKeyAscii))

            If Asc(sKey) < 65 Or Asc(sKey) > 90 Then
                Beep
                nKeyAscii = 0
                Exit Sub
            End If

        Case "N"
            If nKeyAscii < 48 Or nKeyAscii > 57 Then
                Beep
                nKeyAscii = 0
                Exit Sub
            End If

    End Select

End Sub

Private Sub txtValidate_KeyPress(Index As Integer, KeyAscii As Integer)
    ValidateKeyPress txtValidate(Index), KeyAscii
End Sub
```

4 Once you've added the code, run the program. Three text boxes appear on screen, one accepting only alphabetic characters, the second accepting only numbers and the third taking 4 characters of anything that's thrown at it. Try typing some things in.

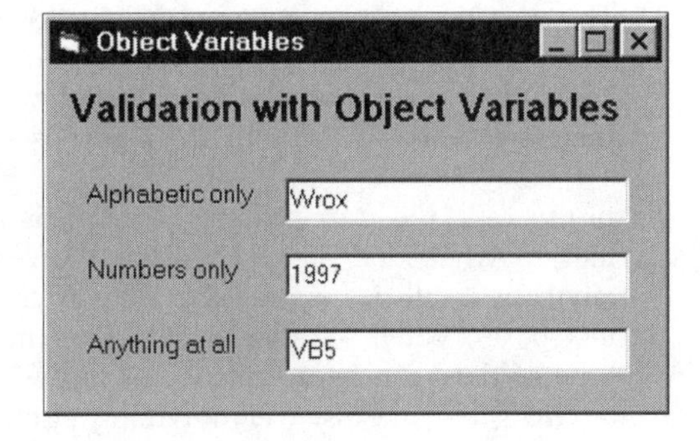

How It Works - Calling the Routine

The main part of this program is deceptively simple. Since all the validation code is held in a routine to which the text box is passed as an **object variable**, only one line of code is needed to handle the validation for all three text boxes.

The routine is called in the normal way with parameters. However, instead of passing a value or variable name as the parameter, you pass a text box control, identified by its index number, and with it, the code of the key that was pressed.

```
ValidateKeyPress txtValidate(Index), KeyAscii
```

How It Works - The ValidateKeyPress Procedure

ValidateKeyPress is a form-level procedure and will be in the (General) section of the code window.

The first line of the subroutine accepts the parameters from the calling statement. Here **txtControl** is our object variable, and we've assigned the key press code to **nKeyAscii.**

```
Private Sub ValidateKeyPress (txtControl As TextBox, nKeyAscii As
Integer)
```

txtControl is declared in the same way as any other variable, except that it's declared as a **TextBox** object. We'll cover exactly how to give these kind of objects their proper names later in the chapter.

The second parameter is the **KeyAscii** parameter given to you by Visual Basic in the **KeyPress** event. Since I've left out the **ByVal** keyword here, the parameter is passed by reference. Setting the value of **KeyAscii** to 0 at any point in the code, which we will do, means that the original **KeyAscii** variable will be reset to 0. In a **KeyPress** event, this has the effect of canceling the key pressed.

> *Passing by reference means that the **KeyAscii** variable that we are dealing with in this procedure is the actual one that the system looks at, as opposed to a copy. If you change its value in the called procedure, it will remain changed when you use it elsewhere. Visual Basic defaults to passing by **ByRef**. We'll cover this in more detail in the next chapter.*

The way the routine determines how to edit the contents of the textbox is by looking at its **Tag** property. This property permits you to store extra data needed for your control. You can assign any value you wish to the **Tag** property and it will be held as a string. You can, therefore, adapt it for your own purposes.

In our case, the **Tag** property is used as a general purpose private label on the controls. It tells us what kind of data will be allowed in each text box. It doesn't actually control anything itself—it's just a label. If you check back at the **Tag** properties we defined for the text boxes, you'll see they're all set up in a similar way. The first character defines what type of data can be accepted—'A' means alphabetic data only, 'N' means numeric, and anything else means, well, anything else! The numbers that follow it determine the maximum characters the text box can accept. We are simply using the **Tag** property to hold the validation rules for each text box.

You can easily change the format of the data that a text box accepts—just bring up the properties window and change the **Tag** property.

The **ValidateKeyPress** code uses the **nKeyAscii** parameter to inform us of the key stroke and the **Tag** property of the **txtControl** text box object variable for validation instructions. Since **nKeyAscii** is passed **ByRef**, any changes to it will change the **KeyAscii** in the calling text box **KeyPress** event.

The first stage of the program checks **nKeyAscii** for special keys (such as *BkSp* or the arrow keys). If one of them was pressed, then that key is not checked and is allowed to pass:

```
If nKeyAscii < 32 or nKeyAscii > 126 Then Exit Sub
```

After this line, the code is certain that it's got a key press which needs to be checked.

The next line places the numbers from the back end of the **Tag** property into the variable **sMaxLength**. This is done using the **Right** function to return all but the first character in the **Tag** property:

```
sMaxLength = Right$(txtControl.Tag, Len(txtControl.Tag) - 1)
```

Once we've determined the maximum length allowed in the text box, a check is made to see if we've exceeded this limit.

```
If Len(txtControl.Text) > Val(sMaxLength) Then
    Beep
    nKeyAscii = 0
    Exit Sub
End If
```

If we are over the limit, then the **nKeyAscii** value is set to 0. Since this parameter is passed to the procedure by reference, the 0 is automatically fed back into **KeyAscii** in the **KeyPress** event. This, effectively, cancels the key press.

The remaining code uses the **Chr$** and **Asc** functions to check whether the keys pressed are valid for the text box, basing the check on the **Tag** property. The **Chr$** function converts the numeric **nKeyAscii** character code into a string containing the appropriate character. The **Asc** function does the reverse and returns the numeric ASCII code of a given character.

```
Select Case Left$(txtControl.Tag, 1)

    Case "A"
        sKey = UCase(Chr$(nKeyAscii))

        If Asc(sKey) < 65 Or Asc(sKey) > 90 Then
            Beep
            nKeyAscii = 0
            Exit Sub
        End If

    Case "N"
```

```
            If nKeyAscii < 48 Or nKeyAscii > 57 Then
                Beep
                nKeyAscii = 0
                Exit Sub
            End If

    End Select
```

For example, if the `Tag` property is set to `N5`, indicating that you can only enter numbers (and only a 5 digit number), then the `Select Case` statement will reject alphabetic or punctuation keys.

*If you use the routine in your own code, bear in mind that it's supposed to be called from a **KeyPress** event, so each key is checked as it's typed. However, this approach isn't foolproof—the user can paste text in to your text box and avoid all the rule processing.*

Declaring Object Variables

You declare an object variable **explicitly** in the same way that you would a regular variable, by stating the type of control it is. For example, to declare an object variable as a `TextBox` (one of the explicit object variable types that Visual Basic recognizes), you write:

```
Dim txtControl As TextBox
```

Your code is more efficient, easier to debug, and will run faster if you declare object variables explicitly. However, Visual Basic will also let you declare an object variable **implicitly**, by simply saying that a variable name relates to a `Control`. For example:

```
Dim ctlControl As Control
```

Function and subroutine parameters can be declared in this way. This enables you to pass any control you like to them at run time. Visual Basic provides a special clause for the `If...Then` statement which allows you to check the type of control an object variable relates to. This is the `TypeOf` statement. We'll take a look at this in more detail in just a moment.

Types of Object Variables

`TextBox` is just one of the explicit object variable types that Visual Basic recognizes. The full list is as follows:

```
CheckBox        ComboBox       CommandButton    MDIForm
Data            DirListBox     DriveListBox     FileListBox
Grid            Frame          HScrollBar       Image
Label           Line           ListBox          Menu
OptionButton    OLE            PictureBox       Shape
TextBox         Timer          VScrollBar       Form
```

These are the standard objects. If you add more controls, then they too can be used as object variables. You may recognize the above as the names that Visual Basic places next to the names that you give your controls in the combo box at the top of the properties window:

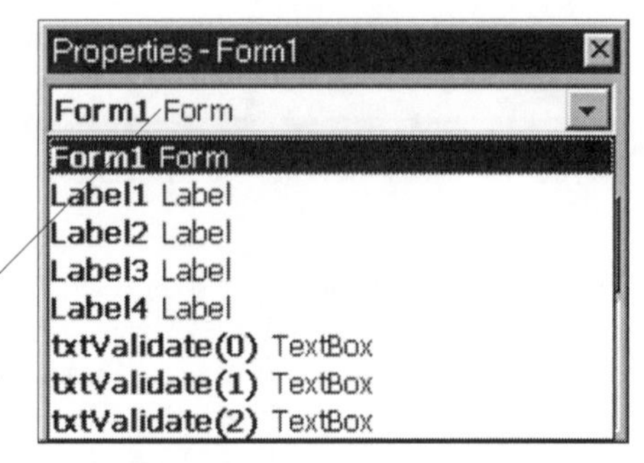

This is the explicit variable type name.

Explicit vs. Implicit Declaration

Although implicit declaration is easier and gives greater flexibility, it does have distinct drawbacks:

- Your code is harder to understand
- Visual Basic has less chance of trapping errors
- It's a lot slower

Your code is harder to understand because you tell future readers of your code less about what's going on. Picture the situation where you have a function that validates data. If you simply declare the object parameter at the head of the function as a **`Control`**, it can be very confusing. The reader can't tell whether you are validating records in a data control, in text boxes, in combo boxes or in the latest hi-tech widget from Visual Basic Add-ons Inc.

Declaring variables explicitly also makes debugging easier. If you declare an object as a specific type, such as a **`TextBox`**, Visual Basic automatically knows which properties are valid for that **`TextBox`**.

For example, if you declare the object variable **`ctlControl`** implicitly as a generic **`Control`**, rather than as a **`TextBox`**, then Visual Basic will allow you to enter the following line of code:

```
ctlControl.Peter = "Some Text"
```

Visual Basic won't spot the error until your program runs; until that time all Visual Basic knows is that you have an object which is some kind of control. It could be any kind of control, however VB has no idea of the properties and methods attached to it until run time. The line may be in a function or a piece of code that you missed in testing, and there's nothing more embarrassing than having a user call to tell you that that the run-time Visual Basic DLL is reporting syntax errors.

> *Visual Basic only checks the properties of a generic* **`Control`** *object at run time, whereas with explicit controls, it reports property errors at compile time.*

As for the difference in speed, the best way to appreciate it is to try it.

Try It Out - Comparing Implicit and Explicit Declarations

1 Time to start on a new project. Add a form as usual and drop some controls on to the form so that it looks like the one shown here. Note that the control to the right of the Time Taken label is itself a label with the **Caption** deleted and the **BorderStyle** property set to 1-Fixed Single.

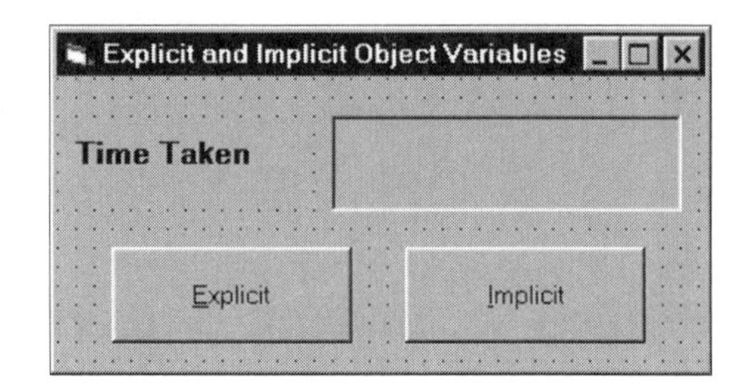

2 Name the blank label control **lblTime**, and the command buttons **cmdExplicit** and **cmdImplicit**.

3 OK—all we need now is the code. Bring up the code window for the form and type in the following procedures. The first two are event handlers, the first being for the Explicit command button:

```
Private Sub cmdExplicit_Click()

    Dim varTime As Variant
    Dim nIndex As Integer

    varTime = Now

    For nIndex = 1 To 15000

        Time_Explicit cmdExplicit, nIndex

    Next

    cmdExplicit.Caption = "&Explicit"

    lblTime.Caption = Minute(Now - varTime) & " Mins, " & Second(Now -
        ↳ varTime) & " Secs"

End Sub
```

The second being for the Implicit command button:

```
Private Sub cmdImplicit_Click()

    Dim varTime As Variant
    Dim nIndex As Integer
```

```
    varTime = Now

    For nIndex = 1 To 15000

        Time_Implicit cmdImplicit, nIndex

    Next

    cmdImplicit.Caption = "&Implicit"

    lblTime.Caption = Minute(Now - varTime) & " Mins, " & Second(Now -
        ↳ varTime) & " Secs"

End Sub
```

The second two are subprocedures that you need to type in the (General) section of the code window.

```
Private Sub Time_Explicit(cmdCommand As CommandButton, nNumber As
    ↳ Integer)

    cmdCommand.Caption = nNumber

End Sub
```

```
Private Sub Time_Implicit(cmdCommand As Control, nNumber As Integer)

    cmdCommand.Caption = nNumber

End Sub
```

4. When you completed typing in the code, click on the Start button on the toolbar or press *F5*, and let's take a look at exactly what the code is doing.

5. When the form appears on screen, click on the Explicit command button. The program shows the time taken to assign 15000 different captions to the command button. The routine it uses to do this accepts the command button as an explicitly declared object variable.

6. Now click on the Implicit command button. This does the same thing, only this time the command button is declared implicitly as an object variable.

If you try this, you will see that the implicit click is slower than the explicit one; the difference isn't massive—it's perhaps 10% slower—but if your career is riding on a big application, that's a lifetime.

How It Works

The two command buttons have very similar **Click** events. First, **varTime** is set to the current system time and then the central loop calls the **Time_Implicit** or **Time_Explicit** procedure 15000 times, passing the command button and the loop counter as parameters.

```
varTime = Now

    For nIndex = 1 To 15000

        Time_Explicit cmdExplicit, nIndex

    Next
```

The difference is in the way the command button is accepted in the two subroutines. In one we accept **cmdCommand** explicitly as a **CommandButton**.

```
Private Sub Time_Explicit(cmdCommand As CommandButton, nNumber As
    ↳ Integer)

    cmdCommand.Caption = nNumber

End Sub
```

Whereas, in the other, we accept it implicitly as a **Control**.

```
Private Sub Time_Implicit(cmdCommand As Control, nNumber As Integer)

    cmdCommand.Caption = nNumber

End Sub
```

Once the loop has run the subprocedure 15000 times, we reset the caption and determine the time elapsed between **Now** and the start time in **varTime**.

The Controls Collection

Every form in your application has something known as a **controls collection** built in. This is conceptually similar to an array. You can use the controls collection at run time to gain access to the controls on a form. You don't have to know the name of each control, or even what type of control it is. It differs from the control array we used earlier in that it's built in to Visual Basic. You don't have to declare it, and all the controls on the form are automatically part of it. Visual Basic assembles and maintains it as you design the form. As controls are added and deleted from the form, VB takes care of adding and removing the controls from the collection.

The elements of a controls collection are accessed in the same way that you access the elements of a normal array.

The controls collection can be useful for data entry forms. For example, you can write a generic routine to go through a controls collection looking for only data controls and then change their database properties to point to the appropriate path and file name for the customer's database.

Unlike regular control arrays, the controls collection does not support any events. However, as the controls that are part of the collection are just the controls that you have been happily adding on to forms, completely oblivious to the existence of the collection object, they do support individual events, properties and methods.

The Controls Property

You can gain access to the controls collection through the **Controls** property of the form. This isn't something you can get at through the properties window—you need to do it through code. The **Controls** property is actually an array of object variables, where each element of the array is a single control; element 0 is the first control on the form, element 1 is the second, and so on.

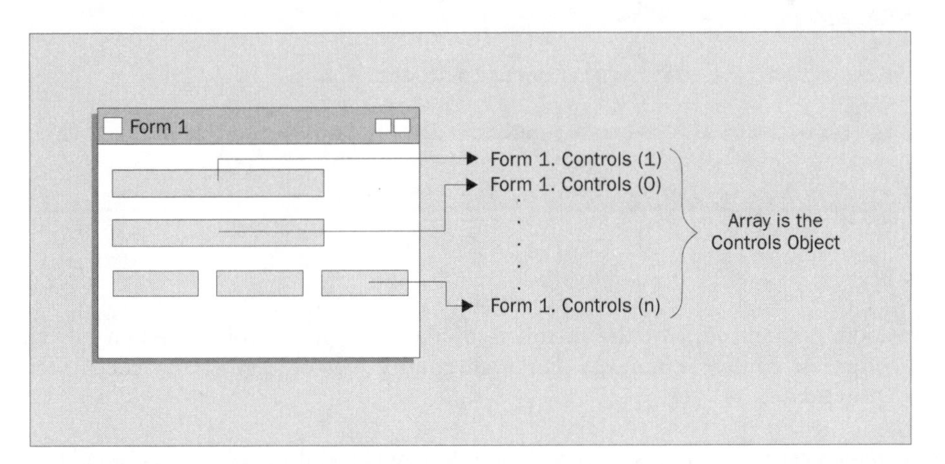

These numbers are assigned to the controls automatically at design time, according to the order in which the controls are drawn on the form.

If you had a simple form with only two text boxes on it, you could change the **Text** property of each with this code:

```
Form1.Controls(0).Text = "Control 0"
Form1.Controls(1).Text = "Control 1"
```

The general format for this is:

```
<form_name>.Controls( <number> ).<property> = <a value>
```

To really make this feature useful, we need to know how many elements there are in a controls collection, and be able to identify them individually.

Identifying Controls on the Form

The **Controls** array has a property of its own called **Count**. This lets you know how many controls are on the form. Be careful, though, if you use this in code. The elements of the control array are numbered from 0. Therefore, if the **Count** property tells you that there are 3 controls on a form, these controls will be numbered 0, 1 and 2 in the **Controls** array, not 1, 2 and 3.

Unfortunately, you have no real way of finding out which control corresponds to which number until run time. However, there is an easy way of identifying specific members of a control collection at run time.

You can use the **TypeOf** method to deal with groups of similar controls. This doesn't let you single out individual controls, but you'll find that most of the time you just want to address all the controls of a certain type. The best way to understand this is to look at some code:

```
For nControlNo = 0 to Form1.Controls.Count - 1

     If TypeOf Form1.Controls( nControlNo ) Is TextBox then
    :
    :
     EndIf

Next
```

Here, we loop through each of the members of the built-in controls collection on **Form1 from 0** to the last control, **Count-1.** For each control we use **TypeOf** to check whether or not it's a **TextBox**.

However, referencing their index numbers is a somewhat clunky way of cycling through the controls in the controls collection. You can do this more elegantly using the **For Each...Next** construct:

```
For Each objControl in Form1.Controls

     If TypeOf objControl Is TextBox Then
    :
    :
     EndIf

Next
```

This approach eliminates much typing, is more efficient, intuitive, and is much cooler.

Now let's get down to business.

Try It Out - Changing Colors

A common facility in today's applications enables users to decide what colors they want to see on the screen. Control arrays let you change the colors of controls throughout a form. And that's exactly what the next project does.... Time to get typing.

1 Start up a new project and drop some controls on the form so that it looks like this. Note that you should start by placing the two frames on the form, and then add the other controls on top of the frames. That way, if you move the frame, its controls will go with it. The controls are contained by the parent frame.

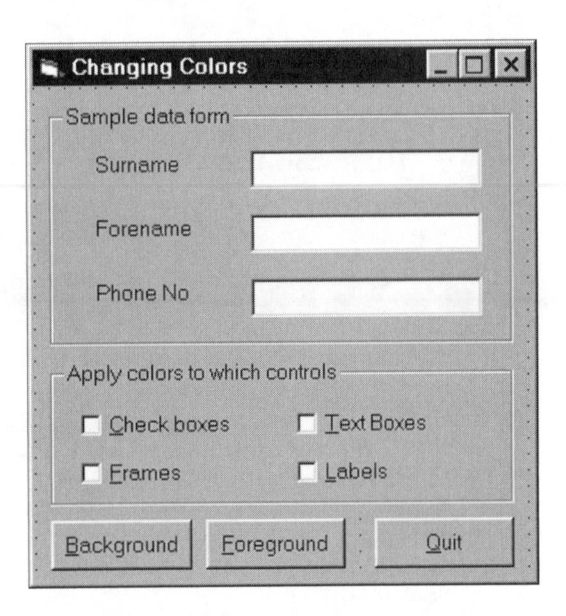

2 You now need to name the controls. Name the form **`frmColors`** and the command buttons **`cmdBackground`**, **`cmdForeground`** and **`cmdQuit`**. Also name the check boxes **`chkCheckBoxes`**, **`chkFrames`**, **`chkTextBoxes`** and **`chkLabels`**.

3 Next add a common dialog control to the form and name it **`dlgColors`**. Remember, if the control isn't in your toolbox, you can add it by selecting Project | Components... and then checking Microsoft Common Dialog Control 5.0.

4 Now for the code. First enter the code for the Background button:

```
Private Sub cmdBackground_Click()

    Dim nColor As Long
    Dim FormControl As Control

    On Error GoTo BackcolorError

    dlgColors.CancelError = True
    dlgColors.Flags = &H1&
    dlgColors.ShowColor

    nColor = dlgColors.Color

    For Each FormControl In frmColors.Controls
        If TypeOf FormControl Is TextBox And chkTextBoxes.Value = 1 Then
         ↳ FormControl.BackColor = nColor
        If TypeOf FormControl Is Frame And chkFrames.Value = 1 Then
         ↳ FormControl.BackColor = nColor
        If TypeOf FormControl Is Label And chkLabels.Value = 1 Then
         ↳ FormControl.BackColor = nColor
        If TypeOf FormControl Is CheckBox And chkCheckBoxes.Value = 1
        ↳ Then FormControl.BackColor = nColor
    Next
Exit Sub
BackcolorError:
    MsgBox("You pressed the cancel button.")

End Sub
```

5 The code for the Foreground button is very similar:

```
Private Sub cmdForecolor_Click()

    Dim nColor As Long
    Dim FormControl As Control

    On Error GoTo ForecolorError

    dlgColors.CancelError = True
    dlgColors.Flags = &H1&
    dlgColors.ShowColor

    nColor = dlgColors.Color

    For Each FormControl In frmColors.Controls
        If TypeOf FormControl Is TextBox And chkTextBoxes.Value = 1 Then
         ↳ FormControl.ForeColor = nColor
        If TypeOf FormControl Is Frame And chkFrames.Value = 1 Then
```

```
            ↳ FormControl.ForeColor = nColor
            If TypeOf FormControl Is Label And chkLabels.Value = 1 Then
            ↳ FormControl.ForeColor = nColor
            If TypeOf FormControl Is CheckBox And chkCheckBoxes.Value = 1
            ↳ Then FormControl.ForeColor = nColor
    Next
Exit Sub
ForecolorError:
    msgbox("You pressed the cancel button.")

End Sub
```

6 Finally, add the code for the Quit button:

```
Private Sub cmdQuit_Click()

    ' Quit the application by unloading the form
    Unload frmColors

End Sub
```

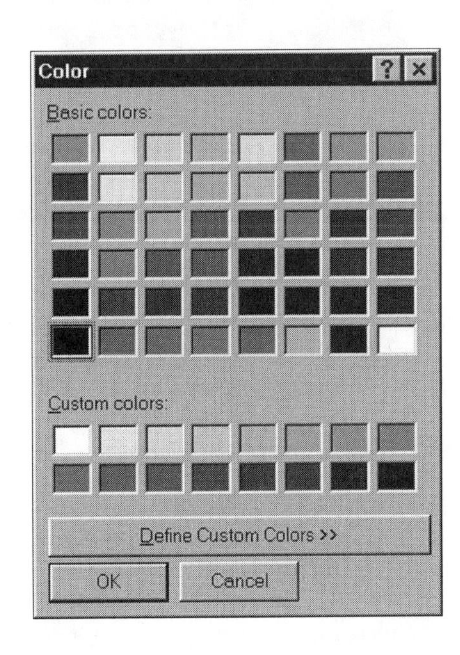

7 Now you're done so run the program. Choose which type of control you want to change the colors on by clicking the appropriate check box. Then press either the Background or Foreground command button. The color dialog comes up:

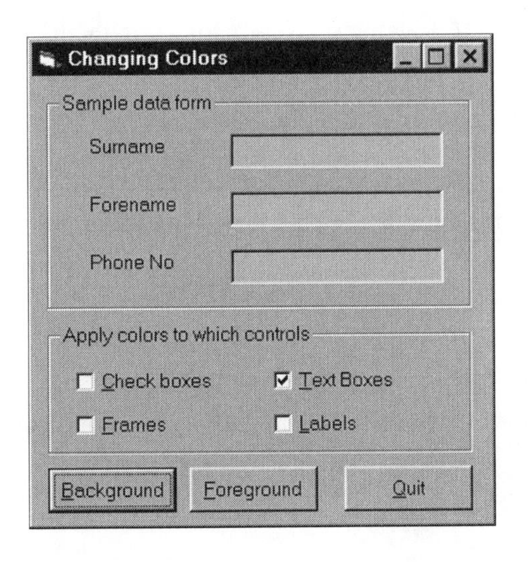

8 Choose a color and the controls change on the form.

How It Works

The code behind the Background and Foreground buttons is very similar. It starts by displaying a colors common dialog and storing the selected color in the **nColor** variable. By setting the **CancelError** property of the common dialog box to True, an error (error number 32755) is generated that will send the code directly to our error handler.

```
dlgColors.CancelError = True
dlgColors.Flags = &H1&
dlgColors.ShowColor

nColor = dlgColors.Color
```

The code then uses a **For Each...Next** loop to move through each control on the form using its controls collection, and places each element into the **FormControl** object variable which was declared at the start of the procedure. The **If TypeOf** statement checks the type of the control. There are four of these tests, one for each type of control that the program is interested in: **TextBox**, **Frame**, **Label**, and **CheckBox**.

```
For Each FormControl In frmColors.Controls
        If TypeOf FormControl Is TextBox And chkTextBoxes.Value = 1 Then
        ➥ FormControl.BackColor = nColor
        If TypeOf FormControl Is Frame And chkFrames.Value = 1 Then
        ➥ FormControl.BackColor = nColor
        If TypeOf FormControl Is Label And chkLabels.Value = 1 Then
        ➥ FormControl.BackColor = nColor
        If TypeOf FormControl Is CheckBox And chkCheckBoxes.Value = 1
        ➥ Then FormControl.BackColor = nColor
    Next
```

Note that you must use the **Is** *keyword when dealing with* **TypeOf** *rather than the = sign.*

Once a matching control has been found, a second **If** statement is used to see if the appropriate check box is set, i.e. if it's one of the controls that the user wants to set the colors on. If it is set, then the **BackColor** property is loaded with the color selected from the common dialog.

There are many uses for the controls collection, such as setting a new font on all controls, resizing all controls to adapt to various monitor resolutions, or enabling / disabling all controls.

MDI Applications

All the applications we have looked at so far are what Microsoft calls **SDI (Single Document Interface)** applications. It's a fairly hefty name for a simple concept. All the forms in the applications we've written so far are independent of each other. They can be resized to whatever size your users want, moved in front of or behind other applications, and so on.

However, it doesn't take very long before an SDI application with multiple visible forms begins to look confusing. Where did I put that customer entry form? Oh yes, it's over there behind Word for Windows, but in front of the order entry form!

An **MDI** (**Multiple Document Interface**) tidies up these kinds of applications. Again, it's a hefty name for a simple concept. In MDI you have one large MDI form (a **parent** form) which acts as a container for all the other forms in your program. The MDI form acts like a virtual form—windows are displayed inside it (called **child** forms) and these can't be moved outside of the MDI form. They can only be maximized to the inside size (client area) of the MDI form. When minimized, they appear as an icon on the MDI form, not on the Windows taskbar.

If you've used other Windows packages, for example Microsoft Word or any of the other components of the Microsoft Office suite, then this will be a concept that you have come across before—probably without even thinking about it.

Parent window

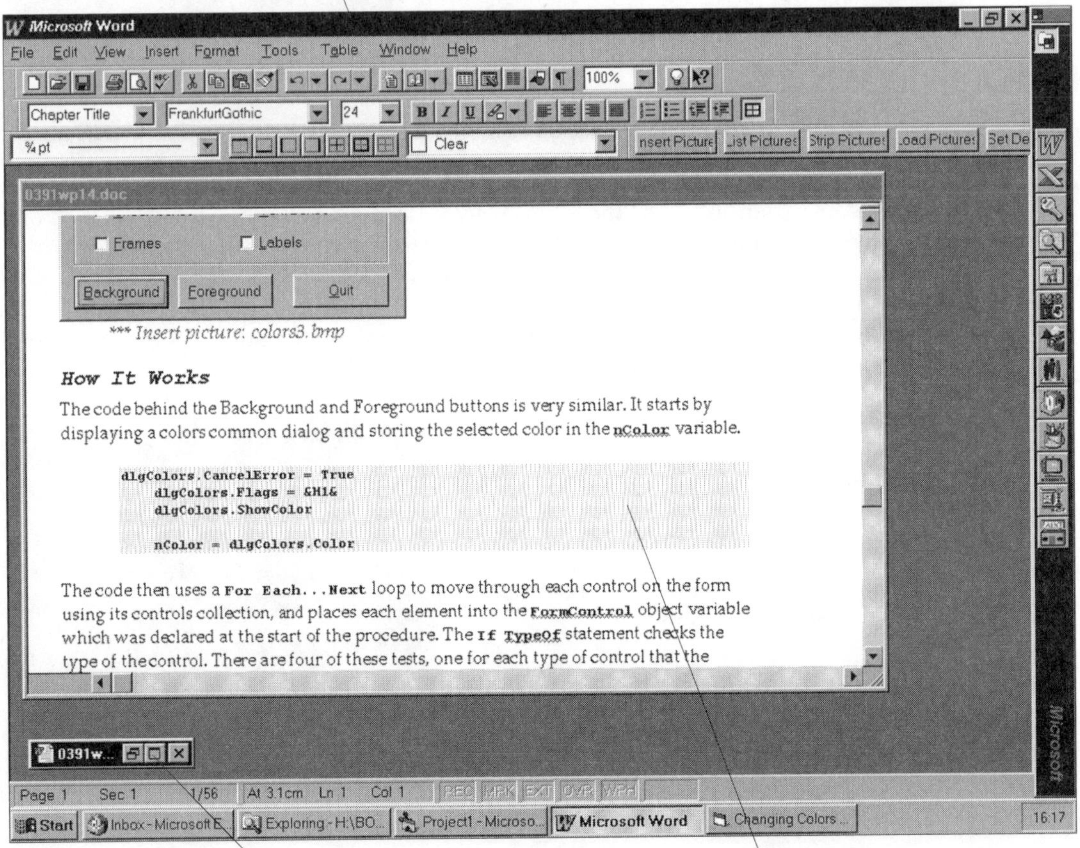

Minimized child window

Child window always inside parent

MDI Forms With Visual Basic

MDI forms are very useful. They can bring order to your application by providing a convenient way for you to group all the forms and functions of your program into one big container window. However, despite its power, MDI under Visual Basic does have some limitations. Let's explore some of them now.

Try It Out - Limitations of an MDI Form

1 Start a new project and from the Project menu, select Add MDI Form.

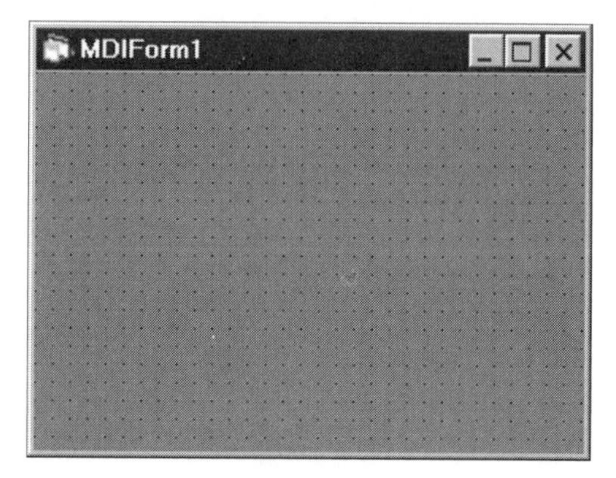

2 When the Add MDI dialog appears, select MDI Form and click Open. Your new MDI form will then appear.

3 Let's put some controls on to the form. Select a command button from the toolbox and try to draw it on the form. Nothing happens. There are only a small number of controls that can be dropped on to an MDI form, including the timer and picture boxes and if you have the Professional or Enterprise editions of Visual Basic, the status bar and toolbar controls. You can't put stuff like command buttons, text boxes, combo boxes (and so on) on to an MDI form.

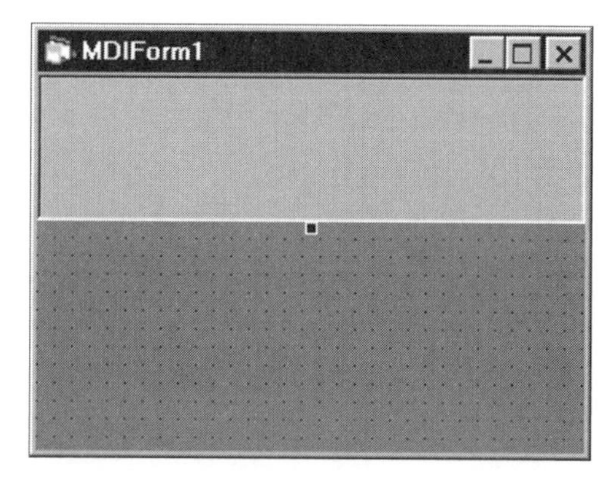

4 Select the picture box from the tool palette and draw that on the form.

The box automatically sits at the top of the form and assumes the same width as the form. You can't change this. Picture boxes drawn on an MDI form are always the same width as the form and attached to either the top or bottom of the form. If you try to align the Picture box to the left or right, it takes up the entire area of the MDI parent form.

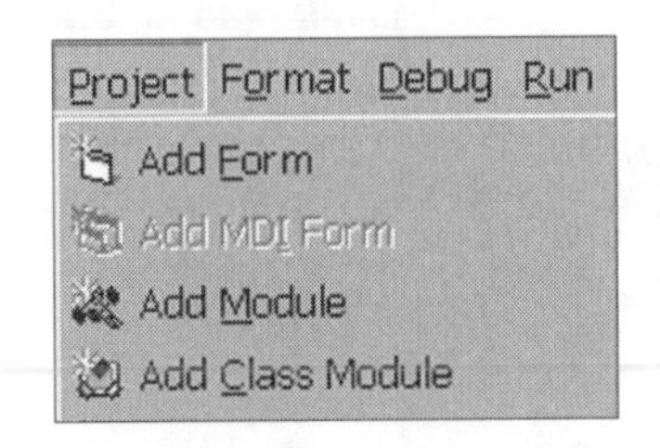

5 Now go to the Project menu again and try to create a second MDI form. The Add MDI Form option is disabled. You can only have one MDI form per application.

Despite these apparent limitations, MDI applications really *are* worth the effort. Imagine what a Windows word processor would be like if you could only open one document at a time, and these couldn't share the same menu structure or toolbar. The bottom line is that MDI applications look good, are comfortable for your users to use, and are an all-round good idea for many types of applications.

Child Forms

When you start to use MDI forms, the other normal forms in your program refuse to fit within the MDI frame. They still float about on their own, happily disrupting the overall karma of windows. You need to tell a form that it's a child form before it will start to behave itself.

Luckily, this is a simple process. The **MDIChild** property of a form can be set to either true or false to tell it that it now belongs to an MDI form. Since Visual Basic only allows you to have one MDI form per application, the child form automatically knows who its parent is, so that when the program runs, it stays within the confines of the MDI form. At design time, there's no visible way to tell the difference between a child form and a normal independent form, other than by checking the form's **MDIChild** property.

Although you can view and set the **MDIChild** property at design time, the property is strictly off-limits at run time. Try setting it to true or false in your code and you'll get an error from Visual Basic before your program crashes.

Try It Out - Child Forms in Action

Let's see all this in action.

1 Start up a new project and name the normal form that appears **frmChild**. Change its **MDIChild** property to True.

2 Next, go up to the Project menu and add an MDI form to the project and name it **frmParent**.

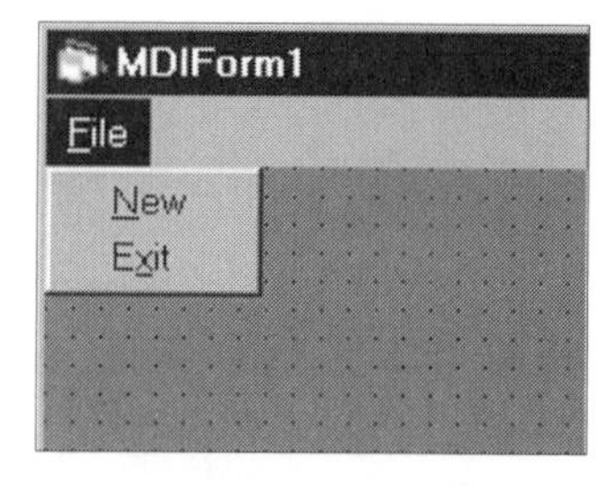

3 Now add a menu to the MDI form that looks like the one shown here. So that the code that we are going to type in works, make sure that the menu items are named **mnuFNew**, and **mnuFExit**.

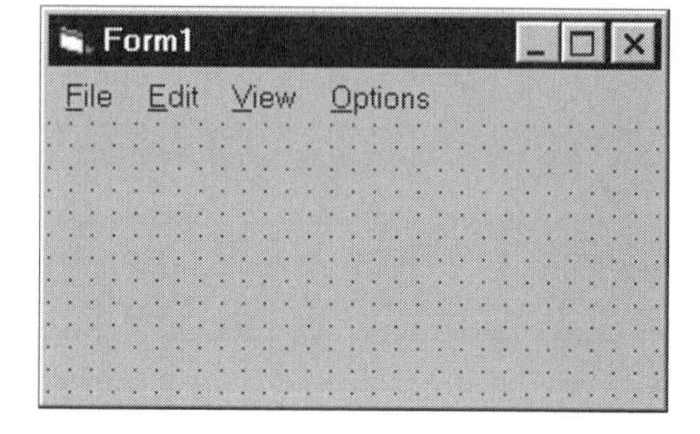

4 Next add some menu headings to the child form so that it looks like this.

5 Bring back the MDI form and add code to the New menu item's **Click** event so that it looks like this:

```
Private Sub mnuFNew_Click()

    Load frmChild

End Sub
```

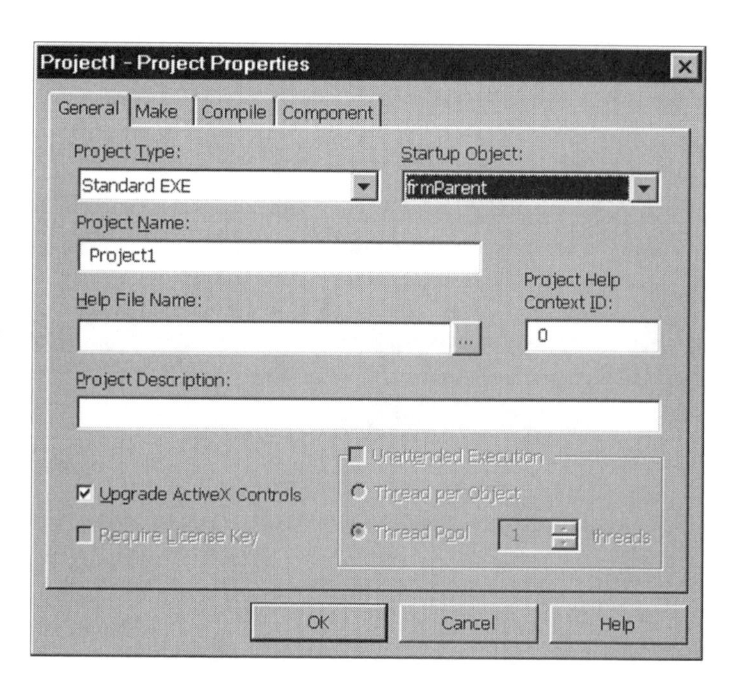

6 Finally, select Project1 Properties from the Project menu and set the start up form so that the first form to appear when the application runs is the MDI form, not the MDI child.

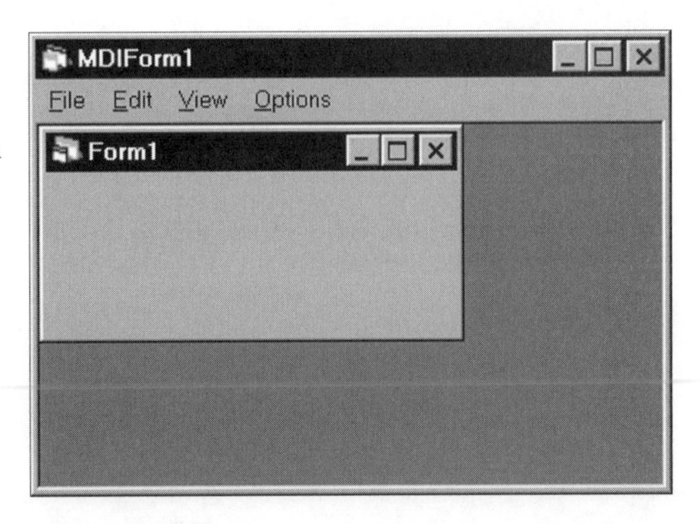

7 Now run the program. When the MDI form comes into view, it has no child windows, so it displays and uses its own menu structure. If you select the New menu option from the File menu, the child form is displayed.

When the child form comes into view, the menu structure of the MDI form changes: it becomes the menu structure of the child window. Once the child window is loaded, you have to shut it down using the title bar or the control box. Only then are the parent menus reinstated.

8 Save the project as **`MDIChild.vbp`**—we'll be using it again in a moment.

Instances of Forms

The previous example only lets you load one child form on to an MDI form. This isn't very useful if you are developing the next Excel.

This is where form **instances** come into play. Using object variables you can create multiple copies, or instances, of a form. Each copy of the form has exactly the same controls on it, and an identical menu structure, but each can hold different data. Although the code and the variable and control names it contains are identical, the actual data each form deals with is stored in a different place in your PC's memory. You had a feeling that MDI forms had something to do with object variables, didn't you?

Try It Out - New Form Instances

Let's put this into action.

1 Stop the **`MDIChild.vbp`** project and using the project window, select the MDI form itself—**`frmParent`**.

2 Select New from the MDI form's File menu to bring up the code window. At present, the code looks like this:

```
Private Sub mnuFNew_Click ()

    Load frmChild

End Sub
```

3 We can create instances of the **frmChild** window using an object variable. Change the code so that it looks like this:

```
Private Sub mnuFNew_Click()

    Dim OurNewForm As New frmChild
    OurNewForm.Show

End Sub
```

4 Back in the project window, select the child window. When the window appears, bring up the menu editor and delete all the menu items. This will make the code a little less complicated for now.

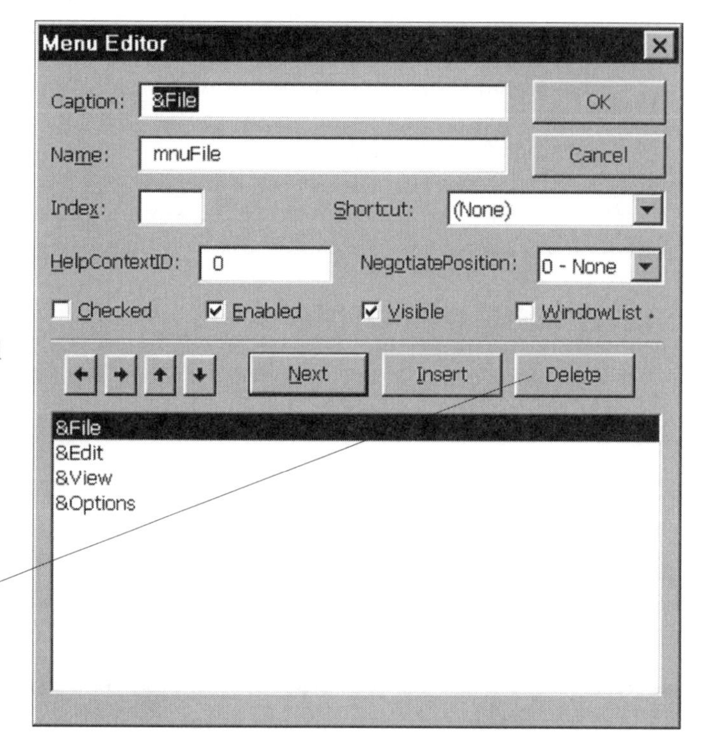

Click on the Delete button four times to remove all the menu items.

5 When all the child form's menus have gone, run the program and select New from the MDI form's File menu. Do it again, and again, and again—each time a new child window is created

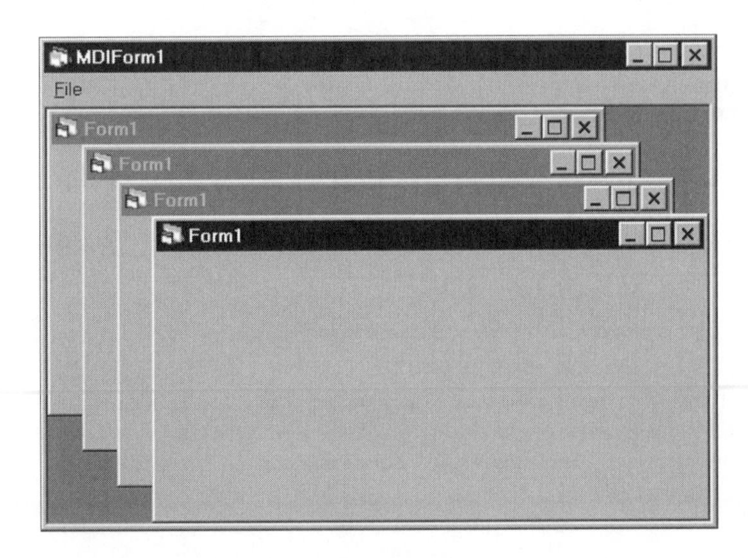

6 When you're done playing, stop the program. Save it by selecting Save File As and Save Project As from the File menu. Rename both the form and the project so that you can always come back to the originals. Call the new project **MDIChild1.vbp**.

How It Works

The first line of code in the **mnuFNew_Click** event is a variable declaration. It sets up an object variable for a **New** form. The form in this case is a copy of the child form called **frmChild**. Confusing, isn't it! We created new command buttons in the same way earlier on in the chapter.

```
Dim OurNewForm As New frmChild
```

We already have a form called **frmChild** in the application. What we want to do is create new copies of it. These new copies all have their own data and variables, but share the same event code.

So, **OurNewForm** is actually an object variable set up to hold a new instance of the **frmChild** object. Once the object variable has been set up, we can treat it just the same as any other form. The command **OurNewForm.Show** shows our new form on the screen.

> *Another way to look at this is to think of* **OurNewForm** *as being a variable of type* **frmChild**. *It, therefore, inherits the properties of* **frmChild**.

Now for the tricky bit. Take another look at the object variable declaration:

```
Dim OurNewForm As New frmChild
```

It's a simple **Dim**, so that means that the object variable is a local variable—as soon as the subroutine finishes, so does the life of the variable. But why does the form you've just created stay in existence?

What we've done here is create an object variable for a new form. If you destroy the object variable, you just destroy the variable itself, **not the new form that was created**. So how do you refer to the new form and the controls on it in your code?

Addressing Your New Form or Talking to Me

Since we now have an application that could theoretically display ten identically named forms, Visual Basic kindly gives us a special keyword called **`Me`** which can be used in your code to refer to the currently active form. Visual Basic keeps track of the currently active window, or form. This is the current window that has focus, or, in other words, the window where any keystrokes or mouse clicks will be sent. It's easy to tell because the active window will always be the window in the forefront and has a highlighted title bar. We can communicate with the window by using **`activeform.txtEmployee.text = "Peter Wright"`**. But even easier is to substitute **`activeform`** with the keyword **`me`**.

A line of code that says:

```
Me.txtEmployee.Text = "Peter Wright"
```

sets the **`Text`** property of a text box called **`txtEmployee`** on the current active form. In the same way, if you need to unload the form from inside one of its events, just type **`Unload Me`**.

I had great problems with this when I first started learning VB. It seems too easy and logical to be right, but believe me it's fine! The key is to remember that, in an MDI application, you can only have one active form. Therefore, you don't need an array to be able to reference the child forms.

Creating Window List Menus

Once you start dealing with MDI forms and child windows, things can get very out of hand on your screen. Your user can get lost in a sea of similar looking child windows, not knowing which is which, or where the first form they created has gone to.

Visual Basic provides a simple way of dealing with this problem—the **Window List Menu.**

Try It Out - Creating a Window List Menu

1 Load the **`MDIChild1.VBP`** that you saved just now. Then bring up the menu editor for **`frmParent`**.

2 Create a Window option on the menu bar:

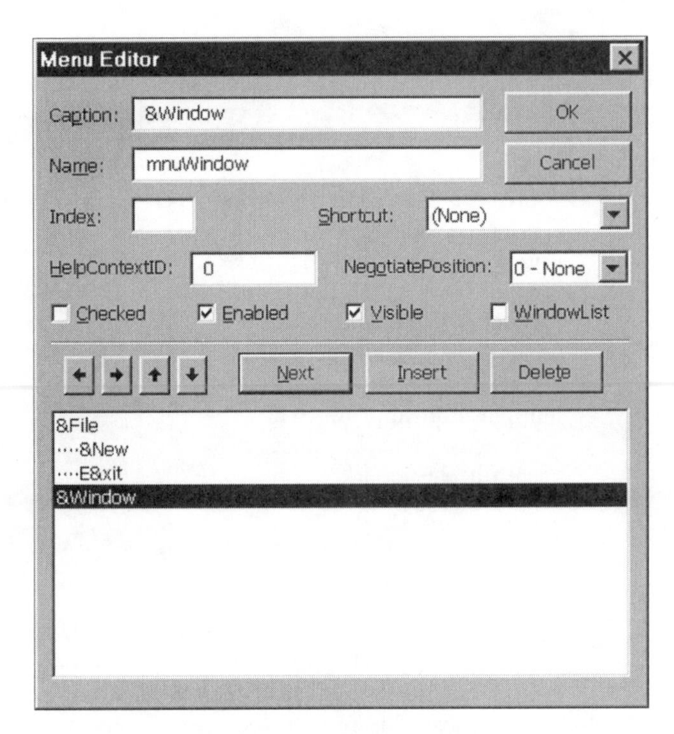

3 Create another item underneath this and set the Caption. Make sure it's named **`mnuWList`** and check the WindowList check box.

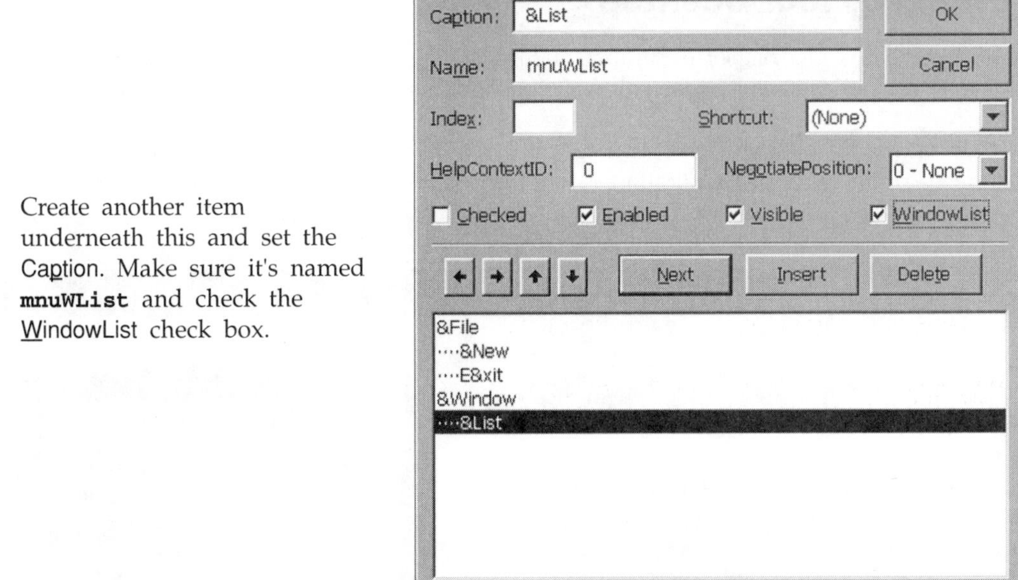

4 Press OK to accept the new menu structure and then run the program.

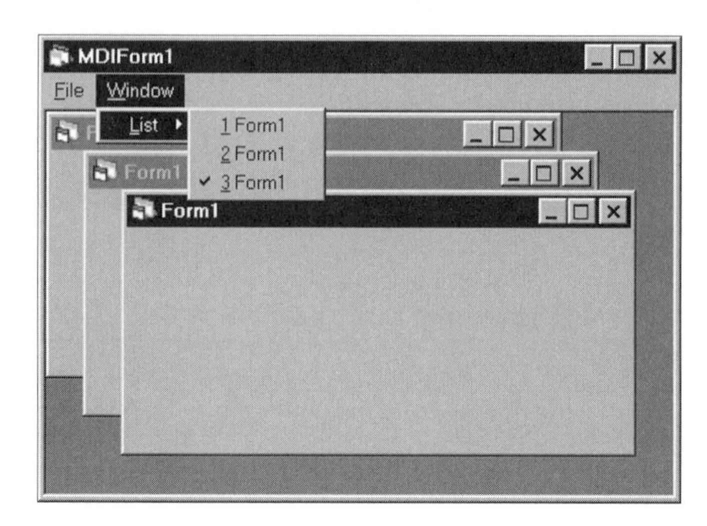

5 Create a few child windows using the File/New menu item on the main MDI form. Now go to the new Window menu and select the List item. A list of all the child forms in the application appears, with the active window marked with a checkmark.

6 If you select any of the items on this list, then that form becomes the current active form. Pretty neat, huh? No code involved!

Don't close this project yet—we're going to use it again in just a moment.

Arranging Your Desktop

WindowList is just one of a number of time saving features of Visual Basic that you have at your disposal when dealing with MDI applications. Another is the **`Arrange`** method.

The **`Arrange`** method allows you to give your users features similar to those on the Window menu of an Office 97 application. Using **`Arrange`**, you can tile and cascade child windows, and arrange the child window icons in a neat and orderly fashion.

Try It Out - Using Arrange

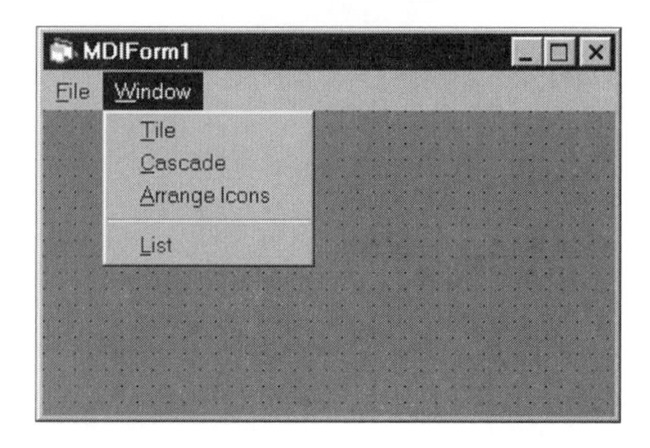

1 Add some more menu items to the Window menu on **`frmParent`** as shown here. Name them **`mnuWTile`**, **`mnuWCascade`** and **`mnuWArrange`**

2 Then open the code window and write their **Click** events

```
Private Sub mnuWTile_Click()

    frmParent.Arrange vbTileHorizontal

End Sub

Private Sub mnuWCascade_Click()

    frmParent.Arrange vbCascade

End Sub

Private Sub mnuWArrange_Click()

    frmParent.Arrange vbArrangeIcons

End Sub
```

3 And that's all there is to it. Run the application and play around with the new menu items to see how they work (don't forget to create some child windows first though).

Different Window Arrangements

The **Arrange** method is very easy to use. You simply type the name of the MDI form, in our case **frmParent**, in front of the **Arrange** method. Then, after the word **Arrange**, type one of the parameter options which govern how the forms are arranged. The VB built in constants **vbTileHorizontal**, **vbCascade**, and **vbArrangeIcons** do all of the work for us.

The options you have for the **Arrange** parameter are as follows:

Value	VB Constant	What It Does
0	**vbCascade**	Cascades all open MDI child forms from the top left to the bottom right of the screen.
1	**vbTileHorizontal**	Tiles all open MDI child forms above and below each other down the screen.
2	**vbTileVertical**	Tiles all open MDI child forms side by side across the screen.
3	**vbArrangeIcons**	Lines up the icons of any minimized child forms.

The first three actions also affect any child forms you may have minimized. Although the results are not immediately visible, they can be seen as soon as the child form is resized.

Summary

It may not appear so to you immediately, but in the Learning Edition of Visual Basic the uses of object variables are fairly simple. However, the Professional Edition of Visual Basic makes very heavy use of them. Databases in Visual Basic Pro, for example, can be dealt with through code, without the need for a data control. The tables of your database themselves are represented as object variables.

If you know how to use object variables, you can write reuseable code. For example, you now know how to write a generic routine for text validation. The code doesn't have to know the name of a specific text box, because you pass the text box to the validate code as an object variable. In fact, it you put your text validation routine in a code module, it can be used by all forms in your project.

In this chapter you have learned:

- What object variables are and how to use them
- How to write efficient code that deals with a lot of controls by referring to them as object variables
- How to create and use an array of objects
- What an MDI application is
- How to create and manage MDI applications

Why Not Try...

1 Can you name three purposes that object variables can be used for?

2 Create a control array of a single label type. Create four more when you click on the label. When you click again, remove the "created" labels. Be sure to display the array number in the label's caption.

3 Create a function that passes an object variable as an argument. Have the function return the object's `Top` property.

4 Explicitly declare an object variable as type Label. Set it equal to a label control What happens if you try to assign a value to a property that does not exist in the label control?

5 Implicitly declare an object variable as type Control. Set it equal to a label control. What happens if you try to assign a value to a property that does not exist in the label control?

asic Visual Basic Visual Ba
al Basic Visual Basic Visual
Basic Visual Basic Visual Ba
ual Basic Vi
Basic Visu
ual Basic V
l Basic Vis
isual Basic Visual Basic
l Basic Visual Basic Visua
Visual Basic Visual Basic Visu
l Basic Visual Ba
l Basic Visual
ic Visual Basi
Basic Visual B
ic Visual Basi
l Basic Visual
ual Basic Visual Basic Visual Ba
Visual Basic Visual Basic Visu
sual Basic Visual Basic Visu
Visual Basic Visual Ba

Using DLLs and The Windows API

Visual Basic does a good job of shielding developers from the nitty-gritty details of Windows. However, there comes a point where you can no longer hide behind the safe walls of VB. Windows is out there, waiting to talk to your program.

Windows provides a number of function calls, in the form of DLLs, that are useful to VB programmers. You can also co-opt DLLs from other programs to do work for you. We'll concentrate on using the Windows DLLs here, but what we learn is widely applicable.

In this chapter you'll learn:

- How to declare API and DLL functions in your programs and how to utilize the underlying power of Windows
- How to use the API to harness the power of multimedia in your VB applications

In this chapter we're really going to focus on the issues surrounding calling code that lives in the Windows API. There's also something known as DLL Callback facilities available in Visual Basic 5 which, instead of you calling code in the API, allows you to make use of certain API calls that will call your code as part of their working process. Believe me—this can be really useful, but it is alas a little beyond our scope here.

Enough with the waffle—on with the show.

How VB and Windows Fit Together

In this chapter we're going to look at how to use tools that lie outside what you might consider as Visual Basic, meaning functions and procedures that are actually part of Windows itself. These are pieces of code that Windows has at its disposal to do what it has to do: manage your applications and provide a consistent user interface and operating environment for your programs.

This sounds complicated, but it isn't. The first thing to note is that we've effectively used part of the Windows code already, without really knowing it, when we used the common dialog control. Let's consider for a while what's really happening when we do this.

DLLs the Easy Way - The Common Dialog

You remember the common dialog. It's that great little control that is a window on to a load of different dialogs. Here's the file open dialog:

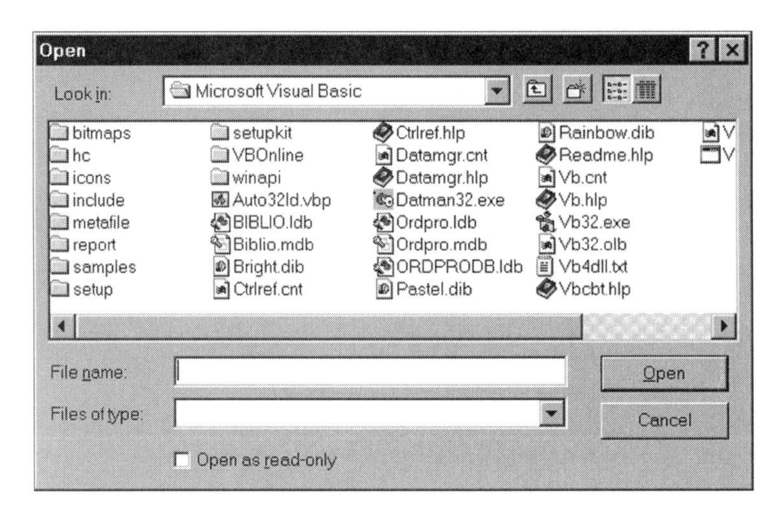

These dialogs not only save us time, but also give our programs the look and feel of a real Windows application. The reason they're called *common* dialogs is that they look the same in all Windows applications. So what's the story (morning glory)? It makes you wonder whether they aren't really part of Windows after all....

Well actually they are. If you load up Explorer and take a look in your **`Windows\System`** directory you'll see a file named **`Comdlg32.DLL`**.

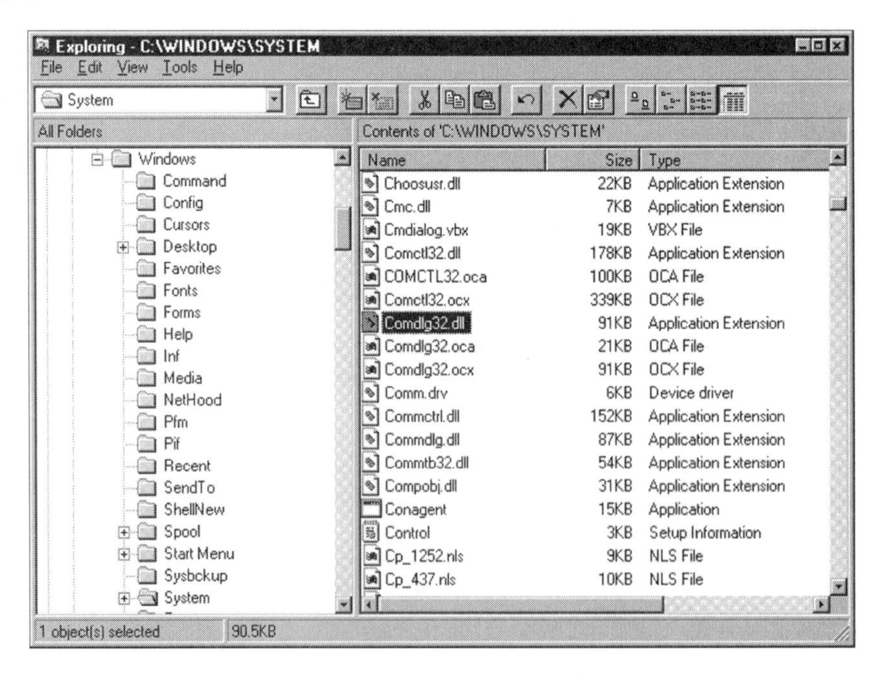

This file contains all the code needed to create the various common dialogs that Windows supports. Lumping all this code together in a file stored in a shared directory makes it accessible to all Windows programs, including Windows itself.

You can't look inside it—it's a compiled lump of C/C++ code and would look like gobbledygook. What interests us, of course, is how we can talk to this little monster and tell it what to do, from our VB code. To understand that, we'll have to take a quick lesson in how Windows works. Bear with me—there is a point.

Dynamic Link Libraries

The `Comdlg32.dll` file is what's known as a **dynamic link library**, hence the file extension. To you and me, this means that it's a block of code containing procedures and functions that are useful for more than one program; it is available to any program that wants to use it. The question is, of course—how?

Let's take a quick lesson in the history of programming. If this really is your first toe in the water of programming, then you don't need to bother to read this. Think yourself lucky you got into the game at the right time, and skip this next bit and jump straight to the bit titled the Windows API.

What is 'Linking'?

Traditional programming languages such as C, when you use them outside an environment like Windows, like to operate as stand-alone blocks. This means that when you compile the program, you end up with an executable file that is self-contained, and doesn't need any other files to run (unlike say a `.vbp` file which requires Visual Basic to run). All the code it needs is 'hardwired' into the body of the program.

This doesn't mean you can't use prewritten code—there are lots of C libraries out there that are very widely used. The question, then, is how do you get the prewritten code into *your* program. This is what is meant by linking, and it can be done in two ways—**static linking** and **dynamic linking**.

Static Linking

In static linking, you provide fixed links between your program and the prewritten modules at design time, just like when you create a module in a VB project and call procedures in it from other parts of your code. However, in order to use these prewritten lumps of code, you have to effectively copy them into your final file at compile time in a process called **static linking**. After that, they are part of your program, locked away in your executable file.

Dynamic Linking

This is the opposite of static linking, and if you understand how it works, you'll see why **dynamic linking** is a good plan. In dynamic linking, the external library file never gets bound into the final executable file. It remains outside the program as a DLL, hopefully in a place where the executable file can find it and send it messages. At run time, these messages are function or procedure calls, requesting that certain parts of the DLL code are executed.

To link your executable and the DLL it needs to run, you just tell your program where the DLL is, and which bit of code you want to run from inside it. It's up to your program to make the connection when the big moment arrives. It is, as they say, dynamically linked.

The Visual Basic DLLs

Perhaps the most graphic illustration of dynamic linking is Visual Basic itself. Take a peek into your Windows **`System`** directory and you should see a set of files that comprise VB's run-time engine. For example **`VB5DB.DLL`** contains some of the code necessary to link to the Data Access Objects at run time should your application choose to look at a local database.

When you write a database application and compile it, even if you compile to a fully independent compiled application rather than simply an interpreted one, the resulting **`EXE`** file knows nothing about databases, what they do or how to deal with them. Instead, your application includes a block of code provided by Visual Basic itself, which at run time loads up that **`VB5DB.DLL`** file and uses the functions contained within.

The Advantages of Dynamic Linking

Of course, with dynamic linking, you have the hassle of making sure that all the DLLs a program needs are present, in the right place, and in the right version. However, while this is not a trivial problem, you are well taken care of by Windows and VB in this respect. And the advantages of dynamic linking are real and important.

Consistency

Users like Windows because it has a more or less common user interface across applications. To achieve this, it helps if you generate as much of your user interface as possible from common code. The common dialog, along with the new Office 97 menus, toolbars, etc., are good examples of this.

Maintenance

By having a lot of common code in one place, you can update and amend that code centrally, and the changes are reflected in all the applications that use it. That's why, when you run Windows 3.1 applications on Windows 95, they inherit some user interface features of the new system. This applies to Visual Basic as well.

Smaller Executables

By moving a lot of the back room business out to another file, rather than statically linking the functions and procedures, you can reduce the size of your executable. The flip side of this is that the DLL files tend to be massive as they need to contain every possible piece of code they support, not just the ones you need. However, they are shared across many applications, so there's still a net gain.

The Windows Architecture

Dynamic linking is fundamental to the design of Windows. Windows is really just a bag of DLLs that the various applications you run use to do their jobs. In fact, even things that you think of as being Windows itself, like the desktop and Explorer, are just applications that run like any other program, calling the procedures from the intrinsic Windows DLLs as you need them.

The great news is that they aren't the only ones that can tap into the Windows DLL goodie bag. All those DLLs are sitting there waiting to work, and they'll work for anyone who shows up with the right program code. If the mood takes you, you can even replace the Windows desktop with your own version, although I'd suggest we leave that one for a rainy day.

There a lot of DLLs that ship with Windows to give it all the functionality it needs. Inside each of these is anything from a handful, to hundreds of available functions and procedures. Collectively, these 1000+ individual routines are called the Windows API.

The Windows API

The Windows **Application Programmer's Interface (API)** is a collection of ready-made functions and procedures. These have traditionally been the domain of C and C++ programmers—the way that the connections to the API operate are more intuitive for C and C++ programmers, for whom arcane and incomprehensible syntax are a stock in trade.

Visual Basic was created to free us from the kind of drudgery that bedevils C/C++ Windows development, and this extends to the API as well. Most of the API calls are already implemented in Visual Basic in the form of VB commands, keywords, methods and properties. These are translated into the corresponding API calls inside VB. In a way, VB is a friendly wrapper around the Windows API.

However, there are still some API functions for which Visual Basic has no substitute. For example, standard Visual Basic has no way for the programmer to get real control of the Windows multimedia system. OK, you can embed files in OLE controls, or use other custom controls. But with the API you can achieve great effects without the overheads of lots of other controls.

Working with the Multimedia API is easy. Well, relatively speaking. Although there's nothing to be frightened of, using API calls in VB is a little fiddly at times. However, armed with a clear understanding of what to do and why you're doing it, you can unlock the power of the API.

API Wrappers and Custom Controls

An alternative to diving around in the API is to look for a **custom control** that does what you want to do. Many custom controls (OCXs or ActiveX controls) are themselves a wrapper around a particular bit of the API, which deliver that functionality to your program in a VB-style, user-friendly manner.

Having said that, more and more ActiveX controls go much further than this, for example, a mapping control. These can really extend the feature set of your applications, without requiring huge programming effort on your behalf. I can tell you now that there's no `DrawAmerica` function call in the API, no matter how hard you look.

ActiveX Controls and OLE Automation Servers (collectively **ActiveX Components**) actually represent the most useable way to distribute code in an API-like format between projects, without having to go to all the hassle of dropping into a compiler and writing a true DLL. We cover them in a little more detail, and discuss how to create your own, in the next chapter.

Another approach is to enclose some API calls into a Visual Basic class module of your own, which brings the power of the API into a VB object. We'll have a look at doing this ourselves later in this chapter.

Finding and Using API Calls

We said that Windows has a lot of DLLs in it—some large, some small. There's no point in trying to take all these in at one go, let alone all of the 1000+ calls they contain. The best strategy for working with the API is to get to know a few common API calls and then fan out your knowledge from there. In this chapter, we'll look at a couple of API calls, and leave you to find out more at your own speed. Often magazines publish these—there are a few listed in the VB Help file, and there are some very good reference books available which list the majority of them.

The Text API Viewer

Depending on which version of Visual Basic 5 you've splashed out all your hard-earned cash on, you may find that it includes a useful utility to help you find the correct declarations for API routines. What the Text API Viewer doesn't do, however, is give you any real help as to what the routine does, exactly what values it expects, and what values it returns. You'll need to buy a reference book to learn more.

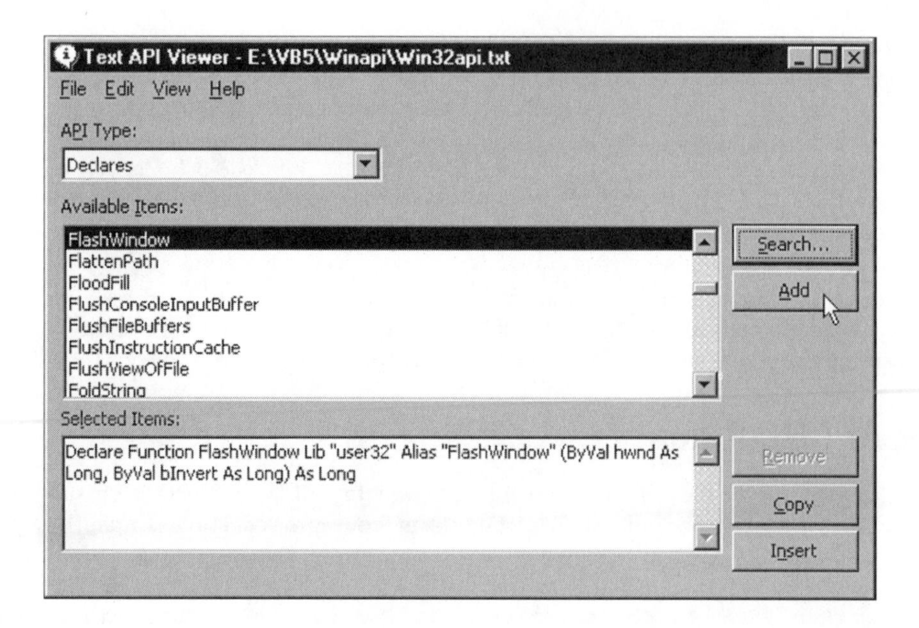

Still, it can help you get the declarations correct, and find out the types and constants it requires. It can even copy them to the clipboard, so you can paste them directly into your code.

Some Windows DLLs

If it helps, think of each API call as a subroutine or function. Given the number of API calls that make up Windows, Microsoft wisely decided to group them together into four main libraries.

KERNEL32	The main DLL, **Kernel32**, handles memory management, multitasking of the programs that are running, and most other functions which directly affect how Windows actually runs.
USER32	Windows management library. Contains functions which deal with menus, timers, communications, files and many other non-display areas of Windows.
GDI32	Graphics Device Interface. Provides the functions necessary to draw things on the screen, as well as checking which areas of forms need to be redrawn.
WINMM	Provides multimedia functions for dealing with sound, music, real-time video, sampling and more. This is a 32-bit only DLL. The 16-bit equivalent is called **MMSYSTEM.**

You can see these files in your **Windows\System** directory. There are also many other smaller, less frequently used DLLs which provide specialist services to applications.

Those listed above are the 32-bit DLL names. If you have been reading this so far with the idea that you are going to support the millions of 16-bit Windows users out there with your application, then I'm afraid I have some bad news for you. In the past, Microsoft have always released a version of Visual Basic that's useable on 16-bit Windows platforms, such as Windows for Workgroups, or Windows 3.1. However, Visual Basic 5 is the first ever 32-bit-only version of VB, with Visual Basic 4 being the last incarnation of a 16-bit development tool from Microsoft.

Having done our homework, now comes the fun part. We're going to check out some common API calls and, along the way, make sure we know everything we need to know about using the API in general. After that, it's up to you to explore away.

Calling API Routines

Calling a procedure in the API is really no different to calling a function or subroutine that you've written yourself and added to a module in your project. For example, if you have this piece of code:

```
Public Sub FindText(objDataControl As Control, sFieldName As String)

' Code to implement function does here.

End Sub
```

To invoke the procedure, you could use this code:

```
FindText datTitles, "Titles"
```

Let's apply the same logic to an API call, which is a subprocedure that isn't only outside our current module, but also outside VB.

A Quick Look at Declaring an API Call

Before a DLL routine can be used, it needs to be declared. Visual Basic needs to be told:

- The name of the subroutine or function
- Which DLL file it can be found in
- The parameters it expects to receive
- The type of value that it can return if the routine is a function

You still use the word **Sub** or **Function** to start the code off, but it must be prefixed with the word **Declare**. Because we're calling an API function, the code isn't directly in our VB program after the declaration, it's off in the DLL we indicated. Apart from that, the declaration is the same as for a function that you wrote yourself.

Once the function is declared, calling it is straightforward. Let's take a look at how this works, using a quick example of an API call.

Try It Out - Flashing a Window with an API Call

1 Create a new project in Visual Basic.

2 Draw a timer control on the form and set the timer **`Interval`** property to **`10`**. This will cause a timer event to occur every 10 milliseconds.

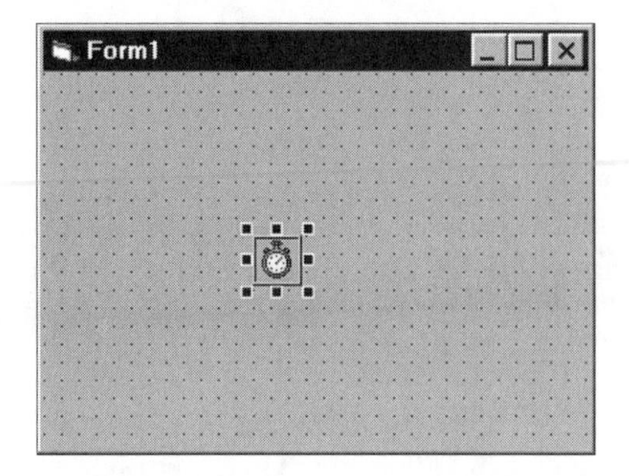

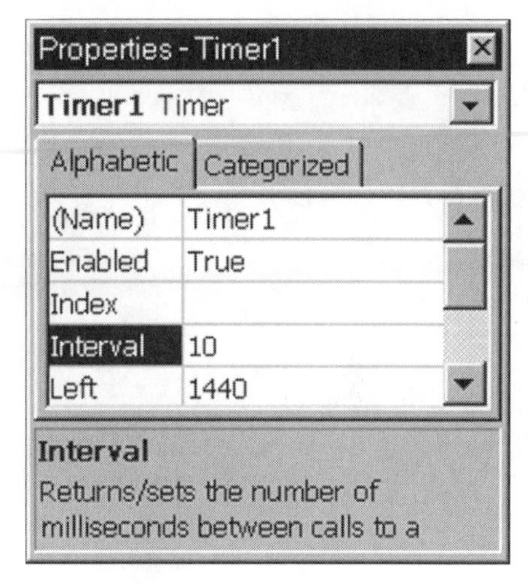

3 Double-click on the timer control to display its code window. Then type in code so that it looks like this:

```
Private Sub Timer1_Timer()

    Dim nReturnValue As Integer
    nReturnValue = FlashWindow(Form1.hWnd, True)

End Sub
```

4 Now declare the **`FlashWindow`** function in the general declarations section as follows:

```
Private Declare Function FlashWindow Lib "user32" Alias "FlashWindow"
    ↳ (ByVal hWnd As Long, ByVal bInvert As Long) As Long
```

5 Now run the program. When the form appears, its caption should be flashing.

This is a very simple program, but flashing the caption of a window using pure Visual Basic code is extremely difficult and requires a lot of code—try it at your own peril!

How It Works - The API Declaration

The function declaration itself is fairly straightforward once you understand its constituent parts. It helps to have a Windows API reference manual handy to determine whether the API call you're about to use is a subroutine or function, which DLL it's contained in, and what the parameters to be passed to it should be.

The word **`Declare`** *tells Visual Basic that we're declaring a DLL routine.*

Immediately following **`Declare`** *is the word* **`Sub`** *or* **`Function`***, which declares either a subroutine or a function. Of course, you can't declare subroutines and functions indiscriminately.*

The **`Lib`** *keyword tells Visual Basic the DLL in which the function we want is contained. In this case, it's the* **`user32`** *DLL file.* **`Alias`** *tells VB what the actual name of the function inside the library is—this could be different from the name we assign to it before the* **`Lib`** *keyword.*

```
Private Declare Function FlashWindow Lib "user32" Alias "FlashWindow"
        ↳ (ByVal hWnd As Long, ByVal bInvert As Long) As Long
```

Finally, the parameters which are to be passed to the function are declared, along with the type of value that the function will return.

The parameters we're passing here are:

```
(ByVal hWnd As Long, ByVal bInvert As Long) As Long
```

The first parameter, **`hWnd`**, is a **handle** that identifies the window we want to blink. It's important that you understand the concept of handles in Windows, and we'll come back to it later. The second parameter, **`bInvert`**, switches the flashing property on and off. If **`bInvert`** is set to **`True`** by the calling statement, then the bar flashes. To return it to its original state, you need to call the function again, with the value **`False`**.

In many API routines, the **`Alias`** is the same as the actual routine name, such as in **`FlashWindow`**. In these cases, we can omit the **`Alias`** part altogether, for example:

```
Private Declare Function FlashWindow Lib "user32"
    ↳ (ByVal hWnd As Long, ByVal bInvert As Long) As Long
```

However, some have names that are illegal in VB, such as **`_lopen`**, and other come in different versions—sometimes with an **`A`** or **`W`** appended to the name. In general, it's safer to use the definition as it is. Some programmers use the **`Alias`** to change the name that the refer to the routine by, or even to declare two different versions of a routine which accept different parameter types—but we'll steer clear of these techniques for now.

How It Works - Calling the API

We called the function in this way:

```
nReturnValue = FlashWindow(Form1.hWnd, True)
```

Once you've declared an API call, it's used in almost exactly the same way as a normal call to a Visual Basic function or subroutine. In the above example, the **FlashWindow** call is a call to a function held in a DLL. Just as with Visual Basic functions, API functions return values which must then be stored somewhere. We store the value that the **FlashWindow** function returns in a variable called **nReturnValue**.

Again, just as with Visual Basic functions, you don't *have* to do anything with the values returned by API functions. But you *do* need to store them somewhere, even if you intend to ignore them, by assigning them to a variable. Almost every API function returns a numeric error code, which you can use to see if everything worked correctly.

In fact, ignoring these values is not only a bit lazy—it can actually be dangerous if you're using more than one call in your code. In this straightforward example, however, it's fine to just store the return value in a variable that we never subsequently use.

Using Windows API calls can potentially crash Windows, if not your machine. When you come to the more complex API calls, such as those which are responsible for allocating vast amounts of memory and system resources, woe-betide the programmer who casually ignores the return code. Since the DLL functions live outside of your application they handle all their own error checking—your only indication that something might have gone wrong is that return code. Remember that, and ignore it at your peril later on!!

Windows' Handles

Visual Basic provides you with a nice soft buffer between your code and the underlying Windows DLL calls. One of the areas where this is most evident is in a control's properties.

Take the form as an example. Windows uses something called a **structure** to hold information about a form. This information is almost identical to the information contained in the form's properties window. However, whereas you or I can easily check a window's properties—we just click on a form and press *F4* to bring up its Properties window—Windows stores each window's structure in a large list of data structures which relates to every window of every program actually running. To determine which structure relates to which window, it uses something called a **handle**. It can't use the name of the form to find it, because the name is just a property of that form. The handle is Windows' own shorthand ID for an object.

As you start to use API calls more and more, particularly those that deal directly with your Visual Basic forms, you'll find handles cropping up again and again. Conveniently, Visual Basic stores handles as read only properties, which you can use to pass to Windows functions when required.

The property is called **hWnd** (handle to a window) and can only be accessed at run time. The property means nothing to your Visual Basic code, but it can be read, and passed as a parameter, to those API calls that need it. You'll find that almost any API call that could do something to a displayed window will need you to pass it an **hWnd** parameter so that the function knows exactly which window you want to deal with.

Declaring Parameter Types

When you declare the type of parameter that a DLL subroutine or function needs, it's important to make sure that the **ByVal** keyword is used whenever necessary.

With regular Visual Basic code, if you pass a parameter to a function **by value**, it tells Visual Basic that the function can only deal with a copy of the parameter you pass it. This is how you do it with a regular function:

```
Function Square(ByVal Number As Double) As Double
```

The alternative to passing by value is to pass the variables **by reference**. Here, you effectively send the whole variable to the routine, not just a copy of its contents. Therefore, if the routine changes the parameter, those changes are also reflected in the original variable. If you don't specify **ByVal**, the variable will be passed by reference automatically. Have another look at Chapter 8 for a reminder of these keywords.

If you write an internal Visual Basic function or subroutines and you miss out the **ByVal** keyword, as long as you pass the correct number of parameters to the code, nothing serious will go wrong. Sure, you may get cases where variables passed as parameters are changed, causing your program to have weird results, but nothing *really* serious will happen. Windows won't crash, for example!

However, with DLLs, the situation is a little more serious. If you omit the **ByVal** keyword, Visual Basic actually passes a pointer to the variable. This number tells the function being called where the variable is stored in memory. It's then up to the function to go to that memory location and retrieve the value itself. This is also what happens in Visual Basic-only situations—but since, in that case, the functions and subroutines are all written in Visual Basic code, Visual Basic can cope. DLL code, written in a language like C, expects things to happen in a certain way, and can get quite upset when they don't.

If a DLL function expects a number, let's say between 0 and 3, and you pass it a variable by reference, the actual value passed could be something like 1,002,342, which would be the address in memory where your variable lives. The DLL function would then try to deal with the number 1,002,342 instead of a number between 0 and 3, the net result of which would be that your system crashes.

There are no nasty error messages here; you know when a DLL call is wrong because your system generally misbehaves, or locks up completely! One of the golden rules of messing about with API calls is ***save your work****! Since you're venturing outside the protected world of Visual Basic, when things go wrong, it can easily result in the* *whole system crashing. Always save your project* before *running code with API calls in it. The best way to do this is to check the* Save Before Run *box in the* Options | Environment *menu.*

Using Classes with the API

It goes without saying that the API is a powerful weapon in the VB programmer's arsenal. However, if you were to put API calls throughout your VB apps, you would pretty soon end up with a garbled mass of code that makes no sense to anyone, except perhaps you. I can't count the number of times I have frantically hunted through a huge VB app in search of a certain function only to realize after much angst that the programmer is using an API call.

The solution with VB5 is to turn the Windows API into easily reusable classes (or ActiveX controls—but more on them later). Each API call can be categorized according to which part of Windows it deals with. These categories can, in turn, be translated quite effectively into VB classes.

For our examples, how about a multimedia class that encapsulates the functionality of the multimedia API calls and, thus, the entire Windows multimedia system? That's what we'll look at next.

We'll start off by seeing how the class that I've put together works, then delve inside and see what's really happening.

Using the Multimedia Class

I have a great reuseable class module here which neatly wraps up a lot of the functionality of the multimedia API in Windows. Use it in your apps to provide access to sound and video files without the overhead of the heavyweight multimedia control that comes with Visual Basic. Let's do some typing.

Start a new Standard EXE project in Visual Basic, and then go to the Project menu and add a brand new class into your application. Then, bring up the code window and type this little lot in...it looks huge but it really isn't—I've padded the whole thing out with comments to make it a lot easier for you all to see what's going on.

```
Option Explicit

'------------------------------------------------------
'   Name      :   MMedia.cls
'   Author    :   Peter Wright, For BG2VB4 & BVB5
'
'   Notes     :   A multimedia class, which when turned
'             :   into an object lets you load and play
'             :   multimedia files, such as sound and
'             :   video.
```

```
'--------------------------------------------------------

' -=-=-=- PROPERTIES -=-=-=-
' Filename       Determines the name of the current file
' Length         The length of the file (Read Only)
' Position       The current position through the file
' Status         The current status of the object (Read Only)
' Wait           True/False...tells VB to wait until play done

' -=-=-=- METHODS -=-=-=-=-
' mmOpen <Filename>    Opens the requested filename
' mmClose              Closes the current file
' mmPause              Pauses playback of the current file
' mmStop               Stops playback ready for closedown
' mmSeek <Position>    Seeks to a position in the file
' mmPlay               Plays the open file

'------------------------------------------------------------------
' NOTES
' -----
'
' Open a file, then play it. Pause it in response to a request
' from the user. Stop if you intend to seek to the start and
' play again. Close when you no longer want to play the file
'-------------------------------------------------------------------

Private sAlias As String         ' Used internally to give an alias name
                                 ' to the multimedia resource

Private sFilename As String      ' Holds the filename internally
Private nLength As Single        ' Holds the length of the filename
                                 ' internally
Private nPosition As Single      ' Holds the current position internally
Private sStatus As String        ' Holds the current status as a string
Private bWait As Boolean         ' Determines if VB should wait until
                                 ' play is complete before returning.

'------------ API DECLARATIONS -------------
'note that this is all one code line:
Private Declare Function mciSendString Lib "winmm.dll" _
    Alias "mciSendStringA" (ByVal lpstrCommand As String, _
    ByVal lpstrReturnString As String, ByVal uReturnLength As Long, _
    ByVal hwndCallback As Long) As Long

Public Sub mmOpen(ByVal sTheFile As String)

    ' Declare a variable to hold the value returned by mciSendString
    Dim nReturn As Long
```

```
    ' Declare a string variable to hold the file type
    Dim sType As String

    ' Opens the specified multimedia file, and closes any
    ' other that may be open
    If sAlias <> "" Then
        mmClose
    End If

    ' Determine the type of file from the file extension
    Select Case UCase$(Right$(sTheFile, 3))
       Case "WAV"
          sType = "Waveaudio"
       Case "AVI"
          sType = "AviVideo"
       Case "MID"
          sType = "Sequencer"
       Case Else
          ' If the file extension is not known then exit the subroutine
          Exit Sub
    End Select
    sAlias = Right$(sTheFile, 3) & Minute(Now)

    ' At this point there is no file open, and we have determined the
    ' file type. Now would be a good time to open the new file.
    ' Note: if the name contains a space we have to enclose it in quotes
    If InStr(sTheFile, " ") Then sTheFile = Chr(34) & sTheFile & Chr(34)
    nReturn = mciSendString("Open " & sTheFile & " ALIAS " & sAlias _
          & " TYPE " & sType & " wait", "", 0, 0)
End Sub

Public Sub mmClose()
    ' Closes the currently opened multimedia file

    ' Declare a variable to hold the return value from the mciSendString
    ' command
    Dim nReturn As Long

    ' If there is no file currently open then exit the subroutine
    If sAlias = "" Then Exit Sub

    nReturn = mciSendString("Close " & sAlias, "", 0, 0)
    sAlias = ""
    sFilename = ""

End Sub

Public Sub mmPause()
    ' Pause playback of the file
```

```
    ' Declare a variable to hold the return value from the mciSendString
    ' command
    Dim nReturn As Long

    ' If there is no file currently open then exit the subroutine
    If sAlias = "" Then Exit Sub

    nReturn = mciSendString("Pause " & sAlias, "", 0, 0)

End Sub

Public Sub mmPlay()
    ' Plays the currently open file, from the current position

    ' Declare a variable to hold the return value from the mciSendString
    ' command
    Dim nReturn As Long

    ' If there is no file currently open, then exit the routine
    If sAlias = "" Then Exit Sub

    ' Now play the file
    If bWait Then
        nReturn = mciSendString("Play " & sAlias & " wait", "", 0, 0)
    Else
        nReturn = mciSendString("Play " & sAlias, "", 0, 0)
    End If
End Sub

Public Sub mmStop()
    ' Stop using a file totally, be it playing or whatever

    ' Declare a variable to hold the return value from mciSendString
    Dim nReturn As Long

    ' If there is no file currently open then exit the subroutine
    If sAlias = "" Then Exit Sub

    nReturn = mciSendString("Stop " & sAlias, "", 0, 0)

End Sub

Public Sub mmSeek(ByVal nPosition As Single)
    ' Seeks to a specific position within the file

    ' Declare a variable to hold the return value from the mciSendString
    ' function
    Dim nReturn As Long

    nReturn = mciSendString("Seek " & sAlias & " to " & nPosition, "",
                              0, 0)

End Sub
```

```
Property Get Filename() As String
' Routine to return a value when the programmer asks the
' object for the value of its Filename property
   Filename = sFilename
End Property

Property Let Filename(ByVal sTheFile As String)
' Routine to set the value of the filename property, should the
' programmer wish to do so. This implies that the programmer actually
' wants to open a file as well so control is passed to the mmOpen routine
   mmOpen sTheFile
End Property

Property Get Wait() As Boolean
' Routine to return the value of the object's wait property.
   Wait = bWait
End Property

Property Let Wait(bWaitValue As Boolean)
' Routine to set the value of the object's wait property
   bWait = bWaitValue
End Property

Property Get Length() As Single
   ' Routine to return the length of the currently opened multimedia
   ' file

   ' Declare a variable to hold the return value from the mciSendString
   Dim nReturn As Long, nLength As Integer

   ' Declare a string to hold the returned length from the mci Status
   ' call
   Dim sLength As String * 255

   ' If there is no file open then return 0
   If sAlias = "" Then
      Length = 0
      Exit Property
   End If

  nReturn = mciSendString("Status " & sAlias & " length", sLength, 255,
                          0)
  nLength = InStr(sLength, Chr$(0))
  Length = Val(Left$(sLength, nLength - 1))
End Property

Property Let Position(ByVal nPosition As Single)
' Sets the Position property effectively by seeking
   mmSeek nPosition
End Property
```

```
Property Get Position() As Single
    ' Returns the current position in the file

    ' Declare a variable to hold the return value from mciSendString
    Dim nReturn As Integer, nLength As Integer

    ' Declare a variable to hold the position returned
    ' by the mci Status position command
    Dim sPosition As String * 255

    ' If there is no file currently opened then exit the subroutine
    If sAlias = "" Then Exit Property

    ' Get the position and return
    nReturn = mciSendString("Status " & sAlias & " position", sPosition,
                                        255, 0)
    nLength = InStr(sPosition, Chr$(0))
    Position = Val(Left$(sPosition, nLength - 1))

End Property

Property Get Status() As String
    ' Returns the playback/record status of the current file

    ' Declare a variable to hold the return value from mciSendString
    Dim nReturn As Integer, nLength As Integer

    ' Declare a variable to hold the return string from mciSendString
    Dim sStatus As String * 255

    ' If there is no file currently opened, then exit the subroutine
    If sAlias = "" Then Exit Property

    nReturn = mciSendString("Status " & sAlias & " mode", sStatus, 255,
                                        0)

    nLength = InStr(sStatus, Chr$(0))
    Status = Left$(sStatus, nLength - 1)

End Property
```

When you're done typing this in, go to the Properties window and change the name of the class to MMedia. Then save it to your hard disk and call it **MMedia.cls**. Save the main project's form as **TestMM.frm**, and the project itself as **TestMM.vbp**. We'll be using this project later—and you never know, you may want to use the class again in your own projects.

This class turns a set of common multimedia calls into a stand-alone class. When an object is created from this class, it functions in exactly the same way as a control—in that it has properties you can set and examine, along with methods that actually make the object do something. This fits in well with the way we think about controls, and makes using the API calls invisible.

The methods that the class supports are as follows:

Method	Description
`mmOpen`	Opens a file (video, sound, music etc.) ready for playback.
`mmClose`	Closes the open file down, preventing any more playback.
`mmPause`	Pauses playback of the current file.
`mmStop`	Stops playback permanently.
`mmSeek`	Seeks a specific position within the file.
`mmPlay`	Take a guess; plays the open file, more often than not causing your speakers to burst into life.

These methods are all individual routines in **`MMedia.cls`** and all make use of the multimedia API calls in some way. We'll take a more detailed look at some of them in a moment to give you a feel for how the code actually fits together.

The following properties are implemented as property procedures in the source file:

Properties	Description
`Filename`	The name of the currently open file.
`Length`	The length of the currently open file.
`Position`	The current position through the file—you can use this in conjunction with the **`Length`** property to give the user some visual feedback as to the status of playback.
`Status`	A text word indicating the status of the file (playing, paused, stopped etc.).
`Wait`	Set this to true to make your code stop until playback has completed, or false to multitask.

Before we take a look at how the class does its thing, let's take a look at how to use the class itself. Along the way, you'll also see how seamless incorporating API calls into an app can be if you wrap the calls up nicely in a VB class.

Try It Out - Using the Multimedia Class

1 Open the **`TestMM.vbp`** project we just created if it isn't already open.

2 Resize the main form and draw a command button and common dialog control on it so that it looks like this:

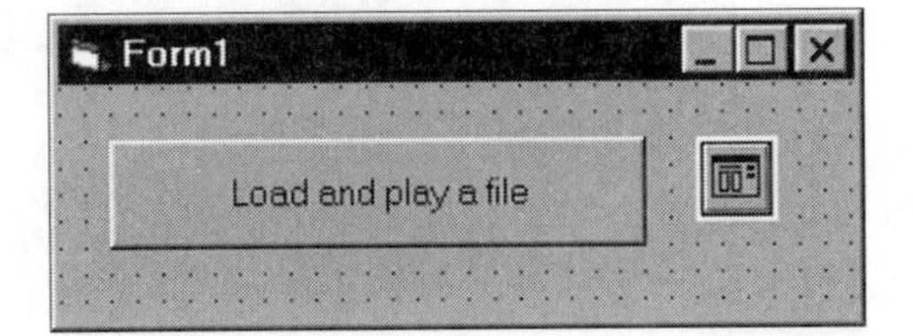

3 We want to pop up the common dialog when the command button is pressed, so that the user is able to select a file name. Bring up the code window for the command button's **Click** event, and type in this little lot:

```
Private Sub Command1_Click()

    With CommonDialog1
        .Filter = "WaveAudio (*.wav)|*.wav|Midi (*.mid)|*.mid|Video
          ↳ files (*.avi)|*.avi"
        .FilterIndex = 0
        .ShowOpen
    End With

End Sub
```

4 If you run the program now and click on the command button, you'll see the familiar file open dialog appear, asking you to select a multimedia file.

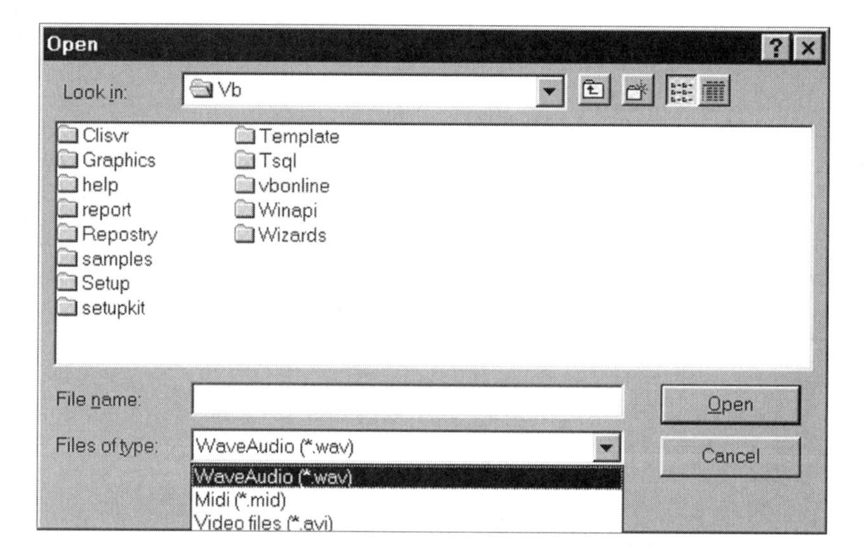

5 Quick and painless so far—all that remains is to bring the multimedia class into being as an object, and actually make use of it. Cancel the dialog and drop back into design mode, so that you can enter just a little more code. Bring up the command button **Click** event again and change it so that it looks like this:

```
Private Sub Command1_Click()

    Dim Multimedia As New MMedia

    With CommonDialog1
        .Filter = "WaveAudio (*.wav)|*.wav|Midi (*.mid)|*.mid|Video
            ↳ files (*.avi)|*.avi"
```

```
        .FilterIndex = 0
        .ShowOpen
    End With

    If CommonDialog1.Filename <> "" Then
        Multimedia.mmOpen CommonDialog1.Filename
        Multimedia.mmPlay
    End If

End Sub
```

6 Run the program. Find a multimedia file on your hard disk (there should be a few in **Windows\Media**) and have a play.

7 Save this project, because we'll be using it again in a while.

Of course, you'll need to have a sound card installed to play **WAV** *and* **MID** *files.*

How It Works

In the first line of the command button **Click** event code, we create a multimedia object which is derived from the **MMedia** class. This turns a class (which at this point is something ethereal and theoretical) into an object (something that can be used).

For the more technically minded amongst you, this process is normally referred to as ***instantiation****.*

```
Private Sub Command1_Click()

    Dim Multimedia As New MMedia
```

The four lines of code we added at the bottom make use of our new multimedia object by opening the selected file using the class' **mmOpen** method, and playing it using the class' **mmPlay** method.

```
If CommonDialog1.Filename <> "" Then
        Multimedia.mmOpen CommonDialog1.Filename
        Multimedia.mmPlay
End If
```

As you can hopefully see from this, wrapping API calls up in a nice class makes life a whole lot easier. If this class were used in a commercial organization, then the programmers using it wouldn't have to know anything about the underlying API calls—they would only need to be trained in how to use the multimedia class.

And of course, it has one other major attraction. Once you've been through the ritual of regular system reboots, as you find and eliminate the bugs in your API calling code, you don't want to have to do it all again in another project. Wrapping the API part in a class provides a safe, tested, and 'plug-in' capability—reducing the number of the API's customary three-fingered salutes that you'll need!

Understanding the Multimedia Class

While Visual Basic is great at detaching a programmer from some of the underlying complexities of Windows itself, there are still certain areas in which the API just can't be beaten, multimedia being one of them.

For example, the multimedia class you just wrote uses just one API call, **mciSendString**. Before we take an in-depth look at the code itself, it's probably a good idea to look at this particular API call in a little detail.

The Multimedia Control Interface

Windows itself actually consists of a number of subsystems: separate units within Windows that handle entire areas of functionality. One such area is something called the **MCI**. MCI stands for **Multimedia Control Interface**, which provides a device-independent way to use the multimedia features of Windows through code.

Device-independent? OK! In the bad old days of DOS, a programmer writing a video game, for example, would have to cope with every possible standard and type of sound and video cards in order to satisfy the games market. Device-independence, and the device drivers that Windows provides, let you hit any sound card, video card, and so on with the same code, just so long as it's supported by Windows.

The MCI provides this layer of independence, putting a neat bunch of functionality between you, the programmer, and the devices which would normally be used to handle multimedia data, namely the video and sound cards.

All this theory is great, but how exactly does the MCI work, and how does it provide this independence? The answer to both questions is that the MCI is responsible for talking to the Windows device drivers, and ultimately the multimedia hardware. You, the programmer, issue commands to the MCI using the API call **mciSendString**. These commands are then translated into calls to the appropriate Windows device driver, something that you no longer have to worry about.

To put it into VB terms then, the MCI is a built-in Windows class, which we have essentially super-classed in the earlier example.

Hang on a minute—programmers issue commands to the MCI. A little strange? Well, yes. Normally, when you deal with API calls, you are actually calling the subroutines and functions embedded in Windows in order to do something. The MCI really is an independent object. It can be programmed, and has its own programming language. When you use **mciSendString** you are in fact programming the MCI—just as easily as if you were firing VB commands out of the debug window.

Using mciSendString

The format of **mciSendString** is quite simple

```
<ResultCode> = mciSendString("<Command>", <ReturnString>, <ReturnLength>,
                             <CallbackHandle>)
```

This needs a bit of explanation. The **<ResultCode>** is a long integer, and varies depending on the command issued. The **<Command>** part (notice it is in quotes, so it's passed as a string literal) is the command you're sending to the MCI—such as **Play** to play a file, **Open** to open one, and so on. We'll look at exactly which commands the MCI understands later on, but for now let's cover the rest of the parameters.

Some MCI commands actually return a string value to your program. The MCI **Status** command, for example, can return a string telling your code whether a file is **Stopped**, **Paused**, **Playing** and so on. The string variable you place here will contain that return string.

The API call needs to know just how much data it can put in this string variable, so the next parameter passed is a number that is the length of the string. For this reason, if you are issuing a command to the MCI which returns a string, you must pass a fixed length string variable to the call and tell the **mciSendString** just how long that string is.

```
Dim sReturnString As String * 255
Dim nReturn As Long

nReturn = mciSendString("status waveaudio mode", sReturnString, 255, 0)
```

Don't worry about what this specific command does at this point, but notice the use of the fixed length string. Adding the *** 255** to the declaration of **sReturnString** tells VB to fix its length to **255** characters.

The final parameter, the **<CallbackHandle>**, is something a bit specialist, which we're not going to be using in this book. However, to satisfy your curiosity, here's a brief description of what it means.

Callback Functions in Visual Basic

Callback functions really only used to apply to those writing code in C, C++, Delphi, or some other low-level compiled language—and not Visual Basic. However, as of version 5, Visual Basic now lets you use callbacks in your code, without requiring special add-ins that were the only way to make it work in earlier versions.

When you use API subroutines and functions normally, your code has no way of knowing what's going on while that routine is running. You have to wait until it ends, then examine the return value. The principle idea of a callback is that an API function can call routines that are inside *your* Visual Basic code, while the API routine is running.

To do this, you have to create a **Public** function inside a VB code module, which has the correct number and type of parameters—as expected by the API routine. Then, when you call the API routine, you send it a **pointer** (the address in memory) of your VB callback function. To do this, you make use of the new Visual Basic **AddressOf** operator:

```
nResult = SomeAPIFunction(ParamOne, ParamTwo, AddressOf MyCallback)
```

As the API routine executes, it will call your VB function and send it the relevant parameters. This is often used to update status bars, get lists of system fonts, and other varied tasks.

As I said earlier, we won't be covering callbacks in this book. They provide an extra layer of complexity in your code, and even more ways to crash your system. However, the Visual Basic help files do give some examples if you'd like to experiment further.

Opening the Media File

Before you can tell the MCI what to do, you have to tell it which file you want to do it on. This is like using disk files. You must start by sending the **Open** command before you can do anything else.

The first part of this code should be self explanatory: you tell the **Open** command the name of the file that you want to open. This is a standard filename like **c:\video.avi**.

```
Open <filename> Type <typestring> Alias <aname>
    ...
    ...
    'Issue commands to do something to the file
    ...
    ...
Close <aname>
```

After the **Type** keyword, you need to tell Windows what kind of file you are dealing with. The standard Windows ones are **WaveAudio** for **WAV** files, **AVIVideo** for **AVI** files and **Sequencer** for **MID** files.

Finally, you can tell the MCI to give the file you just opened a name, an **Alias**, which you will use from now on to refer to the open file. It's rather like naming a variable, in that the name can be almost anything you want. For example:

```
Open c:\video.avi Type AVIVideo Alias Peter
```

If you sent this to the MCI with **MCISendString**, it would tell the MCI to open a file called **c:\video.avi** as a Microsoft video file and that, in future MCI commands, we'll refer to this file using the name **Peter**.

Once opened, normal MCI commands can be issued using the alias to play the file, stop it, pause it, find out its status and so on. For example:

```
Play Peter
Pause Peter
Stop Peter
```

There are literally hundreds of combinations of MCI commands that you can use, and we'll take a look at the most common a little later.

Once you have done your stuff with a file, you need to close it down by sending the **Close** command, followed by the alias of the file you are dealing with.

```
nReturn = mciSendString("Close Peter", "",0,0)
```

Let's take a look at how the code does what it does now, and see more of what our new class can do.

Try It Out - Displaying Status and Position for a Multimedia File

1 Open the **TestMM.vbp** project we just created if it isn't already open.

2 We're going to add some controls to see how the **Status** and **Position** properties of our **MMedia** class can be used. Add a **ProgressBar**, a **Label**, and a **Timer** control to your form, so it looks like this:

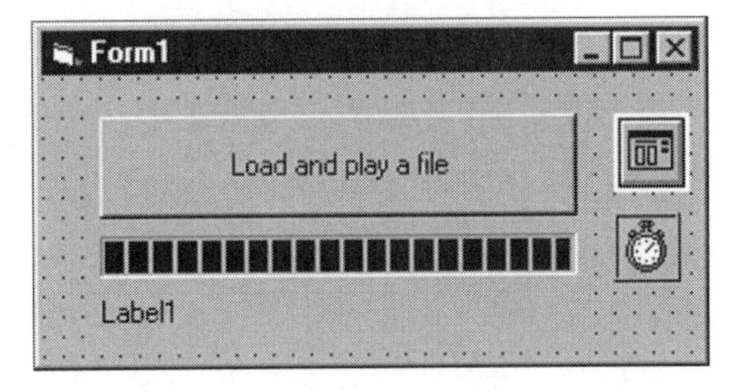

If you can't find the progress bar in your toolbox, add it by selecting Components *from the* Project *menu, and check the* Microsoft Windows Common Controls 5.0 *option box.*

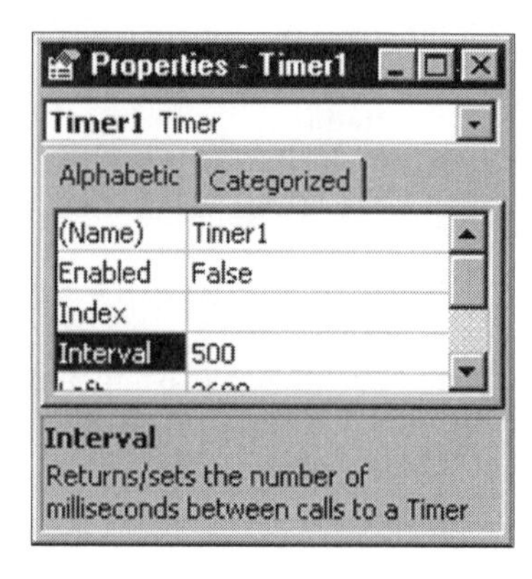

3 Open the Properties window for the **`Timer`** control, and set its Enabled property to **`False`**, and its Interval property to **`500`**. Clear the caption for the Label control at the same time.

4 Double-click on the Load and play a file button to open the Code window for its **`Click`** event. Add these highlighted lines to the code:

```
Private Sub Command1_Click()
   ...
   'other existing stuff here
   ...
    If CommonDialog1.Filename <> "" Then
         Multimedia.Wait = False
         Multimedia.mmOpen CommonDialog1.Filename
         ProgressBar1.Value = 0
         ProgressBar1.Max = Multimedia.Length
         Timer1.Enabled = True
         Multimedia.mmPlay
    End If
End Sub
```

5 Back in the form, double-click the **`Timer1`** control to open the Code window for its **`Timer`** event. Add this code to it:

```
Private Sub Timer1_Timer()

   ProgressBar1.Value = Multimedia.Position
   Label1 = "Status: " & Multimedia.Status
   If ProgressBar1.Value = ProgressBar1.Max Then
      Multimedia.mmClose
      Timer1.Enabled = False
   End If

End Sub
```

As it stands now, we have a minor problem. We defined the variable that refers to instance of our **MMedia** class within the **Command1_Click()** event routine. Now we want to refer to it from our **Timer1_Timer()** event routine as well.

6 In the **Click** event for the command button, select the line that declares the **Multimedia** variable, press *Ctrl-X* to cut it to the clipboard. This removes it from the **Command1_Click()** event routine. Then select (General) in the top left drop-down list in the Code window, and hit *Ctrl-V* to paste it into the General Declarations section, where it will be available to all the code in this form.

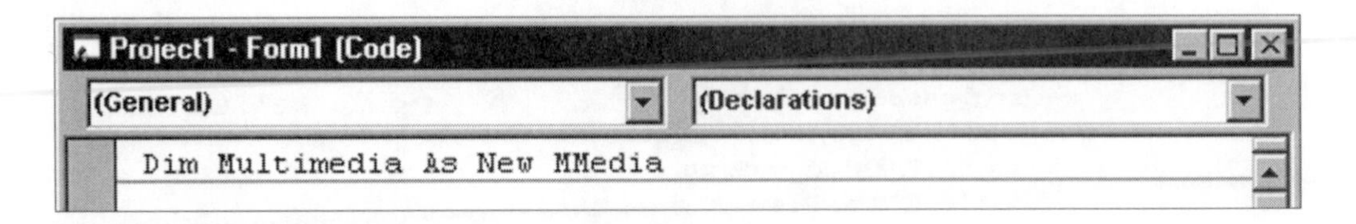

7 OK, we're ready to go. Click the Load and play a file button, and select a multimedia file as before. For a change this time, we've chosen one of the 'Welcome to Windows 95' videos from the Windows CD-ROM.

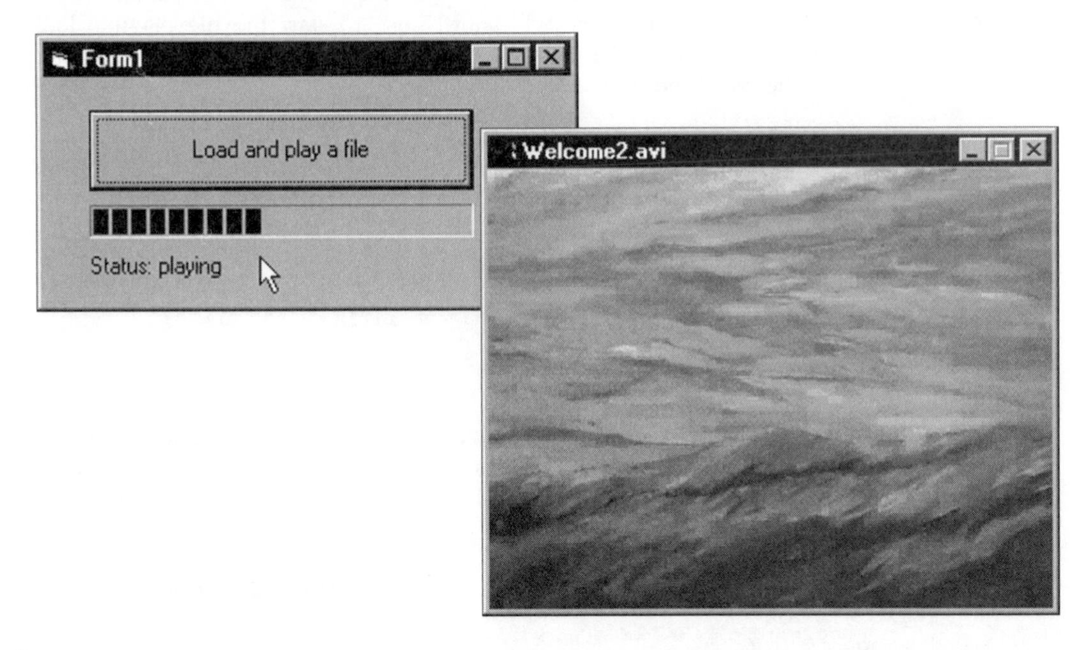

8 You can see the progress bar now shows how far through the file we are, and the status—in this case playing. When the video is finished, you'll see this change to stopped.

How It Works

We'll use this example to show you in more detail how some parts of the **MMedia** class work, and how we've used them. Firstly, the code that runs when you click the Load and play a file button.

We added four lines to the routine you saw in the earlier example. These are all concerned with setting up the controls on the form, and the properties of the **Multimedia** object, before we start playing the file.

```
If CommonDialog1.Filename <> "" Then
        Multimedia.Wait = False
        Multimedia.mmOpen CommonDialog1.Filename
        ProgressBar1.Value = 0
        ProgressBar1.Max = Multimedia.Length
        Timer1.Enabled = True
        Multimedia.mmPlay
    End If
```

Our **MMedia** class, and hence our **Multimedia** object, has a property named **Wait**. This determines if the code in our VB program will continue to run (multitask) while the file is playing, or just stop and wait for it to finish, like it did in the earlier example. The **mmPlay** method of the class, which we will shortly use to start the file playing, looks at the value of a private variable in the class named **bWait**. If it's **True**, it includes the command **wait** in the **mciSendString** call:

```
Public Sub mmPlay()        'in the MMedia class
    Dim nReturn As Long
    If sAlias = "" Then Exit Sub
    If bWait Then
        nReturn = mciSendString("Play " & sAlias & " Wait", "", 0, 0)
    Else
        nReturn = mciSendString("Play " & sAlias, "", 0, 0)
    End If
End Sub
```

And how does **bWait** get set to the correct value? Remember from our discussions on class modules, that we can supply property routines which allow the values of the internal variables to be set and read just like a normal Visual Basic control's properties:

```
Property Get Wait() As Boolean
    'Routine to return the value of the object's wait property.
    Wait = bWait
End Property
```

```
Property Let Wait(bWaitValue As Boolean)
    'Routine to set the value of the object's wait property
    bWait = bWaitValue
End Property
```

The next step is to open the file we want to play. To do this, we use the **MMedia** class' **mmOpen** method.

Opening the File

First off, we declare a couple of local variables to hold temporary values. We'll see what these are for shortly. Then there's a lot of code devoted to building up the command string, before we send it to the MCI.

```
Public Sub mmOpen(ByVal sTheFile As String)
    Dim nReturn As Long
    Dim sType As String

    If sAlias <> "" Then
       mmClose
    End If

    Select Case UCase$(Right$(sTheFile, 3))
       Case "WAV"
          sType = "Waveaudio"
       Case "AVI"
          sType = "AviVideo"
       Case "MID"
          sType = "Sequencer"
       Case Else
          Exit Sub
    End Select

    sAlias = Right$(sTheFile, 3) & Minute(Now)
    If InStr(sTheFile, " ") Then sTheFile = Chr(34) & sTheFile & Chr(34)
    nReturn = mciSendString("Open " & sTheFile & " ALIAS " & sAlias _
                                  & " TYPE " & sType & " wait", "", 0, 0)
End Sub
```

First the **mmOpen** routine checks a class level/module level variable called **sAlias**.

```
If sAlias <> "" Then
   mmClose
End If
```

Whenever you deal with the MCI, it's a good idea to assign aliases to each file you have open. Here, the **MMedia** class works out a name for the alias for you and stores it in **sAlias**. When you next go to open a file with **mmOpen**, or set the file name property, the code can check this and call another routine which closes the first file down. Closing multimedia files down when they are no longer needed frees up memory and speeds up playback, so it's always a good idea.

A familiar **Select Case** construct is then used to figure out the file type. When you open a file with the MCI, you need to tell it what type of data the file holds. The **Select Case** construct here does that, storing the MCI type name in the **sType** variable declared at the start of the routine.

```
Select Case UCase$(Right$(sTheFile, 3))
   Case "WAV"
      sType = "Waveaudio"
   Case "AVI"
      sType = "AviVideo"
   Case "MID"
      sType = "Sequencer"
   Case Else
      Exit Sub
End Select
```

At this point, any previously opened file has been closed, and the type name of the new file has been stored in **sType**. All that remains is to decide on an alias for the file, and then open it.

Aliases must be unique, since the MCI can cope with having more than one file open—and even playing. Since we don't want to force unnecessary complexity on the user of the class, it makes sense if the class decides on its own alias.

```
sAlias = Right$(sTheFile, 3) & Minute(Now)
```

It does this by taking the right three characters of the file name and appending the minutes part of the current system time. So if it was 16:15 when you opened **c:\video.avi**, then the alias the class would come up with would be **AVI15**. The newly calculated alias is then stored in the **sAlias** module level variable that we checked when the procedure first started. The value in **sAlias** is then used throughout the rest of the module whenever we need to do something to the open file—like play it.

So, armed with the file type in one variable, the alias in a second, and the file name in a third, we can finally send the **Open** command to the MCI. The only fly in the ointment is the need to surround file names which contain spaces with quotation marks (**"**):

```
If InStr(sTheFile, " ") Then sTheFile = Chr(34) & sTheFile & Chr(34)
nReturn = mciSendString("Open " & sTheFile & " ALIAS " & sAlias & " TYPE
                   ↳     " & sType & " wait", "", 0, 0)
```

The command sent is **Open**, followed by the file name, followed by **ALIAS** then the new alias (held in **sAlias**), followed by **TYPE** and the type, and finally, the word **wait**.

The **wait** statement on the end here tells the API not to let our VB code continue running until it has finished loading the file. Without this, on a fast machine with a slow hard disk, problems can occur—you might try to play the file before it has loaded, simply because the code is running a lot faster than the hard disk. Notice that this isn't the same as the **Wait** property that we looked at earlier, which controls whether our program continues to run while the file is *playing*, and not while it's *loading*.

So, now, we can set up the progress bar ready to show the progress of the file's playback. But we need to know how long it is, so that we can set the progress bar's **Max** value. And of course, we'll need to know the relative position in the file at regular intervals so that we can update it while the file is playing. To recap, here's the **Command1_Click** event again. So far we've only managed to open the file that we want to play:

```
If CommonDialog1.Filename <> "" Then
     Multimedia.Wait = False
     Multimedia.mmOpen CommonDialog1.Filename
     ProgressBar1.Value = 0
     ProgressBar1.Max = Multimedia.Length
     Timer1.Enabled = True
     Multimedia.mmPlay
End If
```

The highlighted code above is the bit that looks after setting up the progress bar. We set it's current **Value** to **0**, which resets it from the last time it was used (i.e. if another file has been played previously). Then we set its **Max** value to the length of the file we've just opened, using the **Length** property of our **Multimedia** object.

Getting the File Length

We can use **mciSendString** to *return* values, as well as to *set* them. The **Length** property of our **MMedia** class is read-only, because we haven't provided a **Property Let** routine. We wouldn't expect to be able to set the length of the file anyway. However, we do have a **Property Get** which returns the length of the currently open file:

```
Property Get Length() As Single
    Dim nReturn As Long, nLength As Integer
    Dim sLength As String * 255
    If sAlias = "" Then
       Length = 0
       Exit Property
    End If
    nReturn = mciSendString("Status " & sAlias & " Length", sLength, 255,
                               ↳ 0)
    nLength = InStr(sLength, Chr$(0))
    Length = Val(Left$(sLength, nLength - 1))
End Property
```

First **sAlias** is checked to see if a file has been opened. If it hasn't, then the value returned from the property procedure is **0**. If a file has been opened, then the MCI **Status Length** command is used to find out how long it is.

You needn't worry about how the length of the file is measured, since any unit of measurement will be suitable for setting up the progress bar. Just for your interest, though, you can set the unit of measurement to various values, ranging from frames in a video clip to milliseconds in a sound file. However, a complete rundown of the options is a little beyond the scope of what we are trying to achieve here.

The **Status** command is a rather special MCI command and can be used in conjunction with keywords like **Length**, **Position**, and **Mode** to find out a great deal of information about the current file. It returns this information in a fixed length string variable which is passed to **mciSendString** after the MCI command. In this example, the return string is called **sLength** and is declared to be **255** characters long.

Of course, you're not always going to get **255** characters back from the **Status** command, especially if you only want to know the length of the file. The unused space in the string is filled with the character **0**, making it easy for us to use VB's **InStr** function to find out exactly how long the returned data is, and pull it out.

```
nReturn = mciSendString("Status " & sAlias & " Length", sLength, 255,
                        ↳ 0)
nLength = InStr(sLength, Chr$(0))
Length = Val(Left$(sLength, nLength - 1))
```

Here, the position of the first **Chr(0)** is stored in **nLength**, since **InStr** returns the character position at which the search data is located, or **0** if it can't find what you are looking for. This now gives us enough information to pull the characters from the left side of the fixed length string, convert them to a number (rather than a string) and return that value ready to go into the **Length** property.

Getting the Current Position

When the file is actually playing, the **Status Position** command can be used repeatedly to find out exactly where in the file playback has reached. The code to return the value of the **Position** property looks strangely familiar:

```
Property Get Position() As Single
    Dim nReturn As Integer, nLength As Integer
    Dim sPosition As String * 255

    If sAlias = "" Then Exit Property
    nReturn = mciSendString("Status " & sAlias & " Position", sPosition, _
                            255, 0)
    nLength = InStr(sPosition, Chr$(0))
    Position = Val(Left$(sPosition, nLength - 1))
End Property
```

The only real difference this time is that instead of sending **Status Length** to the MCI, we are sending **Status Position**.

Getting the Current Status

To get the text message for the status, sometimes called the **mode**, we query the class' **Status** property. This is done using another **Property Get** routine, almost identical to the **Position** property we've just seen.

The only differences are that we send the command **Status Mode** instead of **Status Length** or **Status Position** to the **mciSendString** function. And, of course, we don't need to convert the result to a number, because it's supposed to be a text string:

```
...
nReturn = mciSendString("Status " & sAlias & " Mode", sStatus, 255, 0)
nLength = InStr(sStatus, Chr$(0))
Status = Left$(sStatus, nLength - 1)
...
```

OK, let's go back to that **Command1_Click** event again, and see where we are. So far, we've set the **Wait** property, opened the file, and set up the progress bar. Before we actually start playing the file, we'll set our **Timer** control ticking. You'll see what it does in just a moment. Then, finally, we'll play the file by calling the **mmPlay** method of our **Multimedia** object:

```
If CommonDialog1.Filename <> "" Then
        Multimedia.Wait = False
        Multimedia.mmOpen CommonDialog1.Filename
        ProgressBar1.Value = 0
        ProgressBar1.Max = Multimedia.Length
        Timer1.Enabled = True
        Multimedia.mmPlay
    End If
```

Starting the File Playing

Here, again, is the complete code for the **mmPlay** method of our **MMedia** class. To execute it, we just need to call it in our **Multimedia** object. It first checks to see we have a file open by examining the **sAlias** variable, then if all is well it executes the MCI **Play** command. We've already seen the way we set and use the **Wait** property, which controls whether the command is actually **Play Wait** or just **Play**.

```
Public Sub mmPlay()        'in the MMedia class
    Dim nReturn As Long
    If sAlias = "" Then Exit Sub
    If bWait Then
        nReturn = mciSendString("Play " & sAlias & " Wait", "", 0, 0)
    Else
        nReturn = mciSendString("Play " & sAlias, "", 0, 0)
    End If
End Sub
```

Updating the Progress Bar and Label Controls

Our final task is to update the progress bar and the label on the form, as the file is playing. We've already covered all the stuff we need to do this with. Before we set the file playing, we enabled a **Timer** control with an **Interval** of **500**. So it will fire every half a second. Each time it does, the code in the **Timer1_Timer()** event routine runs:

```
Private Sub Timer1_Timer()
    ProgressBar1.Value = Multimedia.Position
    Label1 = "Status: " & Multimedia.Status
    If ProgressBar1.Value = ProgressBar1.Max Then
        Multimedia.mmClose
        Timer1.Enabled = False
```

```
    End If
End Sub
```

You're probably well ahead of me by now. All this code does is take the value of the **Multimedia** object's **Position** property and assign it to the **ProgressBar** control's **Value** property, updating the display on the form. Then it gets the **Multimedia** object's current **Status** property, which is a text string, and pops it into the **Label1** control on the form. Remember, this is happening twice a second.

Simply retrieving these properties, of course, runs the **Property Get** routines we wrote in the class, which in turn use the MCI **Status Position** and **Status Mode** commands each time.

The only other thing is to stop it all happening when we get to the end of the file. This is done by comparing the progress bar's current and maximum values. When they're the same, it's time to close the file using the **Multimedia** object's **mmClose** method, then disable the timer to prevent this routine running again until another file is opened.

Our MCI Commands Summary

To end, here's a list of the MCI commands used in our **MMedia** class:

Command	Description
Play	Plays a file.
Pause	Pauses playback, ready to start up again at any time.
Stop	Stops a file—you need to seek to a position to continue playback.
Seek	Followed by a number, seeks to that position in the file.
Status Mode	Returns a string indicating what the file is doing (i.e. Stopped, Paused, Playing, Ready).
Status Position	Returns a number indicating the position through the file that playback has reached.
Status Length	Returns the length of the file and helps to put the number returned from **Status Position** into some meaningful context.
Close	Closes the file and frees up the memory it previously occupied.

The MCI supports a few more commands than this, and also a number of specialized ones for each file format.

What I hope to have shown you is how even apparently complex topics, such as multimedia, really aren't that hard if you drop down to the API. Also, that the API itself is not the daunting mother of all nightmares that many VB programmers make it out to be.

Summary

This chapter should have provided you with a glimpse of the power that lies beyond the strict limits of Visual Basic, as defined in the language itself. This is a huge subject, and so what we've done is touch on the main principles of using the Windows API.

With power comes responsibility, because once you choose to operate outside the confines of Visual Basic, you have to look after yourself. It pays to develop a deep understanding of all the components of Windows, so you can write Visual Basic programs that are truly well-behaved members of the Windows desktop community.

In our brief tour we covered:

- How Windows and Visual Basic fit together
- The Windows API
- How to use the Windows API to extend the power of Visual Basic
- How to write well-behaved Windows applications

Why Not Try...

1. Using the Windows API is a two step process. What do you need to call DLL outside of the Visual Basic environment?

2. When passing a string argument from a VB application to a routine in a DLL, should the argument be passed by reference or by value?

3. In your Visual Basic window, there is an icon for an API Text Viewer. This contains the name of the functions and procedures contained in the various DLLs that comprise the API. Experiment with this just a bit. Load the Win32API Text file. You should receive a message indicating that This API file will be loaded faster if it is converted to a database. Would you like to convert it now. Select Yes. The text file will be converted to an Access database. Notice that there are 3 categories of viewable items---Constants, Declares, and Types. See if you can find an API that will tell you what kind of drive a drive letter is associated with. For instance, is drive D a fixed drive, CD-Rom, or network drive.

4. Now that you've found the function to determine the type of drive, can you find the values that are returned by this function.

5. Create a project with a single form and a command button. When the button is clicked, display an input box that prompts the user for a drive letter. Use the Windows API to determine the type of drive associated with the drive letter.

asic Visual Basic Visual Ba

al Basic Visual Basic Visual

Basic Visual Basic Visual Ba

ual Basic Vi

Basic Visu

ual Basic V

l Basic Vis

isual Basic Visual Basic

al Basic Visual Basic Visua

Visual Basic Visual Basic Visu

l Basic Visual Ba

l Basic Visual

ic Visual Basi

Basic Visual B

ic Visual Basi

al Basic Visual

ual Basic Visual Basic Visual Ba

Visual Basic Visual Basic Visu

sual Basic Visual Basic Visu

Visual Basic Visual Ba

Visual Basic and Components

Huh? We already did this, back when we looked at programming with controls, right? Well, kind of! Component development with Visual Basic actually goes far beyond simply dropping controls from the toolbox on to a form at design time.

What we're going to take a look at in this chapter is the whole picture surrounding the use of ActiveX. In earlier chapters we took a peek at using ActiveX controls, the new replacement for OCX and VBX controls that Visual Basic 5 now supports. In this chapter, though, we go beyond that and take a look at ActiveX components, ActiveX documents and linking and embedding with OLE. We even show how you can actually create a component with Visual Basic 5.

You'll learn:

- What ActiveX really is, and what happened to OLE 2
- How to use ActiveX components, such as those provided by Microsoft Office
- How to create your own ActiveX component servers
- Everything you ever wanted to know about ActiveX, OLE, in-process and out-of-process components and much more besides

Of all the areas of VB5's functionality, its ActiveX support is by far the most exciting and engrossing. Although in this chapter we look mainly at ActiveX components, if you have the Control Creation, Professional or Enterprise editions of Visual Basic, then you'll probably want to take a look at the next chapter as well, where we cover how to create your own ActiveX controls. So, let's get stuck in...

DDE, OLE, ActiveX – I Can't Take Any More!!!

Confusing isn't it? Programmers just love their jargon, not least because it makes the whole job seem so complex and so far out of reach of the average mortal that they no longer feel threatened. The truth of the matter, however, is that programming is easy—and in general, the more confusing the acronym, the easier the subject matter it surrounds. MS-DOS stands for Microsoft Disk Operating System—but it actually came from a humorous name given to the very foundation code that formed it—Messy Dos. That in turn came from something known as the Quick and Dirty Operating System (Qdos). Still worried by acronyms? <G>

All the slightly worrying acronyms in the heading above relate to the same common goal: to provide developers with a way to share functionality and information between applications, and thus increase the possibility of code re-use. In English—each of them helps you cheat by using other peoples' code to develop your own applications.

The one we're most interested in is, of course, ActiveX, but it's worth taking a little stroll down memory lane in order to see how we got to where we are.

DDE – The Dynamic Data Exchange

Ah—the dulcet sounds of babies sleeping. WAKE UP!! This thing was great, but its usage overhead only served to propel us closer to the ActiveX standard that we can now enjoy.

DLLs provided a great way for applications to share a common code base, such as the common controls you already find in Windows 95 for example, but what about these applications sharing information at run time. Wouldn't it be great, the developers at Microsoft mused, if that VB guy could grab some information from that Excel spreadsheet, or better still, update the Excel spreadsheet based on what the user does with the VB app.

DDE provided a way to do just that, allowing two applications to set up a very simple 'conversation' between each other, with one feeding data into a preset area of the other. Great stuff. It came with a price though, as many programmers found when their brains started to melt under the complexity of setting the darn thing up...there had to be an easier way. There was...let the users do it themselves, and let the developers do nothing more than provide the users with the necessary tools to undertake the task. Enter stage left...

OLE – Object Linking and Embedding

Now we're getting somewhere. DDE was just too constrictive, not robust enough, and too difficult for the average programmer to set up, let alone to let the average user loose on. So, in keeping with the point and click, drag and drop philosophy of Windows, OLE was introduced—and whether you like it or not, its pronounced OH LAY, not O. L. E.

With the first incarnations of OLE, users had the ability—with OLE enabled applications, of course—to literally drag and drop data from one application right into another. How many times have you seen the ad where a user drops an Excel graph right into their Word document, for example: that's OLE.

Technology moves on though, and over the years since its release, OLE has been heavily enhanced and extended to support many really neat features, like **in-place activation** and **automation** (formerly known as OLE automation).

These sound scary, but in fact they're so simple that the chances are that you've probably already used them a lot without even knowing it. With in-place activation, users would be able to double click on the data that they have in one app from another, and in turn run up the second application within the first. Confused? Imagine having that Excel graph inside your Word document and double clicking it. In-place activation causes the menus and toolbars in Word to change, without removing your document from view, and lets you edit and change all the properties and look and feel of that graph using Excel, but without ever leaving Word or losing sight of your original document.

Automation, on the other hand, is a different kettle of fish. If you think about it, most users have a suite of applications on their desktop that do almost everything that they need to do, and use custom developed applications to augment their functionality to do things that those shrink-wrapped packages can't do out of the box. For example, Excel is great at dealing with numbers, but the chances are that it won't handle your invoices for you in the format that your business needs and so you make use of invoicing software supplied by the IT department.

In the past, this would have meant that the IT department would have to spend a lot of time writing an application that includes code to print, calculate, look at your stock and customer databases and so on. With Automation they don't have to. If your stock and customer databases are in Access format, then using Automation, you could run up the Access forms and reports that you have already designed, and then, still using Automation, run up Excel to format the numbers and data from Access into a printable invoice with all the necessary calculations and so on handled by Excel. Automation is really all about reusing the objects on the desktop, and always making use of the best tool for the job. With Visual Basic 5 you can create objects for others to use, in addition to using objects that other people have written.

Why knock up a grid and write reams of VB code to perform arithmetic calculations on it, when that's something that Excel does really well?

ActiveX – Building the Future on the Foundations of the Past

ActiveX (don't ask me what it means—I have no idea) really builds heavily on the foundations of OLE and, in the process, replaces it. You'll still hear a lot about OLE 2, but let there be absolutely no mistake—ActiveX is the next generation.

Sure we can still do linking and embedding with Visual Basic in the same way that users expected to see with Version 1 of OLE. Sure we can still take control of a remote application and program it, using the properties and methods of the objects that it makes available, using the same techniques and ideas that define Automation. Both of these technologies are ActiveX technologies, but this isn't all that ActiveX is.

ActiveX is really all about component software—enabling software developers to seamlessly add powerful prebuilt blocks of code to their applications, without having to worry about where they came from or how they operate. ActiveX components can be built with a variety of computer languages, including C, C++, Pascal, and, now, even Visual Basic. They can be used in an even wider array of containers, this time including VB, C++ and Pascal applications, Web browsers, even Office 97 documents and applications.

What about making your own forms and objects available to all within the boundaries of the user's web browser? Or reducing the size of or adding Internet functionality to the components you design? Ask these questions and a myriad of others along the same lines at the next Microsoft conference you attend and they'll smile back 'Ah—you wanna be looking into ActiveX'.

...and that's just what we're going to do now.

Taking a Peek at ActiveX Really Working

One of the many cool things you can do with ActiveX is to front end Microsoft Office, and develop entire applications based around reusing the objects that Office exposes. I'm going to focus on Office in this section (this is suitable for both Office 95 or 97).

For those of you who don't have Office, don't panic. There's still plenty you can do with ActiveX components, particularly since Visual Basic lets you create your own and then access them just like any other. We'll take a peek at how this works in a little while.

For now though, let's take a stroll through Office—or more precisely, Excel.

Try It Out – Building the Application (Office 95 or 97 Compatible)

Before we go through a big explanation of every intricacy in ActiveX, let's take a look at an (almost) real-world example of how you might use it, just to introduce some of the concepts. What we're going to do here is get our VB app to work with the **`Biblio`** database. It will accept two years from the user and then, in Excel, display a count of all the titles published in those years by each publisher.

1 Start a new standard EXE project.

2 Drop some controls on to the form and set them up so that the form looks like this:

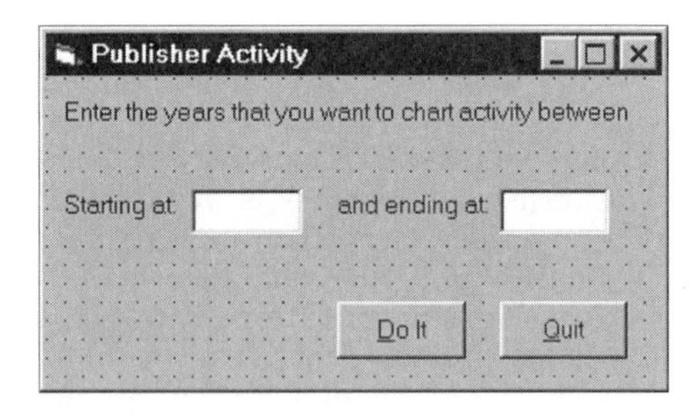

3 Name the text boxes **`txtStart`** and **`txtEnd`**, and the command buttons **`cmdDoIt`** and **`cmdQuit`**. Also set the **`Default`** property of the Do It button to **`True`** and the **`Cancel`** property of the Quit button to **`True`**.

4 So far so good. Now, we need to put in some kind of link to the database. With a little SQL magic we can get away with just one data control to deal with grabbing the publisher names and counting the number of titles that they released in a year. Drop a data control on to the form, like this

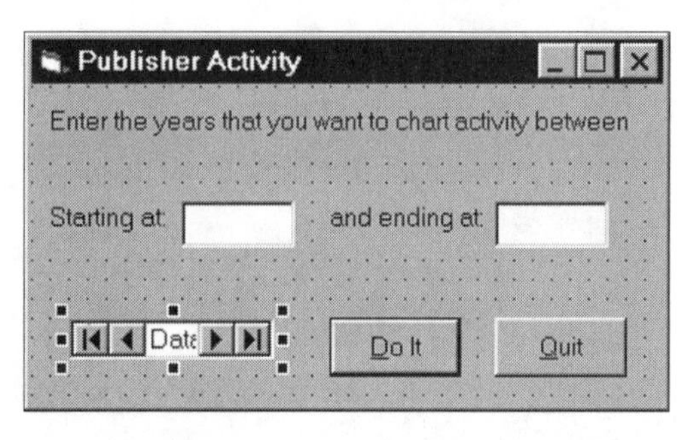

5 Set the **Visible** property of the data control to **False** (we're going to navigate through the recordset using code), set its **Name** to **datTitles** and point the **DatabaseName** property at the **Biblio** sample database that comes with VB. We don't need to set up the **RecordSource** property at this point because we're going to do that at run time based on the information entered into the two text boxes.

6 Let's add some code to that Do It button to walk through the records in the database. Bring up the code window for its **Click** event and type this in.

```
Private Sub cmdDoIt_Click()

    Dim CurrentRow As Integer
    Dim sLastPublisher As String

    Screen.MousePointer = 11
    Plot_Titles txtStart, txtEnd

    datTitles.RecordSource = " SELECT DISTINCT Publishers.[Name],
         ↳ Titles.[Year Published], Count([ISBN]) AS Count FROM Titles
         ↳ INNER JOIN Publishers ON Titles.[PubId] = Publishers.[PubId]
         ↳ " & " WHERE Titles.[Year Published] >= " & txtStart & " AND
         ↳ Titles.[Year Published] <= " & txtEnd & " GROUP BY
         ↳ Titles.[Year Published], [Name] "
    datTitles.Refresh

    CurrentRow = 2
    sLastPublisher = ""

    With datTitles.Recordset

    If .RecordCount > 0 Then
       .MoveFirst
       Do While Not .EOF
           If .Fields("Name") <> sLastPublisher Then
               sLastPublisher = .Fields("Name")
               CurrentRow = CurrentRow + 1
               Plot_The_Name CurrentRow, .Fields("Name")
           End If
```

```
            Plot_The_Value CurrentRow,
               ⇘ datTitles.Recordset.Fields("Count"),
                ⇘ datTitles.Recordset.Fields("Year Published") - txtStart
            .MoveNext
        Loop

    End If
    End With

    Screen.MousePointer = 0

End Sub
```

7 Now add a line of code to the Quit button to make sure that it works as it should:

```
Private Sub cmdQuit_Click()

    Unload Me

End Sub
```

How It Works

Although it looks totally horrendous, it really isn't. What's happening here is that a SQL query is being built up to join the **Titles** and **Publishers** tables together, and then get a count of all the titles published in the years between the two that were entered into the text boxes on the form.

```
Screen.MousePointer = 11
Plot_Titles txtStart, txtEnd
```

We start by using the **MousePointer** property of the **Screen** object to set the mouse pointer to an hourglass—our Automation code may take a while and we don't want our users to think that nothing's happening. We then make a call to the **Plot_Titles** subroutine. We'll look at this in a moment.

```
datTitles.RecordSource = " SELECT DISTINCT Publishers.[Name],
    ⇘ Titles.[Year Published], Count([ISBN]) AS Count FROM Titles
    ⇘ INNER JOIN Publishers ON Titles.[PubId] = Publishers.[PubId]
    ⇘ " & " WHERE Titles.[Year Published] >= " & txtStart & " AND
    ⇘ Titles.[Year Published] <= " & txtEnd & " GROUP BY
    ⇘ Titles.[Year Published], [Name] "
datTitles.Refresh
```

Next, the SQL query does an inner join between the **Titles** and **Publishers** tables, returning the publisher name and book title for each record that resides in both tables where the year published falls between the dates given by the user. The records are ordered first by the year published, and then by the publishers name. The statement **Count([ISBN]) AS Count** returns the number of books published by the given publisher for the given year.

```
    CurrentRow = 2
    sLastPublisher = ""

    With datTitles.Recordset

    If .RecordCount > 0 Then
        .MoveFirst
        Do While Not .EOF
            If .Fields("Name") <> sLastPublisher Then
                sLastPublisher = .Fields("Name")
                CurrentRow = CurrentRow + 1
                Plot_The_Name CurrentRow, .Fields("Name")
            End If
            Plot_The_Value CurrentRow,
                ↳ datTitles.Recordset.Fields("Count"),
                ↳ datTitles.Recordset.Fields("Year Published") - txtStart
            .MoveNext
        Loop

    End If
    End With
```

Once the query is built up, a loop is used to move through all the records retrieved, printing the name of the publisher each time a new one is located, and then printing the number of books published in each year on each new record retrieved.

```
    Screen.MousePointer = 0
```

Finally, once we've completed the processing, we set **MousePointer** back to its default value.

The application will now do everything that we need it to do except, of course, dump the results out to Excel. Time to add that ActiveX code.

Try It Out - Adding the ActiveX Code (Office 95 or 97 Compatible)

There are a number of steps that need to be followed when dealing with ActiveX.

1. The first thing we need to do is to make sure that we're referencing the relevant ActiveX server. From the Project menu, select References.... In the dialog that appears, make sure that the checkbox to the left of the Microsoft Excel 8.0 Object Library (or Excel 5.0 Object Library if you have Excel 95) is checked, and then click on OK.

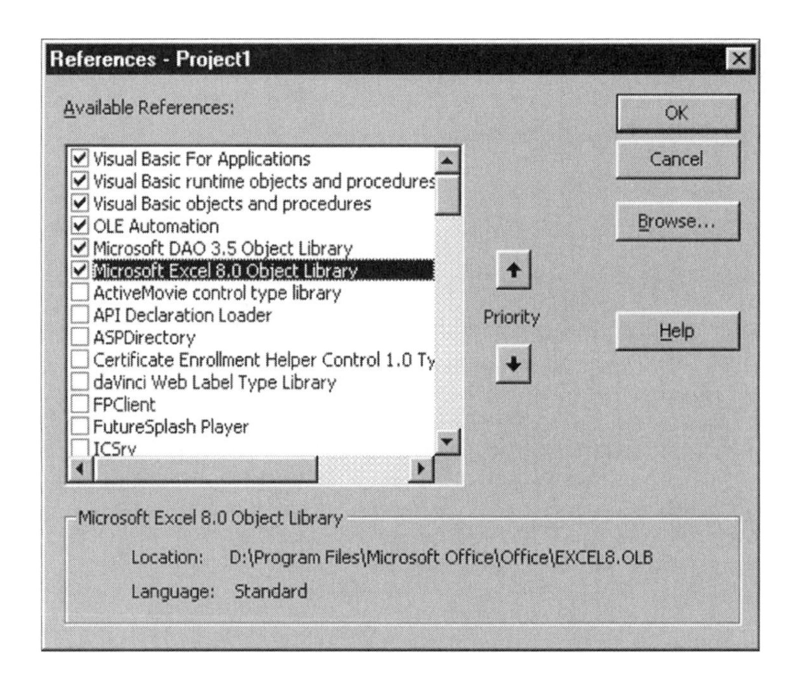

> *Many of the ActiveX component servers that you'll encounter come equipped with something called a* **`TLB`** *or* **`OLB`** *file. This is nothing more than a small file which ActiveX enabled applications, like VB, can load up to get a list of the objects supported by a server, and their properties, methods and events.*

When the VB screen returns to normal, you'll see that nothing really has changed; at least when you add a new ActiveX control into the environment it appears on the toolbox. Don't panic though—plenty has happened and VB is now ready for you to write code to deal with Microsoft Excel.

2 The next thing that we need to do is actually create an ActiveX object. We could do this every time the user clicks on the Do It button, but as you will see, there's actually quite a delay each time you create a new object, and so it's best to keep the number of times you do this to a minimum.

The first coding stage in dealing with ActiveX components is to declare a variable. Add the following declarations to the **`General Declarations`** section of the form:

```
Option Explicit

Dim Active_Excel As Object
Dim Active_Workbook As Object
Dim Active_Worksheet As Object
```

3 So far so good, but as you may remember from our work with object variables before, declaring the object is only part of the story. The next bit is to actually bring the object to life by setting it to something. The code to do this needs to go into the **Form_Load** event.

```
Private Sub Form_Load()

    Set Active_Excel = CreateObject("Excel.Application")
    Set Active_Workbook = Active_Excel.Workbooks.Add
    Set Active_Worksheet = Active_Workbook.Worksheets.Add

End Sub
```

4 As with any other object variable, before the program finishes we have to clear those variables up. Bring up the form's **Unload** event and clear the object variables we just created like this:

```
Private Sub Form_Unload(Cancel As Integer)

    Set Active_Worksheet = Nothing
    Set Active_Workbook = Nothing
    Set Active_Excel = Nothing

End Sub
```

5 Now bring up the code for the **Click** event of the Do It button again. To make Excel appear magically on the screen when the report is done, we need to change a property of the Excel **Application** component that we have in our **Active_Excel** object variable.

```
    :
    :
    :
Loop

    End If
    End With

    Screen.MousePointer = 0

    Active_Excel.Visible = True

End Sub
```

6 Nearly there. All that we need to do now, to get the application running, is feed the information that we're pulling in the loop into the Excel sheet. Again, this involves nothing more than using the methods and properties of the various objects that we have in our object variables. We're now ready to write the code for the **Plot_Titles**, **Plot_The_Titles** and **Plot_The_Value** subprocedures. Here goes:

```
Private Sub Plot_Titles(ByVal nStart As Integer, ByVal nEnd As Integer)

    Dim nYear As Integer

    For nYear = nStart To nEnd

        With Active_Worksheet.Cells(1, (nYear - nStart) + 2)
            .Value = nYear
            .Font.Bold = True
        End With

    Next

End Sub
```

```
Private Sub Plot_The_Value(ByVal nCurrentRow As Integer, ByVal nCount As
Integer, ByVal nYear As Integer)

    Active_Worksheet.Cells(nCurrentRow, nYear + 2).Value = nCount

End Sub
```

```
Private Sub Plot_The_Name(ByVal nCurrentRow As Integer, ByVal sName As
String)

    With Active_Worksheet.Range("A" & nCurrentRow)

        .Value = sName
        .Font.Bold = True

    End With

End Sub
```

If you've used Excel before, then this should look strangely familiar. However, if it doesn't, then don't panic too much. Remember—we're just using the methods, properties and subobjects within Excel to do things with it.

7 Now run the application and you'll see the whole thing working properly. Because the line of code that creates our Excel object is in the **`Form_Load`** event, we won't see a form until Excel has completed loading. When the form does appear, though, try keying in 1990 and 1996 as the start and end date respectively and click Do It. After quite a pause, Excel will appear with all the values in it.

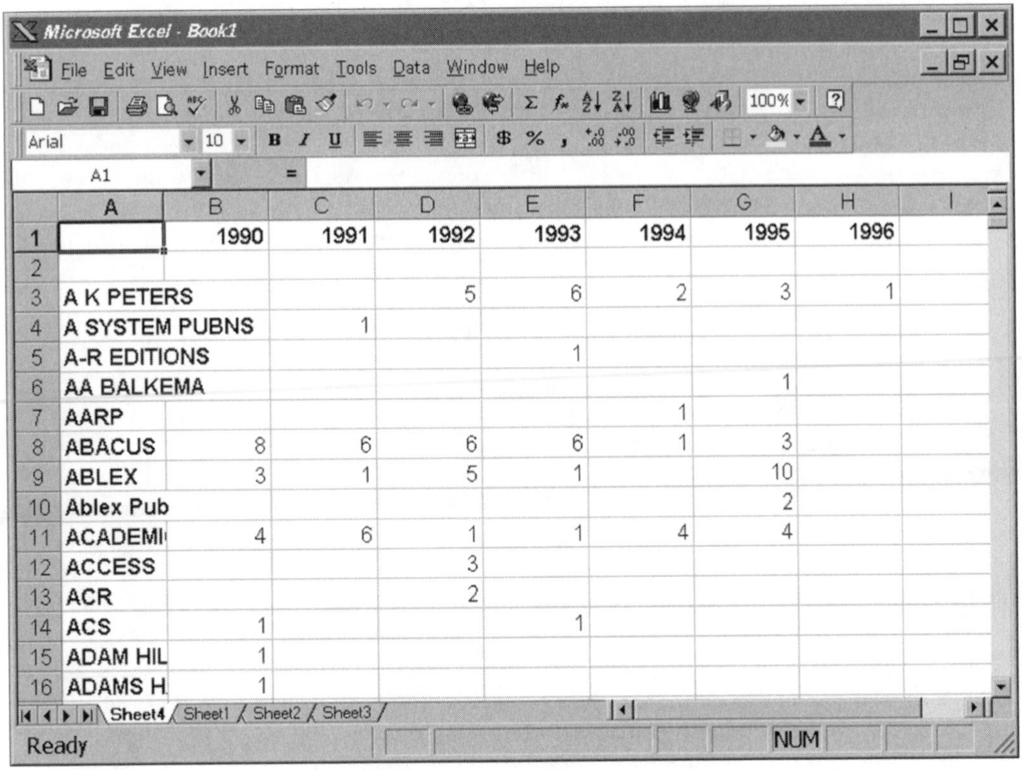

Microsoft Excel - Book1

File Edit View Insert Format Tools Data Window Help

	A	B	C	D	E	F	G	H	I
1		1990	1991	1992	1993	1994	1995	1996	
2									
3	A K PETERS			5	6	2	3	1	
4	A SYSTEM PUBNS		1						
5	A-R EDITIONS				1				
6	AA BALKEMA						1		
7	AARP					1			
8	ABACUS	8	6	6	6	1	3		
9	ABLEX	3	1	5	1		10		
10	Ablex Pub						2		
11	ACADEMI	4	6	1	1	4	4		
12	ACCESS			3					
13	ACR			2					
14	ACS	1			1				
15	ADAM HIL	1							
16	ADAMS H	1							

Sheet4 / Sheet1 / Sheet2 / Sheet3

Ready NUM

How It Works

Since we're dealing with Excel here, we started by declaring 3 variables: one for the application, one for the Excel workbook, and one for the sheet within that workbook that we're going to deal with. We need to keep these variables alive for the duration of the program, so we declared them in the **General Declarations** section of the form.

```
Dim Active_Excel As Excel.Application
Dim Active_Workbook As Excel.Workbook
Dim Active_Worksheet As Excel.Worksheet
```

We then set the variables in the **Form_Load** event:

```
    Set Active_Excel = CreateObject("Excel.Application")
    Set Active_Workbook = Active_Excel.Workbooks.Add
    Set Active_Worksheet = Active_Workbook.Worksheets.Add
```

The first line should be pretty clear: we're telling VB to create a new **Application** component from the Excel component server and store it in our object variable **Active_Excel**. What about the other two lines though? Well, they will look pretty strange since, at this point, we're no longer dealing with straight VB code as such. What you see here is two calls to methods within Excel. It's just like when you declare an object variable to instantiate a class; once the variable has been set up, you can then call the methods and use the properties of that object as defined in the original class.

The second line here is using the **Add** method of the **Workbooks** collection in Excel to add in a new workbook for us to use. The result is then assigned to our **Active_Workbook** variable ready for the third line, which does almost the same thing, only this time it's using the **Worksheets** collection of a workbook to add a new sheet into Excel.

Don't worry too much if this all looks a little confusing. As I said, this is all Excel stuff, but it represents a good demonstration of VB's abilities to call methods and properties in ActiveX components, something we're going to be doing quite a bit more of in a little while.

Next, in the form's **Unload** event, we cleared the object variables:

```
Set Active_Worksheet = Nothing
Set Active_Workbook = Nothing
Set Active_Excel = Nothing
```

Nothing new there, but there is a catch. Normally, this would be all we need to do to get rid of an object after we have created it, freeing up the memory that the object took up and returning the system to the state that it was in before the object was created. However, with ActiveX components the story is a little different. The above lines do nothing more than 'disassociate' the object variables and the component. The component itself stays alive.

> *Note that we set our object variables to nothing in the reverse order to that in which they were declared. This is because it may happen that one or more of the objects depends on the existence of another object to operate correctly (although this shouldn't happen). Telling the server we're not using the objects in the opposite order to that in which they were declared avoids this problem.*

What this means is that at run time, after clicking on the Do It button to run up and display Excel, if the user stops our code running, Excel will carry on running. If you need to close down a component served from an application like Excel, then you need to make sure that you call the relevant method in that server to close it down. For example, in Excel, we could call the **Quit** method to close the **Application** down.

> *Note that this is not how you would normally handle components: generally, you just want to set your object variable to nothing and let the server itself decide when to shut down. You can understand why this is the best way to do things: what if another application happened to be using an object from the same instance of Excel that you're using? If you shut down Excel, you'll shut down their object and break their program. In this case, though, we know we're the only application using Excel, so we can safely shut it down with the **Quit** method.*

We then changed the **Visible** property of our Excel Application object to True, so that it appears on the user's screen. One of the beauties of component development is that you can actually hide from the users the fact that you are cheating somewhat—many component servers, in fact all of the servers included with Office (except Access), will not appear on the screen unless you explicitly tell them to.

You can see how it's looking more and more like dealing with a control on a form. All we need to do to make Excel show itself at run time is change the **`Visible`** property of the application to **`True`** and it will show itself. It's no good changing the **`Visible`** property of the workbook and worksheet though, since all they will do is show and hide the workbook and sheet inside the currently invisible Excel application.

> *One more thing... if you set your object variable to nothing and didn't make Excel visible, you would lose your ability to quit Excel with code or with a simple mouse click on the application itself. The only way to kill an application in this state is to use the Windows task manager to find the application and shut it down.*

Finally, we added the code for the subroutines that place the information extracted from the database into the Excel worksheet. **`Plot_Titles`** loops through each year the user has selected and adds them all to the top of the Excel sheet. This routine is called once *before* we start looping through the recordset in the data control. To print the publisher names and book counts we use the **`Plot_The_Name`** and **`Plot_The_Value`** subroutines. **`Plot_The_Name`** is only called once for each row, when the **`Name`** field in our recordset isn't equal to the last publisher book count we printed. **`Plot_The_Value`** is the simplest of them all, with one line of code that sets a cell in the Excel sheet with the count value it is passed.

Of course, at this point when you run the program, the information is still not formatted very well—the first column is a little too narrow to display some of the publisher names. We could add code to format this column on the fly, or we could leave it to the users to do it by hand. However, if we take the code route, how do we know what methods and properties there are available for us to use? In fact, how did I know about all those other methods and properties in the code?

Well, that's where the object browser comes into play.

The Object Browser

The object browser is an extremely handy tool that you should get used to if you're going to be using objects or controls from other applications. It shows you every object and class that's available to you in your code, along with their properties, methods and events.

Hit *F2* to open it up:

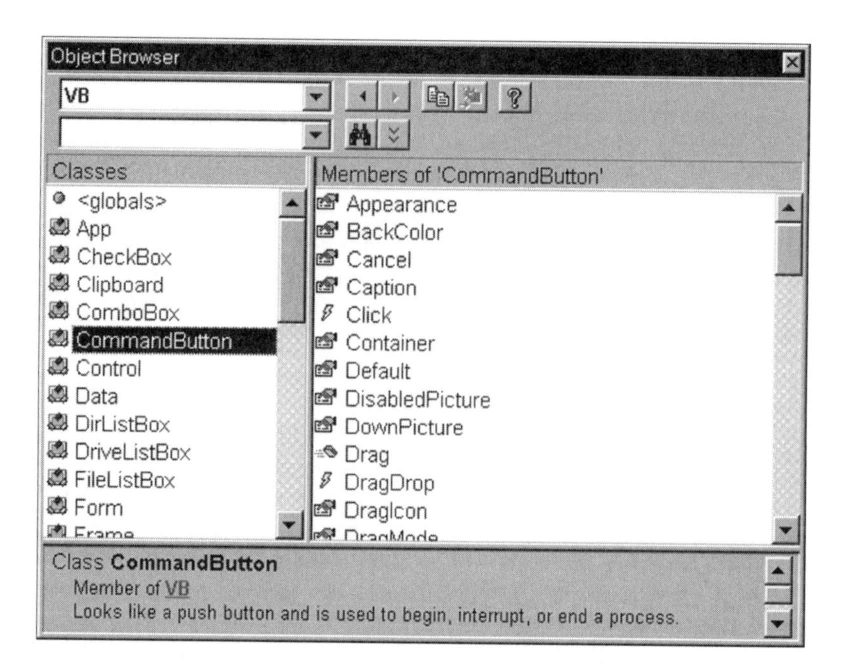

As you can see, the bulk of the display is taken up with a split window, the left half showing you the names of any objects and classes in the current library, and the right showing the properties and methods that belong to that class.

Library? Look at the top of the browser. See the combo box that in my screenshot says VB? Visual Basic groups objects according to their reference source. In the screenshot, for example, I am looking at normal VB objects, hence the combo says VB. However, drop it down and you should see all the reference sources that are currently defined in your project—including, of course, the Excel library that we referenced earlier (assuming that you still have the example code open).

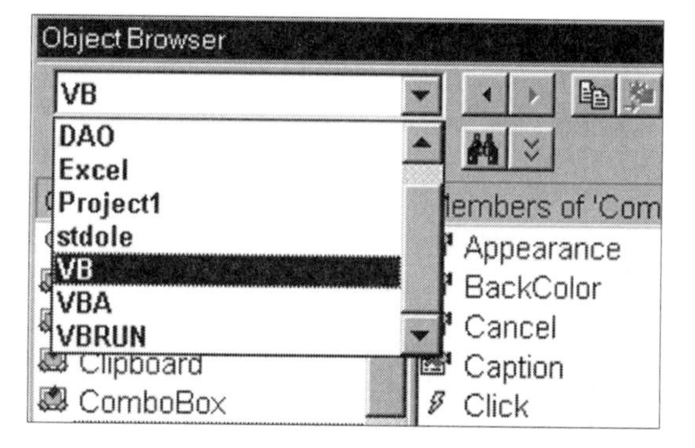

By default, that list should always include at least StdOle, VB, VBA and VBRUN, as well as the name of your project, so that you can easily get at the definitions of any objects and classes in your project. The default selection, All Libraries, shows you a complete alphabetical list of all the objects and classes, without segregating them by category.

Each line in the browser, either on the object side or the members side, has an icon against it. These are the same icons that you would normally see in the project explorer window, showing you at a glance if something is a class, a form, a property, a method or an event. Have a browse around for a bit to see what I mean.

For example, in the VB library find the Screen object.

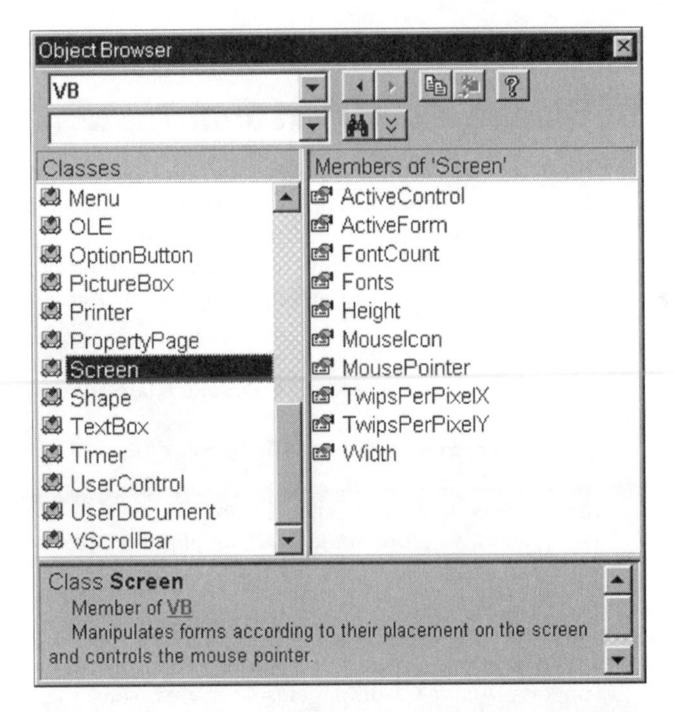

VB's Screen object doesn't have any methods or events that you can deal with, and so all that you can see on the right are property icons, with the name of each property beside them. Click on the Listbox object though and what you see is a different matter.

As you already know, the list box has events that it can respond to, as well as methods like **`Clear`** and **`AddItem`**, and a whole host of properties. It also has events like **`Click`**. That's exactly what the object browser is telling you.

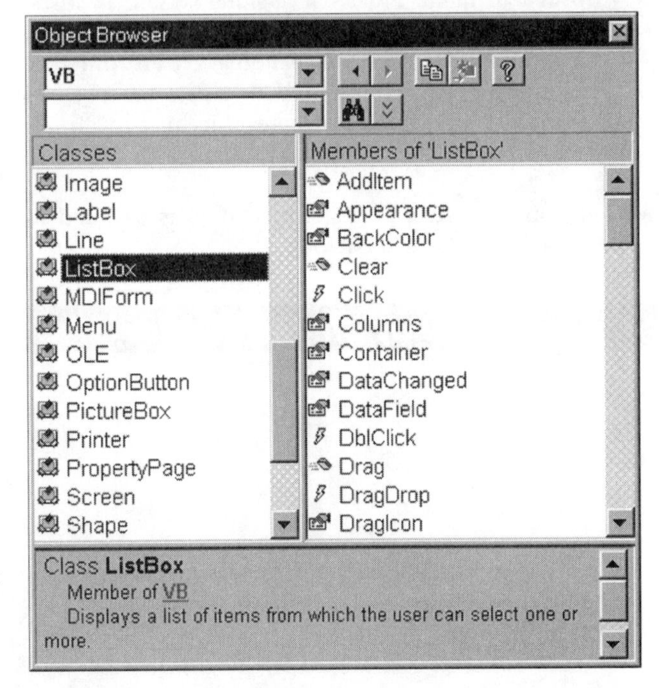

If ever you need to look up an object's member list, or even the syntax for using a member, then the object browser is where you want to be. Get used to it—it can be a real godsend at times.

Enough digression for now, let's go back and look at some more code.

Of Bindings and Personal Taste

There are actually two ways to get an object to look at an ActiveX component in Visual Basic, and which you choose depends on the binding method that you choose. Bindings? Like so many things in computing, ActiveX comes with a whole set of terms and new words for you to get your teeth into and binding is just one of them. The process of declaring an object and setting it to be an ActiveX component is known as **binding**. Simple.

Visual Basic gives you two ways to bind object variables to components: **late** and **early** binding. What we did earlier is called late binding. When you declare an object like this:

```
Dim Active_Excel As Object
```

then that is said to be late binding. What this means is that we're telling Visual Basic that we're going to store some kind of object in there—but until the program runs, we can't tell VB what its going to be.

This can be a particularly useful way of working if, for example, you're unsure which versions of the server applications are running on the target machine. For example, Office 97 supports ActiveX Components—which means that if we wanted, we could use early binding to talk to them. Previous versions of Office do not support this, offering only a limited version known as Automation. Because the objects made available to you from an application that supports Automation are different to those available from ActiveX component servers, we need to create the object at run time. In general though, you will receive greater help and more efficient code from VB if you stick with apps that support ActiveX components, such as Office 97.

If you have that package, then now is as good a time as any to take a look at what it can do for you. Let's try it out.

Try It Out – Early Binding (Office 97 Only)

1 Create a standard VB project and drop a button on to the default form.

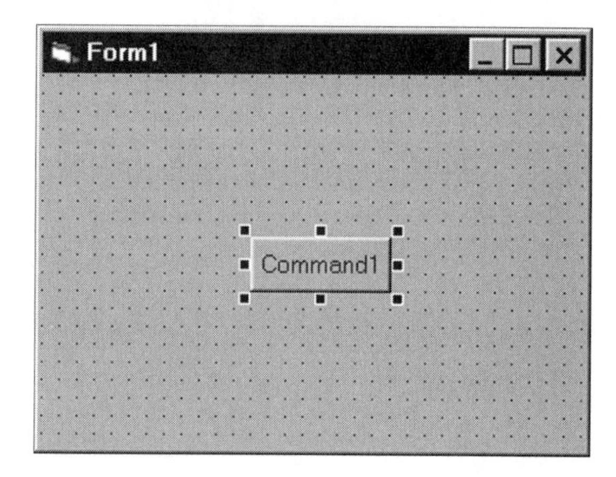

2 Now bring up the code window and type this small block of code into the command button's **Click** event:

```
Private Sub Command1_Click()

    Dim objExcel As Excel.Application

    Set objExcel = New Excel.Application
    objExcel.Visible = True

    Set objExcel = Nothing

End Sub
```

3 From the Project menu, select References.... In the dialog that appears, make sure that the checkbox to the left of the Microsoft Excel 8.0 Object Library is checked, and then click on OK.

4 Now run the program.

How It Works

When dealing with ActiveX Component servers we can actually declare variables specifying the application and component that we are most interested in using, which for now is **Excel.Application**. This comes with a number of benefits, not least of all that the Visual Basic AutoFill wizards will display a list of the properties and methods applicable to that object as you type in your code.

After declaring an object and specifying the type of component that you want, you still need to create a new instance of that object which, as you can see, is done using the **New** Keyword in the code above.

That's really all there is to it, the rest of the code is working just as you would expect a late bound object to work. Let's compare the two forms of binding to assess the different benefits they offer.

Early Binding vs. Late Binding

Early binding means that VB can help you out with the AutoFill wizards as you write code, and you can also refer to the object browser for a complete list of all the properties, methods and events of an object. Since VB knows more about what you're doing and what the component you're using expects, it can flag errors at design time that wouldn't be caught until run time with a late bound component. Finally, early binding is much faster than late binding since VB knows exactly what you are planning to do and can optimize the compiled code that it produces to help you out. Late binding is slower at run time than early binding, although you do have the advantage that you can pick and choose which components to use at run time rather than forcing the user to use a specific one.

As I mentioned earlier though, it's important to note that you'll get the most benefits—in terms of help from VB itself as you write the code, and in terms of execution speed—if you make use of Early Binding. However, you should always remember that you can only early bind to components exported from Microsoft Office 97 or later.

Building Servers

So far, we've looked at the world of ActiveX from the client side: writing programs that make use of ActiveX components in order to leverage their functionality into our VB apps. But that's only half the story. Those ActiveX servers have to come from somewhere.

If you are using the Control Creation, Professional or Enterprise editions of Visual Basic 5, then you have the power on your desktop to create ActiveX controls. However, no matter what edition of VB5 you have, you all have the power to create ActiveX component servers, just like Word or Excel.

Processes – It's all a Question of Delegation

Tiny bit of theory for you before we get into building our own server. As you may or may not know, Windows 95 and NT are multitasking operating systems, which basically means that they can run more than one application at a time. In reality they can't (unless they have more than one processor); all active applications share processing time, but that's a whole new book. When we create ActiveX servers then, we have a choice as to whether we want to provide our component users with objects that run as independent processes, or whether they bolt on to the component users' applications.

This can be a little confusing, so let me explain. If you run a one man business then you have a number of roles. One moment you are the secretary, the next the chief executive and the next the accounts clerk. Normally you are quite happy doing all of these tasks, even though they're totally unique and follow their own rules and requirements—but because you're all on your own you have to stop dealing with one role, in order to take on the next.

In ActiveX terms, undertaking each separate task is known as running a component **in-process.** If you create an in-process component server (one which when compiled becomes a DLL), then any code which uses it has to load in the code from your DLL and run it, the main flow of that calling application stopping while the component does its thing.

The alternative is an **out-of-process** component. As your business grows, you hire staff, and at that point find that you can yell across the room to them the things that you would like them to do. If you hired well, then the chances are that you're free to get on with whatever you're doing, while they simultaneously get on with the task that you just assigned them.

In ActiveX terms again, this means that you compile your component serving application as an executable program, like Excel. Any code which uses your component then runs alongside the application. Each time it calls a method or deals with a property of yours, it continues to run, and expects your code to get on with what it needs to do in the background.

Just as with the businesses though, this does have downside. Anyone who has tried to get a decision out of a huge organization in a hurry will find that no matter how hard they try, things take a lot longer than they would with a smaller outfit.

The same applies with ActiveX. If you give your users in-process components then they'll find that they're fast and neat, whereas give them an out-of-process component and they may suffer a big speed hit. With efficient coding you can reduce the performance difference between in-process and out-of process servers, but you'll never eliminate it.

Why Bother Choosing, and Which to Choose?

If in-process component servers are so much faster and better than the alternative, then why bother worrying about the decision at all? Why not simply dish out DLL servers to your component users?

Well, the idea of ActiveX components is not so much to provide a way for you to service other developers, but more for other developers and users to benefit from the components in your application. Let's say you are developing an Internet stock forecasting application. You may have a class in that application that works very nicely in terms of grabbing a stock quote off the net and storing it in a database.

Your goal here is to simply write a stock forecasting application, not provide developers with a neat way to do what you can do, so there's no question that you're going to ship the application as an EXE. Now, let's say that someone calls you up and says 'You know... that application is great, but it would be even better if I could use it to grab stock information in your app and dump it into my spreadsheet'. At which point, you're looking at telling that user how to use your out-of-process stock component. There's no point in developing an in-process DLL here, since the users are just interested in the fringe benefits of reuse that come from buying your application, and didn't just buy your application because of its components.

There is, of course, also the point that almost anything that deals with the Internet is slow and clunky, so an out-of-process component that can afford to sit idly online waiting for information while the other person's application goes about other tasks is just what the doctor ordered.

Since out-of-process servers, by definition, run in their own process space, they can be considered completely separate applications from any clients that may use them. Out-of-process servers can be accessed by multiple clients at the same time, and they can enable data sharing by allowing internal members to be set and retrieved by different applications.

OK – So How Do I Do It ?

Creating an ActiveX component server is surprisingly easy, in fact there really isn't that much more to it than there is to creating a normal Visual Basic application. In Chapter 17, where we look at building ActiveX controls, you'll come across a couple of new rather neat features of classes and Visual Basic which can really extend the usefulness of your ActiveX work. For now, though, we're going to keep it simple.

Building Your First Server

Once you've decided whether you're going to create an in-process or out-of-process server, the first step to building it is to create either an ActiveX EXE or ActiveX DLL project. Simply select New Project from the File menu, and choose the appropriate type of project from the new project dialog that appears.

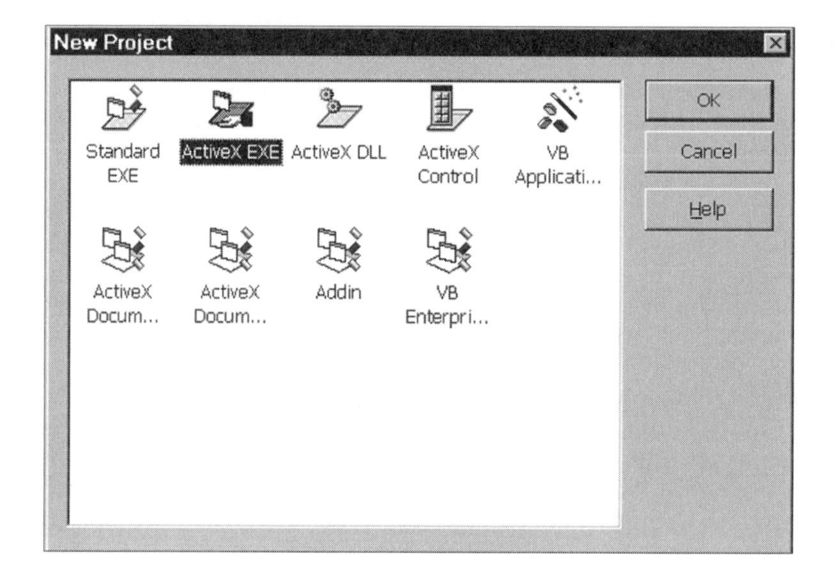

For now, choose ActiveX EXE to create an out-of-process server application. After a short pause, just as when you create a Standard EXE project, your new empty project will appear. The big difference, though, is that there are no forms in this project

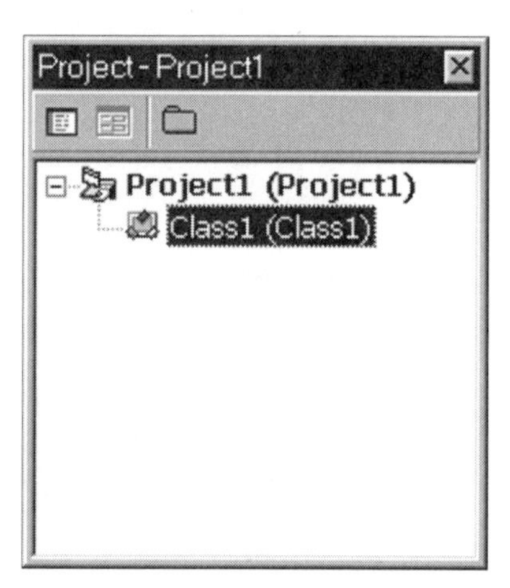

Don't panic. Visual Basic thinks that because you want to create an ActiveX server that you aren't going to want to have any forms in your project, and so instead it gives you a new project with nothing more than a single class inside it. At run time, it's the classes in your ActiveX EXE which become the components that others can use. You're still free to add forms to the project in the normal way if you want, and can at this point add forms and other modules to the project to create what appears to be a normal VB application. In fact the only difference is that this one, when it's compiled, includes a little extra code to let other applications see and use its objects.

You tell VB which classes you want to expose as components at run time with the properties of the class modules. Take a look at the properties window.

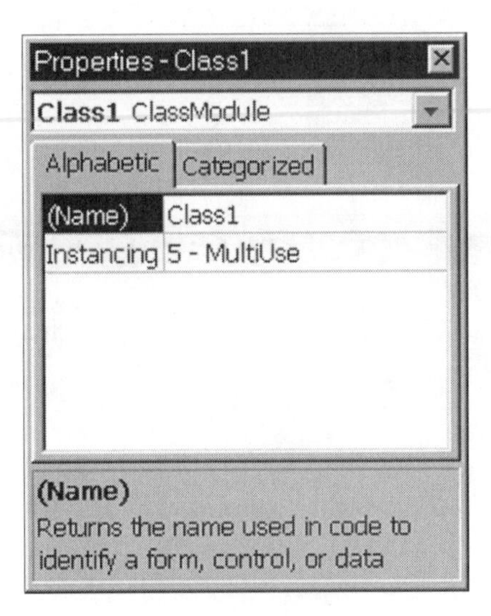

The important property here is the **Instancing** property. This tells VB how others can use the class as a component. **Instancing** can be set up to any of the following values:

Value	Description
Private	This class cannot be accessed at all outside of the application that contains it.
PublicNotCreatable	Objects created from this class can be used, but component users cannot create their own objects from this class. For example, if an object of this class was returned from a function then that would be fine, but if another application tried to create an object of this class then they would find themselves with problems.
SingleUse	(Not allowed in ActiveX DLLs.) Other applications can create objects from this class, but each new object created starts up its own copy of the component server—very memory hungry.
GlobalSingleUse	(Not allowed in ActiveX DLLs.) This is the same as **SingleUse** except that your properties and methods in the class will be available to component users just as if they were global methods and functions

Value	Description
`MultiUse`	This is the opposite of `SingleUse`. Other applications can create objects from this class, but each new object created will be served by the same running copy of your application
`GlobalMultiUse`	Same as `MultiUse`, but again, the properties and methods of the class are available to the component user as if they were global functions and methods.

Creating an ActiveX EXE or DLL project and setting the **`Instancing`** property of the classes in that project is really all you need to do to create a component server in Visual Basic—apart from make it actually do something of course. Let's now add some life to this server.

Try It Out - Creating a Component Server

1 Create a new project, choosing ActiveX EXE from the New Project dialog.

2 Set the class' **`Instancing`** property to **`SingleUse`**, and set the **`Name`** property to **`Cname`**.

3 The next step is to write some code to make the class do something. Bring up the code window for the class and type in these few lines.

```
Private m_sName As String

Property Let Name(ByVal sName As String)
    m_sName = sName
End Property

Public Sub ShowName()
    MsgBox "Hi there, " & m_sName
End Sub
```

This should all be fairly self-explanatory; we're just creating a single property called **`Name`**, and a method in the class called **`ShowName`** which displays the contents of the **`Name`** property in a message box on the screen. This is not going to set the component world on fire just yet, but it's a good starting point.

4 The last step is to set up the project name. Select Project1 Properties from the Project menu and key in **`TestServer1`** as the project name.

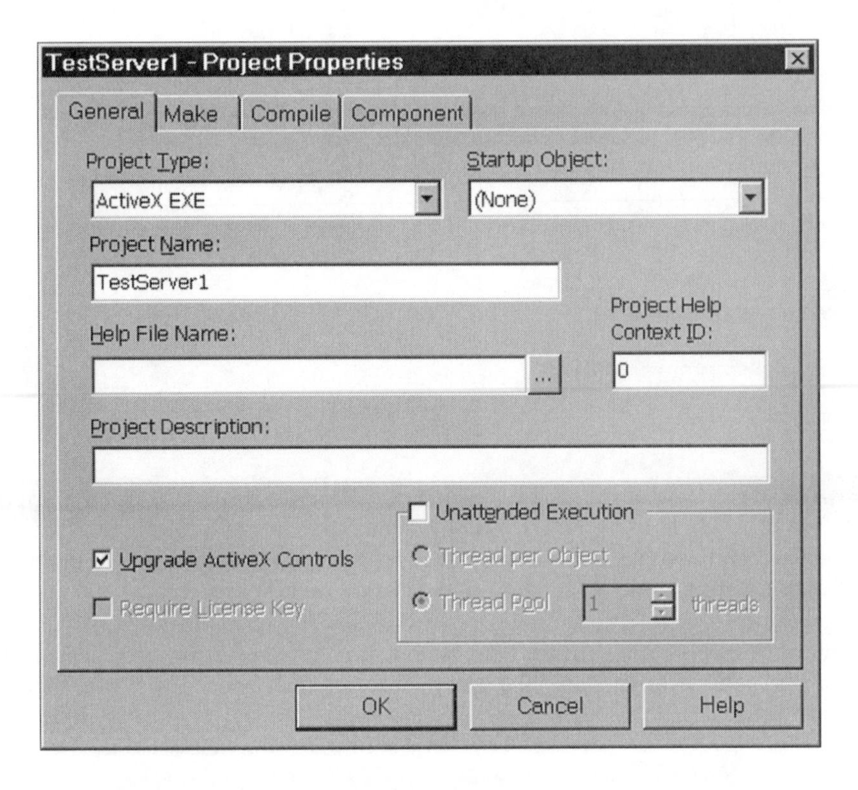

5 All that remains is to compile the application, by selecting Make TestServer1.exe from the File menu. Once you've chosen a name for your new EXE file, a flurry of disk activity will occur and, provided you typed in all the code correctly, your new ActiveX server will be created on your hard disk.

6 So far so good—we have the server. However, it isn't really all that impressive yet since it still doesn't do anything. We need to knock up a quick little application to actually use it.

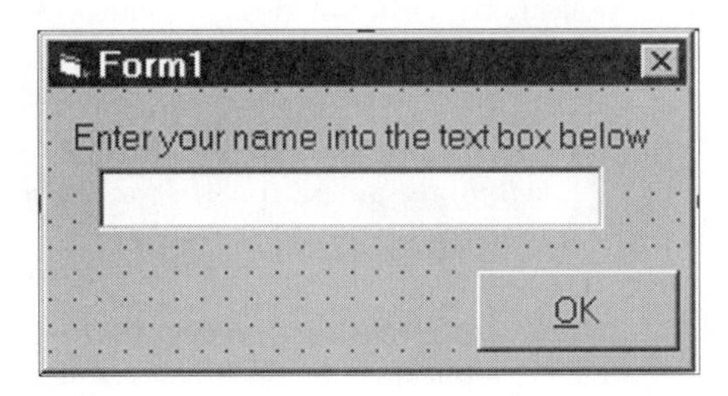

Save the project files for your server before going on! Then you can start up a standard EXE project and drop some controls on to the form so that it looks like this:

7 Name the text box `txtName` and the command button `cmdOK`, and then add this code to the command button's `Click` event

```
Private Sub cmdOK_Click()

    ' At this point the user has entered their name, so we can
    ' pass it out to our remote server
    Dim MyServer As Object

    Set MyServer = CreateObject("TestServer1.CName")

    MyServer.Name = txtName
    MyServer.ShowName

    Set MyServer = Nothing

End Sub
```

Just as in the previous examples where we were creating objects from components, the first step is to declare the object variable. Once that is done, the world is our component, and we can start to play around with the properties and methods of the component just as easily as if they lived in our own source code.

8 Try running the program to see it in action: key in your name and click on the OK button and after a brief pause the external component shows you your name in a message box.

That's really all there is to it at this stage. When we cover ActiveX controls, though, you'll see a lot more of the power of ActiveX.

The OLE Container Control

The final piece in the ActiveX/OLE puzzle is the OLE container control.

This versatile little tool enables you to place linked or embedded objects in your applications, either at design time or at run time.

> *Linking is where a reference (and only a reference) is placed into the parent file to where the data file is stored. Embedding is where the actual data is stored within the parent file. It's far easier to demonstrate the differences than to explain them—which is what we're going to do next.*

Linking and embedding allows us to give a portion of our application's screen real estate to another application to do whatever it pleases. For example, if we link or embed a Word document in an OLE container control in our application, then a user can click on the control to start up Word and edit the document inside our application. This may sound complicated, but it isn't—it's simple, as you'll see in a second. There are only three properties that need setting up, and even these are handled by common dialogs both at design time and run time. Let's try it.

Try It Out - Creating a Linked Object at Design Time

1 We're going to create a link to a Word document so start by firing up Word (or WordPad if you don't have Word) and create a document. Anything will do. Save it as `Sample.doc` and close it.

2 Now switch back to VB and create a new standard EXE application and add an OLE container control to the form. After a short pause, one of the OLE common dialogs will appear.

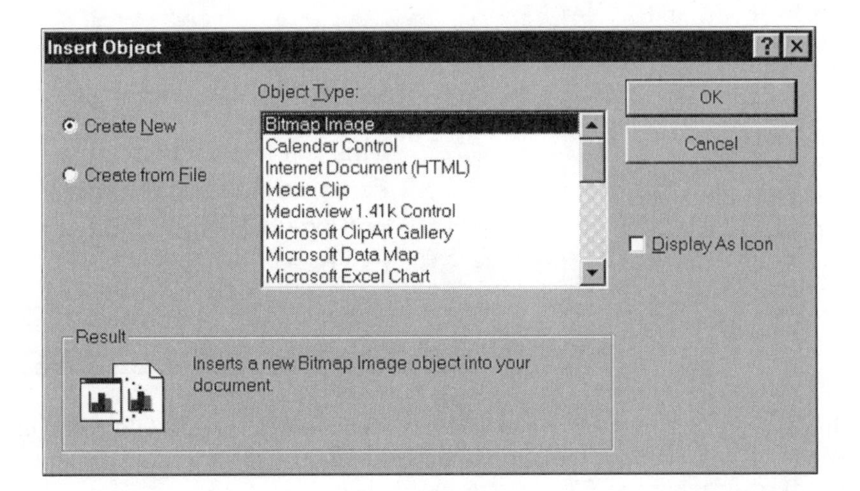

3 Click on the Create From File checkbox—the dialog will change.

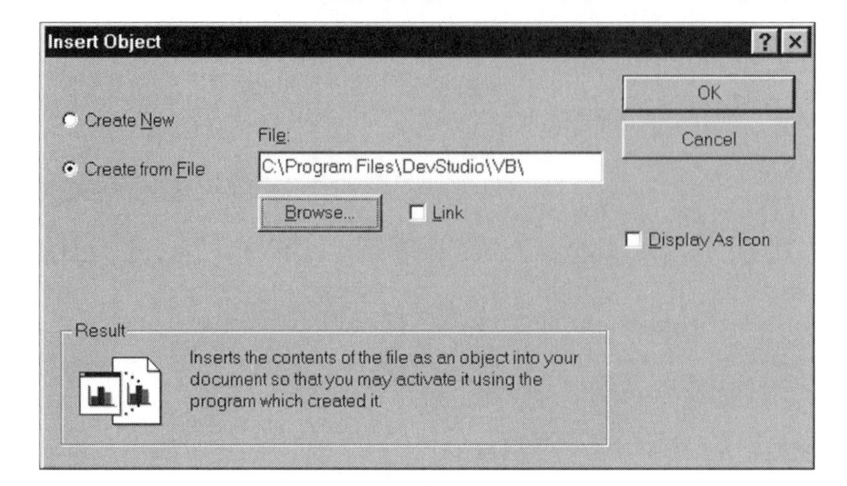

4 Click on the Browse button and find the Word file that you just created. Once you have selected the file and selected Insert button to return to the previous dialog, and then check the Link check box on the dialog, and then click on the OK button.

5 At this point you'll return to Visual Basic in design mode, and you should see your file displayed on the form. You may have to resize the form and OLE container control to make all the text visible.

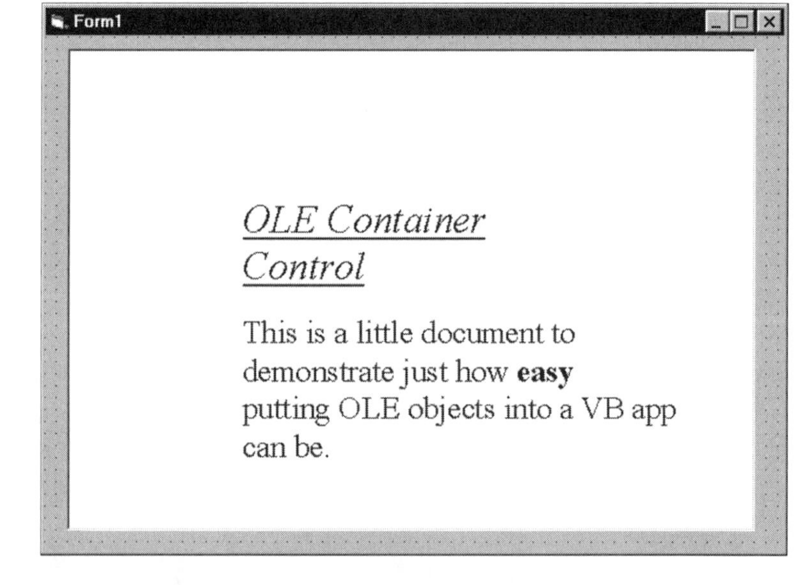

6 Run the application, and when it starts, double-click on the OLE container control. Windows will start up the application associated with DOC files (on my system this is Word), displaying the file you created earlier.

How It Works

Because we've created a linked object here, the container control simply holds a pointer to the file containing the data. So, when the user double clicks the OLE object, the original application is run as a totally separate application. It's responsible for handling any changes any application decides to make to the file, as well as for saving the file itself.

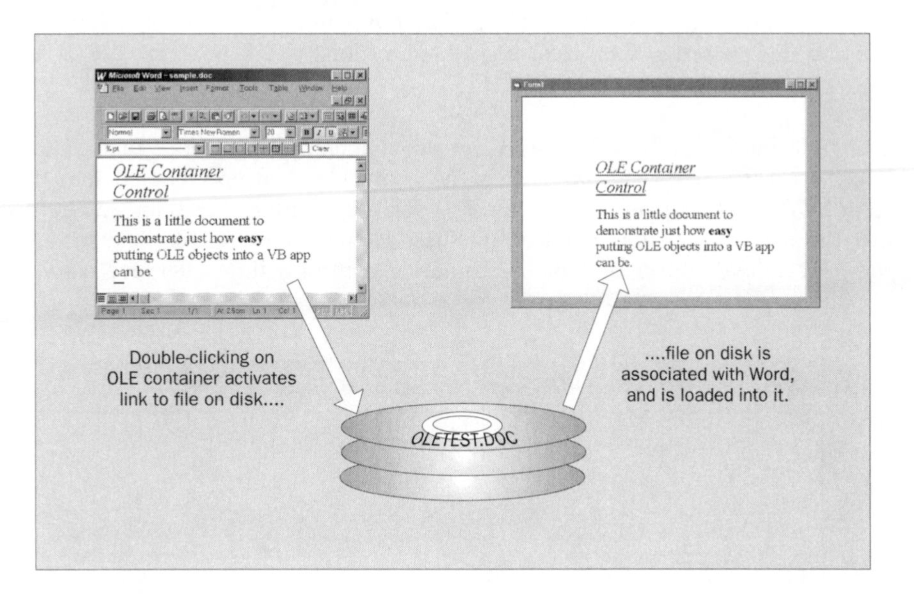

With Word or WordPad running, you can now make changes to the document. However, for those changes to be reflected in the OLE container control, you must first tell Word or WordPad to save the document back to disk. The OLE container will then automatically notice that the file has been changed and update its image of the file.

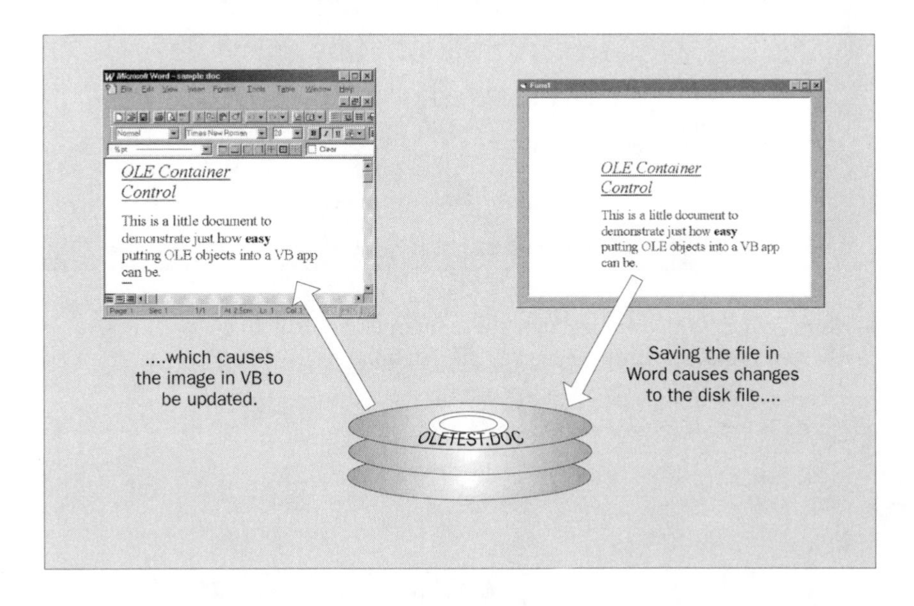

Try It Out - Creating an Embedded Object at Design Time

Embedded objects work in a quite different way to linked objects. Let's take a look.

1 Create a new project in Visual Basic and, once again, draw an OLE container control on the default form. As before, when the common dialog appears, select Create from File and find **Sample.doc**. This time, though, don't check the Link box before clicking OK.

2 This time the object is embedded in the container control, rather than simply being linked to it. What this means is that the entire object is now copied into the container control. Your VB app is now responsible for maintaining that data, saving any changes that the user may make, and loading these changes back in the next time the program runs. We'll cover this aspect of the container control a little later; for now, though, just run the application.

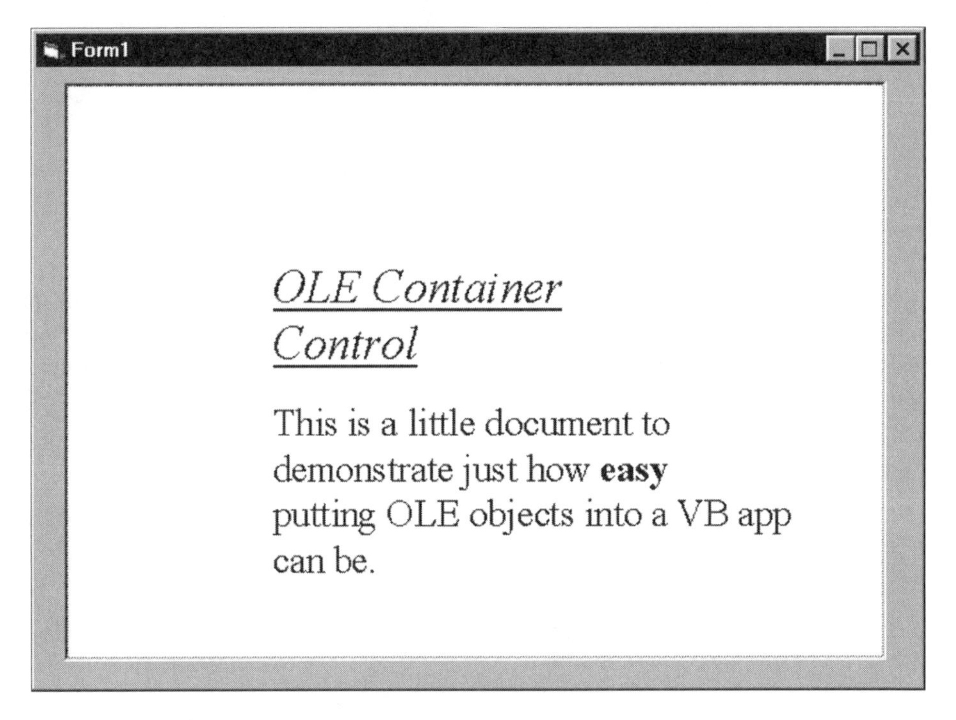

3 This time, when you double click the container control to activate the object, editing actually takes place within your VB application.

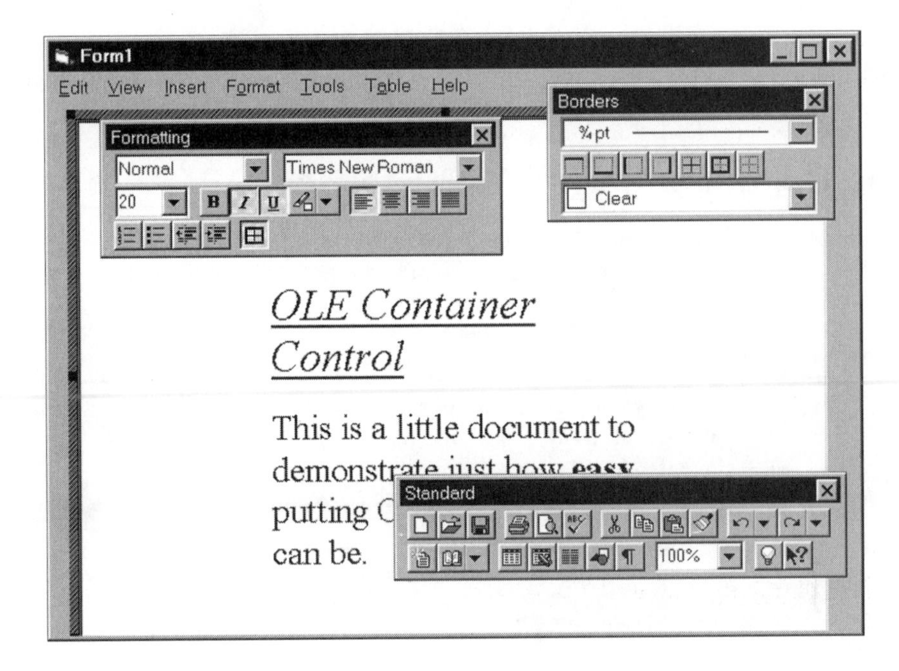

How It Works

When you create an embedded object at design time, VB loads in an image of the file into its own memory space. This is a snapshot of the data at this point in time.

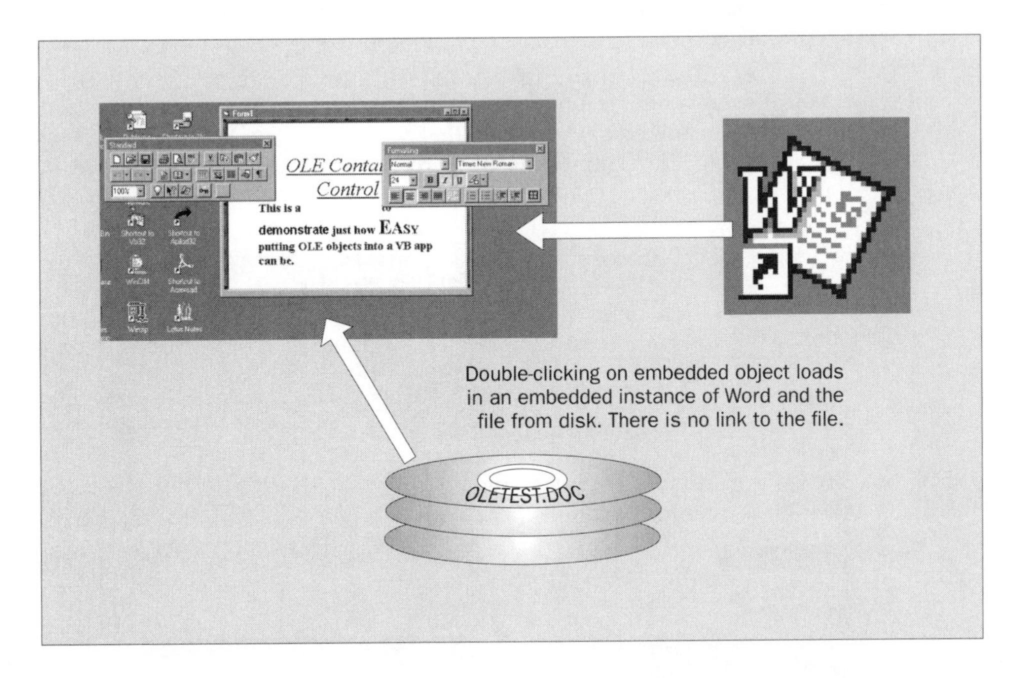

When VB runs, it creates an object inside itself of the Word class and then uses this to edit the chosen file. This is fundamentally different from linking, which is like glorified shelling out.

Using the Container Control's Properties

Rather than using the OLE container control's common dialogs to set up a common control, you could do it the hard way and make use of the OLE control's properties:

Property	Description
`Class`	Sets or returns the class name of an object. This property determines the application that created and maintains the data on display.
`SourceDoc`	The source document that you want to turn into an OLE object.
`SourceItem`	Can be used to select only a part of the source document when creating a linked object—no use for embedded objects.

Let's create a new object and see these properties in action.

Try It Out - Using the Container Control Properties

1. Create a new project. Draw a container control on the form again, but this time cancel the OLE dialog when it appears. Click on the control to select it and press *F4* to bring up its properties window.

2. Find the **`Class`** property in the properties window. This defines the application that is used to create and later maintain the data that you intend to either link or embed. Click on the ellipses to the right of the property to bring up a list of known document servers.

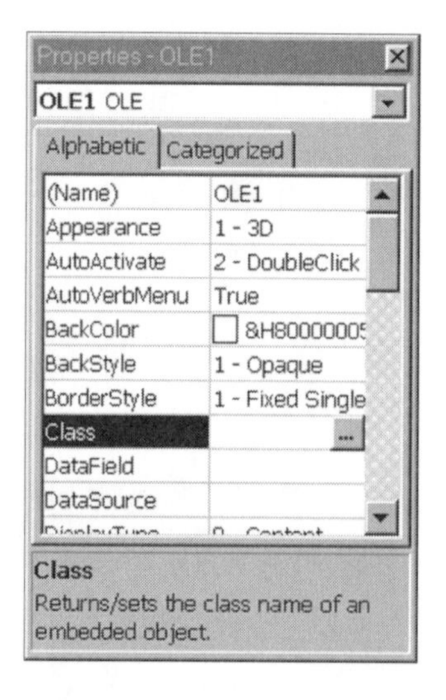

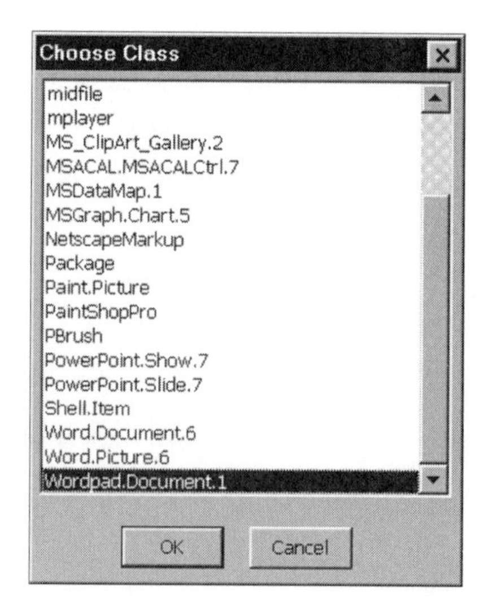

3 Find the WordPad entry at the bottom of the list. Notice how it reads Wordpad.Document.1. This indicates that you are opening a WordPad document and the command that the container control needs to send to the application (commonly known as the verb) is 1. For now, just select the WordPad entry and click OK.

4 Now find the `SourceDoc` property. This is used to tell the container control exactly which document we intend to deal with Click on the ellipses to the right of the property to bring up the standard OLE dialog, then select your `Sample.doc` file using Browse. We want this object to be embedded so don't click the Link checkbox.

5 Finally, run the program and double click on the OLE container control.

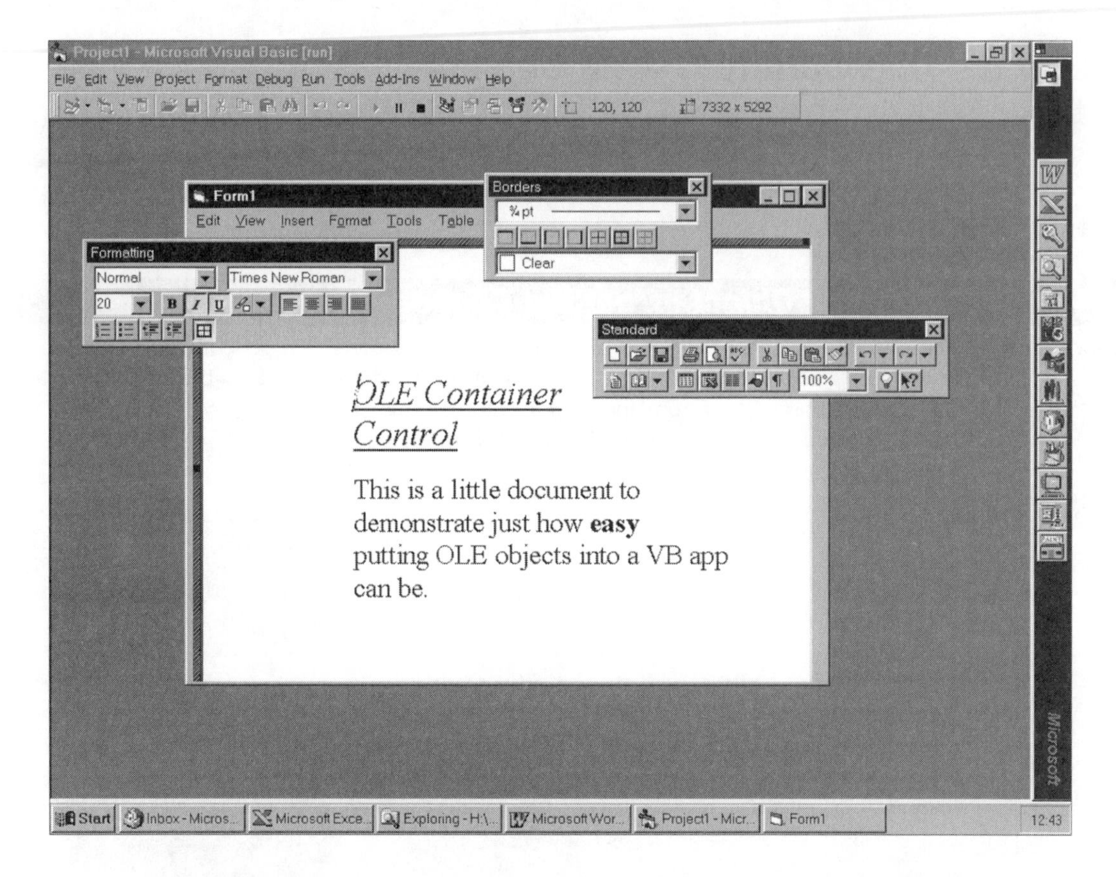

In this example, we set the properties using the properties window. Note that these properties could be set equally well with running code. This is useful if you want to change what you're linking to or embedding at run time, possibly in response to some action your user takes.

We didn't set the final property—**SourceItem**. This allows you to specify a part of the file to use as the OLE object, using whatever notation the source application supports. For example, if we had just linked an Excel sheet, then we could set the **SourceItem** property to something like R1C1:R12C100 to select a range of cells in the sheet. If you have Excel, then you can try it out—go through the same processes we just covered to link an Excel sheet, but this time put in a range specification in the **SourceItem** property.

Notice how the property that names the application which will be embedded is called a class. VB declares an object variable of this type to access all the methods and properties of the Word application.

Using the Clipboard to Create Objects

You can also create linked or embedded objects at design time using data on the clipboard. For example, many OLE applications allow you to cut or copy data to the clipboard and subsequently use a Paste Special option in a different program to create an OLE object. Visual Basic is no exception.

Try It Out - Creating Objects from the Clipboard

1 Open up your **Sample.doc** file and drag the mouse over the text in the document to select it. Then choose Copy from the Edit menu. At this point, you have a document in the clipboard which can be pasted into an OLE container control.

2 Back in Visual Basic, start a new project and draw an OLE container control on the default form. Cancel the OLE common dialog when it appears—we don't need to use it to paste data in. Now right click on the container control and a pop-up menu will appear.

3 Notice how the Paste Special... option is enabled. If you select this, the OLE paste dialog will pop up.

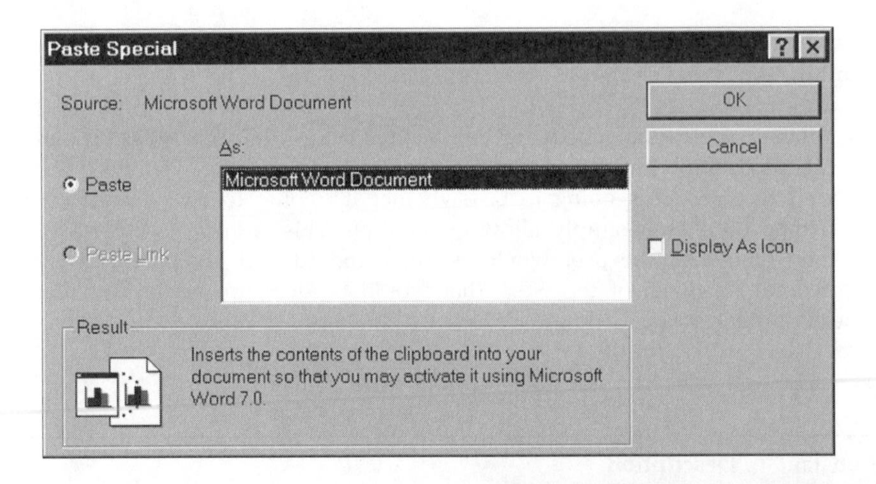

4 The OLE object contains a link to the source application, so the dialog knows the name of the source application, as well as the source document file name. Click on the OK button on this dialog to paste the data into the container control.

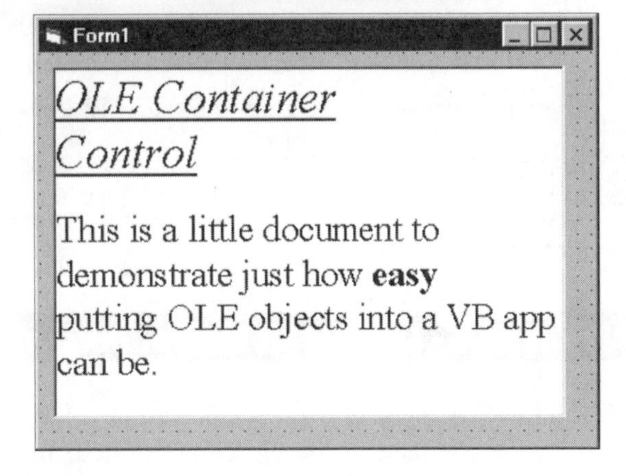

A little later, we'll see how to use the clipboard to paste objects into your container control from within your code.

Linking and Embedding at Run Time

Of course, being able to link and embed objects at design time is only half the OLE story. The real power of OLE comes from being able to do the same at run time, and more than that, from being able to link and embed data without having to worry about the format of the server application.

The **`CreateLink`** and **`CreateEmbed`** methods let you link and embed at run time. Both methods work on OLE container controls, and as their names suggest, one creates a linked object, the other creates an embedded one.

The syntax of the two methods is simple:

```
OLEContainer.CreateLink <Filename>
OLEContainer.CreateEmbed <Filename>
```

There's one other property that needs dealing with, though: the **OLETypeAllowed** property. Before you can place an object into a container control at run time, you need to tell Visual Basic what kind of object it is going to be—whether it's going to be a linked or embedded object, or whether VB should simply allow either type. This is because, unless you code your application otherwise, the user won't see the standard OLE dialog that we can use in VB at design time. So, much of the work that would be done manually with that dialog, you now need to take care of through code.

The **OLETypeAllowed** property can take the following values:

Value/Constant	Description
vbOLELinked	Tells VB that the container control will only hold linked objects.
VbOLEEmbedded	Tells VB that the container control will only hold embedded objects.
VbOLEEither	Go on—take a wild guess! Allows the control to hold either type of object.

Actually using these properties and the **CreateLink** or **CreateEmbed** methods in code is really easy.

Try It Out - Linking or Embedding at Run Time

1 Start up a new project in VB and drop a container control, two command buttons and a common dialog on to the form so that it looks like this. Click Cancel when the OLE common dialog appears—we'll insert the object through code.

2 Name the command buttons **cmdLink** and **cmdEmbed**, the common dialog **dlgFileOpen** and leave the container control as **OLE1**.

3 Now let's add some code to the command buttons to breathe a little life into the project. Double-click on the Link button to bring up its code window. Change the **cmdLink_Click** event so that it looks like this:

```
Private Sub cmdLink_Click()

    With OLE1
        .Class = ""
        .SourceDoc = ""
        .SourceItem = ""

        dlgFileOpen.ShowOpen

        If dlgFileOpen.Filename <> "" Then
            .OLETypeAllowed = vbOLELinked
            .CreateLink dlgFileOpen.Filename
        End If
    End With

End Sub
```

4 The code for the Embed button is similar. Type the following into the **cmdEmbed_Click** event:

```
Private Sub cmdEmbed_Click()

    With OLE1
        .Class = ""
        .SourceDoc = ""
        .SourceItem = ""

        dlgFileOpen.ShowOpen

        If dlgFileOpen.Filename <> "" Then
            .OLETypeAllowed = vbOLEEmbedded
            .CreateEmbed dlgFileOpen.Filename
        End If
    End With

End Sub
```

5 Now, if you run the program, the buttons will work. You can click either to display a common file dialog, and from there select a document that you want to turn into a linked or embedded object.

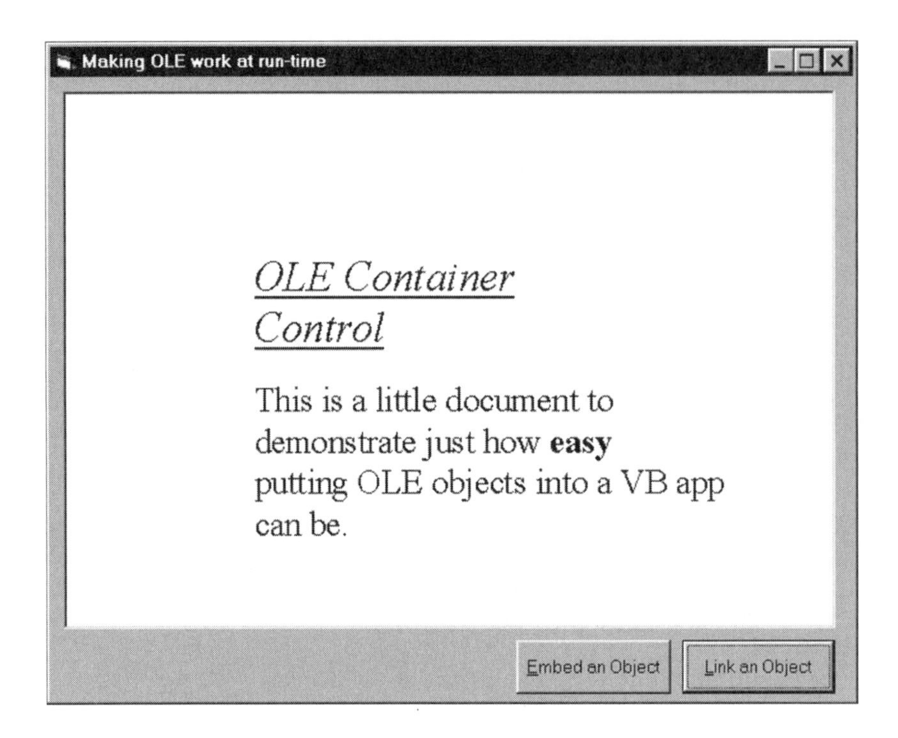

How It Works

The code itself is a little more verbose than it would probably be in the real world—I've written it like this to illustrate the concepts more than anything else.

For both buttons, the first three lines of code inside the **With** block reset the OLE container control, clearing the **Class**, **SourceDoc** and **SourceItem** properties, ready for new data.

```
With OLE1
        .Class = ""
        .SourceDoc = ""
        .SourceItem = ""
```

With that done, the file open dialog can be shown by calling the **ShowOpen** method of the common dialog control.

```
dlgFileOpen.ShowOpen
```

Finally, we check to see that the user actually selected a file before setting the **OLETypeAllowed** property. Finally, the **CreateLink** or **CreateEmbed** method is called.

```
        If dlgFileOpen.Filename <> "" Then
            .OLETypeAllowed = vbOLELinked
            .CreateLink dlgFileOpen.Filename
        End If
```

A slightly easier way to do this would have been to set the **OLETypeAllowed** property to 2—Either at design time.

Loading and Saving Embedded Data

I mentioned earlier that, with embedded objects, your VB application is responsible for maintaining the integrity of the object's data, including accepting responsibility for loading and saving it to disk.

Luckily, this is nowhere near as complex as many developers think it is. VB has two wonderful built-in methods to handle the whole task for you: **SaveToFile** and **ReadFromFile**. Take a look at this code:

```
Sub SaveOLEControl()

    Dim nFileNumber As Integer

    nFileNumber=FreeFile
    Open "Test.OLE" For Binary As #nFileNumber
    Ole1.SaveToFile nFileNumber
    Close #nFileNumber

End Sub
```

This code would save the contents of an OLE container control to a file called **Test.OLE**. How does it work?

First of all we use the **FreeFile** function to return the next available file number. We then open the file on disk that we're going to save the data to.

```
Open "Test.OLE" For Binary As #nFileNumber
```

Since we're saving OLE data, which could easily be a mix of binary, textual and numeric information, the file needs to be opened telling VB that it will contain **Binary** data. This line opens a file called **Test.OLE** as a binary file, and tells VB that from now on we'll refer to the file using the file number held in our **nFilenumber** variable.

Once we've opened a file, we can then save data out to it, using the **SaveToFile** method:

```
Ole1.SaveToFile nFileNumber
```

The syntax is quite simple. Since the **SaveToFile** method works on an OLE container control, the name of the control must be placed before the method. In this example I have assumed that the control is called **Ole1**. All that remains is to specify the number of the open file that you want to save to, which you do using **nFilenumber**.

The final step the program takes is to close the file down.

```
Close #nFileNumber
```

Loading data into an OLE container control from a file is equally easy—in fact the code is almost identical:

```
Sub LoadOLEControl()

    Dim nFileNumber As Integer
    nFileNumber=FreeFile
    Open "Test.OLE" For Binary As #nFileNumber
    Ole1.ReadFromFile nFileNumber
    Close #nFileNumber

End Sub
```

Apart from the obvious difference in the name of the subroutine, the only other difference is the use of the **ReadFromFile** method instead of the **SaveToFile** method. The rest of the code follows the same pattern that we saw in the previous example: get file number, open file, perform operation, close file. Simple!

Linking and Embedding with the Clipboard

The clipboard object itself has no specific methods for checking whether the data held on the clipboard is, or could become, an OLE object. However, the OLE container control does—the **PasteOK** property.

The **PasteOK** property returns true if the data in the clipboard can be pasted into the OLE container control, false if it cannot. In the event that a true is returned, you can invoke the **Paste** method on the container control to actually get the data out of the clipboard.

An alternative to using the **Paste** method, and a much more professional method too, is to pop up the Paste Special dialog that so many applications, including Visual Basic, make use of. This can be accomplished with a call to the **PasteSpecialDlg** method.

> *Before we look at the nuts and bolts of using the clipboard with OLE, a little programming theory fits here quite well. The **Paste Special** menu item is usually placed inside an application's **Edit** menu. However, it is standard procedure to only enable this menu item if there is an object on the clipboard that can be pasted.*
>
> *The problem for novice programmers comes in deciding where to put the code to enable and disable the menu item. I have seen a number of approaches to this within my company, ranging from idle loops that check the clipboard whenever the computer has a spare moment, to timer-based code which checks the clipboard once every n milliseconds, to complex DLL based code that takes the strain away from VB totally. None of these is what I would consider the correct solution.*

The trick with stuff like this is to remember that you're programming in an event-driven development system—the bulk of your code will run in response to events that either the user or the system triggers. When deciding where to put code like this, try to figure out which natural event would suit your code best. In this particular example, the best event to use is the Edit *menu item's* `Click` *event.*

In order to drop down a menu, the user must click on the menu heading. By putting a little code in that item's `Click` *event, we can enable and disable menu items only when they are about to come into view. This is by far the most elegant approach and illustrates a good programming point—never overcomplicate your code.*

Try It Out - Pasting OLE Objects

1 Start up a new project in Visual Basic and drop a container control on the form as before—don't bother to link or embed any documents into it since we are going to do that from the clipboard in a moment. Also, add an Edit menu to the form called **`mnuEdit`**, with a single Paste Special item on it called **`mnuEPasteSpecial`**.

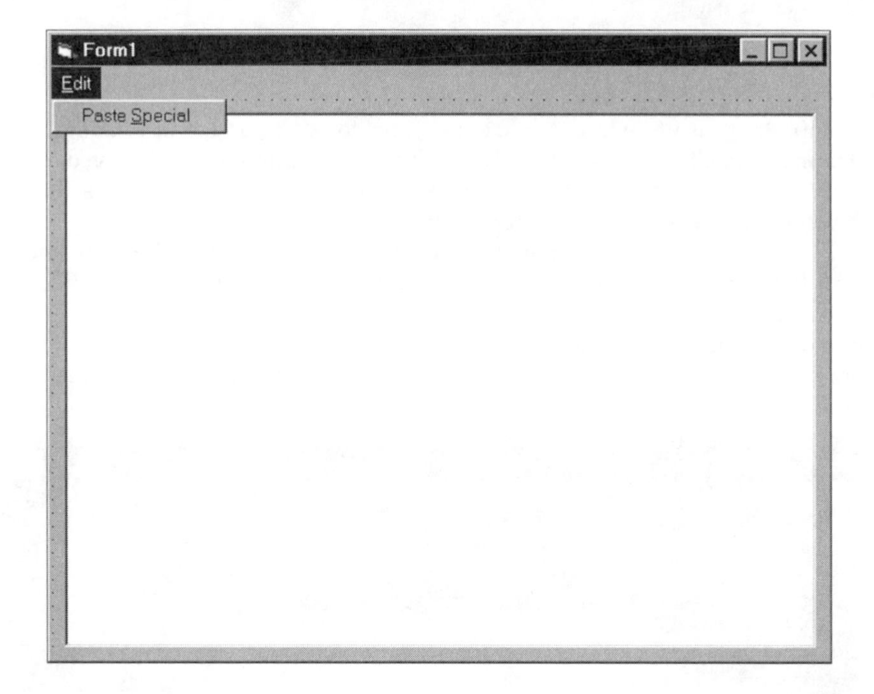

2 Next up, bring up the code window and type in some code to deal with those two menu items.

```
Private Sub mnuEdit_Click()

    mnuEPasteSpecial.Enabled = OLE1.PasteOK

End Sub

Private Sub mnuEPasteSpecial_Click()

    OLE1.PasteSpecialDlg

End Sub
```

3 That's all there is to it...run up the application and you'll find that you have a Paste Special item that only enables itself when there is something on the clipboard that can be pasted, and that also lets you actually paste data into the container on the form.

To put something on your clipboard, try copying some text from Word for instance.

Suitably shocked? With the exception of the lines that mark the start and end of the event procedures, there are only two lines of actual code in the application. Once again, Visual Basic blows the myth that dealing with OLE is a complex issue out of the water. It isn't!

How It Works

The first important bit of code is the **Click** event for the Edit menu heading. When this menu is clicked, directly before the rest of the menu is displayed, the code copies the value of the **PasteOK** property into the **Enabled** property of the Paste Special menu item. Therefore, if **PasteOK** returns true, indicating that the data on the clipboard can be pasted into the container control, the **Enabled** property of the Paste Special menu item is set to true. If the contents of the clipboard cannot be pasted, the menu item is disabled. Since the Paste Special menu item can only be clicked when it's enabled, no further checking of the clipboard is required in the **mnuPasteSpecial _Click** code. All that event procedure does is run the **PasteSpecialDlg** method, which displays the Paste dialog shown below.

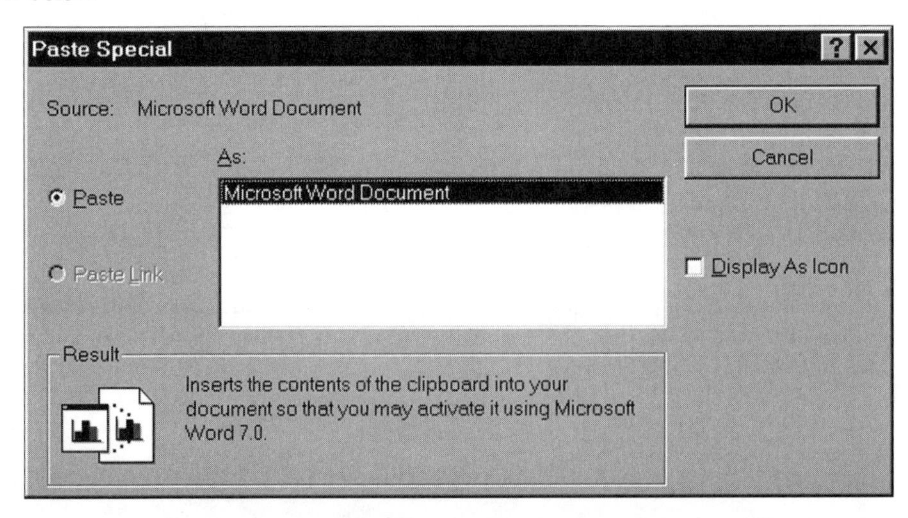

Remember how, in Chapter 1, I said that VB programming was essentially providing your user with the tools to do their job, and then letting them do it? This is a case in point.

The dialog shows the user the class of the object, in this case a Microsoft Word document. They can then choose to either link or embed the data into the container control. The actual pasting of the data from the clipboard into the control is handled for you, as is setting the control's properties and displaying the data on screen.

You should have seen, by this point, how VB can make seemingly complex tasks simple. Many C and Pascal programmers have avoided OLE in their applications like the plague, simply because, on the surface, it seems a nightmare to implement. As a VB programmer, though, you can walk into any programming circle, look the god of OLE in the eye and honestly say 'Linking and embedding... no problemo!'

Summary

A large part of Visual Basic's popularity is due to its ability to create and use components. Each ActiveX control you've used relies on OLE and the Component Object Model that lies beneath it. The components provided by Microsoft Office are also based on OLE. In this chapter we've talked a little more about what OLE and ActiveX are. Specifically, we've covered:

- The similarities and differences between DDE, OLE, and ActiveX
- Using some ActiveX components that are a part of Microsoft Office
- The terms in-process, out-of-process, early-binding and late-binding
- Creating a very simple ActiveX code component with Visual Basic 5.0
- Using the OLE container control to host ActiveX documents

In the next chapter, we'll talk even more about creating components with Visual Basic 5.0 when we cover ActiveX control creation.

Why Not Try...

1. What's the difference between an in-process component and an out-of-process component? What makes one more advantageous than the other?

2. What properties of a class are not permitted in an ActiveX DLL?

3. Create an ActiveX out-of-process component server with two properties and two methods. The server will be used to display the name and age of a user who invokes it.

4. Create a standard project to access the properties and method of the ActiveX server you created in Exercise 3. Have the project contain a single form, a command button, two text boxes and two labels. When the command button is clicked, invoke the server, and use it to display in a message box the name and age of the user.

5. What is the difference between an embedded and linked OLE object? Is one better than the other? What are the advantages and disadvantages of each?

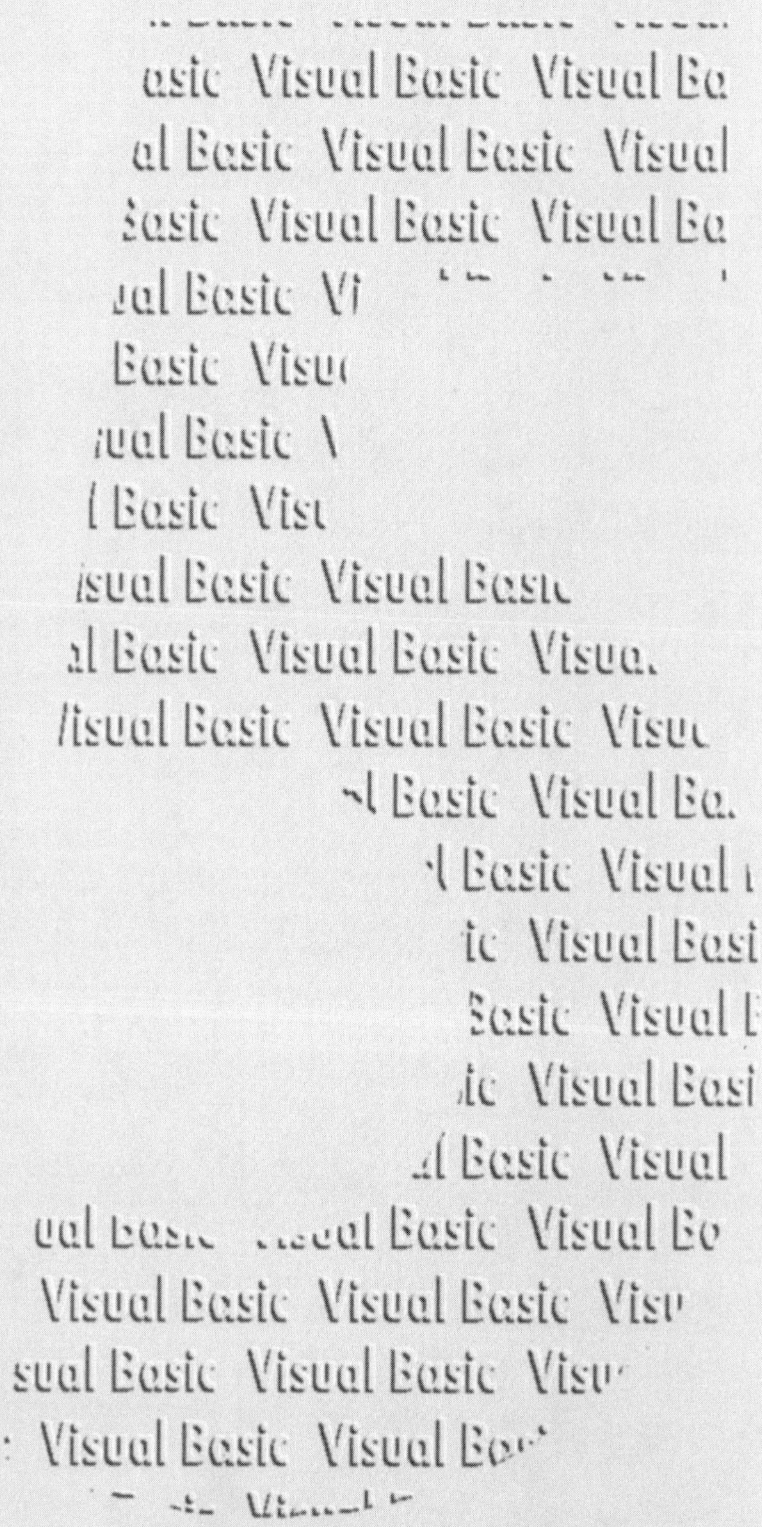

asic Visual Basic Visual Ba
al Basic Visual Basic Visual
asic Visual Basic Visual Ba
ual Basic Vi
Basic Visu
ual Basic V
l Basic Vis
isual Basic Visual Basic
al Basic Visual Basic Visua
Visual Basic Visual Basic Visu
l Basic Visual Ba
l Basic Visual
ic Visual Basi
Basic Visual B
ic Visual Basi
l Basic Visual
ual Basic Visual Basic Visual Ba
Visual Basic Visual Basic Visu
sual Basic Visual Basic Visu
Visual Basic Visual Ba

Creating Your Own Controls

So far in the book we've relied on using the controls that come with Visual Basic out of the box to build our applications. However, one of the big improvements that Microsoft made to VB5 is the addition of the ability to create your own ActiveX controls.

This obviously enables you to produce controls with functionality that the normal VB ones don't have, but there are other benefits too. More and more applications, particularly those from Microsoft it would seem, are beginning to include support for ActiveX controls. What better way to share the hard work you've done coding up your business rules, than to put them into ActiveX controls that everyone can use. In addition, you can also add life to web pages by embedding ActiveX controls in them, or even enter the growing market for ActiveX controls with one of your own.

You should note that to create ActiveX controls, you must have the Control Creation, Professional or Enterprise editions of VB5.

In this chapter we are going to cover:

- How to create an ActiveX control from scratch
- How to use the ActiveX control wizard to have one built for you
- How to change the icon that appears on the toolbox
- How to get the new control to appear in the toolbox

> *Of course, given the space of just one chapter we can only hope to give an introduction to creating your own controls here. However, if you're interested in taking this further, check out* **Instant Visual Basic 5 ActiveX Control Creation**, *also from Wrox Press.*

Now, without further ado, on with the show....

A Color Control

By now you should be comfortable with the common color dialog which allows your user to select a color. Suppose you decided that you wanted a button that the user could click to bring up that dialog. Not too hard right? Now suppose that you're developing an application and you want this same button on a lot of different forms. This still isn't too hard, but wouldn't it be nice to have a pre-built color dialog button that you could put on each form just like any other control? Let's take a look.

Try It Out – A Color Button Control

1 Start up a new project in Visual Basic, but this time, instead of selecting Standard EXE as the type of project, choose ActiveX Control from the list.

At first glance, it looks just like a regular project. However, if you look closely at the project window, you'll see that the display indicates we're working with a control rather than a regular project.

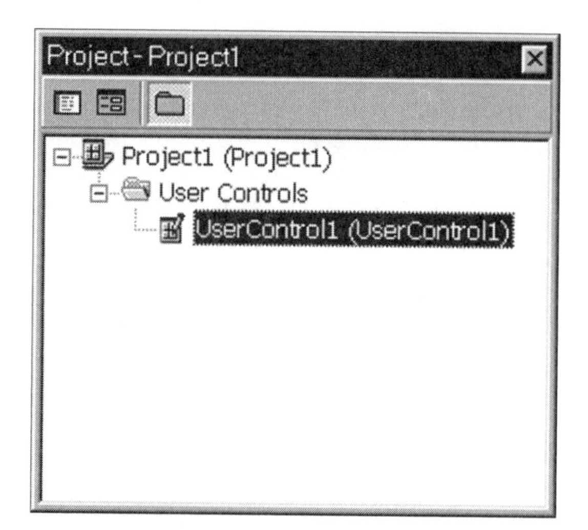

2 Click on UserControl1 in the project window and use the properties window to change the **Name** property to **ColorButton**.

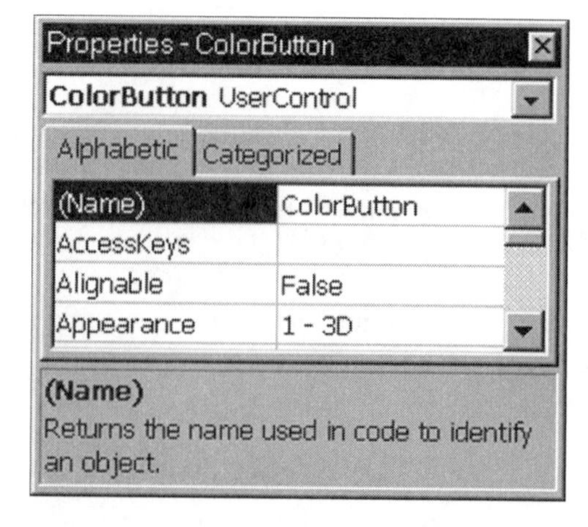

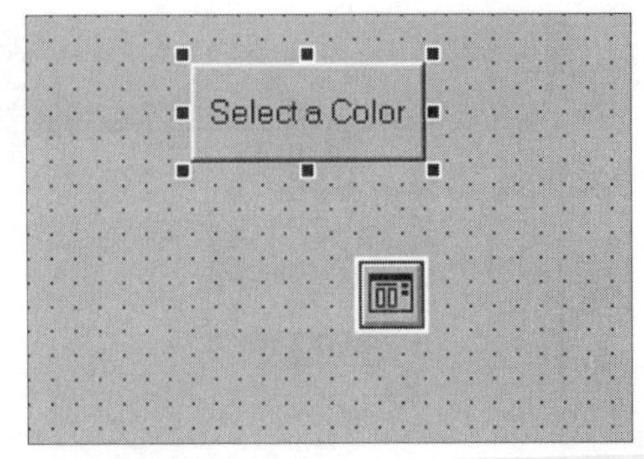

3 Now place a button control and the common dialog control onto the form. Change the button's caption to Select a Color.

4 Bring up the code window and type in the following code:

```
Event Click()

Private Sub Command1_Click()
  CommonDialog1.ShowColor
  RaiseEvent Click
End Sub

Public Property Get Color() As Long
  Color = CommonDialog1.Color
End Property

Private Sub UserControl_Resize()
  Command1.Move 0, 0, ScaleWidth, ScaleHeight
End Sub
```

Our control is done at this point. Testing controls is a little trickier than the other projects we've done so far though. To test a control we've got to use it in another project.

5 The first thing to do is compile our control. First, save this project as **ColorButton.vbp**. Then, choose Make ColorButton.ocx from the File menu option to compile the control.

6 Next, make sure you close the design window (not just the code window) for this control by clicking the close button in the menu bar. Visual Basic won't let us use our control while the design window is still open—VB doesn't want us changing the control out from under it.

7 Now select Add Project from the File menu and create a standard EXE project. Take a look at the project window. There are two different projects listed:

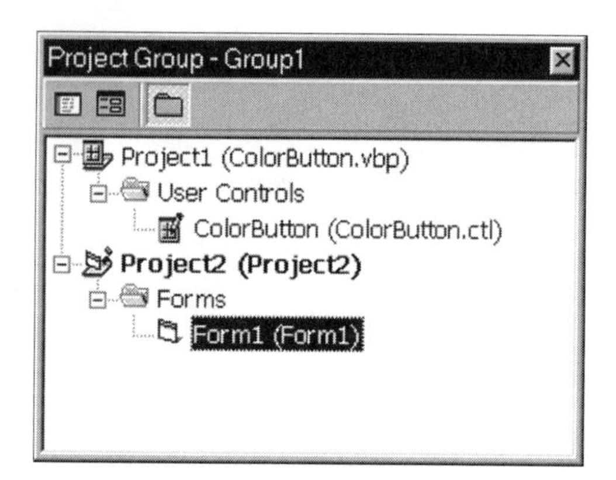

What we've done here is add a second project into the Visual Basic environment where we built our control project. **Project1** is our control, and **Project2** is the new project we just created.

8 If you look in the toolbox you'll see that there's an icon listed for our color control. Place one of these controls on the form, just as you would any other control.

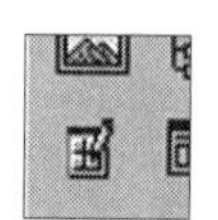

9 Now bring up the code window and type in the following code:

```
Private Sub ColorButton1_Click()
  BackColor = ColorButton1.Color
End Sub
```

10 Finally, run the project and click on the button. Up pops the familiar color dialog. If you select a color and click OK, the form's background color will change to the one you chose.

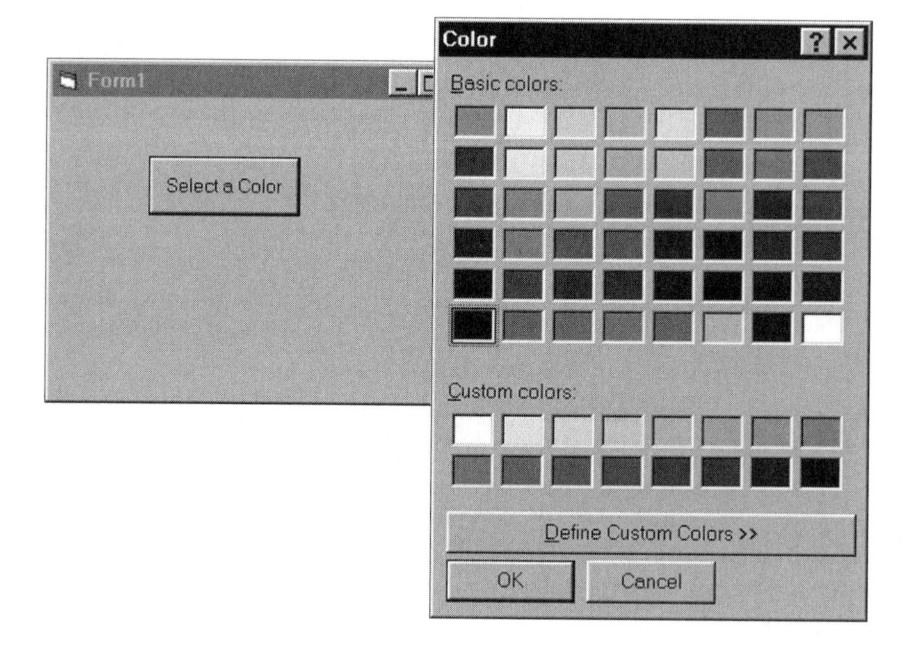

Pat yourself on the back, you've created your first control!

There wasn't much code involved to make all this work. And even the code we did type in is similar to some we've used earlier in the book—in fact that's the whole idea. Creating controls isn't supposed to be much more effort than regular programming.

Let's take a closer look at all that code to see exactly what's going on with it.

How It Works - Getting the Right Size

First, let's look at the code you entered to size the control:

```
Private Sub UserControl_Resize()
  Command1.Move 0, 0, ScaleWidth, ScaleHeight
End Sub
```

This should be pretty straightforward by now. When a control is resized, a **Resize** event happens and you can put code in your control to react to that event. That's exactly what we've done here. **Move** is a command that can be used on most controls to both move and resize the control. In this example, **Command1.Move** is used to move the control to coordinates 0, 0 and to set the control's width and height to match that of our custom control. All we're doing is resizing the command button so it fills the whole of our control, regardless of how our control gets stretched.

At first glance this can seem confusing—after all, don't controls just handle sizing automatically? Well, yes they do—but only because the programmer who created the control made it work that way. Since we're creating this control ourselves, we'll have to make the sizing work right.

> *The whole process of developing controls means you need to change your mind set. Instead of being a control* user, *you've now become the control* creator. *You'll soon find that controls don't do much of anything unless the programmer who made the control puts in some effort.*

How It Works - Getting the Color

In our test project we had a line to set the color of the form:

```
BackColor = ColorButton1.Color
```

But where did that ColorButton's **Color** property come from? Well, if you look at the code you typed into the control, you'll see the following:

```
Public Property Get Color() As Long
  Color = CommonDialog1.Color
End Property
```

This is the code that gives our control a **Color** property. You can see that all it does is pass on the **Color** property from the common dialog control—about as easy as you could hope for.

How It Works - Handling the Clicks

Of course, almost all controls have events so that programs that use them can respond when something happens. In our test program we used the ColorButton control's **Click** event:

```
Private Sub ColorButton1_Click()
  BackColor = ColorButton1.Color
End Sub
```

And as with the **Color** property, the **Click** event is only there because of the code you typed in:

```
Event Click()

Private Sub Command1_Click()
  CommonDialog1.ShowColor
  RaiseEvent Click
End Sub
```

Now this gets a little more confusing. Did you notice the **Event** and **RaiseEvent** commands in the code?

The **Event** command tells Visual Basic that this control might cause some certain event to happen. In this case we've told it that our control might cause a **Click** event. This is very much like declaring variables at the top of our program, only in this case we're declaring events. Of course, just declaring an event doesn't mean it will happen, it just means that it could happen. You have to tell the event to actually happen using yet another command.

RaiseEvent is, as you might have guessed, the command that actually causes our control to fire a **Click** event. You can see that we cause our **Click** event to happen inside the command button's **Click** event. This is because when the user clicks on the button, we want it to seem to our test program that they clicked on the ColorButton control.

Of course, before we cause our **Click** event to happen we want to present the color dialog to the user, so we place the **RaiseEvent** command after the **CommonDialog1.ShowColor** command. This way, the ColorButton's **Click** event gets fired after the color dialog has been displayed and the user has clicked the OK button.

The ColorButton control is about as simple as you can get. Creating more complex controls can get to be a lot of work. However, luckily for us, Microsoft has made it easy by supplying, what else, a wizard! Read on, and we'll create a full-featured control using the ActiveX Control Interface Wizard.

An Improved Combo Box

Microsoft has provided us with a number of ways to work with lists of information, including the combo box control. This control doesn't take up much space on the screen until the user expands it, when they get to choose from a list of options.

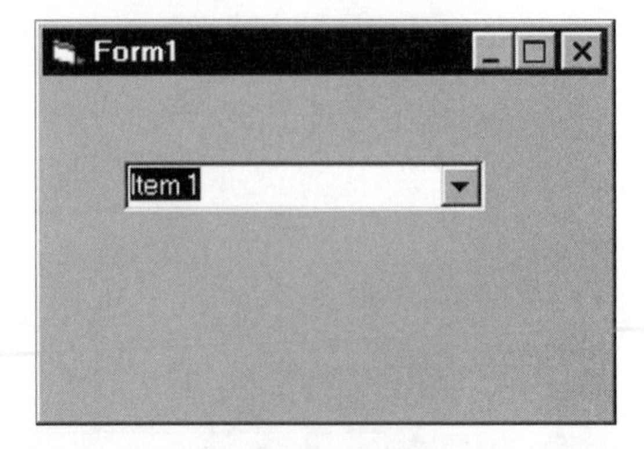

Unfortunately, the combo box isn't great from the user's point of view when the lists of data become very long. This is because the user only gets to see a few items from the list at any time—they have to scroll up and down to see the rest. Imagine a combo box with over a thousand entries and our poor user having to page down or use the mouse to scan the list to find the line they want to choose. If you set the list's **`Sorted`** property to **`True`**, the user can effectively press the first letter of a word and jump to the first instance. Still, there may be hundreds of entries with that same first letter and so this is hardly a good solution.

Some programs solve this problem by having a similar control that allows the user to enter the first *few* characters of a word and the list will scroll to any matching entry. This type of functionality allows you to present hundreds or thousands of entries to the user in a simple, but effective, list control.

In VB5, we can not only create new controls from scratch, but we can also base new controls on ones that are provided by Visual Basic. So we can make a new, improved, combo box control of our own.

There are a fair number of steps to this process, so bear with me as we walk through it all. Once we're done, though, we'll have a useful control to use.

Try It Out – Preparing the Control

1. Create a new project, making sure that you select the ActiveX Control project type.

2. From the Project menu, select Project1 Properties... and change the project name to **`WComboBoxControl`**. While we're here, let's also make the project description read **`Searchable ComboBox`**. This description will show up in the Component list and object browser, providing a more readable description of our control.

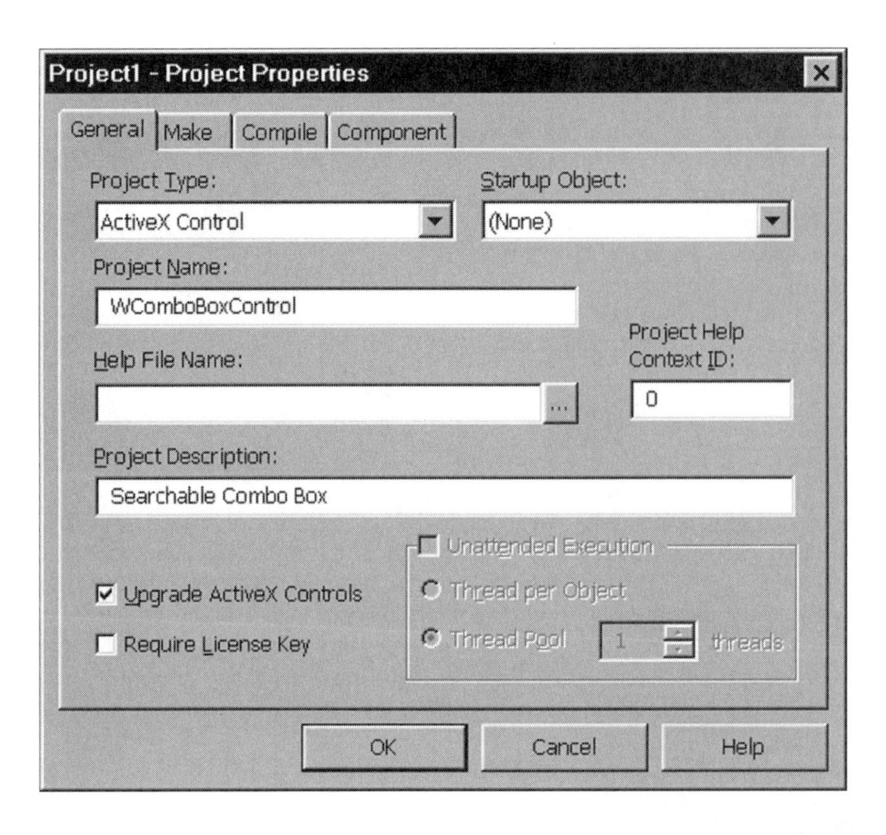

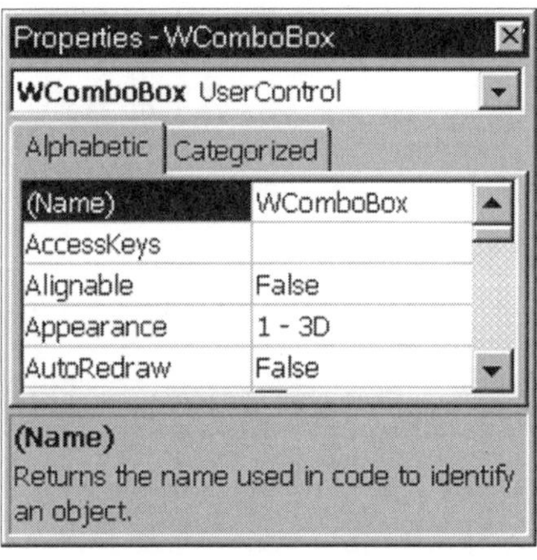

3 Next, select **`UserControl1`** and change its **`Name`** to **`WComboBox`**. This is the control name that will be seen and used by programmers who use our control in their projects.

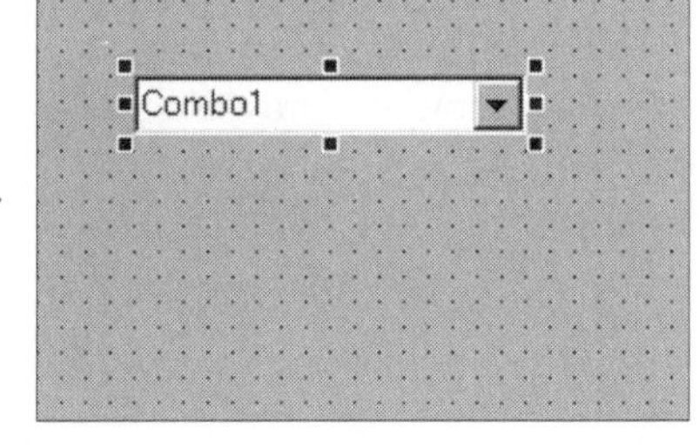

4 Now add a combo box control to the custom control.

You needn't worry about where the combo box appears in the design window, since we'll be repositioning and resizing it through code. We want it to respond to the programmer just like a regular combo box control, so we'll need to create some code to handle that.

5 Name the combo box **`cboCombo`**. Remember that the combo box we've added is *inside* our control. Since we're defining our control's programming interface, our combo box subcontrol won't be directly accessible to a programmer unless we allow it. They will only see **`WComboBox`**, the name of our control.

At this point you can compile the control and test it if you want to. Use the same process you used to test the color control earlier. You'll soon see that the control is very far from being complete. In fact, it's almost impossible to do anything useful with it at all as yet.

The ActiveX Control Interface Wizard

Now that we have the basics of our control set up we can use the ActiveX Control Interface Wizard. The wizard won't do everything for us, but it will at least create the skeleton of our interface—and it'll be much quicker and easier than doing all the work by hand.

As we saw in the earlier ColorButton example, you normally would have to provide each property, method and event for the control by hand. It's no good putting a combo box or button in a control if we don't give the programmer some way to interact with it. Essentially what the wizard does is add this code automatically. It doesn't do everything perfectly, but it sure can save a lot of typing.

Try It Out – Adding the Wizard to the Menu

1 By default, the wizard isn't set up to be used. Before we can use it to help us out, we need to tell Visual Basic that it's there. From the Add-Ins menu, select Add-In Manager and select the VB ActiveX Control Interface Wizard option. Then click OK.

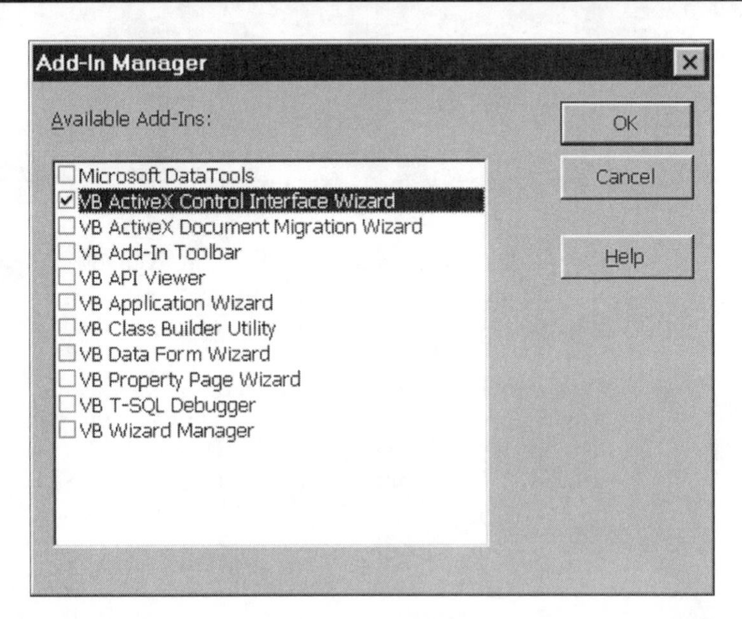

> *This is something you should only have to do once. Once you've added the wizard to your add-ins menu it should stay there, even if you close Visual Basic and start over.*

2 Now when you go to the Add-Ins menu, you should see the ActiveX Control Property Wizard option. Select this.

3 The first panel of the wizard is just an introductory screen with an overview of the wizard's capabilities. Read this then click Next to move on.

4 This next panel is where the fun begins. The wizard has already made a number of guesses about the interface for our control.

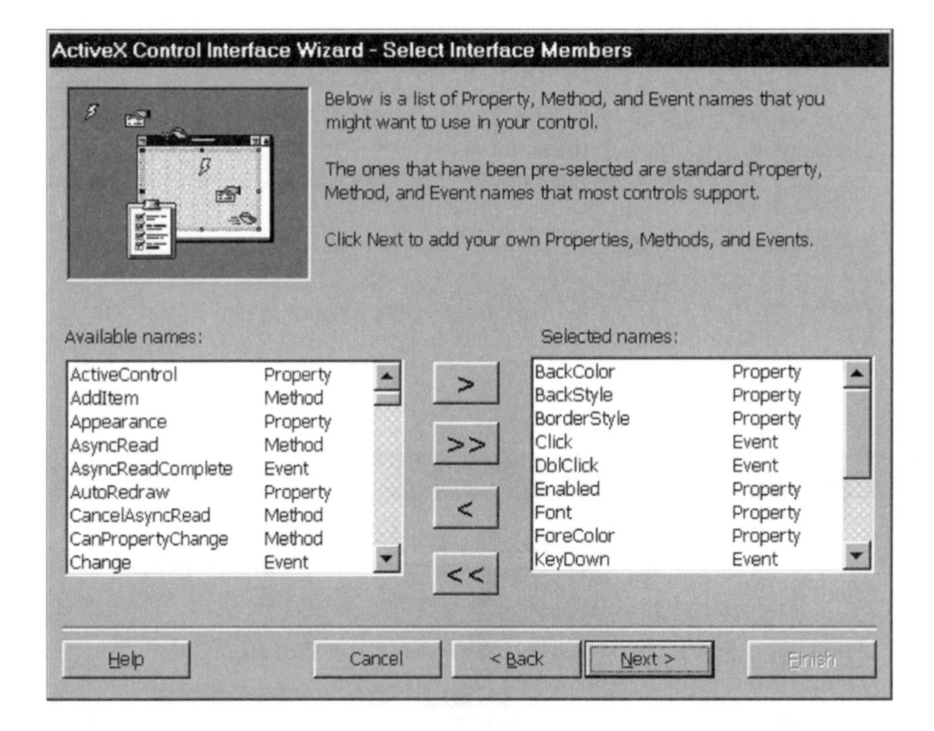

On the left the wizard lists all of the available properties, methods and events from the user control itself and from any subcontrols we've added to our user control. In this case, it has added all the interface elements for our combo box subcontrol.

On the right the wizard lists all the names of the properties, methods and events that it will include in the final control. Initially the wizard creates a default list of items that are typical to most controls. This is the list we need to modify, removing the items we don't want and adding those that we need.

5 Let's start by trimming out the names on the right that we know we don't want. The wizard's default list contains some interface elements which aren't appropriate for our control. In particular, these are elements which aren't supported by a normal combo box control with its **`Style`** property set to **`0`**:

```
BackStyle    BorderStyle    Click    DblClick    MouseDown
MouseMove    MouseUp
```

To remove an item from the list, click on the item with the mouse and then click the '<' button.

6 Once these are removed, we can add in additional interface elements from the left-hand list. The ones we need to add are those that are specifically supported by the combo box control so we can have an interface that matches as closely as possible:

```
AddItem         Appearance  Change       Clear         DropDown
FontBold        FontItalic  FontName     FontSize      FontStrikethru
FontUnderline   hWnd        ItemData     List          ListCount
ListIndex       Locked      MouseIcon    MousePointer  NewIndex
RemoveItem      SelLength   SelStart     SelText       Sorted
Style           Text        ToolTipText  TopIndex      WhatsThisHelpID
```

To add an item to the list, click on the item with the mouse and then click the '>' button.

At this point we have all the normal properties, methods and events we will support for our control.

7 Now click Next to move to the next panel of the wizard. This one allows us to enter new properties.

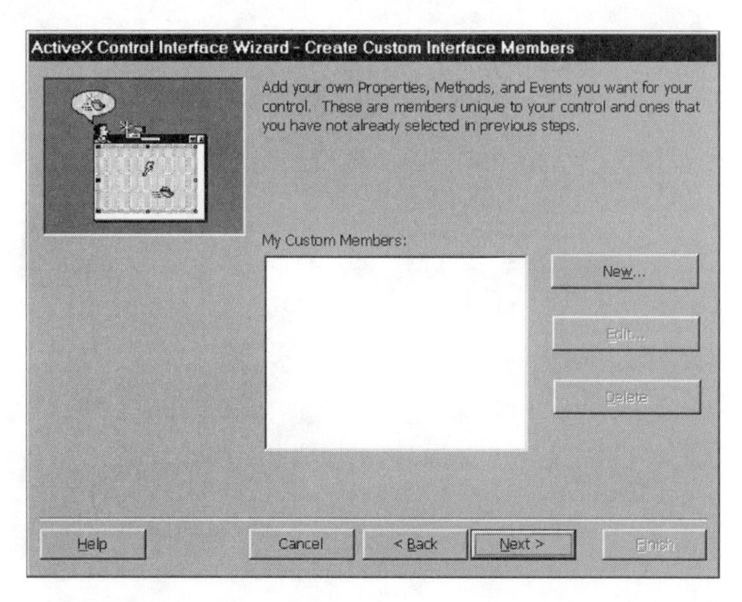

The normal combo box control, with **`Style 0`**, lets the user enter anything they want. Our control should also accept user input, but we also want it to only allow the user to enter items that are in the list. To do this, we'll add a **`LimitToList`** property to our control. This is a new property, so it is not in the list on the left. We'll have to add it ourselves.

8 Click the New... button and type in **`LimitToList`** as the name of the property. Then click OK.

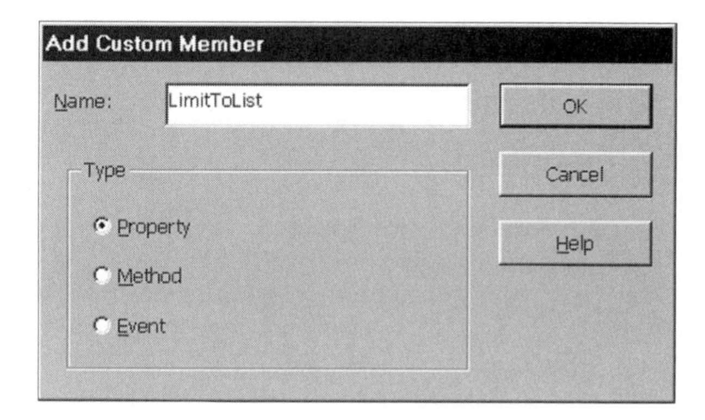

To add methods or events, you use the same technique and just make sure the relevant option button is selected. For this example, though, we're happy with just one new property.

9 Now click Next to move on. The next panel in the wizard lets us **map** our properties, methods and events to our control or subcontrols. Mapping means that we will tell the wizard to automatically cause each property, method or event to be handled by another property, method or event that is supported directly by our control or our combo box subcontrol.

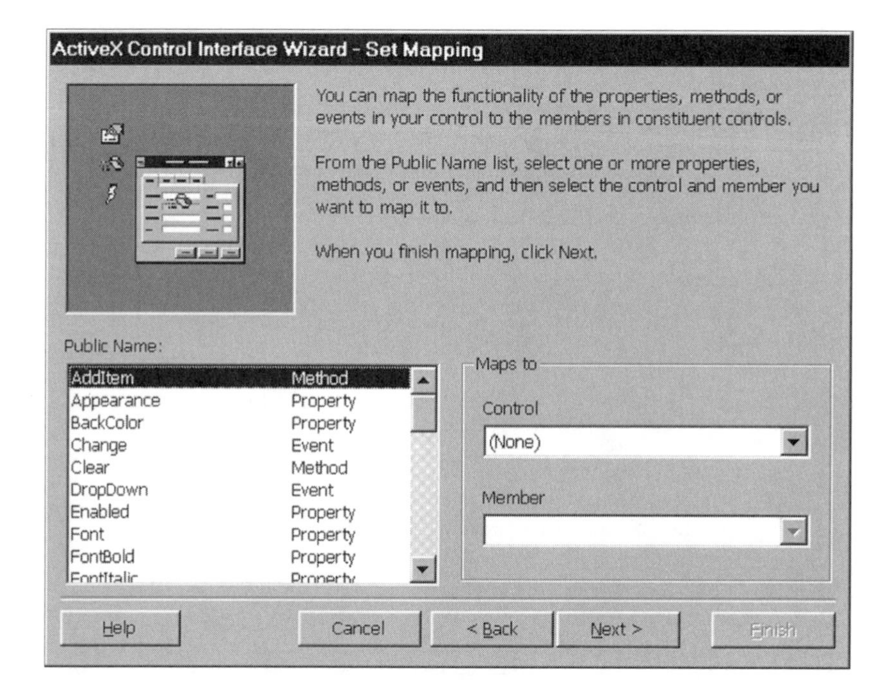

We'll map our control's entire interface to **`cboCombo`** except for the **`LimitToList`** property which we'll talk about later. Since **`cboCombo`** doesn't have a matching **`LimitToList`** property, we can't map this property to the subcontrol. The wizard helps us out here, in that custom interface elements aren't even listed on this panel.

10 Since we want our entire interface to be mapped to our combo box control, we can use a shortcut technique. Using the mouse or keyboard, highlight all the items in the list on the left. Then click on the Control box on the right and choose **`cboCombo`**. The wizard will automatically map all the items to the properties, methods and events from **`cboCombo`** since they have the same name.

If you click on the top item in the Public Name list you'll see that it mapped **`AddItem`** to **`cboCombo`**'s **`AddItem`** method. You can now move down through the list of items and see that each one was mapped to the corresponding item in **`cboCombo`**.

Our control's **`AddItem`** *method.....*

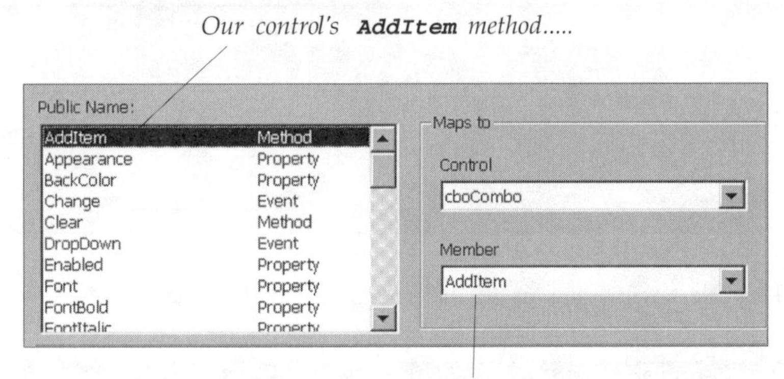

....is mapped to the **`AddItem`** *method of* **`cboCombo`**

This technique can be very useful to identify which interface elements are supported by a given subcontrol. After doing this global mapping, you can move through the items in the Public Name list. If any of the items in the list have no corresponding match in your subcontrol, they will show up as being mapped to Control '(None)' with the Member field being blank.

11 Click Next. The wizard now needs more information about any elements that aren't mapped (in our case, the **`LimitToList`** property). In particular, it needs to know the data type of the property, what its default value will be and whether it is read-write, write-only, read-only or unavailable at both design and run time.

We can also specify a description for our property. This description will be used in the various help windows and browsers throughout Visual Basic.

Set the attributes as shown in the screenshot.

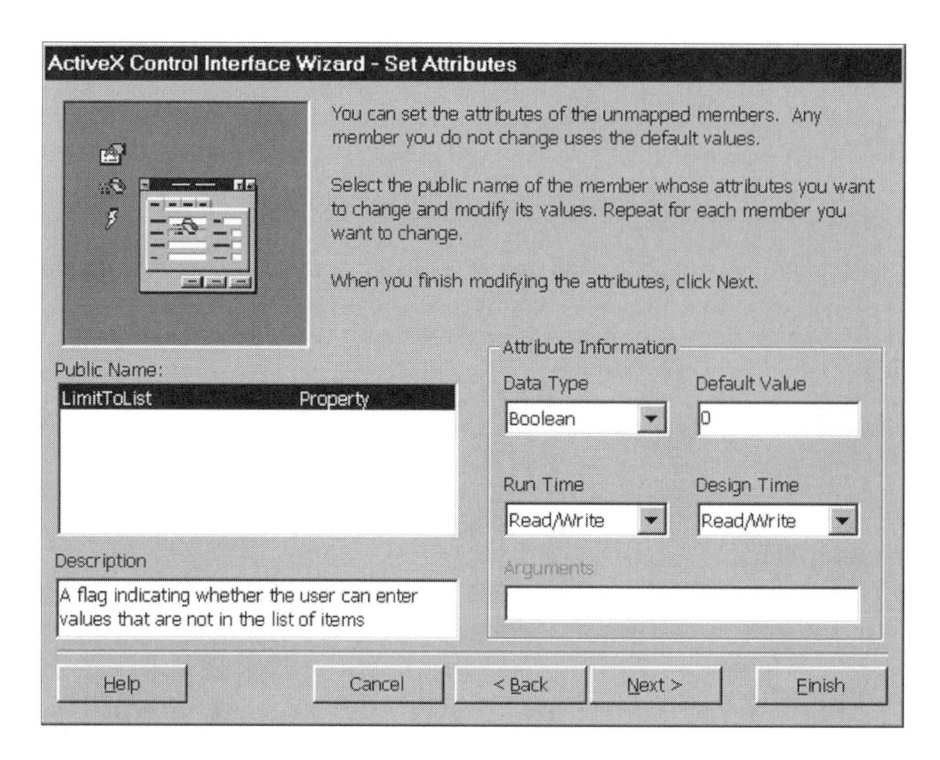

12 Clicking Next will bring us to the final panel of the wizard.

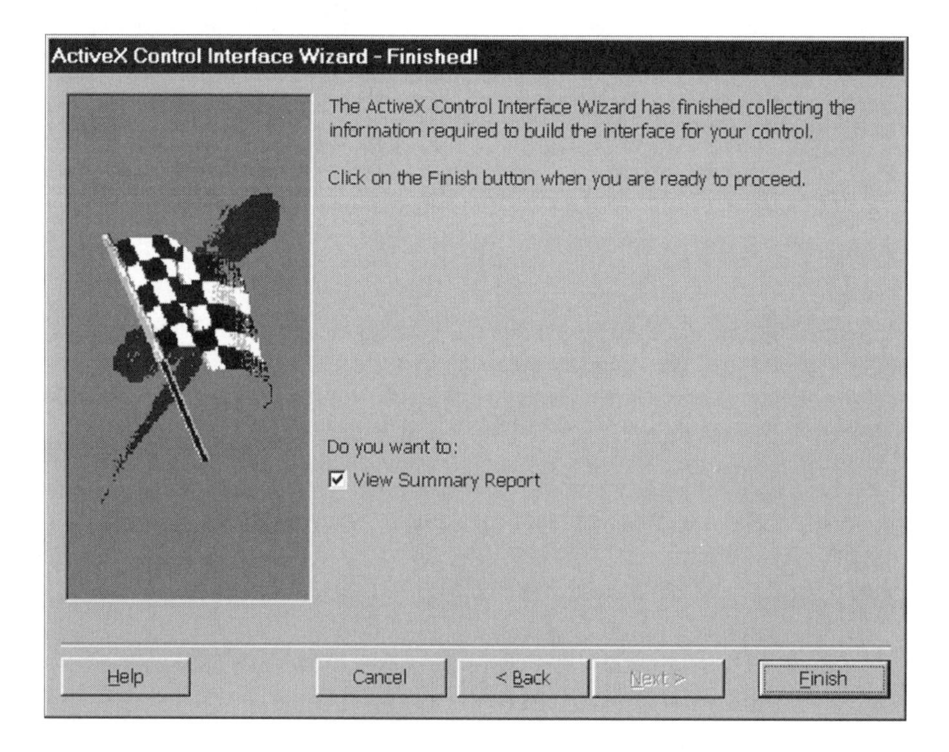

Click the Finish button and the wizard will generate all the code to manage our control's interface and will insert that code into our control's code window.

The summary report that you can choose to view will give you a list of activities you now need to perform. We'll walk through those activities in the remainder of this chapter.

The wizard does a lot of work for us, but there's still a fair amount of work left to do. I am going to step you through what needs to be done without much explanation so we can get our control working. Towards the end of the chapter I'll walk back through many of the steps and explain why we had to do everything we did.

Try It Out – Cleaning Up After the Wizard

1 Open up the control's code window and you'll see that it's full of wizard-generated code. The wizard has created code so that each property, method and event of our control's interface is automatically passed through to the **cboCombo** subcontrol to be processed.

WComboBoxControl - WComboBox (Code)

UserControl | InitProperties

```
'Initialize Properties for User Control
Private Sub UserControl_InitProperties()
    m_LimitToList = m_def_LimitToList
End Sub

'Load property values from storage
Private Sub UserControl_ReadProperties(PropBag As PropertyB
Dim Index As Integer

    cboCombo.BackColor = PropBag.ReadProperty("BackColor",
    cboCombo.ForeColor = PropBag.ReadProperty("ForeColor",
    cboCombo.Enabled = PropBag.ReadProperty("Enabled", True
    Set Font = PropBag.ReadProperty("Font", Ambient.Font)
    cboCombo.FontBold = PropBag.ReadProperty("FontBold", 0)
    cboCombo.FontItalic = PropBag.ReadProperty("FontItalic"
    cboCombo.FontName = PropBag.ReadProperty("FontName", ""
```

2 In the **UserControl_ReadProperties** routine, remove the following lines of code:

```
'TO DO: The member you have mapped to contains an array of data.
'  You must supply the code to persist the array.  A prototype
'    line is shown next:
  cboCombo.ItemData(Index) = PropBag.ReadProperty("ItemData" & Index, 0)
'TO DO: The member you have mapped to contains an array of data.
```

```
'    You must supply the code to persist the array.  A prototype
'    line is shown next:
  cboCombo.List(Index) = PropBag.ReadProperty("List" & Index, "")
```

3 In the `UserControl_WriteProperties` routine, remove the following lines of code:

```
'TO DO: The member you have mapped to contains an array of data.
'    You must supply the code to persist the array.  A prototype
'    line is shown next:
  Call PropBag.WriteProperty("ItemData" & Index,
cboCombo.ItemData(Index), 0)
'TO DO: The member you have mapped to contains an array of data.
'    You must supply the code to persist the array.  A prototype
'    line is shown next:
  Call PropBag.WriteProperty("List" & Index, cboCombo.List(Index), "")
```

4 Change the `Property Let` of the `ListIndex` property to look like this:

```
Public Property Let ListIndex(ByVal New_ListIndex As Integer)
  If Ambient.UserMode = False Then Err.Raise 382
   cboCombo.ListIndex() = New_ListIndex
End Property
```

5 Now make the same changes as shown in step 4 to the following `Property Let` routines:

`FontBold`	`FontItalic`	`FontName`	`FontSize`	`FontStrikethru`
`FontUnderline`	`SelLength`	`SelStart`	`SelText`	`TopIndex`

6 Change the `UserControl_ReadProperties` routine by removing the following lines of code:

```
  cboCombo.FontBold = PropBag.ReadProperty("FontBold", 0)
  cboCombo.FontItalic = PropBag.ReadProperty("FontItalic", 0)
  cboCombo.FontName = PropBag.ReadProperty("FontName", "")
  cboCombo.FontSize = PropBag.ReadProperty("FontSize", 0)
  cboCombo.FontStrikethru = PropBag.ReadProperty("FontStrikethru", 0)
  cboCombo.FontUnderline = PropBag.ReadProperty("FontUnderline", 0)
  cboCombo.ListIndex = PropBag.ReadProperty("ListIndex", 0)
  cboCombo.SelLength = PropBag.ReadProperty("SelLength", 0)
  cboCombo.SelStart = PropBag.ReadProperty("SelStart", 0)
  cboCombo.SelText = PropBag.ReadProperty("SelText", "")
  cboCombo.TopIndex = PropBag.ReadProperty("TopIndex", 0)
```

7 Change the `UserControl_WriteProperties` routine by removing the following lines of code:

```
  Call PropBag.WriteProperty("FontBold", cboCombo.FontBold, 0)
  Call PropBag.WriteProperty("FontItalic", cboCombo.FontItalic, 0)
```

```
    Call PropBag.WriteProperty("FontName", cboCombo.FontName, "")
    Call PropBag.WriteProperty("FontSize", cboCombo.FontSize, 0)
    Call PropBag.WriteProperty("FontStrikethru", cboCombo.FontStrikethru,
        ↳ 0)
    Call PropBag.WriteProperty("FontUnderline", cboCombo.FontUnderline, 0)
    Call PropBag.WriteProperty("ListIndex", cboCombo.ListIndex, 0)
    Call PropBag.WriteProperty("SelLength", cboCombo.SelLength, 0)
    Call PropBag.WriteProperty("SelStart", cboCombo.SelStart, 0)
    Call PropBag.WriteProperty("SelText", cboCombo.SelText, "")
    Call PropBag.WriteProperty("TopIndex", cboCombo.TopIndex, 0)
```

8. Finally, save the project. You've done a lot of work and we're almost ready to test the control—you wouldn't be best pleased if you now lost everything due to a power outage!

Try It Out – Adding Your Own Code

Now that we've sorted through the code that the wizard kindly wrote for us, we can add our own functionality.

1. In order to make our control resize just like the regular combo box control, add the following code into the **UserControl_Resize** event routine:

```
Private Sub UserControl_Resize()
  If Height <> cboCombo.Height Then Height = cboCombo.Height
  cboCombo.Move 0, 0, ScaleWidth
End Sub
```

   This code will keep our control's height the same as the combo box subcontrol (remember that a combo box control has a fixed height—you can't change it). It will also make sure that the combo box control stretches to have the same width as our user control. To the programmer, our control will appear to work just like a regular combo box.

2. Add the following lines into the General Declarations section of the control:

```
'True if FindItem is running
Private bFinding As Boolean

'Current cursor position within the text
Private lPos As Long

'Index value of the last item selected
Private lIndex As Long
```

3. Now we need to add the routine that matches what the user types to what's in our list. Type it all in:

```
Private Sub FindItem()

  Dim lIdx As Long
  Dim sText As String
  Dim lLen As Long
  Dim bFound As Boolean

  bFinding = True
  lPos = cboCombo.SelStart
  sText = cboCombo.Text
  lLen = Len(sText)
  bFound = False

  For lIdx = 0 To cboCombo.ListCount
     If StrComp(sText, Left$(cboCombo.List(lIdx), lLen), vbTextCompare) =
       ↳  0 Then cboCombo.ListIndex = lIdx
       bFound = True
       Exit For
     End If
  Next lIdx

  If m_LimitToList And Not bFound Then
    cboCombo.ListIndex = lIndex
      If lIndex = -1 Then cboCombo.Text = ""
      cboCombo.SelStart = lPos - 1
  Else
    cboCombo.SelStart = lPos
    lIndex = cboCombo.ListIndex
  End If

  cboCombo.SelLength = Len(cboCombo.Text)
  bFinding = False

End Sub
```

4 Now find the **cboCombo_Change** event. This event will get called each time the user presses a key, so it's the ideal place for the code that will make everything happen. The wizard has already placed the **RaiseEvent** line there; add the rest of this code:

```
Private Sub cboCombo_Change()
  If bFinding Then Exit Sub
  If Len(cboCombo.Text) = 0 Then
    lPos = 0
    lIndex = -1
  Else
    FindItem
  End If
  RaiseEvent Change
End Sub
```

5 In our control's **Initialize** event, set the **lIndex** module level variable to **-1** to indicate that no item is selected from the list.

```
Private Sub UserControl_Initialize()
  lIndex = -1
End Sub
```

> ***UserControl_Initialize** is the first event ever fired in a control. It indicates that the client program has created an instance of our control and that they may continue to work with it. This is a good place to initialize internal variables and generally get the control ready for use.*

6 The final thing to do is to ensure that the *Backspace* key will work properly in our control. Go to the **cboCombo**'s **KeyPress** event, and add the following to the line that the wizard inserted:

```
Private Sub cboCombo_KeyPress(KeyAscii As Integer)
  If KeyAscii = 8 Then
    bFinding = True
    cboCombo.SelText = ""
    bFinding = False
  End If
  RaiseEvent KeyPress(KeyAscii)
End Sub
```

And that's pretty much it! To quickly summarize the steps so far, we have:

- Created an ActiveX Control project
- Set up the basics of the project
- Run the ActiveX Control Interface Wizard
- Cleaned up after the wizard
- Added code to make the control really do what we want

To add some polish to our control, we'll want to set the toolbox bitmap for the control so programmers who use our control can easily identify it. As we saw in the Color control earlier, Visual Basic gives us a default icon, but no self-respecting control designer is going to be satisfied with using the same icon as everyone else!

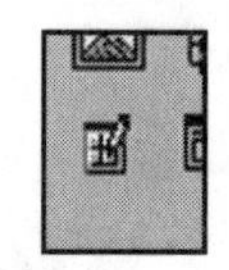

Changing the icon is an easy process—all we need to do is set a property in the control's property window.

Try It Out – Setting the Toolbox Bitmap

1. Bring up the properties window for the WComboBox control and find the `ToolboxBitmap` property.

2. Double-click on this property to bring up a standard file open dialog window and select the bitmap of your choice.

> *You can choose any bitmap which is about the right size to fit on the toolbox. The size of a bitmap displayed on the toolbox is 16x15 pixels. If you choose a bitmap of another size it will automatically be scaled to fit into this size.*

3. Save your project and then compile it by selecting Make WComboBoxControl.ocx from the File menu. Finally, close down the design window and your bitmap will appear in the toolbox. You are now ready to test the control.

Testing the Control

WComboBox is no harder to test than the Color control earlier in the chapter, though since this control is more sophisticated, the testing will be a little more involved.

Try It Out – Testing the WComboBox Control

1. Select Add Project from the File menu and add a standard EXE project.

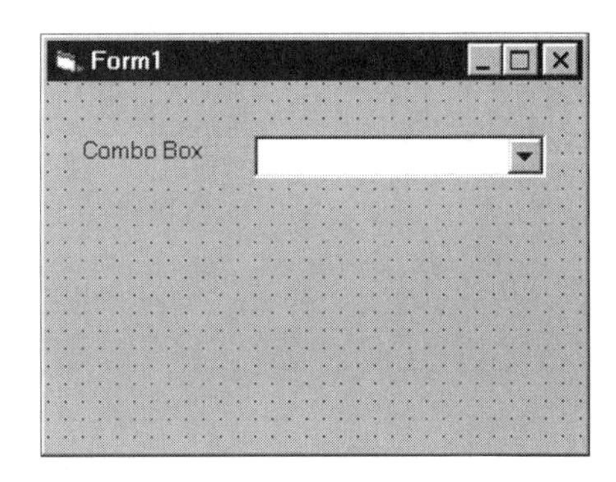

2. Add a regular combo box control to the form for comparison with our new control. Blank out its `Text` property and add a label as shown here:

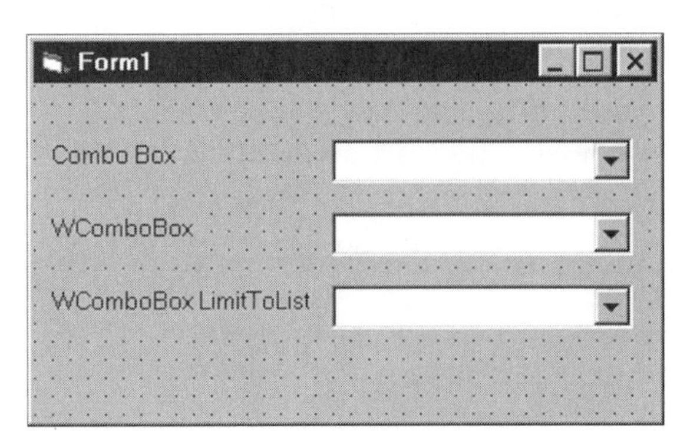

3. Now add two WComboBox controls from the toolbox. Blank out their `Text` properties and add some labels.

Our two new controls should be called **WComboBox1** and **WComboBox2** by default. These names are automatically derived from the **Name** property we used for our control.

4 Now change the **LimitToList** property of **WComboBox2** to True. This will allow us to test whether the control does in fact prevent the user from entering values that aren't in our list.

5 Now that we have the form set up, we can add some code to populate the three controls. To get a decent set of test data, while at the same time avoiding a lot of typing, we'll generate a few hundred random strings for each control by putting the following code in the **Form_Load** event:

```
Private Sub Form_Load()
  Dim Index As Long
  Dim LenIndex As Long
  Dim lLen As Long
  Dim sText As String

  For Index = 1 To 300
    lLen = Rnd * 10 + 1
    sText = ""
    For LenIndex = 1 To lLen
      sText = sText & Chr$(Rnd * 25 + 65)
    Next LenIndex
    Combo1.AddItem sText
    WComboBox1.AddItem sText
    WComboBox2.AddItem sText
  Next Index
End Sub
```

6 Run the program.

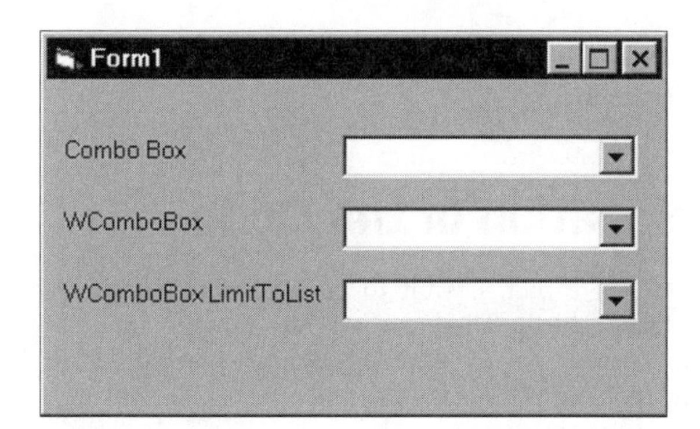

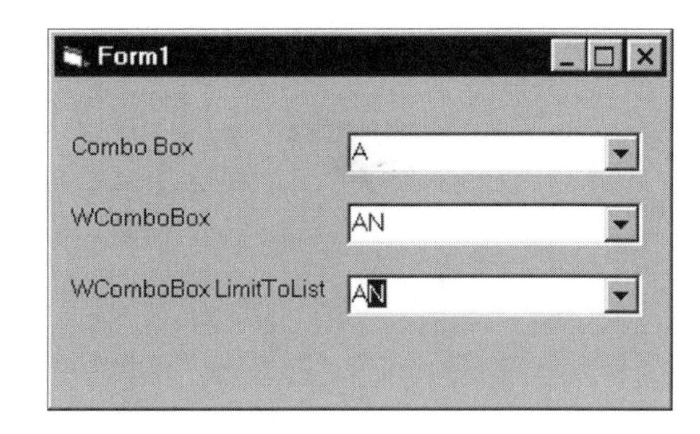

7 First let's try just entering a single character into each control. Type the letter 'A' into each control.

You can see how the normal combo box did nothing special, but our new control found a match and displayed it.

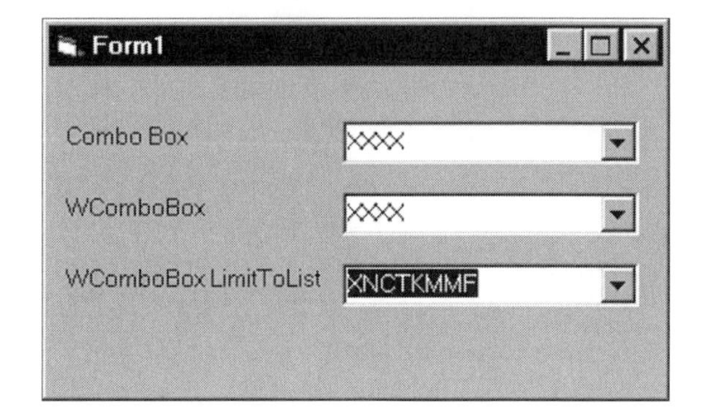

8 Now enter four 'X' characters into each control. Of course, since the list items are random your results may vary slightly.

Notice how the last control limited our entry to the items in the list while the first two controls just let us enter a value with no match.

That's it. You have now completed a control that you can use in your programs as easily as any other control.

An Explanation of the Code

As I promised earlier, I want to go back through much of what we did to make the WComboBox control. There were a lot of steps after the ActiveX Control Interface Wizard completed that I quickly flew through so you could see how the whole process worked. These are very important steps, and some of them are kind of complicated, so it's worth reviewing them in more detail.

If you bring up the code window for our control, you'll see that there's a lot of stuff there. When you were answering all those questions that the wizard asked, it was busy coming up with everything you see here.

I'm not going to go through all the code line by line. Still, I will point out the major sections of the code and describe what's going on in each.

Controls have Standard Properties

All the controls we've worked with so far in the book have had properties. For instance, you've used the **BackColor** property on picture boxes to change the color. Obviously properties are an important way for controls to communicate with programs, so you need properties on your own controls as well.

The wizard creates code for each property that will be supported by our control. For example, this is what it writes for the **ForeColor** property:

```
'WARNING! DO NOT REMOVE OR MODIFY THE FOLLOWING COMMENTED LINES!
'MappingInfo=cboCombo,cboCombo,-1,ForeColor
Public Property Get ForeColor() As OLE_COLOR
  ForeColor = cboCombo.ForeColor
End Property

Public Property Let ForeColor(ByVal New_ForeColor As OLE_COLOR)
  cboCombo.ForeColor() = New_ForeColor
  PropertyChanged "ForeColor"
End Property
```

Notice how the property is actually set and retrieved directly from the underlying **cboCombo** control. Each of the properties of our control is actually handled by the **cboCombo** control with the exception of the **LimitToList** property which I'll talk about next.

Also note the call to the **PropertyChanged** method in the **Property Let** routine. This method is important as it tells Visual Basic that the property value has changed, so any displays such as the properties window can be updated.

The LimitToList Property

The **LimitToList** property is a custom property which isn't supported by the normal combo box control. Because of this, **cboCombo** can't be used to manage this property and so the code is somewhat different.

The wizard creates a local constant to hold the property's default value and it declares a module level variable to hold the current value of the property:

```
'Default Property Values:
Const m_def_LimitToList = 0
'Property Variables:
Dim m_LimitToList As Boolean
```

The wizard writes code in the **UserControl_InitProperties** procedure to set the custom property's initial value to the default defined above.

```
'Initialize Properties for User Control
Private Sub UserControl_InitProperties()
  m_LimitToList = m_def_LimitToList
End Sub
```

*The difference between **`InitProperties`** and **`Initialize`** can be confusing. We used **`Initialize`** in our ColorButton example to set a module level variable for later use and that is a good use for that routine. **`InitProperties`** is intended to be used for setting the initial values of your control's properties, such as setting the **`LimitToList`** property value here.*

The actual code to manage the property simply maintains the appropriate module level variable. It's up to us to actually use the variable to do something useful, which is what we do with the **`FindItem`** subroutine.

```
Public Property Get LimitToList() As Boolean
  LimitToList = m_LimitToList
End Property

Public Property Let LimitToList(ByVal New_LimitToList As Boolean)
  m_LimitToList = New_LimitToList
  PropertyChanged "LimitToList"
End Property
```

Controls have Methods

Like the properties, all the methods are implemented to pass any call to our control's method directly to **`cboCombo`** by calling the method of the same name. For example, this is what we get in the **`Refresh`** method.

```
'WARNING! DO NOT REMOVE OR MODIFY THE FOLLOWING COMMENTED LINES!
'MappingInfo=cboCombo,cboCombo,-1,Refresh
Public Sub Refresh()
  cboCombo.Refresh
End Sub
```

Controls have Events

As you have seen throughout the book, Visual Basic and Windows are event driven environments. You've used events such as **`Click`** to put code in your programs so that things happen when the user clicks on something.

When you create a control, it has to have events too otherwise it won't be able to react to events. The wizard uses the **`Event`** keyword to declare the events that will be supported by our control:

```
'Event Declarations:
Event KeyDown(KeyCode As Integer, Shift As Integer)
'MappingInfo=cboCombo,cboCombo,-1,KeyDown
Event KeyPress(KeyAscii As Integer) 'MappingInfo=cboCombo,cboCombo,-
1,KeyPress
Event KeyUp(KeyCode As Integer, Shift As Integer)
'MappingInfo=cboCombo,cboCombo,-1,KeyUp
Event Change() 'MappingInfo=cboCombo,cboCombo,-1,Change
Event DropDown() 'MappingInfo=cboCombo,cboCombo,-1,DropDown
```

To actually make the events happen when they need to, the wizard puts in code so all the events raised by **cboCombo** are sent back through our control for use by the programmer. This is done using the **RaiseEvent** method as shown here:

```
Private Sub cboCombo_DropDown()
    RaiseEvent DropDown
End Sub
```

Saving Design Properties

When you use a control, you typically set various properties at design time. If you save the project and bring it back up later, you obviously expect those design time properties to have the same values that you entered.

The wizard creates two routines to support this functionality: **UserControl_ReadProperties** and **UserControl_WriteProperties**.

These routines use a couple of new commands: **ReadProperty** and **WriteProperty**. **ReadProperty** is a function that returns the value of a property. The first parameter you send it is the name of the property you're after, while the second is a default value in case the property doesn't have a stored value. **WriteProperty** saves the value of a property. You just need to supply the name of the property, the value to save out and a default value.

Why a default value to write out a value? This is to save space. If the value of your property matches the default value, then Visual Basic won't save the property's value. Of course, you need to make sure you use the same default values on your **ReadProperty** statement for that property or things really won't work right.

These routines are actually methods of a built-in object called **PropertyBag**. The **PropertyBag** object is basically a 'bag' of properties that you can have Visual Basic store for your control until they are needed later. They are actually stored in the **FRX** file associated with the form in which your control is being used.

An example of these routines is shown below:

```
'Load property values from storage
Private Sub UserControl_ReadProperties(PropBag As PropertyBag)
```

```
    cboCombo.ForeColor = PropBag.ReadProperty("ForeColor", &H80000008)
    cboCombo.Enabled = PropBag.ReadProperty("Enabled", True)
    Set Font = PropBag.ReadProperty("Font", Ambient.Font)
    m_LimitToList = PropBag.ReadProperty("LimitToList", m_def_LimitToList)
End Sub
```

```
'Write property values to storage
Private Sub UserControl_WriteProperties(PropBag As PropertyBag)

    Call PropBag.WriteProperty("ForeColor", cboCombo.ForeColor, &H80000008)
    Call PropBag.WriteProperty("Enabled", cboCombo.Enabled, True)
    Call PropBag.WriteProperty("Font", Font, Ambient.Font)
    Call PropBag.WriteProperty("LimitToList", m_LimitToList,
m_def_LimitToList)
End Sub
```

Properties Not Available at Design Time

When we mapped our properties to the **cboCombo** subcontrol we included a number of properties which are available at run time but which aren't supposed to be available at design time. Unfortunately, the wizard does not properly generate code to handle these properties. Worse yet, there's no easy way to know which properties these are, so you'll have to manually compare your control's properties to those of the regular combo box to identify the ones to change.

We fixed this problem in our control by adding the following line to a number of **Property Let** routines:

```
If Ambient.UserMode = False Then Err.Raise 382
```

> ***Error 382 is 'Set not supported at run time'. This is the value the wizard uses if you create a custom property through the wizard and indicate that it isn't available at design time.***

What happens is that Visual Basic will try to put a value into each property. If it gets an error 382, Visual Basic figures that the property isn't intended for design time use and so it doesn't show it in the control's properties window.

So how do we know that we're in design mode? That's where the **Ambient.UserMode** value comes in handy. This value will be **True** when the control is running in a program, and **False** when the control is being used in design mode.

> *The **Ambient** object is a built-in object available to your control. It represents the container that holds your control. This is typically a form, but it could be a picture control or other control that can act as a container. **Ambient** has a number of properties which tell your control about the state of the container that is using the control.*

Property Arrays

The wizard doesn't have enough information to handle properties which are actually property arrays. In our case, this means the **ItemData** and **List** properties.

A property array is just a property that works like an array. The combo box control's **List** property is an excellent example. To work with the **List** property, you would write code like:

```
MsgBox Combo1.List(0)
```

To use the **List** property, you give it an index value just like you would when working with a regular array. This type of property is called a property array.

The actual property code is generated just fine, but the **UserControl_ReadProperties** and **UserControl_WriteProperties** routines aren't fully created. Instead, the wizard puts some **TO DO** comments in these routines.

The code for the **UserControl_ReadProperties** routine is listed here:

```
'TO DO: The member you have mapped to contains an array of data.
'   You must supply the code to persist the array.  A prototype
'   line is shown next:
  cboCombo.ItemData(Index) = PropBag.ReadProperty("ItemData" & Index, 0)
'TO DO: The member you have mapped to contains an array of data.
'   You must supply the code to persist the array.  A prototype
'   line is shown next:
  cboCombo.List(Index) = PropBag.ReadProperty("List" & Index, "")
```

As you can see, there are **TO DO** comments above both the **ItemData** and **List** entries with instructions about how to read in the values for these properties.

In our case, we don't need to worry about this. Neither the **ItemData** nor **List** properties can be altered at design time and so we don't need to save or restore them in these routines. We removed the following code from the **UserControl_WriteProperties** routine:

```
'TO DO: The member you have mapped to contains an array of data.
'   You must supply the code to persist the array.  A prototype
'   line is shown next:
  Call PropBag.WriteProperty("ItemData" & Index,
cboCombo.ItemData(Index), 0)
'TO DO: The member you have mapped to contains an array of data.
'   You must supply the code to persist the array.  A prototype
'   line is shown next:
  Call PropBag.WriteProperty("List" & Index, cboCombo.List(Index), "")
```

Summary

In this chapter, we've seen how we can create new controls that are just as easy to use as the ones supplied with Visual Basic. We also saw how to change the behavior of an existing control to get it to do what we want done. We looked at how to:

- Create a simple control
- Add the ActiveX Control Interface Wizard to Visual Basic's menu
- Use the ActiveX Control Interface Wizard to help create a control
- Test our control, to make sure it does what we wanted it to do

Remember, if you want to explore creating your own controls further, you should take a look at *Instant Visual Basic 5 ActiveX Control Creation* from Wrox.

Why Not Try.....

1. How many different 'types' of ActiveX control can you make?

2. Prototype a control, using a command button and a timer control, which permits the designer to ring a bell for a duration at predetermined intervals. Both duration and interval will at some point be configurable properties.

3. Begin the process of creating an ActiveX control that acts as a bell. Add the appropriate code to give the Bell control properties necessary to specify the interval of the ring (seconds between rings), and the duration of the bell ring (in seconds).

4. Add the code to ensure that the control can deal with the command button being resized.

5. Finally, test out the control. Place a Bell control on a form, set the properties (in the **Form_Load** event) and run the project.

asic Visual Basic Visual Ba
al Basic Visual Basic Visual
Basic Visual Basic Visual Ba
ual Basic Vi
Basic Visu
ual Basic V
l Basic Vis
isual Basic Visual Basic
al Basic Visual Basic Visua
Visual Basic Visual Basic Visu
al Basic Visual Ba
al Basic Visual
ic Visual Basi
Basic Visual B
ic Visual Basi
al Basic Visual
ual Basic Visual Basic Visual Ba
Visual Basic Visual Basic Visu
sual Basic Visual Basic Visu
Visual Basic Visual Ba

Putting It All Together

By now, most of you should be pretty confident with how to use Microsoft's latest development masterpiece. However, as a great many of you will testify, knowing how to use it, and being confident at using it are two very different things. Sure, we've covered how to use controls and write code to take control of them at run time. We've even delved into the murky depths of ActiveX, databases and the API. But actually sitting down at this point and writing a whole application from scratch requires just a tiny bit extra.

In this final chapter we're going to take a whirlwind tour of how to build a complete application from scratch. Of course, in the space of one chapter it's going to be impossible to cover every angle, from design to conception, but you can at least get a feel for what you have to do and, hopefully, enough confidence to strike out on your own.

In particular, we're going to look at:

- Some simple Windows design ideas
- Where to start with building an entire application
- How to make the best use of the tools you have
- Some of the things that are available to help you get it right first time

So, without further ado, let's get stuck in.

Where do I Start?

It's a question that even the pros regularly ask themselves. You've just been given the mother of all applications to develop, and have scribbled down its comprehensive design and detailed specification on a napkin during the lunch meeting you just had with the user. Where do you go from here?

Love it or hate it, and I hate it, the answer is not the computer, but to the nearest large pad of paper and stash of pencils, crayons and pens. The first stage of building the application is to design it.

Maybe you're lucky and work in an organization that has analysts that do this kind of thing for you. Maybe you're a one man band. Whatever the scenario, modern software can still cost every bit as much as a building to develop, and for that reason we need to lay down some foundations.

There are books, seminars, and degree courses aplenty out there, and I can't hope to cover every detail here. However, I can give you some good ideas and point you in the right direction.

Designing the Application

As you will see in a little while, the most important part of any application that you develop is the data that it will manage. There are three parts to this data, and it's these parts that ultimately govern the design of your application.

The first part is **input**. In an invoicing system, for example, the user is going to need to be able to enter invoice details and customer details at the very least, which means that we need to come up with forms to provide that functionality. In addition, you'll probably want some kind of security in there to stop idle passers-by churning out invoices by the bucketload to their worst enemy. This means that there will have to be some kind of login screen in the system and, presumably, a way for users to maintain this security system.

If you think about it then, the first stage of designing your application is simple. Think about the data that you're managing and draw up a list of the forms that you're going to need to get that data into the system. Of course, this is an extremely high level view, but as I said the idea at this stage is just to clear up the clouds of confusion that are hanging over some of you.

In traditional circles, this would be thought of as defining the bounds of the system; at an early stage, we need to be able to say that the system is going to deal with X and Y elements of the business, but not Z. Going back to the invoicing system, for example, it's great that the system can store customer details and their invoices, but does it really need to be able to log the details of the marketing campaign that attracted those customers? That would be beyond the bounds of the system.

The next part of the data is **output**. In the invoicing example, it's obviously going to need to be able to produce invoices, but how about a form to allow the user to list invoices to the screen? How about a customer report and customer search form? Again, this is a case of defining the bounds of the system. We know that the invoicing application is going to produce an invoice, but it wouldn't necessarily be expected to stick the stamp to the envelope.

With these two areas covered, even in a very rough way, we should end up with a list of forms and high level functionality that the user would expect to be able to push their data through.

In a complex system, though, we would actually take these stages a little further. We know that we need an invoice entry form, and that we're also going to need a way to print an invoice, store it in the database, pull it from the database and so on. But rather than simply code subprocedures to do these things, how about coming up with plans for classes to represent the major objects in the system? This way we could have a reusable invoice class that could print itself, automatically store its information in the database, pull its information from the database and so on.

Here we're basically putting in a middle layer between the input and output of the data, giving the data a conceptual form of life, if you like, by defining in classes what each object of data can actually do with itself in the system.

Of course, it's not an absolute requirement that you do this, and in very simple systems (like the one we will start to develop in a little while), this would probably be overkill. In a big system, though, this would mean that you're making your application a lot easier to understand, maintain and debug, as well as identifying objects which could perhaps be reused from other applications in the business, or reused within other developments that are going on.

The third part of the data, which we'll cover a little later, is the **storage** of it: the physical tables in your database that will hold the information.

If you follow the items above then you should have a pretty good idea of the user interface, and maybe even an understanding of some of its underlying functionality. Suddenly the problem looks a little easier to solve.

Some Windows Thoughts for You

Have you ever wondered what it is about Windows that makes it so popular today? The simple answer is that it's easy to use. However, there's nothing simple about making Windows easy to use.

You see, it's not so much that Windows is easy to use, but that all the best applications that run on it adopt a number of pre-set standards that make them all look alike. If all the programs you ever run look and work in similar ways, then your learning curve as a user is likely to flatten out early on and you'll feel a lot happier about using a computer with Windows installed.

This is something you need to pay close attention to when you start to think in a little more detail about your application, what it's going to do and how it's going to do it. For example, a program with no drop-down menus, but oodles and oodles of pop-up ones would probably scare your users witless. A program with no File menu, but an item on a document menu that says Process binary document data on disk would probably not go down quite as well as a File menu with Open on it.

Microsoft have set out a lot of standards for developers to follow, covering everything from the spacing on your toolbars, to the layout of your menus, to the order and position of the OK and Cancel buttons on a dialog. They are all documented in a lot of detail in *The Windows Interface Guidelines for Software Design*, available from Microsoft Press. However, you can get a pretty good feel for what they are all about by just paying close attention to the Microsoft applications you have on your system, such as Word or even Notepad.

Familiarity breeds content—heed that when designing your user interface, and plethora of forms and dialogs that allow your users to deal with their data.

A Note about our Application

Time to move on to the application that we're going to be working on through the course of this chapter.

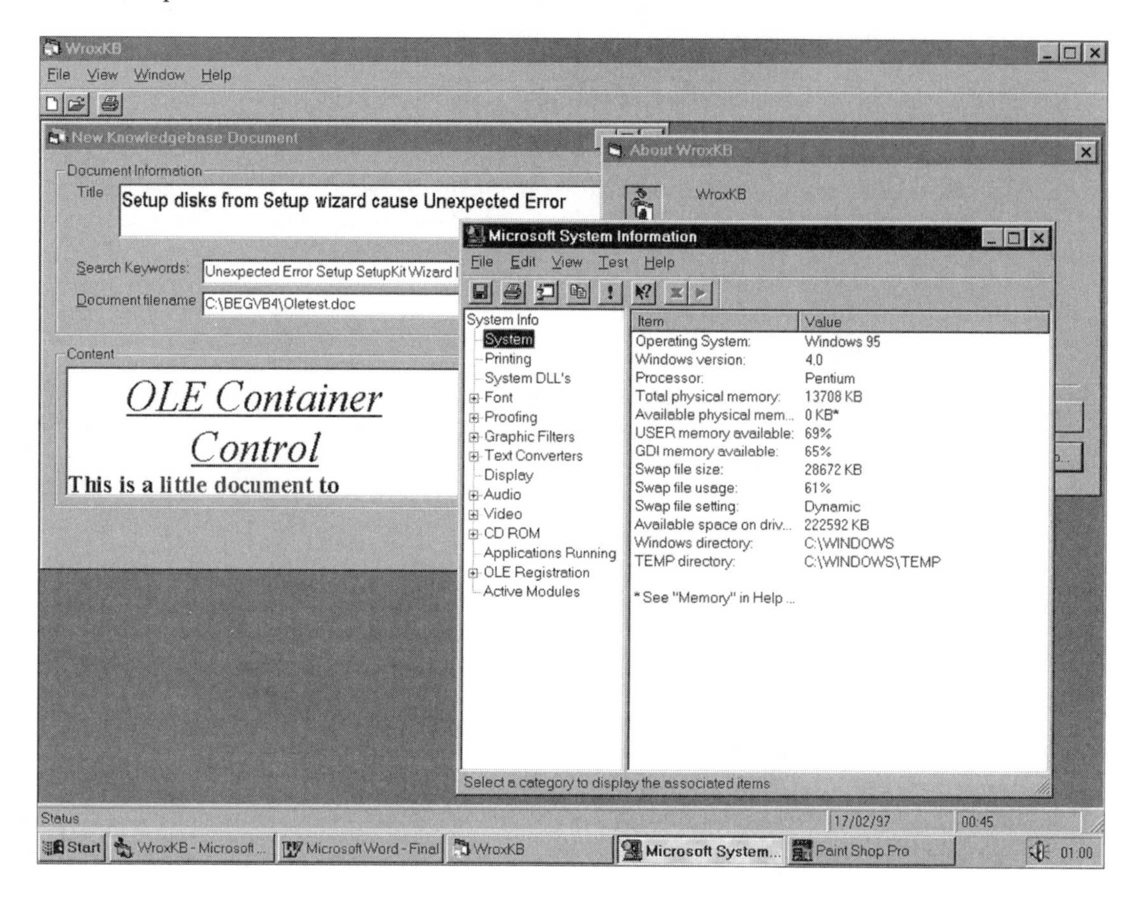

What we're going to be building is a very basic, but useful knowledge base system. The idea is simple. It needs to have the following functionality:

- It should be a multiuser system, so it's going to have to have some security in place, or at least some means of identifying users.
- Users should be able to log in and search the knowledge base for articles on specific subjects, such as problems with software or hardware, bug lists and so on, much the same as a support engineer on the phone might do.
- Users need to be able to store almost any kind of information in the system, from video files through spreadsheets and simple text files. They should be able to enter their own documents and update the ones already in the system.

- In addition, the program should be totally standard in the way it looks and behaves. It should provide a typical splash screen at startup to keep the owners of slower machines happy, and an About form to tell anyone interested all about the product.

Sound easy enough? Let's go.

Step 1 – The Data is All Important

In the bad old days of programming, the program itself was everything, with complex flow diagrams showing the path of execution through your code, even more complex diagrams depicting the algorithms that do calculations in the program and so on. A few years ago, though, some bright spark figured out that at the end of the day, the most important part of any computer program is the data that it manages.

In our application, we have to start by building an Access database to store all that knowledge base information. We're dealing with just one main type of data—knowledge base documents. The easiest way to ensure that we can deal with any kind of data at run time is to use an OLE container control and just store the filename in the database.

We therefore need to start with a **`Documents`** table. This is really quite straightforward, and just needs to hold the document title, the user id of the person who created it, the name of the file holding the data and the date and time that the document was last updated.

Remember the requirements also said that users should be able to search for documents. This search will be based on keywords, so we need to store those keywords somewhere. Since we won't know how many keywords the user is going to want to assign to a document until run time, the easiest way to deal with that is to use a linked **`Keywords`** table... more on this in a little while.

First let's create the **`Documents`** table.

Try It Out - Building the Database

1 In Visual Basic, from the Add-Ins menu choose Visual Data Manager....

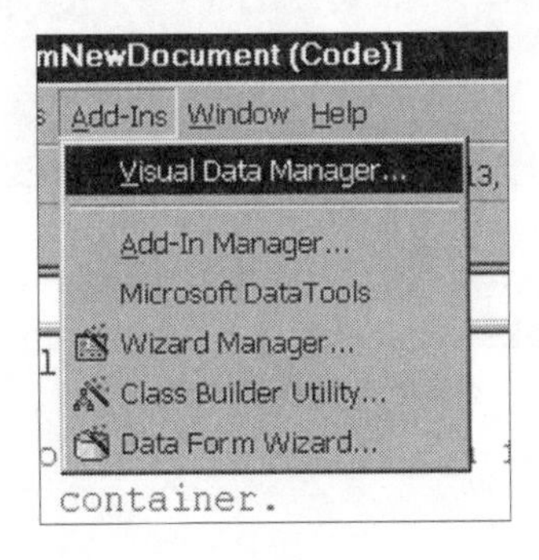

After a pause, Vis Data will appear, just as it did when we used it back in the database chapter.

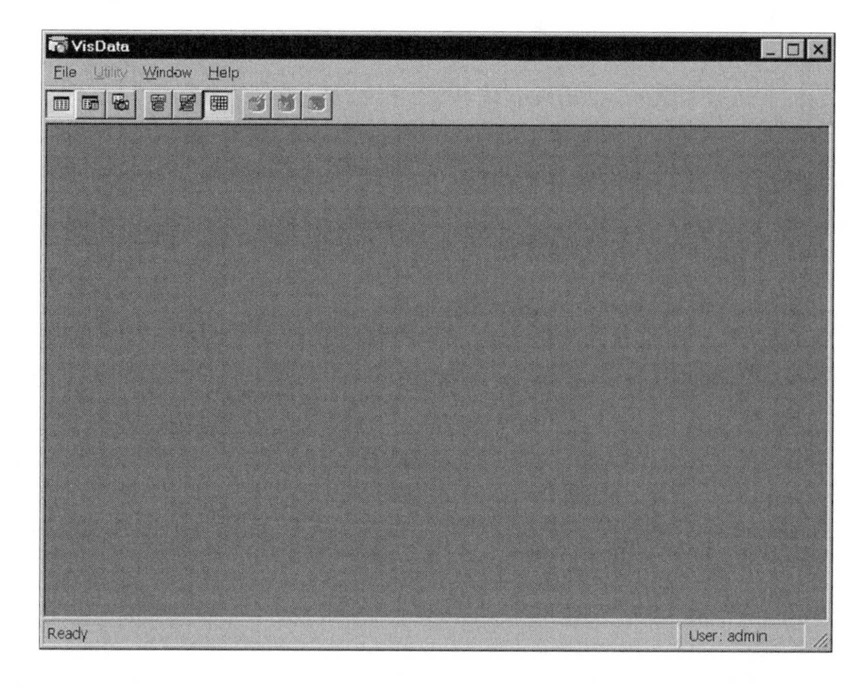

2 Click on the File menu and select the New option. This will display a list of database formats, the top one being Access. Clicking this will, in turn, display another menu, this time listing the versions of Access databases that VisData is able to deal with. Select version 7.0 (or 3.0 if that's what you have).

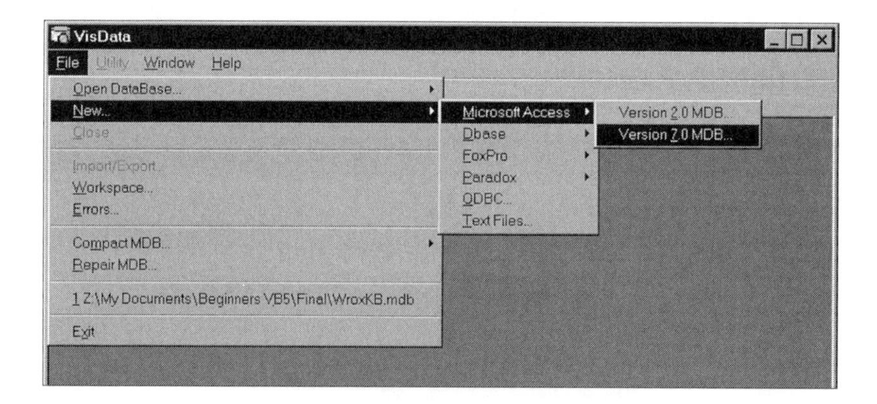

3 When the file dialog appears, name your database and save it. I called mine **`WroxKB`**, so it would probably make sense for you to call yours the same. That way we won't get confused later on with different filenames.

That's really all there is to creating a blank database. After another pause the database and query windows will open up within VisData ready for you to go ahead and start adding the tables that our application will need.

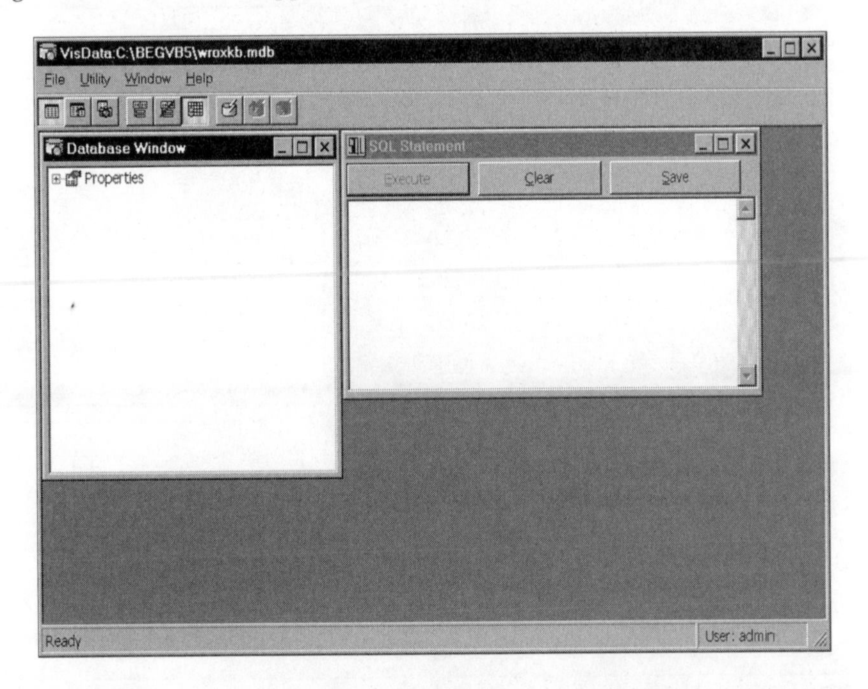

Try It Out - Adding the Tables

I'll lead you step by step through creating our first table, but after that I'm just going to give you the field and index details that I need you to create. That way you get some real hands on experience—so pay attention—it's a jungle out there.

1 Right click in the database window to display a pop-up menu. Select the New Table option and the Table Structure dialog will appear ready for us to add our fields.

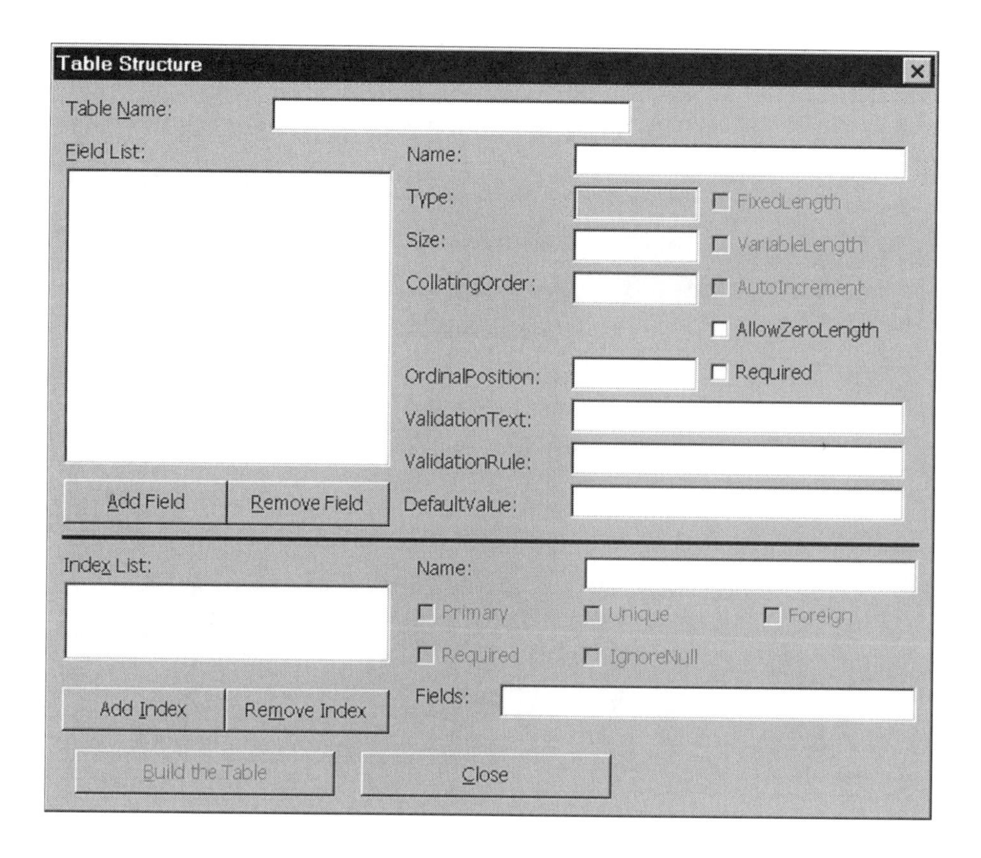

2 Our first table is the **`Documents`** table. Type **`Documents`** in the Table Name text box at the top of the dialog.

3 We now need to add the fields. First up is the **`Document_ID`**. This a special field as we want the Access database itself to assign a unique number to each document we create. This is called an auto incrementing field.

To add this field, click on the Add Field button, and then fill in the dialog for the **`Doc_ID`** field just as I've done here:

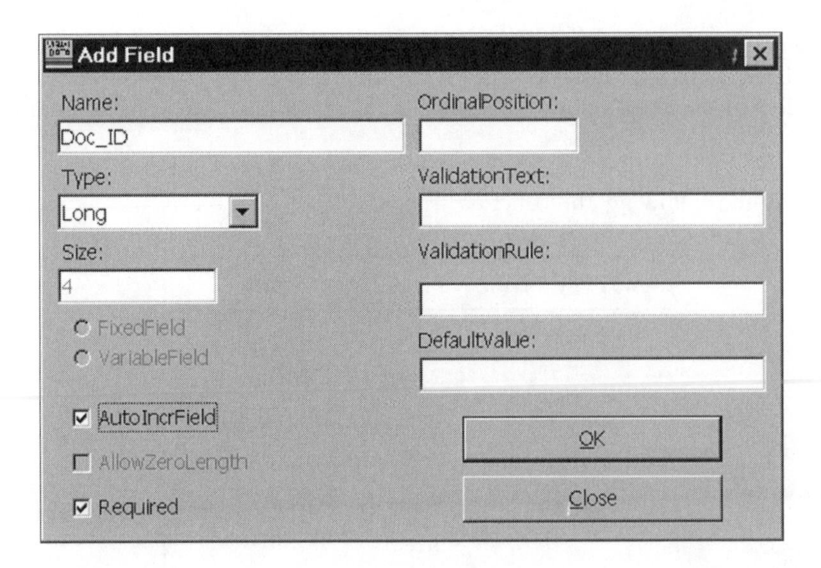

When creating an auto incrementing field, you have to set the type to long. Remember that if there are going to be a lot of records in the database then those auto incrementing IDs can get real big real quick.

The other thing to note is that I set up the required field. This isn't absolutely necessary when we're dealing with auto incrementing fields since all it does it make sure that the user entered some information into the field before saving the record; with an auto incrementing field this is taken care of for us. However, since this is the key field of the **`Documents`** table, it's good practice to make sure that it is a required field.

4 Click on the OK button to save the changes to this field, and the form will blank out ready for a new field to be added.

5 This time we need a field to hold the title for the document—a short description of what it is about. Set the properties of this new field up like this:

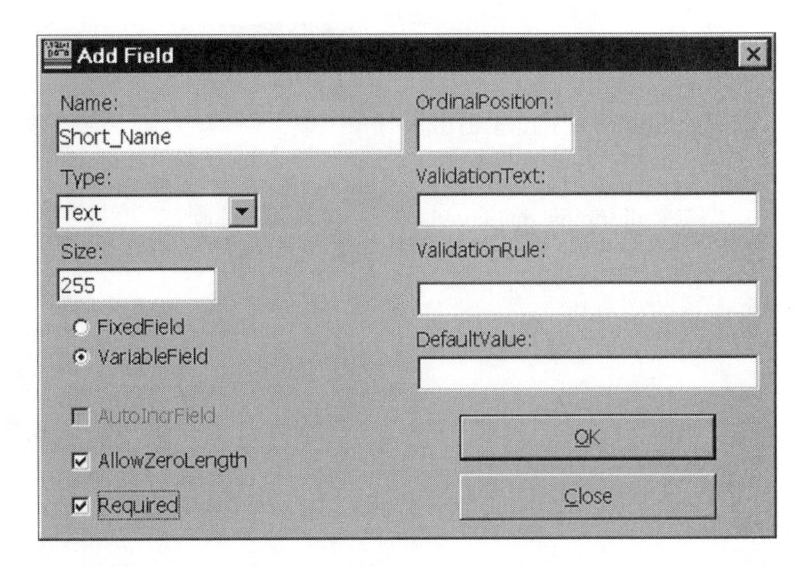

Once again, I've set this as a required field, but this time there's good reason—it would be silly for the user to enter a document into the database and not give it some kind of name. After all, the idea of the database is to convey information, not hide it.

6 Now add the following three fields:

Field Name	Property	Value
`User_ID`	Type	Long
	Required	Yes
`Date`	Type	Date/Time
	Required	Yes
`Linked`	Type	Text
	Size	250
	Required	Yes

We'll see the **`User_ID`** field in action in a short while, but basically it's set to long because it's going to point at a user in the **`Users`** table that we'll create shortly. The **`Date`** field will hold the date and time that the user last modified the page, and finally the **`Linked`** field will hold the name of the disk file that contains the body of the document.

7 Click the Close button on the Add Field dialog to return to the main table editor. You should now see all your fields displayed.

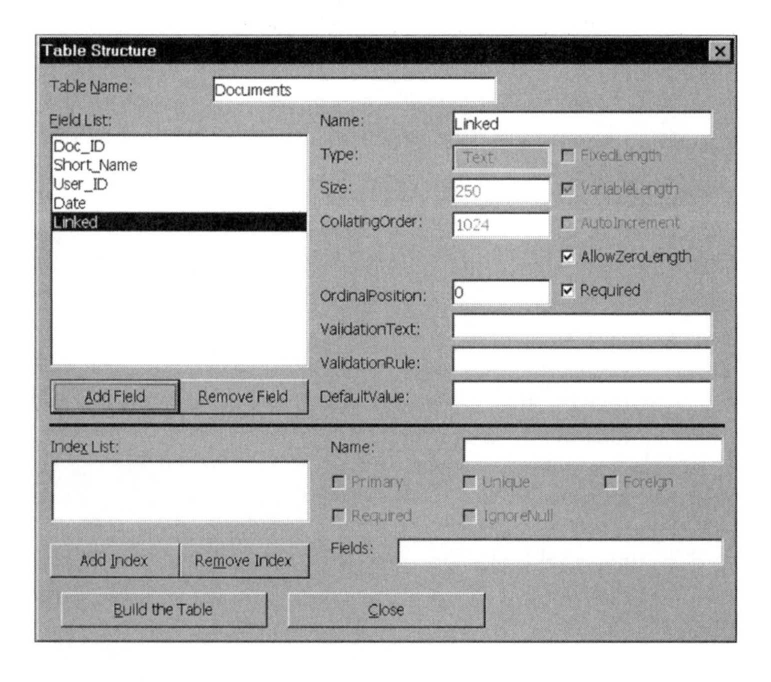

8 We now need to add the indexes. Click on the Add Index button and the Add Index dialog will appear, looking not unlike the Add Field dialog we were just looking at:

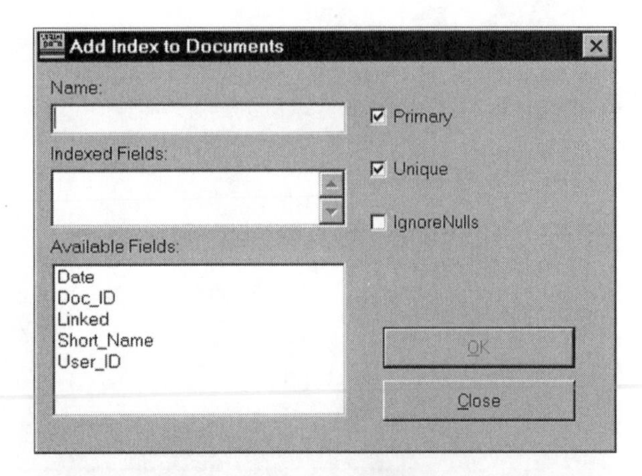

9 The **`Documents`** table needs two indexes: one on the document id, the other on the user id. First type **`PrimaryKey`** in the Name box and then double-click on the **`Doc_ID`** field.

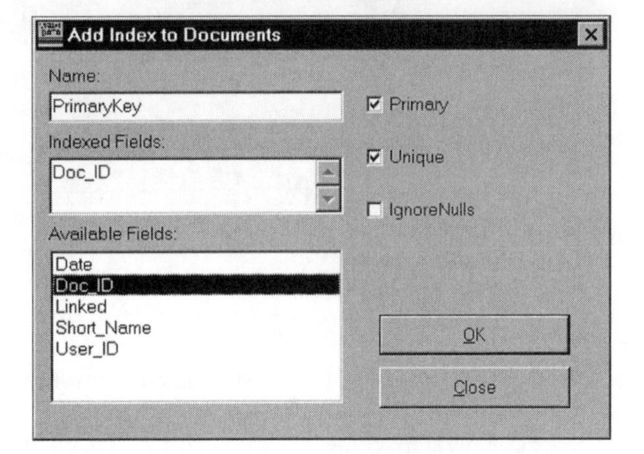

This is the primary key, which effectively means that it's the default index that the table will use. It needs to be unique, but this is OK since we're using an auto incrementing field for **`Doc_ID`**.

10 Click on the OK button and, as with the field dialog, the text boxes will clear out. Add the second index, this time called **`ByUser`** using the **`User_ID`** field. This index should be neither unique nor primary, so clear those check boxes.

11 Now click on OK as before and then click the Close button to take you back to the Table Structure dialog.

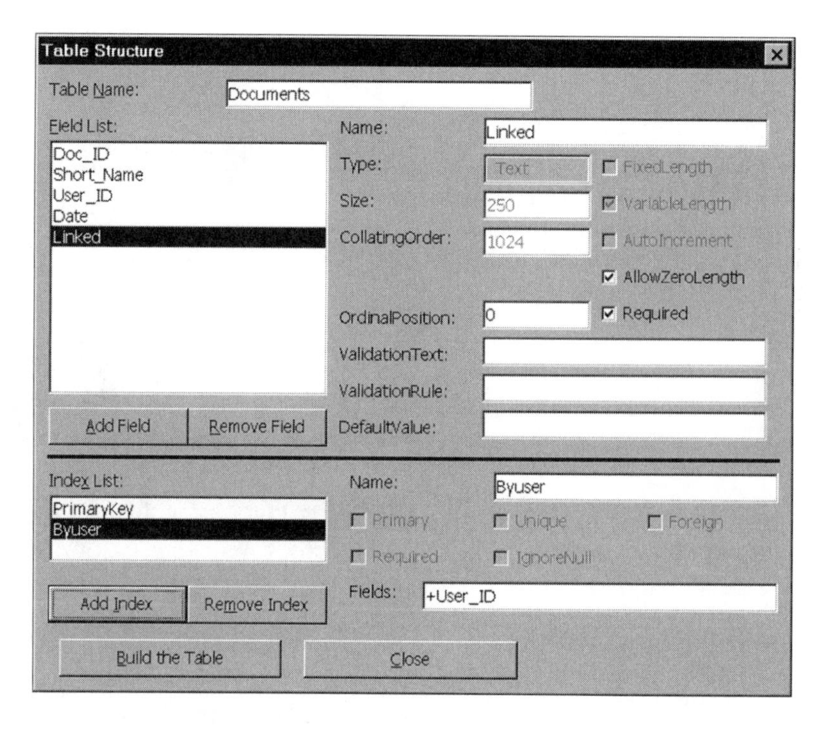

12 Now that you have the structure set up, click on the Build the Table button to put all the fields and those two indexes into effect and cast them in stone.

Well done—you've just created your first table.

13 Now I'm going to leave you to create the other tables on your own. The first is called **Keywords** and contains just three fields: **Word_ID**, **Doc_ID** and **Keyword**. **Word_ID** and **Doc_ID** should both be of type long, with **Word_ID** set to auto incrementing. **Keyword** should be of type text, and 15 characters in length.

The indexes for this table are as follows:

Index Name	Primary	Unique	Field
ByDocument	No	No	**Doc_ID**
ByKeyword	No	No	**Keyword**
PrimaryKey	Yes	Yes	**Word_ID**

14 The final table is the **Users** table. This has 4 fields in it: **LoginName**, **FullName**, **Password** and **User_ID**. The **LoginName**, **Password** and **FullName** fields are all of type text, with the **LoginName** and **Password** fields being 15 characters long, and the **FullName** field being 50 characters long. The **User_ID** field is your old friend, the auto incrementing long field.

The indexes are as follows:

Index Name	Primary	Unique	Field
`PrimaryKey`	Yes	Yes	`User_ID`
`User_Validate`	No	Yes	`LoginName`, `Password`

Note that the `User_Validate` is set up to use first the `LoginName` field and then the `Password` field. This is so that, at run time, it's easy for us to do just one search to match both the user name and password that the user enters when they attempt to log in, and instantly tell from that search whether the user has access.

15 When you have all the tables, fields and indexes set up, you can close VisData down (it automatically saves your work—you don't have to tell it to save the database) and then drop back into Visual Basic. We can now start to build the application proper.

Step 2 – Building the Framework

In the bad old days of VB4 and its predecessors, developers had to do a lot of repetitive work every time they developed a new application (unless they were sensible enough to build up—or buy—a code library that they could reuse). Thankfully, that's no more in VB5. The Application Wizard that we saw briefly back in Chapter 1 will do it all for us, very quickly and very painlessly.

You should find that you can use the Application Wizard to build up an empty skeleton of an application for nearly all your development work, including this project.

Using the Application Wizard

You can get to the Application Wizard by just starting up a new project. One of the items that appears on the new project dialog is an icon for the Application Wizard. Just double-click it and away it goes:

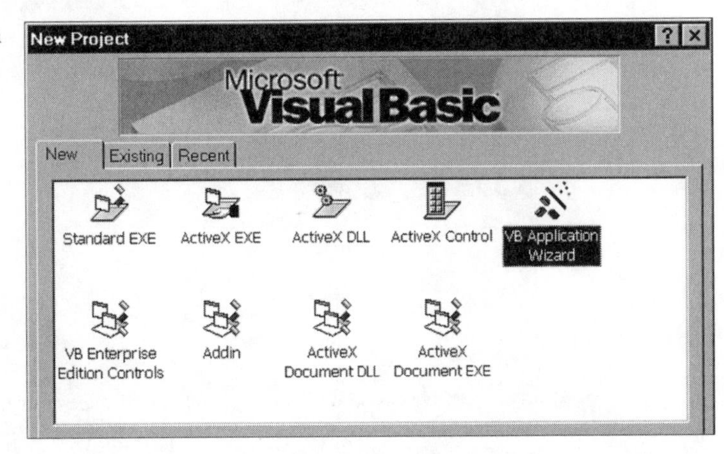

We walked through the application wizard back in Chapter 1 so take a peek back there if you need a quick refresher. If not though, just follow the screen prompts.

Try It Out - Using the Application Wizard

1 Start up the Application Wizard, click Next to skip the opening screen and then choose to create an MDI application.

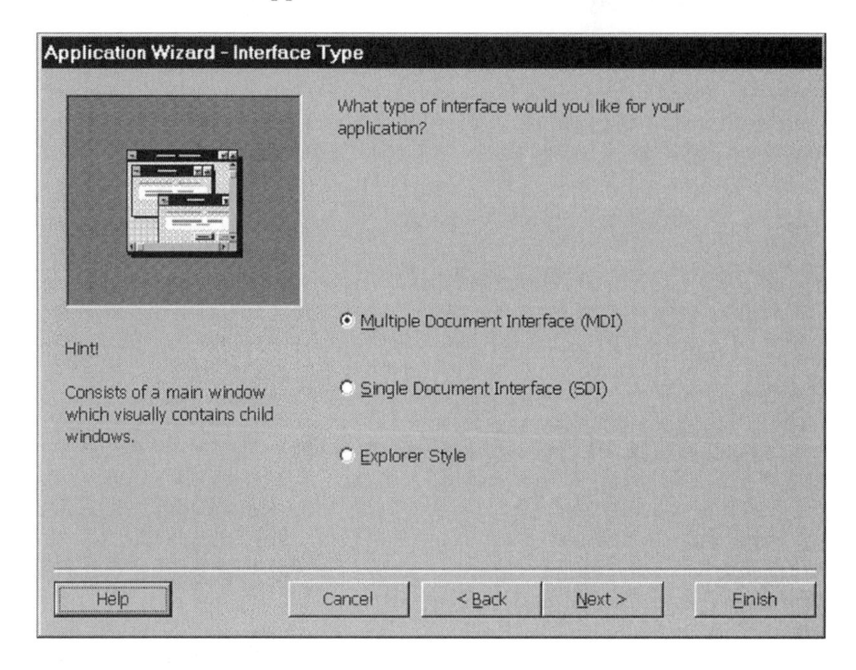

2 Add three menus: File, Window and Help, and click Next.

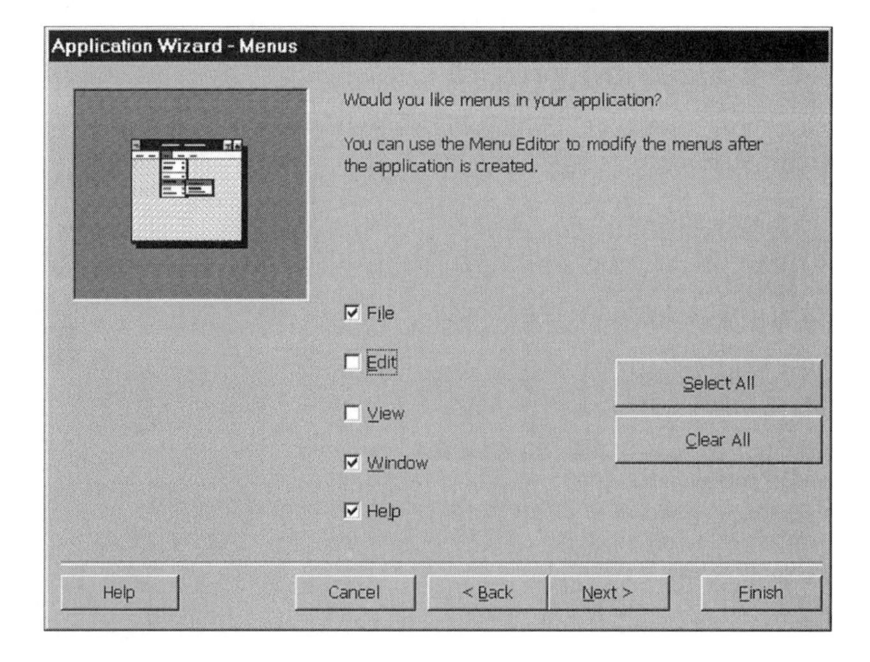

3 We don't want to include resource files, so just skip past the next window.

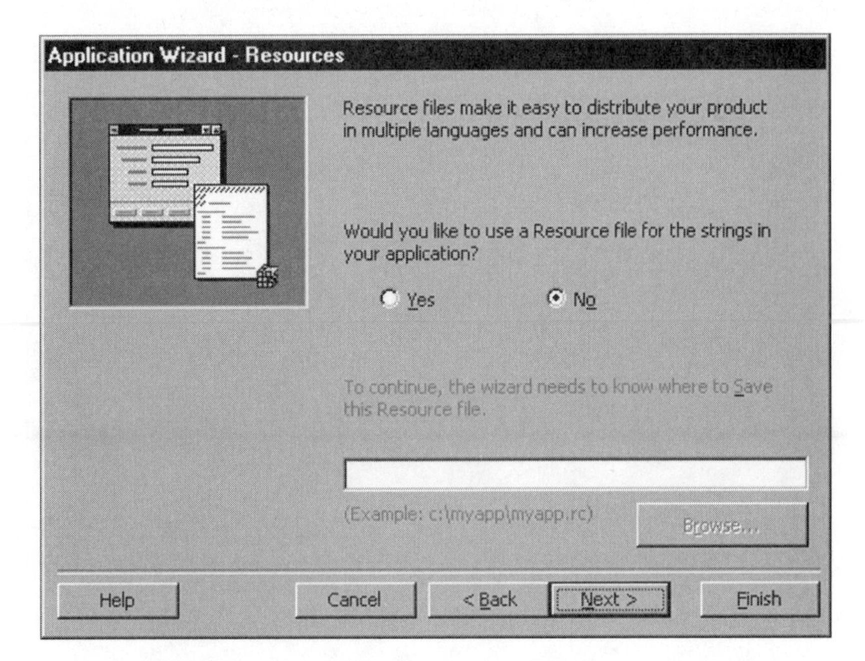

4 Get the wizard to provide Internet access from your application:

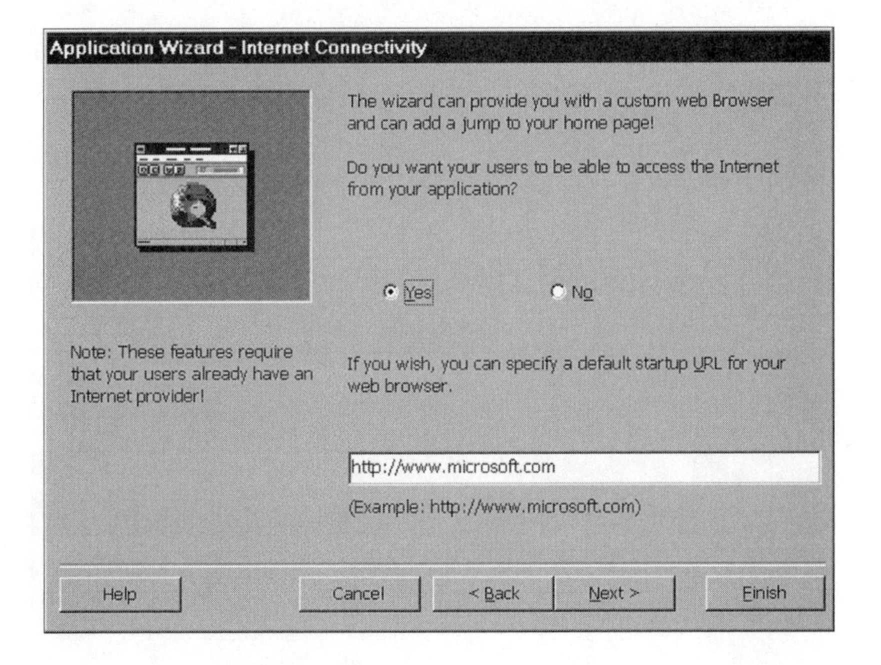

5 Include a splash screen, a login dialog and an About box:

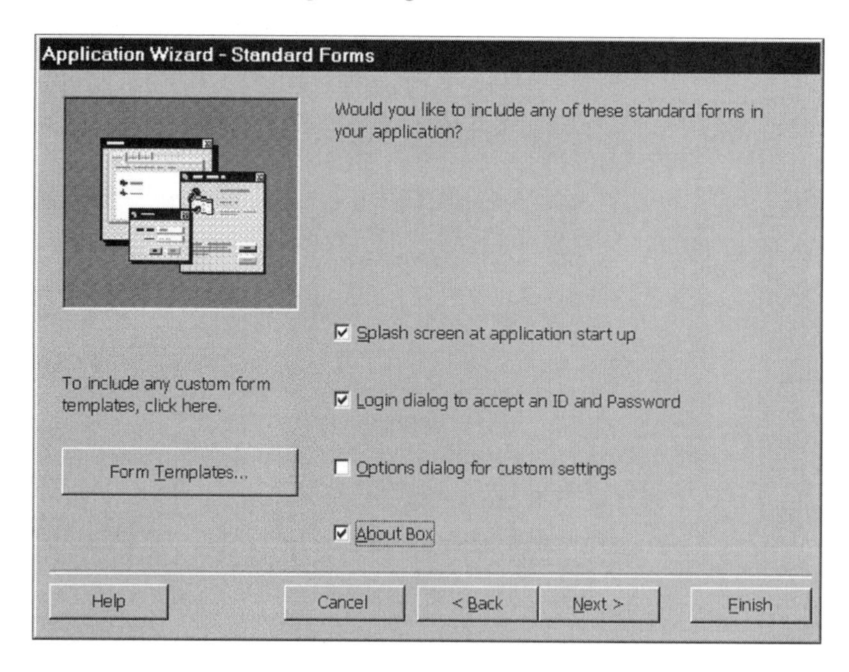

6 We don't need the wizard to create any forms for us, so on the next screen, select No.

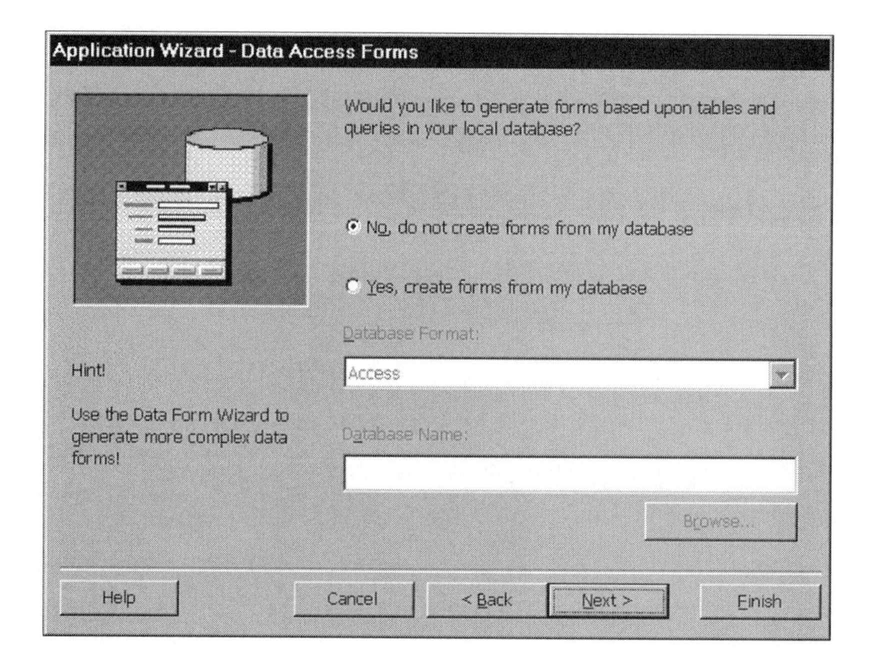

7 Finally, name your application `WroxKB`, get the wizard to generate a summary report and then, with the framework complete, click Finish.

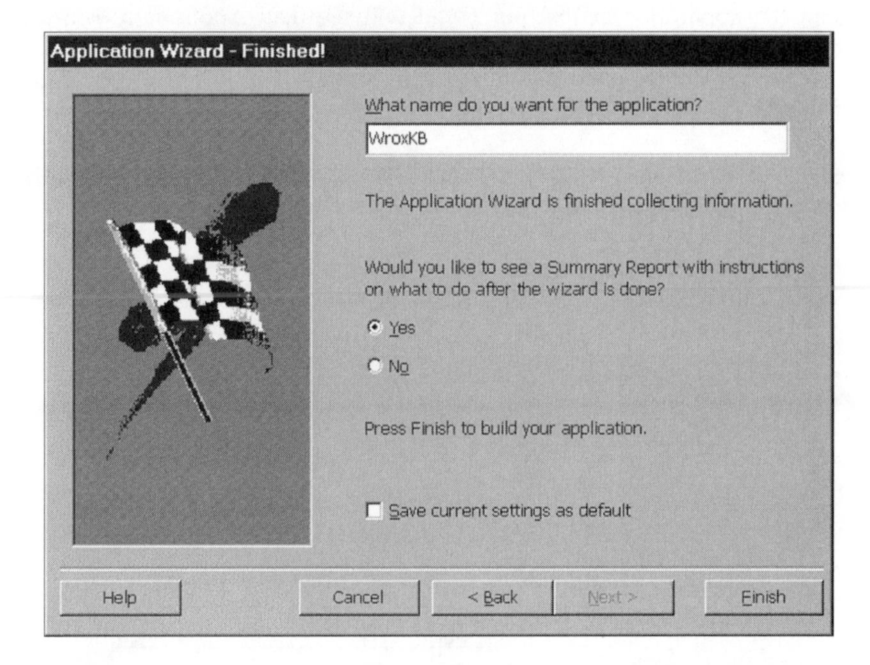

8 VB will now go away and create your application for you, ready for you to customize to your heart's content.

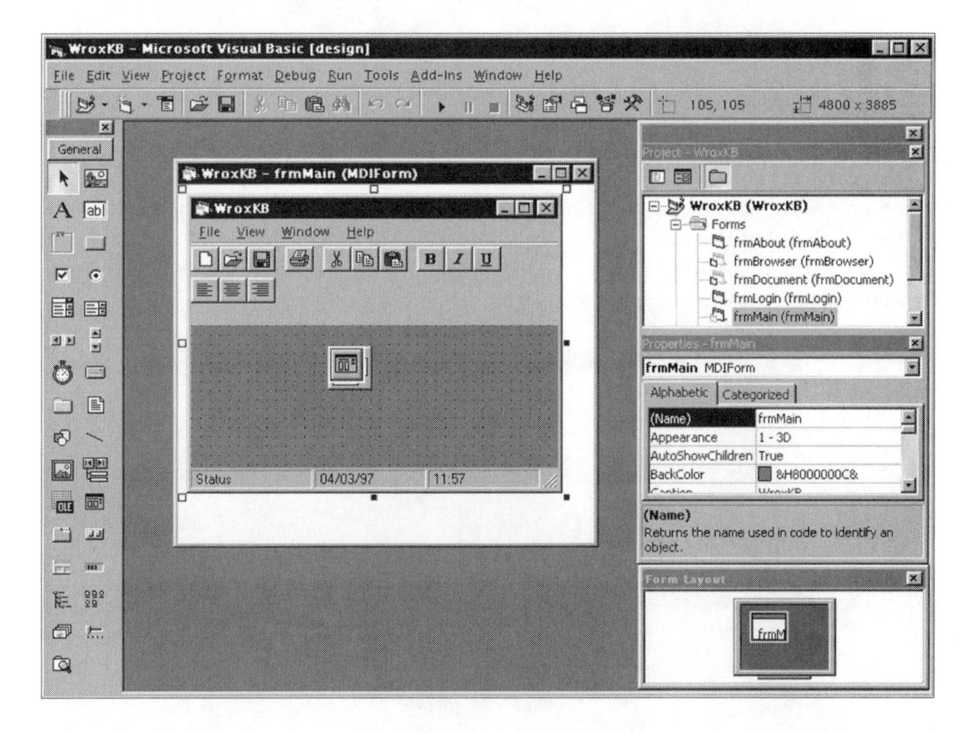

Customizing the Framework Application

If you run the application at this point you will see that Application Wizard has provided you with a very comprehensive framework for your own application. Too comprehensive, in fact, so the last thing to do before we start writing our own code is to remove the unwanted bulk.

Try It Out - Preparing the Application

1 First thing to do is remove the excess buttons on the toolbar. Right click on the toolbar and when the property page is displayed, go to the Buttons tab.

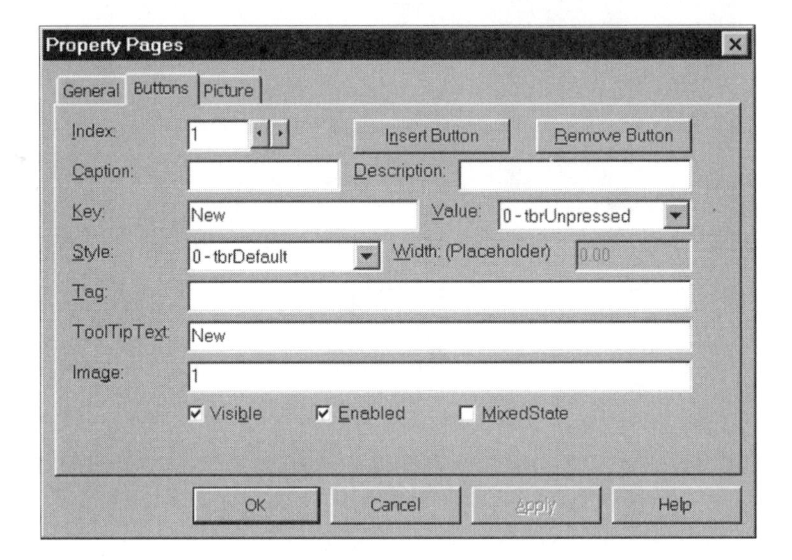

2 We want to keep the New, Open and Print buttons—indexes 1, 2 and 5. Select the others using the Index field, and click Remove Button. Note that there's a separator button before the Print button—that's why it's number 5 not 4. Also note that the index numbers will change once you start removing buttons. You can check which one is the current one by looking at the ToolTip Text or Key field.

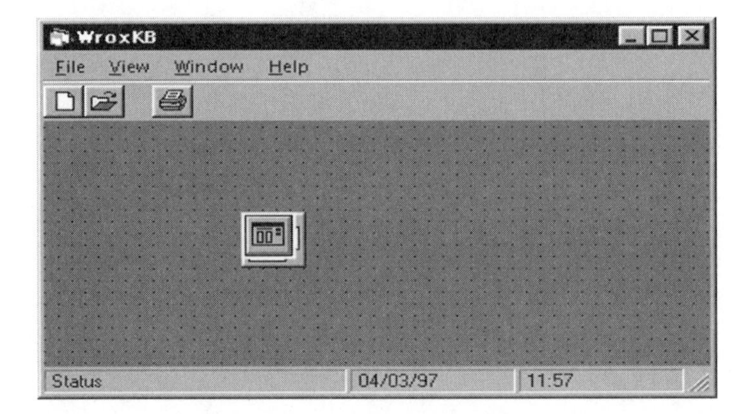

> *You can use the* **Insert Button** *to add new buttons to the toolbar if you accidentally delete the wrong one. However, I don't want to distract you from the matter in hand too much, so if you're curious as to the other stuff that you can do with the toolbar, take a look in the online help at the Toolbar Control and the Image List control. The Image List is a component that holds the images that will be shown in the buttons on the toolbar. When you add new buttons in, you need to fill in the properties of the button in the toolbar dialog to tell it which image to use from the image list.*

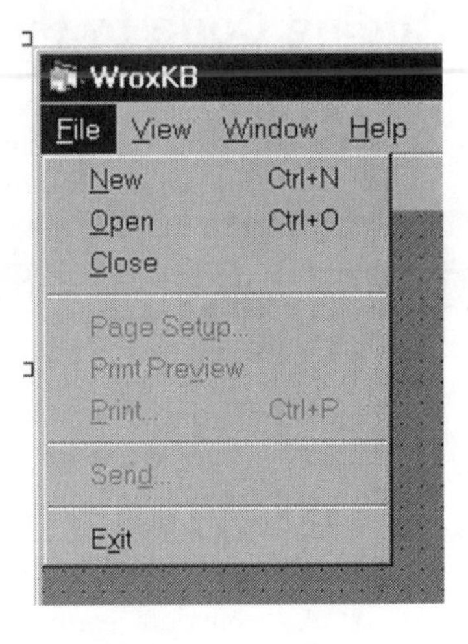

3 Next, bring up the menu editor and remove all the items from the File menu except the ones shown. Also disable the print and send items as shown—you'll see why a little later.

4 Since we'll be adding our own forms into the application to handle data entry and output, remove the form named **frmDocument** from the project. This is the default form that the framework displays within the main MDI window when the application starts.

5 If you now try to compile the application you'll get an error in **LoadNewDoc** subprocedure. This is because we've removed **frmDocument**. Don't panic, this is quite normal and is actually a neat lazy way of finding out what else needs to be given the snip or commented out. Comment out the lines of code that will fall over as a result of objects no longer existing.

```
Private Sub LoadNewDoc()
    Static lDocumentCount As Long
   ' Dim frmD As frmDocument

  lDocumentCount = lDocumentCount + 1
   ' Set frmD = New frmDocument
   ' frmD.Caption = "Document " & lDocumentCount
   ' frmD.Show
End Sub
```

Now, at last we're ready to start building our own application out of the framework.

Step 3 – Building on the Framework

Now that we have a framework that looks quite close to what we're after, we can start to bring it to life by adding in code of our own. 'Out of the box', the framework application has a lot of default behavior and a lot of missing functionality. It's our job to change this by really doing a programming join-the-dots type exercise.

Let's start by getting that login form working.

Adding Code to the Login Dialog

If you take a look at the code behind the OK button on the login form at the moment, you'll see that all it's doing is checking to see that a blank password has been entered, before letting you into the application. This isn't quite what we're after.

Try It Out - Coding the Login Form

We want to be able to store user names and their passwords in our database and have the login form check the database to ensure that the password for a particular user is correct. Only then will the user be allowed to log in.

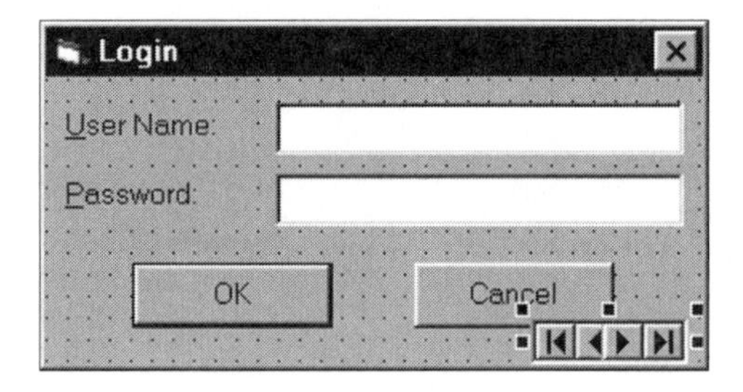

1 Drop a data control on to the login form and name it **datUsers**. Change its **Visible** property to false so it won't show up when we run the form.

2 Set its **DatabaseName** property to point at our **WroxKB.mdb** database (you know, the one we made earlier), set its **RecordSource** property to **Users** and set the **RecordsetType** to **Table**. Note that if you leave the **RecordsetType** at its default setting of **Dynaset**, you'll find that the code that we're about to write doesn't work properly.

3 Now we can write some code to do a **Seek** on the table, using the index that you set up to find a user based on their user name and password. Delete the first few lines of code in the **cmdOK_Click** event, and add the following:

```
Private Sub cmdOK_Click()
  datUsers.Recordset.Index = "User_Validate"
      datUsers.Recordset.Seek "=", txtUserName, txtPassword
```

```
        If Not datUsers.Recordset.NoMatch Then
            OK = True
            gnUserID = datUsers.Recordset.Fields("User_ID")
            Me.Hide
        Else
            MsgBox "Invalid Password, try again!", , "Login"
            txtPassword.SetFocus
            txtPassword.SelStart = 0
            txtPassword.SelLength = Len(txtPassword.Text)
        End If
End Sub
```

4 The above code uses the public variable **gnUserID**, which tells us exactly which user is logged in. We want this variable to be available from everywhere in the application, so make sure that it is declared in the declarations section of Module 1—not just for the form. You can rename this to something more meaningful if you want by selecting it in the project window and then changing its **Name** property. For now, though, Module 1 is fine, since all we're going to do is just stick a global variable in there, no actual code functionality.

```
Public gnUserID as Long
```

5 At this point you can test the application again to make sure that all is well. You'll have to create a user first though, so open up VisData again, double-click on the **Users** table and type the user information into the record form.

How It Works - The Password Check

Although it's initially quite daunting, the code for checking that the user has entered the correct password is really quite straightforward.

We need a way to check whether the user trying to log in actually can, and the easiest way to do this is, of course, to search through the **Users** table. Earlier on, when you set this table up, you added an index to the table called **User_Validate**. This index allows us to search for a unique record based on the user name and password combination. This is exactly the information that the user is entering into the dialog, and so what better way to check if a user has access to the system than to do a seek on this index, using the user name and password that they entered on the dialog.

```
        datUsers.Recordset.Index = "User_Validate"
        datUsers.Recordset.Seek "=", txtUserName, txtPassword
```

The first thing that the code does is set the **Index** property of the recordset to **User_Validate**. Once this is done, we can use the **Seek** method to find a match based on the user name and password entered into the text boxes on the form. Although the password text box is set up to display *** whenever someone types something in, we can still use its **Text** property in code to find out the true value that they entered and use that in the **Seek**.

```
If Not datUsers.Recordset.NoMatch Then
    OK = True
    gnUserID = datUsers.Recordset.Fields("User_ID")
    Me.Hide
Else
    MsgBox "Invalid Password, try again!", , "Login"
    txtPassword.SetFocus
    txtPassword.SelStart = 0
    txtPassword.SelLength = Len(txtPassword.Text)
End If
```

As you may recall from back when we covered databases, there's a property on a recordset called **NoMatch**. If the call to **Seek** manages to find a matching record, then this **NoMatch** property is set to False. On the other hand, if the call to **Seek** fails, then it is set to True. It's a little weird admittedly, but good enough for what we need.

The next part of the code looks at this **NoMatch** property and if it is set to False (meaning that we did manage to find a user with the name and password that were entered) then the global variable that we set up to hold the current user ID is set and the form is hidden. The **OK** variable is also set to True, indicating to the **Main()** subprocedure that it should load the splash form and then the main form.

If on the other hand the seek failed, which means that **NoMatch** would be True, then the standard code that the Application Wizard put in will be run, showing that there was an error and asking the user to enter their information again.

Step 4 – Extending the Framework

Customizing the way that the framework application looks and behaves is really only part of the equation when it comes to building an application of your own. It's quite likely that you'll need to add a lot more forms to the application to deal with your specific data, and probably one or two dialogs as well.

In our case we need to add at least two new windows: one to open up documents in the database and another to create new ones. With a little thought, though, even this stage can be kept fairly painless.

Let's start by taking a look at the New Document form—the form that the user will bring up when he or she wants to add a new document to the database.

Adding the New/Edit Document Window

In order to keep the number of forms and the amount of code down, we can use a single form to handle adding, viewing and editing documents in the database. Surprisingly, the code really is quite simple. Let's create the form first.

Try It Out - Creating the New Document Form

1 From the Project menu select Add Form. When the new form appears, set its **MDIChild** property to True and its name to **frmNewDocument**.

2 Next, drop some controls on to the form so that it looks like this:

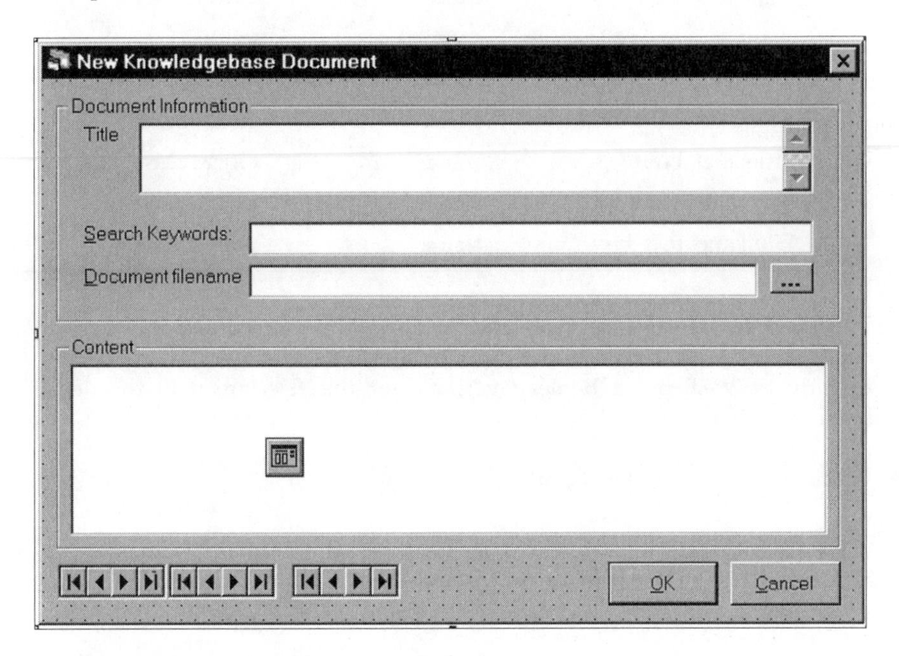

3 Set up the properties on the controls like this

Control	Property	Description
1st data control	**Name** **DatabaseName** **RecordsetType** **Visible**	**datKeywordQuery** **WroxKB** **Dynaset** **False**
2nd data control	**Name** **DatabaseName** **RecordSource** **RecordsetType** **Visible**	**datKeywords** **WroxKB** **Keywords** **Table** **False**
3rd data control	**Name** **DatabaseName** **Recordsource** **RecordsetType** **Visible**	**datDocuments** **WroxKB** **Documents** **Table** **False**

Table Continued on Following Page

Control	Property	Description
Common dialog control	**Name**	**dlgFile**
OK command button	**Name**	**cmdOK**
	Default	**True**
Cancel button	**Name**	**cmdCancel**
	Cancel	**True**
OLE container control	**Name**	**oleDocument**
... button (Browse)	**Name**	**cmdBrowse**
Title text box	**Name**	**txtTitle**
Keywords text box	**Name**	**txtKeywords**
Filename text box	**Name**	**txtFilename**

4 Since the form is used for both adding new data and editing existing data, we need some way of knowing from the code in the form exactly what mode the form is currently in. We'll use a Boolean variable for this. Declare it in the declarations section of the form:

```
Private bInEdit As Boolean
```

5 When the form first gets loaded, we want to set this variable to false, meaning that we're adding a new record to the database by default. Add the following line to the **Form_Load** event:

```
Private Sub Form_Load()
    bInEdit = False
End Sub
```

6 We also need a custom method on the form which can be called after the form is loaded by any other subprocedure that wishes to use the form to edit an existing document:

```
Public Sub Edit(ByVal nDocID As Long)

    With datDocuments.Recordset

        .Index = "PrimaryKey"
        .Seek "=", nDocID

        txtTitle = .Fields("Short_Name")
        txtFilename = .Fields("Linked")

   End With
```

```
    ' Now we need to pull in the keywords themselves
    datKeywordQuery.RecordSource = "SELECT * FROM Keywords WHERE Doc_ID
  ↳  = " & datDocuments.Recordset.Fields("Doc_ID")
    datKeywordQuery.Refresh

    With datKeywordQuery.Recordset
        .MoveFirst

        Do While Not .EOF
            txtKeywords = txtKeywords & .Fields("Keyword") & " "
            .MoveNext
        Loop

    End With

    bInEdit = True

End Sub
```

As you can see, this subprocedure takes a single parameter, which is the ID of the document that the calling code wants the form to edit. This is used in the first couple of lines to do a seek on the **datDocuments** data control to find the specified record, and then pull information from its fields collection into the controls on the form.

Next up the code builds up the keyword list attached to the document. Remember, the database itself stores each keyword associated with a document in a separate record to make searching a lot easier, but this form lets the user enter the keywords separated by spaces into a single text box. So, the code issues a query on the **datKeywordQuery** data control to find all the keywords associated with the selected document and loads them into the text box.

Finally, our Boolean variable is set to true to indicate to the form that we have changed from adding a new record to editing an existing one.

7 While the user is editing the data in the form, two more pieces of code are required in order to ensure that the OLE container control loads up any filename specified.

In the filename text box's **Change** event, we need to check that the file specified exists. If it does, then we can call the **CreateEmbed** method of the OLE container to load the file up and display it to the best of its abilities within our application.

```
Private Sub txtFilename_Change()
    If Dir$(txtFilename) <> "" Then
        oleDocument.CreateEmbed txtFilename.Text
    End If
End Sub
```

8 In addition, we need to make the browse button pop open the common dialog on the form and then feed the results into the filename text box. This in turn will trigger the **Change** event and cause the document to load up:

```
Private Sub cmdBrowse_Click()

    ' Pop open the common dialog and grab a filename, then link that
    ' file into the OLE container.
    On Error GoTo No_File_Selected
    dlgFile.ShowOpen

    txtFilename = dlgFile.Filename

    Exit Sub

No_File_Selected:
   'User clicked cancel so exit the subprocedure
End Sub
```

This is almost exactly the same code that we saw back in the dialogs chapter, and so this shouldn't present you with any difficulties.

9 The Cancel button needs some code to stop users accidentally clicking it and losing all their work. Enter this:

```
Private Sub cmdCancel_Click()

    ' Check before canceling
    If MsgBox("Are you sure you want to stop editing ?", vbQuestion +
↳ vbYesNo, "Cancel ?") = vbYes Then
        Unload Me
    End If

End Sub
```

Here, every time the Cancel button is clicked we just check with the user that that was what they really wanted to do. If the answer is yes, then the form is unloaded, otherwise nothing happens.

10 The OK button is slightly more complex, though, and is really spread across 4 different subprocedures. First type the **Click** event handler in:

```
Private Sub cmdOK_Click()

    ' Before we do anything else, validate the information shown

    ' First make sure that the user actually entered a title.
    If txtTitle = "" Then
        MsgBox "You need to enter a title for this knowledgebase
        ↳    document.  Try again.", 16, "Data entry error"
```

```
            txtTitle.SetFocus
            Exit Sub
        End If

        ' Next, do the same for the keywords and give the user a little
        ' help if they are having problems.
        If txtKeywords = "" Then
            MsgBox "You should enter some keywords so that other users can
            ↳ find your article. Enter the words separated by spaces
            ↳ in the text box provided. ", 16, "Data entry error"
            txtKeywords.SetFocus
            Exit Sub
        End If

        ' Finally, check that we have a linked file selected by the user
        If txtFilename = "" Then
            MsgBox "Enter a filename for the document itself, or click on
the
            ↳ button to browse", 16, "Data entry error"
            txtFilename.SetFocus
            Exit Sub
        End If

        ' If we reach this point then we can go ahead and save the changes

        If Not bInEdit Then
            Add_Data_To_Table
        Else
            Edit_Existing_Data
        End If

        Unload Me

End Sub
```

11 Next we need the subprocedures that will handle the adding and editing of the data:

```
Private Sub Edit_Existing_Data()

        datDocuments.Recordset.Edit
        Copy_Fields_Across

End Sub
```

```
Private Sub Add_Data_To_Table()

        ' Subprocedure to add the information in the form into a new
        ' record in the documents table.
        datDocuments.Recordset.AddNew
        Copy_Fields_Across

End Sub
```

```
Private Sub Copy_Fields_Across()

    Dim sKeyword As String

    ' First do the Documents table
    With datDocuments.Recordset

        .Fields("Short_Name") = txtTitle
        .Fields("Date") = Now
        .Fields("User_ID") = gnUserID
        .Fields("Linked") = txtFilename

        .Update

        .Bookmark = .LastModified

    End With

    ' Before we go any further make sure that there are no keywords on
    ' file for this document. If there are then get rid of them
    datKeywords.Database.Execute "Delete from Keywords where Doc_ID = "
      ⇘ & datDocuments.Recordset.Fields("Doc_ID")

    ' Great, now we can loop through the keywords entered and add
    ' them into the database
    Do While txtKeywords.Text <> ""

        datKeywords.Recordset.AddNew
        datKeywords.Recordset.Fields("Doc_ID") =
         ⇘ datDocuments.Recordset.Fields("Doc_ID")

        If InStr(txtKeywords, " ") = 0 Then
            sKeyword = txtKeywords
            txtKeywords = ""
        Else
            sKeyword = Left$(txtKeywords, InStr(txtKeywords, " ") - 1)
            txtKeywords = Mid$(txtKeywords, InStr(txtKeywords, " ") + 1)
        End If

        datKeywords.Recordset.Fields("Keyword") = sKeyword

        datKeywords.Recordset.Update

    Loop

End Sub
```

12 Finally, we just need to add a couple of lines of code to the New item on the File menu on the main form to bring the form into life at run time:

```
Private Sub mnuFileNew_Click()
    Dim NewDoc As New frmNewDocument

    Load NewDoc

End Sub
```

How It Works - The OK Button

In terms of actual real code in the OK button's **Click** event, it's really quite simple. The bulk of the event just checks each text box on the form to make sure that none of them were left blank by the user. If any were, then an error message is displayed and the focus is moved back to the offending control for the user to try again.

Assuming everything went OK though, these lines are executed:

```
    If Not bInEdit Then
        Add_Data_To_Table
    Else
        Edit_Existing_Data
    End If
```

Here we check to see whether we're in edit mode. If we are, then a call is made to the **Edit_Existing_Data** subprocedure, otherwise it is sent to **Add_Data_To_Table**.

```
Private Sub Edit_Existing_Data()

    datDocuments.Recordset.Edit
    Copy_Fields_Across

End Sub
```

```
Private Sub Add_Data_To_Table()

    datDocuments.Recordset.AddNew
    Copy_Fields_Across

End Sub
```

The only difference between these two is that Edit triggers an **Edit** operation, while Add triggers an **AddNew**. Both subprocedures then call the **Copy_Fields_Across** code to move the data from the form into the fields in the table.

Adding the Open Document Window

The only form which we haven't done yet is the one which is used to find and then edit existing documents. You may be a little shocked to learn that this one is incredibly simple.

Try It Out - The Open Document Form

1 Create a new form in the application and set its **`MDIChild`** property to True and its name to **`frmOpen`**.

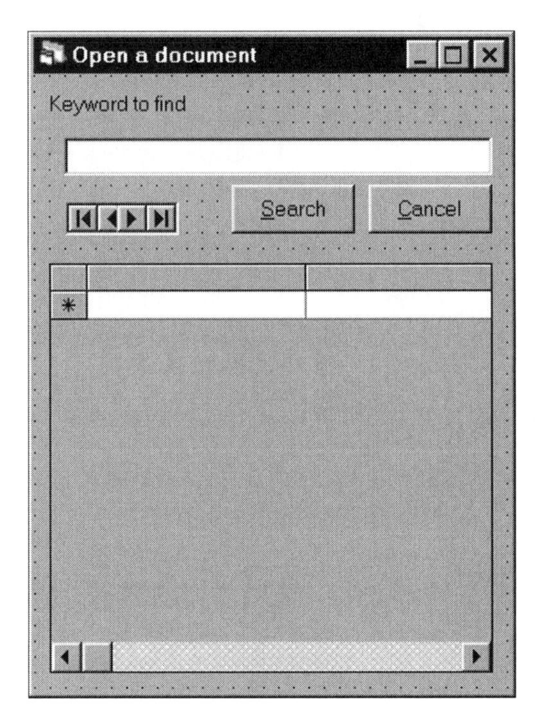

2 Now drop some controls on your new form so that it looks like this. Remember, if the dbGrid control isn't in your toolbox, you can add it by selecting the relevant option from the Project|Components dialog.

3 Next set up the properties on the controls.

Description	Property	Value
Text box	**`Name`**	**`txtSearch`**
Cancel button	**`Name`**	**`cmdCancel`**
	`Cancel`	**`True`**
Search button	**`Name`**	**`cmdSearch`**
	`Default`	**`True`**
Data control	**`Name`**	**`datDocuments`**
	`Visible`	**`False`**
	`DatabaseName`	**`WroxKB`**
	`RecordSource`	**`Select Doc_ID, Short_Name from Documents`**
dbGrid	**`Name`**	**`grdDocuments`**
	`DataSource`	**`datDocuments`**

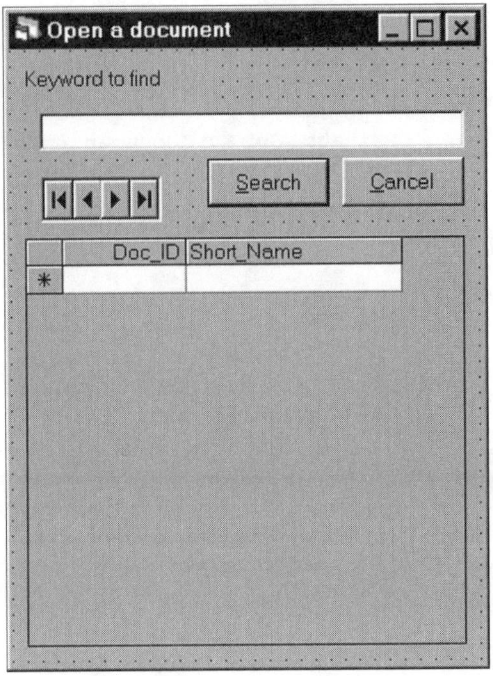

4 Now right click on the dbGrid control and select Retrieve Fields. The column headings will then be filled in.

With that lot set up, there really are only 2 very small pieces of code to bring this form, and thus the application, to life.

4 When clicked, the Search button should take whatever keyword the user entered and tack it on to a **query**. This query can then be issued and the data control refreshed. Add this code to the search button's **`Click`** event:

```
Private Sub cmdSearch_Click()

    If txtSearch = "" Then
        MsgBox "You must enter a keyword to search for. Try again.", 16,
        ➥ "Data entry error"
        txtSearch.SetFocus
        Exit Sub
    End If

    datDocuments.RecordSource = "SELECT Documents.Doc_ID, Short_Name FROM
        ➥ Documents INNER JOIN Keywords ON Keywords.Doc_ID =
        ➥ Documents.Doc_ID WHERE Keyword = '" & txtSearch & "'"
    datDocuments.Refresh

End Sub
```

5 Finally, when an item in the grid is double-clicked we need do nothing more than load up the edit form and call its **Edit** method, passing across the ID of the document that was double-clicked.

```
Private Sub grdDocuments_DblClick()
    Dim EditDoc As New frmNewDocument

    Load EditDoc
     EditDoc.Edit datDocuments.Recordset.Fields("Doc_ID")

End Sub
```

6 Now open the code window for **frmMain** and find the event handler for the Open item on the File menu. Delete the code that was put there by Application Wizard and add the following lines.

```
Private Sub mnuFileOpen_Click()
    Dim OpenDoc As New frmOpen
    Load OpenDoc
End Sub
```

7 Finally, in the **frmOpen** Cancel button code, just put a one-liner in there that says:

```
Unload Me
```

Once that's done, your work is complete—that wasn't too painful now was it?

Try running the application now and have a play with it to get a feel for its strengths and weaknesses.

Although there are a lot of ways in which the application could be further improved, you should now have a very good idea about how to build your own from scratch.

Summary

OK—we covered a lot of ground in this chapter, but hopefully you now have a little bit more courage to strike out on your own. Visual Basic 5 comes with some very powerful features indeed which can make developing a full-blown application a snip, and can also be an extremely good aid to prototyping your own ideas.

In particular though, we covered:

- Using the Application Wizard to create your own application framework
- Modifying the application framework to remove the features you don't need
- Adding your own code and forms to the framework to bring in the functionality you need

That's all there is to it. Take a look through the appendices now for a little insight into coding style, as well as some pointers on where to go now for more information. In the meantime, good luck in your VB travels.

Why Not Try.....

All these exercises build on the application you have just created in the chapter.

1. Customize the look of the About form and Splash form.

2. Use the API function **`GetVersionEx`** to put the Windows version and build number onto the About form. The declaration for the function can be found in the **`Win32api.txt`** file in your VB folder. You will also need to declare a user defined type (**`OSVERSIONINFO`** also found in the text file) to store information from the API call. Use this information to display the Windows version and the variant of Win32.

   Hint: The data structure needs to be passed **`ByRef`** and the first field needs to be set by you to the length of the variable. Use **`Len(MyDataStructure)`** to get this (it will be 148!).

   The data structure has a field called **`dwPlatformId`**. A value of zero indicates Win32, one indicates Win 95 and two indicates Win NT.

3. Set up a filter in the File Open dialog so that the user can only select Office documents (Word, Excel, PowerPoint) to be displayed in the OLE container.

4. If you take a look at the File menu, there are some options on there which could be quite tricky to code. For example, if you have a number of documents open and the user clicks on the Close item on the menu, how are you going to get the code in the MDI form to close down the active child window? The print option needs to be able to tell which child window is open and grab the document information from it so that it can print it.

   We don't want the user to be able to get at the Print and Send options on the File menu without a document window open—since that is the only window relevant to these functions. Set up code so that the options are only enabled when there is a child window open.

5. Word 97 has **`PrintOut`**, **`PrintPreview`** and **`SendMail`** methods which open up some interesting possibilities for the Print, Print Preview and Send menu options. If you have Word 97, have a go at getting these menu options to work.

asic Visual Basic Visual Ba
al Basic Visual Basic Visual
Basic Visual Basic Visual Ba
ual Basic Vi
Basic Visu
ual Basic V
l Basic Visu
isual Basic Visual Basic
al Basic Visual Basic Visua
Visual Basic Visual Basic Visu
l Basic Visual Ba
l Basic Visual
ic Visual Basi
Basic Visual B
ic Visual Basi
al Basic Visual
ual Basic Visual Basic Visual Ba
Visual Basic Visual Basic Visu
sual Basic Visual Basic Visu
Visual Basic Visual Ba

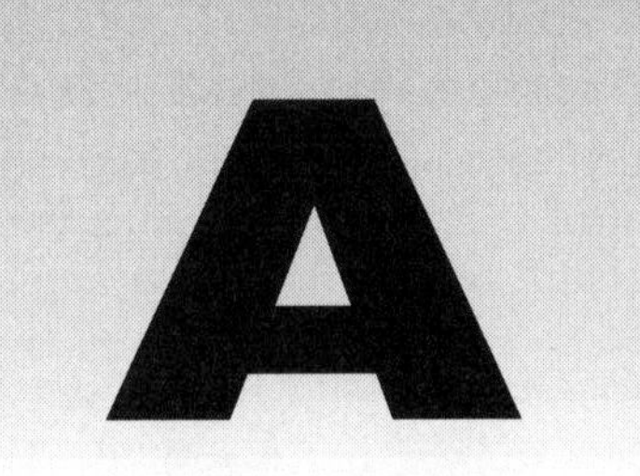

Where to Now?

By now you should have a pretty good idea of how to piece together a Visual Basic application. Well done, you have come a long way and deserve a pat on the back. However, the learning curve does not end here. As many programmers and developers already know, simply learning the semantics of how to use a development environment is but a small step on the path to that most revered title of Programming Guru.

So, what you need to know now is

- What are the tools that I need to empower my VB applications... big time?
- What about the other versions of Visual Basic—will they help me?
- Where can I go for help?

In this appendix you will learn the answers to all these questions and more.

All About the VB Family

If you have followed the book all the way to this point, then you should have got the hang of the basics of the Learning Edition of Visual Basic 5. However, the Learning Edition is only one in a growing family of five. The good news for you is that the skills you have acquired can be translated effortlessly to any of the other four—which you choose will depend on the job you need to do.

VBA (Visual Basic: Applications Edition)

We all know the Microsoft goal—to put a computer running Microsoft software on every desk in every house and business. However, there are number of clear subplots to this goal, one of them it seems is to put a version of Visual Basic inside every one of the above computers.

VBA is just that version of Visual Basic. Microsoft are very keen on everything about the way we use our computers, even down to providing a common programming language with every desktop application. This is where VBA fits in.

VBA is now shipped with every application in the Microsoft Office suite, giving users a standard way in which to control both the applications themselves (Excel, Access, Word, Powerpoint) as well as the ActiveX objects that these applications can export.

VBA is basically the core language of VB5. In fact, to put it the other way around, VB5 is a direct, more powerful descendant of VBA. VBA includes all the facilities you need to make use of ActiveX effectively—ideal since all the applications in Office are ActiveX enabled.

So, who would use VBA? Basically, anyone who needs to breathe more life into the Office suite than is already there, as well as application developers who need to supply applications that are native to any of the Office components.

For example, if you have been assigned the task of producing a complete order entry system making use of Excel for the financial side, Access for the database side and Word for the reporting and documentation side, then VBA could well be the product for you. Many other software companies are also licensing VBA as the language to program their own products. Knowing Visual Basic will help you to create programs for an ever-increasing number of products.

Visual Basic: Professional Edition

In the bad old days of VB3, the Professional Edition was the only place a programmer could go when looking for a more powerful version of Visual Basic. With the advent of the Enterprise Edition, the pro version has really become an in-between step. However, that does not mean that it has lost any of the power gain it represented in VB3. It simply means that it doesn't include certain features of the incredibly powerful Enterprise Edition.

Aside from the convenience of having all the Visual Basic manuals supplied on CD-Rom, the Professional Edition also lets you take control of the Data Access Object (DAO) directly through code. This means that you can create database applications that essentially do away with the need for the somewhat clumsy data control. As a result, database applications run faster and, by taking direct control, you as developer are able to take even more measures to safeguard the data you deal with.

Also related to database development is Crystal Reports, a package not included with the Learning edition. This handy utility and ActiveX control takes all the pain out of creating reports for database applications by letting you draw the report on screen in much the same way as you would draw components on to a Visual Basic form. The result is a saved report file which you simply tell the control to load at run time in order to print your reports out.

The Professional Edition allows you to create fully compiled code to improve the performance of your application. It gives additional help to the programmer with extra wizards that help build custom controls, and the setup wizard is enhanced to support Internet distribution.

Of less significance, but still useful, you'll find that the Professional Edition is supplied with even more controls, components and object libraries than the Learning one, giving you easy access to the serial communications systems in Windows, a powerful way to deal with multimedia files, and various other, smaller, neater controls including some allowing you to use the Internet from your application.

Typically, if you need to create powerful, single-user database systems, or have an urge to dabble in the wacky world of communications (or better still write a powerful single-user database application that communicates occasionally), you need to be looking at the Professional Edition. Those of you with a need to do something more powerful, perhaps a multiuser, distributed client-server application—you'd better take a look at what the Enterprise Edition has to offer.

Visual Basic: Control Creation Edition

This edition is actually a freebie released by Microsoft to allow anyone to create ActiveX controls. It is limited in that it can't produce an executable application itself, just controls to be used by other Visual Basic programs (including Office VBA programs). It does contain some of the features in the Professional Edition specific to creating controls, such as the Control Interface Wizard. It also has the Internet-enhanced Setup Wizard to allow you create controls to be used in Internet Explorer.

If you are planning to upgrade from the Learning Edition, then it is worth while to download this free version just to have a look at some of the extra goodies available in the Professional Edition.

Visual Basic: Enterprise Edition

The mother of all Visual Basics, Enterprise Edition has absolutely nothing to do with Kirk and friends, but is instead an incredibly powerful client-server application development tool.

In addition to everything included in the Learning and Professional Editions, the Enterprise Edition also comes with a whole host of new applications, including an Automation manager for monitoring connections to ActiveX objects, the Component manager for managing all your new controls and ActiveX objects, various client-server database and connection management tools, a multideveloper version control system known as Visual Source Safe, a resource editor and much more besides.

If you work in a large team of VB developers, and need to create supremely powerful and well-connected database applications then you really better get the boss to get the check book out for this little beauty.

The Visual Studio 97 Suite

The crème de la crème, though, of all the Editions, has to be the Visual Tools Suite, particularly if you work in a team that is trying to ship a full commercial product. While VB is great for a good many things, there are still times at which you need the support and power of other tools.

The Visual Tools Suite, again from Microsoft, addresses that need by providing you with full copies of Visual Basic 5, Visual C++ version 5, Visual FoxPro, Internet Explorer, Frontpage, Visual Java and a whole host of technical information and documentation on CD-ROM that you wouldn't normally get without paying a hefty development subscription fee to Microsoft.

Using this little lot you should be able to create almost any kind of application under the sun, including full-blown Internet solutions and support DLLs for desktop applications with the power that comes from Visual C++.

Getting it Out the Door

There comes a point in development where, no matter how much you love your new baby, you can't wait for it to leave home. The downside of this in terms of software is that getting it out the door involves quite a bit more work and invariably a good suite of backup software.

The first hurdle that you are going to have to leap over is Help. All users expect their Windows applications now to come with extensive online help, but producing help files needs tools. By far the best on the market, in my humble opinion, is RoboHelp, a what-you-see-is-what-you-get help editor that quite literally bolts on to Microsoft Word and lets you produce a help file just as if you were producing a printed document for any other purpose.

However, more and more people are turning to HTML for their help files, rather than the somewhat more cumbersome Windows Help standard. If this sounds like you (bearing in mind that Visual Basic comes with the necessary controls to let you read and display HTML/Web pages) then you really have two choices.

The first is Microsoft's Frontpage 97, another what-you-see-is-what-you-get tool, this time aimed at producing web pages but just as useful at producing HTML documentation for your application.

The second alternative, again in terms of ease of use and sheer simplistic power, is Netscape's new Communicator. Get hold of Version 4 of this puppy and you can use the Netscape composer to knock out those web pages in no time.

> *Microsoft are currently also working on an HTML Help tool, an ActiveX control designed to create help files in the HTML file format. Watch this space.*

OK—so now you have your application, and you have your help files, either in standard Windows help format, or in HTML, the next step is to get the application out and into the hands of your users.

Unless you are releasing a commercial product, or have some pretty specific requirements on how your users set up the application, the Setup Wizard that comes with Visual Basic should be fine. If you are releasing commercial software, though, or need your users to be able to choose which parts of your application to install, then you really should be looking elsewhere.

At the time of writing, a good bet is to use InstallShield. This is rapidly becoming the de facto standard for commercial installers, allowing you to specify different configurations of install for your users to choose from (such as Typical, Custom, Notebook and so on) as well as set up a single install file for download over the Internet, or customize the install to run off a CD-Rom. This thing is actually so good that it's now used by all the big boys in the business too, including Microsoft, Netscape and one or two others you may have heard off.

If you want more information, or would like to download a trial copy, then check out **`http://www.installshield.com`**.

Help... I Feel So Alone

... so goes the cry of many a lonely developer, particularly those learning or just starting out with a new development system. Fret not—there are thousands of people out there dying to help you solve your latest coding dilemma, and for free as well. Never be afraid of asking for help, no matter how trivial the problem may seem—there are even times when I have to resort to using the developer community to help me.

The best place to start when you need help is of course cyberspace. If you have a modem, then make sure you are either a member of The Microsoft Network, Compuserve or link to any good Internet Service Provider. If you don't have a modem yet, then please put this book down and go and get one; it's not healthy to have your nose stuck in a book all day.

Compuserve is a good online service to be a member of if you have VB troubles. You can either go to the MSBASIC forum, or the VBPJ forum—both are populated by thousands of VB developers ranging from the complete novice to the total guru (yes, I use Compuserve too;->), all providing valuable hints and tips, support code and some very interesting discussions on nothing more than coding technique, or the rashness of the latest Microsoft decision.

On the Internet, check out the **`comp.lang.visual.basic`** newsgroup. It's a little easier going than Compuserve, but equally well-populated.

If online services are really not your scene, then how about a user group. In the UK you can join the Visual Basic User Group (VBUG) which regularly holds local meetings as well as an annual conference. It also provides its members with a bi-monthly magazine providing some very handy hints and tips. In the US, pick up a copy of The Visual Basic Programmers Journal—an excellent publication again backed up by user group meetings and 4 yearly conferences of astounding quality and reputation.

Both VBUG and VBPJ carry regular reviews of the latest add-in controls and applications to make your choice of these a lot more informed than it may have been previously. In the last edition of this book I listed some of the best controls on the market, however, the market has grown so much since that was released that it is now proving impossible for anybody to keep up with everything that's out there.

If you are looking for a new add-in, or a new set of OCXs then check out either VBUG or VBPJ to see what they think, post a few messages on the Internet to gauge public opinion, or simply check out the magazines to see what they have to say.

Finally, again on the Internet, there are various programmer sites out there which can provide the VB developer with valuable tricks and tips, the most interesting being Microsoft's own site at **`http://www.microsoft.com`**. It's full of support information for VB developers, as well as mailing lists and a host of downloadable goodies.

> *If, like us, you don't really fancy the idea of spending your entire day online, browsing and downloading, then why not take a look at an offline reader, such as Net Mage from Psynet Interactive. With this baby, everyone on the team can queue up requests for web pages and then download them at off peak times and in the process build up a valuable offline library of cool Internet sites that the whole team can browse and share. For more information, send an email* **`admin@gendev.demon.co.uk`**, *or check out the web page on* **`www.gendev.demon.co.uk`**.

And Finally... Bedtime Reading

As you begin to move towards the more complex stuff (client-server databases, multimedia, communications, etc.), you will need to read a fair amount more in order to get the results you want.

First of all, I really do have to make a shameless plug.

Beginning Visual Basic 5 Application Development

You know the basics. You say to your colleagues, in a moment of rash confidence, 'I've learned Visual Basic 5' and then you find yourself writing a full-blown application!

Now, I have every confidence you'll succeed, and that all your work with this book to date will prove invaluable, but, like all languages, there's always something new to learn. You may have the grammar and the vocabulary off pat, but that only serves to open new horizons. It's there, based on the masterly use of the language that you'll learn idiomatic Visual Basic development.

Beginning Visual Basic 5 Application Development (ISBN 1-861000-45-6, to be published July 97) will help you on that road. Written by yours truly (hence the plug) it answers the question, 'How do I start actually developing my own applications?', and many others, by giving you an insider's view on the problems and pitfalls that you are going to have to overcome to develop the next great Windows application.

We cover everything in there from good object-oriented design and in-depth error control, through making full use of ActiveX controls and components, to advanced database techniques and optimizing and packaging your applications. Each step of the way we look at these things in the context of a real-world programming problem (OK, they are really made up programming problems like the ones that occur in the real world—but you get my point) and give you a better overall picture of where to go with VB. 'Lil Johnny needs new shoes—so go buy this book right now' <G>.

Other Notables

If you look at the diagram on the back cover of this book you can see how Wrox Press envisage helping you with your future programming needs. It is, of course, only a snapshot of the current and some forthcoming titles—fill out the reply card at the back of the book for a Wrox Developer journal subscription to keep you abreast of the latest title releases, or visit their web site.

Beginning Visual Basic 5's sequel joins other forthcoming 'Level II' Beginning guides from Wrox, including *Beginning Visual Basic 5 API Programming* and *Beginning Visual Basic 5 Database Programming*. These look at more specialized subjects, but in the same example-laden tutorial style, to further your understanding of key parts of Visual Basic programming.

Then there are the Wrox Instant guides which aim to give you a clear, thorough and, above all, timely grounding in the latest technologies. As you can see they cover quite a variety of related subjects, including VBScript and Visual Basic 5 Control Creation Edition.

Finally, although Visual Basic is a great language, it is useless unless your work in it is backed up by effective design and programming practices. The bible for this is *Code Complete* (ISBN 1-55615-484-4), written by Steve McConnell and published by Microsoft Press. It has no Visual Basic specific information in it at all, but the background information and insight it provides into the entire development cycle is invaluable. His follow-on tome, *Rapid Development* (ISBN 1-55615-900-5), is also extremely useful for gaining an insight into the demons that can cause a project to overrun, as well as keeping a grip on managing a new development.

asic Visual Basic Visual Ba
al Basic Visual Basic Visual
Basic Visual Basic Visual Ba
ual Basic Vi
Basic Visu
ual Basic V
l Basic Vis
isual Basic Visual Basic
al Basic Visual Basic Visua
Visual Basic Visual Basic Visu
l Basic Visual Ba
l Basic Visual
ic Visual Basi
Basic Visual B
ic Visual Basi
al Basic Visual
ual Basic Visual Basic Visual Ba
Visual Basic Visual Basic Visu
sual Basic Visual Basic Visu
Visual Basic Visual Ba

Visual Basic Naming Conventions

This appendix introduces a scheme for naming all the objects in Visual Basic in a way that increases the safety and readability of your code. Some parts of this are taken from standards published by Microsoft, and some are my own.

There are three kinds of object we need to have standard names for in our Visual Basic code:

- Controls
- Variables
- Functions and procedures

Before we come to each of these in turn, let's consider why it's necessary to have a naming scheme at all.

Why Have a Standard Naming Scheme?

Naming standards can help prevent costly and embarrassing mistakes. By adopting a set of standards and sticking to them, you're guaranteeing that in *x* months time, when you return to debug or change some code, you'll understand what you were trying to say back when it was written.

Think about road signs. Imagine how confusing it would be if each town in the country had different designs and standards for their road signs. Each time you came to a new town, you'd waste valuable reaction time trying to understand unfamiliar drawings and symbols; time that's better spent on the job—driving.

The same applies to programming. With a decent set of programming standards, your code can, in many ways, becoming self-documenting; reading such code could be as easy as reading a book about it.

Take a look at this—it's a program that your boss has just given you which has a bug in it, and you have ten minutes to fix it.

```
For a = 1 To z

d(a) = d(a) - cv(d(a))
q(a) = q(a) + d(a)
v(a) = cv(d(a))

next a
```

Impossible! You can't make any sense of it. There's no indication of what the code does, or what the variables are that it deals with. As a contrast, look at the same piece of code, now with some standards applied:

```
For nInvNo = 1 to nTotalNumberOfInvoices

nPrice(nInvNo) = nPrice(nInvNo) - Vat(nPrice(nInvNo))
nBalance(nInvNo ) = nBalance(nInvNo) + nPrice(nInvNo)
nVat(nInvNo) = Vat(nPrice(nInvNo))

Next
```

Here, the code is spaced out to make it easier to read, and the variables now have sensible names. It's obvious that the code is dealing with invoice totals, and in particular, the outstanding balance of an invoice, the amount payable and the VAT (sales tax).

From this it's easy to see that the bug is in the first line. **`Vat`** should be added to the price, not subtracted.

Naming Controls

The objective, when naming a control, is to help anyone reading the text to understand two things about the control that the code refers to:

- What kind of control is it? Each control has a unique three letter **prefix** that tells you what kind of control it is.
- What does the control do? Does this command button exit the form, or print the data? This function is described by the **usage identifier**.

Each control name is, therefore, made up of a prefix followed by a usage identifier:

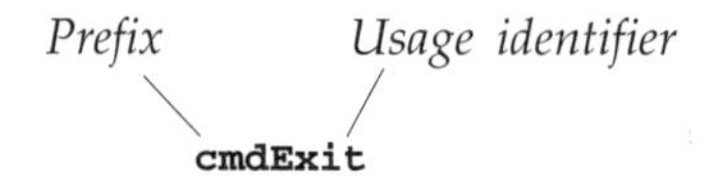

Control Prefixes

A three-letter prefix is used to identify the type of control, and to make it clear which names in your code are variables and which are controls.

The control prefixes that I use are:

Prefix	Control
cboom	Combo box
cfrm	MDI Child Form
chk	Checkbox
cls	Class Module
dat	Data control
dir	Directory list box
dlg	Common dialogs
drv	Drive list box
fil	File list box
fra	Frame
frm	Form
gph	Graphic control (lines, boxes and circles)
grd	Grid
hsb	Horizontal Scrollbar
img	Image control
lbl	Label
lst	List box
mdifrm	MDI Form
mnu	Menu
obj	A generic object, perhaps derived from a class
ole	OLE control
opt	Option/Radio buttons
pic	Picture Box
tim	Timer
txt	Text box
vsb	Vertical Scrollbar

*The **lin** and **shp** names that are in the Visual Basic manuals for Line and Shape have been ignored here. This is purely a question of personal taste; I rarely use the graphical controls so I use the same prefix for all of them, namely **gph**.*

Naming Custom Controls

There's a temptation with custom controls that you're adding to projects, to use the brand name of the product as the prefix. Don't do it! If you decide later on to switch to a control from another supplier, then you'll have to change all your code. The safe way to do it is to use a name that describes the function of the control. For example, if you're using the Image Knife control, don't use the prefix **knf**; instead, use something like **imp** (**im**age **p**rocessing).

Choosing a Control Usage Identifier

When choosing the main part of the name for a control, your aim should be to convey a clear idea about what that control is used for in the code. You can use one or more English words that clearly define this usage. General rules that are worth following include:

- Use capital letters for parts of the name.
- Underscore characters can be used to separate the words of the name (this is left to your personal preference).
- You can make the name as long, or as short, as you like. If it's too short, though, it probably won't tell you anything, and if it's too long, you're giving yourself a lot of typing to do—a sensible limit is about 15 characters.

There are some limitations to the names you can use. For example, you can't create variables that have identical names to Visual Basic keywords. Equally, you can't start a variable name with a number, or with a special character, such as $,%,^,&,*.

Example Control Names

First the bad names. These are all too cryptic to be useful:

```
Text1      Combo     A_Form     txtDSADSXZ chkB
Alfred     Henry     God_Knows
```

Don't laugh! I've seen all these in Visual Basic programs!

These, on the other hand, are much nicer:

```
txtSurname   cboEmployees       frmMainForm
chkSex       txtEmpCode
```

Naming Variables

When naming a variable, there's a piece of information we need to include, in addition to its type and a description of its usage: its scope. Controls are all local to the form on which they're placed, but variables can be either local, global or static.

The format of a typical variable name is:

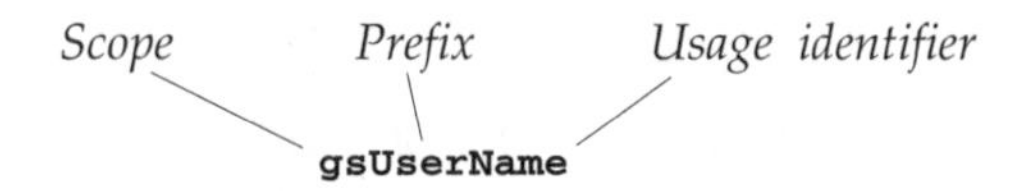

Variable Scope

The scope part of the name consists of a single letter prefix to the variable name:

Prefix	Variable Name
m	Module level variables—defined with **Dim** or **Static** in the declarations section of a fForm (**.Frm**) or mModule (**.Bas**).
no prefix	All local variables—those defined using **Dim**, **Private** or **Static** in a function or procedure—have no prefix.

Variable Type

Just as with scope, a single alphabetic character can be used to define the type of a variable, such as string, integer, and so on. These **type** letters are as follows:

Character	Type of Variable
s	String
i	Integer
l	Long (a large integer)
f	Floating point number, both singles and doubles
c	Currency
var	Variant
b	BooleanByte
d	Date

Choosing a Variable Usage Identifier

The rules for naming variables are similar to those for controls. Never use quick names for variables, such as the traditional **X, Y, I, J, Z**. An experienced programmer knows that **I** means an Integer index in a **For** loop, but a beginner might not. Badly named variables can lead to you using them in the wrong place in your code, such as typing **I** where you meant to type **J**, and so on. If you've taken the time to declare a variable for a particular purpose, then take the time to give it a useful name!

Example Variable Names

To summarize, some examples of variable names are:

`iCounter`	An integer used as a counter of some kind.
`bMale`	A Boolean value; true represents male.
`mdDate`	A module level date.

Declaring Variable Data Types

Although Visual Basic supports the use of type identifiers such as $ for string, and % for integer, they're really only a hang over from the original ANSI specification for BASIC. Type identifiers can easily be mistyped. Notice how $ is next to % on the keyboard. Also, they don't jump out at you when you reread a buggy section of code for the 12th time, and they look cryptic if your code is handed to a beginner.

- When declaring data types, *always* use the data type name, such as **`String`** instead of **`$`** and so on
- Remember to never leave the data type off a declaration, as this results in you defining a variant, which would probably mean your variable name is wrong

Object Variables

Most object variables are controls, so you just go ahead and name them as you would a normal control. However, object variables relating to databases are named along the same lines as controls. The prefixes to use are:

Prefix	Variable
`dyn`	Dynaset type recordset
`tbl`	Table type recordset
`snp`	Snapshot type recordset
`db`	Database
`rec`	Recordset
`que`	Query type recordset

Naming Functions and Procedures

Function and procedure names should reflect the purpose of the procedure or function, using English words.

Naming Functions

Functions always return a value and, where possible, should be given a name that reflects the return value. A function that returns the square root of a number should simply be called **Square_Root**, or **Square_Root_Of**, rather than **Calculate_Square_Root**. You can tell if a function has been given a good name by seeing how the code reads:

```
fRoot = Square_Root_Of ( 36 )' This is good!
fRoot = ClcSqrRt( 36 )' This is bad, read aloud!
```

Naming Procedures

The same amount of thought should be given to procedure names. Procedures generally perform a task, such as clearing a list box, or changing a frame layout. The task the procedure performs should be reflected in the name.

```
Remove_Borders Frame1' Easy enough!
RBF1_V1 Frame1' No idea - bad name!
```

asic Visual Basic Visual Ba
al Basic Visual Basic Visual
Basic Visual Basic Visual Ba
ual Basic Vi
Basic Visu
ual Basic V
l Basic Vis
isual Basic Visual Basic
al Basic Visual Basic Visual
Visual Basic Visual Basic Visu
l Basic Visual Ba
l Basic Visual
ic Visual Basi
Basic Visual B
ic Visual Basi
l Basic Visual
ual Basic Visual Basic Visual Ba
Visual Basic Visual Basic Visu
sual Basic Visual Basic Visu
Visual Basic Visual Bas

Solutions

The next few pages propose solutions to the exercises that were included at the end of each chapter. Don't worry if you've come up with different ways of achieving the same result—there's usually more than one solution to a problem. However, have a read through the answers included here because, more often than not, you'll find some good hints and tips that you can make use of in your own code.

Chapter 1 - Welcome to Visual Basic

1 There are 49 properties in the properties window of a form. The property used to hide a form is the **`Visible`** property.

2 You can find the following key combinations listed under the Global Keys section of help.

Press	To
F1	Open Help.
F5	Run an application.
F8	Execute code one line at a time.
Shift+F5	Restart an application from the beginning after an interruption.
Shift+F8	Execute statements one line at a time without stepping into procedure calls.
Shift+F10	View shortcut menu.
Ctrl+Break	Stop running a Visual Basic application.
Ctrl+C	Copy the selection.
Ctrl+G	Display the immediate window.
Ctrl+X	Cut the selection.
Ctrl+V	Paste the selection.
Ctrl+Z	Undo the last edit.
Alt+F4	Close the active window; if all windows are closed, close Visual Basic.
Alt+F5	Run the error handler code or return the error to the calling procedure.
Alt+F6	Toggle between the last two active windows.
Alt+F8	Step into the error handler or return the error to the calling procedure.
Ctrl+Tab	Switch between windows.

3 A Visual Basic statement is an intrinsic part of the language, such as the word **Let**. A method is a piece of code that is attached to a control that is made available to your project. In essence, it extends your Visual Basic project.

4 Changing the Height and Width grid units affects the density of the grid pattern on the default form in design mode. The grid pattern is there to help you align controls at design time.

5 The default Height and Width grid units are 120 and 120 respectively. Changing them both to 300 increases the distance between the dots. The pattern is saved with the project.

Chapter 2 - Inside a Visual Basic Program

1 Here is the code necessary to hide the button upon startup.

```
Private Sub Form_Load()
    Command1.Visible = False
End Sub
```

Now try this! Use *Ctrl-Break* to halt execution of the program. Use *Ctrl-G* to display the immediate window. You can type commands into this window. Type in the following.

```
Command1.Visible = True
```

Now resume program execution by using *F5*. What happens? The form appears! Suppose you had pressed the *Shift+F5* combination? The program would restart, making the button invisible again.

2 This is your first lesson on debugging. When you press *F8*, you run the program in Step mode, which allows you to watch the effect of each line of code and see the order in which they are run. Here you see the **Form_Load** event being run. You should note though, that **Form_Load** actually occurs after the **Form_Initialize** event. You don't see this event here because there isn't any code for it. More on debugging in Chapter 8.

3 Select File from the main menu. Then select Make Project1.exe. Now switch to Explorer and run the project by double clicking the **exe** file.

4 You can use the Version Number option to display the version number of your application releases. You can use this in conjunction with the Auto Increment check box. These properties are part of the App object and are available to you at run time. By selecting Auto Increment, you specify that each you generate an executable, the revision number of the application should be incremented. It's a good idea both for you and your users!

5 Once the **BIBLIO** project has been opened (you should find it in the **\VB5\samples\PGuide\Biblio** directory), double click on **Form1** in the project window and then click the View Code button (in the project window). Click the arrow in the top left drop down box and find the **Form** object. Then use the right drop down box to find the **Load** event. Now go to the Edit menu and select Find. You can now search for all occurrences of the string "**Unload**" in the current procedure, module and project. Select Find Whole Word Only. You should find one occurrence of the word **Unload** in the **Form_Load** event of **Form1**. By selecting module to perform your search, you should find an additional occurrence (**Unload** is found in the **Click** event of the **MnuExit** option of the menu bar). By selecting project as your search scope, you should find a third occurrence in the **Click** event of the **Command1** command button (on the **frmAbout** form).

Chapter 3 - Common Controls

1 Here is the code necessary to change the caption when the command button is clicked:

```
Private Sub Command1_Click()
    Command1.Caption = "ON"
End Sub
```

2 This is the code that moves the command button 100 twips to the left.

```
Private Sub Command1_Click()

    Command1.Left = Command1.Left - 100
    Form1.Print Command1.Left, Command1.Top
End Sub
```

As you can see, as the command button begins to move off the 'edge' of the form, its left coordinate moves into a negative number range.

3 Here is the code necessary to center the command button on the form (note the use of integer division):

```
Private Sub Command1_Click()
  Command1.Left = (Form1.Width - Command1.Width) \ 2
  Command1.Top = (Form1.Height - Command1.Height) \ 2
End Sub
```

When the button is renamed, the code for the **Click** event is moved to the **general** section of **Form1**!

4 Place this code in the `Click` event for `Command1`. Then use the hot key combination *Alt+T* to trigger it.

```
Private Sub Command1_Click()
    MsgBox "Tom button has been clicked"
End Sub
```

This is the code for the second command button.

```
Private Sub Command2_Click()
    MsgBox "Terry button has been clicked"
End Sub
```

The question we posed is a bit of a trick question in so far as neither message box is displayed, as just pressing *Alt+T* never actually clicks the buttons!

5 `Text1` receives focus at run time (you can see that because `Text1` displays the insertion point). You can change this behavior in several ways. At design time, you can change the `TabIndex` property of `Text2` to 0. This will ensure that `Text2` receives focus at run time. You could also add the following code to the `Form_Load` event of `Form1`.

```
Private Sub Form_Load()
    Form1.Show
    Text2.SetFocus
End Sub
```

Notice how I had to show `Form1` before I could set focus to one of its objects. If you try to set focus to an object that is not visible, you will generate a run-time error.

Chapter 4 - Writing Code

1 As with exercise 3-5, focus can be set to the text box with this code

```
Private Sub Form_Load()
    Form1.Show
    Text1.SetFocus
End Sub
```

This code is then used to check the text in the text box against the secret password

```
Private Sub Command1_Click()
    If Text1.Text = "Kevin" Then
        MsgBox "Congratulations, that is the correct password"
    End If
End Sub
```

Note that this password is case sensitive, so be careful! There are ways to eliminate the case sensitivity of the comparison. You could place the statement **Option Compare Text** in the declaration section of your module. This results in a *case-insensitive* text check. You could also modify the **If** statement in the **Click** event like so...

```
Private Sub Command1_Click()
    If UCASE$(Text1.Text) = "KEVIN" Then
        MsgBox "Congratulations, that is the correct password"
    End If
End Sub
```

2 The modified code for the **Click** event of the **Command1** button looks like this:

```
Private Sub Command1_Click()
    If UCase$(Text1.Text) = "KEVIN" Then
        MsgBox "Congratulations, that is the correct password"
    Else
        MsgBox "Sorry, that password is not correct"
        Text1.Text = ""
        Text1.SetFocus
    End If
End Sub
```

Notice, I have enhanced the project a bit by clearing the text box and setting focus to it if the password entered is incorrect.

3 I chose to check for the character being entered into the text box by using the **Text1_KeyPress** event. This event takes place when a key on the keyboard is pressed. This event returns an integer value (**KeyAscii**) equal to the ASCII character of the key being pressed. This event is a little cleaner to deal with than either the **KeyUp** or **KeyDown** events which also detect function keys and navigation keys. Counting these could have disastrous results in our next exercise.

The returned ASCII integer value can be converted to a character by using the **CHR** function. Note also that I have used a static variable to keep track of the vowels entered into the text box. Without a static variable, the value of the variable would be initialized to 0 each time the event occurred. Notice also that after each keystroke, I clear the entry in the text box. Finally, I use the **UCASE** function to create a *case insensitive* check.

```
Private Sub Text1_KeyPress(KeyAscii As Integer)

Static iVowelCount as Integer

Select Case UCase(Chr(KeyAscii))

Case "A", "E", "I", "O", "U"
    iVowelCount = iVowelCount + 1
    Label1.Caption = "The vowel count is " & iVowelCount
```

```
    Text1.Text = ""
End Select

End Sub
```

4 Very similar to 4-3, except this time we're counting the consonants as well.

```
Private Sub Text1_KeyPress(KeyAscii As Integer)

Static iVowelCount As Integer
Static iConsonantCount As Integer

Form1.Print Chr(KeyAscii)

Select Case UCase(Chr(KeyAscii))

Case "A", "E", "I", "O", "U"
    iVowelCount = iVowelCount + 1
    Label1.Caption = "The vowel count is " & iVowelCount
    Text1.Text = ""
Case Else
    iConsonantCount = iConsonantCount + 1
    Label2.Caption = "The consonant count is " & iConsonantCount
    Text1.Text = ""
End Select

End Sub
```

5 Here we use the **`Form_Load`** event to perform our calculations. We use the **`SendKeys`** method to type into the text box.

```
Private Sub Form_Load()

Dim x As Integer
Dim y As Integer

For x = 1 To 12
For y = 1 To 12

SendKeys x & " x " & y & "=" & x * y & "{ENTER}"

Next
Next

End Sub
```

Chapter 5 - Making Data Work for You

1 The inclusion of a simple **If** statement makes the system impenetrable on the weekends.

```
Private Sub Command1_Click()
    Dim myweekday
    myweekday = WeekDay(Now)

    If myweekday = vbSunday Or myweekday = vbSaturday Then
        MsgBox "Sorry, access denied to the system on Weekends!"
        End
    End If

    If UCase$(Text1.Text) = "KEVIN" Then
        MsgBox "Congratulations, that is the correct password"
    Else
        MsgBox "Sorry, that password is not correct"
        Text1.Text = ""
        Text1.SetFocus
    End If
End Sub
```

2 Some interesting code here. We use the **Mod** operator to determine whether our counter is even or odd. If our counter is odd, we change the character in the string to upper case. If our counter is even, we leave it alone. We use a **For...Next** loop to move through the characters in the string. By using the **Mid$** function, we are able to examine each character in the string, and then write the string out to the new string using string concatenation.

```
Private Sub Command1_Click()

Dim strOld, strNew As String
Dim intLength, intCounter, intRemainder As Integer

strOld = "the rain in spain"
intLength = Len(strOld)

For intCounter = 1 To intLength
    intRemainder = intCounter Mod 2
    If intRemainder = 1 Then
        strNew = strNew + UCase(Mid$(strOld, intCounter, 1))
    Else
        strNew = strNew + LCase(Mid$(strOld, intCounter, 1))
    End If
Next intCounter

Form1.Print strNew

End Sub
```

3 Here is some code that can be used to determine if the text box is empty. We use a message box to display the results. When **Command1** is clicked, we are informed that **Text1.Text** is equal to "".

```
Private Sub Command1_Click()
If IsNull(Text1.Text) Then
        MsgBox "Text1 is null"
    End If

    If IsEmpty(Text1.Text) Then
        MsgBox "Text1 is empty"
    End If

    If Text1.Text = "" Then
        MsgBox "Text1 is "& Chr(34) & Chr(34)
    End If
End Sub
```

Here is the code used to check for the value of a declared variant variable. Again, we use a message box to display the results. When **Command2** is clicked, we are informed that the variant variable has a value of *both* 'Empty' and "".

```
Private Sub Command2_Click()

Dim varX As Variant

    If IsNull(varX) Then
        MsgBox "varX is null"
    End If
    If IsEmpty(varX) Then
        MsgBox "varX is empty"
    End If
    If varX = "" Then
        MsgBox "varX is "& chr(34) & chr(34)
    End If
End Sub
```

Here is the code used to check for the value of a declared integer variable. Again, we use a message box to display the results. When **Command3** is clicked, we're informed that the integer variable has a value of '0'. Does that surprise you? (If we had checked for a value of "" in code, a run-time error would have occurred.)

```
Private Sub Command3_Click()
Dim intX As Integer

    If IsNull(intX) Then
        MsgBox "intX is null"
    End If
    If IsEmpty(intX) Then
        MsgBox "intX is empty"
```

```
    End If
    If intx = 0 Then
        MsgBox "intX is 0"
    End If
End Sub
```

Finally, here is the code used to check for the value of a declared string variable. Again, we use a message box to display the results. When **Command4** is clicked, we're informed that the string variable has a value of "".

```
Private Sub Command4_Click()

Dim charX As String

    If IsNull(charX) Then
        MsgBox "charX is null"
    End If
    If IsEmpty(charX) Then
        MsgBox "charX is empty"
    End If
    If charX = "" Then
        MsgBox "charX is "& chr(34) & chr(34)
    End If

End Sub
```

A final note here: if you want to determine if a text box is truly 'empty', why not use the **Len** function to determine if the length of the text is 0? The code would read:

```
If Len(Text1.Text) = 0 then
    MsgBox "The text box is really empty"
End If
```

4 This is a fun project to work with. We place two buttons on **Form1**. One button, **Command1**, is intended to display a message box with the value of a variable called **intX**. We declare this variable in the declaration section of **Form1** with **Dim**. The second button, **Command2**, is necessary to show **Form2**. It's a good idea to name the button on **Form2** as **Command3**, as Visual Basic will name it **Command1** by default and this can then be confused with **Command1** button on Form1.

Once **Form2** is displayed, we place in **Command3**'s **Click** event the same code found in **Command1** of **Form1** which attempts to display a message box with the value of **intX**. However, we receive a message indicating that the variable has not been defined (this is because variables declared using a **Dim** statement in **Form1** are private to **Form1**—nothing, not even specifying the form name in **Command1** of **Form2** will display the value). Here's the code for the initial setup:

In the General Declarations section of **Form1** we place:

```
Option Explicit

Dim intx As Integer

Private Sub Command1_Click()
MsgBox "The value of intX is " & intX
End Sub

Private Sub Command2_Click()
Form2.Show
End Sub
```

This code was placed on **Form2**:

```
Private Sub Command3_Click()
MsgBox "The value of intX is " & intX
End Sub
```

To make **intX** visible to **Form2**, we need to change its declaration from **Dim** to **Public** in the declarations section of **Form1**. We also need to change the way we reference **intX** from **Form2**. Here's the revised code for the declarations section of **Form1**:

```
Option Explicit

Public intX As Integer
```

Here's the code in the **Command3** button on **Form2**.

```
Private Sub Command3_Click()
MsgBox Form1.intx
End Sub
```

Notice how we prefix the public variable found in **Form1** with the form name.

Finally, in order to maintain a running total of the number of times that **Command1** has been clicked, we need to change the declaration of **intX** to a static variable, and increment its value by 1 each time the button is clicked. Because a static variable can only be declared at the procedure level, we need to move the declaration of **intX** from the General Declarations section of **Form1** to the **command1_click()** event of **Form1**.

```
Private Sub Command1_Click()
Static intX As Integer
intx = intX + 1
MsgBox intX
End Sub
```

5 **Mid$** and **Right$** will both work in this example, although quite honestly we're really stretching things by using **Mid$**. **Right$** is the ideal tool for the job, but **Mid$** will work just as well. Because **Mid$** requires two arguments (the starting position within the source string to extract, and also the number of characters to extract), the code is a little trickier than **Right$**. All we need to do is determine the length of the string that we wish to extract (in this case 1) and pass that value to the function along with the starting point. If we wanted to extract the last two characters in the text box this code would be even trickier.

```
Private Sub Command1_Click()
Dim intLen As Integer
Dim strLastChar As String
intLen = Len(Text1.Text)
If intLen > 0 Then
    strLastChar = Mid$(Text1.Text, intLen, 1)
    MsgBox "The last character of the text box is " & strLastChar
End If
End Sub
```

The **Right$** function is ideal for this task! It merely needs to know how many characters starting from the right of the source string we wish to extract. In this case, that's easy. It's 1!

```
Private Sub Command2_Click()
Dim intLen As Integer
Dim strLastChar As String
intLen = Len(Text1.Text)
If intLen > 0 Then
    strLastChar = Right$(Text1.Text, 1)
    MsgBox "The last character of the text box is " & strLastChar
End If
End Sub
```

Chapter 6 - List Controls

1 This may not seem like much of a challenge. But you'd be amazed at the number of people who prefer to populate their list boxes in this manner, and then are befuddled to find that the **List** property closes each time they press *Enter*. The real challenge here is in adding more than one member to the **List** property without exiting the list. If you add an item to the list and then press *Enter*, you exit the list. To continue adding to the list, press *Ctrl+Enter*.

2 A **For...Next** loop is a quick to way to load the capital letters of the alphabet. **Chr** is a function that returns a string containing the character associated with a specified ASCII code. In this case, we start with ASCII 65 (the letter 'A'), and work our way through ASCII 90 (the letter 'Z').

```
Private Sub Form_Load()
   Dim x As Integer
   For x = 65 To 90
      List1.AddItem Chr(x)
```

```
    Next x
End Sub
```

3 Yes, the combo box does have a **IntegralHeight** property. Like the list box, the default is true.

4 This is an interesting problem, and here's one way I've solved this problem. I use a combination of events to add the new item to the combo box. First, I place a command button on the form and label it Select or something along those lines. In the **Click** event of the command button, I place the following code:

```
Private Sub Command1_Click()
  If Combo1.ListIndex = -1 And Combo1.Text <> "" Then
    Combo1.AddItem Combo1.Text
    Combo1.ListIndex = -1
    Combo1.Text = ""
    Form1.Show
  End If
End Sub
```

If the user selects an item that appears in the list, the value of **ListIndex** will be equal to the position of the item in the list. If **ListIndex** is equal to -1, then nothing from the list has been selected. Additionally, if the **Text** property of the combo box is not empty, then I know that the user has typed something into the combo box. After adding the new item to the list, I reset the **ListIndex** property to -1, and empty the **Text** property of the combo box.

Instead of having the user click on the command button to add the entry, you could set things up so that the entry is added when they press *Enter*. You can do this by placing the following code in the **KeyPress** event of the combo box. If the *Enter* key is pressed (**KeyAscii = 13**), then you can invoke the **Command1_Click** event procedure, which will add their item to the list.

```
Private Sub Combo1_KeyPress(KeyAscii As Integer)
   If KeyAscii = 13 Then
     Command1_Click
   End If
End Sub
```

5 In a combo box, the **Change** event occurs when the text in the text box portion of the control changes. The **Change** event occurs only if the **Style** property is set to 0 (Dropdown Combo) or 1 (Simple Combo). The **Click** event occurs when a user selects an item in a combo box either by pressing the arrow keys or by clicking the mouse button.

Chapter 7 - Creating Your Own Objects

1 Create a new project and then go to Project | Add Class Module. Select the VB Class Builder and then create a new class called **clsTrafficLight**. Remember, at this point, your class can respond to two built-in events: the **Class_Initialize** event and the **Class_Terminate** event.

2 Use the Add New Property button to add the five properties. Class Builder will place the following declarations in the code window:

```
Option Explicit

'local variable(s) to hold property value(s)
Private mvarHeight As Integer               'local copy
Private mvarWidth As Integer                'local copy
Private mvarX As Integer                    'local copy
Private mvarY As Integer                    'local copy
Private mvarRedLight As Boolean   'local copy
Private mvarYellowLight As Boolean          'local copy
Private mvarGreenLight As Boolean 'local copy
```

These properties will be readable and writeable by procedures from outside of the class. To accomplish this, Class Builder writes a **Property Let** and a **Property Get** subprocedure for each property. For example, for the **GreenLight** property, it adds:

```
Public Property Let GreenLight(vData As Boolean)
'used when assigning a value to the property, on the left side of an
'assignment.  Syntax: X.GreenLight = 5

    mvarGreenLight = vData

End Property

Public Property Get GreenLight() As Boolean
'used when retrieving value of a property, on the right side of an
'assignment.  Syntax: Debug.Print X.GreenLight

    GreenLight = mvarGreenLight

End Property
```

A word of warning here. I included properties for red, green, and yellow lights in case, at some future date, a traffic engineer needs to override the behavior of traffic lights as we know them. By making these properties public, we could be asking for problems later on. For this reason, you might want to delete the **Property Let** statements, which in effect creates a read-only property of the class. After all, we've included methods to allow us to change our light colors.

3 In order to establish default values for the properties **Height** and **Width**, when the class is instantiated, I take advantage of the fact that the **Class_Initialize** event is invoked. Use the **Class Initialize** event to set values, properties etc. when the Class first comes alive.

```
Private Sub Class_Initialize()

    mvarHeight = 500
    mvarWidth = 500

End Sub
```

I then fill in the method code. I use the **Line** method to draw my traffic light, passing it an object to draw on and the coordinates for the traffic light are obtained from the **x**, **y**, **Height** and **Width** properties of the class. I initialize the traffic light with all 3 lights (red, yellow and green) lit.

```
Public Sub DrawLight(Canvas As Object)

  Canvas.Line (mvarX, mvarY)-(mvarX + mvarWidth, mvarY + mvarHeight),
  ↳ vbRed, BF

  Canvas.Line (mvarX, mvarY + (1 * Height))-(mvarX + mvarWidth, mvarY +
  ↳ (1 * Height) + mvarHeight), vbYellow, BF

  Canvas.Line (mvarX, mvarY + (2 * Height))-(mvarX + mvarWidth, mvarY +
  ↳ (2 * Height) + mvarHeight), vbGreen, BF

End Sub
```

In the **ClearLight** method, again I use the **Line** method to clear the traffic light by setting its colors equal to the background color of the canvas.

```
Public Sub ClearLight(Canvas As Object)

  Canvas.Line (mvarX, mvarY)-(mvarX + mvarWidth, mvarY + mvarHeight),
  ↳ Canvas.BackColor, B

  Canvas.Line (mvarX, mvarY + (1 * Height))-(mvarX + mvarWidth, mvarY +
  ↳ (1 * Height) + mvarHeight), Canvas.BackColor, BF

  Canvas.Line (mvarX, mvarY + (2 * Height))-(mvarX + mvarWidth, mvarY +
  ↳ (2 * Height) + mvarHeight), Canvas.BackColor, BF

End Sub
```

The **TrafficGo** method sets the green portion of the traffic light on, while setting the red and yellow lights to off.

```
Public Sub TrafficGo(Canvas As Object)

 Canvas.Line (mvarX, mvarY)-(mvarX + mvarWidth, mvarY + mvarHeight),
 ➥ Canvas.BackColor, BF

 Canvas.Line (mvarX, mvarY + (1 * Height))-(mvarX + mvarWidth, mvarY +
 ➥ (1 * Height) + mvarHeight), Canvas.BackColor, BF

 Canvas.Line (mvarX, mvarY + (2 * Height))-(mvarX + mvarWidth, mvarY +
 ➥ (2 * Height) + mvarHeight), vbGreen, BF

End Sub
```

In a similar way, the **TrafficStop** method sets the red light on, while setting the green and yellow lights off:

```
Public Sub TrafficStop(Canvas As Object)

 Canvas.Line (mvarX, mvarY)-(mvarX + mvarWidth, mvarY + mvarHeight),
 ➥ vbRed, BF
 Canvas.Line (mvarX, mvarY + (1 * Height))-(mvarX + mvarWidth, mvarY +
 ➥ (1 * Height) + mvarHeight), Canvas.BackColor, BF
 Canvas.Line (mvarX, mvarY + (2 * Height))-(mvarX + mvarWidth, mvarY +
 ➥ (2 * Height) + mvarHeight), Canvas.BackColor, BF

End Sub
```

Finally, the **TrafficCaution** method sets the yellow light on, while setting the red and green lights off:

```
Public Sub TrafficCaution(Canvas As Object)

 Canvas.Line (mvarX, mvarY)-(mvarX + mvarWidth, mvarY + mvarHeight),
 ➥ Canvas.BackColor, BF

 Canvas.Line (mvarX, mvarY + (1 * Height))-(mvarX + mvarWidth, mvarY +
 ➥ (1 * Height) + mvarHeight), vbYellow, BF

 Canvas.Line (mvarX, mvarY + (2 * Height))-(mvarX + mvarWidth, mvarY +
 ➥ (2 * Height) + mvarHeight), Canvas.BackColor, BF

End Sub
```

4 First, I create a control array of 5 command buttons on the form. Using a control array will simplify the code a little bit. Button 1 (with **Index** 0) is captioned Build Light. Button 2 (with **Index** 1) is captioned Go. Button 3 (with **Index** 2) is captioned Stop. Button 4 (with **Index** 3) is captioned Caution. Button 5 (with **Index** 4) is captioned Destroy Light. When the Build Light button is clicked, I declare a new instance of the class **clsTrafficLight**, and invoke its **DrawLight** method, passing as a single argument the keyword **Me**. When the class instance **MainStreet** is instantiated, the **Class_Initialize** event sets default values for the properties **x**, **y**, **Height** and **Width**.

```
Private Sub Command1_Click(Index As Integer)

  If Index = 0 Then
     Dim MainStreet As New clsTrafficLight
     MainStreet.DrawLight Me
  End If

  If Index = 1 Then
     MainStreet.TrafficGo Me
  End If

  If Index = 2 Then
     MainStreet.TrafficStop Me
  End If

  If Index = 3 Then
     MainStreet.TrafficCaution Me
  End If

  If Index = 4 Then
     MainStreet.ClearLight Me
  End If

End Sub
```

5 The final touch for this project is to enable the class to behave like a true traffic light. The traffic light must cycle through a series of green, yellow, then red. In order to implement this behavior, I place a timer control on the form, and set its **Enabled** property to false, and its **Interval** property to 1. I then place another command button on the form (once again, part of the control array). When this command button is clicked, it sets the **Enabled** property of the timer control to true, which invokes the **Timer** event of the timer control.

```
If Index = 5 Then
  Timer1.Enabled = True
End If
```

Here's the code for the **Timer** event of the timer control:

```
Private Sub Timer1_Timer()

  Dim MainStreet As New clsTrafficLight
  Static Interval As Integer

  Interval = Interval + 1
```

```
    If Interval > 60 Then
      Interval = 1
    End If
    MainStreet.LightOn Me, Interval

End Sub
```

The **Timer** event begins by declaring a static variable called **Interval**, which then becomes the argument to a class method called **LightOn**, which I add to the class.

The **LightOn** method has two arguments. One is **Canvas** which we have seen simply dictates where the traffic light is drawn. The second is **Interval**, which is a value that indicates how long the timer control has been enabled. Depending on the value of **Interval**, the **TrafficGo**, **TrafficCaution**, or **TrafficStop** methods of the class are called.

```
Public Sub LightOn(Canvas As Object, Interval As Integer)

  Select Case Interval
    Case 1 To 25
        TrafficGo Canvas
    Case 26 To 30, 56 To 60
        TrafficCaution Canvas
    Case 31 To 55
        TrafficStop Canvas
  End Select

End Sub
```

Chapter 8 - Debugging Your Programs

1 Here is the code necessary to set up the command button's **Click** event. Notice the use of **DoEvents** here—this passes control to the operating system. If we didn't include **DoEvents** in this loop, the label's caption would never get a chance to be updated, so the first caption to be displayed would be 1000.

```
Private Sub Command1_Click()
Dim Counter As Integer
For Counter = 1 To 1000
  Label1.Caption = Counter
  DoEvents
Next counter
End Sub

Private Sub Command2_Click()
Dim Counter As Integer
For Counter = 1000 To 1 Step -1
```

```
    Label2.Caption = Counter
    DoEvents
  Next Counter
  End Sub
```

2 There are several ways to add a watch expression. One way is to determine watch expressions at design time through the Tools menu. The easiest way to do this is to highlight **Counter** in the loop and then select Debug | Add Watch or right click and select Add Watch. This will automatically populate the expression box with the selected expression. Leave the Watch Type as Watch Expression. Click OK and your Watches window will appear, and you'll see the watch expression in the expression portion of the window. Now run the program and click on **Command1**. Pause the program and you'll see value for **Counter**.

3 Very similar to what we did in the previous exercise. This time we specify a watch for the counter variable in **Command2**. We also want to cause the program to break when the value of this variable reaches 383. As before, highlight the variable or expression that you wish to watch in the code procedure we wish to monitor it in (in this case, **Command2_Click**. Then, select Debug | Add Watch. Modify the expression in the expression box so that it reads Counter = 383. Specify a watch type of Break When Value is True. This will pause the program when the value of the counter reaches 383. Run the program, click on **Command2**, and the program breaks when the counter counts down to 383.

4 A single line of code will allow you to view the value of a changing variable. Note, also, that if you forget to remove this line of code, it's automatically ignored by the compiler when you turn your project into an executable.

```
Private Sub Command1_Click()
Dim Counter As Integer
For Counter = 1 To 1000
  Label1.Caption = Counter
  DoEvents
  Debug.Print Counter
Next Counter
End Sub
```

5 Sometimes I find it easier, during the debugging process, to place either a picture box or a text box on my form, and use it to display any internal values I'm interested in. Either one works fine. The advantage of the text box is that if you set the **MultiLine** property to true, and **ScrollBars** to either both or vertical, the text box is scrollable. Here is the code I use to display the values of **Counter** in a scrollable text box.

I first set focus to the text box, then use two **SendKeys** statements—to display the counter in the text box and then to simulate the press of the *Enter* key to generate a carriage return and line feed. This ensures that in the next iteration of the counter, the value for counter will be displayed on the next line of the text box. I use **SendKeys** here to give the text box the 'scrollable' look. If I had simply set the **Text** property of the text box equal to **Counter**, I would have overprinted the counter each time and lost my running total. **SendKeys** is a great way to simulate something we all try to avoid having our users do—type.

```
Private Sub Command2_Click()
  Dim Counter As Integer
  For Counter = 1000 To 1 Step -1
    Label2.Caption = Counter
    DoEvents
    Text1.SetFocus
    SendKeys Counter
    SendKeys "{Enter}"
  Next Counter
End Sub
```

Chapter 9 - Menus

1 There are 79 shortcuts available. *Ctrl+A* through *Ctrl+Z*. *F1* through *F12*. *Ctrl+F1* through *Ctrl+F12*. *Shift+F1* through *Shift+F12*. *Shift+Ctrl+F1* through *Shift+Ctrl+F12*. *Ctrl+Ins*, *Shift+Ins*, *Delete*, *Shift+Delete*, *Alt+Bksp*.

2 You receive an error message, upon attempting to exit the menu editor, Shortcut key already assigned.

3 In this case, I created a form with a top level menu item called **mnuTop** and a submenu item called **mnuTopTest**. I gave the submenu item an index of 0, which told Visual Basic that it was a member of a control array called **mnuTest**.

I then created a command button, which when clicked, created a new member of the control array, set the checked value of the menu item to true, and changed the caption to its index value. In the General Declarations section of the form, I declared a private integer variable called **intCount**:

```
Private intCount As Integer
```

Here's the code for the command button's **Click** event:

```
Private Sub Command1_Click()

  intCount = intCount + 1
  Load mnuTopTest(intCount)
  mnuTopTest(intCount).Checked = True
  mnuTopTest(intCount).Caption = intCount

End Sub
```

4 Add a second command button and place the following code in its **Click** event. Notice how I check to ensure that we don't unload the menu item created at design time, something we are not permitted to do. Attempting to do so would generate a run-time error.

```
Private Sub Command2_Click()

  If intCount = 0 Then
     MsgBox "Can't unload control created at design time"
     Exit Sub
  Else
     Unload mnuTopTest(intCount)
     intCount = intCount - 1
  End If

End Sub
```

5 The key to creating this type of pop-up menu is to create the menu structure in the normal way. That is, create it and attach it to the form. However, with this type of right click menu, we typically make the menu item invisible. Then, we use the **MouseDown** event to check to see if the user has clicked the right mouse button (**Button = 2**). If they have, we use the **PopupMenu** method, along with the name of the menu that we wish to display. Here is the code for the **MouseDown** event:

```
Private Sub Form_MouseDown(Button As Integer, Shift As Integer, X As
    ↳ Single, Y As Single)
   If Button = 2 Then
     PopupMenu mnuTop
   End If
End Sub
```

Chapter 10 - Dialogs

1 To refresh your memory, here are the list of **Msgbox** constants.

vbOKOnly	0	OK button only (default).
vbOKCancel	1	OK and Cancel buttons.
vbAbortRetryIgnore	2	Abort, Retry, and Ignore buttons.
vbYesNoCancel	3	Yes, No, and Cancel buttons.
vbYesNo	4	Yes and No buttons.
vbRetryCancel	5	Retry and Cancel buttons.
vbCritical	16	Critical message.
vbQuestion	32	Warning query.
vbExclamation	48	Warning message.
vbInformation	64	Information message.

For simplicity's sake, I inserted my code into the **Form_Load** event of the form. It's a simple nested loop. The outer loop controls the buttons displayed, and the inner loop displays the symbol displayed. Adding them together gives us the style argument to the **Msgbox** function. Don't forget, since **Msgbox** is a function, that it returns a value which is stored in the variable **Response**. This return tells us which button the user presses. Here is the code:

```
Private Sub Form_Load()

Dim Msg As String
Dim Response
Dim Style, ButtonValue, Symbol As Integer
Msg = "Exercise 10-1"
For ButtonValue = 0 To 5 Step 1
 For Symbol = 0 To 64 Step 16
    Style = ButtonValue + Symbol
    Response = MsgBox("Button value is " & ButtonValue & "+" & Symbol,
↳  Style)
  Next
Next

End Sub
```

2 Again, for simplicity sake, I inserted my code into the **Form_Load** event of the form. There's nothing terrifically special here. Just an **InputBox** function where I specify a title for the box, a message to be displayed, and a default value. Notice the x and y parameters of 0 to indicate that the input box should be located in the upper left hand corner of the screen.

```
Private Sub Form_Load()
Dim Message, Title, Default, Response
Message = "Good morning. Would you care for Coffee or Tea?"
Title = "Exercise 10-2"
Default = "Coffee"
Response = InputBox(Message, Title, Default, 0, 0)
End Sub
```

Input boxes are a quick way of getting input from the user, but many Visual Basic programmers shy away from them. Why? Well, you're limited to one response per input box. If you wanted to ask the user whether they would like toast or a bagel, you'd have to execute another **InputBox** statement. Also, there is no way to restrict input. We're only serving coffee and tea today, but the user could type in orange juice for all we know. We don't know what they've entered into the input box until they press the *Enter* key, and the entry is placed in our variable **Response**. For programmers who like to use the **KeyPress** event of the text box to 'spy' on the user, this can be somewhat restrictive.

3 Once again, I inserted my code into the **`Form_Load`** event of the form. I modified the **`Value`** parameter of the **`MsgBox`** function by adding 4096 to it. (This is the value necessary to create the system modal box.) Once again, if you run the project, it will display 30 different message box styles, but this time they will all be modal.

With a system modal box, the user can do nothing but click on one of the buttons in the message box. They also cannot access other portions of the application.

```
Private Sub Form_Load()

Dim Msg As String
Dim Response
Dim Style, ButtonValue, Symbol, Extra As Integer
Msg = "Exercise 10-3"
Extra = 4096
For ButtonValue = 0 To 5 Step 1
  For Symbol = 0 To 64 Step 16
    style = ButtonValue + Symbol + Extra
    response = MsgBox("Button value is " & ButtonValue & "+" & Symbol,
➥  Style)
  Next
Next

End Sub
```

4 I placed the code for the display of the color common dialog into the **`Click`** event of the command button. Once the user has made a selection, I set the **`BackColor`** property of the form equal to their selection, which can be found in the **`Color`** property of the command dialog.

```
Private Sub Command1_Click()

CommonDialog1.ShowColor
Form1.BackColor = CommonDialog1.Color

End Sub
```

5 Similar to Exercise 4, this time we use the common dialog to change the font size of the caption displayed in our label. By setting the **`AutoSize`** property of the label to True, we ensure that it will be resized to accommodate nearly every font size that our user selects. However, changing fonts can be more complicated than changing colors. This is because there are more properties to deal with, and because of the existence of the 'Font Object'. In the following code, I use the **`With ... End With`** construct to change the appropriate properties of the font object. Notice also, that I set the **`Flags`** property of the common dialog to designate screen fonts. By adding 256 to this value, I allow the user to choose a color. Finally, notice that color is not a property of the font object, and therefore the color of the label must be set outside of the **`With...End With`** construct.

```
Private Sub Command1_Click()

CommonDialog1.Flags = cdlCFScreenFonts + 256
CommonDialog1.ShowFont

With label1.Font
   .Name = CommonDialog1.FontName
   .Bold = CommonDialog1.FontBold
   .Italic = CommonDialog1.FontItalic
   .Size = CommonDialog1.FontSize
   .Strikethrough = CommonDialog1.FontStrikethru
   .Underline = CommonDialog1.FontUnderline
End With

label1.ForeColor = CommonDialog1.Color

End Sub
```

Chapter 11 - Graphics

1 Not too challenging, but a good exercise for the artistically challenged among us. The line control is a great way to draw shapes of all sorts, and the judicious use of lines in your interface can make it more attractive and efficient. In order to draw the tic-tac-toe board we need to draw two vertical lines and two horizontal lines. Experiment a bit to get the correct layout (it will vary depending on the setup of your machine—so there is no 'definitive' layout). Be sure to experiment with the **BorderWidth** property to adjust the width of your lines. Jot down the X and Y coordinates of your lines for Exercise 11-3. They will come in handy!

2 Instead of using the line control as we did in the previous exercise, here we use the **Line** method. We need two horizontal and two vertical lines. Prior to calling the **Line** method, we set the form to the proper height and width to accommodate our tic-tac-toe board. I experimented to find an appropriate setting for **DrawWidth** which is a property that determines the width of the output of a graphics method.

Then we pass the **Line** method two pair of x and y coordinates. The first pair represents the starting position for the line, and the second pair represents the stopping position for the line. We repeat this method four times for our tic-tac-toe board. I placed the code in the **Click** event of the form.

```
Private Sub Form_Click()
Form1.height = 4635
Form1.width = 6840
DrawWidth = 8

Form1.Line (2265, 420)-(2265, 3360) 'Draw Vertical Line 1
Form1.Line (4465, 420)-(4465, 3360) 'Draw Vertical Line 2
```

```
Form1.Line (500, 1300)-(6000, 1300) 'Draw Horizontal Line 1
Form1.Line (500, 2400)-(6000, 2400) 'Draw Horizontal Line 2

End Sub
```

3 The code necessary to draw the tic-tac-toe board remains the same from Exercise 11-2, with one exception. In order to make the game appear as if it's actually being played, I placed the code necessary to 'play' the game in the **Interval** event of a timer that I placed on the form. I specify an interval of 1000 (1 second) for the timer. After drawing the tic-tac-toe board, I enable the timer.

```
Private Sub Form_Click()

Form1.Height = 4635
Form1.Width = 6840
DrawWidth = 8

Form1.Line (2265, 420)-(2265, 3360) 'Draw Vertical Line 1
Form1.Line (4465, 420)-(4465, 3360) 'Draw Vertical Line 2

Form1.Line (500, 1300)-(6000, 1300) 'Draw Horizontal Line 1
Form1.Line (500, 2400)-(6000, 2400) 'Draw Horizontal Line 2

Timer1.Interval = 1000
Timer1.Enabled = True

End Sub
```

I then place the following code in the **Timer** event of the timer. I know there are more eloquent ways of drawing the X's and O's of tic-tac-toe, but what the heck, the game's rigged anyway!

```
Sub Timer1_Timer()

Static Counter
Counter = Counter + 1
Select Case Counter

Case 1:
Form1.Line (1000, 600)-(1600, 1000), vbBlue
Form1.Line (1000, 1000)-(1600, 600), vbBlue

Case 2:
Form1.Circle (5300, 3000), 200, vbRed

Case 3:
Form1.Line (1000, 2800)-(1600, 3200), vbBlue
Form1.Line (1000, 3200)-(1600, 2800), vbBlue

Case 4:
```

```
Form1.Circle (1300, 1900), 200, vbRed

Case 5:
Form1.Line (5000, 600)-(5600, 1000), vbBlue
Form1.Line (5000, 1000)-(5600, 600), vbBlue

Case 6:
Form1.Circle (3300, 1900), 200, vbRed

Case 7:
Form1.Line (3000, 600)-(3600, 1000), vbBlue
Form1.Line (3000, 1000)-(3600, 600), vbBlue

Case 8:
Form1.Line (800, 800)-(6000, 800), vbYellow

Case 9:
Timer1.Enabled = False

End Select

End Sub
```

Perhaps the most important part of this code is the choice of a variable called 'counter' as a static type. This enables me to keep track of which move has been made. If I had not chosen a static variable, then the same move would have been made indefinitely. Such a game would certainly have bored our alien visitors.

Of course, all of the moves are predetermined. Each case represents a 1 second interval, which accounts for the appearances of a played game.

4 Ok, maybe we have been working too hard. Here is the code necessary to draw and calculate the area of a 1000 twip and 1400 twip diameter pizza. By the way, I was right, the 1400 twip diameter pie has almost twice the area of a 1000 twip diameter pie. What a bargain!

As for the code, I placed it all in the **`Form_Click`** event. Having experimented a bit, I placed two circles side by side on the form by using the **`Circle`** method. This method accepts a starting x and y coordinate, a radius, and (optionally) a color. I calculated the radius as half of the diameter. The area of the circle I calculated as 22/7 (remember Pythagoras) multiplied by the radius of the circle squared. I then displayed the area in the appropriate label. Don't forget to set the **`AutoSize`** property of the label to True.

```
Private Sub Form_Click()

   Dim Radius1, Radius2 As Integer
   Dim Area1, Area2 As Long

   Form1.Height = 5000
```

```
    Form1.Width = 7000

    Radius1 = 1000 / 2
    Radius2 = 1400 / 2

    Form1.Circle (1200, 1600), Radius1, vbRed
    Form1.Circle (4400, 1600), Radius2, vbBlue

    Area1 = (22 / 7) * (Radius1 ^ 2)
    Area2 = (22 / 7) * (Radius2 ^ 2)

    Label1.Top = 3360
    Label1.Left = 470
    Label1.Caption = "Circle 1 is " & Format(Area1, "###,###,###,###") & "
      ↳ square twips"

    Label2.Top = 3360
    Label2.Left = 3780
    Label2.Caption = "Circle 2 is " & Format(Area2, "###,###,###,###") & "
      ↳ square twips"

End Sub
```

5 What a sore loser! All I've done here is add a command button to the form captioned It must have been a mistake!. When the button is clicked, the following code is executed, which obliterates the game. The key to this code is the random function. I use the graphics **Line** method to randomly draw lines of random length and color on the screen. I use the form's **ScaleHeight** and **ScaleWidth** to provide my limits, and to keep things simple, I use the **QBColor** function to provide the color for the **Line** method.

```
Private Sub Command1_Click()
Dim FromX, ToX, FromY, ToY, nIndex, intColor

Randomize
For nIndex = 1 To 2000
FromX = Int(Rnd(1) * Form1.ScaleWidth)
ToX = Int(Rnd(1) * Form1.ScaleWidth)
FromY = Int(Rnd(1) * Form1.ScaleHeight)
ToY = Int(Rnd(1) * Form1.ScaleHeight)
intColor = Int(Rnd(1) * 16)
Form1.Line (FromX, FromY)-(ToX, ToY), QBColor(intColor)
Next

End Sub
```

Chapter 12 - Using Database Controls

1 As a professor of mine once said, the answer is in the question. Verify that you have successfully established a Microsoft database called 'Pizza', which should contain 3 tables called **Customer**, **Inventory** and **Transactions**. The **Customer** table should contain 4 records, the **Inventory** table 5 records, and the **Transaction** table 9 records.

2 This is really pretty simple. Place 4 text boxes on your form. To be really user friendly, it would be a great idea to place descriptive labels next to the text boxes so that your user knows what fields are being displayed. Next, draw a data control on the form. Specify the correct name (**PIZZA.MDB**) in the **DatabaseName** property of the data control. By default, the **RecordsetType** property is set to dynaset. That will be fine for us. Regardless of whether we choose table or dynaset, we'll still be able to update the underlying table. For the **RecordSource** property, specify the **Transactions** table.

At this point, we now have a working data control. By the way, take note of the **ReadOnly** property of the data control which by default is false. If we wanted to prevent updates to the underlying table, we would change this property to True. If we wanted to prevent updates to a particular field, then we could change the **Locked** property of the text box to True. Another alternative would be to use a bound label instead of a bound text box. Also take note of the **EOF** property of the data control. By default, it is set to **MoveLast**. One of the options for this property is **AddNew** which means if the user reaches the End Of File, the user will be able to add a new record. **MoveLast** will prevent us from adding a new record to the underlying table.

What remains to be done now is to bind our 5 text boxes to the data control. This is a 2 step process. First, select the first text box, and specify **Data1** as the **DataSource** for the text box. Then, select **Date** as the **DataField** for the text box. Repeat this process for the other 4 text boxes, and then run the application. You should now see the underlying data in the **Transaction** table of the Pizza database.

3 The first course of action is to add two new data controls to your form. Since you'll be pulling in information from the **Customer** table (**Customer** field) and the **Inventory** table (**Description** field), you'll need to place a data control for each on your form. As we did in Exercise 2, you'll specify the DatabaseName and the appropriate table. What will differ slightly in this case in your choice of **RecordsetType**. For the **Transaction** data control, we specified a dynaset because we wanted to update the underlying table. In this instance, however, both the **Customer** and **Inventory** tables are really being used as a lookup table to display a corresponding value based on a field in the **Transaction** table. We don't want our user updating either the **Customer** table or **Inventory** table by accident. Therefore, the safe thing to do is to specify snapshot as our **RecordsetType**. Also, for aesthetic reasons, we'll want to set the **Visible** property of the two additional data controls to False.

If you now run the application, you'll find that the application works much the same as before, but in addition, you also have two labels that display a Customer Name and an Inventory Description. Unfortunately, they never change! The Customer Name is the first in the **Customer** table, and the Inventory Description is also the first in the **Inventory** table. They aren't synched to the **Transaction** table. We need to place some code in the **Validation** event of the **Data1** (transaction) data control to sync the other two data controls to the correct **Cust_ID** and **Stock_ID**.

The key to this working is to replace, at run time, the **RecordSource** property in the **Data2** (Customer) data control and in the **Data3** (Inventory) data control. Here's the code necessary to do that. I chose the **Data1_Reposition** event to do that. When the reposition event is invoked, **Text2.Text** contains the **Cust_ID** of the **Transaction** table, and **Text3.Text** contains the **Stock_ID** of the **Transaction** table. The SQL statement that's generated is then used as the **RecordSource** for the respective data controls, and the **Refresh** method redisplays the data.

```
Private Sub Data1_Reposition()

Dim SQL2, SQL3 As String

SQL2 = "SELECT * FROM Customer WHERE [Cust_ID] = " & Text2.Text
SQL3 = "SELECT * FROM Inventory WHERE [Stock_ID] = " & Text3.Text

Data2.RecordSource = SQL2
Data2.Refresh

Data3.RecordSource = SQL3
Data3.Refresh

End Sub
```

Before we can run this project, however, we need to add a **Form_Load** event to populate our form before the **Data1_Reposition** event is fired:

```
Private Sub Form_Load()

Data1.Refresh

End Sub
```

4 As we did in Exercise 2, the first thing we do is place a data control on the form. As before, the **DatabaseName** will be **Pizza.MDB**. Specify a **RecordSource** of **Transaction**. Next, place a database grid control on to the form. Specify its **DataSource** as **Data1**. In order to populate the grid, I placed the following code into the **Form_Load** event of our form.

```
Dim SQL1 As String
SQL1 = "SELECT * FROM Transactions"

Data1.RecordSource = SQL1
Data1.Refresh
```

The **RecordSource** property of the data control is a simple SQL statement. If you wish, you can experiment with it a bit.

5 In order to pull in associated information from the **Customer** and **Inventory** tables, all we need to do is make a change to our SQL statement. That's the beauty of the database grid. No new labels or text boxes to add. The grid changes dynamically according to the **RecordSource** property. Here is the code for the **Form_Load** event:

```
Private Sub Form_Load()

Dim SQL1 As String

SQL1 = "SELECT DISTINCTROW Transactions.Date, "
SQL1 = SQL1 + "Customer.Customer, Inventory.Description,"
SQL1 = SQL1 + "Transactions.Quantity, Transactions.Price "
SQL1 = SQL1 + "FROM (Transactions INNER JOIN Customer ON "
SQL1 = SQL1 + "Transactions.Cust_ID = Customer.Cust_Id) "
SQL1 = SQL1 + "INNER JOIN Inventory ON Transactions.Stock_Id = "
SQL1 = SQL1 + "Inventory.Stock_ID"

Data1.DatabaseName = App.Path & "\pizza.mdb"
Data1.RecordSource = SQL1

Data1.Refresh

End Sub
```

A complicated SQL statement to be sure! In fact, we had to break it up into several lines. By the way, you don't need to be a SQL wizard to conjure up statements of this kind. The easiest thing to do is to use Microsoft Access to build your query for you. Once you're sure you're getting what you really want, in Query Design mode, select View SQL. You can then copy and paste the SQL statement that Access generates for you into your code. Try it, and see how easy it can make it for you.

Chapter 13 - Programming Database Access

1 Not too difficult. I replaced the data control's VCR buttons with 4 command buttons. Here's the code. Notice how we handle the possibility of moving beyond the beginning and the end of the table.

```
Private Sub cmdFirst_Click()

Data1.Recordset.MoveFirst

End Sub
```

```
Private Sub cmdPrevious_Click()
```

```
Data1.Recordset.MovePrevious

If Data1.Recordset.BOF Then
  Data1.Recordset.MoveNext
End If

End Sub
```

```
Private Sub cmdNext_Click()

Data1.Recordset.MoveNext

If Data1.Recordset.EOF Then
  Data1.Recordset.MovePrevious
End If

End Sub
```

```
Private Sub cmdLast_Click()

Data1.Recordset.MoveLast

End Sub
```

2 I placed a new command button on the form captioned Find. When clicked, this button displays an input box which prompts for the numeric customer id. (I know, we've said real programmers don't use input boxes, but they're ideal for applications like this!)

The user's response is stored in a variable, and that variable then forms the basic for the recordset's **FindFirst** method. Of course, I check to ensure that the user has not clicked Cancel or merely pressed the *Enter* key. Also, in the event that we don't find a match, the default behavior of **FindFirst** is to position our record pointer to record number 1 of the dynaset. I save the bookmark of the recordset prior to issuing the **MoveFirst** statement. If the customer id is not found, I display an appropriate message, then I move to the saved bookmark.

Here is the code.

```
Private Sub cmdFind_Click()
Dim nresult As Integer
Dim cfind As Integer
Dim sfind As String
Dim cbookmark As String

cfind = InputBox("Enter Customer ID:", "Customer Find")
sfind = Str(cfind)
sfind = UCase(Trim(cfind))
sfind = "[Cust_ID] = " + sfind

If Len(sfind) > 0 Then
   cbookmark = Data1.Recordset.Bookmark
```

```
        Data1.Recordset.FindFirst sfind
    If Data1.Recordset.NoMatch Then
        MsgBox "Can't find Customer " + Str(cfind), 0, "Find Error"
        Data1.Recordset.Bookmark = cbookmark
    End If
End If

End Sub
```

3 Before I start, let me say that there's more than one way to paint a picture. Part of the fun of Visual Basic is designing a user interface such as this. The wonder of it is that if you had a room of 10 programmers, you'd get 10 different interfaces.

Let's start with the code for the Add button. The first thing I do is set a bookmark for the current record. This way, if the user decides to change their mind about adding a new record, I can reposition the record pointer to the record they were working with prior to clicking on the Add button. I also set a Boolean variable called **badding** to True (declare it in the General Declarations section of the form). When the user clicks on the Add button, I disable the Add, the Delete, and Find buttons. I invoke the **AddNew** method of the dataset to bring up a blank record for update. Some programmers would also include an Update button, disable the navigation buttons, and have the user click on that to save the new record. However, in this instance, once the user is done completing the fields on the form, if they reposition the recordset by clicking on one of the navigation buttons (they're still active), the **Validate** event is triggered, and the record is saved.

```
Private Sub cmdAdd_Click()

sbookmark = Data1.Recordset.Bookmark
badding = True
cmdAdd.Enabled = False
cmdCancel.Eanbled = True
cmdDelete.Enabled = False
cmdFind.Enabled = True
cmdQuit.Enabled = False

Data1.Recordset.AddNew

End Sub
```

Let's discuss the Cancel button next. In this interface, really the only thing the user can cancel is the process of adding a record. If our Boolean variable **badding** indicates that the user was in the process of adding a record when they decided to cancel, I set that variable to false. I then re-enable the buttons that I disabled when the user pressed the Add button, except for Cancel, which is then disabled. (It's only enabled when the user presses Add) . The key to this event is the **CancelUpdate** method of the recordset. This method cancels changes to the underlying dataset. When the bookmark method is invoked against the dataset to reposition the dataset to the record the user was working with prior to clicking the Add button, the **Validate** event of the data control is invoked. This does an intrinsic save of the dataset. **CancelUpdate** ensures that the added record is not saved.

```
Private Sub cmdCancel_Click()
If badding = True Then
  badding = False
  cmdAdd.Enabled = True
  cmdDelete.Enabled = True
  cmdCancel.Enabled = False
  cmdFind.Enabled = True
  cmdQuit.Enabled = True
  Data1.Recordset.CancelUpdate
  Data1.Recordset.Bookmark = sbookmark
End If
End Sub
```

Now for the Delete button. This is fairly simple to do. When the user clicks on the Delete button, I display a message box asking them if they are sure. Their response is stored in a variable called **nresult**. If they answer Yes, the return value is 1, and I issue the **Delete** method of the data control. I then simulate the press of the Next button by setting its value property to True.

```
Private Sub cmdDelete_Click()

Dim nresult As Integer

nresult = MsgBox("Are you sure?", 1, "Delete Record")
If nresult = 1 Then
    Data1.Recordset.Delete
    cmdNext.Value = True
End If

End Sub
```

4 The issue of the **Validate** event may be difficult for some to fathom. Thus, this question. To check it out, use the following code. Be thoroughly familiar with the meaning of the data control **Validate** event. Most people are comfortable with the **Action** argument. The **Validate** event's **Action** argument indicates the type of action that caused the **Validate** event to take place. Here are the codes, along with their intrinsic constants:

vbDataActionCancel	0	Cancel the operation when the Sub exits.
vbDataActionMoveFirst	1	**MoveFirst** method.
vbDataActionMovePrevious	2	**MovePrevious** method.
vbDataActionMoveNext	3	**MoveNext** method.
vbDataActionMoveLast	4	**MoveLast** method.
vbDataActionAddNew	5	**AddNew** method.
vbDataActionUpdate	6	**Update** operation (not **UpdateRecord**).
vbDataActionDelete	7	**Delete** method.
vbDataActionFind	8	**Find** method.
vbDataActionBookmark	9	The **Bookmark** property has been set.
vbDataActionClose	10	The **Close** method.
vbDataActionUnload	11	The form is being unloaded.

As you can see, there are twelve different action arguments. Here's code that I placed in the **Validate** event to let me know what is happening.

```
Private Sub Data1_Validate(Action As Integer, Save As Integer)

Select Case Action
Case 0
  MsgBox "Cancel method invoked"
Case 1
  MsgBox "MoveFirst invoked"
Case 2
  MsgBox "MovePrevious invoked"
Case 3
  MsgBox "MoveNext invoked"
Case 4
  MsgBox "MoveLast invoked"
Case 5
  MsgBox "AddNew invoked"
Case 6
  MsgBox "Update invoked"
Case 7
  MsgBox "Delete invoked"
Case 8
  MsgBox "Find invoked"
Case 9
  MsgBox "BookMark invoked"
Case 10
  MsgBox "Close invoked"
Case 11
  MsgBox "Unload invoked"
End Select

End Sub
```

5 This can be a little tricky. I created a list box control at the top of my form. Since we're going to allow the list box to display the customer id's, we no longer need to display that field in the database grid. The **Form_Load** event is a great place to build the contents of the list box, and to build the initial view of the database grid. Thereafter, when the a customer id is selected in the list box, we'll requery our table to build a new view of the database grid. That requery code will be place in the **Click** event of the list box. Here is the code for the **Form_Load** event.

```
Private Sub Form_Load()

Data1.DatabaseName = App.Path & "\pizza.mdb"

Dim sqllist As String

sqllist = "SELECT DISTINCT [CUST_ID] FROM TRANSACTIONS"
Data1.RecordSource = sqllist
Data1.Refresh
```

```
List1.AddItem "ALL"
Do While Not Data1.Recordset.EOF
List1.AddItem Data1.Recordset("CUST_ID")
Data1.Recordset.MoveNext
Loop

Dim SQL1 As String

SQL1 = SQL1 & "SELECT DISTINCTROW Trans_ID, "
SQL1 = SQL1 & "Date, Stock_Id, Quantity, Price "
SQL1 = SQL1 & "FROM Transactions"
Data1.RecordSource = SQL1
Data1.Refresh

End Sub
```

To build the values for list box, I executed a **`Select Distinct`** query against the **`Transaction`** table. The **`Distinct`** option insures that I get no duplicate values in my resultant recordset. I then make the ever popular ALL the first item in the list box. If the user selects ALL in the list box, then I want to display every record in the **`Transactions`** table in the database grid. If they select 1 in the list box, then I only want to display Transactions whose Customer Id is 1.

This code is placed in the **`Click`** event of the list box. Here is the code.

```
Dim SQL1 As String

If List1.Text = "ALL" Then
  SQL1 = SQL1 & "SELECT DISTINCTROW Trans_ID, "
  SQL1 = SQL1 & "Date, Stock_Id, Quantity, Price "
  SQL1 = SQL1 & "FROM Transactions"
Else
  SQL1 = SQL1 & "SELECT DISTINCTROW Trans_ID, "
  SQL1 = SQL1 & "Date, Stock_Id, Quantity, Price "
  SQL1 = SQL1 & "FROM Transactions WHERE [CUST_ID] = " & List1.Text
End If

Data1.RecordSource = SQL1
Data1.Refresh
```

As we noted earlier, when an SQL statement becomes too wordy, break it up on to several lines by using the method you see here. I use a simple **`If`** statement to determine if the user has selected ALL in the list box. If they have, then I return every transaction to the dataset. If not, then I tailor the SQL select statement by using a **`WHERE`** clause, whose argument is the **`Text`** property of the list box.

Chapter 14 - Object Variables

1 Using object variables, you can:

- Create new controls at run time
- Copy controls to produce new instances of existing ones
- Create duplicate forms, all with identical names, controls and code—but each containing and dealing with different data.

2 This code is placed in the click event of the label.

```
Private Sub Label1_Click (Index As Integer)

  Static sNextOperation As String
   Dim nIndex As Integer

   For nIndex = 1 To 5

     If sNextOperation = "UNLOAD" Then
       Unload Label1(nIndex)
     Else
       Load Label1(nIndex)
       With Label1(nIndex)
           .Visible = True
           .TOP = Label1(nIndex - 1).TOP + Label1(nIndex - 1).Height
           .Caption = "This is label " & nIndex
       End With
    End If

   Next

   If sNextOperation = "UNLOAD" Then
     sNextOperation = "LOAD"
   Else
     sNextOperation = "UNLOAD"
   End If

End Sub
```

3 I declared this function (appropriately named **Topis**) in the General Declarations section of the form. It accepts a single argument of type Control, and returns a long value. Notice how the return value is set by assigning a value equal to the function name (**Topis**).

```
Function Topis(myobject As Control) as Long

Topis = myobject.Top

End Function
```

I then placed two controls on the form. A command button and a text box. I placed the following code in both the **Click** event of the command button and the **Click** event of text box. When the controls are clicked, I display their **Top** property in a label I placed on the form.

```
Private Sub Command1_Click()

Dim myobject As CommandButton
Dim nresult As Long

Set myobject = Command1
nresult = topis(myobject)
Label1.Caption = "Called object's top property is " & nresult

End Sub
```

```
Private Sub Text1_Click()

Dim myobject As TextBox
Dim nresult As Long

Set myobject = Text1
nresult = topis(myobject)
Label1.Caption = "Called object's top property is " & nresult

End Sub
```

4 If you explicitly declare an object variable as type label, or if you try to assign a value to a property that does not exist, you'll receive a compile error. You can't run the project at all. Check out this code. This will generate a compile error.

```
Private Sub Form_Load()

Dim myobject As Label
Set myobject = Label1

myobject.Text = "smith"

End Sub
```

5 If you declare an object variable as type control, and then try to assign a value to a property that does not exist for that control, you'll receive a run-time error. This points up the danger in using the generic object variable declaration. It allows you to get much further than explicitly declaring object variable. Check out this code.

```
Private Sub Form_Load()

Dim myobject As Control
Set myobject = Label1
```

```
myobject.Text = "smith"

End Sub
```

Chapter 15 - Using DLL's and the API

1 Before you can use an API call, your Visual Basic application must declare the API procedure or function in the General Declarations section of a form, standard module, or class module. This process isn't much different to writing your own procedure or function, but you use the keyword **DECLARE** to tell Visual Basic that the function or procedure is external to your application.

2 Ordinarily, this won't pose much of a problem if you copy and paste API declarations from the API Text Viewer. However, you might be calling a DLL using documentation from an outside source. In that event, be sure to pass a string variable by value. String variables are handled differently in C than they are in Visual Basic, and since most DLLs are written in C, you might cause your system to crash or hang if you pass a string value by reference. Remember, when you pass any value by reference, whether within Visual Basic or outside of it, you're actually passing an address to a variable, not the value of the variable itself. If the DLL interprets that address as data, you could have a real problem.

Because a DLL is working outside of your Visual Basic environment, if the routine is expecting a value, and you pass it an address, unpredictable results could occur.

3 The function is **GetDriveType**.

4 The answer to this question can be near impossible to find out without the hint I'm about to give you. You can hunt and peck in the Constants area of the API viewer. What I did, after several minutes of frustration, was to use a plain old text editor to view the **WIN32API.TXT** file located in the **WINAPI** subdirectory of the Visual Basic 5 directory. Then I simply searched for drive type and I found these constants. Of course, a manual or book on the Windows API would come in quite handy now.

Here are the values that will be returned by **GetDriveType**. These can also be found listed under the constants section within the API Text Viewer.

2	DRIVE_REMOVABLE
3	DRIVE_FIXED
4	DRIVE_REMOTE
5	DRIVE_CDROM
6	DRIVE_RAMDISK

5 Here's the **Declare** of the function that I found in the API Text Viewer. I placed it in the General Declarations section of my form. When placed on the form, the word **Private** must precede **Declare**. Notice how the function is expecting a single argument of string type called **nDrive**, and will return a value of type long.

```
Private Declare Function getDriveType Lib "kernel32" Alias
"GetDriveTypeA" (ByVal nDrive As String) As Long
```

Here's the code that I placed in the **Click** event of my command button. Notice how I used a simple input box for the input of the desired drive letter. What can give you real problems is the format of the string you need to pass to the function. You can guess all you want, but you'll have to be pretty lucky to guess that the format is **C:**. Most people assume the argument is the single letter designating the drive. Considering the myriad of API calls available to you, where do you get this type of information. Well, of course, you'll need a book on the Windows API, which gives you the definitive answers on formats, argument passing, and return values.

```
Private Sub Command1_Click()

Dim nresult As Long
Dim sdrive As String

sdrive = UCase(InputBox("Enter a Drive Letter"))
nresult = getDriveType(sdrive & ":\")

Select Case nresult
   Case 2
         Label1.Caption = "Drive letter " & sdrive & " is a Removable
type"
    Case 3
         Label1.Caption = "Drive letter " & sdrive & " is a Fixed Type"
    Case 4
         Label1.Caption = "Drive letter " & sdrive & " is a Network Drive"
    Case 5
         Label1.Caption = "Drive letter " & sdrive & " is a CD_ROM"
    Case 6
         Label1.Caption = "Drive letter " & sdrive & " is a RAM DISK"
    Case Else
         Label1.Caption = "That drive letter does not exist on this
system"
End Select

End Sub
```

Chapter 16 - Visual Basic and Components

1 An in-process component server is one which when it is compiled becomes a DLL. Any code which uses it has to load the code from the DLL. An out-of-process component is compiled as an executable program, like Excel. Any code which uses its components runs alongside the application.

2 **SingleUse** and **GlobalSingleUse** are not allowed in ActiveX DLL's.

3 I opened a new project and specified an Active Exe project. I then created two properties and two methods by typing the following code into the class module.

```
Option Explicit

Private m_sName As String
Private m_intAge As Integer

Property Let Name(ByVal sName As String)
    m_sName = sName
End Property

Property Let Age(ByVal intAge As Integer)
    m_intAge = intAge
End Property

Public Sub ShowName()
    MsgBox "Your name is " & m_sName
End Sub

Public Sub Showage()
    MsgBox "You don't look " & m_intAge & " years old"
End Sub
```

You should then bring up the properties for the class and give the class the name **cnAge**. Also, don't forget to bring up the properties window for the project. You'll see that the project type is ActiveX exe. Make sure you give it a project name. I called mine **TestServer2**. I then compiled it into an **.exe**, and called it **TestServer2.exe**.

4 Once the class is created, named, saved, and made into an executable, you then need to create a standard project to access it. I created a standard project, with two text boxes, two labels and a command button. I called one text box **txtName** and the other **txtAge**. and added this code to the **Click** event of the command button:

```
Private Sub Command1_Click()

Dim Myserver As Object

Set Myserver = CreateObject("Testserver2.cnAge")

Myserver.Name = txtName
Myserver.age = txtAge
Myserver.showname
Myserver.showage

End Sub
```

After typing in my name and age into the appropriate text boxes, the server fires up, and displays a message box containing my name and age.

5 Linking is much like shelling out. With linking, the container control simply holds a pointer to the file containing the data. So, when the user double clicks the OLE object, the original application is run as a totally separate application. It's responsible for handling any changes made to the file, as well as for saving the file itself. When you create an embedded object at design time, VB loads in an image of the file into its own memory space. When VB runs, it creates an object inside itself of the OLE class and then uses this to edit the chosen file. The VB app is now responsible for maintaining that data, saving any changes that the user may make, and loading these changes back in the next time the program runs.

Chapter 17 - Creating Your Own Controls

1 You can create three 'types' of ActiveX control. With the first type, the control is drawn from scratch. This requires that you create code to determine how and where the control should be drawn. With the second type, the ActiveX control is derived from a single control, such as the command button example in the chapter. With the third type, the ActiveX control is derived from a group of controls.

2 I prototyped the project by ensuring that it worked outside of a control. I placed a command button and a timer control on a form. I declared the following public variables in the General Declarations section of the form.

```
Public datStartTime As Date
Public lDuration As Long
```

I set the **Enabled** property of the timer control to false, and left the **Interval** set at its default—0. I then placed the following code into the **Timer** event of the timer control.

```
Private Sub Timer1_Timer()

   Beep
   DoEvents
   If DateDiff("s", datStartTime, Now) >= lDuration Then
      Timer1.Enabled = False
   End If

End Sub
```

I changed the caption of the command button to Ring Me and then placed the following code into its **Click** event:

```
Private Sub Command1_Click()

   datStartTime = Now
   Timer1.Enabled = True
```

```
    Timer1.Interval = 1000
    lDuration = 10

End Sub
```

The idea is that when the command button is clicked, we enable the timer control and also set the interval for the 'ring interval' of our bell. Duration is set to be the length of time we want our bell to ring. As soon as the **Timer** event recognizes that the desired duration is equal to or greater than the current time less the start time in seconds, then the **Enabled** property of the timer is set to false. I didn't bother to permit either the duration or interval to be set at run time, since when we design our control in the next step, it will be set via property settings by the designer using our control. All that's lacking now is a visual interface.

3 I started a new project in Visual Basic and chose ActiveX Control from the list that appears at startup. I then clicked on **UserControl** in the project window and, in the properties window, changed the **Name** property to **BellButton.** I then placed a command button and a timer control on the form and changed the **Caption** of the button to Ring Me. I set the timer control's **Enabled** property to false and left its **Interval** property set to 0. I then declared the variables in the General Declarations section of the form. This time though, I included some private variables to be set by the **Property Let** procedures that will be invoked when the property of the control is set.

```
Public datStartTime As Date
Private mvarDuration As Long        'local copy
Private mvarInterval As Integer     'local copy
```

I also included **Property Let** and **Property Get** procedures (to make the properties read/write) for **Interval** and **Duration**. Notice how I set the timer control's **Interval** property at the time the **Interval** property of the control is set.

```
Public Property Get Duration() As Integer

  Duration = mvarDuration

End Property
```

```
Public Property Let Duration(vdata As Integer)

  mvarDuration = vdata

End Property
```

```
Public Property Get Interval() As Integer

  Interval = mvarInterval

End Property
```

```
Public Property Let Interval(vdata As Integer)

   mvarInterval = vdata
   Timer1.interval = vdata

End Property
```

As with the prototype, I then placed the following code into the **Timer** event of the timer control. This time, however, I compared our start time to the private variable **mvarDuration** set by the **Property Let** procedure.

```
Private Sub Timer1_Timer()

   Beep
   DoEvents
   If DateDiff("s", datStartTime, Now) >= mvarDuration Then
         MsgBox "All ringing will now cease..."
         Timer1.Enabled = False
   End If

End Sub
```

I placed the following code into the **Click** event of the command button. Notice that this code includes the **RaiseEvent** statement.

```
Private Sub Command1_Click()

    datStartTime = Now
    Timer1.Enabled = True
    RaiseEvent Click

End Sub
```

Finally, I indicated the events that our control can react to. In this case, it will react to a **Click** event. Add the following line:

```
Event Click()
```

4 To enable the control to deal with the command button being resized (remember, we're designing a control—the designer can place it anywhere and also resize it), I added the following code to the **UserControl_Resize** event:

```
Private Sub UserControl_Resize()
    Command1.Move 0, 0, ScaleWidth, ScaleHeight
End Sub
```

5 Save the project as **BellButton.vbp** then choose the File | Make BellButton.ocx menu option to compile the control.

Close the design window for the new control and then select the File | Add Project menu option and select a standard project.

Now add a bell control from the toolbox to the form and place the following code in the **Form_Load** event:

```
Private Sub Form_Load()
    Bellbutton1.Interval = 1000      'Bell rings every second
    Bellbutton1.duration = 5         'Bell rings for 5 seconds
End Sub
```

Finally, run the project.

Chapter 18 - Putting It All Together

1 You'll just have to use your imagination for this one! Run the program to see the effect of your work. You can view the About form by selecting it from the Help menu.

2 Add three labels to the About form. These will display the Windows version, a caption for the build number and the build number itself. To obtain this information we need to call the **GetVersionEx** API function. We declare it in the general declarations section of the About form. Just paste in the declaration for the function and the needed data structure from the **Win32api.txt** text file.

```
Option Explicit
'This information can be found in the Win32API.txt text
'file that is supplied with VB. We have to add the keyword:
'Private
'to the declaration to use then in a form module. The TYPE we
'are using is a data structure that will be filled in by the
'API function

'It is important that we fill in the first field of the type
'which tells the api function how big the structure
'will be
Private Type OSVERSIONINFO
        dwOSVersionInfoSize As Long
        dwMajorVersion As Long
        dwMinorVersion As Long
        dwBuildNumber As Long
        dwPlatformId As Long
        szCSDVersion As String * 128   '  Maintenance string for PSS usage
End Type
Private Declare Function GetVersionEx Lib "kernel32" Alias
"GetVersionExA" (ByVal lpVersionInformation As OSVERSIONINFO) As Long
```

We also need to declare a variable of this new user defined type.

```
Private udtOSVersioninfo As OSVERSIONINFO
```

We will use the function in the **Form_Initialize** event to determine the operating system that our program is running on.

```
Private Sub Form_Initialize()

Dim lngRet As Long
Dim strVersionNo As String
Dim lngPlatform As Long

udtOSVersioninfo.dwOSVersionInfoSize = Len(udtOSVersioninfo)
lngRet = GetVersionEx(udtOSVersioninfo)
```

It's important that we set the first value of the UDT to be the size in bytes it takes up, so we use the **Len** function. Then we're able to safely call the function. All that remains is for us to extract the information and place it into our labels' captions.

```
strVersionNo = udtOSVersioninfo.dwMajorVersion & "."
    ↳ & udtOSVersioninfo.dwMinorVersion & "."
     ↳ & udtOSVersioninfo.dwBuildNumber
lblVersion.Caption = strVersionNo
Select Case udtOSVersioninfo.dwPlatformId
  Case 0: lblString.Caption = "Win32s Running on Windows 3.x"
  Case 1: lblString.Caption = "Win 32 Running on Windows 95"
  Case 2: lblString.Caption = "Win 32 Running on Windows NT"
End Select
End Sub
```

The values for the **dwPlatforID** field of the data structure have been taken from the Win32 SDK. When the About form is displayed, the new labels will contain OS information.

3 To set up a filter in the File Open dialog, set the **Filter** property of the common dialog in the **frmNewDocument**'s **Form_Load** event:

```
dlgFile.Filter = "Word Documents | *.doc | Excel Sheets | *.xls  "
dlgFile.FilterIndex = 1
```

4 We can enable the menu items when there is an active child window by using our old friend the **Tag** property. A good place to put the code to enable/disable menu options is the File menu **Click** event because when a user goes to select a menu item they have to first click on the topmost menu item. In the **Click** event we can look at a special object variable called **ActiveForm** and use that to examine the **Tag** property. This way, if there's no currently-active child window, we can disable the Print and Send options on the File menu before they even appear.

Open up **frmNewDocument** and set its **Tag** property to **DOC**. Then add the following code to the File menu's **Click** event:

```
Private Sub mnuFile_Click()
    On Error GoTo No_Child
    Dim blnIsWord97Doc As Boolean
    blnIsWord97Doc = (ActiveForm.Tag = "DOC")
    mnuFilePrint.Enabled = blnIsWord97Doc
    mnuFilePageSetup.Enabled = blnIsWord97Doc
    mnuFilePrintPreview.Enabled = blnIsWord97Doc
    mnuFileSend.Enabled = blnIsWord97Doc

No_Child:
   'No Active Document so disable all the menus
    mnuFilePrint.Enabled = False
    mnuFilePageSetup.Enabled = False
    mnuFilePrintPreview.Enabled = False
    mnuFileSend.Enabled = False
End Sub
```

The **On Error** handler catches the instance when there are no child forms active. At this point, checking **ActiveForm** would normally cause a crash, but of course with the **On Error** code in place, that crash is safely stopped and the **Click** event exited after ensuring that all the menu items are disabled.

The rest of the code just compares the **Tag** property of the **ActiveForm**. This comparison will always return True if the **Tag** property is set to **DOC** and False if it is not... just the values we need to feed into the **Enabled** property of the menu items.

5 Rather than waste time writing these functions from scratch, we can just drop into a little ActiveX component work and use the methods which already exist on our users' machines. Take a look at this:

```
Private Sub mnuFilePrintPreview_Click()
    Dim NewDoc As Object

    On Error Resume Next
    If Dir$(ActiveForm.txtFilename) <> "" Then
        Set NewDoc = GetObject (ActiveForm.txtFilename)
    'If the document is not an Office 97 document then
    'The PrintPreview method probably won't exist, so
    'an error will occur which we just ignore here
        NewDoc.PrintPreview
    End If
End Sub
```

```
Private Sub mnuFilePrint_Click()
    Dim NewDoc As Object

    On Error Resume Next
    If Dir$(ActiveForm.txtFilename) <> "" Then
        Set NewDoc = GetObject(ActiveForm.txtFilename)
        NewDoc.Printout
    End If

End Sub


Private Sub mnuFileSend_Click()
    Dim NewDoc As Object
    On Error Resume Next
    If Dir$(ActiveForm.txtFilename) <> "" Then
        Set NewDoc = GetObject(ActiveForm.txtFilename)
        NewDoc.SendMail
    End If

End Sub
```

Here, we take the same steps in each event. First, we declare a late bound object to hold the component that we're dealing with. Then, since there are a number of error conditions that can occur with these methods (such as the printer running out of paper, or the network going screwy), some very simple error handling is initiated:

```
On Error Resume Next
```

This just tells VB to carry on regardless if an error occurs, which means that sooner or later the subprocedures will exit. Crude, I know—but effective.

Next, we use the **DIR$** function to see if the filename specified in the **txtFilename** box on the document form actually exists. If it does, then we can go ahead and create our component by using **GetObject** to load that file in, and the server that created it. At that point, it's a simple matter to just call the relevant component method, such as **Printout** to print the file, or **SendMail** to email it.

With a little careful use of things like this, your development time can be slashed, and your users provided with some very professional applications indeed.

asic Visual Basic Visual Ba
al Basic Visual Basic Visual
Basic Visual Basic Visual Ba
ual Basic Vi
Basic Visu
ual Basic V
l Basic Visu
isual Basic Visual Basic
l Basic Visual Basic Visua
Visual Basic Visual Basic Visu
l Basic Visual Ba
l Basic Visual
ic Visual Basi
Basic Visual B
ic Visual Basi
l Basic Visual
ual Basic Visual Basic Visual Ba
Visual Basic Visual Basic Visu
sual Basic Visual Basic Visu
Visual Basic Visual Ba

A

B

C

D

E

F

G

H

I

M

N

O

P

Q

R

S

U

V

W

asic Visual Basic Visual Ba
al Basic Visual Basic Visual
Basic Visual Basic Visual Ba
ual Basic Vi
Basic Visu
ual Basic V
l Basic Visu
isual Basic Visual Basic
al Basic Visual Basic Visua
Visual Basic Visual Basic Visu
al Basic Visual Ba
l Basic Visual
ic Visual Basi
Basic Visual B
ic Visual Basi
al Basic Visual
ual Basic Visual Basic Visual Ba
Visual Basic Visual Basic Visu
sual Basic Visual Basic Visu
Visual Basic Visual Ba

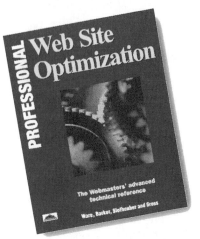

Beginning Linux Programming

Authors: Neil Matthew, Richard Stones
ISBN: 187441680
Price: $36.95 C$51.95 £33.99

The book is unique in that it teaches UNIX programming in a simple and structured way, using Linux and its associated and freely available development tools as the main platform. Assuming familiarity with the UNIX environment and a basic knowledge of C, the book teaches you how to put together UNIX applications that make the most of your time, your OS and your machine's capabilities.

Having introduced the programming environment and basic tools, the authors turn their attention initially on shell programming. The chapters then concentrate on programming UNIX with C, showing you how to work with files, access the UNIX environment, input and output data using terminals and curses, and manage data. After another round with development and debugging tools, the book discusses processes and signals, pipes and other IPC mechanisms, culminating with a chapter on sockets. Programming the X-Window system is introduced with Tcl/Tk and Java. Finally, the book covers programming for the Internet using HTML and CGI.

The book aims to discuss UNIX programming as described in the relevant POSIX and X/Open specifications, so the code is tested with that in mind. All the source code from the book is available under the terms of the Gnu Public License from the Wrox web site.

Professional SQL Server 6.5 Admin

Authors: Various ISBN: 1874416494
Price: $44.95 C$62.95 £41.49

This book is not a tutorial in the complete product, but is for those who need to become either professionally competent in preparation for Microsoft exams or those DBAs needing real-world advice to do their job better. It assumes knowledge of databases and wastes no time on getting novices up to speed on the basics of data structure and using a database server in a Client-Server arena.

The book covers everything from installation and configuration right through to the actual managing of the server. There are whole chapters devoted to essential administrative issues such as transaction management and locking, replication, security, monitoring of the system and database backup and recovery. We've used proven techniques to bring robust code and script that will increase your ability to troubleshoot your database structure and improve its performance. Finally, we have looked very carefully at the new features in 6.5, such as the Web Assistant and Distributed Transaction Controller (DTC) and provided you with key practical examples. Where possible, throughout the book we have described a DBA solution in Transact SQL, Visual Basic and the Enterprise Manager.

Wrox Press
http://www.wrox.com/

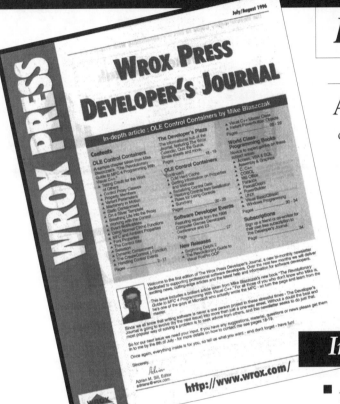

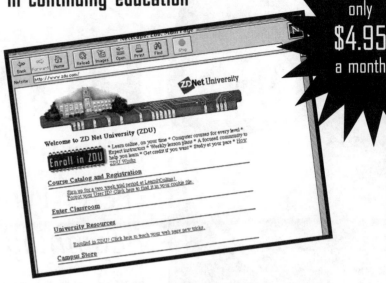

Register Beginning Visual Basic 5 and sign up for a free subscription to The Developer's Journal.

A bi-monthly magazine for software developers, The Wrox Press Developer's Journal features in-depth articles, news and help for everyone in the software development industry. Each issue includes extracts from our latest titles and is crammed full of practical insights into coding techniques, tricks, and research.

Fill in and return the card below to receive a free subscription to the Wrox Press Developer's Journal.

Beginning Visual Basic 5 Registration Card

Name ______________________

Address ______________________

City ____________ State/Region ____________

Country ____________ Postcode/Zip ____________

E-mail ______________________

Occupation ______________________

How did you hear about this book? ______________________

- ☐ Book review (name) ______________________
- ☐ Advertisement (name) ______________________
- ☐ Recommendation ______________________
- ☐ Catalog ______________________
- ☐ Other ______________________

Where did you buy this book? ______________________

- ☐ Bookstore (name) ____________ City ____________
- ☐ Computer Store (name) ______________________
- ☐ Mail Order ______________________
- ☐ Other ______________________

What influenced you in the purchase of this book?

- ☐ Cover Design
- ☐ Contents
- ☐ Other (please specify) ______________________

How did you rate the overall contents of this book?

- ☐ Excellent ☐ Good
- ☐ Average ☐ Poor

What did you find most useful about this book? ______________________

What did you find least useful about this book? ______________________

Please add any additional comments. ______________________

What other subjects will you buy a computer book on soon? ______________________

What is the best computer book you have used this year? ______________________

Note: This information will only be used to keep you updated about new Wrox Press titles and will not be used for any other purpose or passed to any other third party.

ıpport for this book

WROX PRESS INC.

Wrox writes books for you. Any suggestions, or ideas about how you want information given in your ideal book will be studied by our team. Your comments are always valued at Wrox.

Free phone in USA 800-USE-WROX
Fax (312) 397 8990

UK Tel. (0121) 706 6826 Fax (0121) 706 2967

Computer Book Publishers

NB. If you post the bounce back card below in the UK, please send it to:
Wrox Press Ltd. 30 Lincoln Road, Birmingham, B27 6PA

NO POSTAGE NECESSARY IF MAILED IN THE UNITED STATES

BUSINESS REPLY MAIL
FIRST CLASS MAIL PERMIT#64 LA VERGNE, TN

POSTAGE WILL BE PAID BY ADDRESSEE

WROX PRESS
1512 NORTH FREMONT
SUITE 103
CHICAGO IL 60622-2567